PROCEEDINGS

OF THE

AMERICAN ACADEMY FOR JEWISH RESEARCH

JUBILEE VOLUME

AMERICAN ACADEMY FOR JEWISH RESEARCH

PROCEEDINGS

Vols. XLVI–XLVII

1979–1980

JERUSALEM

1980

AMERICAN ACADEMY

FOR

JEWISH RESEARCH

JUBILEE VOLUME
(1928–29 / 1978–79)

EDITED BY
SALO W. BARON AND ISAAC E. BARZILAY

JERUSALEM 1980

AMERICAN ACADEMY FOR JEWISH RESEARCH

Distributed by

COLUMBIA UNIVERSITY PRESS

NEW YORK AND LONDON, 1980

Published with Subvention from the
LOUIS AND MINNA EPSTEIN FUND
ALEXANDER KOHUT MEMORIAL FOUNDATION

PRINTED IN ISRAEL

AT CENTRAL PRESS, JERUSALEM

TABLE OF CONTENTS

ENGLISH SECTION

*deceased

TABLE OF CONTENTS

HEBREW SECTION

THE ROYAL STOA IN THE SOUTHERN PART
OF THE TEMPLE MOUNT

By Benjamin Mazar

The extensive archeological excavations conducted near the retaining walls of the enclosed Temple area in Jerusalem enable us to arrive at certain conclusions regarding the elaborate design of the Herodian construction project, particularly since it was conceived in the area of Robinson's Arch, and the southwestern corner of the Temple Mount.

This was undoubtedly one of the focal points of the metropolis during the period of Herod's Temple. Here was the axis of the paved streets: of the main street, which ran the length of the Tyropoeon valley, and served the large markets; and the streets that branched out from it, eastward — to the gates in the southern and western walls of the enclosed Temple area, and westward — to the Upper City, and Herod's palace. From this point, one ascended from the mainstreet up to the Royal Stoa on a monumental stair-case, which rested on Robinson's Arch, and on the row of arches extending to the south of it, in measured distances, each arch lower than the other.

It is noteworthy that Josephus, in referring to the four gates of the Western Wall, pays particular attention to the fourth gate, which was the most southerly one, and from which one descended, on many stairs, to the Tyropoeon valley. From that point, a row of stairs led to the Upper City (*Antiquities*, XV, 410). Near this site, beside the southwestern corner of the Temple Mount, a large, hewn stone with a niche in its inner side was discovered. Bordering on the niche was a Hebrew inscription: לבית התקיעה להכ[ריז?] "to the House of Trumpeting [*to proclaim*]." This stone must have fallen down from the top of the priests' bureaus, where one

of the priests customarily sounded a trumpet on the eve of the
Sabbath, to announce its advent (Josephus, *Wars*, IV, 582).

   In describing the enclosed area of the Temple Mount, Josephus
devotes considerable attention to the Royal Stoa (βασίλεων
στοά), saying that "It is a structure more worthy to be spoken of
than any other under the sun" (*Antiquities* XV, 411–416). This
magnificent stoa extended from the eastern valley (the Kidron
valley), to the western valley (the Tyropoeon valley). The main
part of it was a long, rectangular Hall of Columns, built in the
design of a basilica. The columns, 162 in number, stood facing
each other, in four rows, the length of the hall. The first, or
southern, row was set into the outer stone wall. Here, a statement
of Rabbi Judah concerning the Temple Mount is of interest:
איסטונית היתה נקראת, סטיו לפנים מסטיו = "It was called *'istônît*
['stoa-like'], one stoa within another." This resembles Josephus'
own description of the stoa's of the Temple Mount, where he
refers to them as διπλαῖ ... αἱ στοαί "the double stoas" (*Wars*,
V, 190).

   According to Josephus, the columns divided the basilica hall,
whose width was about 39 meters, and whose outer wall was
1.5 meters thick. There were three areas of space: the middle, and
two lateral areas. The middle area was one and a half times as wide
as the lateral ones, and twice as high. Josephus is also informative
in stating that it required three men, holding each other with
extended arms, to reach around each column.

   Generally speaking, one receives quite a clear picture regarding
the character of the Royal Stoa from Josephus' descriptions; one
that is borne out with considerable accuracy by the outer measure-
ments that have been made, and by the limited investigations we
have carried out at the Huldah gates. This applies, as well, to the
passages leading from underneath the Royal Stoa to the interior
of the enclosed Temple area, and to the columns, whose diameter
is approximately 1.45 meters, and to the fragments of the Co-
rinthian capitals. The large, and decorated arch-stone, discovered
along with other decorated Herodian building stones, is particularly instructive. It was found in the heaps of debris piled up

outside the southern wall, and adjacent to it, east of the eastern Huldah Gate (the Triple Gate), together with a fragment of a monumental Hebrew inscription, as yet unexplained. One may reasonably suppose that this arch-stone belonged to the apse, which was built adjacent to the rear, eastern wall of the Hall of Columns.

As far as the history of the Royal Stoa is concerned, one may assume that it constituted the most important part of the Herodian construction project undertaken during the first eight years, a phase which included the walls and stoas. (According to *Wars*, I, 40, construction began in Herod's fifteenth year, i.e. 19 B.C.E., and according to *Antiquities*, XV, 380, in his eighteenth year).

We must bear in mind that according to the Gospel of John (2:20), the construction work in the enclosed Temple area continued for 46 years, until the time of the Procurator Pontius Pilate (26–36 C.E.). Actually, construction work of great scope was accomplished during this period, involving the repair of the physical plant, with restorations and additions. This activity was necessitated primarily by the severe damage done to the stoas through fire and devastation, caused by the soldiers of Sabinus during the time of Archelaus (*Wars* II, 49).

Presumably, the construction was executed under the supervision of Gamaliel the Elder (Paul's teacher, according to Acts 22:3). With reference to Gamaliel, it is stated: הָיָה עוֹמֵד עַל הַבְּנִין בְּהַר הַבַּיִת (a Geniza fragment reads: עַל הַבָּנִים —) "He [= Gamaliel] used to supervise the *builders*." (Yerushalmi, *Shabbat*, Ch. 16). S. Lieberman explains this passage as follows:

משמע שהיה רבן גמליאל משגיח על מלאכת הבנאים... בהר הבית. ולפי דרכנו למדנו שבנייני המקדש היו נתונים לפיקוחו של הנשיא בזמן רבן גמליאל הזקן.
This informs us that Rabban Gamaliel used to supervise the work of the *builders*. From this statement, as we understand it, we learn that the temple buildings were under the supervision of the Patriarch during the time of Gamaliel the Elder.[1]

---

[1] S. Lieberman, *Tosefta Ki-fshuṭah*, Part III, *Order Mo'ed* (New York, 1962), p. 204 (Hebrew).

In turn, this correlates with the received tradition that forty years prior to the destruction of the Temple (ca. 30 C.E.), the seat of the Sanhedrin was located in the "stores" (Hebrew: *ḥānuyyôṯ*) within the Temple area:

גלתה סנהדרין מלשכת הגזית לחניות ומחניות לירושלים...

"The Sanhedrin moved from the bureau of hewn stone to the stores, and from the stores to Jerusalem..." (Bavli, *Shabbat*, 15a; *Rosh Hashanah*, 31a; *ʿAbodah Zarah*, 8b; and so forth).

Although the precise sense of the term *ḥānuyyôṯ* is not sufficiently clear (it is a *hapax legomenon* in Jer. 37:16), it appears to derive from Aramaic *ḥānûṭāʾ*, and refers to the basilica hall in the Royal Stoa, which served communal needs, including commerce involved in sacred donations and sacrifices. For the housing of the Sanhedrin, the apse was constructed at the rear wall of the basilica, and it was accommodated for the sessions of the Sanhedrin. Possibly, it was separated from the Hall of Columns by a partition. In any event, it is clear that Herod's architects built the Royal Stoa on the model of the Roman basilicas, which served important communal and commercial functions in relation to the Forum; and it was where the seat of the Sanhedrin was located.

The earliest known example is the Basilica Porcia of Cato (184 B.C.E.), near the Forum Romanum in Rome. In the course of time, the basilica became commonplace in the Roman Empire, and was the plan widely diffused in the eastern provinces. What distinguished the communal basilica, in general, was the hall with four rows of columns, along the length of the hall, with lighting in its upper portion, and a rectangular, or semi-circular platform adjacent to its rear wall, opposite the entrance wall. As an example of a Royal Stoa one may cite the square, enclosed area in Cyrene, surrounded by stoas on all four sides. One of these stoas was a basilica, with an apse adjacent to its rear wall, opposite the entrance. This type of enclosed area, with a basilica, became common in the centers of the Eastern Empire, such as Antioch and Palmyra. As Sjöqvist quite reasonably supposes, its origin is to be found in the Kaisareion of Alexandria, built in the time of Julius Caesar

(48 B.C.E.), and which was intended to serve as an official center for the imperial cult.[2]

On this basis we assume that the Royal Stoa in Jerusalem was erected by Herod as an integral part of the enclosed Temple area, on the model of the basilicas in the eastern provinces of the Roman Empire.

One ascended to the stoa from the markets of the city, located in the Tyropoeon valley to the west, on a monumental staircase, leading up to the Temple Mount. The stoa served primarily for commerce in cultic provisions for the Temple. It is significant, moreover, that the term *ḥānuyyôṯ* was one of the designations for the basilica, where the Sanhedrin was relocated, subsequent to the restoration work accomplished under the supervision of Rabban Gamaliel the Elder. It is probable that the Sanhedrin was housed in the apse, constructed on the eastern side of the Hall of Columns.

In the light of what has been discussed, one should inquire if it was not in this very place in the Temple that the confrontation between Jesus and the purveyors of pigeons, recorded in the known episode from the Gospels, took place. (Pigeons were required for sacrifices offered by women after childbirth, and by those suffering from flux, according to Lev. 12:8, 15:14.) The same would hold true for Jesus' confrontation with the money changers, who exchanged coins bearing the image of Caesar for Jerusalemite coins. Jesus sought to expel such merchants from the Temple area.

This proposal, occasionally suggested with reservations by Dalman, accords well with the previous discussion about the function of the Royal Stoa. Moreover, one should mention the fragment of a vessel, inscribed in Hebrew letters with the word קרבן, "offering," and showing, underneath the inscription, two

---

[2] See E. Sjöqvist, "Kaisareion, a Study in Architectural Iconography," *Opuscula Romana* (Sweden, 1954), I, 86 ff.; J. S. Ward Perkins and M. A. Ballance, "The Caesareum at Cyrene and the Basilica at Cremma," *Papers of the British School at Rome* (London, 1958), XXVI, pp. 137 ff.; G. Foerster, *Art and Archaeology in Palestine, The Jewish People in the First Century* (Amsterdam, 1976), II, 980.

inverted figures of pigeons. This fragment was found in the heaps
of debris on the paved Herodian street, south of the southern wall
of the Temple Mount. Actually, it must have come originally from
the Hall of Columns in the Royal Stoa.[3]

In conclusion, I should raise the possibility that those who built
the great synagogues in the diaspora centers, knew well the design
of the Royal Stoa on the Temple Mount, and that they constructed
the communal installations to resemble it. Religious buildings were
in the form of the basilica, with its hall of columns, including a
semi-circular apse, which was for the elders of the community.
There was also the small, anterior courtyard, apparently re-
sembling the one that stood in the Royal Stoa, between the gate
at its western end, and the entrance in the narrow western wall of
the Hall of Columns. An instructive example is the synagogue
discovered at Sardis (Sepharad), in Anatolia.[4] I am indebted to
Dr. Lee Levine who reminded me what is said about the great
synagogue in Alexandria, in the Tosefta (*Sukkah*, 4b):

אמר רבי יהודה: כל שלא ראה בדפלוסטון של אלכסנדריא של מצרים לא
ראה כבוד לישראל מימיו. כמן בסלקי גדולה היתה, סטיו לפנים מסטיו, שבעים
ואחת קתדראות של זהב היו שם כנגד שבעים ואחד זקן.

    Rabbi Judah said: Whoever has not gazed at the 'double stoa'
[Greek: διπλόστων] of Alexandria in Egypt, has never in his
entire life seen glory reflected on Israel! It was like a large basilica,
a stoa within a stoa; with 71 golden seats, corresponding to the
71 elders.[5]

Therefore, many divergent and complex problems are bound up
with the Royal Stoa in the southern part of the Temple Mount in
Jerusalem. One hopes that additional investigations of this area

---

[3] See B. Mazar, חפירות ארכיאולוגיות בירושלים העתיקה, א, תשכ״ט עמ׳ 8–10
and B. Mazar, *The Excavations in the Old City of Jerusalem* (1969), I, 15–16.

[4] See A. Seager, "The Synagogue of Sardis" [Hebrew], *Qadmoniot* (Jerusalem,
1974), VII, Nos. 3–4, pp. 123 ff.; Andrew R. Seager, "The Building History
of the Sardis Synagogue," *American Journal of Archaeology*, 76 (1972),
425 ff.

[5] See S. Lieberman, *Tosefta Ki-fshuṭah*, Part IV, *Order Mo'ed* (New York,
1962), pp. 273, 889–891.

with comprehensive examination of the relevant literary materials, and the numerous structural fragments uncovered in the heaps of debris outside the retaining walls, will provide further elucidation, and new solutions with respect to the Royal Stoa.

AL-QIRQISĀNĪ ON THE VALUE/WEIGHT
OF THE SHEKEL

By Leon Nemoy

When the publication of the monumental Code of Karaite Law
by Ya'qūb al-Qirqisānī (10th century) was first planned, it was to
have been a joint undertaking. I was to prepare an edition of the
Arabic text, while my classmate at the Yale University Graduate
School, the late Joseph J. Schwartz, was to make an annotated
English translation of it, with constant reference to rabbinic law
and literature. My share of the work was eventually completed
and was published in due course, with the generous help of the
Alexander Kohut Memorial Foundation and its then director,
the late Dr. George Alexander Kohut.[1] Unfortunately for me —
and fortunately for the thousands of Jewish refugees during and
after World War II, to whom Dr. Schwartz gave vital help in his
capacity as European director of the American Joint Distribution
Committee — Dr. Schwartz was at an early date diverted into
the field of social service, and this left him neither time nor energy
to execute his part of the undertaking, which, in my judgment at
least, would have required much more time and labor than my
own part. No one else volunteered or even came to my attention
as a replacement, the sad fact being, now as well as in times past,
that few young scholars care to enter the field of Karaite studies,
and those who are induced to write their doctoral dissertations
on Karaite topics quickly thereafter abandon this field and branch
out into other more popular and more rewarding sectors of
Jüdische Wissenschaft. This is a pity, for Karaite literature is
an integral part of general Jewish literature, and is a rich and

---

[1] *Kitāb al-anwār wal-marāqib, Code of Karaite Law, by Ya'qūb al-Qirqisānī,*
ed. by Leon Nemoy (New York, 1939–43), 5 vols. (Publications of the
Alexander Kohut Memorial Foundation).

multifaceted one, and only a small fraction of it — particularly of the older medieval period — has so far been published and studied.

Be that as it may, a competent annotated English translation of the Code (entitled *Kitāb al-anwār wal-marāqib*) of al-Qirqisānī remains an urgent and unfulfilled desideratum, which again is a pity, for such a translation would make a valuable contribution to our knowledge of the history of both Karaite and Rabbanite law, as well as of many other aspects of tenth century scholarship, such as theology (Jewish, Christian, and Muslim), philosophy, logic and dialectics, medicine (physiology and therapeutics), history and geography, Hebrew and Judeo-Arabic philology, and many others. Of course it would also open to non-arabists this exceedingly detailed and generally very reliable thesaurus of very early Karaite knowledge and thought.

In the meantime I have tried, as much as my overloaded work schedule would permit, to publish from time to time English translations of selected chapters from the *Kitāb al-anwār*, dealing with various, for the most part rather curious and generally interesting (e.g. medical), subjects with brief prefatory remarks and explanatory notes.[2] Needless to say, my contributions to the translated texts had to be brief and could touch only slightly upon rabbinic literature and law, in which my ability to navigate is regrettably limited, and could no doubt be greatly expanded by a specialist in Halakhah. But, to quote an old Arabic literary cliché, "I have done what I could — let him who comes after me do better."

The chapter translated here treats of the value — that is to say, weight — of the ancient Hebrew shekel. As usual, the author discusses the subject briefly but exhaustively, with his customary erudition and sound logic. He quotes, out of his Karaite pre-

---

[2] A register of these translations will be included in a bibliographical list compiled by Sheldon R. Brunswick, of the University of California Library at Berkeley, expected to be published in the near future. Translations of shorter quotations from the *Kitāb al-anwār* appeared in a number of published papers by several authors, of which I need mention here only the excellent series by Georges Vajda, "Études sur Qirqisānī," *REJ*, CVI–CVIII, CXX, CXXII.

decessors and contemporaries, only Anan,[3] and cites the Rabbanite view as well. He opposes both, although in polite scholarly language: his usual procedure, since only rarely does he give way to his temper and his razor-sharp tongue and employ biting satire against Karaite and Rabbanite alike; although, unlike Salmon ben Jeroham, for example, he never condescends to plain curses and maledictions, even against that bête noire of the early Karaites, Saadiah Gaon. He was unquestionably a man of profound learning, in things both Jewish and non-Jewish, with a keen and incisive mind, who permitted nothing to divert him from speaking the truth as he perceived it, letting the chips fall where they may, which is probably the reason for his comparative neglect by the later generations of Karaite savants — they read his Code (or portions of it) and cited it occasionally, but they took no particular care to preserve it in a sufficient number of manuscript copies to insure its survival in toto, and they let his other works disappear entirely, at least as far as we know at present. His commentary on Genesis seems, from citations in the Code, to have been likewise a monumental work, and so was his commentary on the nonlegal portions of the Pentateuch (entitled *Kitāb al-riyāḍ wal-ḥadāʾiḳ*). His opera minora, from their titles alone (e.g. an essay on the art of interpretation and explanation, and another essay on the art of translation), seem also to have been valuable works of scholarship. One can only hope that, *inshallah*, manuscripts of at least some of them may be discovered some day in the exceedingly rich royal and mosque manuscript collections of the newly independent Muslim states, few of which have been as yet properly catalogued.

---

3 Almost certainly meaning that no other Karaite scholar before al-Qirqisānī bothered to deal in detail with this subject. Nor did later scholars. The 14th century encyclopedic savant, Aaron the Younger ben Elijah of Nicomedia, in his Pentateuch commentary כתר תורה (Eupatoria, 1866–67, II, 103b–104a) dismisses *twenty gērāhs* (Exod. 30:13) with the brief remark הם גרגרי חרובין (Ibn Ezra, *ad. loc.*: גלגלות חרוב). A far better Karaite philologian, David ben Abraham al-Fāsī (10th century; *Jāmiʿ al-alfāẓ*, ed. Skoss, I, 345), states flatly that "a gērāh is a *dāniq*," citing the same verse.

CHAPTER XXXVIII[4]
ON THE SHEKEL AND ITS QUANTITY
(*kamīyah*)

1. Many people identify the shekel with the *mithqāl*,[5] even though
they disagree as to its quantity. In fact the shekel may actually
signify a unit of weight (rather than a monetary unit), and weights
vary.

We say, first of all, that the shekel which was in use among the
(Jewish) people was of two kinds, one reserved for the Sanctuary,
since Scripture says in many places *after the shekel of the Sanctuary*
(Exod. 30:13, and elsewhere). Had there been no other kind of
shekel, there would have been no use or sense in specifying (it) in
each of these places as (the shekel of) the Sanctuary — if there
was no other kind of shekel, it could have meant only the known
and familiar mithqāl; why then specify *shekel of the Sanctuary*?
This controverts also Anan's view that the shekel equals the
mithqāl in use today, and none other.

2. Anan then proceeded to seek support for his interpretation
in the next words, *The shekel is twenty gērāhs* (Exod. 30:13),
meaning, according to him, twenty *qīrāts*,[6] and the definite article
preceding the word *shekel* showing that what is meant is the
familiar (present-day) mithqāl, and none other. But this argument

---

[4] From the Sixth Discourse of the *Kitāb al-anwār*; ed. Nemoy, III, 666–668.

[5] An Arabic term (= Hebrew מִשְׁקָל, from the same root as shekel), whose
original meaning is merely "weight" (e.g., Koran 4:44, *mithqāla dharratin*,
"the weight of a mote"), which subsequently came to signify the (perhaps
oldest) Arabic unit of weight, corresponding to the Roman-Byzantine *solidus*.
The Arab imperial gold dinar weighed originally one mithqāl, and the two
terms were sometimes used interchangeably. The silver dirham weighed 0.7
of a mithqāl. "Dīnar" is of course a loan-word, from the Greek δηνάριον
(Latin *denarius*) and so is "dirham" (Greek δραχμή). As usual in coinage, the
weight and precious metal content of both coins varied through the course of
centuries and in the various territories of the Muslim domain. Cf. G. C. Miles'
articles in the *Encyclopedia of Islam*, 2nd ed., II, 297–299, 319–320.

[6] A mithqāl comprised generally 24 qīrāts (qīrāt = carat, the weight of a
small pea or bean; Greek κεράτιον, literally "little horn").

works really against him and not for him, for if it was the familiar shekel, and none other, what need was there to define it (with the definite article) and to describe it as consisting of twenty gērāhs? On the contrary, what made it necessary to define the shekel and its equivalent (in gērāhs) was the presence of another mithqāl of different description and quantity.

3. As for the Rabbanites,[7] they identify the gērāh with the *dāniq*, that is to say, the gold dāniq weighing slightly less than five *dirhams*.[8] The answer to their explanation is that dāniq means nothing more than "one-sixth," whether of the dirham or of the dinar, and is actually used for one-sixth of other things, as for example, one-sixth of a ground-lot or of a parcel of land is likewise called a dāniq. Thus when the Rabbanites say that the mithqāl comprises twenty dāniqs, they actually say that it comprises twenty-sixths, which is absurd, since every (unit of) weight can comprise no more than six-sixths.

4. Another argument against Anan's view is the fact that the number of qīrāṭs in the mithqāl varies from place to place. In Baghdad and its vicinity, up to al-Raqqah,[9] (the mithqāl comprises) twenty qīrāṭs; in other places in Syria (it comprises) twenty-two and one-half qīrāṭs; and in still other places, for example al-Ramlah[10] and the whole of Palestine, Egypt, al-Baṣrah,[11] and elsewhere, (it comprises) twenty-four qīrāṭs. Now the Children of Israel, at the time of their sojourn in the wilderness, had come out of Egypt and were on their way to Palestine. Accordingly, the weights familiar

---

[7] Cf. B. Bekh. 50a; M. Kasher, תורה שלמה, XXI, 11 (for further references). In the biblical terminology, 1 Temple shekel = 20 gērāhs (or me'āhs). In Talmudic times, 1 Temple shekel = 1 sela' = 4 dinar (or zūz) = 24 me'āh. Thus 1 dinar comprises 6 me'āh, a me'āh consequently being one-sixth of a dinar and corresponding to the Arabic *dāniq* (Persian *dānāq*), the sixth part of (usually) a dirham.

[8] Gold being heavier than silver.

[9] Town in North-Central Syria, 105 miles east of Aleppo (Ḥalab).

[10] Town west-north-west of Jerusalem, which served as the administrative center of the province of Palestine (Filasṭīn) under Muslim rule.

[11] In Iraq, an important port on the confluence of the Tigris and the Euphrates.

to them must have been those of these two countries. Had Scripture wished, in describing the mithqāl and in defining it in qīrāṭs, to tell them that it was the same as the one familiar to them, it would have defined it in the same qīrāṭs as were familiar to them, namely it would have equated the mithqāl to twenty-four Egyptian qīrāṭs, current in the land they had just left, or (twenty-two and one-half) qīrāṭs, current in the land toward which they were proceeding, rather than to twenty Baghdadi qīrāṭs, current in a land with which they were unfamiliar and which was not their destination or their aim.

5. As for the Scriptural *twenty gērāhs* (Exod. 30:13), we say that it actually means twenty dāniqs of silver, each equal to one-sixth of the dirham, totaling three dirhams and two dāniqs.[12] This is supported by the Scriptural definitions of the *talent*[13] (*kikkār*) — which is the same as the *badrah*[14] — when we are told that the sum total of the ransom money[15] amounted to one hundred talents and 1,775 mithqāls: *And the hundred talents of silver… and… the thousand seven hundred seventy and five shekels* (Exod. 38:27–28), which is equivalent to 301,775 mithqāls, received from 603,550 souls, at the rate of one-half of a mithqāl per soul.

6. In proof of the talent being equivalent to the badrah, it is well-known that the standard[16] blood money for a man is a badrah,[17] and Scripture says, *Then shall thy life be for his life, or*

[12] $3 \times 6 + 2 = 20$.

[13] See below, note 22.

[14] The Arabic term for 10,000 dirhams. Originally probably the word for the bag or purse holding such a sum of money.

[15] Referring to Exod. 30:11: *Then shall they give every man a ransom for his soul unto the Lord, when thou numberest them, that there be no plague among them.*

[16] *ʿAlā al-iqnāʿ*, literally "up to satisfaction," that is to say, of the relatives of the murdered man, and inducing them to give up their right to vengeance.

[17] The original Arab blood ransom (*diyah*) for a slain adult freeman was one hundred camels, for which a monetary *Wergeld* was later substituted, amounting to 1,000 gold dinars or 10,000 silver dirhams (variant: 12,000 dirhams, probably depending on variations in the relative value of gold and silver bullion). See E. Tyan's detailed article in the *Enc. of Islam*, 2nd ed., II, 340–343.

else thou shalt pay a talent of silver (1 Kings 20:39). This is not strong proof,[18] but it is sufficient, since one cannot find fault with it.[19]

Should one ask, where does Scripture mention the dirham, from which we might conclude that there was (among the Jews) such (a weight) as (one-sixth of it, that is to say), a dāniq, we would refer him to the verse, *And weighed him the money, even seven shekels, (equal to) ten silver (dirhams)*[20] (Jer. 32:9): it is true, down to the present day, that seven mitqāls are equal in weight to ten dirhams,[21] using the common mithhqāl. As for the mithqāl of the Sanctuary, equaling three dirhams and two dāniqs, as stated above, since the talent comprises three thousand mithqāls,[22] and each mithqāl comprised three dirhams and two dāniqs, it follows that the talent equals ten thousand dirhams,[23] which is exactly equivalent to the common badrah.

---

[18] Since it is not Pentateuchal, and is based only on a proof-verse from the Historical Books of the Hebrew Bible.

[19] That is to say, it does not contradict anything enjoined in the Torah, nor is it contrary to sound reason.

[20] Jewish Publication Society Version and King James Version: *even seventeen shekels of silver,* which is the usual interpretation of this phrase.

[21] At the rate of 1 dirham = 0.7 mithqāl (see above, note 5).

[22] 50 shekels = 1 mina; 60 minas = 3,000 shekels = 1 talent (in Babylonia 60 shekels = 1 mina; 60 minas = 3,600 shekels = 1 talent).

[23] 3 dirhams and 2 dāniqs = 20 dāniqs; 20 × 3,000 = 60,000 dāniqs = 10,000 dirhams.

AMÉRICO CASTRO AND HIS VIEW OF THE ORIGINS OF THE PUREZA DE SANGRE

By B. Netanyahu

In the final version of his magnum opus, *The Structure of Spanish History* (1954), which appeared in a revised and broadened edition under the name of *The Spaniards*, 1971, and also in his book *De la Edad Conflictiva*, 1961, as well as in several other places, Américo Castro attempted to show that "the concern for being pure in blood (limpio de sangre), which disturbed Christian Spaniards from the fifteenth century on," sprang from sources much older than those usually associated with the Spanish Inquisition, and, moreover, from such that did not originate in Spain altogether. In fact, he says, the "purity of blood" idea, the way it developed and operated in Christian Spain, was rooted not in Spanish, but in Jewish sources.

If the Marranos, then, were discriminated against, were eliminated from positions of honor and income, were refused intermarriage with Old Christians, and were subject to a variety of other abuses, solely on account of their particular race (which allegedly had a "pollutive" quality), and regardless of their position on religious questions (for religiously they may have been good Christians), the fault really lay not with the Spaniards, or rather, with those Spaniards who promoted that idea, but with the forefathers of the Marranos — i.e., the Jews, as well as with the Marranos themselves. For it is the Jews, says Castro, who carried into Spanish society, as soon as they entered it through their conversion, the "Semitic system of purity of lineage"; and thus, "if from the end of the fifteenth century Spaniards considered it infamous to mix with Hispano-Hebrews and Hispano-Moriscos, it is because they had assimilated the Hebrew belief" — the very belief that "had forced the Jews to maintain themselves as a caste apart."[1]

To see this idea in clearer light, one must bear in mind Castro's similar notion regarding the origins of the Spanish Inquisition, namely, that this famous institution, with its principles, guidelines and modes of procedure, was likewise a product of Jewish influences.[2] Both forms of persecution, the religious and the racial, were, according to Castro, alien to the Spanish spirit, but were well within the framework of Jewish law and Jewish social and religious practices. It would seem unnecessary to deal here with Castro's views on the origins of the Inquisition; this has been done by Prof. Baer who convincingly refuted Castro's assertions on this point.[3] Consequently, this study will be limited to an examination of Castro's arguments concerning the origins of the *limpieza*, and, more precisely, to an examination of the evidence on which these arguments rest.

Castro never gave us a systematic exposition of his theory about the rise of the *limpieza* in its totality, but offered it sporadically, point by point, as he came across documents that seemed to him relevant. Viewed in chronological order, however, these documents may be divided into the following three categories: biblical, Talmudic and medieval. We shall start with the biblical.

I. THE BIBLICAL EVIDENCE

By means of this evidence Castro tried to prove the following three points which are related to his thesis: first, that the idea of the Chosen People, as it was expounded in the biblical sources, was integrally bound with the idea of a "closed caste," which called for the Israelites' separation from the rest of mankind; second, that the Israelites effected this separation by pursuing a policy of

---

[1] Américo Castro, *The Spaniards* (Berkeley, 1971), p. 67.

[2] See on this Castro's *España en su historia* (Buenos Aires, 1948), pp. 547–548, and *The Structure of Spanish History* (Princeton, 1954), pp. 534–544.

[3] Y. Baer, *A History of the Jews in Christian Spain* (Philadelphia, 1966), II, pp. 444–456 (Appendix).

racial purity; and third, that their insistence on this kind of purity was exhibited not only in their relations with other nations, but also in their treatment of individuals and groups within their own ranks.

In presenting his views about the idea of the Chosen People, its origin and implications, Castro cites Deuteronomy 7:6, which speaks of the Election of Israel, and interprets that verse as a reflection of the circumstance that certain primitive peoples "assign a magic and spiritual value to blood."[4] The same verse, moreover, indicates, according to Castro, that the Hebrew people regarded the "communion of its 'spiritual' blood in *extreme form*."[5] What is implied in these assertions is that the concept of the Election emerged from a system of blood evaluation that goes back to the traditions of "certain primitive peoples," among whom the Hebrews stood in the forefront.[6] Neither the premises of these major conclusions, nor the chain of deductions that led to them, however, are indicated by Castro either here or elsewhere, and thus we are left with the unenviable task of deriving Castro's views from the verse he referred to. Deuteronomy 7:6, however, resists, as we see it, any attempt at such a derivation. What it says, in plain language, is that, of all the peoples of the world, Israel was chosen by God to be His people, and furthermore that it was "holy to God" — namely, assigned to be dedicated to His service. As for the *cause* of the Election, as indicated by Castro, there is

---

[4] *The Spaniards,* p. 67.

[5] *Ibid., ibid.* (intalization is mine, B. N.)

[6] Castro's general thesis seems to have been influenced by Renan's remarks on the ancient Hebrews' interest in "purity of blood" and their view of themselves as the "elected race" (see his *Études d'histoire religieuse* (Paris, 1864[7]), pp. 89–92; Spanish translation: *Estudios de historia religiosa* (Valencia, 1901), pp. 74–76). His assertions on the beliefs of primitive peoples in the magical and "spiritual" powers of the blood echo statements made to this effect by W. Robertson Smith, *The Religion of the Semites* (London, 1927[3]), especially pp. 313 ff., and J. G. Frazer, *Golden Bough,* Index, v. blood. As far as we know, however, neither these, nor other scholars who dealt with this matter related the primitive notions on blood to the Election idea of the Hebrews.

no reference in that verse to the "magic of the blood," or its "spiritual" value, or anything pointing to a racial source. Indeed, the *cause* of the Election is not suggested in Deuteronomy 7:6 at all.[7]

The biblical Election doctrine is one of the most complex and most elusive of all biblical ideas. It stemmed from two traditions[8] which have never fully merged and left on it forever the mark of dichotomy, and its development, which continued beyond the biblical period, was marked by constant questioning and controversy.[9] Castro gives us no indication that he studied the evolution of this intricate doctrine, or paid any attention to its various transformations. As we have seen, he presented no evidence for his view that it was rooted in some primitive notions about the blood, and we should add that his very formulation of this view indicates reliance on error. Castro identifies "blood" with "race," doubtlessly on the basis of the common usage of the word in Latin and other Western languages, and then relates the primitive notions about "blood" to the ancient Hebrews. But in ancient Hebrew "blood" did not serve to indicate "race" or racial con-

---

[7] Deut. 7:8, however, gives the question "why Israel was elected" a double answer: God's *love* for the people and the *oath* He gave the Patriarchs. But this answer does not forestall the repetition of the same question (now to assume the form of "why the *love* and why the *oath*"), and for this, as well as other reasons, many students of the Bible came to the conclusion that the Election must be ascribed to divine Grace. Among the medieval Jewish scholars who shared this view, most notable were Ibn Ezra (Comm. on Exod. 23:24) and Maimonides (*Iggeret Teman*, c. 1). The latter also stated that we must confess ignorance of the reasons for the Election (*Guide*, II, c. 25).

[8] The Patriarchal and Sinaitic; see on this K. Galling, *Die Erwählungstraditionen Israels* (Giessen, 1928), pp. 26–63.

[9] Among the various works on the subject see, for the biblical period, H. H. Rowley, *The Biblical Election Doctrine* (London, 1950); for the Talmudic period, E. E. Urbach, *The Sages — their Concepts and Beliefs* [Hebrew] (Jerusalem, 1971), pp. 466–494; for the medieval era, I. Heinemann, "Ha-maḥaloket 'al ha-lĕumiyut ba-agada u-va-pilosofia shel yĕmei ha-beinayim," in *Sefer Dinaburg* (Jerusalem, 1949), pp. 100–132, and his articles on Yehuda Halevi in *Zion*, IX (1944), pp. 147–177, and *Kneset*, IX (1945), pp. 163–200. And see on this further below, n. 24.

tinuity; the term used for this purpose in Hebrew was not "blood," but "seed." [10]

Intermarriage

To the biblical Election doctrine, which he thus conceived, Castro ascribed the policy of *pureza* which the Jews allegedly pursued uninterruptedly from ancient times onward. Evidence to this effect was provided, as he saw it, in the prohibitions for the Israelites to intermarry with the Canaanites (Deut. 7:6), and in the severe restrictions imposed on their intermarriage with four of their neighboring nations (Deut. 23:4–10). Contrary to his habit of quoting the sources in evidence, Castro does not cite the above indicated verses; [11] instead he relies on a "summary" by Pulgar, who does not cite them either.

Speaking of the statute established in Guipúzcoa which prohibited Old Christians from intermarrying with New, Pulgar makes one of his paradoxical statements which, while always interesting, are not always true. Castro cites him: "... These people [i.e., the New Christians] are now paying for the prohibition that Moses made to his people that they should not marry Gentiles." [12] Castro believes that Pulgar here offered us a testimony about the origin of the Spanish *limpieza*. [13] As we see it, however, we do not have a "testimony" here, but a typical pointed speculation of Pulgar which was calculated to serve two purposes. On the one hand, it was meant to jab at the Old Christians for following an

---

[10] Also for family and group kinship the term used was not "blood," but "flesh," or, more commonly, "bone and flesh" (see Gen. 29:24; Judges 9:2, and other places). "Blood," it seems, did not signify any ethnic or racial relationship for the Hebrews.

[11] Cf. below, n. 23.

[12] Fernando del Pulgar, *Letras*, ed. J. Domínguez Bordona (Madrid, 1949), p. 138. The words in brackets ("New Christians") are ours (B. N.). Castro put there: "the Jews," evidently as a more striking parallel to the "Gentiles." The fact, however, that we do not deal here with *Jews* but with *New Christians* reflects the special problem of the situation referred to — a problem that could not be resolved or elucidated by Pulgar's remark, as Castro thought.

[13] *The Structure of Spanish History*, p. 531.

old "Jewish" teaching, while grossly violating Christian law;[14] on
the other, to indicate the irony of history reflected in the Statute of
Guipúzcoa, whereby the conversos became subject to the same
discrimination which their forefathers, the Jews, imposed upon the
Gentiles. The analogy, however, was not altogether fitting, nor
was Pulgar's historical observation.

Pulgar interprets the Mosaic prohibition as if it referred to *all*
Gentiles, and not to *specific* Gentile groups that appeared morally
or religiously unacceptable. Thus, he did not view it as a moral or
religious, but as a purely racial injunction. That he so interpreted
it is also evident from the fact that he accused Moses of inconsistency — of not practicing what he himself decreed — for in the
two marriages that Moses *himself* contracted, he took Gentile
women as his wives.[15] The inconsistency, however, was only in
Pulgar's mind, since the two women whom Moses married were
not members of the proscribed nations.[16] Castro fails to note
Pulgar's remark about the alleged contradiction between Moses'
teaching and behavior — a remark which should have prompted
him to look into the matter and discover the true facts. He cites
only Pulgar's general statement to the effect that Moses forbade
the Jews to marry "Gentiles" (seemingly, *all* Gentiles), and
accepts it without any reservation as *representative of the Mosaic
Law*. Furthermore, Castro believed that this prohibition, like all
other Mosaic laws, was binding upon the Jews for all time. This
seemed to supply the necessary proof of what Castro called
the "racial hermeticism" of the Jews, and thus "establish" the
view that the Jewish people was, racially speaking, a "closed
caste."

From all the indications Castro gives us we must conclude that
he virtually believed that the "closed caste" condition represented
the "historical reality" of Jewish life — that the Jews in ancient

---

14 Pulgar, *Letras*, p. 138: "... grand ofensa ficieron a Dios por ordenar en
su iglesia contra su ley."

15 *Ibid., ibid.*

16 See Exod. 2:21 and Num. 12:1.

times actually secluded themselves racially and socially from all other peoples, and continued so doing throughout their history—at least, to the end of the medieval era. That this view is unrealistic with respect to the post-biblical period can readily be taken for granted; but it is doubtlessly wrong or oversimplistic for biblical times as well. Scholars have differed on the extent of intermarriage that took place between the Israelites and their neighbors in Canaan, but, as far as we know, none of them maintained that the Israelites constituted a "closed caste." Against Stade[17] and others who believed that intermarriage between the Israelites and Canaanites was widespread and protracted, Kaufmann recently expressed the view that the Israelites intermarried with their neighbors *outside* Canaan, while generally refraining from intermarrying with the peoples of Canaan itself.[18] It is difficult to maintain Kaufmann's view in the light of Judges 3:5–6 and in light of the tradition which came down to Ezekiel: "Thine origin and thy nativity is of the land of the Canaanite, thy father was the Amorite, and thy mother a Hittite" (Ezek. 16:3).[19] But whatever the measure of truth in that hypothesis, it is clear that intermarriage between Israelites and non-Israelites was going on throughout the period of the First Temple, and hence, that there was no abhorrence in Israel of foreign blood as such, contrary to what we may gather from Castro. Nor could such an attitude develop in a nation whose consciousness bore with equanimity the facts that four of its tribes, including the strongest and most populous, were descendants of mixed blood;[19a] that the "father of its prophets" twice married Gentile women; and that the founder of its hallowed royal dynasty was himself a scion

[17] See B. Stade, *Geschichte des Volkes Israel* (Berlin, 1887), I, p. 111.

[18] Or, more precisely, of the territory conquered by the Israelites; see Y. Kaufmann, *Toledot ha-Emuna ha-Yisrēēlit* (Jerusalem-Tel Aviv, I [3], 1953), pp. 633–637.

[19] Kaufmann's attempt to interpret Ezek. 16:3 and 16:45 as merely disparaging comparisons of the Israelites to the Hittites and the Amorites (see *ibid.*, p. 638) must be regarded as unsuccessful. It fails to take into account the first part of Ezek. 16:3 with its manifest ethnic connotations.

[19a] See Gen. 41:50–52; Gen. 38:2–5 and I Chron. 4:21–23; and Gen. 46:10 and I Chron. 4:24,

of a mixed marriage.[20] The historical reality in ancient Israel did not conform, therefore, to any racial view of the kind indicated by Castro. In consequence, when the law came to establish sanctions against intermarriage with *certain* peoples, it could not appeal to any racial feeling any more than it could to any racial theory.

This brings us to another point that has a bearing on Castro's contentions. To justify its strictures on ethnic intermixture, the Bible offers a variety of reasons which are not identical in all cases. They are religious, moral, historical, or cultural;[21] but they have a common denominator in that they are not racial.[22] This common feature may be seen as part and parcel of the biblical ideology relating to intermarriage. Like Pulgar, however, Castro ignored this ideology as if it were of no significance, assuming perhaps that it merely served as cover for a distasteful racial policy.[23] Even so,

[20] Further testimony to this effect are such facts that Hiram, the builder of the temple in Jerusalem, is presented as the son of a mixed marriage (I Kings 7:14); that Uriah the Hittite, a partner in a mixed marriage, is described as a highly moral person (II Sam. 11:11); that no fault is ascribed to the Davidic dynasty on account of the fact that Rehoboam, King Solomon's son, was also the son of Na῾ama the Ammonite (I Kings 14:21); that the Bible justifies the conspiracy against King Joash which was led by two sons of mixed marriages (II Chron. 24:25–26); and that the majority of Israel is reported to have followed Absalom, likewise the son of a mixed marriage (II Sam. 3:3), in his rebellion against King David, his father (II Sam. 15:13). Additional evidence of similar import may be adduced from other biblical sources.

[21] See Deut. 7:4; 23:5; Exod. 34:16; Num. 31:15–17; Judges 3:6; I Kings 11:1; Ezra 9:14; Nehemia 13:24.

[22] The only possible exception to this rule is the expression *zera῾ ha-kodesh* (commonly translated as the "holy seed") in Ezra 9:2 which seems to have racial overtones and which, in the centuries following Ezra, was interpreted by many, mostly by sectarian zealots and mystics, in a racial sense (see on this, for the period of the Second Temple, Abraham Schalit, *König Herodes* [Berlin, 1968], pp. 483–512). There is no evidence, however, that Ezra himself saw in *zera῾ ha-kodesh* (literally, "seed of holiness") anything more than *zera Elohim* (literally, "seed of God") of Malachi 2:15 — namely, a "seed" designated by divine plan (by the Covenant and the Election) to be dedicated to the service of God (= Holiness).

[23] It is typical of Castro's peculiar approach to the study of this ideology that while he disregarded all biblical passages which give non-racial explana-

it is obvious that this ideology of the Bible is vital for determining the issue at hand. For what we seek to establish is a *medieval* attitude, and the impact of the Bible on its formation, and it is clear that the Bible's justification of its laws — a justification which was taken at its face value in the Middle Ages — was far more influential in shaping views and attitudes than any contradictory fact it may have hidden. What is more, judged by post-biblical developments, the non-racial ideology triumphed in *life* and formed part of the *mainstream* of Jewish thinking.[24] Therefore it is to it, rather than any countercurrent, that Castro should have turned his main attention, if he wished to understand the historic course of Jewry in post-biblical times.

The post-biblical times, however, seem hardly to have entered the sphere of Castro's interests. He completely shut his eyes to the whole body of literature in Hebrew, Aramaic, Greek and Latin, stemming from the period of the Second Temple and the first centuries of the Christian Era, that could have enlightened him so much on the question that concerned him — i.e., the attitude of the Jewish people toward race. He passed in silence over the great drive for proselytization, which the Jews developed from Hasmonean times on, and which made such deep inroads into the Hel-

---

tions to the laws on intermarriage, he presented the controversial verse of Ezra 9:2 as the sole representative of the biblical position. See *The Spaniards*, p. 69.

G. F. Moore's comparison of Ezra's policy of "seperation" to the segregationist policies of Greece and Rome at the time (see his *Judaism*, I [Cambridge, Mass., 1927], pp. 19–21) may serve as a denial of Castro's assumption that Ezra's actions were typically "Semitic." For the extraordinary considerations that prompted Ezra's moves, see S. W. Baron, *A Social and Religious History of the Jews*, I (New York, 1937²), p. 147.

[24] Pointing to the dominant view in "later Judaism" on the issue under discussion, Kaufmann said that it showed the "complete liberation of Judaism from any ethnic attachment" (*Gola ve-nēkhar* [Tel Aviv, 1929], I, p. 226). Though obviously incorrect with respect to Jews who converted to another faith, it is, however, correct with respect to Gentiles who converted to Judaism. And cf. below, n. 28.

lenistic and Roman worlds that it moved a man like Cassius Dio
to state that he could not define what the Jews were, "except to say
that thay are people of different races who follow the laws of the
Jews."[25] This statement alone could have made a shambles of
Castro's theory about the Jews' "closed caste" and their addiction
to "pureza," and it might have deterred him from espousing that
theory, had he duly considered its true meaning and its historical
and social background.[26] Of that background, however, he
seemed unaware. As we indicated, he believed that the laws of the
Old Testament were binding upon the Jews in all places and for all
time, but he failed to note that they became binding in the framework
of the interpretations given them by the Talmudic Sages. He cited
the biblical strictures on intermarriage as proof of the position of
Spain's Jews on race, but he evidently did not know that, for the
Jews of Spain, these laws were no longer valid. For under the great
sweep of the proselytizing movement and the attitude it advocated
for proselytes of all origins, these laws were questioned, amended
and narrowed,[27] so that they were ultimately replaced by new laws
which actually abolished them altogether.[28]

---

[25] Cassius Dio, *History of Rome*, XXXVII, 17.

[26] What it implied, of course, was that, already at the turn of the 2nd
century, owing to the large influx of proselytes, the western segments of the
Jewish people lost all ethnic distinctiveness. On the numerical significance of
that influx, see, among the studies related to this subject, A. Harnack, *The
Expansion of Christianity in the First Three Centuries*, I (New York-London,
1904), pp. 1–12.

[27] See L. M. Epstein, *Marriage Laws in the Bible and the Talmud* (Cambridge,
Mass., 1942), pp. 204–207.

[28] The final position, as formulated by Maimonides, reads as follows:
"... when nowadays a person becomes a proselyte anywhere, whether he is an
Edomite, an Ammonite, a Moabite, an Ethiopian [black], or of any other
nation, and whether male or female, he is permitted to enter the congregation
at once" (*Code*, Holiness, Forbidden Intercouse, xii. 25). An exception was
taken with respect to one nation by Asher b. Yehiel who maintained that,
insofar as the Egyptians were concerned, the old biblical law should be upheld;
see *Turim*, Even Haezer, Hilkhot Pĕriah u-rĕviah, 4.

Siliceo

This voids, we believe, Castro's major claim that Old Christian opposition to intermarriage with Conversos was prompted by the latter's "biblical" traditions. But it still leaves unchallenged his more limited claim that the policy of *pureza* pursued by Cardinal Siliceo with respect to the Church hierarchy in Toledo (1547) was derived from Jewish views recorded in the Bible. The book of Nehemiah, Castro noted, tells us that certain priests in Judea in Nehemiah's time could not establish their priestly origin by means of genealogical records, and were therefore disqualified from the priesthood. Having quoted these passages, Castro exclaims: "Here is the foundation for the statutes of purity of blood in the 16th century, even though no reference is ever made to it, because it is not a pleasing topic for either Christians or Jews. Cardinal Siliceo purged the Cathedral of Toledo of impure priests in accordance with the model of Ezra and Nehemiah."[29]

That no reference had been made (presumably in scholarly literature) to this assumed connection between Ezra and Nehemiah and the actions taken by Cardinal Siliceo against the Conversos, was not owing to the fact, as Castro put it, that "it is not a pleasing topic for either Christians or Jews," but simply because it had occurred to no one that there was any connection there. Scholars may fail, of course, for various reasons, to surmise or notice the true developments, but the tacitness referred to is fully accordant with both the sources and the historical circumstances. As for the sources, they offer no indication that the Cardinal ever appealed to Ezra and Nehemiah for justification of his policy.[30] And as for the circumstances, so different was the condition of Siliceo's Spanish Church, at the height of the powers of the Inquisition and the Empire, from the pitiful state of affairs of

[29] *The Spaniards*, p. 69.

[30] See Balthasar Porreño, *Defensa del Estatuto de limpieza... 1547*, included partly in Ms. 13048 of Bibliotea Nacional, Madrid, ff. 19–28, 38–47. These sections contain the parts of the original arguments of Siliceo and his followers which include references to the Bible.

small Judea, struggling for survival in the days of Ezra and Nehemiah, that it would, it seems, hardly occur to anyone to draw an analogy between the latter and the former.

"The Cardinal," says Castro, "purged the Cathedral of Toledo of impure priests in accordance with the model of Ezra and Nehemiah." But the Cardinal must have known that Ezra and Nehemiah could in no way serve him as a model for his actions simply because their own actions were based on quite a different principle. He was well aware of the fact that from time immemorial it was established in Israel, and in the Law of Israel, that no one could be a member of the priesthood unless descended from a priestly family; and thus it was quite natural for Ezra and Nehemiah — in that period of transmigration and resettlement — to check the records of all those who claimed to be priests. But of what interest could such a procedure be to a Catholic archbishop? Christianity did away with the hereditary principle as far as the Church hierarchy was concerned; its priesthood was appointed, not inherited; and it was meant to include people of all origins, all nations and all classes, chosen solely on the basis of merit. Cardinal Siliceo did not change this principle, nor did he intend to. What led him, then, to apply hereditary considerations to Christians of Jewish origin? Why were the latter alone deprived of the privilege of being appointed to the priesthood on the basis of their merits, and their merits only? There is a question here, of course, that has to be answered; but it cannot be answered by Ezra and Nehemiah.

II. ORIGIN OF *Hidalgo*

If old rabbinic literature is ignored by Castro as the ultimate interpreter of biblical law (as it was, in fact, seen by the Jews of the Middle Ages), it is used by him to prove that the life system of the *hidalguía* followed the pattern of the Jewish nobility. That pattern was indicated, Castro believed, in the Talmudic and Midrashic references to the *běnei tovim* from whom the Spaniards borrowed, as he maintained, the major concepts of their noble class. One of these concepts was the excellence of lineage which they came to cherish as a supreme asset; and from this view of lineage developed, as from a kernel, the *limpieza* philosophy that was to dominate Spain.[31]

It would be difficult to speak of the nobility in Israel, either in the First or the Second Temple period, in the same sense that one speaks of the nobility in Greece, in Rome, or in the post-Roman Western societies. In Israel, as in other nations, social distinctions were determined by wealth, rank and ancestry, but they were facts of life, not of law, for the law allowed no privileges or exemptions in favor of the rich, the prestigious or the famed. It recognized, in fact, no secular noble class, and consequently could not endow such a class with special rights, hereditary or other. Denied a legal and hereditary status, aristocracy in Israel had inevitably to rely, in greater measure than elsewhere, on public opinion.

The *běnei tovim* are generally supposed to have belonged to the Judaean aristocracy in the first centuries of the Christian Era, and Castro, as we noted, believed that they served as the prototype of the Spanish nobility. To prove this, he cited a few rabbinic sources in which the *běnei tovim* are referred to.[32] What we can gather from these references, however, may offer us some clues for hypothetical constructions, but by no means lucid, adequate information about *who* or *what* the *běnei tovim* were. Thus, we may say with reasonable assurance that most of the *běnei tovim* were affluent people or, at least, belonged to affluent families.[33] But we really know nothing about the level of their wealth or about its social and economic foundations.[34] Similarly, we may

---

[31] See his article "Hidalgo: un injerto semítico en la vida española," in *Papeles de Son Aramdans* (Madrid, 1961), Año VI (t. xx, núm. LVIII), pp. 9–21.

[32] *Ibid.*, pp. 12–15.

[33] See Tosefta, Peah, IV.10; P. T. Shekalim, V.4.

[34] From the Tannaitic references to the *běnei tovim*, we may gather that bankruptcy or the loss of property were common phenomena among them (see sources indicated above, n. 33, and see Tosefta, Shekalim 2.16, from which we gather that in every town there was a fund for the "secret" support of poor *běnei tovim*). This seems to indicate that the *běnei tovim*, while they were members of families of means, did not belong to the high aristocracy that could rely on large-scale landed property.

conclude that the *běnei tovim* were known for their fine manners and good upbringing;[35] but again, we do not know how important a role morality played in determining their status. Above all, we are not certain whether the *běnei tovim* or, for that matter, the *tovim* from whom they sprang, are to be identified with the aristocracy as a whole, or whether they merely constituted a common type in the higher social strata (including the upper middle class). It is also possible that they formed some special élite groups which were recognized on a local, if not a national level.[36] If the latter supposition is historically the correct one, these groups must have been related, in some manner, to the *tovei ha'ir* (the "good people of the town").[37]

What could these *běnei tovim*, who lived in Judaea in the first centuries of the Christian Era, have to do with the appearance of the *hidalgos* in Spain eight or nine centuries later? According to Castro, a great deal. He has no doubt that the ancient *běnei tovim* continued to exist as a "class" in the Middle Ages and continued to function in Jewish life in Spain as they did in the preceding centuries. Castro does not offer us any evidence in support of these far-reaching assumptions; and, consequently, we cannot speak, as he does, with such certainty — or, in fact, with any certainty at all — of the "existence of the institution of the *ben tovim* among the Hispano-Hebrews".[38] Castro does not cite even a single Spanish source in which the expression *ben tovim* appears, and from which we could gather anything about the meaning that was associated with it in the thinking of the Spanish Jews. Nor is any study available to us about the various usages of the phrase *ben tovim* and the frequency of its appearance in Spanish Hebrew literature. It remains, therefore, a somewhat ambiguous term, unrelated specifically to Hispano-Jewish life.

If Castro could not prove by direct evidence the existence of the

---

35 See Midrash Rabba, Numbers, 18; Sifrei, Deut. 26.
36 This seems to be suggested by the sources indicated above, n. 34.
37 See Appendix.
38 See his article "Hidalgo," *loc. cit.*, p. 16.

institution of *běnei tovim* in Spanish Jewry, he nevertheless believed that he could prove it indirectly, by pointing to its influence in Spanish society. That this influence was far-reaching, even decisive, was apparent to him from the very word *hidalgo* — the "basic denomination of the Christian noble class"[39] which, he claimed, was nothing but a literal translation of the Hebrew term *ben-tovim*.[40] Moreover, the Spaniards borrowed from the Jews not only the term which signified their nobility, but also the social concepts it denoted. All this is deduced from a linguistic analysis, to which we shall now turn our attention.

Castro tells us that he began to suspect a foreign influence on the formation of the term *hidalgo* when he noticed that the structure of *hijo de algo* is quite uncommon to occidental languages. *Hijo d'algo* means a "person of noble lineage", but "algo" in old Castilian and Portuguese means "material worth, riches, moral worth (bien)."[41] *Hidalgo* (= *hijo d'algo*), therefore, means, literally, "son of worth" (or: of wealth).[42] Yet the Western mind, Castro believed, would not conceive of a "material or moral object" as a "father" of any lineage. On the other hand, Castro found that "the 'filial' manner of designating the condition or quality of a person" is typical of some Semitic languages.[43] He therefore thought that both the name "hidalgo" and the "conception of the reality" from which it sprang "ought to have been Semitic."[44]

On the basis of this general observation Castro built, as we shall see, a specific theory about the way the term *hidalgo* was fashioned. He found Arabic and Hebrew phrases whose components, he thought, were identical with those of the word *hidalgo*. "The Arabic phrase *awlād ni'mati* ("sons of worth")," he believed, "corresponds exactly to the Spanish *fijos dalgo*" which, as he noted,

[39] *Ibid.*, p. 17.
[40] *Ibid.*, p. 12.
[41] *Ibid.*, p. 10.
[42] *The Spaniards*, p. 266.
[43] "Hidalgo," p. 11.
[44] *Ibid.*, p. 10.

has literally the same meaning.[45] Thus we seem to have an Arabic root for the most common Spanish term for "nobleman."

Nevertheless, it is not in the Arabic phrase that Castro saw the *main* root of *hidalgo*. A parallelism for *hidalgo*, Castro believed, can also be seen in the Hebrew term *ben tovim*; and it is to this term that Castro attributed the real origin of the Spanish designation. Of the various reasons which he offers for this preference, we shall first mention the following two: first, unlike the *awlād ni'mati*, but like the *běnei tovim*, the hidalgos formed a "separate social class";[46] second, the *hidlagos* enjoyed privileges and exemptions "in the same fashion" as did the *běnei tovim*.[47] The linguistic parallelism is thus here supported by a social institutional equivalence.

In view of what we know about the ancient Jewish aristocracy, and the *běnei tovim* in particular, this equivalence must, of course, be questioned. The *hidalguía* indeed formed a "separate social class" whose rights and duties were clearly defined, but we have no such clarity about the *běnei tovim* whose status, constituency and class affiliation can only be matters of conjecture. Nor do we have any evidence to the effect that the latter owned privileges recognized by law, and consequently we cannot say that they enjoyed their privileges "in the same fashion" as did the *hidalgos*. Castro is simply investing the *běnei tovim* with some of the social features of the hidalgos; but, socially, he has thus far shown no analogy which could offer support to his thesis.

There remains, therefore, his claim about the linguistic affinity between the terms *hidalgo* and *ben tovim*, and it is indeed on this assumed relationship that his whole theory rests. How true or valid this assumption is, we shall soon be able to see.

Etymologically, Castro proves his claim as follows: "*Tovim* is plural of *tov*, *tuv* (which means wealth [*bienes* in Spanish], good things, riches, property, precious stones)."[48] *Ben tovim,* therefore,

45 *The Spaniards,* p. 271.
46 *Ibid., ibid.*
47 *Ibid.,* p. 270.
48 "Hidalgo," p. 12.

according to Castro, means literally, "son of wealth" or, in Spanish, "*hijo de bienes*". Nevertheless, he noted that the term *ben tovim* is defined in the dictionaries as "a man of good family, of illustrious birth." Castro concluded that while the literal meaning of the Hebrew term corresponds to that of the Spanish ("son of wealth"), its extended definition likewise agrees with the extended definition of *hidalgo*.[49]

In support of this interpretation, Castro tells us that it fully agrees with the one given to *hidalgo* by Spain's famous code, *Las Siete Partidas*. On the one hand, he tells us, the *Partidas* defined *hidalgo* as *hijo de bienes* ("son of wealth"); on the other hand, it stressed his good descent; the *hidalgos*, it says, "were chosen from good places," which Castro explained as "good families" or "good stock."[50] Thus in the *Partidas'* definition of *hidalgo*, two distinct ideas are expressed: the appreciation of "wealth" and the appreciation of "lineage", both of which, he was convinced, were not of Spanish, but of Semitic, or rather Hebrew origin.

This is Castro's main line of thought and, fundamentally, his main proof, which we may now proceed to examine. Before doing so, however, it would be proper to review two supportive arguments he offers to this proof. Apart from completing Castro's case, such a review will show us more clearly the extent to which Castro was committed to his thesis — that is, to his view that the chief ideals of the *hidalguía* were borrowed from Semitic sources. We shall touch, therefore, first upon his supportive argument which relates to the ideal of "lineage," and then upon the other which relates, correspondingly, to the ideal of "wealth."

Buenos lugares

Castro sees in the expression "good places" (*buenos lugares*), which appears in the *Partidas'* definition of "hidalgo," evidence that its author was himself a Jew, or someone inspired by Semitic thought. "It is not human 'occidentally'," Castro tells us, "that a

49 *Ibid., ibid.*
50 *Ibid.*, p. 16.

person be born *from* a *known place* (solar conocido)." "In places,"
Castro says, "plants spring up or houses are built, but, in the
Western world, men will not sprout from their soil." "This," adds
Castro, "happened to Adam who was fashioned from the clay
of the earth."[51] It follows that, in the Semitic world, according to
Castro, "place" is conceived of as the *physical* origin of man and,
therefore, also as his *biological* origin — that is, in the sense of
"family" and "lineage." Appearing in this sense in the definition
of the *Partidas*, the expression "good places" indicates the Semit-
icism, or more precisely, the "Jewishness" of the lineage idea,
which forms the *base* of the *hidalgo* concept.

If at first glance one may still wonder whether so thin a thread
of linguistic conjecture can sustain Castro's far-reaching hypothesis, on closer examination it can be clearly seen that factually
there is no thread here at all. Whatever support may be drawn for
Castro's thesis from Arabic classical literature, neither in Hebrew
nor in Arabic does "place" serve as a synonym for "family,"
and, besides, we have no evidence whatever that the author of the
Partidas knew any of these tongues. In contrast, we do know that
he mastered Latin and must have familiarized himself with Latin
idioms; and in Latin we do find the usage of "place" in a sense
akin to the one we have noted in the *Partidas*. *Infimo loco natus*
(of the lowest descent) and *summo loco natus* (of the highest
descent) are common phrases in Latin literature, and so are
honesto loco natus and *nobili loco ortus*; in all of these expressions,
locus (place) serves as a synonym of family rank, origin, or status.
The author of the *Partidas* may well have used *locus* (lugar) in the
same sense as his Roman models did — that is, to indicate a
family's place in society.[52] So while the influence of Latin here

[51] *Ibid., ibid.*

[52] As a matter of fact, we find in Spanish literature *lugar* in the sense of
family origin as a direct rendition of the Latin *locus* communicating the same
sense. See, for instance, Valerius Maximus' formulation, *De his qui humili loco
nati clari evaserunt* (*Factorum et dictorum memorabilium libri novem*, Berlin,
1854, p. 276, lib. iii, c. 3) translated by Diego de Valera as *De los que nascidos
de bajo lugar fueron fechos claros, excelentes e nobles* ("Espejo de verdadera
Nobleza," in Valera's *Epistolas*, Madrid, 1878, p. 186).

appears likely, or even probable, the influence of Hebrew or Arabic usages is virtually non-apparent.

It follows that the case made by Castro for the Jewish origin of the hidalgo's ideal of "lineage" is, in fact, no case at all. We shall now pass to the argument he presents on behalf of his other assumption — namely, the Semitic origin of the element of "wealth" we find in the *Partidas'* definition of "hidalgo." Castro offers it in connection with a remark made by Ramón Menéndez Pidal with respect to the beginnings of that term.

Bene nati

Pidal surmised that the word *hidalgo*, which first appears in *The Poem of the Cid* (c. 1140), may already be found about a century and a half earlier in a "strange latinized form" in two Leonese documents dated respectively 985 and 1020. The Latin term referred to is *filii bene natorum* ("sons of the well born") and, in both documents mentioned, it served to designate the nobles in the entourage of King Bermudo II of Leon.[53] Pidal may have been prompted to see in this expression a possible representation of *hijos de algo* because the opening words in both the Spanish and Latin phrases have the identical meaning (hijos = filii = sons). On the other hand, he may have considered the Latin form "strange" because he could not find any such parallel in the closing words: *de algo* and *bene natorum*. In any case, Castro, who accepted Pidal's conjecture, thought that he *could* show a parallelism. In the phrase *filii bene natourm*, he said, the "signifying accent falls on the word *bene*" which alluded to the word *bien* in the *Partidas'* definition of *hidalgo*, as well as to the word *bienes* (wealth), which stands for *tovim* in *ben tovim*, according to Castro's above mentioned translation.[54] No wonder, says Castro, that Menéndez Pidal considered the Latin form "strange": he did not know of the Hebrew term *ben tovim*, its meaning and its influence.

---

[53] See R. Menéndez Pidal, *Cantar de mío Cid* (Madrid, 1895), pp. 690–691.

[54] See "Hidalgo," p. 16.

But "those nobles of about the year 1,000 were considered *well born (nacido bien)* because they were *sons of wealth* (hijos de bienes), because they were thus seen by those who... contemplated on the life around them with a Hebrew mentality."[55]

The "Hebrew mentality" which, Castro was certain, was characterized by a passion for material values, had accordingly so influenced the nobles of Spain that it virtually "replaced" their own mentality when they "contemplated on the life around them." And so, when they called themselves "well born," they actually meant to say that they were "born to wealth," the wealth which is the essence of nobility for the Hebrews and the asset most emphasized in their noble's title. One might conclude from this that a forceful alien view came to dominate the thinking of the Spanish nobility, and via the thinking also its actions (some of which influenced so much Spain's history!), unless one realizes that the theory is unsubstantiated — indeed, groundless — etymologically and historically alike.

Castro treats the expression *bene nati* as if it first appeared in 985, or as if it were coined at about that time in a way "unnatural" to Latin. But *bene nati* (well born) is found in Latin works written centuries before the year 985;[56] and in these works the term does not signify — at least not explicitly — *material* value, but generally the "goodness" or luster of descent. Similarly, when the secretary of King Bermudo II used the expression *filii bene natorum* to describe the barons who attended the issuance of decrees by the king in 985 and 1020, he no doubt assumed that his prospective readers would know precisely what *bene nati* meant. It meant *nobles* and nothing but nobles; and this was its meaning at that very time not only in Spain, but also in England and other countries.[57] We may take it for granted, of course, that if the old Latin

[55] *Ibid., ibid.*

[56] See, e.g., Ennodius, lib. 3, epistles 16, 17; *Novellae*, 78, cap. 2, 1; *Vita S. Caesarii Episcopi Arelatensis* by Messianus and Stephanus, in Migne, *Patrologia Latina*, vol. 67, p. 1028.

[57] Thus the Anglo-Saxon translations of the Bible present *nobilis* by *welboren* = wellborn (see the *Lindisfarne Gospels* rendition of Luke xix:12) and *nobiles* by

authors and the contemporary ones in England and Northern Europe used the adverb *bene* ("well") as suggestive of wealth (and wealth may have been occasionally in their mind as one of the common features of the "wellborn"), they did not do so under the influence of the Hebrew term *ben tovim*, but under the impact of the traditions associated with this concept which go back to early Antiquity.[58]

It is clear, then, that the two marginal arguments with which Castro sought to bolster his thesis offered it no real support. But his *main* proof, we must add, is no better founded. There are simply no grounds for his insistence that *hidalgo* stemmed from the Hebrew *běnei tovim*. His understanding of the literal meaning of the phrase was, from the outset, patently wrong, and it was on this unfortunate misapprehension that his whole theory was originally founded. It is distressing to go into such elementary demonstrations, but what choice do we have in this case? *Tovim* is *not* the plural of "tov" or "tuv," as Castro says, but of "tov" only. "Tuv" may indeed be understood as "wealth" or "riches" or "property" and the like; but "tov" must be translated essentially as "good," and "tovim", in the term under discussion, means literally only "good people" and in no way "riches," "possessions" and the like. *Běnei tovim*, therefore, means "sons of good people," and Castro's assumption that it means "sons of wealth" must be rejected as a glaring error, and with it we must reject also his notion that *hidalgo* was a translation from the Hebrew.

Hidalgos and běnei tovim: Fundamental Differences

It may, perhaps, be argued that, despite his mistranslations and erroneous etymological deductions, Castro hit upon something

---

welborene (in Aelfric's rendition of the Vulgate, Deut. 1:15). These translations date respectively from approximately 950 and 1,000 — that is, from the very time in which the documents cited by Pidal were written (985 and 1020).

[58] The Greek prototype of *bene natus* — εὐγενὲς — is found in Homer, Aeschylos, and other Greek authors. See Little-Scott-Jones, I, 708 (v. εὐγενέτης, εὐγενὲς).

fundamentally true. After all, the *běnei tovim* did come from families that were economically sound or affluent; and so did the *hidalgos*; their social status was based, at least partly, on an honorable and reputable descent, as their very name "běnei tovim" indicates; such, also, was the status of the *hidalgos*; and the *běnei tovim* were expected to be virtuous and well-mannered, following the moral principles of their ancestors — again, just like the *hidalgos*. Thus we have here an array of similarities which entitle one to consider the possibility that one institution — i.e., the older — influenced the rise of the other — the younger. A careful consideration of this possibility, however, must lead us to a negative conclusion.

For the similarities indicated can be found, we should say, not only in the *hidalgos* and the *běnei tovim*, but also in all aristocratic groups of whatever nation or society. Wealth, virtue and praiseworthy ancestry were the hallmarks of nobility in all places and at all times, and this was already pointed out by Aristotle on the basis of common observation. Some people "are thought noble," Aristotle tells us, "because they spring from wealthy and virtuous ancestors."[59] Thus we have here the essential characteristics of both the *běnei tovim* and the *hidalgos*. Indeed, what we have here is the common denominator of all *élite secular groups*. To prove his thesis that one of these groups (i.e., the *hidalgos*) was specifically modelled on another (i.e., in this instance, the *běnei tovim*), Castro should have shown, beyond the aforesaid similarities, some distinct features which were shared by the "hidalgos" and the "bênei tovim" *only* — features which would have distinguished them as groups apart from all other aristocratic bodies. Castro failed to show such common traits, however, perhaps because there were none to be found, which means that he failed to present an analogy that might be suggestive of his contention.

Moreover, Castro ignored some basic differences between the *hidalgos* and the *běnei tovim* — differences that virtually exclude the assumption that the latter served as a model for the former.

[59] *Politica*, V. i (1301b).

To begin with, we must consider the place which *lineage* occupied in the lives of both groups. The *Partidas* tell us that the *hidalguía* was "*a nobility that comes to people by lineage.*"[60] And indeed, from its inception to its dissolution, the life of the *hidalgo* was governed by that principle (i.e., the lineage principle) in a way that bears hardly any resemblance to that of the Hebrew aristocrats. Most significantly, according to the *Partidas*, a *hidalgo* (or a *hidalga*) forfeits the nobility of his (or her) offspring by marriage to a commoner.[61] No such limitations existed in Jewish life and we know of no *běnei tovim* who were of a "pure" or an "impure caste," as Castro suggests.[62] Nor was there in Israel any legal basis for a prohibition of class intermarriage. Lineage simply never played *such* a role in the social life of the Jews.

But just as the *hidalgo* differed from the *ben tovim* with respect to lineage (which is, for Castro's thesis, the decisive issue), so he differed from him with respect to other matters, including the most fundamental principles of conduct. For everything the *hidalgo* did, or was expected to do, was geared to serve one overall purpose: to meet the exigencies of war. Thus, if the *hidalgos* were supposed to be distinguished, among other things, in the "four virtues,"[63] it was because without them, as the *Partidas* tell us, they could not "best maintain the condition of defense for which they were appointed."[64] If they were to be faithful, loyal, dexterous and cunning, firm and, if need be, pitiless, it was because all these qualities were vital to men engaged in war and dedicated to its art.[65] In brief, their entire way of life and all their ideals were suited to the needs of superb fighting men or, as the *Partidas* put it, "for men who were entering upon a career of death."[66] But this

---

60 *Partidas*, tit. xxi, law 3.
61 *Ibid.*
62 "Hidalgo," p. 16.
63 *Partidas*, tit. xxi, law 4 (prudence, fortitude, temperance, justice).
64 *Ibid., ibid.*, end of law 4.
65 *Ibid., ibid.*, laws 9, 8, 12, 5.
66 *Ibid., ibid.*, law 13 (end).

was not the career upon which the Jewish aristocrat of Spain entered, or the one who was known in old Judaea by the designation of *ben tovim*. The latter's moral concepts and ideals of life were predicated on quite different foundations.

Since these conclusions appear inescapable, we remain with the commonly held view, formed long ago by medieval scholars, about the rise and development of the *hidalguía*. The Spanish *hidalgo*, like the French chevalier, the German Ritter and the English knight, was essentially a product of medieval warfare, of the feudal system and the ideal of nobility as it developed in Western Europe. We see nothing in the *hidalgo's* foundations of life that could be borrowed from the Spanish Jewish aristocracy, and nothing that Castro has said or pointed out leads us to change this opinion.

III.   THE MEDIEVAL EVIDENCE

1. *Santob*

If we now turn to the evidence Castro adduces from Spanish Jewish sources, we notice that it consists of no more than four documents, two in Castilian and two in Hebrew, all of which were composed within a century and a half, from 1275 to 1425. Of the Castilian documents, the first, chronologically, is included in a collection of didactic poems known as *Proverbios Morales*. The collection was made public c. 1350 and its author was Rabbi Shem-Tov ben Ardutiel, better known as Don Santob de Carrión.

The *Proverbios* do not deal with such matters as intermarriage, but they occasionally touch upon the theme of the *hidalgo*, and on these occasions they show, according to Castro, that the Spanish Jews attached special importance to the ideas of "lineage" and "nobility." In Castro's opinion, these two concepts were inseparable in the thinking of the Jew. The value of "nobility" was determined for the Jew by the significance he attributed to "lineage," and this, in turn, was determined by his view of "race" and his appreciation of "purity of blood." In Castro's opinion, Santob's *Proverbios* show us that the Spanish Jew upheld that racial set of values and that he "sensed and expressed it with such a force as later did the Christian."[67]

Castro quotes a passage from the *Proverbios* which is supposed to demonstrate this assumption. The crucial part of this passage is the following stanza:

> Fidalgo de natura,
> usado de franqueza,
> e trajol la ventura
> a mano de vileza![68]

In these verses, Castro believed, the poet gave expression to the admiration for nobility which was so deep-rooted in Jewish thinking, and also to his "distress" that the existence of the Jew, the "nobleman by birth," came to be dependent on the men of "low birth," i.e., the Gentiles.[69] In *De la Edad Conflictiva* Castro explains to us that the Jew "considered himself as a *hidalgo* by nature," because he saw himself as a member of a unique people, "the people whom God elected to be His."[70] He further tells us that when Santob wrote those verses (about the nobleman being subjected to a "peasant"), he also "doubtlessly thought of himself"; and thus what they express is not only a collective, but also a personal experience.[71] In sum, according to Castro, what these verses reflect is the Jew's consciousness of the conflict between "his own worth" and "society's resistance against recognizing it."[72]

Where did Castro get the necessary evidence for this double assumption of his? We truly do not know. We do not find any grounds in the *Proverbios* for the assertion that, in the "nobleman," whose fate Santob bemoaned, he was actually portraying himself; and we know nothing about his life from other sources that might

[67] *De la Edad Conflictiva* (Madrid, 1961²), p. 159.

[68] "A hidalgo by nature, /accustomed to giving freely, /was dragged by Chance into the hands of infamy." See Santob de Carrión, *Proverbios Morales,* ed. Ignacio González Llubera (Cambridge, 1947), lines 801–802.

[69] *The Structure of Spanish History,* p. 558.

[70] *De la Edad Conflictiva,* p. 159.

[71] *Ibid., ibid.*

[72] *The Structure,* p. 557.

lead us to conclude that this man, who bore the proud name of Don Santob de Carrión, was ever at the mercy of "villeins" or "peasants." Similarly, the contention that the phrase "nobleman by nature" was intended to indicate the "chosen people," as against the rest of the world which was "naturally" ignoble, goes against the grain of the Election concept which was postulated not on *superiority by nature*, but on superiority by divine choice; and this is quite a different matter. Also, the idea that "fate" (or "chance") had dragged the Jews into the hands of the "villeins" (presumably, the Gentile nations) is not precisely in accord with the conviction of the Jews who believed that it was God (not fate) and, of course, their "sins" (hence their "bad conduct," and not "bad luck") that were responsible for their condition.[73] In fact, this whole cluster of words — "chance," "nature" and "nobility by nature" — does not reflect typical "Jewish" concepts and therefore cannot serve as "obvious" allusions to the Jewish people as such. Consequently, they could not lead Santob's readers to assume that they imply the meaning indicated by Castro.

If the first phrase in the stanza raises doubts about its applicability to the Jews, the second only serves to increase these doubts. "Usado de franqueza" is supposed to indicate an essential characteristic of our "nobleman by nature." But what does it actually mean? It may be understood in either of two senses: it may signify "used to liberties and exemptions," or it may indicate "accustomed to giving freely." Juan Guzmán Álvarez, the latest editor of the *Proverbios*, explains it in the first sense.[74] Castro translates it according to the second.[75]

---

[73] The term *zĕman* (literally, "time") in the sense of "fate," or the unpredictable occurences of time, is commonly used in Spanish Hebrew poetry as indicative of a factor determining man's condition. But in the "sacred" poetry which deals with the historical condition of the Jews, *zĕman* is mentioned only on rare occasions, and then it appears as the cause of some troublesome vicissitudes, but not as the factor that brought about the downfall of the Jewish people.

[74] See Sem Tob de Carrión, *Proverbios Morales*, ed. J. Guzmán Álvarez (Salamanca, 1970), p. 16.

[75] *The Structure*, p. 557.

I believe that Castro's translation is the correct one (as we shall later prove); but if so, what does this characterization have to do with the particular condition of the Jews? To be sure, alms-giving to the poor was urged upon the Jews by all their moral teachers from the prophets on, but the "custom of giving freely," of which Santob speaks, referred not to a teaching, but to a practice, and to one which distinguished the "nobleman" from all others, and especially from those far below him in rank. If we follow Castro's interpretation to its conclusion, the Jews (collectively) were supposed to have exhibited a good deal of generosity toward the Gentiles (that is, before they became subject to the latter), while the Gentiles, when in control of the Jews, always treated them stingily, as peasants do. It is difficult to prove that this set of ideas — in themselves debatable and not precisely true — was, on this occasion, in the poet's mind. It also remains inexplicable why, of all the misfortunes that befell the Jews in their exile, and of all the tragic elements in their condition, Santob chose their subjection to "miserliness" (as contrasted to their own alleged "liberality") to demonstrate their worst plight. Castro, who usually dwells on every word of the texts he cites in support of his theories, passes in silence over the problematic phrase *usado de franqueza*, as if it were marginal to the discussion. But the phrase is central to Santob's description of the *hidalgo* and conveys an idea integrally related to the concept of the nobleman he seeks to present.

In view of the above, it appears probable indeed that Castro's interpretation is altogether wrong, and this probability turns into a certainty when we discover the source of Santob's thought. Like most of the ideas of the *Proverbios Morales*, it was borrowed from one of the collections of aphorisms that Santob freely used for his versified compositions. As Leopold Stein convincingly demonstrated, what we have before us is merely a replica of an idea expressed in the *Choice of Pearls*,[76] a collection of moral sayings derived from many sources (Jewish, Arabic and Greek) which is

---

[76] See Leopold Stein, *Untersuchungen über die Proberbios Morales von Santob de Carrion* (Berlin, 1900), pp. 83–84.

available in a Hebrew translation from the Arabic by Judah
ibn Tibbon and which, despite some uncertainty, most scholars
believe to have been composed by Solomon ben Gabirol.[77]

It should be noted that Santob's proverb does not deal only with
a nobleman's plight. It points out three tragic situations which, in
the opinion of the author, deserve everybody's commiseration.
These situations occur when (a) a nobleman becomes subject to a
peasant, (b) a just man falls into the hands of a wicked person, and
(c) a wise man becomes the servant of a fool.[78] The motif, which
goes back to Arabic sources, is also found in the writings of
Petrus Alphonsus (a younger contemporary of Ibn Gabirol), as well
as in the *Bocados de Oro*, a thirteenth century Spanish translation
from the Arabic of a collection of epigrams.[79] Santob may have been
aware of these and other versions of the same thought; but the
text which he followed and which inspired his muse, was clearly
that of the *Choice of Pearls*. It is only when we recognize this fact
that we can understand Santob's particular presentation.

It may seem strange that while Santob dealt briefly, as the
Choice did, with the themes of the wealthy and the wise man,
unlike the *Choice*, he devoted two full stanzas to the *hidalgo*.
Castro would have argued (it seems almost certain) that Santob's
elaboration on the theme of the *hidalgo* shows the poet's (or the
Jew's) special interest in the subject. But this is not what a careful
reading of the poem leads us to believe. Let us consider the first
of the two stanzas:

---

[77] On the sources of the *Choice* see Stein, *op. cit.*, pp. 35–36; on the provenance of the work, see Alexander Marx, "Gabirol's Authorship of the Choice
of Pearls," *HUCA*, IV (1927), pp. 433–448, and A. M. Habermann, his ed. of
Mivḥar ha-Pĕninim, 1947, Epilogue. It is not unlikely that Santob believed in
Gabirol's authorship of the *Choice*. The tradition about this authorship goes
back to Joseph ben Isaac Kimhi whose poetical rendition of the *Choice* must
have been known to Santob, undoubtedly an expert on gnomic literature.

[78] The Hebrew version of the saying in Ibn Tibbon's translation reads:
שלשה דברים ראוי לחמול עליהם מכל אדם. דעתן שמנהיג [אותו] משוגע. וצדיק
שמושל בו רשע. ונדיב שהוא צריך לנבל. See *A Choice of Pearls* by Salomon ibn
Gabirol, ed. B. H. Ascher (London, 1859), no. 488 (p. 96).

[79] See Stein, *op. cit.*, pp. 84–85.

> Fidalgo que menester
> Ha al honbre villano
> Y con mengua meter
> Se viene so su mano.[80]

Prima facie, it would appear that the basic idea (of a nobleman who must resort to a villein) is already expressed in this first stanza, so that the second, quoted earlier,[80a] appears superfluous; but if we examine the Hebrew source more closely, we soon see that this is not the case. Santob obviously struggled with the problem of how to present in rhymed Spanish verse all the shades of thought he found expressed in the original. He produced two formulations of the same idea, neither of which satisfied him completely, because neither expressed Gabirol's thought fully; and so he decided to keep them both. While the first formulation (the first stanza), presents the *core* of the problem discussed (a nobleman's need of a peasant), it missess the fullness of the contrast between the two, and thus does not suggest the full depth of the nobleman's misfortune.

Santob's main difficulty lay in the need to transmit the connotation of the Hebrew term *nadiv* which Ascher translated into English as *noble-minded* and Stein into German as *Edler*.[81] In like manner, Santob translated it in the first stanza, as we have seen, by *hidalgo*.[82] Yet this embodied only *one* sense of the term, the one which appears in such biblical verses as I Samuel 2:8 and Numbers 21:18 (where *nadiv* is a synonym of nobleman = a people's leader). The other sense was that of the *generous giver*, whose giving comes not from habit or duty, but from goodness of heart, from natural disposition. Santob wanted to explain to his readers what kind of *hidalgo* he was speaking of — an *hidalgo* whose magnanimity was part of his nature. The importance of this dis-

---

[80] "An hidalgo who is in need/ of a rustic person/ and out of want/ puts himself in his hands." See Llubera's ed., lines 799–800.

[80a] See above, note 68.

[81] See Ascher, *op. cit.*, p. 97; Stein, *op. cit.*, p. 84.

[82] See above, n. 80.

position loomed large to him, not only because it was so intimately related to Ibn Gabirol's *main* idea, or rather, to that idea in Ibn Tibbon's translation, but also because it was contrasted in that translation with the quality which is its very opposite. Opposed to the *nadiv* in the Hebrew aphorism is the *naval*, and the *naval* is not only a stingy person, but an outrageously evil one. Santob was thinking of all the aspects of the *naval*, represented in the abstract by the Hebrew word *nevala*,[83] when he translated the latter into the Spanish *vileza*. In short, while in the first stanza Santob tells us how dire need brought a nobleman to subject himself to a peasant, in the second he gives us the full sense of the conflict when he confronts natural largesse with vicious miserliness.

This is the explanation of the rather expanded presentation of Ibn Gabirol's brief saying. By deeply delving into the meaning of every word of his Hebrew counterpart, Santob broadened his poetic sweep and gave full expression to Gabirol's idea. What we have here, then, is no more and no less than an inspired translation of Gabirol's words with an attempt to communicate his ideas faithfully. But just as Gabirol did not refer in his saying to a particularly Jewish phenomenon, neither did Santob de Carrión. There is no discussion here, as Castro imagined, of the Jew who is noble by nature against the Gentile who is ignoble by birth. Here, quite evidently, Santob is commenting on phenomena of a different order, phenomena that belong to all nations and are observable in all societies.

Consequently, the aforementioned verses do not reflect the Jews' infatuation with "lineage and nobility," as Castro thought. Nor do we find evidence of this elsewhere in the *Proverbios*. Among Santob's many counsels and reflections on man's life, not one points out the significance of "ancestry" or rather, of "illustrious" ancestors, or the need of maintaining "purity of blood lines." Neither does he uphold such values as "wealth," which were usually associated with nobility. On the contrary, wealth is presented by him as ephemeral, as a doubtful asset on which a wise

83 Cf. I Sam. 25:25; Isaiah 32:6.

man should not count.[84] The aspiration for high social status is likewise devalued by Santob's pointed observation that the "higher they climb, the harder they fall."[85] Nowhere do we see in Santob's work a reflection of the "punctilious sense of honour" that Castro saw in it.[86] Instead, we find him preaching "humility," which is so highly praised in Jewish moral teachings.[87] Even when catalogued according to subject and considered from a purely quantitative standpoint, Santob's proverbs fail to support Castro's thesis. Of the 2743 verses of the *Proverbios*, only two more brief passages, besides the one cited,[88] discuss the *hidalgo*, or the "noble" person. Where, then, are the signs of the "Jewish preoccupation" with this particular subject? We find no such signs in the *Proverbios*! Castro's attempt, therefore, to present Santob's poetry as reflecting the Jewish *infatuation with lineage* must be regarded as a failure.

2. *Arragel*

We shall now turn to another Jewish author who, like Santob, wrote in Spanish and in whose work Castro found additional evidence for the validity of his theory. I refer to Rabbi Moses Arragel who, between 1423 and 1433, translated the Bible into Castilian, and also composed a Castilian commentary on it, at the request of Don Luis de Guzmán, the Grand Master of the Order of Calatrava.[89] Beyond this fact and a few more items that we can glean from his exchange of letters with the Master, we know nothing about Arragel's life, nor of his activity as a Jewish scholar. To be sure, Guzmán says that Arragel was spoken of as "very

---

[84] See Llubera's ed. of the *Proverbios*, lines 607–636.

[85] See *ibid., ibid.*, and lines 67–90.

[86] As was correctly noted by Guzmán Álvarez in his introduction to the *Proverbios*, 1970, p. 16. And cf. *The Structure*, p. 557.

[87] *Proverbios*, ed. Llubera, lines 637–654.

[88] *Ibid.*, lines 577–584 (Álvarez has here *notable* instead of *noble*; see his edition, verse 1064 . And see also Álvarez' ed., verses 1616–1623).

[89] *Biblia* (*Antiguo Testamento*), translated by R. Moses Arragel of Guadalfajara, published by the Duke of Berwick and Alba (Madrid, 1918–1921), I, p.1 (cited below as *Biblia*).

learned in the law of the Jews,"[90] but Arragel himself belittled this "rumor" and insisted on his "inadequacy" as a scholar and his "unworthiness" to be entrusted with the translation of the Bible.[91] Since Hebrew literature bears no trace of Arragel's activity or even existence, we shall probably not be wrong in concluding that Arragel was not widely known as a scholar, and that his self-evaluation, while over-critical, was, nevertheless, fundamentally correct. Arragel was, in fact, unequal to the task. He was, to be sure, a learned man, but his learning lacked depth and his style inspiration. His translation of the Bible is too pedestrian, while his commentary appears pale and shallow, and altogether over-popular. Perhaps his annotations yield this impression partly because of his self-imposed limitations: his eagerness to please his Christian lords, or his desire not to displease them. He dodged many issues which could be embarrassing to a Christian, and often phrased his comments in such terms as to blur the contrast between Judaism and Christianity. Antonio Paz y Mélia, who studied the commentary, points out, quite correctly, the "docility of the Jew" in stating opinions "dictated by his censors" and in "temporizing with the ideas of his lord, Don Luis de Guzmán."[92] This does not mean, of course, that Arragel's work has no historical value, or does not mirror views that prevailed among Spain's Jews; but obviously, we must use it with great caution. We cannot take it as a true, free expression of Spanish Jewish opinion.

From Arragel's commentary, Castro cites a passage which, in his judgment, reflects the view of race that he attributed to the "Hispano-Hebrews." The comment in question is on Ezra,

---

[90] *Ibid., ibid.*

[91] *Ibid.*, p. 2 (Ch. I: "... *concluyo que en la tu villa de Maqueda, sy de mi sson imprenssionados yo ssabio ser, yo como que cognosco la mi insuficençia e indignidat...*" . He repeats this at the end of the same chapter: "cognosco la mi insufiçençia," p. 2, and in Chapter XV, p. 13.

[92] See "La Biblia puesta enromance por Rabi Mose Arragel de Guadalfajara," in *Homenaje a Menéndez y Pelayo* (Madrid, 1899), II, pp. 24, 26 (also appears in English translation as introduction to the *Biblia* of the Duke of Alba).

Chapter 9, which deals with intermarriage of Israelites with other peoples. Arragel says that from this chapter we gather that "he who takes a *wife* from an alien nation causes much sorrow and anger to God."[93] He further notes that Solomon "took wives from alien nations," and that this fact "caused all the woe of Israel and their falling into captivity."[94] He also asserts that Ezra said (explicitly!) that "the sin of *sleeping* with women of other nations and begetting sons upon them was alone sufficient [justification] that no remnant of Israel should survive."[95] Castro, after citing the latter remark, with the omission of the words "and begetting sons upon them," concludes: "It is clear that long before Christian literature talks of 'purity of blood', the concern over maintaining that purity was con-substantial with the very existence of the Hebrew."[96]

What Arragel was talking about was indeed a relationship that concerned Spain's Jews long before Christian literature in Spain began to talk of "purity of blood." But that relationship had nothing to do with "blood," or any other biological factor, and as such it concerned Arragel's Christian no less than Jewish contemporaries. Moreover, it concerned both Jews and Christians centuries before and after his time. For what he was talking about was simply the prohibition against Jews marrying and cohabiting with Christians, a prohibition that, in Christendom, was expressed in harsh laws more than a thousand years before Arragel's time,[97]

[93] *Biblia*, II, p. 868 (note 33): quien toma muger de agenas nasciones... fase muy fuerte pesar e enojo a Dios.

[94] *Ibid., ibid.*

[95] *Ibid.*: e dijo que solo este pecado de dormir con mugeres de otras nasçiones e en ellas fijos engendrar era bastante para que en Israhel non quedase ningund remanente.

[96] *The Spaniards*, p. 69, n. 35.

[97] As is known, it was Emperor Constantius I who issued (in 339) the first law forbidding Jews to marry Christian women under the penalty of death to both spouses; and it was Theodosius I who broadened that law so that it included, under the same penalty, also the marriage of Jewesses to Christians. See on this, and some of the subsequent developments, J. Juster, *Les Juifs dans l'empire Romain*, II (Paris, 1914), pp. 47–48.

and in Judaism, still earlier.[98] None of these laws, however, had any force or meaning in Christendom for *ex*-Jews who turned Christian, or in Jewry for *ex*-Christians who became Jews, which makes it quite obvious that the purpose of these laws was, on both sides, to guard, not the purity of race, but the purity of religion — or the religious uniformity, unity and wholesomeness of the communities involved.

Castro simply misunderstands Arragel when he reads racial arguments into his comments. Perhaps what misled him was Arragel's repeated use of the term "alien nations" (instead of "alien religions") to indicate the prohibited spheres of relationship. But to Arragel, who discussed the matter from *his* standpoint — that is, from the standpoint of rabbinic law, "alien nations" and "alien religions" were co-extensive and threfore interchangeable. More precisely, he knew that, according to Jewish law, a Gentile, once converted to Judaism, becomes *ipso facto* a member of the Jewish nation, while as long as he remains *unconverted* to Judaism, he cannot but be a member of an "alien nation." By using the latter term, Arragel, as a Jew, did not bend the truth or compromise his conscience, even though he was fully aware of the fact that, insofar as Jewish law was concerned, what prevented "aliens" from cohabiting with Jews was not their different race, but their different religion.

In a country where not only Christians were forbidden to convert to Judaism (under penalty of death), but also Moslems (under penalty of slaveiy),[99] a Jew who addressed himself to Christian readers would naturally refrain from saying anything that might be viewed, or interpreted, as advocating proselytization. And so Rabbi Arragel was reluctant to state that Jews were forbidden to take women from other nations *unless they were*

[98] Jewish law, however, committed the Jewish culprits neither to death, nor to excommunication (as did several Christian Councils — such as that of Orléans, 533, and Rome, 743 — for Christian offenders), but to flagellation; yet it permitted zealots to kill a Jew if, and while, he copulated with a gentile woman "publicly." On the other hand, the gentile partners were subject do the death penalty (the man only if he slept with a *married* Jewess). See Maimonides, Forbidden Intercourse, XII, 1–5, 9–10; and see below, n. 104.

[99] See Baer, *Die Juden im christlichen Spanien*, II (Berlin, 1936), p. 49.

converted to Judaism, for such a provision might be interpreted by some as an encouragement or invitation for non-Jews to become Jews, which would place the law of Moses in direct conflict with the laws of Spain. Obviously, Arragel sough⁴ to avoid, as much as possible, the suggestion of such conflicts, and tried to circumvent the difficulty in question by ignoring the above-mentioned provision. For the same reason, we may assume, he did not use the term "heathen," as Rashi did, to define the "peoples of the lands." [100] Such a term would have either indicated that Ezra's prohibition applied to "heathen" *only,* and not to Christians and Moslems (which would be untrue from the standpoint of Jewish law), or it would have suggested that Christians, too, were defined by Jewish law as "heathen" — which would have been offensive to the Christians and, consequently, damaging to the Jews. To avoid both horns of the dilemma, Arragel used the term "alien nations" [101] — a term which would make him more acceptable to the Christians without rendering him less acceptable to the Jews.

That he was trying to please his Christian readers may also be gathered from another word which he employed in the same comment. As we have noted, Arragel came out, first, against the crime of "marrying women from alien nations," and then against the crime of "sleeping" with them; and it is in connection with the latter transgression that he attributed to Ezra the statement that "it alone was sufficient for Israel to deserve annihilation." Ezra, however, did not speak of *this* transgression (i.e., of "sleeping" with foreign women). He clearly and exclusively referred to *intermarriage,* [102] and it is the crime of intermarriage that he considered so grave as to justify the aforementioned punishment. [103] What, then, moved Arragel to go beyond the text and thus double

100 See Rashi on Ezra 9:2.

101 Which he could also justify by its similarity to Ezra's term: "the peoples of the lands" (Ezra 9:1, 2, 11).

102 See his three statements on the subject in Ezra 9:2, 12, 14. Nehemiah, too, complained of *intermarriage,* and not of extra-marital relations, as is evident from Nehemiah 13:25. The term *hoshivu nashim,* used in Neh. 13:23, is therefore correctly interpreted by Rashi as "married."

103 See Ezra 9:14.

the target of Ezra's denunciation? No doubt Arragel bore in mind the fact that Rabbinic law did not recognize intermarriage, whereas it sharply reproved and formally prohibited sexual relations between Jews and non-Jews.[104] But, it also stands to reason, Arragel did not want his Christian readers to assume that Ezra's famous prohibition did not apply to *extra*-marital relations between Jews and "alien" women — relations which the Christians and Christian law in Spain viewed as abhorrent and intolerable. By lumping together *all* relations with "foreign women" and by treating them as crimes of equal severity, Arragel, in all likelihood, wished to show that the Mosaic — or Jewish — law was, in this instance, in general agreement with the Christian law.

Whatever the reason for that interpolation on "sleeping with women from alien nations," it is clear that, in making it, Arragel did not espouse a policy of "racial purity," just as he did not do so in his remarks on Ezra's prohibition on intermarriage. We have seen that, in support of the latter prohibition, he mentioned the sin of Solomon and the disaster that ensued;[105] and the nature of that sin was, of course, known to every reader of the Bible: the "alien women" that Solomon married *worshipped foreign gods* and *seduced him to support that worship*;[106] his crime, therefore, was religious, not racial.[107] In like manner, when Arragel discusses the misdeed of "sleeping with women of alien nations," he had a *religious* transgression in mind. This is evident from his comment on Malachi 2:11, where the prophet denounces sexual intercourse between an Israelite and a "daughter of a foreign god." Arragel says there: "The text goes on to reveal how Judah and... Israel *slept with alien women*, that is, *we have to note*, who served alien gods."[108]

104 See Maimonides, *Code, loc. cit.*, c. xii, 2, 4, 7.

105 See above, notes 93 and 94.

106 I Kings 11:4–8.

107 In referring to Solomon in this connection, Arragel of course followed Nehemiah (13:26) who likewise emphasized the religious reason for the prohibition on intermarriage.

108 *Biblia*, II, p. 454 (n. 20): ... e va declarando el testo como Iuda e los diez tribus de Israhel durmieron con agenas mugeres, es de notar, *que servieron a agenos dioses* (italization is mine, B. N.).

So "sleeping with alien women," like marrying them, is to Arragel a *religious* crime, and by no means one of racial import; and he made it crystal clear in his "note" to the effect that the term "alien women" (used by Nehemiah) means "women who wor-shipped alien gods."

If carnal attachment to "alien women" by an Israelite is for-bidden for clearly religious reasons (for these women, as we have seen, may seduce the Israelites to follow their faith, their worship and their customs), what about "begetting sons upon them," which Arragel censured as a consequence of that attachment, or perhaps as an independent crime? It is probable that in this latter censure which, although he did not cite, he undoubtedly noticed, Castro saw a clearly racial motivation — a refusal to bring into the Jewish fold people of mixed or not purely Jewish blood. And it is possible that it was owing to that censure that he saw in Arragel's above comment proof that the "concern over maintaining purity of blood was con-substantial with the very existence of the Hebrew." In any case, Castro failed to sense or correctly define Arragel's thought. Arragel knew, of course, that, according to Jewish law, the son of a Gentile woman and a Jew was considered a complete gentile, while the son of a Jewish woman and a Gentile was regarded as a Jew. Since no consideration of mixed blood motivated the latter decision, it would appear unlikely that such a consideration would be involved in the former. As a matter of fact, it did not. What prompted Arragel to combine the sin of "sleeping with alien women" with that of "begetting sons upon them" was Maimonides' treatment of both these transgressions as parts of *one* severe crime. Maimonides, however, explained the severity of that crime, including the begetting of Gentile children, by strictly *religious* reasons — that is, by the claim that intercourse with a Gentile woman "equals marriage into foreign worship,"[109] since it "leads us to cleave to the Gentiles" and thereby "abandon God."[110]

[109] Following Shabath 55b.
[110] Maimonides, *Code*, Forbidden Intercourse, c. XII, 6, 7, 8.

No, we can see no preaching of *pureza de sangre* in Arragel's comments on Ezra 9. Nor is any such philosophy to be seen in the other passage Castro cites from Arragel. Reflecting on the condition of the Spanish Jews, Arragel said in his letter to Guzmán that the Jews of Spain were the "most learned" and "most honored" of all the Jews in the dispersion because of their distinction in the following four properties: lineage, wealth, goodness and knowledge.[111] On the basis of this statement, Castro says: "The greatest advantage that Rabbi Arragel assigned the Castilian Jews was that of 'lineage,' of having nobler blood than the non-Spanish Jews."[112] Castro, no doubt, derives this conclusion from the fact that "lineage" is listed first by Arragel among the assets of the Spanish Jews. But can one find in this any real proof that he valued lineage more than anything else? That he mentioned *lineage first and knowledge last*, that he put *wealth and magnanimity before knowledge*, is certainly a departure from Jewish tradition, in which knowledge ("wisdom") and morality precede all other values.[113] But it must be recalled that he addressed his letter to one of the leading Spanish noblemen of his time, and while mentioning the virtues, he may have listed them in accordance not with his, but the latter's scale of values. Indeed, there is no doubt that to the great nobles of Spain and, for that matter, of all European nations, lineage, wealth and the show of magnanimity far outweighed, for all practical purposes, the virtue of knowledge (i.e., learning), in which, ordinarily, they could easily be outmatched by many a friar of plebeian origin. But as for Rabbi Moses Arragel, there is really no evidence in the above that, in his opinion, lineage ranked highest of all virtues. As a matter of fact, in the same letter to Guzmán, he pointed out that at the time of writing (i.e., in 1422) the Jews of Spain found themselves in "much misery and poverty," and that "the best, the most learned and the *fijos de algo* among us

[111] *Biblia*, I, p. 3.
[112] *The Spaniards*, p. 73.
[113] See the impressive list of ancient and medieval sources compiled in support of this conclusion by N. Sokolow, *Baruch Spinosa and his Time* [Hebrew] (Paris), p. 341.

have departed from us or died."[114] Arragel refers, of course, to what happened to the Jews of Spain from 1391 onward; "goodness" (which relates to the sphere of morality) is listed first, "wisdom" (*los mas sabios*) second, and nobility (*fijos de algo*) third[115] — that is, in the last place. So where is the proof that lineage was considered by Arragel the most important of all qualities?

This is not to say that a feeling of superiority did not permeate the thinking of the Spanish Jews when they came to compare themselves to other Jewish communities — or that Arragel did not share that feeling. Such a feeling could be nurtured by the objective facts, for no other Jewish group equalled Spanish Jewry in its wealth, social status and the development of learning in so many fields, both Jewish and general. No wonder that they considered themselves the "crown and diadem of the entire Hebrew exile," as Arragel said.[116] But this does not mean that they attributed their successes primarily to the excellence of their stock, by which they allegedly differed fundamentally from the other Jewish communities. Judging by Arragel's second statement (cited above from his letter to Guzmán), he seems to have believed that the great material wealth which the Spanish Jews managed to amass was the primary cause of their unique achievements, and that, once their wealth was gone, all their other distinctions soon disappeared with it. This means that Arragel did not ascribe to Spains' Jewry some special inherent qualities of race by which they differed from the rest of the Jews, but a combination of certain properties which distinguished them in the period preceding their downfall. What he seems to have said, or meant to say, was that among the Jews of Spain there was, in that period, a larger number of learned, rich and aristocratic families than could be found among other groups of Jews; and this is quite a different thing from saying that "lineage" was their greatest advantage.

---

[114] *Biblia*, I, p. 13.
[115] Actually fourth, for by "misery and poverty" he refers of course to the "wealth" which was taken from Spanish Jewry.
[116] *Biblia*, I, p. 13.

But it was not a minor matter either — that is, from the standpoint of Arragel; and none of the above should be taken to indicate that lineage was not rated by him highly. The precedence of the nobles over the commoners was a major fact of medieval life, recognized and respected by all the inhabitants of Spain — Moslem, Jewish or Christian — as it was in all other European countries. Arragel referred to that fact insofar as it related to the Jewish society. But this is not at all identical with the assumption that the Jewish community *as a whole* belonged, in his opinion, to a superior ethnic brand.[117] Had this been the case, Arragel would not

[117] To be sure, in Moslem times some Spanish Jews claimed (on the basis of Obadiah 1.20) that they stemmed from the ancient inhabitants of Jerusalem, whereas the other Jewish communities of the Diaspora descended from the dwellers of Judaea's other towns. Arguing for this claim was Moses ben Ezra who limited it, however, to the Jews of Andalusia (see his *Shirat Israel*, transl. B. Halper, Leipzig 1924, p. 64); but a generation later Abraham ibn Daud, who was well acquainted with Hispano-Jewish traditions, limited it still further when he presented it as peculiar to the Jews of Granada (*Sefer ha-Qabbala*, ed. G. D. Cohen, p. 71). In the following centuries (until the Expulsion) we find no Jewish author of Christian Spain imputing a "Jerusalemite" origin to Spanish Jewry, or to any part thereof. No wonder that Arragel ignores the whole idea in both his letter to Guzmán and his Commentary on Obadiah.

It should be noted that Obadiah's famous phrase: "the Captivity of Jerusalem that is in Sefarad", which served as the starting point for the whole contention, may mean, or may be interpreted to mean *that part of the captivity*, etc., while the related sources (commentaries and chronicles) are not only equally ambiguous or uncertain (see, e.g., Kimhi's three different interpretations for Obadiah 1.20), but occasionally also directly contradictory of the theory referred to. If from Ibn Daud we may gather quite clearly that mo.t Spanish Jews were not "Jerusalemite" in origin, or rather did not consider themselves as such, other sources indicate that the "Jerusalemite exiles" did not settle in Spain *alone* (see Josippon, ed. D. Flusser, Addenda A and B, pp. 432–433; Abravanel, Comm. on II Kings, conclusion). A composite of all these indications was probably the view that came to prevail in Spanish Jewry and was expressed, summarily, by Solomon ibn Verga. In the original Jewish settlers of Spain, the latter saw "exiles from Jerusalem and *the* [*other*] *towns of Israel*," as apparently were, in his opinion, also the Jews of Germany and France (see *Shevet Yehuda*, ed. A. Shohat, p. 120).

have said that, when he wrote his letter, the Jewish community of Spain was the "opposite" of what it "had been" in the time of its "prosperity,"[118] when it possessed the four distinctions mentioned above (including a number of *hijos d'algo*), distinctions which it lost with the change of its fortunes. Surely if the Jewish community *as a whole* was of "nobler blood than that of the non-Spanish Jews," that special quality (its inherent ethnic excellence) could not disappear under whatever circumstances (let alone change into its opposite), and therefore it would still be, by virtue of that fact, the élite of the entire Jewish diaspora. Evidently, this was *not* what Arragel had in mind; and of course we do not hear him argue for any *pureza* policy to be pursued by the Jews of Spain toward other Jews.

But whatever his thinking on this particular subject, it is entirely unwarranted — and of course most far-fetched — to conclude from the above references of his that it was from the fragile Jewish aristocracy that the Spaniards learned the value of noble birth, when their own nobility was infinitely more powerful, incomparably more prestigious, and historically far more deep-rooted and entrenched. What inspiration could the so-called Jewish *hijos d'algo* provide to a nation whose foremost noble houses divided the whole land among themselves and some of whose *ricos hombres*, great barons and magnates could trace their bloodlines to the days of the Goths? To the Spaniards, indeed, lineage *was* the foremost factor in determining their social status and consequently in dictating the course of their lives; and one requires therefore a peculiar imagination to accept Castro's thesis that it was from the Jews that they acquired the appreciation of its great value, and that statements such as those cited from Arragel provide proof or evidence of the verity of this thesis.

3. *Rosh*

We shall now pass to the testimonies in support of his theory which Castro presents from Hispano-Hebrew literature, and we shall first examine the evidence he adduces from a document

[118] *Biblia*, I, p.13.

composed in 1320. It consists of a question which R. Yehuda ben Wakar, personal physician to Don Juan Manuel (then Regent of Castile for Alfonso XI) addressed to the famous rabbinic authority, Rabbenu Asher ben Yehiel of Toledo (the Rosh). The question concerned a Jewish widow in Coca (a town between Toledo and Valladolid) who bore twins — a boy and a girl — to a Christian who was her steady consort. Shortly after birth the boy died and the girl was baptized in the Christian faith.[119] These developments, as well as the fact that the woman gave the Christian most of her property, were condemned by the Jews as scandalous and were the talk of the town among Jews and Christians. Yehuda ben Wakar felt that punitive measures should be taken against the delinquent woman, and he asked R. Asher whether mutilation of her face would be considered by him an appropriate punishment.[120]

Yehuda offered two reasons for the harsh sentence he proposed: the need to prevent an attitude of contempt on the part of the Gentiles toward the Jewish law, and the need to deter other Jewish women from following the example of the "harlot."[121] Castro, in his citation, omits the second argument and gives a wrong interpretation to the first. "The Law of the Jewish caste," says Castro, "emphasized the effect of transgressions on public opinion, and identified the reputation or honor of the individual with the honor of the community."[122] Whether this was generally so or not, it was certainly not the issue here, and it is important that we understand the issue before we consider the judgment proposed by ben Wakar. Castro believed that what the judgment indicated was the concern of the community for its own reputation, while what ben Wakar was concerned with was the reputation of the Law. This is no small difference.

We may assume that a community which tolerated such sins, or

---

[119] Undoubtedly in accordance with the Spanish law (*Fuero Real*, III, 8.3) that children born out of wedlock by a Christian father and a Moorish or a Jewish mother must be reared by the father. See also Baer, *op. cit.*, II, p. 39.

[120] Asher ben Yehiel, *Responsa*, 18.13; cf. Baer, *op. cit.*, II, pp. 138–139.

[121] Asher b. Yehiel, *op. cit.*, 18.13.

[122] *The Spaniards*, pp. 76–77.

the presence of such a sinful woman in its midst, could be regarded as sinful. Yet this fact in itself (that a community might be sinful) would not necessarily mean that its *Law* was at fault. In the case of the Coca scandal, however, the developments were such, Yehuda argued, that the stand to be taken by the Jewish community might have precisely such implications. For in response to an appeal that he protect the Jewish widow from the threat of prosecution by the Jews, Don Juan Manuel declared, Yehuda tells us, that her case was outside his jurisdiction and that she ought to be judged by a Jewish court and according to Jewish law.123 This placed the whole resposibility for judging her, openly and squarely, upon the shoulders of the Jews, and whatever decision they might make in the case would be viewed by the Christians as a *legal* decision, reached in full accordance with the *Law*. Consequently, if the sentence of the Jewish court were to involve a *light* punishment for the woman, the Christians would gather from this that the law of the Jews was permissive in such matters; and such a law would arouse their contempt, since their own penalties for such offences were extremely severe.124

Castro tries to show that the judgement of ben Wakar testifies to the policy of the "closed caste" which the Jews of Spain followed rigidly, and that it is from them that the Christians borrowed it. In actual fact, what is reflected here is the occasional influence of Christian law and opinion on the position the Jews took in such cases. Castro, who translated the question of ben Wakar from Baer's German translation, ignored or failed to see Baer's correct comment: "The punishment proposed [by Yehuda ben Wakar] naturally corresponds not to the Jewish, but to the Christian medieval penal law."125 In contrast, Castro says: "The law in the *Partidas* put a relatively moderate penalty upon illicit relations between Christian women and non-Christian men, reserving severe punishment only for those who offended repeatedly."126

123 Asher b. Yehiel, *op. cit.*, 18.13.
124 *Ibid.*
125 Baer, *op. cit.*, II, p. 139.
126 *The Spaniards*, p. 76.

But the penalty imposed by the *Partidas* in such cases was not moderate at all. Taken as a whole, it may, indeed, be viewed as more severe than the punishment suggested by ben Wakar. For according to the *Partidas* (VII. 25. ix), a Jew or a Moor who slept with a Christian virgin or widow, should be put do death (see also VII. 25. 10) for the *first* offense, while the Christian woman, the partner in sin, should pay with her life for the second offense. Castro passes in silence over the *death* penalty which the *Partidas* decreed for the non-Christian offender, and greatly diminishes the punishment they imposed upon the Christian woman (a virgin or a widow.) According to him, her punishment for the first offense was the loss of *half* her property, for the second offense the loss of *all* her property, and only for "a subsequent recurrence" of the offense was she condemned to death.[127] The *Partidas*, however, do not refer in such cases to "subsequent occurrences" at all. They already impose the supreme penalty on the guilty woman for the *second* offense: the loss of life *in addition* to the loss of her entire property.

This form of double punishment is noticeable also in ben Wakar's proposed sentence; for in addition to the mutilation of the woman's face, he suggested that she be charged a "small monetary fine" to be paid to the lord of the town of Coca.[128] We can scarcely assume that he considered her case as that of a first offender. No doubt, he regarded her as a persistent sinner whose relationship with the Christian was of a permanent nature and who had no intention of breaking it. If we thus consider his view of the case, the punishment he proposed, both financial and bodily, was considerably lighter than that of the *Partidas*.

But something else which is of even greater importance ought to be noted in this connection. Whatever conclusion we may reach by a comparison of the positions taken by the *Partidas* and ben Wakar, it is clear that the *Partidas* were not the sole representative of Christian-Spanish law at the time. The *Partidas* were

[127] *Ibid., ibid.,* n. 54.
[128] Asher b. Yehiel, *op. cit.,* 18.13.

adopted as the law of the country only in the middle of the four-teenth century — that is, *after* Yehuda ben Wakar issued his aforementioned judgment, while the ruling Christian law in *his* time for such cases was that expressed in the *fueros* of the towns; and these already dictated the death penalty for *both* the Christian woman and her non-Christian consort for the *first* offense. This is evident from the formulation of the law, which does not mention a second or a third offense. Thus, the *fuero* of Sepúlveda decreed that any Jew who slept with a Christian woman must be con-demned to death by being hurled from a precipice, while his Christian partner should be burned to death;[129] and the law of Sepúlveda was both old and widespread. Already in 1076, it was "confirmed" by Alfonso VI,[130] and it was later extended, directly or indirectly, to many towns in Castile and Aragon.[131] Further-more, it was ratified by Fernando IV in 1309, just eleven years before Yehuda ben Wakar proposed his sentence.[132] Prior to the acceptance of the *Partidas*, therefore, Christian law in Spain protected the Christian community against sexual relations with members of other faiths by imposing the death penalty on both parties, the man of the other faith and the Christian woman, for the first offense. The Jewish community could not punish both sides, and consequently its ability to deter such relations and protect itself against them was far more limited. Even so, we do not hear of any death sentence imposed in such cases by any Jewish court on any guilty Jewish woman. Jewish law did not warrant it, and the sentence of face mutilation is in itself an imitation of forms of punishment then current among the Christians.[133]

---

[129] Todo judio que con christiana fallaren sea despennado y ella quemada; see *Los Fueros de Sepúlveda*, ed. Emilio Saez, Segovia, 1953, p. 90, par. 71; cf. Baer, *Die Juden*, II, p. 115.

[130] *Los Fueros de Sepúlveda*, Introduction, p. 5.

[131] *Ibid.*, pp. 32–38.

[132] *Ibid.*, pp. 17–18. And cf. the fueros of Cuenca (ed R. de Ureña, p. 332b) and Teruel (ed. M. Gorosch, § 497) which decree death by fire for any christian woman who had sexual relations with a Jew or a Moor, as well as for her partner in crime.

[133] See *Partidas*, vii. 28.4; for blaspheming God or Holy Mary the *Partidas*

Castro thus overlooks many basic aspects of the sentence he cites from the Responsa of R. Asher when he tries to relate it to a Jewish tradition of guarding racial purity. What we have before us are two parallel traditions, Christian and Jewish, both attempting to prevent sexual relations between members of different religions (and not different races!) — relations which were looked upon with deep resentment by both Christians and Jews. In fact, if we may gauge the intensity of this resentment by the punishments laid down in the different laws, the intolerance of the Christians for such relations was far greater than the intolerance of the Jews.[134] Why, then, should an opinion of a Jewish rabbi, unrepeated and unbacked by any other source, be seen as having greater influence on the Spanish mind than a more general, more ancient and more authoritative opinion already crystallized in laws that were binding upon the Christians? Assuming that such decrees — or laws — reflected, in a way, the "purity of blood" policy (in reality they reflected only religious segregation), what, in this regard, could the Spanish learn from the Jews that they could not learn from their own sources?

impose the penalty of 50 lashes for the first offense, the *branding of the culprit's lips with a hot iron* for the second, and *cutting of the tongue* for the third. Similarly, Asher, *Responsa*, 17.8 (and see on this Graetz, *Geschichte*, VII, 2nd ed., p. 274). Here, too, Yehuda b. Wakar was involved. The idea was to punish the part of the body which was instrumental in the commission of the crime; Yehuda ben Wakar proposed to mutilate the face of the sinful woman on the assumption that it was her beautiful face that enchanted her Christian lover (see Asher, *Responsa*, 18.13).

[134] Indicative of this intolerance is also the order for Tortosa which was issued in 1393 by Juan I of Aragon, and which states that "if a Jew be caught with a Christian woman in a place where he might be *suspected* of having had sexual intercourse with her, both will be burned without mercy" (see Baer, *Die Juden*, I, p. 717). The decree was aimed at separating the Conversos from the Jews, and in referring to a "Christian woman" the law giver no doubt had in mind a "Converso woman." Nevertheless, while in all other paragraphs of the decree the Conversos are specifically mentioned, the change of designation from "Converso" to "Christian" in the stipulation cited above indicates that the law giver considered it necessary and possible to place that stipulation on a general basis.

4. *Adret*

Just as Castro shows no awareness of the attitude of Jewish law toward the question just discussed — i.e., that of extra-marital relations between Jews and Gentiles, he indicates no sign of familiarity with its attitude toward marriage between Jews and slaves — more precisely, slaves of Gentile origin.[135] While Jewish law ordered Jewish owners of Gentile slaves to encourage the latter to be baptized and circumcised, and also to perform some commandments, it did not consider the Gentile slaves as proselytes even if they fulfilled all the above requirements and openly declared for Judaism. [136] To become true proselytes, which meant full-fledged Jews, such slaves had first to be freed from their bondage, be baptized again for the sake of conversion and thus opt for Judaism as free men.[137] We touch here, incidentally, upon one of the great differences between Judaism and Christianity in this regard (Judaism did not accept slaves to its ranks, while Christianity did!), and also upon one of the major factors which hindered Judaism in its competition with Christianity in the first centuries of the Christian Era.

To return to the problem that concerns us at the moment: as long as he was not freed and converted, the Gentile slave remained, from the standpoint of Jewish law, with the double status of slave and non-Israelite. Needless to say, like all other non-Israelites, the slave, even if circumcised and baptized, had no right to contract marriage with a Jew or a Jewess, and if he or she did, the marriage was invalid, like marriages between Jews and Gentiles. Also, with respect to extra-marital relations, the situation was essentially the

---

[135] Among the various works on this subject, see S. Asaf, *Bĕ-Oholei Ya'akov* (Jerusalem, 1943), pp. 223–256; E. E. Urbach, "Hilkhot 'Avadim ke-Makor la-Historia ha-Ḥevratit, etc.", in *Zion*, XXV (1960), pp. 141–189.

[136] Such slaves were no longer considered as Gentiles, but neither were they considered real Jews. See Maimonides, Forbidden Intercourse, XII, 11 and XIV, 17 (יצאו מכלל הגויים, ולכלל ישראל לא באו).

[137] Some authorities maintained, however, that if a freed slave who failed to rebaptize married a Jewess, the marriage was valid. See *Maggid Mishne*, on Maimonides, Forbidden Intercourse, XII. 12.

same. While children of a slave and an Israelite woman were legally regarded as Jews, those of an Israelite father and Gentile bondwoman were regarded as both non-Jews and slaves. No such limitations or disadvantages, however, were encountered by a Judaized slave who was freed. Summarized by Maimonides, the law in this matter clearly reads as follows:

> All gentiles, without exception, once they become proselytes and accept all the commandments enjoined in the Torah, including the [Gentile] slaves [who had already accepted Jewish law], *once they are freed*, are regarded as Israelites in every respect, as it is said: As for the congregation, there shall be one statute for you and for the *stranger* [גֵּר] (Numbers 15:15), and they may enter the congregation of the Lord immediately — the proselyte and the manumitted [Judaized] slave may marry a daughter of an Israelite and an Israelite may marry a female proselyte or a manumitted [Judaized] bondwoman.[138]

It would lead us away from the subject under discussion if we were here to consider the various reasons for the Jews' refusal to accept slaves as full-fledged proselytes. But whatever the reasons, it is quite apparent that the preparedness of the Jews to marry freed slaves, of whatever nation and whatever origin, excludes any racial motive from the area of their considerations in this matter. Indeed, if there is anything that runs counter to the theory that the historical development of Judaism and the Jewish people was inspired by doctrines of "racial superiority" or "purity of blood" or "closed caste," as Castro so emphatically claimed, it is this legal and practical acceptance by the Jews of former Gentile slaves in their midst; for unlike other Gentiles, all Gentile slaves were assumed to have no legal paternity. [139] Thus, by its readiness to absorb former slaves, Judaism has clearly demonstrated its openness to all the blood strains of the human race.

All this must be borne in mind when we come to assess the following evidence which Castro offers for his assumption that "long before the 'purity of blood' idea appeared among the Christian Spaniards, the Jews of Spain were possessed by the same

---

138 Maimonides, *Code*, Holiness, Forbidden Intercourse, xii.17.
139 B.T. Kiddushin, 69a.

idea and had actually followed it as a guiding principle." The evidence referred to is included in a *responsum* of the famous Rabbi Solomon ben Adret of Barcelona to a question addressed to him on a matter which concerned the legitimacy of a certain Jewish family.[140] Castro cites Adret's *responsum* from the English translation made by Abraham A. Neuman and included in the latter's *The Jews of Spain*. To be fully understood, however, Adret's *responsum* must be read in the original Hebrew, for some of its terms are pregnant with meanings which are not always reflected in Neuman's translation. In fairness to Castro, one ought to admit that several phrases used by Neuman in his translation may have led Castro to his erroneous conclusion, although, in my judgment, he could have saved himself from error had he exercised more circumspection in the matter.

Now the case that was brought to the attention of Adret concerned two Jewish brothers who were charged with having a bondwoman among their ancestros. This could have meant that all the offspring of that woman, including the two brothers, may have been legally both slaves and Gentiles. Such an accusation, whether true or false, was regarded by Jewish law as an extremely grave matter; even "one who merely called another Israelite a slave was to be placed under the ban." If the stigmatized man did not protest, he was automatically considered suspect as charged, and the accusation would, in consequence, necessitate an inquiry into the family origins.[141] As is evident, what was involved in such cases was not the "value of the blood," as Castro thought, but the double value of "Jewishness" and "freedom" as related to the Rabbinic laws on slavery. Obviously, such a matter concerned not only the person (or persons) of the family involved, but the whole Jewish community, each of whose members could be affected by marriage with individuals of that family.

[140] Solomon ben Abraham ben Adret, *Responsa*, I, no. 386 (ed. 1958, pp. 136–137).

[141] B.T. Kiddushin 28a, Ketubot 14b and Maimonides, Code, Forbidden Intercourse, XIX. 22. In his *Criticisms* of the Code (*ibid.*), however, Abraham ben David denied the continued validity of this ruling.

The two brothers appealed to Solomon ben Adret, requesting
that he express his opinion on the case, hoping thereby to clear
their name and restore the legitimacy of their status. They accompanied their request with the opinions of five rabbis who had
examined the case and come to the conclusion that the accusation
was concocted with malicious intent. The family tree of the accused,
said the rabbis, was carefully checked and found to be flawless;
the man who originated the vicious rumor deserved to be placed
under the ban.[142]

In translating the opinion of one of these rabbis, Neuman
abridged it, paraphrased its contents, and presented it in the
following manner:

> I certify over my signature to all whom this document may reach
> that witnesses appeared before my teacher, Rabbi Isaac son of
> Rabbi Eliakim, who was presiding at the court session, and that he
> received proper and legal testimony from aged and venerable men
> of the country concerning the family of the brothers David and
> Azriel to the effect that they were of pure descent, without any
> family taint, and that they could intermarry with the most honored
> families in Israel; for there had been no admixture of impure blood
> in the paternal or maternal antecedents and their collateral relatives.
> Jacob Issachar, son of R. Shalom."[143]

Now, the expressions "pure descent" and "no admixture of
impure blood" *are not found in the original text.* Neuman included
them in his paraphrase of the *responsum* as reflective, in his
opinion, of its content. But what the opinion of the rabbi actually
stated was that the family of the accused brothers was found to be
free of any "element of slavery" (צד עבדות) and was therefore
"fit" to marry Jews.[144] Nor are such expressions as "pure descent"
or "admixture of impure blood" found in any of the other opinions
which accompanied the question addressed to ben Adret or in
the *responsum* of ben Adret himself.

Neuman's translation of Adret's *responsum* is free of such
racial terms, or rather, terms that could be seen by Castro as

[142] Adret, *Responsa*, I, 136b–137a.
[143] A. A. Neuman, *The Jews of Spain*, II (Philadelphia, 1944), pp. 5–6.
[144] Adret, *Responsa*, I, no. 386 (ed. 1958, p. 137a).

indicative of a racial policy, but it is considerably abridged; and part of what Neuman omitted in his abridgment is of interest for this discussion. Ben Adret begins his *responsum* by saying that "clearly the family must be considered fit [for marriage with Jews] from several standpoints." And it is noteworthy that the reason he presents first is that "all [Jewish] families must be held as fit and as emanating from the children of Israel."[145] And "if some fool slanders [any of these families] he must be viewed as a wicked man" who will pay for his sins. "There is no need to pay attention to such defamations, for wherein lies the superiority of the defamer" that he ought to be heeded? Indeed, "if we take seriously the authors of such libels, there will remain not a single family [in Israel] that will be considered fit from the standpoint of its ancestry."[146]

This remark is of special importance for the examination of Castro's thesis, as it indicates quite clearly that while the great rabbi regarded the vilification referred to him as a crime, he did not consider an investigation mandatory, and was satisfied to rely upon the statements of the accused and the general opinion of the Jewish community prior to the vilification. Accordingly, he did not urge any further inquiry into the family tree of the accused, and was not at all "possessed" by the issue of *genealogy*, as might appear from Castro. On the contrary, he believed that if slanders such as this — i.e., relating to the origins of Jewish families — had to be carefully investigated, and if the flawlessness of these families had to be established, all Jewish families could end up as "unfit," or suspect of being so, because he evidently considered it very difficult, owing to the paucity or absence of records, to prove the absolute legitimacy of all the forbears of any Jewish family.

But Castro, who did not read the original *responsum* and relied

---

[145] Cf. Kid. 76b and Maimonides, Forbid. Intercourse, XIX. 17.

[146] Adret, as above, n. 144. Like Nahmanides and Isaac of Dampierre, it should be noted, Adret minimized the scope of the related ruling (see above, n. 141) so that cases of the kind he now examined were excluded from its applicability (see Turim, Even Haezer, II, and Caro's *Beth Yosef, ibid.*).

only on Neuman's translation and abridgment, into which he read much of what the original did not say, hastened to declare on ben Adret's *responsum*: "We have before us the earliest text of a proof of purity of blood in Spain, with witnesses examined in different places, a text without parallel among the Christians at that time."[147] Indeed, witnesses *were* examined, but not on the question of race; the examination revolved round the question of slavery as related to Jewishness according to Jewish law, and such an examination could not be held among Christians — either at that time or at any other time — inasmuch as the Christian law with regard to marrying slaves differed radically from the Jewish law. Castro defines the document under discussion as the "earliest text" of its kind that provides proof for the "purity of blood" policy among the Jews. We do not know how he came to the conclusion that this was the "earliest" text of its kind. But since Castro evidently believed that it was, it is remarkable that he failed to ask himself: What happened to all similar testimonies in all the preceding centuries? Surely Jewish law was not established at the time of Solomon ben Adret! Why, then, was this the "earliest" record? Furthermore, the word "earliest" suggests that Castro was aware of the existence of "later" documents which involved the same procedure. But can we doubt that if Castro had had evidence of such cases, he would not have failed to adduce it?

One more point will complete our remarks on Castro's aforesaid conclusions. In ben Adret's *responsum* he saw, as we have noted, definite "proof" that the Jews of *Spain*(!) were adherents of the "purity of blood" principle and that, furthermore, to establish the "blood" condition of a person, they would "examine witnesses in different places" (as was done in Spain several centuries later by the Old Christians). This was supposed to show that Spain's Jews were dedicated to the practice of genealogical inquiries and hence, it was from *them* that the Christians learned their methods of establishing the "*limpieza*" of a person. But had Castro read the *responsum* in the original, he would have noticed that the case which was submitted to ben Adret, and the "witnesses examined

147 *The Spaniards*, p. 76.

in various places," did not relate to Spain at all. The question was addressed to "Rabbi Solomon of Barcelona" from "a place called Austerlitz" in Bohemia.[148] So we do not have here "the *earliest* text of a proof of *purity of blood* in *Spain*"; we do not have here, in fact, such a proof at all. Again, we can understand why Castro erred here. He *assumed* that the case related to Spain because Neuman, in discussing ben Adret's *responsum*, failed to indicate that the question came from Bohemia; and since Neuman was supposed to be concerned in his work with the mores of the Jews of Spain, and the *responsum* considered was of a famous Spanish rabbi, it would not ordinarily occur to Castro that the case did not relate to Spain. Yet, while we can understand *why* Castro erred, this does not diminish the seriousness of his error. The fact is that he attributed to the Jews of Spain a far-reaching policy on a major issue on the basis of a document whose original he had not read, of which he had only a partial free translation, and which he mistakenly considered to be of Spanish origin. And once he "established" on the basis of such evidence the position of the Jews on the issue of race, he did not hesitate to use this assumed position as proof for his other, even more extreme contention — namely, that it was from the Jews that the Spaniards borrowed their *pureza de sangre* policy.

SUMMARY

If we wish to summarize what we gathered from our examination of Catro's theory about the origins of the *"pureza,"* we may put it briefly as follows.

Castro's view that "the thousands of converts who came over to the Christian caste" injected into it the "biblical idea" of "purity of blood" appears to be wrong on all counts. To begin with, there was no such "biblical idea," or rather, one which the Bible promoted. Insofar as the *Law* itself was concerned. it never took any racial position against the marriage of Israelites with

---

[148] Adret, *Responsa* ‚I, ed. 1958, p. 136a (מה ששלחו לי מבהם ממקום הנקרא אושטלריש). Cf. B. Bretholz, *Ouellen zur Geschichte der Juden in Mähren* (Prague, 1935), p. 8 (§ 8).

members of other nations. The position it took was religious or moral, and this non-racial view lay no doubt at the basis of the vision of the universalistic expansion of Judaism which was projected and steadily nurtured by the Prophets. Whatever diversion from this line occurred, therefore, it was bound to yield — as it actually did — to the general thrust of the biblical ideology.

If Castro's reading of the Bible is wrong, and his understanding of its message on race erroneous, his assumption that the Jews in the Middle Ages believed that the Bible wished them to be racially a "closed caste" is clearly misconceived and patently untrue. Castro ignores the fact that the Jews in the Middle Ages understood the Bible the way their exegetes did, and that the latter leaned heavily on the Talmud which all, or most of the Jews followed. Yet the Sages of the Talmud who determined the reasons, the meaning and intent of the biblical instructions, not only abolished almost all the limitations which the Bible ever placed on intermarriage, but also formally equalized all races with the Israelites, once the former adopted the religion of the latter. Whatever vagueness or doubt, therefore, may have attached to the position of the Bible on this issue, it was swept away by the clarity of the records of the post-biblical period.

Castro's failure to consider this development, which made the Jews a conglomerate of all races, only highlights the flimsiness of his assumption that the Jews of Spain carried the theory of *limpieza* into Spanish society. Since proselytes were welcome, according to Jewish law, to join the ranks of the Jewish people, it is obvious that Spain's Jews, no less than other Jews, in no way upheld, adhered to, or practiced a policy of purity of blood; and since they did not uphold such a policy, how could the Spaniards borrow it from them, or adopt it in reaction to the policy of the Jews?

No firmer foundation can be ascribed to Castro's claim that the special importance which the Spanish nobility attached to the principle of *lineage* was due to the example of the Jewish aristocracy and the place which lineage occupied in its ranks. The arguments he advanced to uphold this view were based, as we have seen, on imaginary assumptions and bore little relationship to the historical facts. Neither the name of the Spanish nobility, nor its customs, ideals, laws, and way of life, were influenced by or borrowed from Jewish sources. If either of these groups imitated the other, it seems certain that it was the Jewish aristocracy that emulated the Spanish, and not vice versa.

The evidence Castro adduces from Hispano-Jewish literature in support of his view on the origins of the *pureza* is likewise, as we demonstrated, untenable. His interpretation of the documents he cites is fanciful and often based on misapprehension of their meaning. Castro fails to differentiate between illegitimacy of marriage due to *prohibited racial intermingling* and illegitimacy of marriage for *various other reasons*, and he confuses respect for families of high repute — a respect which is "human, all too human" (and therefore existed in all nations at all times) — with the determined national or class policy, backed by ideology, law and custom, of keeping the blood lines pure.

To be sure, Castro says: "Among the medieval Christians we do not find the preoccupation with what was later called 'purity of blood'. If it had existed, the strong racial mixture maliciously denounced in the *Tizon de la Nobleza* would not have been possible."[149] But the "strong racial mixture" to which Castro refers — i.e., the one which took place in the course of the fifteenth century — could not have occurred without the cooperation of the New Christians who were, of course, full-fledged partners in that mixture. It is true that while intermarriage between the groups was making headway, the movement opposing it was growing, too; but that movement was not of Converso origin. The statutes against intermarriage, such as the one of Guipúzcoa, were enacted by Old Christians, not by New, while among the Conversos we hear of *protests* against these statutes, such as the one expressed by Pulgar. In brief, the policy of *pureza de sangre* was born among Old Christians and was pursued by them alone; no counterpart existed among Jews or Conversos that might have stimulated an imitation.

[149] *The Spaniards,* p. 74.

When Castro says, therefore, that "the purity of blood was the answer of a society animated by anti-Jewish fury to the racial hermeticism of the Jews,"[150] he sees some moral and social equilibrium where no such equilibrium existed. The hermeticism of the Jews on the issue of intermarriage was not *racial* but *religious*, precisely as was the hermeticism of the Christians with respect to the same issue. Just as the Jews would not marry non-Jews (religiously speaking), so would the Christians not marry non-Christians. The *pureza de sangre* introduced, however, a trend not toward religious, but toward *racial* segregation — and this within the bosom of a Christian society which, both by its ideology and traditions, ought to have been anti-racial. Castro understood there was a problem here, and believed he had found its solution. But while the question he posed was right and to the point, the answer he gave was wrong and misleading. Obviously, the answer lies in a different direction. But this subject is beyond the limits of the present paper.

---

[150] *The Structure,* p. 531.

APPENDIX

THE "GOOD PEOPLE"

The foregoing criticisms of Castro's assertions about a Jewish influence on the rise of the *hidalguía* relate to the views expressed in his article "*Hidalgo: un injerto semítico*," which appeared in 1961.[1] During the next ten years, however, and before he published his book *The Spaniards* (1971), Castro discovered that *běnei tovim* means literally "sons of good people" and, in this connection, he also learned of the existence of such a concept as *tovei ha'ir* (the "good people of the city").[2]

It would appear that at this point Castro should have abandoned his previous interpretation and all that he derived from it. But rather than do so, he retained his old view and merely tried to combine it with his new find. Thus *ben tovim* is now translated by him either as "son of wealth," *or* as "son of good people," *or* as both at one and the same time.[3]

Etymologically, the combination is, of course, untenable, and cannot be justified by any ingenuity; but Castro simply ignored the discrepancies and used the correct meaning (i.e., *ben tovim* = son of good people) as a point of departure in search of new arguments in support of his old theory. Fortune seemed to favor his effort. He found that "the good people" (*los buenos*) appears in the sense of "nobles" in several works of the sixteenth century.[4] In one of them, by Francisco de Villalobos, there also appears the phrase *hijos de buenos* ("sons of good people"),[5] and on the basis of this single occurrence Castro declared that "all of the aforesaid Spanish phrases were copied from *běnei tovim*."[6]

Since we are concerned with the *origins* of the *hidalguía* it may be questioned, of course, whether the evidence offered here is altogether adequate, or even relevant. Phenomena belonging to the sixteenth century can hardly serve as proof for what happened in the eleventh, or probably even earlier, in the tenth. If, therefore, "los buenos" as a synonym of nobility dates from the sixteenth or the fifteenth century, the usage is of little interest to us, even if it were *proven* to have been borrowed from the Jews, directly or indirectly (through Converso

[1] See above, n. 31.
[2] *The Spaniards*, p. 270.
[3] *Ibid.*, pp. 269, 270.
[4] *Ibid.*
[5] *Los Problemas de Villalobos*, in Bibl. de Autores Españoles, XXXVI, p. 425.
[6] *The Spaniards*, p. 269.

channels). What Castro seeks to indicate, however, is that the sixteenth century expression was not an innovation, but a recurrence of an old usage — that is, one that went back to the beginnings of the *hidalguía* and the formation of its basic concepts. Since Castro offers no proof for this assertion, we may dismiss it as an unproven assumption. But this would not help us to determine the issue. "Unproven" is, after all, not "disproven," and in itself it cannot tell us whether Castro's contention is fundamentally true or not. Obviously, to come to grips with this question, we must try to broaden our knowledge of the "good people" as reflected in both Jewish and Spanish sources.

We have referred to the "good people," and not to "sons of good people," because it is only in the former expression that we are offered a semblance of a recognized social phenomenon in Spain. While the use of the expression "*hijos* de buenos" in the passage cited from Villalobos may be purely coincidental, the word *buenos* ("the good people") in the same phrase may be taken to indicate an institutional phenomenon, since it also appears independently (without "hijos") in Mateo Alemán,[7] and since from another work, by Vélez de Guevara, we may gather that *buenos* stood for "noblemen," and more particularly, for the "noblemen of the Mountain" ("los buenos de la Montaña").[8] Castro reminds us that "in Hebrew, the good people (*los buenos*), the leaders of the city, are called *tovei ha'ir.*"[9] In view of these assertions, the question arises: were the Spanish "good people of the Mountain" a replica of the Jewish "good people of the city"?

To be sure, in ancient Israel, the "seven *good men* of the city" signified the city's leading residents, or those who headed the city's administration. But the "good men" in the city were not limited to seven, as may be gathered from other sources,[10] and they may have represented the kind of people from whom the city's leaders were chosen. The Jewish communities in Spain, however, preferred to designate their leaders by other titles, even though the title *tovei ha'ir* was not entirely excluded.[11] From Rashba's *Respona*, it appears certain that the old institution was not operative in Aragon — at least, not under the old designation — and, furthermore, that the old designation was understood as referring to a small group of leaders only.[12]

[7] In *Guzmán de Alfarache*, III, ii.5.
[8] *The Spaniards*, p. 270.
[9] *Ibid.*
[10] Soferim 19.10.
[11] See Baer, *op. cit.*, II, Index, v. Gemeinde.
[12] When Solomon ben Adret sought to determine the function of the *mukademin* (adelantados), he said that the latter were identical with those

Somewhat different, however, was the state of affairs with respect to the *tovei haʻir* in Castile.

In a document from Toledo, dated 1112, the *tovei haʻir* appear, next to the *elders* and the *magistrates*, as participants in the determination of a legal dispute.[13] They again appear as judges in a Castilian document: the famous set of regulations of 1432.[14] Whereas in the former instance they are seven in number, following the model of the ancient institution, in the latter instance they are three, the three being described as "*of* the *tovei haʻir*" and the "most qualified among the students of the Law in that place."[15] From this we may gather that the title *tovei haʻir*, i.e., the "good men of the city," was not limited — or at least, no longer limited — to some elected or selected leaders, but indicated a segment of the community's population that was distinguished, among other things, in Jewish learning. It is not impossible, of course, that the "seven good men of the city," mentioned in the Toledan document of 1112, were likewise chosen from the élite of the community — that is, from a group that was commonly regarded as constituting the *tovei haʻir*.

This deduction brings to mind the groups of "good men" that existed at that time in the towns of Christian Spain — the *boni homines* in Aragon and the *buenos hombres* in Castile, who were also engaged in magisterial tasks. The identity of the description used in all these cases (i.e., the "good men"), the association of this description with the Spanish *cities*, and its reference in all instances, to the *higher layers* of the burghers, tempt one to hypothesize that the above-mentioned Spanish terms were coined under the influence of the Hebrew טובי העיר. A survey of the usage of these terms, however, must lead us to a different conclusion.

In his definitive study of the municipal regime in Catalonia from about the year 800 C.E. to the end of the Middle Ages, José M. Font Rius has clearly demonstrated that the institution of the "good people" (*probi homines*), which was later to assume a character of communal representation (at least, from the middle of the twelfth century, in the

whom the Sages called the "seven good men of the town" — a sure sign that the term *tove haʻir* was not used to designate the communal leadership in Aragon (see his *Responsa*, III, no. 394). According to Adret, the "seven good men" mentioned in the rabbinic sources were appointed by the community as guardians over its affairs, but they were not the most distinguished members of the community "in learning, wealth, or reputation" (*ibid.*, VII, no. 450).

[13] Baer, *op. cit.*, II, p. 10.
[14] *Ibid.*, p. 285 (*takana* ii.2).
[15] *Ibid.*

chief cities of Catalonia), goes back to the beginning of the ninth century, when it passed to Catalonia from the Carolingian Empire, with the latter's extension into the borders of Spain.[16] Historical studies of Frankish law, moreover, pointed to the presence of the same institution in Gaul already in the Merovingian period, while other researches relating to Italy traced its existence to Roman times. "We can find the *probi homines* — or their predecessors, the *boni homines* or the *boni viri*," says Font Rius, "in almost all the Southern countries of Europe."[17] We also find them indicated in the Theodosian Code, which applied to the Eastern Roman Empire.[18]

The Eastern Roman Empire, however, extended beyond the "Southern countries of Europe"; it also embraced Palestine, and thus the survey of the history of the *boni homines* brings us in touch with the Land of Israel in which the term *tovei ha'ir* was current. Moreover, since the Theodosian Code applied that term to the *leaders* of the city (the *decurions*) and since the term itself was known in Rome at least from the last days of the Republic,[19] it was, perhaps, not without Roman influence that the notions of the *tovim* and *tovei ha'ir* (and consequently of the *běnei tovim*) were fashioned in Judaea, judging by our sources, about the beginning of the Christian Era.

The common elements we may find in these Hebrew social concepts and the aforementioned Spanish urban institution may be explained, therefore, by their common Roman origin. In any case, it is evident that the designation of the "good people," which appears in Spain in the beginning of the ninth century, was not borrowed from its Hebrew counterpart, but from Christian-Roman sources. We may even assume that the Jews revived its usage under the influence of the institution of the "good people," as it progressively developed in the Spanish cities. In any case, it is obvious that there was no need for the *hidalgos* to borrow their view of themselves as "good people" from the Jews or from the latter's *tovei ha'ir*. They could take it from the Christian Spanish burghers.

Moreover, until the middle of the twelfth century (that is, until the term *hidalgo* became current, which means until after the birth of the *hidalguía*), the term *boni viri* was used to designate in Spain also the

---

[16] See J. M. Font Rius, "Orígenes del régimen municipal de Cataluña," in *Anuario de Historia del derecho Español*, XVII (1946), pp. 334–335.

[17] *Ibid.*, p. 328.

[18] Lib. VI, tit. xxi, 1.i.

[19] See Cicero, *De officiis*, I, vii.20; and the conception may go back to earlier times (see Cato, *De agri cultura*, 144).

nobility as such,[20] perhaps because in accordance with the old traditions, noblemen were held there, as elsewhere, to be "good," or perhaps because the nobles refused to see this title exclusively appropriated by the urban upper class. It follows that if the notion of the "good people" was associated with the *hidalguía* from its inception, the *hidalgos* did not have to borrow or inherit it from the Christian — let alone the Jewish — urban élite; they could have acquired it directly from the Christian nobility whose ranks they joined and whom they sought to emulate. In brief, there was nothing that the *hidalgos* could learn or adopt from the Jewish "good men of the cities" that they could not find in their own *probi homines* or *buenos hombres*.

This, then, it seems, does away with the notion that the sixteenth century expressions cited by Castro offer support for his thesis. If they reflect old medieval usages, we know what their sources might have been. If, on the other hand, they were of late origin, they teach us nothing about the rise of the *hidalguía*. As late adaptations, they may have stemmed from various origins (including Converso and anti-Converso sources) and have been used for purposes quite different from those which are relevant to this discussion.

[20] Font Rius, "Orígenes," *loc. cit.*, pp. 342–343.

SCRIPTURE AND MISHNAH:
THE EXEGETICAL ORIGINS OF *MADDAF*

By JACOB NEUSNER

The concept of *maddaf*-uncleanness is stated in M. Zabim 5:2:

> Whatever is carried above the Zab is unclean. And whatever the Zab is carried upon is clean, except for something which is suitable for sitting and lying, and except for man.

This rule is illustrated with cases in which the finger of a Zab is underneath stones and a clean person is above them. The clean person is made unclean so that he imparts uncleanness at two removes and unfitness at one still further remove. If food and drink, a bed or a chair, and a *maddaf*-article — an article not used for sitting and lying — are located above the stones with the Zab below, they impart uncleanness at one remove and unfitness at one remove. If the bed and chair are below, and the Zab above, they impart uncleanness at two removes and unfitness at one. If food, drink and *maddaf*-objects are below and the Zab is above, they remain clean. Now this rule is treated as beyond dispute, and its details are taken for granted. Tosefta's version (T. Zab. 5:1A) concurs that food, drink, and *maddaf*-objects above a Zab are subject to a more stringent rule than food, drink, and *maddaf*-objects underneath a Zab, while a bed or chair underneath a Zab is subject to a stricter rule than a bed or chair located above a Zab.

In asking about the origins of this rather complex notion, we find no assistance whatever either in attributions, for all parties agree on the matter, or in attestations, for there is no reference to the matter in the whole of Seder Tohorot in which the principle of *maddaf* is at issue. The important point, then, is the distinction between what is carried above the Zab and what is carried below. If something not used for lying or sitting, inclusive of food and drink, is located above a Zab, it is unclean, while if it is located below the Zab, it is clean. Only a bed or chair located below a Zab will be unclean, because of bearing his weight even without directly touching him (I here omit all reference to man).

Philological Facts

Let us first ascertain the meaning associated with the word in the earliest assigned pericopae.[1] *Maddaf* is familiar as the name of an object, which we have translated *bird trap* in M. Kel. 23:5 (Part[2] II, p. 220); as *the smoker of the bees* (M. Kel. 16:7, Part II, p. 78), required by context in both cases. Zabim by contrast, knows that word to mean "an object, not used for lying or sitting, located above the Zab" (M. Zab. 4:6, 5:2). The third meaning is "a status as to uncleanness," a definition to be made more precise when we return to M. Par. 10:1–2, and M. Toh. 8:2. The former (Part X, pp. 164–171) requires the meaning, "A status as to uncleanness related to *midras* but of lower degree of uncleanness than *midras.*" Thus M. Par. 10:1 states: "Whatever can become unclean with *midras*-uncleanness is regarded as actually unclean with *maddaf*-uncleanness so far as the purification-rite is concerned." (There is a further dispute, M. Par. 10:1, assigned to Yavneans, on what can be made unclean with corpse-uncleanness and whether that sort of object likewise is unclean with *maddaf*-uncleanness.) Accordingly, in the context of M. Par. 10:1–2, *maddaf* can only mean, "a status of uncleanness," which, we know, is uncleanness in the first remove, effecting uncleanness for food and liquid. This same meaning is absolutely required at M. Toh. 8:2 (Part XI, p. 186): If someone deposits with an *'am ha-areṣ* a box full of clothing, Yosé says, "When it is tightly packed, it is unclean with *midras*-uncleanness, and if it is not tightly packed, it is unclean with *maddaf*-uncleanness." Accordingly, once more, *midras*-uncleanness is set into contrast with *maddaf*-uncleanness. In this

[1] Chayim Yehoshua Kasovsky, *Thesaurus Mishnae* (Jerusalem, 1958), IV, 353a.

[2] *Part* = Neusner, *A History of the Mishnaic Law of Purities* (Leiden, 1974–1977), I–XXII.

instance the point is that the *'am ha-areṣ* is unclean as a Zab. If a Zab shifts an object not used for sitting or lying, we know the object suffers *maddaf*-uncleanness and renders food and drink unclean. M. Ed. 6:2[3] further has a dispute of Joshua and Neḥunya b. Elinathan with Eliezer, in which it is taken for granted, tangentially and within the structure of argument: "The uncleanness of living beings is greater than the uncleanness of corpses, for a living being imparts uncleanness, by lying and sitting, to what is underneath him, so that it conveys uncleanness to man and utensils, and also conveys *maddaf*-uncleanness to what is above him, so that it conveys uncleanness to food and liquid, a mode of transferring uncleanness which a corpse does not convey." The same authorities — Joshua and Eliezer — are at M. Par. 10:1–2, and, moreover, Yosé continues the matter, at M. Toh. 8:2, taking the rule for granted, just as do Joshua and Eliezer. We need not review in detail Tosefta's usages of the same word, since all occur in the context of the correlative Mishnaic pericopae (T. Par. 10:2, 3; T. Toh. 9:4; T. Zab. 3:3, 5:1).

The two senses in which the word is used (now omitted: reference to the occurrences in M. Kel.) of course are complementary. M. Par. and M. Toh. know *maddaf* as a status concerning uncleanness contrasted to *midras*, and M. Zab. uses the word to refer to objects which can enter that very same status as to uncleanness. What can become unclean with *maddaf*-uncleanness — an object not used for lying and sitting and hence not susceptible to *midras*-uncleanness (a point familiar throughout our order, e.g., M. Kel. 24) — here is called *maddaf*. And M. Par. and M. Toh. know *maddaf* as that uncleanness imparted to something which can become unclean with *maddaf*-uncleanness, as distinct from something (used for lying and sitting) susceptible to *midras*. Zabim, moreover, hastens to add: The status of *maddaf*-uncleanness is attained when an object not used for lying or sitting (also food or drink, explicitly included as well) is located above a Zab.

---

[3] See my *Eliezer b. Hyrcanus. The Tradition and the Man* (Leiden, 1973), I, 339–340.

Maddaf as the opposite of *midras*, of course, is contained in the pericopae of M. Toh. in particular, but also, with slight eisegesis, at M. Par.

We shall now see that the contrast between *midras* and *maddaf*, strikingly, is precisely the same as the contrast I hypothetically impute to the exegetes of Lev. 15:10a in the following exercise. Indeed, *midras* and *maddaf* express exactly the same idea as is spelled out in what is to follow. Our invocation, at that point, of the rule of opposites therefore is justified by the result of the present analysis of the consistent contrast, drawn in M., between *midras* and *maddaf*. The concept of *maddaf*, in its two, complementary senses, most certainly is attested by Joshua and Eliezer at M. Ed. and M. Par. Because of the givenness of the idea of M. Par., at both pericopae assigned to Eliezer and Joshua, I am inclined to suppose that the concept of *maddaf*-uncleanness and of objects susceptible not to *midras*, because they are not used for lying and sitting, but, under the specified circumstance, to *maddaf*-uncleanness, hence *maddaf*-objects, originates before 70, probably long before that time.

Analogical-Contrastive Exegesis: The Hypothetical-Logical Method

When, in Mishnah, we find a conception clearly present in the foundations or originating at the earliest strata of Mishnaic thought, we have to ask whether or not the said conception may originate in Scripture. In the present case, by a very brief series of logical steps, I shall show that the conception of *maddaf*-uncleanness, with its distinction between a chair or a bed below, and objects not used for sitting or lying below a Zab, and a chair or a bed above, and objects not used for sitting or lying above, a Zab, emerges from Scripture itself. The process by which this rather complex conception emerges, moreover, is not through formal exegesis, as is the claim of Sifra Zabim III:3–7 (below), but through the hypothetical-logical reconstruction of the analogical-contrastive mode of exegesis which I shall lay forth. That mode of exegesis rests upon the perfectly simple supposition that, when the exegetes who contribute to Oral Torah read Scripture, they come with a single, two-sided conception: rules derive from Scripture by either analogy or contrast. That is, something (1) either is like or (2) unlike something else. If (1), it is like that other thing, it follows its rule. If (2), it is unlike that other thing, it follows the exact opposite of its rule. If, again, Scripture states a rule and its condition, then the presence of the opposite condition will generate the opposite of the stated rule.

Let us now proceed to the relevant Scriptural passage. At the left hand I specify the verse itself, and, to the right of it, simply restate what the verse says. Then I produce what I call a *secondary* meaning, which is simply a restatement of the contents of the Scriptural passage in more general language. There then follows a *tertiary* meaning, at which level I reproduce not the stated rule but its exact opposite: *now the method not of analogy, but of contrast.* At the *fourth* level, we then state the opposite of the opposite of the third level, that is, what clearly is implied by the negative of the rule at the third level of meaning. At this point, a mere three stages of reasoning away from the simple sense of Scripture, we find that we have stated what is at issue in M. Zab. 5:2.

Lev. 15:9: *And any saddle on which*   *The saddle ridden upon by the Zab*
he who has the discharge rides shall   *is unclean.*
be unclean.

SECONDARY MEANING

Since the saddle is dealt with apart from the bed and chair, it is subject to a distinctive set of rules.

Lev. 15:10a: *And whoever touches*   *An object located underneath a Zab*
anything that was under him shall   *is unclean.*
be unclean until the evening.

SECONDARY MEANING

I take it that the simple meaning is derived by treating Lev. 15:10a as a continuation of Lev. 15:9, which is to say, "A saddle on which a Zab has ridden is unclean, and whoever touches anything on which a Zab rides (or: has ridden) is unclean." But if we read the verse disjunctively, then it bears a different meaning. Mere *location* of an object beneath a Zab — even if he is not touching it, and even if he is not riding on it — imparts uncleanness to the object. Accordingly, we take account of the spatial relationships of objects to a Zab. And this yields the clearly-required notion that an object used for sitting, lying, or riding which is located beneath a Zab is unclean, even though the Zab has not sat, lain, or ridden on said object.

TERTIARY MEANING

Touching or carrying the saddle produces uncleanness, as specified. Touching an object located underneath a Zab, even though said object is not touched by the Zab and even though said object is not directly sat, lain, or ridden upon by the Zab but merely bears the weight of his body, imparts uncleanness so that the formerly clean person is made unclean and furthermore makes his clothing unclean, and, by extension, imparts uncleanness to utensils in general.

FOURTH LEVEL OF MEANING

1. An object used for sitting and lying which is located underneath the Zab is subject to the uncleanness imparted by the Zab to objects upon which he has sat or lain, and so forth. It follows that the same sort of object located *above* the Zab is *not* subject to the uncleanness imparted by the Zab to objects used for sitting and lying.

2. An object *not* used for sitting and lying located *beneath* the Zab (but not touched by him or subjected to the pressure of his body-weight) is *not* unclean.

3. And, it follows in the rule of opposites, an object not used for sitting and lying which is located *above* the Zab *will* be unclean.

Let us now relate the foregoing to Mishnah, specifically M. Zab. 5:2.

M. Zab. 5:2: Whatever is carried above the Zab is unclean. Whatever the Zab is carried upon, but

The important point here is the distinction between what is carried *above* the Zab and what is carried

which is not touched by him, is clean, except for something used for sitting and lying (Lev. 15:10a) and except for man who carries the Zab (Lev. 15:10b).

below him, without touching him. In the former case, there is uncleanness, and this applies, specifically, to food, drink and objects not used for lying and sitting (*maddaf*). If these are carried below the Zab, they are clean. Only man and bed and chair below the Zab are made unclean because of their serving to carry his weight even without directly touching him. The illustration, M. Zab. 5:2L–M, further indicates that what is unclean above the Zab — food, drink, *maddaf* (an object not used for lying and sitting) — is unclean in the first remove.

The principle is dual: (1) What is carried *underneath* the Zab is unclean, except for an object used for lying and sitting. (2) What is carried *above* the Zab is unclean. The relationship to Scripture is not self-evident. On the one side, we may readily account for the first principle. That an object used for lying and sitting which was under the Zab is unclean is specified at Lev. 15:10a. But the rule excludes objects not used for lying and sitting. To review what has been suggested: The distinction begins at Lev. 15:9. The saddle on which the Zab rides is unclean. Lev. 15:10a, continuing this point, then specifies that whoever touches anything that was under him — thus, that has served him for sitting — is unclean. And, by exclusion therefrom, whoever touches something which has been located under the Zab but which the Zab has *not* used for sitting is not unclean. Accordingly, the object itself, if not used for sitting, does not become unclean if the Zab is located above it.

But whence the notion of *maddaf*? That is, how do we know that an object *not* used for lying and sitting and located *above* the Zab is unclean? We come to the fourth level of meaning imputed to Lev. 15:10a. (1) What is unclean beneath the Zab is not unclean above him. (2) Then: What is *not* unclean beneath the Zab *is* unclean above him. Objects not used for sitting and lying, food and drink (2) are unclean above, because they (1) are clean below, the Zab. Thus: Objects used for sitting and lying are clean above, because they are unclean below, the Zab.

Formal Exegesis: The Method of Sifra

There is a quite separate theory of the origins of Mishnaic law in Scripture. It is that of Sifra, which insists that *only* through formal exegesis of Scripture, not through logical inquiry into the character of abstract principles of law, do we reach the principles of the law. This systematic polemic of Sifra[4] has the larger purpose of proving that it is solely through revelation, and not through logic, that we reach firm knowledge of Torah. Logical exegesis of Scripture's facts therefore is explicitly rejected in favor of *formal* exegesis of Scripture's language. Mishnah is based, Sifra insists, upon formal exegesis of Scripture, and not on the working of logic. That is why the sort of hypothetical-logical exegesis I have set forth never is attempted in Sifra's repertoire of exegetical foundations of the law of Mishnah. The relevant passage in Sifra, interestingly, meets head on the sort of hypothetical-logical exegesis I have laid forth, and rejects it on rather solid grounds, I must admit.

    A. *And every vessel of wood shall be rinsed in water* (Lev. 15:12b).

    B. Said R. Simeon, "What does this verse come to teach us?

    C. "If its purpose is to teach that he imparts uncleanness to a rinsable vessel through touching it, is that not already stated in the following: *And he who touches that which the flesh of the Zab has touched will wash his clothing?*

    D. "If he who touches him makes unclean the rinsable vessel through contact, he himself could surely impart uncleanness to a rinsable vessel through contact.

    E. "If so, why is it said, '*And any vessel of wood shall be rinsed in water*'?

    F. "But these are food and drink and utensils [not used for sitting and lying] which are above the Zab." [They are made unclean if they are located above him.]

            Sifra Me'ṣora Zabim III:3.

    G. And is [the contrary proposition] not a matter of logic:

4 Part VII. Negaim. Sifra, pp. 1 ff.

H. Now if in a situation in which he makes unclean a bed which is under him, he does not make unclean a *maddaf* [utensil not used for sitting and lying] which is under him,

I. In a situation in which he did not impart uncleanness to a bed which is above him, is it not logical that we should not treat [as unclean] a *maddaf* [utensil not used for sitting and lying] which is above him?

J. [Accordingly] Scripture [is required] to state, *And every vessel of wood shall be rinsed —*

K. Teaching that he [add: *does not*] impart uncleanness to a *maddaf* [utensil not used for sitting and lying] which is beneath him [Rabbenu Hillel: teaching that he imparts uncleanness to a *maddaf* (utensil not used for lying or sitting) which is above him].

III:4

L. It is an argument *a fortiori* that he should render unclean a bed which is above him:

M. Now if in a situation in which he does not render unclean a *maddaf* [utensil not used for sitting or lying] which is below him, he renders unclean a bed which is below him, in a situation in which he does impart uncleanness to a *maddaf* [an object not used for sitting and lying] which is above him, is it not logical that he should impart uncleanness to a bed which is above him?

N. Scripture says, *And every bed on which the Zab shall lie shall be unclean —*

O. A bed does he make unclean below him, but he does not make a bed which is above him unclean.

III:5

P. It is an argument *a fortiori* that he should make unclean a *maddaf* [an object not used for lying or sitting] which is below:

Q. Now if in a situation in which he did not impart uncleanness to a bed which is above him, he does impart uncleanness to a *maddaf* [an object not used for lying and sitting] which is above him, in a situation in which he does impart uncleanness to a bed which is below him, is it not logical that he should impart uncleanness to a *maddaf* [an object not used for lying and sitting] which is below him?

R. Scripture [accordingly is required] to state, *And every bed on which the Zab will lie is unclean —*

S. To a bed which is below him does he impart uncleanness, but he does not make unclean a *maddaf* [an object not used for lying and sitting] which is below him.

III:6

T. It is an argument *a fortiori* that he should not make unclean a bed which is below him:

U. Now in a situation in which he imparts uncleanness to a *maddaf* [an object not used for lying or sitting] which is above him, he does not impart uncleanness to a bed which is above him, in a situation in which he does not impart uncleanness to a *maddaf* [an object not used for lying and sitting] which is below him, is it not logical that he should *not* impart uncleanness to a bed which is below him?

V. [Accordingly] Scripture [is required] to state, *And every bed on which the Zab will lie will be unclean* —

W. This teaches that he imparts uncleanness to a bed which is below him.

III:7, Weiss, pp. 77a, b

This exercise reverses the ground of argument time and again, but its main points are clear. M. Zab. 5:2 refers us to a *maddaf*, that is, an object not used for lying and sitting but susceptible to uncleanness along with food and drink. Simeon's unit, A–F, includes food, drink, and "utensils" above the Zab, and shows that the cited passage is inclusive of such objects. If they are located above the Zab, they are made unclean. The remainder takes up this proposition, but is not integral to Simeon's exegesis, introducing *maddaf* in place of Simeon's "utensils." We first ask, How do we know that objects not used for sitting and lying are unclean when above the Zab? Perhaps they should be deemed clean when located above the Zab. After all, a bed under the Zab is made unclean, but if the bed is over the Zab, it is clean. If objects not used for sitting and lying are under the Zab, they are clean. Then all the more so should they be clean when located over the Zab, since they are subject to a less stringent rule than the bed, which is clean when located over the Zab. Accordingly, J–K, Scripture alone can prove the proposition stated by Simeon at F.

The remainder then flows in the expected dialectical movement. If we have shown, on the basis of Scripture, that objects not used for lying and sitting located on top of the Zab are unclean, then surely a bed should also be unclean when located on top of the Zab, so L–O. That proposition would be logically true, and accordingly, Scripture limits the matter by stating that a bed is unclean when *below* the Zab but not when *above* the Zab. Naturally, we again reverse the course of argument, P–S. If a bed is not unclean when over the Zab, why should an object not used for lying and sitting when below the Zab *not* be unclean? After all, the bed above the Zab is clean but an object not used for lying and sitting above the Zab is unclean. Then the object not used for lying and sitting is subject to a more stringent rule than the bed. If the bed is unclean — below the Zab — said object also should be unclean. Scripture is introduced once more. It specifies that the bed under the Zab is unclean, and since bed is specified, that excludes something not used as a bed. Of necessity, we go on, at T, to reverse the matter once again, with exactly the same reasoning.

Conclusion

This exercise can readily be repeated for the principles and generative rules of three tractates, Negaim, Niddah, and the remainder of Zabim, all of which[5] to begin with draw out and spell out Scripture's rules and principles for the *mesora'*, the menstruating woman, Zabah, woman after childbirth, and, finally, for the Zab, respectively. All deal with sources of uncleanness.[6] Here the Oral Torah is contented to restate and develop through logical exegesis (not merely through formal exegesis, such as at Sifra, which is post factum) what is said in the Priestly Code. The reason is that at the outset the people among whom the Oral Torah, that is, Mishnah, originates have no intention whatsoever to augment and enrich the laws of the *sources* of uncleanness and even those of the transfer of the uncleanness of those sources of uncleanness to men and utensils, food and drink, objects purified by immersion and objects purified by breaking,

---

[5] See Parts VI, VII and VIII. Negaim; XV, XVI, Niddah; and XVIII, Zabim.

[6] The same is so of M. Ohalot Chapters 1–3 and 16–18, that is, the prologue and epilogue of Ohalot, which deal with such unclean substances as the corpse.

food which is unconsecrated, which is heave-offering, and which is Holy Things.

Their original and fresh proposition concerns the *locus* of uncleanness, which is the world as well as the cult, and the means of removing uncleanness, in the world as well as in the cult. Accordingly, tractates on these matters begin in conceptions wholly autonomous of, and alien to, the Written Torah, because the Priestly Code, in its ultimate redaction, claims that cleanness and uncleanness are categories of the cultic metaphysic, not of the world outside the cult. The ultimate redactors who make such a claim in behalf of the Temple of course obscure the worldly locus of the laws of uncleanness, e.g., the corpse which lies in the tent imparts uncleanness to the utensils which are in the tent, and this without regard to the use of said utensils in the cult. Menstrual impurity has primary implications for the home, not only for the cult, despite the ultimate redactional claim stated in connection with the pericope of the Zab, the menstruating woman, and the Zabah at Lev. 15:31, *Thus you shall keep the people of Israel separate from their uncleanness, lest they die in their uncleanness by defiling my tabernacle that is in their midst.*[7]

It would be an error, however, to conclude that the Oral Torah represented by Mishnah bears an essentially dual relationship to the Written one, that is, partly exegetical, partly autonomous. Even though Kelim, Ohalot, Parah-Yadayim, Tohorot-Uqsin, Miqvaot-Tebul Yom, and Makhshirin begin in conceptions essentially autonomous of Scripture, while Negaim, Niddah, and Zabim (merely) spell out and develop rules laid down in Scripture, all the tractates, whatever the character of their fundamental pre-suppositions in detail, share an approach which is distinctive to Mishnah in its very origins. All of them take an intense interest in details of cleanness. This fact is what marks them all, whatever their relationship to Scripture, as particular and Pharisaic. Even though everyone in the Land of Israel concurred that the Zab was unclean, not everyone developed the layers of exegesis, the sec-

7 See Part XVI, pp. 208–211.

ondary and tertiary conceptions, producing a tractate such as Zabim. So far as our extant sources tell us, whether or not others, e.g., in the Essene community at Qumran, observed the purity-laws, no one else took equivalent interest in developing the laws of Leviticus Chaps. 12–15. The detailed principles of Negaim, Niddah, and Zabim in no way express conceptions definitive of and distinctive to Pharisaism, such as we observe in Kelim, Parah, Tohorot, Miqvaot, and Makhshirin, and (possibly), at the shank of Ohalot (M. Oh. 3:6–16:2), as well. Authorities before 70, whom we assume are Pharisees, devote time and attention to the elucidation and extension of Scripture's rules. Extant evidence does not suggest that others did so. What is distinctive to the "Oral Torah" which we assume characterizes Pharisaism is detailed attention to matters of uncleanness. Others either took for granted and observed them or took for granted and ignored them. Accordingly, there are two aspects to the analysis of the relationship of Zabim to Scripture, exegetical and eisegetical. Exegesis of a straight-forward, and (hypothetically) highly logical, sequential character produces Zabim. Not exegesis, but eisegesis imparts such importance to Lev. 15:1–15 that the exegetical enterprise is undertaken in the first place.

ARNOLD WHITE,
BARON HIRSCH'S EMISSARY

By Moshe Perlmann

The explosion of the *furor judophobicus* in Russia in 1890–91 gave rise to reports, indignation and protests in the foreign press, and in social and political circles, especially in Britain and the United States.[1] The position of Russian Jewry at the time became the subject of two inquiries initiated in the West. One was by a governmental agency of the United States: two commissioners of immigration, J. B. Weber and Dr. Walter Kempster, were sent to Russia to report "upon the causes which incite immigration to the United States."[2] The other was by Arnold White, a British public figure, on behalf of Baron Maurice Hirsch, who was planning mass settlement of Jews from Russia in the Argentine Republic.[3]

[1] Simon Dubnow, "Furor judophobicus in the last years of the reign of Alexander III," *Evreiskaia Starina* (1918), 27–59; in his *Weltgeschichte des jüdischen Volkes*, X (Berlin, 1929) chapts. 18–20, treat the same subject, and follow the *History of the Jews in Russia and Poland*, tr. by Israel Friedlaender (Philadelphia, 1916–20), II. Cf. his memoirs, *Kniga Zhizni* (Riga, 1934), I, chapts. 25 and 27. Cf. P. A. Zaionchkovskii, *Rossiiskoe samoderzhavie v kontse XiX stoletiia* (Moscow, 1970).

[2] *52d Congress, 1st Session, House of Representatives, Executive Doc. 235*, Pt. I (Washington, 1892), 331 pages, and Pt. II, pp. 107–109 (hereafter called Report).

[3] The report to Hirsch was printed in White's volume, *The Modern Jew* (London, 1899), pp. 294–301, and other data collected by him are given in the chapter "The Problem in Russia," (pp. 11–33), and in substance in the article, "The Truth about the Russian Jew" in *The Contemporary Review* (1892), 695–708; the journal had published an anti-Jewish article by an Anglo-Russian, 1891, pp. 309–326. Cf. White's article in *The New Review*, London (August, 1891), 97–105; it is followed by an article by E. B. Lanin (E. J. Dillon, 1855–1933) who wrote against the Russian regime in general, and against the treatment and persecution of Jews in particular, in his *Russian Characteristics* (London, 1892).

Indeed, the inquirers of both parties met in Russia on August 19, 1891.[4]

To conduct their inquiries both the Americans and the Briton made contacts with Russian authorities and public figures and also secured the assistance of knowledgeable Russian Jews.

White's assistant was David Feinberg (1840–1916), a St. Petersburg community leader. He accompanied White to Moscow (May 8), Kiev and other centers of Jewish population. White and Feinberg arrived in 'the Jewish capital,' Berdichev, on the eve of the Shavuot festival. Clean houses, white tablecloths, and wall portraits of the Czar, Montefiore, Rabbi Isaac Elchanan Spector (of Kovno) impressed the Briton. But he intimated to his assistant that the Jews were materialists, worshiped the golden calf, and would sell anything for money; to which Feinberg's reply was: if the Jews were materialists, nothing would be simpler for them than to embrace the Orthodox Christian faith, become full-fledged citizens, and rid themselves of disabilities. White seemed duly impressed by this retort.[5] Their language of communication was French.

---

[4] Report, p. 32; White, *Modern Jew*, p. 40: "... The American Commissioners... had made up their minds before any of the facts had been examined. No doubt, Messrs. Kempster and Weber are accurate and conscientious observers, but from conversations held with these gentlemen in St. Petersburg before they set out on their journey through Russia to collect facts, it was evident to me what their report would be ...."

Weber and Kempster had met Baron Hirsch too in Paris on July 27 and learned about White's activity in Russia (Report, p. 15). White was also critical of Harold Frederic whose *The New Exodus, A Study of Israel in Russia*, appeared in London in 1892.

Frederic in turn felt that White had reported as facts about Moscow a pack of lies which had been told him by the officials of the Holy Synod (re: cruelties in March 1891). Cf. pp. 14, 214, 236.

[5] "David Feinberg's Historical Survey of the Colonization of the Russian Jews in Argentina," tr. by Leo Shpall, in the *Publications of the American Jewish Historical Society*, XLIII (1953), 37 ff., esp. p. 47.

On Feinberg, cf. S. M. Ginsburg, *Amolike Peterburg* (New York, 1944), pp. 111–124 and G. Sliozberg, *Dela minuvshikh dnei* (Paris, 1933), II, 107. An earlier part of his memoirs was translated in *He-Avar*, IV (Tel Aviv, 1956).

The Americans secured the assistance of the jurist Henry (Genrikh) Sliozberg (1863–1937), and the medium of communication was German.[6] Thus two inquiries were conducted simultaneously by non-Jews with Jewish assistants. Both produced very positive reports about Russian Jewry. The American report saw in this community a source of immigrants to the United States, while the White report saw in them prospective settlers under the Hirsch colonization scheme.

The present study is centered on White and his activity. Arnold White (1848–1925) was a man with a political and literary record. A public spirited man of independent means, the son of a clergyman, he became associated with the movement against the immigration of destitute aliens (which meant at the time Russian-Polish Jews) to Britain. He belonged to the group of writers who studied urban problems in London; later he wrote on imperial problems, and (in the new century) joined in the anti-German chorus. Recent studies of the anti-alien movement mention him as a (even if unconscious) social Darwinist, a rather muddle-headed, better class politician sliding toward mob agitation. His statements about the Jews sounded judophobic. What made him suspicious of the Jews was that they (except for a tiny aristocratic crust) refused to intermarry with non-Jews, and thus remained outside the main bloodstream of the country. Yet White was very afraid of being called an anti-Semite.[7]

White mentions (*Modern Jew*, p. 55): "During my journey I was accompanied by a Russian-Jewish gentleman who speaks the 'jargon' — half Hebrew and half German — of the Chosen People, and to whose help and ever-ready energy I am deeply indebted," and in the report to Hirsch (*ibid.*, p. 296) Feinberg is mentioned by name.

[6] In his memoirs that appeared in 3 volumes in Paris in 1933, he discusses the period of Alexander III in I, 249 ff., and the Hirsch project and his own work with the Americans in II, 31 ff. Cf. the *Russian Jewish Encyclopedia* and the *Encyclopaedia Judaica s.v.* Sliozberg. On the assistance given by Jews to Weber and Kempster, see the note on p. 33 of the *Report*. A French summary of their report appeared under the title *La situation des Juifs en Russie*.

[7] John A. Garrard, *The English and Immigration 1889–1910* (New York and London, 1971); according to Bernard Gainer, in his *The Alien Invasion*

Four times he stood unsuccessfully for Parliament (1886–1906).
The *Times* obituary of White had this to say:

> But it was as "Vanoe" in the *Referee* that Mr. W. was best known.
> For years he set forth, week by week, the strong, sometimes extreme,
> views which he ardently held on the questions of the day. They
> were substantially the views of the average Englishman, the "man
> in the street," who delighted to see his own rather hazy ideas and
> prejudices presented in clear form and with a compelling plausi-
> bility. Probably W. never wrote a line in which he did not himself
> most fervently believe, and there can be no doubt that it was this
> intense conviction, added to no slight skill in effective literary
> expression, which accounts for his long tenure of the position of a
> popular oracle. Many, perhaps most, of his views were fundamentally
> sound and healthy. The light of his patriotism always burned high
> and clear; he stood, for example, unfalteringly for a strong Empire
> and a strong Navy. But, like most enthusiasts of this type, he was
> apt to ride his hobbies too far and too hard, and thereby give
> handles to the cynic and the mocker. He was too fond of shortcuts
> and neat solutions, hardly realizing the extraordinary complexities
> of our social and political problems. For this reason it may be
> doubted whether his influence as a publicist was in the long run as
> great as might have been imagined from the number of his readers.
> He was profoundly convinced of the reality of subterranean
> influences in our social, political, and industrial life... While his
> attitude towards the activities of the Jews was extremely critical.
> He was known to an immense number of people — very largely

(New York, 1972), p. 3 the actual number of Russian-Jewish settlers in England
was: over 7,000 in 1891, about 3,000 in 1892, and fewer than 3,000 in 1893.
For the rest of the decade — about 2,500 annually. The first reference to
immigration in *The Times* was a letter from White. Gainer, *ibid.*, p. 81.

He felt that immigration depressed the Englishman's standard of comforts
(p. 79). He was painfully honest and well-meaning, but hasty-tempered, overzealous, and woefully unsystematic (p. 82).

Every year for the six years following 1884, he visited South Africa to plant
settlements of English laborers and artisans among the Dutch in Cape Colony,
and in the intervals, investigated Continental emigration schemes. Emigration
was his panacea for the moral, economic, and physical maladies of a congested
nation, and, moreover, the best practical aid he could devise to "the true
federation of the Empire" (p. 108).

This reminds one of Foggartism in John Galsworthy's *The Silver Spoon*
(pt. 2, chapts. 1, 2, 4).

through his letters which *The Times* has been wont to publish, for his persistent concern in everything that affected the welfare of the Empire and of all humanity....[8]

In 1899, after a decade of writing essays on the Jews, he published a volume of new articles, *The Modern Jew*. Filial piety prompted him to include observations by his father on biblical prophecies (pp. 283–294). His trips to Russia and visits with the Jewish communities, especially in the rural settlements, are discussed anew (he had done it before in journals), and some documents pertaining to the trips are published: Hirsch's letter of introduction to Pobedonostsev (pp. 26–27); White's memorandum to the Russian authorities citing desiderata for operations under Hirsch's scheme (pp. 46–48); the first report to Hirsch (pp. 294–301).[9] The Russian situation reviewed, White goes into Austrian affairs (pp. 67–81): an alarmist survey of Jewish numbers and successes in banking, the press, commerce, education, landed estates; and the anti-Semitic movement (pp. 82–91). White saw in the Dreyfus affair the decadence of France (p. VIII).

"Captain Dreyfus as a hero and a man adds one more to the long line of Jewish worthies whose annals adorn the history of the race." Yet he quotes in earnest German anti-Semites, and even repeats the stories that in 1840 Jewish elders assembled in Prague decided that the press must be seized in order to blind and deceive the people, and that a decade later a French Jewish leader had declared that the wealth of the world would belong exclusively to the Jews (p. 87).[10]

The alarming growth of Jewish materialism and cosmopolitan

[8] *The Times* (London), February 6, 1925, p. 14. *The Times*, March 4, 1925, p. 10: A fund for cancer research in his memory was started.

[9] *The Jewish Chronicle*, April 7, 1899, pp. 10–12 — necrology of Baroness de Hirsch; pp. 12–13: In memoriam by A. White. Here mention is made of *several* reports discussed by White and the Hirsches.

[10] Elie Halevy, *Imperialism and the Rise of Labour* (vol. V, *A History of the English People in the Nineteenth Century*), tr. by E. T. Watkin (London, 1951), pp. 371–375. Here in the note on pp. 372–373, White is characterized as an anti-Semite. S. Bayne touches on White's activity in *Jewish Leadership and Anti-Semitism in Britain 1898–1918* (Columbia thesis, 1976).

indifference to family and national development seems to call for a redress from a source that is neither to be bought nor influenced. In the growth of the woman's movement I look for the healthiest antidote to Jewish materialism [p. 279].

A place will have to be found for the persecuted or the undesirable Jews. White is inclined to take up a suggestion of some Russian grandees: Jews might be settled in Armenia depopulated by Turkish massacres (of the Semitic race, Armenians). Therefrom the Jews would expand to Palestine and it would not be long before "the fulfilment of prophecy would come about by the operation of natural and economic law" (p. 277).

The author is outspoken against Jewish financiers for their support of Russian loans, and inaction in the face of Russian persecution of the Jews. For a time the publication *Darkest Russia* enjoyed support of Jews but that was later withdrawn (pp. 223–236).

It occurred to some that what may have moved Hirsch to turn to White and employ him for repeated visits to the Czar's empire, was not only White's experience in colonizing in South Africa, but also White's unimpeachable judophobia that assured him a hearing with the fanatical Jew-baiters who dictated Russia's Jewish policy.[11]

In St. Petersburg White kept in touch with the British Embassy. His negotiations with the Russians and his report to Hirsch were in confidence communicated to the ambassador who in turn brought them to the knowledge of the cabinet[12] which sent them for perusal to Queen Victoria and the Prince of Wales.[13]

We thus have here a set of archival data about Hirsch's initi-

[11] Gainer, *Alien Invasion*, p. 25. The view was expressed by Sliozberg, (*op. cit.*, II, 34), who adds that if so, Hirsch made no mistake by selecting White to be his emissary. Sliozberg mentioned White's readiness to assist the Russians against their "detractors" in the new century, in the era of pogroms.

[12] Eliyahu Feldman, "The Moscow Expulsion of 1891 in the Reports of British Ambassador in Russia," *He-Avar*, XVIII (Tel Aviv, May 1971), 55–62.

[13] The future King Edward VII only began to receive cabinet material at about this time, since by the queen's order he had been kept out of state affairs for many years.

ative, White's negotiations and the British Embassy's reporting thereof. A survey of these follows.

Hirsch gave White a letter to Pobedonostsev, the influential figure of the Russian regime.[14] Writing (May 7, from Paris) about his colonization scheme and the difficulties encountered, Hirsch appeals to the generosity of the Russian to obtain a respite, a delay in executing measures concerning the Jews. Such relenting would enable a number of the unfortunate to find a new life in the colonies.

On June 11, the British ambassador in St. Petersburg, Sir R. Morier, reported to London White's arrival with a letter from Lord Salisbury (Britain's prime minister and foreign secretary), and mentioned that the Russian ambassador in Britain (Staal) had addressed a letter to the Russian minister of foreign affairs (Giers) warmly commending White. Morier presented White to the Russian minister for foreign affairs,[15] as well as to other Russian personages. The emperor received a report on the subject, proved "well disposed to the plan, though he did not believe in the possibility of its success."

The British ambassador was particularly impressed by Hirsch's letter to Pobedonostsev: "a letter of extreme astuteness and admirably written." He then proceeds with the story of the million francs Hirsch had left earlier in the hands of Pobedonostsev who appropriated the sum, allegedly for Orthodox priests' seminaries. This gave Hirsch an occasion to address Pobedonostsev. Giers and the minister of finances, Vyshnegradsky,[16] cooperated against

[14] Robert F. Byrnes, *Pobedonostsev* (Indiana, Bloomington, 1968). On P's position on Jews, see pp. 104 f., 203–209.

[15] Nikolai Karlovich Girs or Giers (1820–1895) worked in the Russian foreign service in Rumania, Turkey, Persia, Switzerland and Sweden. He became senator in 1875 and minister of foreign affairs in 1882. Originally he supported an alliance with Austria and Germany, tried to avoid clashes with Britain (re: Central Asia and India), but was instrumental in bringing about a rapprochement with France. His attitude toward the Jews deserves separate treatment.

[16] Ivan Alekseevich Vyshnegradsky (1832–95) was an eminent scientist, technologist and inventor. He served as minister in 1882–92. Cf. the Brockhaus-

Pobedonostsev, to secure some relenting in the anti-Jewish scheme of action.

On July 10, 1891, White's successful negotiations are reported, and copies supplied of some documents. One is a statement on what is requested of the Russian government to enable the Hirsch organization to act in the Empire;[17] the other is the report to Hirsch.[18] "Sunshine and sweat" will give the Jews of Russia a better life in the new colonies.

"In short, if courage — moral courage — hope, patience, temperance, are fine qualities, then the Jews are a fine people. Such a people, under wise direction, is destined to make a success of any well-organized plan of colonisation, whether in Argentina, Siberia, or South Africa."

The tour de force of Balaam. The ambassador summarizes White's success: in less than two months Mr. White has attained first the initiatory consent of the Russian government for his inquiry; second, the completion of his tour of inspection (in Russia, not Poland). "These are results far transcending anything I had expected or could reasonably have hoped for, and I am still at a loss fully to account for them."

He proceeds to indicate what might partly explain such results, and concludes with a dithyramb for the Hirsch plan and its impact on Jewish fate and future:

> The moment of Mr. White's arrival was a singularly opportune one, and nobody could have been so well fitted to use the opportunity as Mr. White. The Moscow persecutions had been a "tchihnovnik" *boutade*, in which the police employés of the sacred city, who for years had vied with each other in receiving bribes from the chosen people, now vied with each other in competitive brutality. They had been initiated *ab irato*, without any definite plan or object, and the whole so-called patriotic press hounding on, a sort

Efron *Encyclopaedia* (1892), VIIa, 595–601 and the *Bol'shaia Sovetskaia Encyclopaedia* (3rd ed., 1971), V, 574 f. He was definitely opposed to the persecution.

[17] This is identical with the letter printed in *The Modern Jew*, pp. 46–48 (dated June 16–28).

[18] *Ibid.*, pp. 294–301.

of anti-Semitic frenzy seized hold of superficial public opinion. But a strong reaction had set in. In the upper Government circles there were many who had all along been against the movement. The deep emotion produced in Europe by the undoubtedly exaggerated and often ignorant reports of the public press outside of Russia increased the numbers of these day by day, even amongst strong anti-Semitics, and, as if with one consent, all began asking "*Cui bono*? What is all this to lead to? How, by driving these people, odious as they are, from pillar to post, will you get rid of them?"

It was at this juncture that Mr. White appeared, and, with a singularly happy metaphor, which soon went from mouth to mouth and became classical, answered the question. "Your Government," he said, "gives me the impression of a man in a close and stuffy room with all the doors and windows shut, martyrized by swarms of flies. He gets up furious and goes about flapping at them from right to left. He creates infinite buzzing, but leaves things as they were before. I have come on behalf of Baron Hirsch with the modest request to be allowed to open a window. The flies will not all go out, but many of them will, and all feel they have the chance. They will cease to madly buzz in their endeavours to escape your terrible flapper." This, I think, gives the key-note to the auspicious *entrée en scène* of Mr. White. But this *entrée en scène* was undoubtedly in the first place due to the extraordinarily astute introduction which he brought to M. Pobedonostzew from Baron Hirsch, writing as the Baron did to a man who had received a 40,000*l.* bribe, had not fulfilled his share of the bargain, and was now standing in the full blaze of an indignant public opinion. Mr. White, who has a most happy knack of calling a spade a spade, used his ground of vantage and boldly told the great Proctor of the Holy Synod that not in Europe only, but in the whole civilized world, he was regarded as the moving spirit, the *fons et origo*, of this nineteenth century revival of the days of Moorish persecution and expulsion. The Proctor denied this, swore he had nothing to do with it personally, but felt the reproach to the quick. "You have a chance," argued Mr. White, "of at least weakening this impression by putting your shoulder to the wheel and using all your efforts to secure success to Baron Hirsch's enterprise. You will get the credit and appear in another light." The hint was not lost, and M. Pobedonostzew did everything in his power to render assistance. All the rest is due to the skill and energy with which the negotiator used the opportunities afforded him. Mr. White is far too good a wine to require any bush to advertise him; but I may remark incidentally, as a matter of psycho-

logical interest, that he possesses in an eminent degree two qualities — exceptional enthusiasm, burning with a clear dry light, and
extraordinary practical knowledge of whatever subject he takes up,
combined with a rare power of work. Now, the Russians possess the
former in a high degree, the latter they are entirely incapable of.
To understand details, and to work, their souls abhor. The result
was that to one class of Russians, and that the best, he succeeded
in thoroughly imparting his own enthusiasm, whilst another class,
the practical "tchinovniks," he fairly magnetized by the wealth of
his knowledge in connection with the art of colonization, and the
way in which all the practical difficulties suggested by them in connection with the scheme seemed to vanish by a few common-sense
explanations showing how the plan had already in its minutest
details been worked out.

In conclusion, I would observe that, although it is impossible to
forecast what will be the practical outcome of the scheme, there is
one side to it which must not be allowed to go unnoticed, because it
has already evoked a force which will have to be reckoned with,
viz., the great excitement and emigration thirst caused throughout
the entire Jewish community by the reports in the press of Mr.
White's mission, and still more by the impact of his visits to the
Jewish centres.

At present the Jewish people are dwelling in the Dantesque
hell — "Ye who enter leave hope behind" — in the impenetrable
darkness of a cavern without issue. The prospect of a land of
promise beyond the seas, to which free access will be open, is
the return of hope, the small ray of light bursting through the
darkness; and this is the answer to those who argue that there can
after all be no practical result to the scheme, for, admitting its
utmost success, and that within the next decade some 200,000 or
300,000 Jews are settled in Argentine, what is that to the 5,000,000
who remain behind?

It is true that, for a long while, only a very small percentage will
leave the land of bondage, but with the first emigrant-ship that
leaves Hamburgh hope will come to all, and the difference of living
with hope and without hope is the difference between living in
Paradise or in hell.[19]

In the course of his tour of the Pale of Settlement, White visited
Odessa (June 15–17).[20] Among his engagements in that city, we

[19] An archival piece from the Public Record Office. It bears the imprint:
"printed for the Cabinet" and was meant to be confidential.

[20] Thomas B. Sandwith, consul general, wrote from Odessa to London on

learn from a report (sent June 18), was "an interesting interview with the members of the Committee for aiding the poor Jews established in Palestine, in common with which Committee he is adverse to the scheme of colonising that country with Jews."

The meeting with the heads of the "Odessa Committee," i.e., the Center of Hibbath Zion headed by Pinsker, was mentioned in Feinberg's account.[21] The above quotation from the British consular report is the only reference to the tenor of the discussion. It is known that Pinsker (who died toward the end of the year) was full of pessimism about Palestine's prospects and must have been inspired by the scope and vigor of Hirsch's plan.[22] It is therefore

July 25, requesting permission to inspect the Jewish colonies in the government of Kherson. In view of White's reported positive opinion of these colonies, Sandwith remarks, "The view commonly held here is curiously adverse to that... held by Mr. White." The reply from London (July 31) was negative: no obstacle should be put in the way of the Hirsch scheme, and controversy should be avoided.

[21] See Israel Klausner, *Mi-Kattowiz ad Basel* (Jerusalem, 1965), p. 96. Upon Pinsker's initiative, a meeting of Jewish public figures was convened at the home of Abraham Greenberg.

[22] Cf. M. Perlmann, "Pinsker's Testament," *Bitzaron*, XLVI (1962), 16–22; A. Böhm, *Die Zionistische Bewegung* (Tel Aviv, 1935), I, 114 f. Apparently Pinsker began to think of a territorial center in Argentina, and of Palestine as a spiritual center. The *initial* impact of the Hirsch scheme and the munificence supporting it was tremendous. The British ambassador refers to it, and Pinsker's attitude presumably was due to it. *Ha-Maggid* of Sept. 17, 1891 (N37):

בא היום שקוינוהו, הגיעה העת אשר נכספה וגם כלתה לה נפשנו! כאגלי טל על ארץ עיפה כן היא הבשורה אשר הגיעה לאזנינו מלונדון, כי סוף סוף עבר רעיון הבארון הירש לטובת אחינו האומללים תקופת החזיון והדמיון וירקם עליו עור וילבש תמונת מעשה חי וקים.

The anti-emigration line of *Voskhod* changes after the weekly and the monthly were closed for six months by a decree of the ministry of the interior (March 13, 1891). Renewing publication (N11 of the weekly) on Sept. 22, the editor wrote:

"In the course of the six months that elapsed since our last talk with our readers, a turning point was reached in the so-called Jewish problem in Russia: The focal point shifted now to the problem of emigration, which is on everybody's lips, and is the only one in which people take interest.... But now the problem has been solved...."

fully possible that the report is not incorrect about the tragic defeatist attitude of the members of the Odessa Committee when confronted with the energetic and eloquent "Argentinian."

Hoveve Zion were following Hirsch's activities for years, discussing them, and aspiring to gain his sympathies for the national cause and for colonization in Palestine.[23]

Eight students from Russia, studying in Berlin and Dresden, wrote a memorandum to White urging him to find out how attached the Jewish masses were to the land of their ancestors and to the idea of colonization of Palestine, and how this idea was steadily gaining loyalty and support both in the East and the West (including America). He, White, has a chance to play an historical role by persuading Baron Hirsch to apply his energy and means to the cause of national regeneration in Palestine.[24]

* * *

A telegram was dispatched from the Foreign Office to the Embassy on September 18, 1891:

> Mr. Arnold White states that two nihilist delegates called upon Baron Hirsch in Paris to endeavour to enlist the assistance of the Jewish community for the nihilist cause. They asked for a subvention of one million francs in furtherance of their new plan of action. They had decided to desist from any attempts in Russia itself where they felt they were powerless, and intended to watch

---

I.L. Perez was at the time the editor of די יודישע ביבליאטעק. In it we find an appendix: The portrait of Hirsch, a son of whom his people may be proud. A quote combined from a biblical passage (II Sam., 7:23; I Chr., 17:21) and from a passage of Minḥa for Sabbath clinches it:

‟אתה אחד ושמך אחד ומי כעמך ישראל גוי אחד בארץ״

[23] A. Druyanov, ed., *Ketavim Letoldoth Hibbath Zion* (Tel Aviv, 1925), II, cols. 264 (1887 1), 311 f., 326, 330, 336 f, 397, 415 f, 420–422, 432 f.; III, 952, 954.

In the Zionist Archives (A g 171/10) there is a Russian letter from Vasilii Berman to M. Ussyshkin, dated Oct. 30, 1891: "Argentina is becoming a fact, and it is time to think of smuggling the seed of Jewish nationalism into Argentina."

[24] Zionist Archives (A 126/15), in Russian.

for purposes of assassination all the members of the imperial family
who might be travelling abroad... .[25]

On September 25 Henry Howard reported from the embassy in
St. Petersburg that on the 19th he had read the dispatch to Giers
who thanked Lord Salisbury for the information.

"His Excellency remarked that he saw that he was partly indebted to Mr. Arnold White for this communication, and said that
he had been much pleased with that gentleman when he had met
him this summer; that he considered that Mr. White was not only
clever and energetic but also very fair, unbiassed, and broad-
minded."

"Mr. de Giers then said that the Jewish Problem was a very
difficult one to solve; in England we had comparatively few Jews,
but that in Russia there were millions; they were an energetic,
persevering and remarkably clever race, so clever that, if not under
disabilities, every post from the lowest to the highest would be
filled by Hebrews within a very short space of time."

"On the other hand, being under the above named disabilities,
and thus never being able to rise in any profession, nor hold any
official post of trust, the Jews become morose and discontented,
and liable to throw themselves into any plot or conspiracy, and
were for these reasons a very dangerous element in the Empire.
He had known some Jews who were excellent and loyal subjects,
but His Excellency feared that they were exceptions to the general
rule."

The cloak and dagger anecdote notwithstanding, this gives us
another glimpse of White's activity and conversations.

* * *

White was impressed by the fact that despite poverty and under-
nourishment, the Jews were sober, gentle to women and children,
and intent on schooling for the young. He learned from observation
and statistics that the various arguments against the Jews were

[25] A group of Russian revolutionaries was arrested in Paris on March 29
1890.

based on malice, distortion, and ill-will. But what is behind that
ill-will? The Russian rational argument was that the Jews were
dangerous to the mass of simple minded Russians, especially the
peasants.

> The intellect of the Jew is masterful. His assiduity, his deadly
> resolve to get on, his self-denial and ambition surmount all natural
> obstacles. If all careers in the Russian Empire were thrown open to
> the Russian Jew, not a decade would go by before the whole Russian
> administration from Port Arthur to Eydtkuhnen and from Arch-
> angel to Yalta must pass into Hebraic hands. This is a sober
> statement of fact. The Russian nature is self-indulgent, impulsive,
> kind-hearted, generous, and passionate. Russians would have no
> chance of survival against the cold determination of a people that
> exists only when living as a parasitic growth on another race. What
> Tsar in his senses, what sane Russian Minister would permit his
> country to commit suicide by ceding the civil administration to a
> Jewish minority? England does not invest the Bengali with power in
> India because he passses difficult examinations with the greatest
> ease.

Jewish disabilities are "the most extravagant compliment ever
paid by one race to another" (*The Modern Jew*, p. 19).

> The main object pursued by the governing classes in repressing
> the Jew in Russia is sheer self-defence. Russians hold that the bright
> Jewish intellect, if allowed free play, would contaminate the whole
> Empire within a short space of time. It has been calculated that if
> the repressive laws of Russia were repealed, and the Jews allowed
> access to any and every post in the service of the Empire, eight years
> would not pass before every post worth having outside the army
> and navy would be filled by an official of the Hebrew faith. I believe
> the statement to be little if at all exaggerated.[26]

White did try hard to see the two sides of the picture, in Russia
and elsewhere. But he could never suppress a layer of antipathy
toward the Jews as subject of his enquiry.[27]

[26] "The Truth about the Russian Jew," 697.

[27] White had no luck with the national biography and with Jewish encyclo-
paedias. Only the *Russian Jewish Encyclopaedia* mentions him in the article
on Hirsch (VI, 564). In 1891 his trips were frequently mentioned in the press,
in general as well as in Jewish publications.

* *
*

Baron Hirsch to Pobedonostsev:

Paris
le 7 mai 1891
2 rue de l'Elysée

Excellence,

Je prends la liberté de remettre la présente lettre à M. Arnold White, Président d'une Société Anglaise de colonisation dans l'Afrique Australe, qui se rend en Russie et que j'ai prié de profiter de cette occasion pour faire, en mon nom, auprès de Votre Excellence la démarche dont je vais avoir l'honneur de lui indiquer l'objet.

Peut-être Votre Excellence a-t-Elle appris que je m'occupe de trouver au delà de l'océan, notamment dans la République Argentine, des étendues considérables de territoire où puissent être installés une partie de mes coréligionnaires de Russie. J'ai envoyé dans ce but à Buenos Ayres, des fondés de pouvoir chargés de procéder aux acquisitions nécessaires et de prendre les mesures préparatoires destinées à organiser l'oeuvre de colonisation que j'ai conçue. Mais, malgré la célérité que j'ai apportée à ces opérations, elles exigent, Votre Excellence le concevra sans peine, des délais assez considérables et il s'écoulera necessairement un certain temps avant qu'elles soient accomplies.

Dans cette situation j'ai pensé pouvoir m'adresser aux sentiments de générosité de V. Ex. pour qu'Elle veuille bien employer sa haute influence auprès des autorités compétentes afin d'obtenir sursis à l'execution des mesures récemment décidées et concernant les israëlites établis dans certaines régions de l'Empire. Je n'entreprends nullement, M. le Procureur Général, d'invoquer l'intervention de Votre Excellence en vue de retrait de ces mesures, sachant bien qu'une demande de ma part serait denuée de toute chance de succès. Mais les terribles effets qu'elles doivent produire seraient au moins en partie atténués si l'exécution en était ralentie de manière à permettre à un certain nombre de malheureux de trouver les conditions d'une vie nouvelle dans les colonies que je m'occupe d'installer et à leur épargner dans l'intervalle l'existence de privations, de vagabondage et d'affreuse misère à laquelle ils seraient condamnés en l'absence de toute ressource et de tout domicile assuré.

J'ose compter que V.E. ne voudra pas refuser sa puissante entremise pour cette œuvre d'humanité et je la prie d'agréer dans cette espérance l'assurance de ma haute considération.

(sé) M. Hirsch.

Translation

Excellency,

I am taking the liberty of entrusting this letter to Mr. Arnold White, president of a British society for colonization in Southern Africa, who is proceeding to Russia and whom I have asked to approach Your Excellency, in my name, concerning a matter which I shall have the honor to present to you.

[The rest is the translation of Arnold White in *The Modern Jew*, pp. 26 f.]

"Perhaps your Excellency has learnt that I am occupying myself in finding on the other side of the ocean, especially in the Argentine Republic, some large tracts of territory for the purpose of settling some of my co-religionists who are Russian subjects. I have sent with this object to Buenos Ayres money and authority to proceed with the establishment of all things that are necessary for the preliminary organisation of the colonies which I have determined to start, but notwithstanding the speed with which I am carrying on these operations, they involve, as your Excellency may well understand without difficulty, considerable delays, and there must elapse a certain time before they can be actually accomplished.

Under these circumstances, I have thought myself able to appeal to your Excellency's feelings and generosity that you would be good enough to apply your high influence with the authorities concerned in order to obtain a suspension in the execution of the measures recently decided with regard to the Israelites established in certain parts of the Russian Empire.

I am not in any way invoking your Excellency's intervention for the withdrawal of these measures, knowing well that such a step on my part would be denounced beforehand and would have no chance of success, but the terrible effects which the suspension of the May Laws will produce suggest that their execution should be at least in part relaxed in such a way as to allow a certain number of these unhappy people to obtain conditions of a new life in the colonies which I am now engaged in preparing for them, and also to spare them in the interval the existence of privations, a life of mendicancy, and the frightful misery to which they will be subjected in the absence of any resources and any assured domicile.

I venture to count on your Excellency not to refuse your most powerful assistance in this work of humanity, and I pray you in this hope to believe in the assurance of my high consideration."

* *
*

The Institute for Advanced Studies
The Hebrew University
Jerusalem, 1977

A LETTER OF RECOMMENDATION ON BEHALF OF THE PROSELYTE MEVORAKH FROM THE GENIZA

By ALEXANDER SCHEIBER

As late as two decades ago, Professor S. D. Goitein wrote the following: "I hope to treat the rather frequent references to proselytes in the Geniza in a separate paper."[1] Most recently he has added: "I have not yet carried out this intention — fortunately, for new material is cropping up all the time and the entire question needs to be studied in a wider context."[2]

Since the eleventh to thirteenth centuries were the Golden Age of proselytism, we should not be surprised to find references to proselytes in all kinds of places.[3] Not long ago Ben-Sasson revived the theory that one of Maimonides' correspondents was the Norman proselyte Obadiah.[4] As late as the thirteenth century there are references to converts to Judaism. In 1234, the son of a proselyte in Egypt is mentioned (בן אלגר).[5]

It is thus easy to understand why an entire tract (now lost) was devoted to the proselytes; this figures on one of Joseph b. Jacob Habavli's book-lists: מאמר על גרים) (מקאלה אלגר.[6]

[1] S. D. Goitein, "The Geniza Collection of the University Museum of the University of Pennsylvania," *Jewish Quarterly Review*, XLIX (1958/59), 46, n. 28.

[2] Goitein, *A Mediterranean Society* (Berkeley, Los Angeles, London, 1971), II, 311.

[3] Judah Rosenthal, "Polemical Tractates" (Hebrew), *Salo Wittmayer Baron Jubilee Volume* (Jerusalem, 1974), III, 370–371; also his "Excerpts of Polemics from the Book of Yoseph Hameqanne" (Hebrew), *Kobez Al-Yad*, VIII (Jerusalem, 1975), 320.

[4] H. H. Ben-Sasson, "Jewish Uniqueness in the Writings of the 12th Century" (Hebrew), *P'raqim* (Jerusalem, 1969–1974), II, 180, n. 108.

[5] M. Gil, *Documents of the Jewish Pious Foundations from the Cairo Geniza* (Leiden, 1976), 438, No. 131.

[6] Nehemiah Allony and Alexander Scheiber, "An Autograph Book-List

Let me draw attention to a new proselyte. The ENA New
Series, based on Geniza material, recently found in the Jewish
Theological Seminary of America (New York) and arranged by
Dr. M. A. Friedmann, Professor S. D. Goitein[7] and Professor
M. Schmelzer, contains many significant items. It was there that
I found the following letter of recommendation (21:10). The
author is unknown. He describes how a good, God-fearing soul
has come to the seat of Rabbenu Menaḥēm, where he adopted
the Jewish religion and the name Mevōrākh. The writer commends
him to R. Yehuda and David, the two "praiseworthy and pure"
brothers: perhaps to ask them to give him material help, or to
introduce him to the local Jewish community.

Rabbenu Menaḥēm is certainly identical with the great Rav of
Cairo, the Chief Judge in the first third of the thirteenth century.
The son of Isaac b. Sāsōn, he was a man of liberal views who
helped all who sought his aid.[8]

Mevōrākh ("the blessed one") or Mubārak as a name adopted
by proselytes is not unusual; several persons bearing this name
are known.[9]

We cannot identify R. Yehuda and his brother. The former's
title "השר הגדול בישראל" does not reveal much, for it is quite
frequent;[10] we do not even know, therefore, where they lived.

Nevertheless, the letter enriches our knowledge about thirteenth
century proselytes. It shows, too, the ethical caliber of those who
adopted the Jewish faith in the Middle Ages.

of R. Josef Rosh-Haseder" (Hebrew), *Kirjath Sepher* XLVIII (1972–73),
153, 161.

[7] S. D. Goitein, "The Rabbi..." (Hebrew), *Tarbiz*, XLV (1975/76), 65, n. 5.

[8] Goitein, *Mediterranean Society*, II, 514, n. 26; and his *Letters of Medieval
Traders* (Princeton, 1973), pp. 65, 68–69.

[9] Norman Golb, "A Study of a Proselyte to Judaism who Fled to Egypt at
the Beginning of the Eleventh Century" (Hebrew), *Ṣefunot*, VIII (1964), 104;
Goitein, *Mediterranean Society*, II, 306–307.

[10] Jacob Mann, *The Jews in Egypt* (Oxford, 1920), I, 260; David Z. Baneth,
"Geniza Documents on Jewish Communal Affairs in Egypt," *Alexander Marx
Jubilee Volume* (New York, 1950), Hebrew Sect., p. 93; J. Mann, *The Collected
Articles* (Gedera, 1971), III, 456.

Ena N.S. 21:10

בששון ועלצון

וסואה אעלאמה דאם ע[זה   אן חא[מלהא
אלשיך מ[בו]רך גר הצדק כ[אדמ]ה כאן מן
עדה סג[ני]ן פי זמאן רבינו מנחם זק̇ל̇ חצ̇ר
5 אלי מגלסה ו[מ]לו אותו לפניו וטבלו אותו והו
אנסאן חסן דיין כייר מא צהר מנה אלא אלדין
ואליראה וקצד כתב כתאב אלי בין ידין מגלס
אלסאדה אלאגלא שני האחים המשובחים
הצחים האזרחים כ̇ק̇ג̇ מרנו ורבינו
10 יהודה השר הגדול בישראל... חם ודוד

תרגום

בששון ושמחה

זולת זה עלי להודיעו, יתמיד כבודו, כי נושא מכתב זה
השיך׳ מבורך גר הצדק עבדך היה לפני
מספר שנים בזמן רבינו מנחם זק̇ל̇ בא
5 אל מושבו ומלו אותו לפניו וטבלו אותו והוא
אדם טוב, ירא שמים, חסיד, לא נראה ממנו אלא חסידות
ויראה ורצה לכתוב מכתב אל מושב
האדונים הנעלים שני האחים המשובחים
הצחים האזרחים כ̇ק̇ג̇ מרנו ורבינו
10 יהודה השר הגדול בישראל... חם ודוד

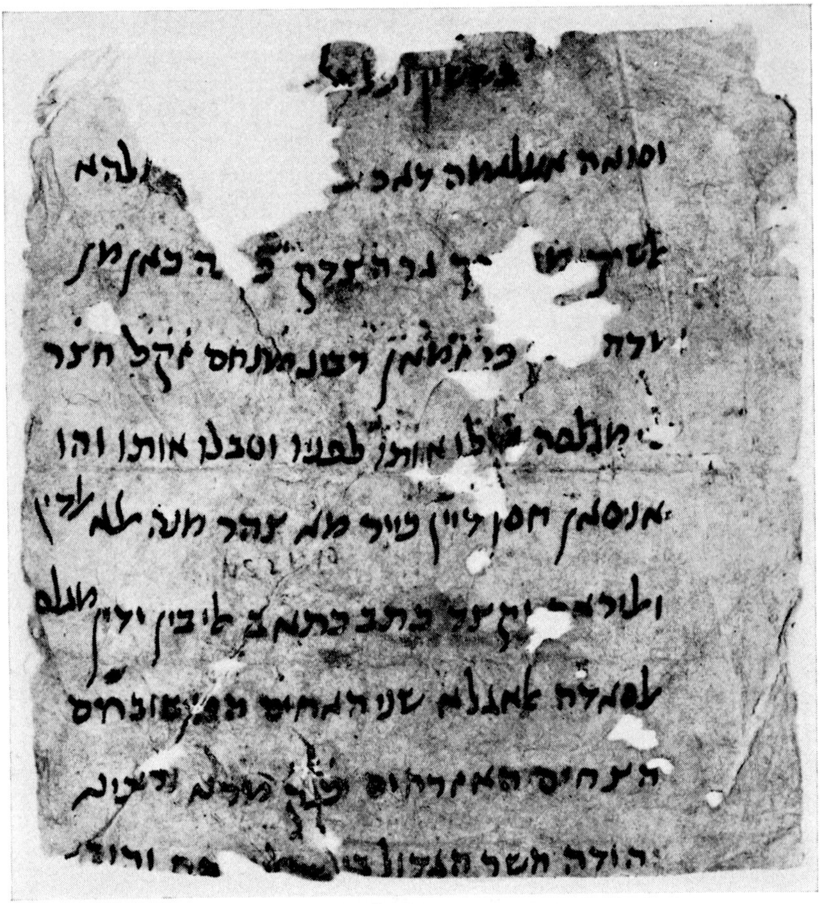

JUDAH MONIS
IN LIGHT OF AN UNPUBLISHED MANUSCRIPT

By Eisig Silberschlag

More than two hundred and fifty years have elapsed since Judah
Monis (1683–1764) was appointed "Instructor of the Hebrew
Language" at Harvard College on April 30, 1722 at a salary of
£50 a year and awarded an M.A. in 1723.[1] Yet an aura of mystery

---

[1] Not in 1720 as Professor Moore maintains. See George Foot Moore,
"Judah Monis" in *Massachusetts Historical Society, Proceedings LII* (Boston,
1919), 290. The reason for the error of such a careful scholar: "Monis's
name was placed at the foot of the class of 1720" in the Triannual Catalog, but
the candidates received the degree in 1723. See Clifford K. Shipton, *Biographical Sketches of Those Who Attended Harvard College in the Classes 1722–1725*
in *Sibley's Harvard Graduates VII 1722–1725* (*Massachusetts Historical
Society*, Boston, 1945), 642, n. 12. The error reappears in Wolfson's sketch
of Judah Monis in *Dictionary of American Biography VII*, ed. Dumas Malone
(New York, 1934), p. 86; also in *Sibley's Harvard Graduates VIII*, 107.
Since Monis resigned from his instructorship on November 12, 1760, he had
served Harvard University for thirty-eight years.

As for Monis's annual salary: it was not "a proper support and main-
tainance" (!) — to use his style in a letter to Harvard's overseers who promptly
increased his salary to an annual £70. See Moore's "Judah Monis," p. 295.
But the increment did not suffice. The resourceful Monis who had engaged in
trade in New York kept a shop in Cambridge and tried to combine an academic
career with a business venture. Later he complained in a petition to Governor
Shirley that, without a grant from the public treasury, he will be "reduced to
want." *Ibid.*, p. 299. The Rev. Benjamin Colman who pronounced a discourse
based on John 5:46 before Monis's conversion on March 27, 1722, hoped that
the overseers of Harvard would appoint Monis "Hebrew professor." But that
was "a hint they did not take," *ibid.*, p. 293. The first to hold a Harvard professorship of Hebrew was Stephen Sewall, a student of Monis who came to be
regarded as the most distinguished Orientalist of his time in America. The
professorship, made possible by the will of Thomas Hancock, was officially
designated "Hancock Professor of Hebrew and other oriental languages
in Harvard College in Cambridge." It was established by the vote of the

surrounds the enigmatic personality: was he an Italian or an
Algerian Jew? Was his conversion to Christianity at the age of
39 — the conversion of a man who had served as rabbi in the
New World and who "… continued till his death to observe [the]
seventh day as the Sabbath"[2] — an act of faith or an act of

president and fellows on June 12, 1765 and "consented to by the… overseers"
on June 14. See *Harvard Overseers Records*, II (1744–68), 211. For the interesting
"Statutes, Rules and Orders relating to the Hancock Professor of Hebrew and
other Oriental Languages in Harvard College in Cambridge," see *ibid.*, pp.
211–214, 217–219. Mr. Sewall was publicly introduced into his office on
June 19, 1765, *ibid.*, p. 214. And he was removed from his professorship on
September 23, 1785 by a vote of the corporation, for "having for nearly three
years past, been rendered incapable of performing the duties of his office, by
bodily indisposition, and being apparently so debilitated in his mental powers
that there is little or no probability of his ever being able to discharge these
duties to the honor and advantage of the University, or to his own reputation."
See Lee M. Friedman, "A Contemporary Appraisal of Judah Monis, Harvard's
First Instructor in Hebrew," *Publications of the American Jewish Historical
Society*, XXXVIII, Pt. 2 (December, 1948), 146, n. 2. For a biographical
sketch of Stephen Sewall, see *Sibley's Harvard Graduates XV — 1761–1763*
(Boston, 1970), pp. 107–114.

   [2] The quotation is from Hannah Adams in George Alexander Kohut,
"Early Jewish Literature in America," *American Jewish Historical Society*,
III (1895), 113. The allusion to the baptism of "Rabbi Judah Monis, M.A." is
mentioned in his epitaph. And a poem on his tombstone — reprinted several
times in the literature on Monis — records his origins in the Jewish faith:

> A native branch of Jacob see,
> Which once from off its olive broke,
> Regrafted from the living tree
> Of the reviving sap partook.
>
> From teeming Zion's fertile womb,
> As dewy drops in early morn,
> Oh rising bodies from the tomb
> At once be Israel's nation born.

Even Increase Mather was impressed by Monis's conversion. In the Preface to
Monis's Discourse before his baptism he wrote: "God Grant that he (who is
the first Jew that I ever knew Converted in New England) may prove a Blessing
unto many, and especially to some of his own nation…". See the Preface to
R. Judah Monis, *The Truth, Being a Discourse Which the Author Delivered at*

opportunism, a chance to win an academic post with a secure, though meager, salary? What brought him to America: adventurism or the search for "filthy lucre?" Unless some new documentary evidence comes to light, the answers to these questions will rely on hypothetical inferences from existing sources, published or unpublished.

Among the unpublished manuscripts of Judah Monis, *Nomenclatura hebraica*[3] offers some interesting insights into his knowledge — and the attempt to transmit that knowledge — of Hebrew and English. It also affords a glimpse into the teaching methodology of classical languages which, at some universities, has not changed to this day. Grammar and acquisition of a modest vocabulary were the primary goals. The texts often served as means to achieve these goals.

Grammar was a beloved preoccupation of Monis who was the author of the first Hebrew grammar in North America.[4] But the

His Baptism (Boston, 1722), p. IV. Increase Mather was wrong. Twenty years before Monis, a Jew by the name of Simon was baptized in Charleston, Massachusetts. See Lee M. Friedman, "Joshua Montefiore of St. Albans, Vermont," *American Jewish Historical Society*, XL[2] (December, 1950), 119. Monis seems to have "protested" too much: "Christianity... is the only Religion wherein I thought I could be saved..." *The Truth*, p. II of the Dedication. His Christian friends certainly thought so. For conversion of the Jews was part and parcel of a millenarian eschatology which inflamed the minds of Puritans in the seventeenth century, the inheritors of their feverish expectations in the New World and particularly in New England. Though the conversion of one Jew was a negligible event, it could have been regarded as a prophetic portent of mass conversion. On English millenarianism, see Margaret C. Jacob, "Millenarianism and Science in the Late Seventeenth Century," *Journal of the History of Ideas*, XXXVII[2] (April-June, 1976), 335-341.

[3] For the publication of the first and last page of the *Nomenclatura hebraica*, see the author's: "Hebrew Literature at the Tercentenary: Prospect and Retrospect," *Jewish Quarterly Review*, XLV (April, 1955), pp. 432 and 433. Monis's Hebrew phrase for Nomenclature is *Sefer Shemot*. See *Nomenclatura hebraica*, p. 16 and 27. The phrase is identical with the Hebrew title for the second book of the Pentateuch. The manuscript of the *Nomenclatura hebraica* was discovered by Professor Moore in the spring of 1919 in the Harvard College Library. See his "Judah Monis," p. 310.

[4] Judah Monis, *A Grammar of the Hebrew Tongue* (Boston, 1735). The full

subject was less beloved by his students who were often bored by the instructor and the subject matter, frequently voicing their protest against his method which was "so tedious as to be discouraging." They even threw "Bricks, Sticks, Ashes... at the door of the Hebrew school, while he was instructing."[5] As for vocabulary: Monis prepared a brief Anglo-Hebrew noun dictionary, *Nomenclatura hebraica*, in twenty-seven pages for the use of his students. The nouns — to the exclusion of all other parts of speech — are arranged alphabetically, but they do not follow an alphabetical arrangement within any given letter. Thus, the letter L begins with *Lord* and is immediately followed by *Light, Lake, Lightning*. A postscript on page twenty-eight describes the work and notes its importance in hyperbolic statements: it is intended for Monis's pupils and for people who wish to acquire knowledge of Hebrew; it also may help to understand not only "sacred oracles in the original but even any Jewish author." Finally, a third claim was made, namely, that "it was a work altogether new." There is no doubt that the "sacred oracles" referred to christological interpretations of Hebrew prophets. But the meager dictionary was certainly inadequate in providing help for the understanding of any Hebrew author. Nor was it "a work altogether new": Hebrew-Latin dictionaries were common before and especially after the invention of printing.

The *Nomenclatura hebraica* has two columns to each page — one in English, one in Hebrew — and, contrary to modern usage, two words in each line. There is no attempt at definition, quotation of selected passages where the words appear, or multiple explication. Each English word has usually one Hebrew equivalent.

The choice of words rests on no evident principle of selectivity.

title reads: *A Grammar of the Hebrew Tongue, Being an Essay to bring the Hebrew Grammar into English, to Facilitate the Instruction of all those who are desirous of acquiring a clear Idea of this Primitive Tongue by their own Studies; in order to their more distinct Acquaintance with the Sacred Oracles of the Old Testament, according to the Original. And Published more especially for the Use of the Students of Harvard College at Cambridge, in New England.*
[5] Clifford K. Shipton, *Biographical Sketches*, p. 643.

It seems to be a haphazard list of common vocables and such uncommon neologisms as *Tannuriyi* for "baked" and *Lehem Kasheh* for "biscuit" ("*Bisket*" in Monis's spelling), *Metaheret* for "Brush," *Komitiyah* for "Comet." Was "Cider" for *Shekar* a bow in the direction of New Englanders who enjoy the brew made of their native apples to this very day? And "damsel" instead of "girl" for *Na'arah* — a *Kamaz* under the *Nun* — is perhaps a word of excessive modesty. Interestingly, the *Nomenclatura* contains postbiblical words like *Avir* and *Sanegor* and *Androgynos*. These words are largely loanwords from the Greek like the three aforementioned ones in addition to *Gammatria, Kategor, Kalamos, Okeanos, Epicurus* (*Afikoros* in Monis's vocalization) or from the Latin *Ispaklariah, Quaestor, Caesar*.

The vocalization is sloppy, shoddy and defective; even the spelling of English words leaves much to be desired; the translations into Hebrew are imprecise and often erroneous. Instances of defective vocalization are too numerous to cite. One or two examples will suffice: מְדְקְדָק on page 9, צוּצֶנַת and זָאב for "gold" on the same page. Monis seems not to have been able to distinguish between *Segol* and *Zereh*, between *Alef* and *He*. He sometimes spelled as he pronounced: מְזָה for "unleavened bread," for instance; and he often misplaced the *Dagesh* as in שְׁבָּט or discarded it as in תַּמּוּז. He has his own way of spelling "breast" and "bosom" and "heretic": "*Brest*" and "*Boosom*" and "*Heritick*."

As for imprecise translations: Monis gives "ashes" instead of "soot" for *Piah* and "adverb" for *Millah*. Church is translated *Kahal* or *'Edah*, imagination is *Mahashavah*, funeral is *Avelut*, Hebraism is *'Ivrit*. Christological terms were first and foremost in Monis's mind. The *Nomenclatura hebraica* begins with the pair of words: Angel, Apostle. Though not specifically Christian, the terms were also Christian. And such words as Baptist, Baptizer, Bishop, Catechize, Catechizer, Christian, Church, Evangelist, Holy Ghost, Jesus, and Lord's Table are purely Christian. Then there are also words of a general theological nature, such as Atonement, Atheist, Arch-Angel, Blessing, Creator, Devil, Excommunication, Infidel, Incubus, Lord, Oblation, Providence,

Penitence, Preacher, Prophet, Prayer, Psalms, Pentecost, Redeemer, Repentance, Religion, Transgression, Guilt, Unbeliever. In a noun dictionary which contained some thousand vocables and which was designed to further understanding of religious texts, there is a surprisingly small percentage of theological terms in general and christological terms in particular. Significantly, the sixth word in Monis's *Dictionary* refers to *Apostate*; and conversion as an awkward translation of *Shinnui* occurs on page 4. What Freud would make of this "confession" is anybody's guess.

An interesting insight into the understanding, or rather mis-understanding, of mythological concepts is afforded by the iden-tification of Apollo with the biblical Yuval: Apollo the Musagete and Yuval, "the ancestor of all who play the lyre and the flute."[6] Bacchus is identified with Noah, probably because of the incident of inebriation connected with Noah,[7] Jupiter with Shem or Baʿal or Ẓedeḳ. This tendency mistaken identities was not an invention by Monis; it was a common misconception among Hebraists of the eighteenth century.

There are many oddities in the *Nomenclatura*. The entry: "Mouse, Mocker" is translated: שׂוֹחֵק or מוֹלֵץ: עַכְבָּר. There is no quarrel with the "mouse" and its Hebrew equivalent, but Monis created a grammatical monstrosity: מוֹלֵץ instead of לֵץ.

The manuscript cannot have been copied by Monis. Too many mistakes of an elementary nature attest to the handwriting of a student struggling with words in a foreign tongue. Monis could not have written גֶּס instead of נֵס for "Standard," מֹאֲגִים for מֹאֲזְנַיִם, כּוֹל instead of קוֹל for "thunder" or נְכוּדוֹת for "vowels." The substitution of ג for נ and נ for ג, כ for ק and ק for כ are com-mon among beginners studying Hebrew in the twentieth century as they were common in the eighteenth century.

The erudition, displayed in the *Nomenclatura*, is not of a high and immaculate character. But it impressed Benjamin Colman who, in a preface to an essay by Monis, declared that "His diligence

---

6 Gen. 4:21.
7 *Ibid.,* 9:20–27.

and industry together with his ability is manifest unto many who
have seen his Grammar and Nomenclator in Hebrew and English."[8]
It must also have given spiritual satisfaction to the learned divines
of New England who were able to read and enjoy the prime
documents of Christianity — the Creed and the Lord's Prayer — in
his Hebrew versions.[9] Contemporary reactions of Jews to Monis
and his work have not been recorded.

[8] See Colman's preface to Monis's essay *Nothing But the Truth: Being a
Short Essay, Wherein the Author proves the Doctrine of the Ever Blessed and
Adorable Trinity, Both out of the Old Testament, And with the Authority of
the Cabalistical Rabbies, Ancient and Modern: And that said Doctrine is not a
novelty, as his Country-Men do think, but as ancient as the Bible itself* (Boston,
1722).

[9] Monis published them at the end of his Hebrew Grammar. In the Preface
he boasted: "At the end I present you a Translation of the Lord's Prayer, and
the Apostle's Creed, according (as I think) to the true idiom of this Primitive
Language." A manuscript miscellany which contains the Ten Commandments
in the Exodus version as well as the Lord's Prayer and the Creed in Hebrew
exists in the Harvard College Library. The documents are titled respectively:
"*Iḳḳare Emunah*" and *Tefillat Adon.* Monis also announced in the Preface
to his Hebrew Grammar: "A Significant and a Plain Nomenclature, and the
Short and Large Catechisms, in Hebrew and English, with some other works
that I have prepared for the Use and Benefit of Young Beginners, I propose to
Publish as soon as Providence will permit." Since Providence has not permitted,
we can speculate but we cannot know of the "other works."

APPENDIX

Nomenclatura hebraica, preserved in the Manuscript Collection of Harvard
and published with the kind Permission of the University.

Hebrew	Nomenclatura hebraica
A I	*Nomenclatura hebraica*
מַלְאָךְ ׃ שָׁלִיחַ	Angel. Apostle:
אֲוִיר ׃ תֵּבָה ׃	Air. Ark.
פֶּחָם ׃ מוּמָר ׃	Ashes. Apostate.
זְרֹעַ ׃ קוֹף ׃	Arm. Ape.
קוֹר ׃ נְמָלָה ׃	Ague Ant:
כַּפָּרָה ׃ כֹּהֵן ׃	Atonement. App.
אַף ׃ קַרְדֹּם ׃	Anger. Ax.
יוֹבֵל ׃ תַּפּוּחַ ׃	Apollo. Apple-Tree
צְדָקוֹת ׃ יִנְבֵּיתָ ׃	Alms. Acre
אִצְטַגְנִינוּת ׃	Astrology. Arrow. חֵץ
אִצְטַגְנִי ׃ יָגוֹן ׃	Astrologer. Anchor.
שַׂר־פְּנֵי ׃ בָּיִן ׃	Arch-Angel. Atheist.
סַנֵּגוֹר ׃ אֲבִיר ׃	Advocate. April.
חֲמוֹר ׃ אֱלוּל ׃	Ass. August.
עַיִר ׃ אֲדַם הַט ׃	Ass-Colt. Armenia.
פֶּרֶה ׃ לְבַד ׃	Ass-wild. Alone.

Nomenclatura hebraica, preserved in the Manuscript Collection of Harvard and published with the kind permission of the University.

אָתוֹן ; תְּשׁוּבָה :	Ass-Feemale. Answer.
מִלָּה : קָתֵגוֹר :	Adverb. Antagonist
חֲגוֹר : שָׂטָן :	Apron. Satan.
קָהָל : ה ; עֵצָה :	Assembly. Advice
צָבָא : עֲבַטְרְיָא :	Army. Arithmetik.

B

זָקָן ; חָזֶה :	Beard. Brest.
חֵיק : כֶּרֶס :	Boosom. Belly.
חַגְמוֹן ; גָּדוֹל : דָּם	Bishop-Arch. Blood
גּוּף : כִּיס :	Body. Bladder.
צִוֹּף : אָב : עֲבוּעַ :	Bird. Blister.
גֶּשֶׁר : יוֹפִי :	Bridge. Beauty.
נַחַל : בּוֹשָׁה :	Brook. Bashfulness.
נֵחָ : סַנְוֵר :	Bacchus. Blind.
אָח : שָׁחוֹר :	Brother. Black.
חָתָן : טְבִילָה :	Bridegroom. Baptist

כָּלָה׃כֹּבֵל׃	Bride. Baptizer.
שׁוּשָׁבֵן׃ חֶמְאָה׃	Brideman. Butter.
שׁוּשָׁבָן׃ הַמִּכְנָסַיִם	Bridemaid. Breeches.
חֶדֶר חָתָן׃	Bride-Chamber.
גִּיס׃בָּשָׂר׃	Brother in Law. Beef.
מַמְזֵר׃מְבוּשָׁלִי	Bastard. Boiled.
עֶצֶם׃הַנֶּאֱפֶה׃	Bone. Baked.
שִׁדְרָא׃לְבֵנָה׃	Back-Bone. Brick.
לֶחֶם or פַּת׃	Bread.
לֶחֶם קְשֵׂה	Bisket.
מִשְׁתֶּה׃הָאֵזוֹב׃	Banquet. Bottle.
גָּבִיעַ׃דְּלִי׃	Bowl. Bucket.
סַל or סַלְסַל׃	Basket.
בִּנְיָן׃בְּרִיחַ׃	Building. Bolt.
מְגוּרָה׃גּוֹרֶן׃	Barn. Barn-Flour.
אָרוֹן׃טִיט׃	Box. Broom.
נַפּוּחַות׃מִטָּה׃	Bellows. Bed.
כְּסֻת׃מִטְהֶרֶת׃	Blanket. Brush.
סֵפֶר׃הֶגְמוֹן׃	Book. Bishop.

בְּרָכָה ׃ טֶבֶלָה ׃	Blessing. Bier.
נְחֹשֶׁת ׃ גָּפְרִית ׃	Brass. Brimstone.
דְבוֹרָה ׃	Bee.
	6

בּוֹרֵא ׃ בְּרוּאָה ׃	Creator. Creature
בְּרִיאָה ׃ קוֹמֵיטָּה ׃	Creation. Comet.
עָנָן ׃ לֶחִי ׃	Cloud. Cheek.
מְלַפְפוֹן ׃	Cucumber.
קְלָלָה ׃ אָרוּר ׃	Curse. Cursed.
בֵּן ׃ כֶּתֶר or עֵלֶט ׃	Child. Crown.
חִינוּךְ ׃ הוֹנֵךְ ׃	Catechize. Catechism
שִׁיעוּי ׃ סִיבָּה ׃	Conversion. Cause
קֶשֶׁר ׃ עִיר ׃	Conjunction. City.
צְדָקָה ׃ שֵׁכָר ׃	Charity. Cider.
כּוֹס or גְבִיעַ ׃ חֶדֶר ׃	Cup. Chamber.
כֵּס ׃ מָעֵץ ׃	Chair. Cushing.
אָרוֹן ׃ אֲחָה ׃	Chest. Chimney.
נֵד ׃ מְעוֹרָה ׃	Candle Do Stick.

5

מִסְרֵק׃ גַּלָּב׃	Comb. Chirurgeon.
נוֹצְרִי׃ פֶּרֶק׃	Christian. Chapter.
חָתוּל׃ בָּקָר׃	Cat. Cow.
עֵגֶל׃ אֶפְרוֹחַ׃	Calf. Chicken.
סָהַר׃ תַּרְנְגוֹל׃	Cage. Cock. (Crow)
יָצַר צוּר׃	Cock. (to Draw)
קִנָּמוֹן׃	Cinnamon.
בֵּית־הַמִּדְרָשׁ	College.
עֲגָלָה׃ רֹאֵשׁ	Cart. Captain.
נֵסֶה׃ מֶרְכָּבָה	Coronet. Chariot.
קָהָל׃ עֲדָה׃ כְּנֵסֶת	Church.
גְּבִינָה׃	Chees

D

מַבּוּל׃ אָהוּב׃	Delluge. Dear.
טִפָּה׃ יוֹם׃	Drop. Day.
יוֹנָה׃ נַעֲרָה׃	Dove. Damsel
טַל׃ כָּוֶת׃ מִיתָה	Dew. Death.
נַנָּס׃ מֵת׃	Dwarf. Dead.

בַּת׃שַׁעֲשׁוּעַ	Daughter. Delight.
חֲלוֹם׃נֵזֶר	Dream. Diadem.
חוֹלֵם׃גֵּשׁ	Dreamer. Divorce
מַעֲלָה׃מוּס	Degree. Defeat.
שִׁכּוֹר׃נִדְכָּר	Drunchard. Defeat.
סַכָּנָה׃מַחֲלֹקֶת	Danger. Dispute.
אֲרֻחָה׃קְעָרָה	Dinner. Dish.
דֶּלֶת׃פֶּתַח	Door. yᵉ opening Doore.
רָקִיד׃מְרַקֵּד	Dance. Dancer.
פֶּתִי׃חוֹב	Dunce. Debt.
חַיָּב׃כֶּלֶב	Debter. Dog.
פֶּלֶךְ׃זַיִן	Distaff. Dagger.
שֶׁלָה׃טֵבֵת	Dark. December.
שֵׁד or שָׂטָן	Devil.

E

מִזְרָח׃קֶדֶם	East
אֲדָמָה׃קֵיסָר	Earth. Emperer.

7

עַיִן ׃ גַבֹּ֫ת ׃	Eye. Eyebrows.
אֹוֶזן ׃ שָׁלִי֫חַ ׃	Ear. Evangelist.
שׂוֹנֵא ׃ פֶּרֶט ׃	Enemy. Epocha.
קַדְרוּת ׃ כּוּשִׁיִּי ׃	Eclipse. Ethiopian.
כּוּשׁ ׃ מָשָׁל ׃	Ethiopia. Example
נֶזֶם ׃ זָקֵן ׃ קָשִׁישׁ	Ear-Ring. Elder.
נִדּוּי ׃ חֵרֶם ׃ שַׁמְתָּה ׃	Excommunication.
מַס ׃ רָחֵל ׃	Excise. Ewe
בֵּיצָה ׃ חֶלְמוֹן	Egg. Egg yolk.
חֶלְבּוֹן ׃ הֵד ׃	Egg-white. Echo.
עֶרֶב ׃ רֵיק ׃	Evening. Empty.
יָצַח ׃ בְּחִירָה ׃	Elegant. Election
מַרְפֵּק ׃ חִידָה ׃	Elbow. Enigma.
סָרִיס ׃ רַעַשׁ ׃	Eunuch. Earth-Quack
אֶפִּיקוֹרוֹס ׃ רָע ׃	Epicure. Evil.
עֵדוּת ׃ סוֹף ׃ קֵץ ׃ גָּם	Evidence. End.
רָחָם ׃ נֵס ׃	Eagle Geir. Ensighn
פֶּסַח ׃ קַדְמוּת ׃	Easter. Eternal.

B	F
וְרָצוֹן׃ רְחִינָה׃	Free-will.
אָב׃ שֵׁד or רוּחַ׃	Father. Fiend.
אֵשׁ׃ לַפִּיד׃	Fire. Fire-Brand.
מַעְיָן׃ קֶרַח הַנָמֵל	Fountain. Frost.
בָּשָׂר׃ חָם ☐	Flesh. Father in law.
פָּנִים׃ רֶגֶל׃	Face. Foot.
אֶצְבַּע׃ נֵץ׃	Fore-Finger. Falcon.
גוּדֶל׃ אֶצְבַּע׃	Thumb-Finger.
אַמָּה׃ קְמִיצָה׃	Finger middle. Finger-Ring
זֶרֶת׃ אֶגְרֹף׃	Finger Little. Fist.
קַדַּחַת׃ דַּלֶּקֶת׃	Feaver. Feaver Burning.
אֱמוּנָה׃ כְּסִלוּת	Faith. Folly.
כְּסִיל׃ מְחִילָה׃	Fool. Forgiveness.
יִרְאָה׃ בְּחִירָה	Fear. Free-Choice
תַּעֲנִית׃ צוֹם׃	Fast.
אֲדָר׃ מָזוֹן׃	February. Food.
יְסוֹד׃ פֶּנִים	Foundation. Frontier-piece
תְּאֵנָה׃ אֲבֵלוּה	Fig-Tree. Funeral.

9

זְבוּב ׃ שׁוּעָל ׃	Flie. Fox.
צְפַרְדֵּעַ ׃ נוֹצָה ׃	Frog. Feather
עוֹף ׃ פַּרְעֹשׁ ׃	Fowl. Flea.
דָּג ׃ דָג ׃ מָלוּחַ ׃	Fish. Fish-Salt.

G

אֵל ׃ אֱלוֹהַּ ׃ אֱלֹהִים	God.
אֱלָהוּתִ ׃ לֵאדֹנָי	God-Head.
רוּחַ ׃ גַּנַּת ׃	Tho. Garden.
בַּבַּת ׃ עָנָק ׃	Giant. Giant.
טוּב ׃ טוֹב ׃	Goodness. Good.
מֵעַיִם ׃ חֵן ׃ חִינָה	Guts. Grace.
טוֹב ׃ מְאֹד ׃	Good- Exceeding.
דִּקְדּוּק ׃	Grammar.
מְדַקְדֵּק ׃	Grammarian.
אֶכְלֵךְ ׃ הוֹד ׃	Glutter. Glory.
מִרְמָה ׃ עֵנָב ׃	Guile. Grape.
צְנְצֶנֶת ׃	Glass-Bottle.
קְבָּה ׃ שֶׁחָט ׃ ת׳ שָׁאוּל	Grape.
זָאבַ or דְהַב ׃	Gold.
אַוָּז ׃ קֻרְקְבָן ׃	Goos. Gizard.

זַנְגְּבִילָא חֶסֶד!	Ginger. godlyman.
מַתָּנָה גּוֹי עוֹלֵם	Gift. Gentile.
חִנָּם כַּרְקְלִינָן	Gratis. Glover (Leather)
קְסְיָא	Glover. (of yarn)
כְּאֵב	Grief
	H.
רוּחַ הַקֹּדֶשׁ	Holy-Ghost.
שָׁמַיִם בַּיִת	Heavens. House.
גִּבְעָה הַטְּחוֹרִים	Hill. Hamorhoids.
חוֹם בָּרָד	Heat. Hail.
בַּעַל יוֹרֵשׁ	Husband. Heir.
שֵׂעָר רֹאשׁ	Hair. Head.
לֵב שׁוֹק	Heart. Hip.
עָקֵב כַּפּוּר בַּצֶּדֶק	Heel. Heritick.
אַנְדְּרוֹגִינוֹס	Hermophrodite.
יָד רָעָב	Hand. Hunger.
בִּטָּחוֹן עִבְרִית	Hope. Hibraism.
עֵת שָׁעָה	Hour. Horse Jocky

אֹשֶׁר ׃ חֲלָלָה ׃	Happiness. Harlot.
כַּרְבְּלָה ׃ קַרְדֹּם ׃	Hat. Hatchet.
חָבִית ׃ דְּבַשׁ ׃	Hogshead. Honey.
קָצִיר ׃ גּוֹי ׃	Harvest. Heathen.
עוֹר ׃ קֶרֶן ׃	Hide. Horn.
אַיָּל ׃ אַיָּלָה ׃	Hart.(mas) Hart.(Fem)
אַרְנֶבֶת ׃ סוּס ׃	Hare. Horse
נֵץ ׃ עֶגְלָה	Hawk. Heifer.
תַּרְנְגֹלָה ׃ אַמְבָּרְבָּס	Hen. Hopper-grass.
יַעֲרָה ׃ נֹפֶת ׃	Honey-wild Do Comb.
מַקֶּבֶת ׃ הַס ׃	Hammer. Hush.
	J
יְהוֹנָתָן ׃ חָנָן ׃	Jonathan. John.
רֶמֶשׂ ׃ שֶׁמֶ□□□ צֶדֶק	Insect. Jupiter.
נַחֲלָה ׃ יְרוּשָׁה ׃	Inheritance
חֶרֶס ׃ יֵרָקוֹן ׃	Itch. Jaundice
סְבָרָה ׃ שֶׁגָגָה ׃	Judgment. Ignorance
גִּילָה ׃ שָׂשׂוֹן ׃ שִׂמְחָה	Joy.
בְּאֵר ׃ אַסְטִיס ׃	Interpretor Indigo.

12

סוֹרֵר : שֵׁבֶט :	Infidel. January.
תַּמּוּז : אָב :	June July.
בְּשַׁמַּרְתִּי : מַחֲשָׁבָה :	Incubus. Imagination
וְחוּשַׁ : לוּחַ : הֹדוּ :	Index. Indies
תִּינוֹק : יֵשׁוּעַ :	Infant. Jesus.

K

מֶלֶךְ : כְּלָיוֹת :	King. Kidneys.
בִּרְכַּיִם : מַפְתֵּחַ :	Knees. Key.
נָשַׁק : חָרִיף :	Kiss. Keen.
דַעַת : סַכִּין : מַאֲכֶלֶת	Knowledge. Knife.
גְּדִי : חַרְצָן :	Kid. Kernel.
שְׁאָר : כְּנֵסָה : עֵדָה :	Hin. Kirk.
יַלְקוּט : כִּיּוֹר	Knap-sach. Kettle
חֶסֶד :	Kindness.

L

יְהֹוָה : אוֹר :	Lord. Light.
אֲגַם : בָּרָק בָּזָק :	Lake. Lightning.
שָׂפָה : מָתְנַיִם :	Lip. Loins.
שׁוֹבֶל : רֵיאָה :	Leg. Lungs

i

13

דַּק: פִּסֵחַ:	Lean. Lame.
אִטֵּר: צָרַעַת:	Left-handed. Leprosy.
דְּרוֹר∞ פְּדוּת∞ הָפְשִׁי:	Liberty.
שָׁקֵרוּ∞ כָּזָב∞ בָּדָּא:	Lye.
תּוֹרָה∞ דָּת∞ אֶלְחִיק	Law. עַב צִיָּה:
עֲשֶׂרֶת הַדְּבָרִים:	Law-moral.
שֻׁלְחַן הַמָּשִׁיחַ	Lords - Table
חַיִּים-נִצָחִיִּים חַיֵּי∞	Life - Eternal. חַיָּיו:
קַו∞ שִׂטָה:	Line
קַו-יָשָׁר:	Line-Streight.
הָכְמַת-הַגָּיוֹן:	Logick.
הָכָם הַהִגָּיוֹן:	Logician
שָׁווּעַ: מְלָל:	Literality. List. eClot
שַׁקְרָן: כֶּבֶשׂ: גְּדִי	Liar. Lamb.
הָבֵץ:	Leaven'd-Bread.
מַצָּה:	Unleavened-Bread.
נָעַל: מַסְגֵּר:	Latch. Lock.
שִׂיד: כְּסוּת:	Slime. Lid.
אַסְפַּקְלַרְיָא:	Looking-glass.

4

אִגֶּרֶת ׃ אִוֶּרֶת ׃	Letter. Letter(a).
סֵדֶר הַתְּפִלּוֹת ׃	Liturgy.
עוֹפָרֶת ׃	Lead
אַרְיֵה אֲרִי שַׁחַץ	Lion.
כְּפִיר ׃ לַיִשׁ ׃	Lion-young. old. Do~
לָבִיא ׃	Lion Decreped.
וְעִדָּר ׃ מְנוֹרָה ׃	Leap-year. Lamp.

M

אָדָם אִישׁ אֱנוֹשׁ	Man.
הַר ׃ טִיט ׃	Mount. Mud.
כֶּסֶף ׃ מִצְווֹתָמִים	Money.
יָרֵחַ לְבָנָה ׃ נַעַר ׃	Moon. Yong-Man.
זָקֵן ׃ יָשִׁישׁ ׃	Man-old. very Do.
אֵם ׃ פֶּה ׃	Mother. Mouth.
חָלָב ׃ רַחֲמָנוּת ׃	Milk. Mercy.
דֶּרֶךְ ׃ אֶרֶץ ׃	Manners.
זִכָּרוֹן זְכִירָה ׃	Memory
חַלָּמִית ׃ מִדָּה ׃	Mallou. Measure
רְצָל ׃ תוּתִים ׃	Muff. Mulberys.

15

חַרְדָּל׃ רֳב׸מָר׃	Mustard. Master.
צֵד׃סְנוּלָח׃	Martyr Mine
רֵחַיִם׃אָתוֹן׃	Mill. Mare
צִפֹּר׃מִל׸עשׂוֹחֵק	Mouse Maker
בְּכָאִים׃	Mullberry-Tree
טוֹחֵן׃ חֹדֶ	Miller. Month.
נִיסָן׸אָבִיב׃	March.
סִיבָן׃בֹּקֶר׃	May. Morning.
רֶגַע׃שָׁחוֹר׃	Moment. Moor
תּוֹלַעַ׃עֶבֶד׃	Maggot. Man-Serv.
אָרוּס׃	Mint. Can herb).

N

צָפוֹן׃מֵנֶקֶרת׃	North. Nurse (wet)
פַּרְתָּם׃אָף׃	Noble (by Blood Nose
נְחִירַיִם׃צַוָּאר׃	Nostril. Neck.
דַּד׃טִיבּוּר׃	Nipple Navel
צִיפוֹרֶן׃מַסְמֵר׃	Naile (finger) Nailiron

טֶבַע: לַיְלָה: לֵיל:	Nature: Night.
וו אומ כְּיָה: קֵיסְטור	Nation. Notary.
עָצֵל: הִירוֹשׁ:	Negligent. New-coin.
קֵן: שָׁכֵן:	Nest. Neighbour. -
כִּסְלֵו: צָהֳרַיִם	November. Noon.
שׁוֹעַ: בְּלִיַּעַל:	Noble (Liberal) Naught
אֳנִי: חָח:	Navie. Needle.
סֵפֶר שֵׁמוֹת:	Nomenclature.
	O
יָתוֹם: נְתוּכָה:	Orphan. ...Dove
שֶׁמֶן: זַיִת:	Oil. Olive.
דַּרְשָׁן: שׁוֹר:	Orator. Ox.
חֹק: עֲצָנָה:	Ordinance. Owl
כּוֹס: אַלּוֹן:	Owl. (little) oak Tree
פַּרְדֵּס: בְּצָלִים	Orchard. Onion.
חוֹתָר: עֻגָּב:	Oar. Organ
חֶשְׁוָן: בּוּל:	October
שְׁבוּעָה: אָלָה:	Oath,

צ׳וּלָ׳חַ: חִיוּב:	Oblation. Obligation.[17]
פְּקוּדָה:	Office. P.

מֵזֶל: שְׁבִיל:	Planate. Path.
אֲנָם: שַׂר~ אַלוּף:	Ponder Prince.
חֵן: רוֹפֵא: כָּפָּרָה:	Pallate Physician.
דֶּבֶר~ נֶגַע סְלִיחָה:	Plague. Pardon.
הַשְׁגָּחָה:	Providence.
הַשְׁגָּחָה כְּלָלִית:	Providence (general)
תְּשׁוּבָה: מוֹרֶה:	Penitance. Preceptor.
רֹאשׁ יְשִׁיבָה:	} President.
רֹאשׁ בֵּית הַמִקְדָּשׁ	
רֹאשׁ הַמִשְׁנָה:	
תֵּיבָה: תַּלְמִיד:	Pulpit. Pupil
לְבָנָה: כּוֹכָב:	Luha. Mercury.
נוֹגַהּ: חַמָּה: מַאֲדִים	Venus. Sun. Mars.
צֶדֶק: שַׁבְּתַּי:	Jupiter. Saturn.

קְצָרָה: הַקְדָּמָה'!	Porringer. Proposition..
בֵּינוֹנִי:	Present. Tense
עָבַר: רֶשׁ:	Preter Do. Poverty.
עָנִי דַּל: שׁ אֶבְיוֹן	Poor i man's
שָׁלוֹם: חֶלֶק:	Peace. Piece.
זָדוֹן: גִּאוֹן: כִּיס:	Pride Pocket.
סִיר: קְדֵרָה: אַרְמוֹן:	Pot.
הֵיכָל: מִסְדְּרוֹן:	Pallace. Porch.
עַמּוּדִי: מַרְצֶפֶת:	Pillar: Pavement.
כַּדָּה: דְּלִי:	Pitcher. Pail.
הַמַּהְפֶּכֶת בֵּית הַמַּטָּרָה:	Prison.
הַסֹּהַר: הַמַּסְגֵּר:	
עֱלִי: אֲבִיק:	Pestle. Pump.
רֶפֶק: נְיָיר:	Pulse. Paper.
עֵט: יָאלְד:	Pin. Pen-knife.

19

קְלָמוֹס ⸱ עֵצֶר: שֵׁבֶט	Pencil.
נְקוּדָה: מְדַקְדֵק:	Quint. Paper.
מָשָׁל: דַּרְשָׁן:	Proverb. Preacher.
נָבִי: תְּפִילָה:	Prophet. Prayer.
שְׁאֵלָה: מִזְמוֹר	Petition. Psalm.
נָבִישׁ: מְדִינָה:	Pearl. Province.
יוֹנָה: רְנַן:	Pigeon. Peacock.
דָּנָר: תֻּכִּי:	Partrige. Parrot.
חוֹל: פַּלְמֵל:	Phœnix. Pi--er.
נֶטַע: אָסוּר:	Plant. Prisoner.
יוֹצֵר: שְׁבוּעוֹת:	Tower. Pentecost.
טָהוֹר ⸱ בַּר: כֹּהֵן	Pure. Parson.
אָדָם: זֵרְעוֹנִים	Person. Pulse(hed)
סוֹף: אָמֵן:	finis.

20

מַלְכָּה or שֵׁגַל ׃ — Queen.

זוֹנָה ׃ — Quean.

רוֹגֵז or רוֹעֵד ׃ — Quaker.

שְׁאֵלָה ׃ — Question.

שִׁעוּר ׃ — Quantity.

אֵיכוּת ׃ — Quality

נֹצָה ׃ — Quill.

כֶּסֶף חַי ׃ — Quick-Silver.

רַבִּי צִיִי ׃ — Quarter-master.

פְּרִישִׁיִן ׃ — Quinas.

שְׂלָוִים ׃ — Quails.

תְּקוּפָה ׃ — Quarter-(of a year).

חִידָה ׃ — Question. (Dark)

מְחֵרָה ׃ — Quickly.

דְּמָמָה ׃ — Qualm.

מְנַגֵּן ׃ — Quirister.

R

גּוֹאֵל or פּוֹדֶה ׃ — Redeemer

יָצוּר ׃ נֶשֶׁם ׃ — Rock Rain.

21

יְאֹורֵ״אְצֵלָע:	River. Rib.
אַיָּה׳חַכְלִל:	Rump. Red (wine)
דַּעַת׃גְּעָרָה:	Reason. Reproof.
גַּזְלָן׃רָשָׁע:	Rober. Rogue.
חֲרָטָה:	Repentance.
צְבִי״שֹׁרֶשׁ:	Robuck. Root.
אֹון״עשֶׁר:	Riches.
עָשִׁיר:	Rich-man.
חֶרְפָּה:	Reproach.
גַּג׃צָנֹון:	Roof. Radish.
שַׁרְבֹיט:	Rule.
שֵׁבֶט״מַטֶּה:	Rod
אֱמוּנָה׃מָאֹוס:	Religion. Reprobate.
אַיִל׃צָדָב:	Ram. Raven.
תַּעַר:	Rasor.

בֵּן:	a son.
דְכוּר״בַּר:	the son.
רוּחַ:	a spirit.
בֵּיהֿ־הַלִימוד:	a school.
נַחָשׁ:	a serpent
בְּשֹׁוכִים:	Spies of all sorts?
רְקִיעַ:	the skye.

22

כּוֹכָבִישׁ ׃	a Star
הַשְׁרֵי ׃	September
שֶׁמֶשׁ ׃	the Sun
יָמִים־דָרוֹם ׃	South
נֶפֶשׁ ׃	Soul (vegetable)
רוּחַ ׃	Soul (sensative)
נְשָׁמָה ׃	Soul (rational)
אַיָּל ׃	Stagg
חוֹל ׃	Sand
יָם ׃	Sea
יָם־אוֹקְיָנוֹס ׃	Sea (ocean)
יָם־סוּף ׃	Sea (Red Sea)
עָשָׁן ׃	Smoak
סְעָרָה ׃	Storm
שֶׁלֶג ׃	Snow
יוֹנֵק ׃	Sucking Child
אָחוֹת ׃	Sister
גִּיד ׃	Sinew
סְפָר ׃	Slap (ing. face)
צוּר ׃	Skin
גוּלְגוֹלֶת	Skul
כָּתֵף	Shoulder
שִׁכְמָה ׃	Shoulder (Blade)
צַד ׃ פַּהיגל	Side. Stomach
יִצֵחַ ׃	Sweat

25.

קוֹל: אֲנָחָה:	Sound. Sigh.
מוֹקֵשׁ: נַחֲרָה:	Snare. Snorting.
בּוּשָׁה: חוֹלֶה:	Shame. Sick-man.
חֵטְא: עָוֹן:	Sin. iniquity.
פֶּשַׁע: אָשָׁם;	Transgression. Guilt.
שֵׁנָה: תָּם:	Sleep. Sincere.
תְּמִימוּת:	Sincerity.
תַּפְתִּיָּא:	a Sheriff.
רוֹמַה: רִיב:	a Spear. Strife.
שְׁגָגָה:	a Sin (of Ignorance)
אוֹן:	Substance.
זֹהַר:	Splendour.
זָרַת: בַּלְקוֹהַ:	a Span. a pair of Snuffers.
כֶּתֶם: מֶלַח:	a Spot. Salt.
שָׁוִים:	Synonymous.
נֵס:	a Standard.
עֶבֶד:	a Servant.

עֵת: כּוֹל: רַעַם:	Time. Thunder.
שֵׁן: לָשׁוֹן:	a Tooth. a Tongue.
גָּרוֹן:	the throat.
יָרֵךְ:	the Thigh.
הוֹדָה:	Thankfulness.
צוּרָה: גָּנָב:	a Type. a Thief.

24

שֻׁלְחָן׃	a Table.
מִגְדָּל׃	a Tower.
נָמֵר	a Tiger.
פֻּנְדָּק׃	a Tavern.
זָנָב׃	a Tail.
מַעֲשֶׂה	a Tale.
בְּדִיל; מַס׃	Tin. Tribute.
צָב; עֵץ;	a Toad. a Tree.
כִּסֵּא; דַּרְדַּר׃	a Throne. a Thistle.
קוֹץ׃	a Thorn.
שׁוֹפָר׃	a Trumpet.
אֹהֶל׃	a Tent (to live in)
נִזְבָּר; קֶשֶׁר׃	a Treasurer. Treason.
חֵלֶב; צְלֹחִית	Tallow. a Tankard.
מִשְׁכָּן׃	a Tabernacle.
כְּפִלוּת	Tautology.
דֶּמַע; חוּט׃	a Tear a Thread.
רַכִּי; רַבָּא; מוֹרֶה; רַךְ׃	a Teacher Tender.
טַעִימָה׃	Taste
זְמַן; מְעַט׃	Time a little.
גְּבוּלִים׃	Terms.
נוֹף׃	the Trunk.
שׂוֹכֵר׃	a Tenant.

יִחוּד׃	Unity. 25.
כֵּלִים׃	Utensils.
נָגִיד׃	Usher.
רִבִּית or נֶשֶׁךְ	Usury.
טָמֵא׃	Unclean.
אֲבַעְבֻּעֹת׃	Ulcers.
כּוֹפֵר חֶסֶד שׁוֹדֵר׃	Unbelievers
עוֹלָם׃	Anger.
כְּלָל׃	Universal.
שָׁנִי לֹל מֶלֶךְ׃	Viceroy.
אֵד׃	Vapor.
בְּתוּלָה חֲצִלְקָיְה׃	Virgin.
נְכוּדוֹת תַּנוּעֹת׃	Vowel.
קוֹל רְשָׁעוֹת הָל	Vote. Voting
רְדִיד מַסְוֶה׃	Vail.
צֵיד׃	Venison.
חוֹמֶץ׃ גֶּפֶן׃	Vinegar. Vine
מְגִילָה׃ פָּס׃	Volum. verse
הַצְדָּקָה הִ׃	Version
שָׁוְא׃	Vanity.
מוּם׃ נֶדֶר׃	Vice vow.
מֵיצָר זֶמִים׃	West. water.
בּוֹר גַּלְגַּל׃	Well. wave
חוֹם רוּחַ׃	Warm wind.

אִשָׁה ׃ יָאַלְמוֹן woman. widower. 26

אֵשֶׁת ׃ חוּרְבָּן wife. while

הָכְכִיהַ ׃ סְתָיו ׃ wisdom. winter.

שָׁבוּעַ ׃ חַלָשׁ ׃ week. weak.

שָׁתִי אוֹ עֵרֶב ׃ warp (webb) woof.

אָרֵג ׃ מַסֶכֶת ׃ weavers webb.

יַיִן ׃ תִּירוֹשׁ wine. wine (new)

גַּת ׃ עֵץ ׃ winepress. wood.

קָנֶה ׃ Wine-pipe.

רָפָּה ׃ Worm-seed.

זוֹנָה הָ הֲלָלָה ׃ Whore.

רָשָׁע ׃ Wicked-man

דַּיְסָא ׃ Water-gruel.

אוֹצָר ׃ Warehouse.

חָטָה ׃ שַׁעֲוָה Wheat. Wax

קוּם ׃ צֶמֶר ׃ Whip Wool.

זְאֵב ׃ Wolf.

חַלוֹן ׃ אֲרוּבָּה Window.

סְרוּס ׃ כָּנָף ׃ Wether. Wing.

אֱגוֹז ׃ אוֹפָן ׃ Walnut. Wheel.

שׁוֹטוּ מִכְשֵׁפָה ׃ Whip. Whitch.

רֶחֶם ׃ תּוֹלַעַ ׃ Womb. Worm.

מִלְחָמָה ׃ אָרוֹן War. Whithe.

אֶבֶן וְורי ׃ Weight to a block

טוֹב ׃ נָכוֹן ׃ עֵד ׃ Well. West. Witness

הַשְׁתַּחֲוָיָה ׃ מִתְפַּלֵל ׃ Worshiping. Worshiper

בְּמִקְוֹה: שָׁנָה: Yarn. year.
כָּנָמִים נְלְמִיקָה yearly.
נַעַר: youngman.

_____

אוֹפֶק־הָצִי־גוּל: Zodiack.
נְקוֹדָה־הָראֹשׁ: Zenith.
קַנָּאָה: Zeal.
קַנָּא: Zelot.

The twelve Sighns.

טָלֶה: Aries.
שׁוֹר. Taurus.
הַתְאוֹמִים: Gemini.
סַרְטָן: Cancer.
אַרְיֵה: Leo.
בְּתוּלָה: Virgo.
מיֹאֹגְנַיִם: Libra.
עָקְרָב:קֶשֶׁת: Scorpio. Sagitarius.
גְּדִי: Capricornus.
דְּלִי: Aquarius.
דָּגִים: Pises.

the fruit Trees not mentioned in esal
Nomenclators are Called by qᵗ
as qᵗ fruit themselves. _____

סֵפֶר־עֻמּוֹת: Hom

Short Nomenclator or vocabular in English
and hebrew, Composed Alphabetically, for ye use and
benefit of my Pupils in particular, and for ye advantg
of these who are Desirous to obtain ye knowlege of ye
hebrew Tongue in general; which may be that great
help to understand not only ye sacred oracles in their
original, but even any Jewish author (so far as
betwcen now) as also it may give great insight
in ye tongue to these, as to Compose it. ——
a work altogether new.

by Judah Monis

Women when good the best of saint.

That bright, Seraphic & lovely

She, who nothing of an Angel

wants but truth & jm mortality

Chose 2

Who, like a limbs & Charm g

face, keeps their warm

NOTES ON THE OCCUPATIONAL STATUS
OF FRENCH JEWS, 1800–1880

BY ZOSA SZAJKOWSKI

In an earlier study on Jewish occupational problems during the French Revolution, I have tried to show that it was difficult to suddenly change the occupational structure of a minority, long oppressed by economic restrictions. Poverty and deeply rooted habits made the process of occupational change slow, often impossible. First only occupational diversification was achieved; later occupational change could be attained through general and vocational education of the younger generation.

The impractical and questionable theories about "productivity" versus "unproductivity" regarding certain occupations, much debated by physiocrats and radical *maskilim* during and after the Emancipation followed by generations of Utopian Socialists and Marxists, Zionists and anti-Zionists, did not take the Jewish reality into consideration. In my opinion, "productivity" cannot be used as a yardstick for achievement, although many researchers will disagree with my assumption; for them achievement and progress are only to be measured in terms of outlived notions of "economic naturalism."

For the period when Jews were already emancipated and legally able to change their occupations, judgment concerning the degree of their productivity cannot be rendered on the basis of a census of Jewish workers, employers or merchants. Such judgment would ask of Jews more than of others. In fact, the French Revolution of 1789 took the special condition of Jews into consideration. The law of January 11, 1795 permitted the return of those émigrés who, at the moment of their departure from France, had previously made a living by working with their hands, such as the peasants, artisans, and so forth. This posed a very special problem for the Jewish émigrés;

531

how could they prove in what way they had made a living? In some cases the authorities decided that Jewish émigrés who were peddlers, merchants, and such, should still benefit from the law because they had been forced to make a living from "dishonest" professions before their Emancipation and were not permitted, for instance, to till the land. In still other cases the authorities found a way to enable Jewish peddlers and merchants to benefit from the law by declaring that their occupations were useful to the local population.[1]

After the Revolution, when Jews were permitted to enter "productive" occupations, many of them were too old to give up the money-lending, peddling, or horse and cattle trading, to which they had previously been restricted. In France widespread industrialization had not yet begun. Productivity was no longer conceived as inherent only in the status of a worker. The trend away from the village to the city, from agrarian society to urbanization with the ownership of a piece of land, a business for oneself, a small factory, or a store, had already started. The proper way to judge productivity among French Jews is to see in what segments of commerce and industry they were occupied, and not how many of them were workers, manufacturers or merchants. A Jew who could give up peddling in the villages and become a busy merchant with a store, employees, and large orders in factories, was considered productive. In short, advancement, progress, improvement and diversification, would be more appropriate terms than "productivity" in a study of the occupational status of the Jews in France. I believe that the same is true for Germany and other countries.[2]

On June 3, 1806, the Jews of Moselle wrote to the Prefect of Police that they were unable to benefit immediately from the citizenship which had been granted them in 1791, because the Revolution

[1] Zosa Szajkowski, "Occupational Problems of Jewish Emancipation in France, 1789–1800," *Historia Judaica*, XXI (1959), 109–132; also my "Jewish Emigrés during the French Revolution," *Jewish Social Studies*, XVI (1954), 331–332. On the "productivity" theories, see my *Jews, War, and Communism* (New York, 1972), I, 410–414, 608.

[2] "La régénération ne pouvait s'opérer que peu à peu," ed., I. Bédarride, *Les Juifs en France, en Italie et en Espagne* (Paris, 1859), pp. 399–400.

had destroyed most of their fortunes. The continental blockade of 1807–1810 was a period of great development for Alsace, mainly in the city of Strasbourg, which served as a storehouse for imported goods. This role of the province declined, however, after the requirement of import licenses was introduced. Until about 1860 the entire province suffered from this economic protectionism.[3] Many Alsatians, including Jews, left their businesses for other occupations, only to return to commerce at a later time. In spite of the emigration to other regions and abroad that took place during this period, the Jewish population of Alsace increased from 19,624 in 1784 to 35,814 in 1866. Yet, commerce and industry in Alsace experienced so many serious crises during the nineteenth century that it hardly offered an opportunity for Jewish economic initiative.

The "productivization" process was even slower in the villages. In 1845, for example, 48 families (240 individuals) lived in the 6 localities of Ay, Emmery, Flévy, Talange, Trémery and Vigy, near Metz. Of the thirty-nine heads of families, twenty-one were engaged in cattle and horse trading. Seldom was a village artisan able to live on the earnings from his trade alone; after a while he had to turn to the occupation of his parents: peddling. Nearby Switzerland was a positive factor in the development of the Alsatian economy, especially in the textile industry. However, the restrictions against Alsatian Jews in Switzerland are well known. During the 1850s and 1860s nine Alsatian Jews conducted their affairs in Basel under the cover of Christian names.[4] The economic rehabilitation of the Jews was difficult; nevertheless one can cite many examples of great accomplishments. Although this may seem an apologetic approach, it is still necessary to bring out these facts.

---

[3] Departmental archives of Moselle, V 149; *Société d'encouragement des arts et métiers parmi les israélites de Metz. Séance générale, 8 janvier 1825* (Metz, 1825), p. 14. A. Barthelmé, *Le Développement des courants commerciaux de l'Alsace* ... (Strasbourg, 1931), pp. 7–15.

[4] JTS [The Library of the Jewish Theological Seminary]; Szajkowski, *Poverty and Social Welfare among French Jews, 1800–1880* (New York, 1954), p. 11; *Note sur la position et les titres des israélites français expulsés du territoire de Bâle et Bâle-Campagne* (n.p., n.d.), 4 pp.

In 1793 there were only two Jewish manufacturers and fifteen workers and day-laborers in Nancy; by 1808 these figures increased to ten and forty-seven respectively. In 1809 there were twenty-eight Jewish workers in the factories of ammunition at Mutzig, twelve manufacturers of soap, and ten of potash, in the Lower Rhine. Fifty-nine Jews were agriculturists; seventy-five worked for employers, seven were artisans, eight were employed at offices owned by Jews, nineteen were bakers and butchers, four were manufacturers and thirty were employers.[5]

In 1848 Jan Czyński, a Fourierist activist but also a Judeophobe, wrote that French industry developed rapidly owing to the Jews. In 1860, Dr. J.-P. Gellavardin, a physician of Lyons, wrote that the Jews of France numbered only 25 percent of the inhabitants of one of the departments but the number of influential Jews in various fields of activities was as great as two or three entire departments. Joseph Cohen, who played a role in the emancipation of Algerian Jewry, wrote that as a result of anti-Jewish persecution, Jews were prepared to adopt the ideas of the nineteenth-century economic revolution quickly, including the building of railroads, the opening of credit facilities, and so forth.[6]

The role of Jewish Saint Simonians as well as the Rothschilds in the construction of French railroads is well known. Thanks to their initiative France was not left behind in economic development. Less known is the pioneering role of Jews in the construction of smaller but equally essential railroad lines. Following are a few examples:

In 1830–1831, Siméon Worms, a former merchant, was the first to study the possibility of constructing a Metz–Sarrebruck route which was the beginning of an important line in three directions: to Paris; to the center of France; and to the North of Germany. Most probably because he was a Jew, his role was later ignored. The

[5] S. Posener, "The Immediate Economic and Social Effects of the Emancipation of the Jews in France," *Jewish Social Studies*, I (1939), 299; Archives Nationales, F19–11009; JTS.

[6] J. Czyński, *Le Réveil d'Israël* (Paris, 1848), p. 2; Dr. Gellavardin, *Position des Juifs dans le monde* (Lyons, 1866), p. 7 (reprinted from the *Revue du Lyonnais*); *La Gerbe* (Paris, 1890), p. 26.

Possibility of building a line from Lyons to St. Etienne was studied by the industrialists, Jules Albert Schlumberger and Emile Koechlin of Mulhouse. One year later, J. S. Blum of the Epinal mines renewed the Schlumberger-Koechlin plan for a Nantes–Strasbourg line via Paris. In 1832 Blum was the first to express the idea of a Strasbourg–Basel line and his efforts were later continued by Jacques Javal. In 1837, the Strasbourg banking firm Ratisbonne tried to obtain a concession for building a Strasbourg–Sarrebruck line. In 1848, R. Lippmann renewed Blum's project which subsequently was realized by Jacques Javal, father of the deputy Léopold Javal, together with the Alsatian industrialist, Nicolas Koechlin. Léopold Javal joined Emile Koechlin of Mulhouse and constructed the Mulhouse–Cernay line, which preceded the Paris–St.Germain line, considered to be the first of France. At a time when France possessed only 50 or 60 steam-engines, Jacques Javal imported such machinery from England despite the prohibition of such export. He also imported an entire engraving workshop from that country. Since 1824 he had been a pioneer in organizing credit for industry. His son started an agricultural school in the department of Yonne where the first agricultural exhibition in France took place.[7] Another Alsatian Jew, Hartzfeld, a former army officer, was an initiator of modern navigation in Alsace and the neighboring provinces. He owned the boat "Le Rhin," the first to sail from the Marne Canal to the Rhine. Shortly before 1800, Thomas and his Jewish partner, Worms, suggested the transportation of coal through a canal, instead of using

[7] Siméon Worms, *Chemin de fer de Metz à Paris par Sarrebruck, vers le centre et le nord de l'Allemagne* (Metz, 1852), 7 pp.; *Courrier de la Moselle*, July 22, 1845; *L'Univers israélite*, II (1845), 205–207, XXXV (1880), 369; Jean Braun, "Les Débuts du chemin de fer en Alsace," *Deux siècles d'Alsace française* (Paris, 1948), 315–350; André Lefèvre, *La Ligne de Strasbourg à Bâle* (Strasbourg, 1947), xiii; R. Lippmann, *Compagnie du chemin de fer de Strasbourg à Bâle . . . Plan . . .* (Strasbourg, 1849), 8 pp.; Tisseron, *Nécrologie, Jacques Javal* (Paris, 1858), 8 pp., reprinted from *Archives biographiques et nécrologiques*, XXXII (1858); D. Schornstein, in *Revue israélite*, III (1872), 261–264; *Archives israélites*, XXXII (1872), 355–359; Fr. E. Sitzmann, *Dictionnaire de biographies des hommes célèbres d'Alsace* (Rixheim, 1909), I, 849.

the more expensive land route. The General Council of Mosell encouraged their initiative but progress was very slow. During the nineteenth century the above noted Jacques Javal was a pioneer in navigation of French boats to China and other countries.[8]

The increasing role of the Jews in the textile industry is a good example of their rapid advance in the course of a relatively short time from peddling to manufacturing, given the turbulent times of the post-Napoleonic Restoration Era, the protective tariff barriers, the lack of modern machinery and credits, and the traditional Alsatian dislike of Jews.

At the beginning of the Revolution, Hayemson Crépange established a textile factory in Sedan.[9] During the continental blockade, a decree of May 14, 1810 promised a reward of a million francs to the inventor of a machine for spinning flax. Emmanuel Bloch created such a machine, but the decree was forgotten as a result of the war and Restoration.[10] In Bischwiller, the textile factory of Aaron Blin (later Blin and Bloch) was opened in 1827; it operated eighty looms. In the same city, the factory of Ruef and Bicard employed 200 workers.[11] At the exhibitions of 1834 and 1844 the textile products of Morel Beer of Elbeuf, B. Javal and J. May of the same city, Ruef and Bicard of Bischwiller and Gondchaux-Picard of Nancy received recognition. The textile manufacturers Beer and Javal were noted for their inexpensive fabrics in seven colors; until then the Elbeuf fabrics were considered to be too expensive. The factory of Paraf in Mulhouse also produced inexpensive dyed fabrics. Elie Lantz of the same city owned a large factory of colored textiles which was later enlarged by his sons. One of them, Lazare Lantz, president of the Upper Rhine Consistory for fifty years, was nicknamed "the minister of finances" of Mulhouse. (Many years

[8] *Moniteur de la Meurthe*, July 27, 1867; *Archives israélites*, XXVII (1867), 744–747; Albert Eiselé, *Le Charbon mosellan. Etude historique et économique* (Paris, 1936), pp. 73–74; Sitzmann, *op. cit.*, I, 849.

[9] *Archives israélites*, V (1844), 754.

[10] Isaie Bloch, "Découverte remarquable due à un Israélite de Metz," *Archives israélites*, XIV (1853), 492–493.

[11] *Archives israélites*, V (1844), 754; XVI (1855), 506.

later, after 1918, Emile Lantz became chairman of the association of producers of printed textiles).[12] Solomon Moyse Lévy of Nancy played an important role in textile commerce with Switzerland and Germany.[13]

From the beginning of the seventeenth century, Bischwiller was a textile center with a mainly Protestant industrial element as in Mulhouse. Its Jewish population of 7 in 1826 increased to 216 by 1861. From 1815 until the 1860s, as a result of the protective policy, the Bischwiller textile industry had to work for the French market only, and there was no room for much initiative. Nevertheless, Jews played an important role in the Bischwiller industry, especially after the 1860s. (A problem for further investigation is whether the Upper Rhine with its Protestant industrialists encouraged the hiring of more Jews in industry than the Lower Rhine and other departments.) Jewish textile factories also existed in Liebfauenthal (Blum and Son), Haguenau (Aron), and other places.[14] During the Revolution, the Brothers Lipman and Théodore Cerfherr established a large textile factory in Tomblaine. During the Restoration, L. Borach of Turkheim (Upper Rhine) also owned a textile factory.[15] In 1819 Jacques Javal founded a factory of printed textiles in the

[12] Ibid., V (1844), 523; XVI (1855), 509; Musée industriel. Description complète de l'exposition des produits de l'industrie française faite en 1834 (Paris, 1835), I, 113–114, 124; Archives israélites, XVI (1855), 509. Among the owners of cloth mills in Mulhouse were Astruc and partners (1847), David Bloch (1867), Henri Bloch (1820), Joseph Bloch (1830), Jules Bloch Son (1863), S. and P. Dreyfus (1859), Raphaël Dreyfus (1850), Dreyfus and the Wallach brothers (1852), Dan Lévy and Sam (1857), Lévy, Picard and Mannheimer (1841), S. Lévy and partners (1857), Mathias Paraf (1826), etc. Société industrielle de Mulhouse. Histoire documentaire de l'industrie de Mulhouse et de ses environs au XIXe siècle (Mulhouse, 1902). See also David Singer, Situation de l'industrie cotonnière en France en 1828 (Paris, 1829); see Archives israélites, VII (1846), 100–102.

[13] J. Godechot, "Les Juifs de Nancy de 1789 à 1795," Revue des Études Juives (hereafter called REJ), LXXXVI (1928), 5.

[14] Jules Camus, Le Développement économique et social de Bischwiller (Strasbourg, 1939), pp. 2, 12, 23–27, 34–35, 42–43; August Kocher, Die Aemter Offendorf und Bischweiler ... (Strasbourg, 1907), p. 122.

[15] Godechot, op. cit., p. 4; sample of a factory stamp of Borach (JTS).

Paris suburb, Saint Denis, where 500 workers were employed. Benoit Samuel of Strasbourg had a factory of handkerchiefs and neckties, where he used the Milan and Elberfeld method. In 1820 he opposed granting import licences for such products as he had manufactured for many years in Alsace. In the 1860s Michel Alcan, a member of the Paris Consistory and professor at the school of arts and crafts, was considered the greatest textile industry expert in France. In 1805 Cerf Lanzenberg opened a shirt factory in Strasbourg, following the modern shirt-making techniques developed there by H. Oppenheim.[16]

In 1800 Siméon Worms was the first to introduce in Metz the use of oil for heating. Later he played a role in local coal-mining. In 1869, E. Javal suggested strengthening the Moselle production of coal, thus alleviating dependence on imports from Germany. In 1820–1863 the Moselle department had 11 concessions of coal mines with 20,750 hectares. Four of them, with 8,628, belonged to Jews and their Christian partners.[17]

N. C. Bloch of Duttlenheim was one of the first producers of glucose. Another Jew, Lippmann, bought a partnership in the Meinau factory for 100,000 francs; he promised to cultivate eighty hectares of sugar-beets. In 1841 Nephtali Cerf Bloch opened the first starch factory in the Lower Rhine, which greatly helped local agriculture.[18] Prosper Trenel played an important role in the printing industry of Lorraine.[19]

[16] *Journal des Débats*, Jan. 11, 1855; *Archives israélites*, XVI (1855), 506–507; XIX (1858), 114–115; Me. Briffault, *Mémoire pour le Sieur Benoît Samuel, négociant à Strasbourg ... contre le Sieur Jean-Philippe Schuster* (Strasbourg, 182–), 40 pp.; *Moniteur*, Dec. 4, 1863; Sitzmann, *op. cit.*

[17] *Univers israélite*, II (1845), 366; *Archives israélites*, VI (1845), 691, 757–758 and XV (1854), 234; *L'Indépendant de la Moselle*, Aug. 29, 1845; Eiselé, *op. cit.*, p. 98.

[18] *La Presse israélite*, I (1869); *Courrier du Bas-Rhin*, June 12, 1869; *Archives israélites*, XVI (1855), 506; XXX (1869), 412; *Réponse de M. Lippmann au rapport de l'assemblée générale des actionnaires de la fabrique de sucre de Meinau, tenue le 15 mars 1842* (Strasbourg, 1842), 12 pp.; *Les Dictionnaires départementaux. Les Alsaciens-Lorrains* (Paris, 1896), I.

[19] *Moniteur de la Moselle*, July 31, 1868.

Over one-half of the products of the leather factories of the brothers Goudchaux and Picard in Nancy and Elbeuf were exported abroad.[20] Weil and his nephew, of Montagne-Verte near Strausbourg, pioneered in the production of inexpensive crystal.[21] The Alsatian partners Lippmann and Mayer were among the leading merchants of lead in France. Louis Lang exported his tin products to America, while in Paris Gustave Lévy of Mulhouse owned an important bronze factory. Auguste Dupont, member of the Metz Consistory, was one of the first industrialists who saw a future in mines on the south banks of the Moselle. By 1846 he had established the metallurgical forges of Ars-sur-Moselle which opened new perspectives for Metz, a city, which because of its large garrison, was leaning too much toward free professions and commerce. Owing to the German occupation in 1870, Nancy profited from such perspectives. The forges of Ars-sur-Moselle were then transferred to Pompey, near Nancy.[22] In Strasbourg the soap factory of Weill and Co. was famous.[23]

I shall not enumerate here all the well-known Jewish bankers of France, but will limit myself to only a few of the less known local bankers and their roles in various industries. Lazare Lantz (1823–1909), chairman of the Mulhouse savings bank, founded the Banque de Mulhouse. Aaron Veil Picard started with a small store of textiles in Besançon, which he expanded into the largest textile business of the province. Later he founded a bank. He was the first to understand the importance of a branch of the Banque de France for the industry and commerce of Besançon. In 1848, when it was difficult to obtain credit, he gave 9 million francs of credit to local industry and thus saved many factories from closing, among them

---

[20] *Musé industriel* (Paris, 1835), I, 120–121.

[21] *Archives israélites*, IV (1843), 290–292; XVI (1855), 507.

[22] *Affaire entre MM. Lippmann et Mayer et MM. Figuéroa et Guillardet* (Paris, 1845), 17 pp. (by de Vaupré); *Conclusions motivées* (Metz, 1853), 6 pp. (by de Fautrier and Rémond); *Archives israélites*, XVI (1855), 507; XXX (1869), 283; *Les Alsaciens-Lorrains*, II; H. Contamine, *Metz et la Moselle de 1814 à 1870* (Nancy, 1932), I, 34–36.

[23] *Archives israélites*, XVI (1855), 506–507.

the factory of Audincourt which employed some 2,000 workers.[24]

What was the effect of Jewish participation in French industry and in large-scale commerce upon the Jewish masses (if one may use such an expression for a population of only about 70,000)? Did the number of Jewish industrial workers increase as a result of Jewish factory ownership? According to a report of 1810 there were, in the Lower Rhine, 165 Jewish factories and 144 workers; in other words, most workers in these factories were not Jewish. In fact, on December 21, 1808 the minister of the interior wrote to Napoleon that the Jewish textile manufacturers employed many Frenchmen; no mention was made in the report about Jewish employees. When a Paris journal wrote in 1847, that Rothschild mainly employed Jews in the administration of the northern railroad line, it was more anti-Jewish gossip than reality. In 1872, only eight native Jews of Paris and one foreign Jew were employed by railroads.[25] The occupational structure of French Jewry was little affected by the activities of the Jewish elite; the majority of the Jews had little to do with the Saint Simonians, Rothschilds and others. For a long time they continued to be influenced by old habits as well as by prior and new restrictions. Before 1880, Jewish participation in the building of railroads and the development of textile and other industries was a phenomenon limited to the Jewish elite alone.

In a study about the Rothschilds and other bankers, Michael Graetz tried to examine the thesis of some historians that during the Industrial Revolution of the nineteenth century there existed an interrelationship between the Jewish economic elite and the ruling powers; that old-fashioned *shtadlanut* (intercession) was of great importance. His conclusion was that not the personal connection

[24] R. Hirchler, *Les Juifs à Mulhouse* (Mulhouse, 1938), p. 11; *Archives israélites*, XXIX (1868), 929–933; *L'Union Franc-Comtoise*, June 4, 1864. When his son, Adolphe Veil Picard, died in 1877, 10,000 inhabitants of Besançon followed the funeral, *Archives israélites*, XXXVIII (1877), 691–692, 718–722.

[25] Paul Fauchille, *La Question juive en France sous le Premier Empire* (Paris, 1884), p. 73; A. E. Halphen, *Recueil des Lois . . .* (Paris, 1851), p. 323; *L'Esprit public*, Jan. 8, 1945; census of 1872 (Archives of the Paris Consistory).

with the regime but Jewish initiative, willingness to take risks, and the ability to adapt to the economic changes played the most important role. The same conclusion is true of both the Jewish economic elite and the less important Jewish industrialists. Despite Emancipation, Alsatian Jews remained victims of the restrictions of the old regime and of succeeding modern, active anti-Semitism. This was also true of other regions. It took more than a half century to overcome these disabilities. When the brothers Lippmann purchased the crystal factory of Baccarat (Meuse) in 1806 they had to face not only an economic crisis but also the opposition of the Catholic Church which tried to prevent the purchase. Nevertheless, the two brothers were able to overcome the difficulties and to provide a living for over one thousand inhabitants. The problems encountered by the Jews of Saint-Esprit, a suburb of Bayonne, in expanding their activities to Bayonne, are well known.

At a time when the interrelationship between intellectual and industrial advancement was very strong and decisive, Jews had little access to liberal professions. A number of Jews then chose conversion as a means to facilitate their advancement. On the other hand many young Jews preferred to fight the combination of social, economic and Church opposition. Among them were a few of the founders of the Alliance Israélite Universelle in 1860.[26] In spite of

[26] Michael Graetz, "Changes in the Interrelationship between the Jewish Economic Elite and the Rulers of Western Europe," *Studies in the History of the Jewish People and the Land of Israel* (Haifa, 1974), II, 191–225; see André Neher, "La bourgeoisie juive d'Alsace," *La bourgeoisie alsacienne. Etudes d'histoire sociale* (Strasbourg–Paris, 1954), p. 436; S. Posener, "Lippmann Lippmann de Baccarat. Fragment de l'histoire économique des Juifs en France," *Festschrift zu Simon Dubnows siebzigstem Geburtstag* (Berlin, 1930), pp. 207–214; H. Léon, *Histoire des juifs de Bayonne* (Paris, 1893), p. 394; Alexandre Weill, "Les Juifs de Paris," *La Gerbe* (Paris, 1890), p. 51; Szajkowski, "The Founding of the Alliance israélite universelle (1860)," *Yivo Bleter*, XVIII (1941), 8, 10; and my "Anti-Jewish Riots during the Revolutions of 1789, 1830 and 1848," *Zion*, XX (1955), 101–102. In the research on important Jewish manufacturers, the economic Jewish elite, mere statistics are often not enough. The difficulties encountered by them can best be illustrated by the records of the many judicial conflicts as

the difficulties, the progress shown by Jews was most impressive; but it took a good deal of physical and intellectual stamina to surmount these obstacles.

At regional, national, and international exhibitions a large number of Jews obtained medals. At the Paris exhibition of 1827, a total of 1,631 manufacturers (or one per 19,000 inhabitants) exhibited their products; among them were fifteen Jews, or one per 4,000 Jews.[27] In 1850–1876, four Jews were elected members of the Academy of Medicine,[28] and in 1836–1875 seven Jews became members of the Institut de France.[29] According to a survey com-

recorded in the *factums* (briefs), which should not be disregarded by researchers.

[27] At the Metz exhibition of 1861 there were forty-four Jews: eleven textile industrialists, six metallurgists, four clothiers, three agriculturists, eleven furniture manufacturers; six Jews exhibited their graphic products, two their military products, six their works of art, three their musical instruments, etc. At the Paris International Exhibition of 1855 there were 140 industrialists from the Lower Rhine, including 10 Jews. At the three Paris International Exhibitions of 1855, 1867 and 1878, a total of ninety-eight Jews received prizes. In addition, between 1840 and 1877, seventy-seven Jews, who were active in the fields of banking and commerce, were decorated on other occasions or were nominated to high administrative posts. Cerf-Mayer received prizes in 1834 and 1844 for his oil-cloth; Javal and May of Elbeuf, Goudchaux-Picard of Nancy, and Picard of Strasbourg for exhibiting cloth in 1834, 1839 and 1844; Vitalis for exhibiting cloth in 1823 and 1844. In 1844 the following were honored: locksmith Block; clockmaker Neuman; leather manufacturers Lanzberg and Co.; the producer of sealing-wax Zegelaar; Wolf, who was active in the toy-trade; Helbronner, who exhibited his tapestries; the manufacturers of arms, Javal and Co., etc. Léon Kahn, *Les Professions manuelles et les institutions de patronage* (Paris, 1885), 25–26; *L'Univers israélite,* I (1844), 95–98, 134–135; Isaac Lévy, "Défense du judaïsme...," *Archives israélites,* XVI (1855), 205–206; XXVIII (1867), 891–892; Elie Lambert, "Expositions de Metz," *Univers israélite,* XVII (1861), 107–114; Isidore Loeb, "Documents de son enquête sur le judaïsme" (Archives of the Alliance Israélite Universelle, corresp. No. 433/2).

[28] Michel Lévy (1850), Germain Sée (1868), Mathieu Hirtz (1873), Nathan Oulmont (1876).

[29] Fromenthal Halévy, Adolphe Franck, Achille Fould, Solomon Munk, Joseph Derenbourg, Maurice Loewy, Michel Bréal.

piled in 1833, on the basis of characteristic Jewish names in the Bottin directory, Isidore Loeb found in Paris twenty-five Jewish lawyers, forty-eight physicians, twenty-two engineers, twenty-two publishers and owners of book stores, and twelve composers and professors of music. Loeb also counted over 450 manufacturers (it may be assumed that many of them were also trading their own products). A total of 1,278 economically active Jews were engaged in an amazingly large number of 175 occupations; they were important enough to be included in the Bottin. In 1889 Léon Kahn listed a very impressive number of French Jews in Paris who occupied high administrative posts, or were engineers (42), physicians, chairmen of associations of industries, and so forth.[30]

Maurice Bloch wrote about "the disproportion between French Jewry's numbers and achievements." In 1906, the Paris correspondent of the London *Jewish Chronicle* noted that the French government had bestowed the highest distinction on no fewer than forty Jews, in connection with the exhibitions at St. Louis and Liège.[31] What brought about these exceptional accomplishments? Undoubtedly, education played a major role. But this means of advancement was often prevented by active anti-Semitism and by extreme poverty of the first post-Emancipation generation. Only when parents bettered their economic position, mainly through commerce, were they able to provide an education for their children which often went beyond primary school. Léon Werth (1795–1877), the well-known nineteenth-century Jewish leader of Alsace, was born to a poor family in Wintzenheim. He was a peddler, a laborer, and a tutor in the home of Léopold Javal. In 1819, he invested his meager savings in the purchase of a small weaving plant in Kaiserberg. Between 1827 and 1830, he had a dyeing plant in Bonhomme, in which he was the first to use red dye from Adrianople. In time,

---

[30] Loeb's survey; Kahn, *Les Professions*, pp. 21–22; and his *Les Juifs à Paris depuis le VIe siècle* (Paris, 1889), pp. 183–189.

[31] Maurice Bloch, "French Judaism since the Revolution. The Disproportion between its Numbers and Achievements," *The New Era* (New York), II (July, 1904), 155–166; "Participation of French Jews in Commercial and Industrial Developments," *Jewish Chronicle*, Oct. 19, 1906.

he owned one of the largest dyeing plants in the country.[32] Often, however, the road to progress bypassed industrial initiative either as manufacturers or workers.

Most recipients of relief from the Jewish Charitable Committee in Paris were not professional beggars, but hard-working people who could not exist on their meager earnings. In 1843 the heads of 409 families receiving relief were engaged in 76 occupations; 44 were listed as day-laborers; 151 were peddlers or in related occupations.[33]

True, for a long time in some places most Jews remained outside the industrial advances. Nancy, for example, was not a center conducive to "productivization." On the eve of the 1848 Revolution, 7,000 people — one half of the male population — was engaged in liberal professions. The same was true for Metz, a city famous for its large garrison. Perhaps this induced Jews to join the ranks of army officers. In 1859 there were 221 Jewish officers in the French army, mostly Alsatian Jews. Among the 4,000 students of the École Polytechnique in 1830–1860, over 100 were Jews. According to one source, in 1867 there was one officer for every 8,260 inhabitants, but the percentage of Jewish officers, in relation to the Jewish population was much higher, despite the fact that army careers really only became open to Jews after the Revolution of 1830. Strasbourg was always a more commercial than industrial center. The same could be said about Alsace in general, with the exception of Mulhouse and a few smaller centers.[34]

No definitive conclusions can be drawn on the basis of our Appendix, which is only a recapitulation of more detailed, though

[32] *Univers israélite*, XXXIII (1877), pp. 52–53; *Archives israélites*, XXXVIII (1877), pp. 661–662.

[33] Kahn, *Les Professions*, pp. 21, 93.

[34] Pierre Braun, "Le département de la Moselle à la fin de la Monarchie de Juillet," *La Révolution de 1848*, XV (1920), 146; Contamine, *op. cit.*, I, 34–36; "Officiers israélites français," *Archives israélites*, XX (1859), 351–353, 458–461; *La Vérité israélite*, I (1860), 37; *Moniteur de la Meurthe*, July 27, 1867; *Univers israélite*, XXIII (1867), 28–31; Henry Bruschwig, *Les subsistances à Strasbourg pendant les premières années de la Révolution française* (Strasbourg, 1932), p. 7.

not always reliable tables. The categories are too interrelated and cannot easily be separated or manipulated; they can mislead or confuse. The researcher must, of course, take into consideration the specific situation of each region. The criteria cannot be the same for Ashkenazic Jews of Alsace, Metz, and Lorraine, and even more so for Ashkenazic, Sephardic or Comtadin Jews.[35]

In all official and consistorial registries of Jews the heading "occupational status" often contains the qualification *rentier* (a man with a small private income, a stockholder), or *propriétaire* (proprietor, a landlord or owner of some other property). According to a 1810 report of the Central Consistory, there were then 46,663 Jews in France, occupied territories not included. 630 served in the army, 374 were listed as proprietors, 189 as industrialists, and 1,257 as children in schools and "useful professions." The ownership of a house was no sign that one had enough to live on. On May 13, 1806, the prefect of Meurthe wrote in the instructions for the preparation of a report on the Jews that in filling in professions, those reporting should only designate as proprietors Jews who had enough invested in houses to allow them to live on the rents, independent of other income. Following instructions, the sub-prefect of Château-Salins recorded 78 Jewish families (400 individuals). Of these, two-fifths had houses of their own, but only one Jew, Lazare Lévy, was to be considered a proprietor. In a census of Jews in the regional Consistory of Marseilles (1809), one encounters the following qualifying remarks about Jewish proprietors "without fortune": Montpellier—nine, including one destitute; Alpes-Maritimes—thirty-one, including four without fortunes; and Rhône—seven, four of them without fortune.[36]

[35] In the 1856 census of Saint-Esprit-lès-Bayonne an artist, an engineer, a railroad employee, a veterinarian, a manufacturer and a horse-dealer who did not figure in the previous census of 1850 are listed. But then, further research is required to find out whether these additions were local people who grew up there or newly settled Jews from other localities. In the 1849 census of Gironde a new mason, a blacksmith, a roofer, a boat captain, a block-maker (or vendor) are recorded, *Archives Nationales*, F19-11050-51.

[36] A.-E. Halphen, *Recueil des lois* ... (Paris, 1851), pp. 307–328, Departmental archives of Moselle; JTS.

One should not imagine that *rentiers* or proprietors owned much property or stocks accounting for large amounts of money. Most of them were far from being wealthy; indeed they even were poor, living on a few small savings. They had to peddle or work to keep from starving, but somehow they proudly preferred to be listed as *rentiers*. Before the Revolution, Jews were not permitted to trade in *rentes*, which was the most profitable form of money-lending, so *rentes* were a relatively new and not always profitable form of trade for them. In 1829, the Jewish Consistory of Metz stated that in all of Metz there was not even one rich Jew whose annual *rente* amounted to 15,000 francs. This was not only true for the Jews, but also for all of France. In 1815–1830, there were 10,000 stockholders who had stocks valued at 30 frs. on the average, 36,000—at 76 frs.; 76,000—at 400 frs., 15,500—at 2,675 frs., 5,000—at 5,460 frs. and 1,600—at 19,000 frs. In 1865, the stockholders of France possessed a total of 1,100,000 stocks, each stockholder averaging 365 frs. There were almost as many *rentiers* of government, city or foreign bonds, of bank or postal savings, as there were voters in France.[37]

This did not mean that the *rentier* or proprietor did not have another occupation. In fact, if one studies such records carefully one can find that the same person was listed one year as a *rentier* and a few years later as a shopkeeper. Such changes were often made for the purposes of taxation, the prestige of belonging to the respectable class of *rentiers*, or simply by the caprice of the communal secretary.

In all records there is a large percentage of *marchands* (merchants, persons who buy and sell goods; *Kaufmann* in German) and *négociants* (negotiators, dealers with other persons; *Haendler* in German). There was a basic difference between the two terms. The first applied to qualified businessmen, wholesale dealers (*Grosskaufmann* in German), while the second referred to petty

---

[37] Szajkowski, *Poverty*, p. 16; and my *The Economic Status of the Jews in Alsace ... 1648–1789* (New York, 1954), pp. 83–86 ("Usury through rentes"); Eymard, *La politique financière sous la Restauration, 1815–1830* (Paris, 1924), p. 156; Ernest Brelay, *Les Classes agricoles avant et après la Révolution* (Paris, 1882), pp. 35–36.

merchants, retail dealers. One year the Jew was registered as a
négociant and a few years later as a *marchand*. It seems that in
the eyes of the persons who compiled the registries the *négociant*
was of a lower level of respectability. This makes any conclusion
on the occupational status of French Jews even more difficult.
Much more detailed research is needed in order to determine if
a Jew who attained the status of a *marchand* had first to pass
through the status of *négociant*. In many cases *commerçant* was
noted, which may mean both *marchand* and *négociant*.

Often a *négociant* was also an artisan, or even a manufacturer.
In a lawsuit, Benoît Samuel of Strasbourg called himself *négociant*, although he had a handkerchiefs and neckties factory. Artisans who were forced by hard times to become wanderers were
noted in registries as peddlers. Gabriel Schrameck of Issenheim
(Upper Rhine), born in 1795, described his father as a skilled
upholsterer who travelled through towns and villages seeking
work at his trade. He returned home only on the Sabbath. Gabriel
was so poorly clothed that his father was ashamed to take him to
work with him. He bought one pair of pants made of old clothes,
and a pair of torn shoes. In order to pay the tailor and the shoe-
maker, this six-year-old boy had to peddle junk in school. Many
small manufacturers sold their products in stores, at the markets,
or were wandering with their products from village to village.
L. Lyon Cahen wrote that his father was a *marchand tailleur*. Out
of 323 individuals in Carpentras in 1846, only 29 were listed as
workers and 4 as *marchand tailleur*. The same situation prevailed
in Avignon.[38]

The *ancien regime* was often tolerant toward Jews by allowing
them to deal not only in second-hand merchandise but also in
imported new merchandise, but only as *marchand forain* (itinerant
merchants, stall keepers at markets, peddlers), i.e., keeping the
merchandise in *magasins* but not in open stores. For a long time

---

[38] Briffaut, *op. cit*; *Erlebnisse von Gabriel Schrameck, geboren in Isen-
seim (Ober Elsass) im Jahr III der Republik, 1795* (Bar, 1907), pp. 3, 6–7;
L. Lyon Cahen, *Souvenirs de ma jeunesse* (Paris, 1912), pp. 8–9; JTS.

after the Emancipation many Jews continued as such businessmen without stores.[39]

The research in the field of Franco-Jewish economic statistics is greatly handicapped by the lack of precise information on employers and employees, manufacturers and workers. In 1809 there were 2,908 Jews in Paris. According to Léon Kahn, 420 (14.4 percent) were engaged in small commerce, the vast majority in peddling; 229 in various professions (*métiers*), which can mean anything, artisans or businessmen; 145 in various occupations; 43 in banking and large scale commerce; 40 in liberal professions. Among the 229 engaged in *métiers,* 36 were listed as workers, 7 as manufacturers and about the others, no information was available whether they were manufacturers, workers or employees. In the original census, 78 were listed as military men. Of the manufacturers and workers, all were in small industries. Among the 963 notables, listed in 1845, who had the right to participate in the consistorial election, 380 were recorded as manufacturers or merchants. Only for the regional Paris Consistory were they listed in separate categories (98 merchants and 38 manufacturers). About the 137 Jews who were employed in Paris in 1846, and the 305 in 1872, it is not known if they were workers, manufacturers or merchants. About the 694 in 1846, and the 1,025 in 1872 who were employed in various industries, we do not know if they were employers or employees. For a long time in their reports to the authorities, the Jewish Consistories used the term *arts et métiers,* without distinction between liberal arts and manual work.[40]

Often, only emigration abroad or to other parts of France afforded some prospect of advancement. One should have expected that this process was also a factor in the industrialization among Jews. However, the facts seem to prove the contrary. In 1809, most of the newly established Jewish communities consisted

[39] E.C.M., *Notice sur l'état des israélites en France* (Paris, 1821); Kahn; *Les Professions,* p. 10.

[40] Kahn, *ibid.,* pp. 65–67; JTS; *Archives israélites,* VI (1845), 831–833; report of the Bouches-du-Rhône Consistory for 1808, Departmental archives of Bouches-du-Rhône, 112 V 1.

principally of peddlers. In Dijon (Côte-d'Or) there was only one manufacturer with 8 workers, or people who could be considered as such, among 236 Jews of the new community. There was not a single worker or manufacturer among the 45 Jews of Dunkerque and the 136 Jews of Lille (nord); most Jews there were peddlers. Among the 66 Jews of Rouen (Seine-Intérieure) there were 2 workers; all the others were peddlers. In the rosters of 1842 and 1853, for the purpose of liquidating the debts of the Metz community, *rentiers* who remained in Metz had their fortunes estimated at 600 and 800 francs, while the fortunes of those who settled in Paris were worth ten times as much. It can be observed that while fortunes increased, the occupations remained the same. Baruch Prager's fortune rose from 200 francs in 1842 to 1,200 in 1853, and Baruch Ettinger's, both bakers, from 200 to 500 francs. Very often the real meaning of one's occupational status can be understood when it is studied together with his estimated or real fortune. In the same roster for 1853 a tailor's fortune was listed as 12,000 francs, a shirtmaker's (or seller's)—as 10,000. Surely, they were not workers or artisans, but manufacturers with or without stores.[41]

It should be noted that industries and large scale commerce developed outside the former ghettos. A description of Jewish life in the former ghetto of Metz from the 1820s to 1860s mentioned the existence of four Jewish restaurants, two bakeries of bread and two of cakes, six butchers, a few stores of fine foods, three jewelry stores, six furniture stores, and so forth. No industries were mentioned.[42]

In 1816 there were 1,288 consistorial tax payers in the department of Lower Rhine and in 1827—1,304. The majority were

---

[41] JTS: *Rôle de la répartition pour l'extinction des dettes de l'ancienne communauté des Juifs de Metz. Année 1842* (Metz, 1843), 32 pp.; *Liquidation des dettes de l'ancienne communauté juive de Metz. Mise en recouvrement du rôle de 1853...* (Metz, 1854), 76 pp.

[42] Général J. Dennery, "La Communauté israélite de Metz avant 1870," *La Famille israélite*, suppl. of *l'Univers israélite*, II (1925), 289–292, 295–298, 305–308.

intermediaries or peddlers, engaged in trading on a small or large scale, with or without stores. Of course, the tax registries did not take note of the entire Jewish population. People of the lowest social status, those who could not afford to pay taxes, were not included. For 1816, only three day-laborers and not even one domestic were listed. However, the data is important for the changes that occurred or did not occur. There were fourteen *rentiers* in 1816, twenty-two in 1822, eighteen in 1826 and not one in 1827. In Strasbourg, five Netters and five Samuels, who were noted earlier as *rentiers*, changed their occupation to that of *négociants* (dealers). The *rentiers*, Isaac Apfel of Fraeschwiller and Samuel Winter of Groesdorf, became merchants. The number of peddlers fell from seventy-five in 1816 to seventy-three in 1818, down to forty-two in 1827. We do not know, however, if they were stricken from the taxation lists or whether they had advanced in their social status. The number of merchants rose from 251 in 1816 to 329 in 1827; the number of horse and cattle dealers rose from 361 to 406. Times were unstable and people who had advanced in their social status were forced to take a step backward. Abraham Kaufman of Bouxwiller was a rolling merchant in 1816 and a merchant in 1827; the peddler Lévy Marx became a merchant of grain. On the other hand Abraham Lévy, a soap manufacturer in 1816, was a peddler in 1827.[43]

In the Marseilles regional Consistory, which comprised eight departments (including Lyons), the number of those engaged in manual labor decreased, while the number of those occupied in trade and free professions increased. At the same time that the number of peddlers and other petty traders decreased, the number of businessmen on a larger scale increased.[44]

For 1872 in Paris we noted 1,025 engaged in various industries as manufacturers, or 16.31 percent of the 6,284 Jews available for our survey and 5 percent of all 23,284 Jews then living in Paris. Only 11 of the 1,025 were noted as manufacturers and 70 as day-

[43] JTS.

[44] Szajkowski, "The Decline and Fall of Provençal Jewry," *Jewish Social Studies*, VI (1944), 49–50.

laborers or common laborers (*homme de peine*), 16 as mechanics, and 44 as plumbers and locksmiths. All the others were listed by their professions, without information about their status either as manufacturers, workers or employees. In addition to 173 jewelry and diamond dealers, 52 were listed as jewelers; most probably some were workers, but we don't know how many. Something can be said about the 219 tailors. One, engaged as a *confectionneur*, may have had a store of ready-made clothes, or worked in such a store. The sixteen *ébénistes* may have been cabinet-makers fabricating and selling furniture, or self-employed artisans, with or without workers; the same could be said about the sixty-five shoemakers and saddlers.[45]

Often it is necessary to speak of employment in general, instead of professions. Since the idea that only workers and peasants were productive is unacceptable, the number occupied in any profession as workers or peddlers should be investigated. Of the 2,908 Jews (women and children included) who resided in Paris in 1809, not less than 889 (30.57 percent) had an occupation, which represented a very high percentage of economically active individuals.[46]

The history of vocational schools in France was already the subject of a detailed study by this writer. Here it should be noted that in spite of the many trials and errors experienced and committed by these institutions, over 6,500 students graduated from these schools between 1827 and 1900, but not all of them remained workers or artisans. Many used the skills acquired in the schools for positions in commerce.[47]

The number of Jewish agriculturists was very limited. Before the Revolution, Jews were not permitted to be farmers. In an earlier study we tried to explain the reasons why Jews bought nationalized properties for resale only during the Revolution. Many Jews who were anxious to become agriculturists were too poor to buy land; they preferred to become tenant-farmers. In the

45 Archives of the Paris Consistory.
46 Kahn, *Les Professions*, pp. 65–67.
47 Szajkowski, "Jewish Trade Schools in France in the 19th Century," *Yivo Bleter*, XLII (1962), 81–120.

Bordeaux region it was fashionable to become owners of parcels of land on which summer homes were built.[48] Some nineteenth century Franco-Jewish leaders were not too enthusiastic about the idea of propagating agriculture among Jews. While a few excellent Franco-Jewish vocational schools existed, all efforts to open an agricultural school failed. Adversaries of such a project claimed that as agricultural workers Jews would not be able to observe the Sabbath and dietary laws. Moreover, they predicted that, as a result of the development of railroads, Alsatian agriculture would suffer from competition by foreign imports. They further contested the idea that a profession demanding greater physical strength was more honorable than one demanding lesser strength. In the 1850s a society to propagate emigration of Alsatian Jews to America, founded by Alphonse de Rothschild, Achille Ratisbonne, and others existed in Strasbourg. Léon Werth protested the aim of the society whose leaders, he thought, tried to rid themselves of the poor Jews, instead of ameliorating their status through vocational training and agriculture.[49]

Alsace and the neighboring departments were approaching a period of economic stabilization, when the Franco-Prussian war broke out and the region was annexed by Germany. A number of industrialists, often together with their businesses, left this German territory for France, even going to Belgium, Luxemburg and the American lands. The number of Jewish families in Besançon rose

[48] Szajkowski, "Jewish Participation in the Sale of National Property during the French Revolution," *Jewish Social Studies*, XIV (1952), 291–316; M. Betting de Lancastel, *Considérations sur l'état des juifs dans la société chrétienne, et particuliérement en Alsace* (Strasbourg, 1824), p. 87; George Weill, "Metz au temps français (1830–1870)," *Revue des études napoléoniennes*, XIII (1918), 211; "Parfois la terre est chère, et alors nos coreligionnaires pas trop aisés, hésitent à s'imposer des dettes pour devenir propriétaires; mais alors ils prennent résolument un autre parti, et deviennent fermiers d'un ou plusieurs champs." Isaac Wurmser, in *La Presse israélite*, I (1869), 362.

[49] Szajkowski, "Some Facts about Alsatian Jews in America," *Yivo Bleter*, XX (1942), 314; see also my *Poverty*, p. 31; and my "Jewish Trade Schools," pp. 106–109.

from 80 in 1869 to 200 in 1879. R. Weil moved his factory of textiles from Strasbourg to Blainville, near Nancy. Bloch and his sons of Bischwiller, Louis Fraenckel and his four sons, the brothers Blin and their partners, Picard, Blum, Meyer and others moved to Elbeauf, Roubaix, Tourcoing and other centers, often bringing their workers with them. Most had to start their economic activities in exile and on a limited scale; instead of former factories they rented ateliers. Some peddlers even settled in France, where they had to start their professions in an unfamiliar environment. Although German Jewish bankers and industrialists who came to Alsace played a very important role in the Alsatian economy under German occupation, the war did disrupt the Alsatian Jewish industrial activity.[50]

Because of the inconsiderable Jewish population in general, the number of Jewish proletarians was too small, almost invisible, to play an influential role. Already during the 1860s and 1870s there were Jewish revolutionaries; rarely workers. Most were leftist intellectuals interested in the political struggles in which the Jewish artisans, peddlers and poor could not be of much help. This lack of a visible Jewish working class helped to propagate the legend of Rothschild as "King of the Jews." There were a few excellent surveys on Jewish poverty,[51] but they were unknown to the public at large or even to the intellectuals. The historian, Isidore Loeb, wrote in 1890 that the Jews were not rich; indeed, they were poor, terribly poor. A few wealthy Jews created the illusion that all the

[50] Archives Nationales F19–11019 (Doubs); H. Laufenburger, "Les migrations dans le textile d'Alsace," *La Vie en Alsace*, IX (Sept., 1926), 197; Camus, *op. cit.*, pp. 60–66; André-E. Sayous, "L'évolution de Strasbourg entre les deux guerres," *Annales d'histoire économique et sociale*, VI (1934), 5, 16, 127–128; *L'Univers israélite*, XXX (1875), 347; *Archives israélites*, XXXII (1871), 90; E. About, *Alsace 1871–1872* (Paris, 1875), p. 19. See *Erinnerungen, eurer, an unseren unvergesslichen Herrn Isaac Adler, Lederfabrikant, Mitglied des Consistoriums fuer Unter-Elsass, geboren am 15. Oktober 1837 zu Obergrimpern (Baden)...* (Strasbourg, 1898).

[51] Gerson Lévy, *Du paupérisme chez les juifs...* (Paris, 1854); L. J. Reboul-Deneyrol, *Paupérisme et bienfaisance dans le Bas-Rhin* (Paris–Strasbourg, 1858). See also the bibliographical notes in my *Poverty*.

Jews were wealthy. Of about 8,000 Jewish families in Paris, 5,000 were unable to contribute to communal expenses.[52] The organized Franco-Jewish community treated the problem of Jewish poverty mostly as a problem of philanthropic activity. Curiously, among the radicals one could even find Jews who were active in communal Jewish life, such as Gaston Crémieux, the leader of the commune of Marseilles in 1871.[53] However, they completely separated the Jewish community from their political ideologies and thus were unable to grasp the importance of the specific economic aspect of Jewish life.

During the anti-Jewish stage of his life, Bernard Lazare used the term *Israélite* for laborers, professionals, shopkeepers, and soldiers. The rich, "dishonest," Orthodox he called *Jews*. Thus, Lazare was then more interested in ethics than in poverty or "productivity." A Jewish working class, a Jewish proletariat, came into being after 1881, when the mass immigration of East European Jews into France started. When Bernard Lazare met an organized group of Jewish proletarians in Paris, it was an unexpected and pleasant surprise.[54]

[52] Isidore Loeb, "Les Juifs de l'histoire et le Juif de la légende," *REJ*, XX (1890), xi.

[53] Szajkowski, *Jews and the Commune of Paris* [Hebrew] (Paris, 1956), pp. 32–35.

[54] Nelly Jussem-Wilson, "Bernard Lazare's Jewish Journey: From Being an Israelite to Being a Jew," *Jewish Social Studies*, XXVI (1964), 150. T. A. Tcher-Ski [Elias Tcherikower and Z. Szajkowski], "The Dreyfus Affair, the Immigrant Workers and the Franco-Jewish Leaders," *Jews in France* [Yiddish] (New York, 1942), pp. 164–167. On the Jewish immigrant proletarian groups, see my *Studies in the History of the Settlement of Immigrant Jews in France* [Yiddish] (Paris, 1936 and 1937), 2 vols.

STALIN'S ZIONISM

By Bernard D. Weinryb

. . . .

MARSHAL STALIN then said he thought more time was needed to consider and finish the business of the conference.

THE PRESIDENT answered that he had three Kings waiting for him in the Near East, including Ibn Saud.

. . . .

MARSHAL STALIN said the Jewish problem was a very difficult one — that they had tried to establish a national home for the Jews in Virovidzan but that they had only stayed there two or three years and then scattered to the cities. He said the Jews were natural traders but much had been accomplished by putting small groups in some agricultural areas.

THE PRESIDENT said he was a Zionist and asked if Marshall Stalin was one.

MARSHAL STALIN said he was one in principle but he recognized the difficulty.[1]

This conversation about Zionism between President Roosevelt and Marshal Stalin took place at the tripartite dinner meeting on February 10, 1945 in Yalta on the penultimate day of the conference in which Roosevelt, Churchill, and Stalin (each accompanied by two aides) participated. The text, from the minutes of the meeting, seems to have been truncated. One might justifiably suppose that after President Roosevelt insisted on ending the conference because on his way home he had to meet three Near Eastern kings to discuss

[1] R. G. 43. National Archives. World War II Conferences. Box 3. Folder: Yalta Conference Reports and Documents (Memos of conversations and meetings). C. Bohlen's minutes of the Big Three Conference at Yalta are among his records: Lot File 74 D379 (Record Group 59). A part is printed in *Foreign Relations of the United States. The Conferences of Malta and Yalta, 1945*. I am indebted to the National Archives and Record Service, Washington, D.C. for the text and information pertaining to this matter. The text of the conversation was also reprinted in *The New York Times* of March 17, 1955 where the Record of Yalta was reproduced.

with them the Palestine problem, some further talk about Jews and Palestine developed of which only a few sentences found their way into the minutes.

President Roosevelt's "Zionism" stemmed mainly from the election campaign of 1944, when both political parties in the United States came out in favor of unrestricted Jewish immigration to Palestine, and a free democratic Jewish commonwealth there. This was also the gist of the Democratic platform's Palestine Plank, and the President made it known that he backed it, promising "if elected I shall help its realization." [2] Roosevelt was careful not to openly favor a Jewish Palestine because the American activities in the Middle East during the war advanced the idea of military bases there as well as the exploration and exploitation of oil in the area. It was this "Zionism" that made him rush off to meet King Ibn Saud aboard a United States navy vessel in Great Bitter Lake at the Suez Canal, after which he declared that he had learned from Ibn Saud a great deal which he did not know about the problem and promised that no decision would be made without consulting both the Arabs and the Jews. He confirmed his promise in a letter written a week before his death.

Stalin's declaration that he was a "Zionist," however, was an entirely different thing. The admission, even though qualified, by the Russian Communist leader seems to have had something to do with his postwar plans, since, up to that time, Zionism had been taboo for the Communists.

COMMUNISTS OPPOSE ZIONISM

When the Bolsheviks became the rulers of Russia in 1917, they brought with them two negative attitudes toward Zionism: one was their inherent opposition to what they called the ideology of a nationalistic bourgeois movement, and the other involved Russia's political position vis-à-vis the Middle East.

---

[2] Robert Feis, *The Birth of Israel* (New York, 1969), p. 16; *The New York Times*, October 12 and 16, 1944. Feis maintains that Roosevelt apparently cherished the illusion... that he... as head of the U.S., could bring about a settlement between Arabs and Jews.

Despite their class-struggle ideology, theoretically at least, Social-ists and Communists had generally adopted the humanistic dream of liberalism and equality. However, they relegated the realization of that dream to a future post-capitalistic society. Only in such a society would the real emancipation of the Jews become a fact and the Jewish problem would inevitably disappear (together with the Jews). Thus, discrimination against Jews, and even pogroms, seemed to be temporary phenomena not necessitating such radical measures as the removal of Jews to a land of their own (emigration). In addition, as internationalists, at least officially, the Bolsheviks were opposed to Zionism's implied nationalism. It appeared much simpler to "solve the Jewish problem" in the abstract, as it were, by denying that Jews constitute a nationality. While there were some social democrats on the European Continent and Laborites in England who in later years did accept Zionism, the Bolshevik group of the Russian Social Democratic organization which was formed in 1903, later to become the Communist party, was anti-Zionist from the outset.

Lenin stated in 1903: "... the Zionist idea of a Jewish nation is absolutely false and reactionary. ... It is absolutely untenable scien-tifically and is reactionary politically." Quoting Carl Kautsky and an assimilated Jew from France, Alfred Naquet (1834–1916), Lenin reiterated that Jews, lacking a territory of their own, ceased to be a nation. Zionism, he held, was reactionary, since it resisted assimilation while in Europe emancipation was followed by assimi-lation.[3] Zionism was also thought to conflict with the interests of the Jewish proletariat. Ten years later (1913) Lenin denounced the Jewish national culture as "the slogan of rabbis and the bourgeoi-

[3] Lenin, *Sochineniya* (fifth ed.), VII, 100; VIII, 27, 72–76, 100; XXIV, 122–124. It should be mentioned that in the same year (June 24, 1903) the Tsarist minister of Internal Affairs, V. Pleve, released a secret circular forbidding Zionist activities in Russia. His reasons were similar to the ones used by Lenin except that instead of unity of the proletariat, Pleve was concerned with unity of the Russian state. He argued that Zionist organizations hamper assimilation and aid segregation which is against the principles of the Russian state. The circular was later reprinted in *Evreyskaya Starina*, VIII (1915), 212–214.

sie — our foes." He contrasted these Jews with Jewish Marxists who assimilated and joined in creating a culture of the labor movement, thereby carrying on the best of Judaism's tradition by fighting the idea of a "national culture."

In the same year Stalin, in *Marxism and the National Question* (1913), similarly denied that the Jews constitute a nation, on the grounds that they lack the necessary basic traits. "All they still have in common is their religion, their common origins, and a few remaining characteristics... [while] their social-economic surroundings... inevitably lead to assimilation." [4] Lenin's opposition to Zionism in 1903 and in subsequent years, his branding it as bourgeois, was not formulated solely for its own sake but was used (or misused) to discredit the Jewish labor party "Bund" — *a strong anti-Zionist group* — with whom Lenin and the Bolsheviks were at that time engaged in a running battle about the make-up of the Russian Socialist party.

In addition, the Communists' anti-Zionist attitude was related to the old Russian pressure for an outlet to the warm waters of the Mediterranean and beyond, that were "guarded" by the Turkish Dardanelles and by Great Britain in the Suez Canal and Gibraltar. The last thing Tsarist Russia did in this connection prior to the Bolshevik Revolution was to sign, after protracted negotiations, the April 1916 secret treaties with the Allies confirming Russia's claims to Constantinople, the Bosporus Straits, and the Dardanelles.

Immediately following the 1917 revolution the Bolsheviks opposed imperialism in general, or pretended to, and disavowed the Tsar's plans to acquire Constantinople. By printing some of the secret documents about this matter, found in the Tsarist archives (December 7, 1917),[5] the Bolsheviks sought to discredit the Tsarist

---

[4] Stalin, *Sochineniya*, II, 299–300, 335. According to him Jews lacked a stable community of language, territory, economic life, or psychological makeup (*ibid.*, p. 296).

[5] The Communist historian, M. Pokrovski, published some additional materials in his writings (1918, 1920). A comprehensive collection of the documents was subsequently published in *Konstantinopol i Prolivy* [Constantinople and the Straits], vols. 1–2 (Moscow, 1925–26).

regime and its Western allies. But the Communists' expansionist policies soon came to the fore in a variety of forms: the support of Mustafa Kemal Pasha of Turkey in his struggle against the Allied occupation; the signing of a Russian-Turkish Friendship Treaty [March 16, 1921]; the attempt to sponsor a separatist regime in Iran and the march on Teheran; the organization of a Congress of the Peoples of the East in Baku [1920] which claimed to represent Asian and African countries from Manchuria to Morocco; and the passing of a resolution there to wage a holy war against British imperialism.

However, all this notwithstanding, by the beginning of the 1920s the Soviets had achieved very little. British rule had been reestablished in Egypt; Mandates by Great Britain and France were being set up in the Fertile Crescent, while in Turkey and Iran nationalist regimes were being consolidated. For the young Soviet state it meant again that Great Britain ("British Imperialism") held the key to the Mediterranean.[6] In the eyes of the Soviets this put the onus of British imperialism on Zionism. Great Britain had issued the Balfour Declaration, had occupied Palestine, and in 1920, had been granted a Mandate by the League of Nations with the goal of building a Jewish (Zionist) homeland there. Not long after this, apparently to counteract the (British) imperialism, a Communist party that was later progressively arabized, was sponsored in Palestine.

IN SOVIET RUSSIA

The Soviet position on Zionism, as on a number of other questions, such as their attitude toward Jews and anti-Semitism[7] and toward

---

[6] Dankwart A. Rustow, *The Appeal of Communism to Islamic Peoples.* Reprint 90 (The Brookings Institute, 1965); Richard H. Ullman, *The Anglo-Soviet Accord* (Princeton, 1973).

[7] During the years 1918–1922 and again in the second half of the 1920s the Soviet state undertook an active attack on anti-Semitism by means of oral propaganda, and the publication of pamphlets and books (about 100 items appeared). The central themes in these writings were the assertions that anti-Semites are class foes whereas Jews are good proletarians and anti-capitalistic. During the same years about 50 publications also appeared against the Jewish religion. The main emphasis in these is on the capital-

the nationality problem, was at first ambiguous and sometimes
contradictory, though the negative approach predominated. Domestically the government at first wavered between leaving the Zionists
alone and harassing them by the Cheka's searches and arrests and
by closing of Zionist institutions in different localities or regions
(in the Ukraine 1919); between arresting some individuals, who
were brought to trial, and "negotiating," in 1925, for some form of
legal organization; between permitting some emigration to Palestine
and increasing persecution of Zionists in Russia. One exception —
up to 1928 — was the left-wing of the Poale Zion party which
seceded from the Russian Jewish Poale Zion (Workers of Zion)
party and formed a "Communist Poale Zion," and also, to some
extent, the Ḥalutz (pioneer) group which cultivated the land. At the
same time the Soviets sought to "Bolshevize" the Jews in Russia
by creating the Jewish Commissariat (*Yevkom–Yevreyski Komis-
sariat*), founded in 1918 in Petrograd (later Leningrad) as a subdivi-
sion of the Peoples' Commissariat for National Affairs under Stalin,
and the Jewish Sections of the Communist Party (*Yevsektzia*). On
the other hand they dissolved the Jewish communal institutions and
harassed religious institutions.

Whether the Jewish Communists voluntarily undertook this task
because of their own anti-Zionism, or whether it was officially or
semi-officially assigned to them by the State and/or party leadership, they were often far more extreme than the government itself.[8]

istic origin and function of religion and its functionaries. See B. D. Weinryb, "The Concept of 'Anti-Semitism' and its Meaning in Soviet Russia,"
Gratz College Annual of Jewish Studies, I (1972), 86–88; the publications
are listed in *Russian Publications on Jews and Judaism in the Soviet Union
1917–1967: a Bibliography* compiled by B. Pinkus and A. A. Greenbaum,
eds. (Jerusalem, 1970), pp. 51–66 and *passim*.

[8] In Jewish historiography the idea prevailed that these Jewish organizations, staffed as they were with former members of Socialist and anti-
Zionist parties that had been liquidated and integrated into the CPSU, had
been independently initiating anti-Zionist actions. (The concept of a Member of the Jewish Section of the Communist Party *Yevsek*, became to Jews
abroad a derogatory expression for an extreme assimilationist and a de-
stroyer of Jewish group life.) Considering the conspirational tactics of the

They began their attack on Zionism by reviving the pre-revolution-ary characterization of it as reactionary, petty bourgeois or anti-revolutionary. Occasionally a new theme was added, such as that Zionism was serving British foreign policy objectives by dividing the land between Jews and Arabs. This theme was especially elabo-rated upon by Commissar Dimantshtein, head of the Jewish Com-missariat, in his speeches and articles. More rhetorical was another theme, namely, that the Zionists sacrificed the Jewish masses on the altar of counter-revolution. (Themes of this sort, albeit with varia-tions, continued to be used for many years.)

On the basis of these accusations, the Jewish Sections and Com-missariats demanded, at the conferences in June 1919 and July 1920, the liquidation of the Zionist organization. The same accusa-tions, plus additional verbiage, were made in the indictment of the delegates of the *Tseire Zion* (Young Zionists) faction arrested by the Cheka in Kiev at their conference on May 4, 1922. Only in this case the imperialists with whom the Zionists allegedly cooperated were identified as "Poincare, Lloyd George, and the Pope." The *Yevkom* was dissolved in 1924 together with the Peoples Commis-sariat for National Affairs, and the Jewish Sections of CPSU were in the forefront of the attack upon Zionism and often took the initiative in trying to induce the State and party authorities to in-crease the pressure, though the latter did not always comply.[9] One

Communist party retrospectively, however, it may appear possible that the initiative came, in fact, from the CPSU leadership which for numerous reasons, among them the possibility of concealing the objectives or to whitewash themselves, or for foreign consumption, wanted rather to be, as it were, "pushed" into anti-Zionist action. See Guido G. Goldman, *Zionism under Soviet Rule 1917–1928* (New York, 1960); Zvi Y. Gitelman, *Jewish Nationality and Soviet Politics. The Jewish Sections of the CPSU 1917–1930* (Princeton, 1972).

[9] The Soviets, at least for a number of years, were somewhat sensitive about the opinion of Zionists in the West concerning their policy toward Zionism. Hence the attempt to make believe that Zionism was not being persecuted in the USSR or the suggestions — in the 1920s — that visas be granted Russian Zionists to participate in the Zionist Congress held abroad, on condition that once there they would deny any oppression in the USSR. It seems justifiable to suppose that both the Western Allies —

such case which deserves to be mentioned here is the so-called Jabotinsky-Slavinsky agreement of 1921.[10] It gave the Jewish Communists a grand opportunity to accuse the Zionists of counter-revolution. On September 4, 1921, Vladimir Jabotinsky, later founder and leader of the revisionist "right wing" Zionist faction, signed in Karlsbad an agreement with Maxim Slavinsky who was representing Simon Petlyura, to organize a Jewish gendarmerie designed to operate in the rear of the Ukrainian army, to assure the safety of Jews in towns that might be occupied by the Ukrainians. This was a precaution in case Petlyura's army, then in exile in Polish Galicia, might reinvade the Soviet-held Ukraine in the spring of 1922.

Nothing, in fact, came of this invasion nor of the plan for a Jewish gendarmerie. But the Slavinsky-Jabotinsky agreement loosed a flood of indignation in leftist and Communist circles (to some extent also among Russian-Ukrainian Zionist emigrés in Europe). The next year and a half witnessed newspaper attacks, demands for Jabotinsky's resignation from the Zionist Executive, and the appointment of a committee to investigate the affair. Jabotinsky resigned from the Zionist Executive in January 1923, but claimed that his resignation was not connected with the Slavinsky agreement.

By far more extreme was the reaction to this affair by the Jewish Communists in Soviet Russia. The Yiddish daily, *Emes*, ran head-

Great Britain and France during World War I — and Soviet Russia in the 1920s overestimated the Jewish influence. This led to the Allies' attempt to draw Jewry — mainly American — to their side, thereby contributing to the issuance of the Balfour Declaration in 1917, and the abovementioned Soviet efforts to appear to favor the Zionists in the 1920s.

[10] During 1917–20, the period of the Ukraine's struggle for independence, Simon Petlyura (1879–1926), a Ukrainian leader, in February 1919, became the head of the newly-established provisional government of an independent Ukraine and chief commander of its forces. In the course of fighting the Bolshevik forces and retreating before Communist pressure, his units became bands making pogroms on Jews in many places. Petlyura was accused of having done nothing to stop these pogroms. (He was assassinated on May 26, 1926 by a Jew named Shalom Shwarzbard in Paris where Petlyura lived as a refugee after 1924. The Paris court acquitted Shwarzbard in 1927, on the grounds that he had sought revenge for the Jewish pogroms.)

lines reading: "The Zionists are plunging a knife into the Revolution's back," or "Jabotinsky had aligned himself with Petlyura to wage war against the Red Army." And the organ of the Commissariat for National Minorities, *Zhizn Natzionalnostey*, printed an appeal to the government "to liquidate the Zionist counter-revolutionary hydra" and to close down its sport organization Maccabee on which Jabotinsky allegedly counted heavily "in his project to collaborate with Petlyura."

Itzhak Rabinovitch,[11] a leading Russian Zionist and the head of the Maccabee, was summoned before the Cheka to give evidence. The case was later transferred to a special Committee of the War Ministry's "Division for Sport and Military Preparedness for Youth" to which Maccabee was directly subordinated. After long deliberation, the Committee exonerated the Maccabee and concluded that the Jabotinsky-Slavinsky agreement was apparently not motivated by counter-revolutionary intentions on the part of the Jews but by a desire to protect the lives of Jews. The Committee's resolution was later accepted at a meeting with the Soviet authorities, among whom were Peter Smidovich, vice-chairman of the Council of the Soviet Republic, and Felix Dzherzhinsky, head of the GPU. Subsequently other Soviet authorities also adopted this approach.

After the occupation of eastern Poland by the Soviets beginning in September 17, 1939, in the course of the new partition of Poland between the Nazis and the Soviets, the Kharkov Yiddish-communist periodical *Shtern* again raised the specter of "The Counter-Revolutionary Face of Zionism," accusing Jabotinsky of having organized Zionist detachments in support of the "bandit Tiutiunik" to fight the Red Army. (Jabotinsky was charged with *actually organizing*, not promising or wanting to organize, detachments.)*

---

[11] Itzhak Rabinovitch, "Heskem Jabotinsky-Slavinsky bifnei ha-Bolshevikim" [The Jabotinsky-Slavinsky Agreement Before the Bolsheviks] in *Haolam* (Hebrew), August 5, 1943; Joseph B. Schechtman, "The Jabotinsky-Slavinsky Agreement," *Jewish Social Studies*, XVII (1955), 289–306.

* By that time neither the *Yevkom* nor the Jewish Sections (*Yevsektsya*) of the CPU were any longer in existence, the latter having been dissolved

Again, with the Nazi invasion of Poland and Soviet Russia's participation in the partition of that country in September 1939, Zionists and Zionist youth reappeared in the USSR. They had been living in the Russian occupied parts or had arrived there as refugees. Many of these Zionists were either suppressed and forced underground or were deported to the northern and eastern parts of Soviet Russia.

In the Lithuanian SSR Zionism was simply classified as "Jewish nationalist counter-revolution." In the spring of 1941, while deportations from Soviet Lithuania (Lithuanian SSR) were in progress, the commissar for State-Security ordered the preparation of systematic reports using prescribed forms (in Russian) on deportees who were to be classified according to nationality and crime. The part dealing with Jews was called "Jewish nationalist counter-revolution" and heading the column was "Zionism." [12]

While all this was taking place inside Soviet Russia, the PKP, the Communist party in Palestine, founded in 1923, directed its energies toward the struggle against the "Anglo-Zionist conquest." At Moscow's insistence, and certainly not without Moscow's approval, the party lent its support to the Arab riots and killing of Jews in 1929, 1933 and 1936, hailing these outrages as the "heroic war of the Arab people." The PKP — probably again with the knowledge and consent of Moscow — met with the Mufti of Jerusalem, Haj Amin el-Huseini, and endorsed Communist cooperation with the Arab National Movement.

WORLD WAR II

The Nazi attack on Soviet Russia (June 1941) caused the Soviet

---

in 1930 with the rationalization that it had become too nationalistic, and some of the leaders had actually been jailed or liquidated. The Jabotinsky-Slavinsky "affair" has been dealt with at length here because it was revived in recent times and plays quite an important part in the general anti-Jewish, anti-Zionist and anti-Ukrainian writings.

[12] The form is reprinted in Josef Gar, *Azoy is es Geveyn in Lite* [So it was in Lithuania] (Tel Aviv, 1965).

regime to change many of its policies and tactics both externally and internally. Soviet agitation against British imperialism ceased. Stalin may also have soon had his doubts about the reliability of the Arab liberation movement. The movement's main champion, the Mufti Haj Amin el-Huseini, took refuge in Berlin in November 1941 and cooperated with the Nazis against the Allies by organizing Arab broadcasts and recruiting Nazi agents in the Arab countries. In some of the Middle Eastern countries clandestine, and not so clandestine, anti-Allied trends became apparent with attempts to cooperate with the Germans (e.g. revolt in Iraq, French Vichy government in Beirut, Egyptian officers' attempts to make contact with Rommel in the desert, and even demonstrations in the streets and chants of the slogan "advance Rommel"). By implication, such a pro-Nazi slant in 1941–42 meant opposition to Soviet Russia and could hardly have been regarded favorably by Stalin.

Internally the Soviet regime undertook total mobilization of resources for the struggle against the invaders. Policies were relaxed a little and certain taboos lifted in an effort to gain the collaboration of various groups through "appeasement." Thus a reconciliation with the Greek Orthodox Church was effected in Russia in 1942–43; the government promulgated this new policy in the hope of gaining the support of pro-Church people who harbored religious sentiments. Similarly, religious and nationalist feelings were encouraged among ethnic and other groups with the aim of promoting unity and bolstering resistance to the enemy.

Committees such as the all-Slav Committee, Soviet Women, and Soviet Youth, were concerned with specific groups. The Jews, too, were induced, in April 1942, to form a "Jewish Anti-Fascist Committee" whose function was to appeal to world Jewry and to seek to influence Jewish opinion toward shaping public opinion at home and in the West in favor of Soviet Russia. Before long the JAC began to publish a Jewish periodical, *Einikeit* (Unity), of which the first issue appeared in June 7, 1942 (initially there were three issues a month; later, three a week). First Director of the JAC was Solomon Lozowski, deputy of the Soviet Information

Bureau, while Solomon Mikhoels, the known Jewish actor, became its chairman, and the leading membership was made up of such Soviet Jewish worthies as the writer Ilya Ehrenburg and General Jacob Kreiser.

The JAC made its appeals to Jews the world over by radio, through publications, and through a delegation consisting of the abovementioned Mikhoels and the Yiddish writer Itzik Feffer, who embarked on a mission to the Jewish communities in the United States, Mexico, Canada and Great Britain. During their stay abroad, which lasted about seven months, the delegates continually emphasized the closeness felt by Russian Jews to "their brethren" elsewhere, the distress over the Jewish losses in Nazi-occupied Europe that they shared with them, the religious and cultural heritage common to all Jews, and the hope, sometimes expressed with exaggeration, for a mutually better future. These tendencies, coming out of Moscow and promulgated by radical Jewish groups in many a country, created among Jews an atmosphere of goodwill toward the Soviets and added to the appreciation of their fight against the Nazis — the foes of the Jews. Concurrently this atmosphere helped to foster the Jews' ethnic consciousness within Soviet Russia.

The same trends underlay the Soviets' seemingly changed attitude toward Zionism, mostly their political attitudes outside the USSR, and especially their responses to the efforts made by Zionists and other Jews to offer support for the USSR's struggle against the Nazis.

The Palestinian Jewish leadership and the Zionists sought "direct contact" with the Soviets in order to promise them political and/or material support, to express appreciation of their conduct in the war, or to explain the Zionist goals and achievements in settling Palestine. Less than a month after the Nazis attacked Soviet Russia, American Zionist leaders met with the Soviet ambassador, Umansky, in Washington (July 17, 1941).

Many contacts developed with the Soviet Embassy in London (Ivan Maisky was ambassador until 1943), some began even before the Nazi-Soviet war, in connection with Lithuanian and Polish

Jewish refugees who found themselves on Soviet territory.[13] During the war a number of Zionist leaders, including Dr. Chaim Weizmann and David Ben-Gurion, who represented the Jewish Agency or Histadrut, came in contact with the Soviet representatives, explaining to them the facts and goals of the Zionist work in Palestine and at times pleading for Zionist refugees from Poland stranded on Soviet territory to be allowed to proceed to Palestine. Memoranda were submitted to Maisky by Weizmann and Ben-Gurion.

Some contacts were of more concrete character. Thus, in August 1942 a check for £10,000 was presented to the Embassy in London for the Soviet Red Cross. More such "concrete connections" were made by the Palestinian Yishuv. Concurrently, radical Jewish groups in Palestine, pro-Communists and leftist Zionists, established a "Committee for the Support of the USSR in its War Against Fascism." Later (May 1942) the Committee was absorbed into a broader organization, League "V" (for victory), founded for the purpose of collecting funds and materiél for Russian war relief. This League sent money, medical and other supplies, such as ambulances, medical equipment and medicines, which were handed over to the Soviet authorities in Teheran, occupied by the Allies for the purpose of delivering American war materiél to the Soviets. The Palestine Potash Company, for example, donated bromide and other Dead Sea minerals to Russia. Other interchanges that developed were an exhibition in Tel Aviv with the title "The USSR and Palestine in Wartime" (July 1943), and an exhibition showing the progress of Jewish colonization in Palestine that was admitted to Russia in January 1944. Other indicators along the lines of Jewish-Soviet cooperation was the voting of Russia's delegates to the World Trade Union Conference in Lon-

---

[13] The Chief Rabbi of Palestine, Herzog, appealed to Maisky for release of religious-school students in Vilna. Maisky reacted by obtaining permission from Moscow to release them. There were a number of similar cases [Jacob Hen-Tov, "Contacts between Soviet Ambassador Maisky and Zionist Leaders During World War II," *Soviet Jewish Affairs*, 8 (1948), 46–55].

don for a resolution in favor of a Jewish Palestine, and an article by the secretary of the JAC in Moscow published in the Palestinian *Mishmar* in favor of a Jewish homeland in Palestine.

In most of these and similar contacts with the Russians, the representatives of the Palestine Jewish community and the Zionists emphasized both the joint struggle against the Nazis and the hope of Russia's support for the Zionist enterprise in Palestine. They did so at the first national convention of the V-League in Jerusalem in August 1942 to which the Soviet legation in Ankara, Turkey, sent two Soviet representatives, as well as on other occasions. The Russians listened to both ideas, but talked mainly about the mutual anti-Nazi and anti-Fascist war effort, though here and there they lauded the achievements in Palestine or voiced approval of a Kibbutz. In other conversations, too, between Zionists or Palestinian Jewish representatives and high Soviet officials, the Russians remained, one might say, for the most part "neutral" about Zionist hopes or any future Soviet position on Jewish Palestine.

Diametrically opposing attitudes could be observed among the Russians. The two representatives from the Embassy in Ankara who visited Palestine in 1942, particularly the secretary of the embassy, Sergey Mikhailov, *intentionally* avoided having anything to do with the Zionist Jewish Agency in Jerusalem. He concentrated on the local Jewish Council (Vaad Leumi). He also visited and participated in Arab gatherings, emphasizing to the Jews the need to cooperate with the Arabs and to employ them. Mikhailov assured the High Commissioner of Palestine, H. A. MacMichael, that the USSR would "never, never" let the Polish Jewish refugees in Soviet Russia leave for Palestine "to stir up additional trouble by exciting the animosity of the Arabs." [14] On the other hand, Ivan Maisky who visited Palestine in October 1943 upon completion of his tenure as USSR ambassador in London, had many conversations with the Jewish leaders in Palestine, after touring Kibbutzim and other places. The comprehensive report of

[14] *Soviet Jewish Affairs*, 4 (1974), 80–89.

his visit to the Kremlin, was regarded by two objective individuals as having been favorable. It is said that the Zionists even contemplated having Churchill arrange for Stalin to receive Chaim Weizmann, president of the Zionist Organization, at the time of the Yalta meeting in February 1945. Churchill, however, did not consider this feasible.

At that time, early in 1945, Soviet Russia had already established itself in southern Europe and somewhat in the Middle East and had plans for further expansion. During 1943–44, legations were opened in Egypt, Syria, Lebanon, and Iraq and were, to some extent, manned by specialists in Oriental languages and/or by Muslims. They attempted to emphasize that the USSR, too, is a Muslim country while, on the other hand, the Russians sought restoration of Soviet citizenship to about 10,000 Russians who had been anti-Soviet refugees in the Middle East, to reestablish relations between Russian and Greek Orthodox Church groups in the Middle East, and to bring the pre-World War I Greek Orthodox religious properties in Jerusalem, as well as the monks, under the authority of the Metropolitan in Moscow.[15] At the meeting with Churchill in Moscow (October 9, 1944) Stalin made his first demand for revision of the Montreux Convention on the Straits because, he claimed, "if Britain were interested in the Mediterranean, then Russia was equally interested in the Black Sea."[16] In retrospect one would surely not be wrong in assuming that by then (or a few months later at Yalta, in February 1945) Stalin was already thinking about taking further steps to assure his position in the region. His pressing to gain control of the Straits, forcing his way into Iran, and obtaining a base in Libya, which came to the fore a little later, were already then in the planning stages. Britain, greatly weakened during the war, was, to be sure, the main barrier to such expansion on the part of the USSR (British

[15] Bernard D. Weinryb, "Palestine in the Changing Middle East," *Contemporary Jewish Record*, 8 (1945), 119–121.

[16] Albert Reiss, "The Churchill-Stalin Secret 'Percentages' Agreement on the Balkans, Moscow, October 1944," *American Historical Review*, 83 (1978), 373.

Secretary Bevin visualized "Russia coming right across the throat of the British Commonwealth"), while in America tensions developed between advocates of the preservation of Great Britain's monopolistic stand, and the economic and oil interests who wanted to take over a share.[17]

Stalin's admission at the dinner in Yalta on February 10, 1945 that he, too, was a Zionist may have been simply intended to placate "the naïveté and vanity" of President Roosevelt, as Stalin had done successfully on other occasions. At this juncture Stalin may have felt an increasing need for such tactics in view of Roosevelt's remark a few months earlier that the United States "no longer pursued a passive policy toward Southeastern Europe." At that time (October, 1944) Stalin told Churchill in Moscow that he did not like Roosevelt's message, for "it seemed to demand too many rights for the U.S. leaving too little for the Soviet Union and Great Britain."[18] Therefore he may have thought it wise to agree verbally to something that hardly seemed important. Or Stalin may have mistaken Roosevelt's Zionism as an intention to dismantle Great Britain's world-wide status and expel her from the Middle East, and he was expressing his wish to participate in this process of dissolution of the British Empire.

As a speculation one could also assume that the abovementioned report from Mikhailov to his superiors about his visit to Palestine in August 1942 contained the information that many Jews applauded his Russian speeches showing, in the words of the abovementioned Itzhak Ben-Zvi, that "thousands and tens of thousands of Jews in Palestine know Russian." While this gave Ben-Zvi a reason to fear the possibility of "wide Soviet activity...

[17] *The Times*, November 30, 1944; John Mac Cormac, "Partners or Rivals," *Asia and the Americas*, April 1944; B. D. Weinryb, "Britain's War Debts in the Middle East," *Asia and the Americas*, February 1945; and my "The Arab League Tool or Power," *Commentary*, March 1946, 50–57; Harry N. Howard, *Turkey, the Straits and U.S. Policy* (Baltimore, 1975).

[18] Albert Reiss, *op. cit.*, pp. 385–386.

[and] treason, subversion and betrayal," [19] it may have come through the Soviet bureaucratic mill in a highly exaggerated form [20] spelling out for Stalin the possibility of using the Jewish settlement as a nucleus for anti-English rule in the Middle East, and for penetrating the Jewish community through "subversion and betrayal." Another hypothesis, albeit an unlikely one, might be that Ivan Maisky (a Jew), then vice-commissar for Foreign Affairs (1943–46) who served as an adviser to Stalin at the Yalta Conference,[21] suggested that Stalin become a "Zionist" (or that the positive report by Maisky brought "Zionism" to Stalin).

Mikhailov's efforts to avoid (or perhaps his fear of) dealing with a Zionist organization in Jerusalem may indicate that in 1942 Zionism was still taboo in official Soviet circles. At the same time it becomes clear from the story told by Stalin's daughter, Svetlana Alliluyeva, that during the war years her father became more anti-Semitic and more suspicious of Jews than he had been before. This extended even to the Jews in his own family. Thus, when his son Yakov was taken prisoner by the Nazis, Stalin suspected betrayal by his Jewish daughter-in-law (she was actually arrested and spent a few years in jail). Stalin disliked Svetlana's Jewish husband because "he was Jewish," refusing resolutely to see him and accusing him of the standard anti-Semitic stereotype of shirking military service (a few years later, after Svetlana had divorced her husband, Stalin told her that the Zionists had surely induced

---

[19] *Soviet Jewish Affairs*, 4, p. 85. (These materials were published by Dr. L. Hirszowicz).

[20] The following may serve as a sample of exaggeration in another matter: David Ben-Gurion asserted many years later that he had been told by "a French friend" that Stalin said at one meeting with Roosevelt and Churchill: "it was essential to establish a Jewish State because the Jewish people deserve an independent state" *Maariv*, March 4, 1971.

[21] According to the American records he participated in all meetings of the Big Three, in a few luncheons or dinners, in a meeting of the foreign ministers. His name is always placed after Molotov and Vishinsky and before Gromyko. There is no information about his rank in the secret Russian meetings or about his participation in them.

the man to marry her for some ulterior motive). Such profound Jew-hatred can hardly be equated with Zionism.[22]

Whatever the truth of the matter, it is not unlikely that Stalin's "Zionism" in Yalta served as the first link in the tangled and twisted chain of Soviet policy that led a few short years later to Andre Gromyko's speech at the United Nations on May 14, 1947, in favor of a Jewish state "to ensure the defense of the elementary rights of the Jewish people." This marked the beginning of Russia's aligning herself with the United States in the United Nations and led to the resolution on the partition of Palestine and the establishment of a Jewish state.[23]

[22] Svetlana Alliluyeva, *Twenty Letters to a Friend* (New York and Evanston, 1967), *passim*; Robert C. Tucker "Svetlana Alliluyeva as Witness of Stalin," *Slavic Review*, 23 (1968), 298–312; Bernard D. Weinryb, "Antisemitism in Soviet Russia," *The Jews in Soviet Russia Since 1917*, ed. L. Kochan (London and New York, 1970), 308–310.

[23] Domestically this was the time when restrictions were introduced on admission of Jews to the higher educational institutes and Jews were excluded from military academies and higher party and state positions. *Foreign Relations of the U.S. (1947)*, vol. 4: *Eastern Europe: The Soviet Union* (Washington, 1972), pp. 584, 629; בן חורין, מה קורה שם ?, translated from Russian (Tel Aviv, 1970), p. 36. But contradictions between domestic and foreign policies are not infrequent in Soviet Russia; such contradictions became more pronounced in the following years.

I wish to express appreciation to the Russian Research Center of Harvard University for their support in the collection of materials, some of which were used here.

GENEALOGIES OF TWO WANDERING
HEBREW MELODIES

By Eric Werner

Dedicated to my dear friend
J. Schirman, Jerusalem

I

It is well known that tunes of songs, no less than their texts, often
provide an historical mirror of an exceedingly sharp focus.
A special category of such songs are the so-called "migrating" or
"wandering" tunes. What wanders is, of course, usually the tune,
or a motif of it, not the text itself. Ever since J. G. Herder alluded
to such migrations, the students of folksongs, especially the German
romanticists, have singled out common motifs of content or form,
rarely of melodic resemblances. Thus, the brothers Grimm were
already aware of the wandering *literary* motifs of the Hebrew
Ḥad Gadya, and a little later the first courageous monograph on
wandering songs and melodies appeared: Wilhelm Tappert,
"Wandernde Melodien," in his *Musikalische Studien* (Berlin, 1868).
He was so bold as to attack, indeed, to refute the favorite romantic
dogma that all folksong is the result of an anonymous, quint-
essential and collective creation of the national spirit. It may be
noted in passing that the entire Haskalah uncritically accepted
this postulate and occasionally even embraced ideas of "racial
characteristics" in a tune or a text (e.g. P. Minkowski, S. Rosowsky,
et al.).

While wandering tunes frequently reveal the cultural (or sub-
cultural) interrelationship between two or more countries, it is
often difficult to decide in a given case, who was the lender and
who the borrower, since both versions of the tune continue to
co-exist, and the go-between-group, if there ever was one, can but
rarely be established.

Judaism, a wandering nation and a "minority-civilization," has ipso facto left many traces in the folklore of the nations with which it came into long-lasting contact. On the other hand, Jewish folksong has absorbed many, today forgotten, tunes and songs of olden times, from the various host-cultures, be it in raw or in stylized versions. The tunes were invariably stylized, if they were incorporated in the liturgical chant: they had to be "actively assimilated" into the existing style of the Jewish musical tradition.

A classical example of such a wandering tune was provided by A. Z. Idelsohn in his examination of the *Hatikvah*-tune.[1] Following his teachers, the German romanticists, he juxtaposed the *Hatikvah*-tune with a great number of other, parallel melodies of most diverse origins, without endeavoring to establish their age, provenance, primary source or appearance, or their (hypothetical) connection with the *Hatikvah*. Aside from this regrettable omission, his study bears the stamp of a true pioneering effort. The wandering tune, common to the Spanish, Polish, Czech, Hungarian, German, Armenian, Basque and Portuguese folksong, has an ancient history that seems to reach back to the fifteenth century and perhaps to even earlier times.

Two celebrated tunes of the Ashkenazic liturgical chant will be studied in this article. However, they will be examined in a different way from the method used by Idelsohn: that is, not simply presenting parallels, whose history is usually obscure, but by investigating their genealogies. As in a family's genealogy, one may differentiate between a main stem and its branches, so in a musical genealogy, there is the main variant that has changed but little in the course of time, and its many branches, that often deviate noticeably from the main stem.

The two tunes under consideration are both "archetypes," in the sense that they should be considered as models of many similar and cognate tunes. The archetype is viewed or thought to be the simplest, (not necessarily the oldest) version of the related variants. They are:

---

[1] A. Z. Idelsohn, *Jewish Music in its Historical Development* (New York, 1929), Table XXVIII, pp. 222 ff.

(1) The tune of *Eli Tziyon*, a melody that in the Ashkenazic tradition is chanted during the so-called "Three Weeks" (between the 17th of Tammuz and the 9th of Ab, the anniversary of the Temple's destruction). It is sung to various liturgical texts, such as "לכה דודי", "קדיש", "תרחם ציון כאשר אמרת", "מי כמוך", "אדון עולם" and others.

(2) The family of tunes, rhythms, or melodic motifs engendered by, or closely related to, the prototype of Ashkenazic "לדוד ברוך" [Ps. 144] and its main variants.

*　*　*

Neither the poet of *Eli Tziyon* is known, nor has the exact age of the poem been established. There are, however, some signs that might hint at the time of its origin. It is certainly a post-biblical *qinah*, whose structure includes the following pattern in the scheme of the rhymes:

1st quatrain	2nd	3rd	4th	5th	6th	
a	c	d	a	a	a	
a	a	a	a	a	a	etc.
b	d	e	f	g	h	
a	a	a	a	a	a	

The metric scheme is arranged in 4-line stanzas; in fact, the entire poem is based upon one suffix rhyme on the penultimate *-eyha*. In each stanza — usually in the last word of the third line — a new word appears that does not rhyme with *-eyha*. Each line contains 3 or 4 words and approximates the old metrical idea of isosyllabism. The meter is not always consistent, inasmuch as the third line (through the new non-rhyming word) sometimes has the accent on the last syllable. The entire poem is an extension of the literary motif וּכְבְתוּלָה חֲגוּרַת שַׂק עֲלֵי [sic] בַּעַל נְעוּרֶיהָ (Joel 1:8).

Although the *piyyut* and its tune follow the rule laid down by Abraham Ibn Ezra: והחרוזים שיש להם טעם נגינות ראים להיות משקל כל חרוז וחרוז שמה... (צחות 7b), it does not necessarily indicate that it is more recent than the rule, for the (foreign) melody was applied to the original text;[2] but according to the musical rhythm it is always the *last* syllable that is stressed; this contradicts the grammatical rules and suggests that the person who set or arranged (not yet in any written form) the Spanish tune to the Hebrew text, did not care about correct stress of the syllables. The germinating cell of the tune is clearly established in the following motif:

Music Ex. 1

Cod. Calixtinus, Santiago di Compostela

Jo - cun - de - - tur ___ et lae - te - tur.

This is found in the ancient *Codex Calixtinus* in Santiago di Compostela, in the liturgy of the patron saint of Spain, St. James (Jacobus maior).[3] This Codex must interest us also for other reasons: it contains a hymn consisting of Latin, Hebrew, and Greek words; its function seems to have been to sound familiar to the myriads of pilgrims from many European and perhaps African countries. Moreover, the monastery was a center of the mission to the Jews, especially during the thirteenth and fourteenth centuries, and was engaged in proselytizing Jews. A few lines of the hymn may demonstrate its character:[4]

Prosa sancti Jacobi

1 (a). Letabunda et cemeha (שִׂמְחָה) gaudeat Yspania.

2. In gloriosi Jacobi almi profulgenti nizaha (נצחון).

2a. Qui hole (עוֹלֶה) celos haiom (הַיּוֹם) in celesti nichtar (נִכְתַּר) gloria.

---

    [2] The Hebrew text might be paraphrased, following Zunz' interpretation, in this way: "in a poem, the verses of which are set to music, the meter of the verses must remain equal, verse by verse." Cf. Zunz, *Synagogale Poesie*, p. 116, n(h).

    [3] P. Wagner, *Die Gesaenge der Jacobusliturgie zu Santiago de Compostela* (Fribourg, 1931), p. 64 (hereafter called PWCC).

    [4] *Ibid.*, pp. 36/7 (fol. 118a Codex Calixtinus.)

3. Hic Jacobus Zebedei achiu (אָחִיו) meuorah ((?מְבוֹרָךְ)) johannis,
supra jamah (יְמָא) Galilee a salvatore nicra (נִקְרָא)... .

The Codex Calixtinus (hereafter called Cod. Cal.) was written
(or compiled) shortly after 1100, and some of its tunes seem to
antedate even the turn of the century, as they can be found in
older French mss., written in the so-called Aquitanian notation.
Many famous clerics belong to the authors of the texts, named in
the Codex, but it is widely assumed that these hymns or narratives
were falsely attributed to them. There is no doubt, however, that
the entire Codex was written and made up in Compostela, the
shrine of St. James, the older brother of Jesus and first bishop
of Jerusalem. Among others one finds contributions by a Patriarch
Guilelmus of Jerusalem (as legal successor of St. James) which
follows immediately upon the "Prosa sancti Jacobi" quoted
above.[5] Therein the saint is asked to attend to the many pilgrims
who have come to visit his shrine. Indeed, the multinational
character of the Cod. Cal. is asserted in these words:

> Hunc codicem primum ecclesia Romana diligenter suscepit.
> Scribitur enim in compluribus locis, in Roma scilicet, in Hirosoli-
> mitanis horis, in Gallia, in Italia, in Teutonica in Frisia et praecipue
> apud Cluniacum [Cluny].[6]

The ms. was certainly not written by Pope Calixtus II, who
died in 1124, but in his honor for authenticating Santiago de
Compostela as the central shrine of St. James. St. James' day was
and is celebrated on July 25 which usually falls in the "Three
Weeks." During that period, especially after July 25, thousands
of pilgrims moved about the European streets, and their hymns
were heard by everyone, Christian and Jew alike. Most scholars
assume that a number of texts and tunes of the Cod. Cal. originated
in France or under French influence, probably that of the monks
of Cluny. Thus it appears that Idelsohn's conjecture of the Spanish
origin of the Jewish tune was essentially correct, although he based

[5] PWCC, p. 38.
[6] Cod. Cal., fol. 185r

it solely on a parallel with a Spanish folksong, which, at closer inspection, turns out to be Basquish, not Spanish.[7] The parallel tunes which Idelsohn presents, including a recent (nineteenth century) song with a Czech text, confirm his basic conviction that the source of the tune was a Spanish pilgrimage song. Nowhere does he investigate its origin, its age, or that of most parallel tunes. We shall now examine the genealogy of the main stem and its main branches or variants.

II

The Latin hymn "Jocundetur et laetetur" (PWCC, p. 64) bears the melodic nucleus of the tune of *Eli Tziyon*. The first expansion and stylization of the Latin hymn, which had a fixed meter, seems to have been made by the knightly monk Heinrich von Louffenberg, whose codex (Cod. B 121), destroyed during the siege of Strasbourg in 1870, was written between 1415–1443.[8] Fortunately the renowned hymnologist Ph. Wackernagel had previously copied almost the entire codex. It contains the Latin-German version of a Christmas hymn.

> Puer natus in Bethlehem
> Unde gaudeat Jerusalem   } 8-syllabic trochees

> or, in the pure German version:

> Ein Kind geboren zu Bethlehem
> Des freudet sich Jerusalem,   } 8-syllabic iambs
> Alleluia.

---

[7] Cf. Felipe Pedrell, *Cancionero musical popular Español,* (Barcelona, n.d.), II, No. 315. In a later publication, Idelsohn has somewhat rectified this, but never reached a conclusion.

[8] Cf. F. M. Boehme, *Altdeutsches Liederbuch* (Leipzig, 1877), p. 771, No. 33; also W. Danckert, *Das europaeische Volkslied,* 3rd ed. (Bonn, 1970), pp. 43, 460.

Music Ex. 2   München, 1586

The Strasbourg ms. contained a number of texts and tunes that were quite well known at that time. There are at least 10–12 variants of the text and tune of *Puer natus* in the old hymn-books of Germany, both Catholic and Protestant, all with two exceptions connected with Christmas or the New Year. Two variants, so-called "contrafacts," have the text "Herr, nun heb den Wagen selb" (Koepple's *Gesangbuch* [Strasbourg, 1537]) and still later "Zion, lobe Deinen Herrn" (Cologne, 1638), both versions kept in 7-syllabic trochees. A Parisian version is attributed to a Jacobus de Benedictis(!)[9]

---

[9] Julian, *Dictionary of Hymnology*, II, 1217; see also E. de Meril, *Poésies inédites du Moyen Age* (Paris, 1854), p. 337.

The Latin parallel cited by Idelsohn

> Salve mundi salutare
> Salve, salve, Jesu care,
> Cruci tuae me aptare   8-syllabic trochees
> Vellem tibi me aequare
> Da mihi tuam copiam

belongs, however, to the Easter cycle, and was obviously copied from the *Vorlage* Puer natus. It is contained in the "Sirenes symphoniacae" (1678), a not very popular Catholic hymn-book.[10] In view of the fact that the great majority of the German and English variants are sung as Christmas or New Year's carols, the question arises: why do most of these hymns belong to the Christmas cycle and not to the Post-Pentecostal cycle, when the patron Saint had his day? The answer is simple: In Santiago de Compostela two days of St. James are celebrated: VIII Kalendis Augusti (July 25) and III Kalendis Januarii (*translacio et electio eiusdem colitur*).[11] The first date may explain the chanting of the tune during the "Three Weeks," when the streets resounded from the hymns of the summer-pilgrims while the second date was used for Christmas and the New Year.

The oldest English version may be found in the Heresford Breviary (1505), but the intonation of our tune is most fragmentary. All other versions of text and tune in England originated centuries later. Before plotting the ages and paths of the variants we ought to give due consideration to the meters: The Hebrew text apparently antedates the original (Spanish) melody, for the Hebrew stresses the penultimate syllables of each line (the 7th syllable), whereas the musical rhythm of the tune demands the stress upon the 8th syllable. Musical ictus and textual accents thus conflict with each other in almost every verse. If the melody had preceded the text, the man who adjusted the text would presumably have fitted it better to the metrical stresses.

[10] Karl S. Meister, *Das deutsche kathol. Kirchenlied* (Freiburg i.B., 1862), p. 326.
[11] PWCC, p. 23.

The migration of our tune appears to have taken place in two phases:

1. As a *pilgrimage* song, either after July 25 or during the Christmas-New Year cycle, often *zersungen* (sung to pieces) with many variants.[12]

2. After the sixteenth century the tune consolidated itself in the form structure of the *folia*, beginning about 1630,[13] and the tune reached the level of art-music in Italy, Spain, France and Austria. As the *Folia* by Corelli, it has become a celebrated composition for violin and keyboard.

What is a *folia*? Although the term is well-known among musicians, a strict definition or etymology is still wanting, owing to the fact that the expression has at least three different meanings, i.e., a ritualistic ceremony (fertility), a musical, and a choreographic one. Leaving the first and third meaning aside, and referring to the specifically musical meaning, the *folia* is defined as an 8-measure structure with fixed bass and/or melody. The example of the *folia*-type, as given in the *Harvard Dictionary of Music*, is all but identical with the Jewish version of our tune, and every other variant shows a distinct resemblance to it.

Music Ex. 3

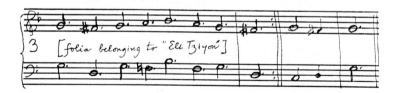

In the foregoing we have sketched the development and the migrations of our tune. Since the *folia* is closely related to the *Moresca*, one senses the Spanish-Arab flavor of our stylized tune.

---

[12] Both of the most recent versions (Basquish and Czech) have secular texts; the tune survived, even after the pilgrimages ceased.

[13] Cf. the article *folia* in *Musik in Geschichte und Gegenwart*.

Before attempting to set down the path of the melody, we must ask ourselves if the Hebrew version is represented in its originally crude form or in a late stylized arrangement. Both the metrical and the prose-texts used in the liturgy for our tune testify that indeed stylization must have taken place: the false stress which the tune sets on the ultimate syllable of the lines of *Eli Tziyon*, disappeared in later poems sung to the same tune, such as e.g., "תְּרַחֵם צִיּוֹן כַּאֲשֶׁר אָמַרְתָּ" as well as in the prose-texts. Moreover, some of the versions in mss. of the eighteenth century, in the Birnbaum Collection of Hebrew Music (at Hebrew Union College in Cincinnati), try, though somewhat timidly, to adjust the proper musical rhythm to the correct metrical stresses. We shall probably not err too much, if we date the time and place of stylization in seventeenth century Germany or Prague, the latter being the "clearing-house" for the export of stylized *ḥazzanut*.

A possible list of the tune's migrations may conclude this first attempt:

A. Likely origin is Cluny, France, the site of the famous abbey from which came tbe religious reform in Christianity of the eleventh to twelfth centuries.

B. Then to Santiago de Compostelo in northwestern Spain, since the ninth century the site of the shrine of St. James.

C. Then to Strasburg, on the border of France and Germany, which became an important religious center after the tenth century.

D. From there, it wandered eastward into the Germanies.

E. Simultaneously, the melody became popular iu both Paris, France, and England.

F. From Paris, it seems to have traveled southward to the Basque area of northeastern Spain.

G. From Germany it spread to Bohemia.

III. THE *Bergamasca*

The *Eli Tziyon* and its variants serve the Ashkenazic liturgy as a "seasonal" leitmotiv preceding the Ninth of Ab exclusively. They are chanted during a particular time of the Jewish year. The tune is, however, not restricted to its original *piyyut*, but is applied to various, not always metrical, texts.

The second melody to be expounded is, however, less an individual tune than a melodic archetype (actually the ideal father of an entire family of related strains), set to a variety of texts, which are chanted on many occasions and seasons. In fact, some of the variants are used all through the year. We shall first quote the textual incipits of the main variants:

Day of rendition	Poet	Incipit
17th of Tammuz	Ibn Gabirol	שָׁעָה נֶאֱסָר
Sabbath Mincha	Ps. 144	לְדָוִד בָּרוּךְ:
Passover	Anonymous (for passover)	אֲדוֹן עוֹלָם
Friday eve	Moshe?	כָּל מְקַדֵּשׁ שְׁבִיעִי
New Year Yotzer	R' E. Kalir	אַדִּירֵי אֲיֻמָּה
Eve of Yom Kippur	Yom Tov of York	אָמְנָם כֵּן
New Year Yotzer	R' Simcha b. Isaac b. Abun	אֶדֶר וָהוֹד

Of the seven texts quoted here, only one is scriptural, although biblical quotations permeate all the other poems. The scriptual text is, of course, *L'David Barukh*, Ps. 144; musically speaking, it is closest to the archetype itself. With the exception of the *Zemirah* כָּל מְקַדֵּשׁ, all other texts belong either to the category of *selihot*, or to *piyyutim* of the High Holidays. Yet these seven texts which are chanted to variants of our mode, are by no means the only verses applied to it. With the exception of *L'David Barukh* (chanted during the *Mincha* service of the Sabbath) all of the other texts, including the numerous ones not quoted here, originated between the eleventh and thirteenth centuries, and were composed by Sephardic as well as by Ashkenazic *peitanim*. The tunes of these texts are by no means fully identical, but they contain certain melodic-rhythmic elements common to all, and characteristic of the archetype. These constants are:

Music Ex. 4[14]

This is the pattern of the Italian *Bergamasca*, a "rogue's dance," that is already mentioned in Shakespeare's comedies (e.g., *Mid-summernight's Dream*, II, 1). A number of German and English songs contain this rhythmic pattern, indicating that the dance was quite popular outside Italy. The incipit of *L' David Barukh* consists of two motifs:

Music Ex. 5[15]

Le - da - vid ba - ruch A - do - nai tsu - ri, ham - la - med ya - dai la - krav

Another variant has the same motifs, but in a different order:

Music Ex. 6

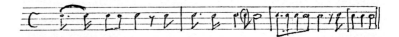

Om-nam ken ye-tser so-khen ye-tser so-khen ba-nu

These melodic deviations are immediately recognizable as simple permutations of the original order, while the rhythmic variants are considerably more differentiated;[16] thus we encounter:

Music Ex. 7: Rhythmic pattern of *Eder vahod*

[14] The first *Bergamasca* in written form is found in the Vienna ms. of Bernhard Schmid Organ book of 1517.

[15] It is reasonable to assume that the German Jews became familiar with the tune in the 17th century.

[16] Permutation of motifs is frequent in folksongs.

Common to all variants is the dance, or marchlike, rhythm.
From where did the Ashkenazic Synagogue pick up this very
merry dance? Although Salomone de' Rossi had written and
published a "Sonata sopra la Bergamasca" (in his *quarto libro di
varie sonate*, 1623), one must not assume that the *hazzanim*, who
did not pay attention to his work under the best of circumstances,
would have liked this rather "highbrow" music, if they were aware
of it at all; the less so, as his synagogal compositions were all but
ignored in *nusaḥ Ashkenaz*.

The most likely sources of foreign tunes, which both *klezmarim*
and *hazzanim* knew and held in high esteem, were military bands
and vagrant singers and musicians (*Fahrende Spielleute*). The
klezmarim, who were in close touch with the latter category,
brought their tunes to the *hazzanim* who paid for them. Yet very
few of them were able to write music or to read it. Hence the
foreign tunes were almost invariably distorted or contaminated.[17]

By far the most famous example of the prototype of these dances
and marches was transmitted to us as a *Gassenhauer* (street song)
by no less a master than J. S. Bach; he ended his celebrated
Goldberg-Variations with a "quodlibet," the dominant tune of
which was the melody of

"Kraut und Rueben

Haben mich vertrieben"

(cabbage and turnips drove me away).[18]

Music Ex. 8

[17] Cf. my *A Voice Still Heard...* (New York, 1977), pp. 97–99.
[18] Cantus firmus of Quodlibet in J. B. Sach's *Goldberg Variations*.

The same motif appears in reverse order as "London Bridge is falling down"

Music Ex. 9

Ken a-nah-nu b'yad'kha he-sed notser (or) falling down, falling down

The motif T is alien to the *Bergamasca* and originated in Jewish tradition; it is the closing refrain of the *Pizmon* "כִּי הִנֵּה כַּחוֹמֶר". This was the way in which foreign tunes were incorporated: the *hazzanim* provided them either at the opening, or, preferably, at the close, with a traditional motif.

That the break in the shape of a tune remained audible to this very day in so extremely drastic a manner as, for example, the elegy for the 17th day of Tammuz, is rare: in the *piyyut* "שָׁעָה נֶאֱסָר" by Solomon Ibn Gabirol, a model of an old German folksong was used for its opening:[19]

Music Ex. 10

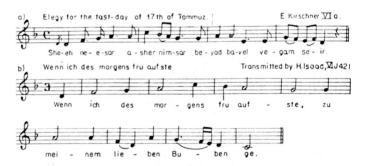

Thus far, the identity of the tunes is evident; but where the German song seems to end, the Hebrew version closes with an elaborate stylized wailing, mindful of the significance of Tammuz 17th:[20]

[19] Cf. A. Baer, *Baal Tefilla* (Goeteborg, reprint New York, 1953/4), No. 1321.

[20] It was the merit of E. Kirschner, the excellent chief cantor of Munich, to have first pointed out these and similar connections between German folksong

Music Ex. 11

Va - ti - ba - kaŗ_____ ha - ir_____
(and breached was _____ the ci - - ty)

thus linking it with the cadence traditional for *qinot*.

In all of these cases one encounters not only borrowings *from* German and Italian sources, and frequently acculturation and adaptation *to* these types, but also, even more significant, demonstrable evidence of (active) assimilation of the borrowed tunes to basic Jewish tradition. The last mentioned case is conspicuous; similarly the old *piyyut* אֶדֶר וְהוֹד by R. Simon b. Isaac b. Abun, the popular *paitan* of the early eleventh century, is another fine example of this mutual assimilation.[21] Both the rhythms and the melodic elements occur in it, but in a different order:

Music Ex. 12

E-der va-hod et-ten be-tsiv-yon she-vah e-e-rokh b'niv ve-higa-yon

Here we find the motif A of *L' David Barukh* inverted, and both B 1' and the final cadence are so shaped that they lead easily into the traditional mode of the יוֹצֵר לְרֹאשׁ הַשָּׁנָה. To alter the motifs in such a way and to such effect, a considerable ability to shape variations was necessary for the *hazzanim*, who had received nothing but the raw material from the *klezmarim* and had to stylize it for use in their synagogues. It had to fit for the proper season or occasion. This was no easy task and deserves closer examination. If the *hazzanim* would have had to live up to A. J.

and Jewish tradition in his fine study, *Ueber mittelalterliche hebraische Poesien und ihre Singweisen* (Nüremberg, 1914).

[21] About R. Simon b. Abun, see I. Elbogen, *Der juedische Gottesdienst,* pp. 328 f.

Heschel's postulate: "I should like to conceive *hazzanut* as the art of *siddur* exegesis...,"[22] they surely should have been happy not to be his contemporaries. They had to please their worshipers, and, at the very least, not offend their rabbis. They were obliged to present not only the established musical tradition, the *nusaḥ*, but also to offer recent, not generally known, material, which they received from their *klezmarim* or their *singers*. They had to compose them for their congregations according to well-known models, carefully observing certain unwritten laws of modes and rhythms; all this and exegesis, too? Nor is Heschel's follow-up tenable: "Words die of routine." This is a general statement, almost a platitude; it may be true of the daily prayers, but it is most certainly not true, when applied to the *piyyutim* for our High Holidays. Their texts, more often recherché rather than simple, to say the least, were not likely to die "of routine." The musical challenge of the medieval and pre-Emancipation *hazzanim* consisted mainly in the acquisition of new music, and its stylization and assimilation to the established *nusaḥ*. Only a few were truly able to fulfill all these demands, and still guard and preserve the dignity of the service. Who would teach them musical taste, when hit songs and vulgar dances inundated the streets outside the ghetto? A. Z. Idelsohn has described their situation exceedingly well in his study on "Songs and Singers of the 18th Century."[23]

Considering that there was no musical school or standard accessible to these cantors, we shall devote the last part of this essay to a brief esamination of the method, by which the best cantors of the eighteenth century varied and stylized the "alien corn," so that it was not immediately recognizable as such.

IV

The phenomenon of "*zersingen*" as well as its practice (sing to pieces by extending either the text, or the melody, or both) is

[22] Cf. A. J. Heschel, "The Vocation of the Cantor," *The Security of Freedom* (New York, 1966).

[23] See A. Z. Idelsohn, "Song and Singers of the Synagogue in the 18th century," *HUCA*, Jubilee Vol. (1925), pp. 357 ff.

well-known among folklorists. The *hazzanim*, while unskilled in
music theory, used this technique in order to conceal or at least
to extenuate the break in style, when a foreign tune was to be
embedded in the Jewish tradition. This was the first and usually
crude way toward a "disguising variation." A good example is
the *z'mirah* כָּל מְקַדֵּשׁ שְׁבִיעִי. Its meter consists of 5 lines, each of
accentuated words, all ending with one rather primitive suffix-
rhyme. The raw material of the tune was taken from an old German
Abendgesang, itself a derivative of an older *Weise*. The *Bergamasca*-
rhythm, familiar to the Jews, which is not compatible with the
German *Vorlage*, was nonetheless added to disguise the foreign
tune, and a bit of *recitativzersingen* followed, so that the similarity
between original theme and variation almost vanished from ear
and sight; the *Bergamasca*-rhythm was still maintained:

Music Ex. 13

We observe here that the Hebrew variation, in this as in most
other cases of originally German tunes, emphatically stresses the
march-rhythm, whereas many of the originals are either in triple
time, or in a quietly fluent 4/4 time, as for example, in the *piyyut*
quoted above, שָׁעָה נֶאֱסָר.[24] A more sophisticated type of variation
is found in the tune of the *piyyut* אַדִּירֵי אֲיֻמָּה (by R. E. Kalir, for
the New Year's Day). It sets pairs of rhymed verses, each of
4 accentuated words, against the congregational response ה' מֶלֶךְ,

---

[24] Even in the so-called hazag-meter, as e.g., in "אֲדוֹן עוֹלָם", the music in
the older tradition always used 4/4 time. Only after 1820 there appeared
versions of it in triple time. Tradition insists on march-rhythm, so did the
Hasidim!

ה׳ מָלָךְ, ה׳ מְלָךְ, ה׳ יִמְלֹךְ. Nothing could be more contrasting with the dialectic poem than the simple love-song:

We juxtapose the two tunes, first the German and then the Hebrew:

Music Ex. 14

This method of "diminution" and "figuration" was well known among the composers of the Baroque, and some of the *hazzanim*

must have been excellent musicians to learn this type of variation "by rote." The German tune is disguished in this way, and the ornaments cover virtually the entire melodic contour of the original.[25] All these borrowings and variations were both necessary and possible under two conditions: (a) the idea of an existent ideal *nusaḥ* had to be maintained; (b) the *hazzanim* were not familiar with musical notation. When the second premise was no longer valid and the cantors learned to read and write music, they were no longer dependent upon the *klezmarim* and could find new tunes either in printed sheet music or else compose their own music and fix it in writing. In the second case they were able to follow the modes and principles of tradition; in the first case they preferred — in Western and Central Europe — melodies from the Italian opera, later from the Vienna classics, while in Poland and Russia the situation was contaminated by the massive influx of Slavonic folksong, mixed with Tartaric and Oriental elements.

* *
*

In the genealogies presented above we encountered in the first tune a saint's hymn, transformed into a dance-form (*folia*) or a pilgrim's song. In the second tune the original songs were again dance tunes, marching or love songs, all secular in character. The marching songs, so eagerly taken up by German *hazzanim*, might be considered the last remnants of the ancient *Heldenlieder*, for which the German Jews had had a considerable flair, as witness the numerous Judeo-German paraphrases of *Gudrun*, the *Nibelungen*, the *Bovo-book*, and the ancient texts and tunes of German folksongs. In sum, what the German Jews used — aside from their old traditional psalmodies and cantillations — were either songs of their Christian environment, often originally religious, then

[25] It is noteworthy that the German song was first written in the celebrated *Lochamer Liederbuch* that bears a Judeo-German dedication by the Jew Wölflin of Locham to his "Gemaken," Barbara. This tune, therefore, antedates 1450; the Hebrew variation, however, is not as old; it probably dates between 1550 and the end of the 16th century.

secularized ones, transformed into a dance-like or march-like variant; occasionally remnants of the old *"Heldenlieder"* were among these songs. These were the styles that breached the walls of the ghettoes and were preserved in the synagogues.[26] To Polish and Russian Jews this kind of heroic or epic song was foreign; the somewhat less alien Italian dances, and the marching melodies, however, were much beloved by *hasidim* as well as *mitnagdim*.[27]

Yet in the end it was the knowledge of musical notation that became the watershed between Eastern and Western Ashkenazic *hazzanut*, even before the Emancipation. The aforementioned great Birnbaum Collection of Hebrew musical manuscripts speaks a most eloquent language concerning this very point. When those early *hazzanim* of around the 1800s first discovered the — for them — "secret" art of musical notation and thereby were exposed to the mainstream of Viennese classical art-music, they simply were unable to resist that powerful impact. It took the repeated warnings and teachings of the young Science of Judaism to stem and regulate the trend toward passive assimilation. Only the genius of a Solomon Sulzer and his disciples was equal to the task of rejuvenating, indeed, of refurbishing the liturgical chant; this time, however, by removing it from German (or Italian) folksong and dance, and orienting it toward a synthesis of Jewish musical tradition and classical form structure.

[26] Cf. *Monumenta Judaica* (Cologne, 1963), pp. 694 ff.

[27] Most interesting is the sharp cleavage that exists between Polish and Czech folksongs. On this question, which also touches on the strong Moravian elements in Ashkenazic chant, see O. Hostinsky, *Mitteilungen ueber das tschechische Volkslied in Boehmen und Maehren*, Vol. III (Vienna, 1909), and Zdenek Nejedly's powerful study, "Magister Zawisch und seine Schueler" (in *Sammelbaende der internationalen Musikgesellschaft* VII, 1905/6); most recent is M. Komma's study, *Das boehmische Musikantentum* (Kassel, 1960).

PHILO'S THEORY OF ETERNAL CREATION: *DE PROV.* 1.6–9

By David Winston

In his discussion of the origin and duration of the world, Aristotle asserts that all his predecessors held it to have had a beginning (γενόμενον), but some (like Plato) had maintained that having begun it was everlasting, others (such as the Atomists) that it was perishable, and others again (such as Empedocles and Heraclitus) that it was subject to an eternal sequence of cyclic genesis and destruction (*De Cael.* 1.10). The Platonic view Aristotle held to be impossible. He was aware, however, that some Platonists interpreted Plato's cosmology differently, though he considered their interpretation to be untrue.

> They claim that what they say about the generation of the world is analogous to the diagrams drawn by mathematicians: their exposition does not mean that the world ever was generated (οὐχ ὡς γενομένου ποτέ), but is used for instructional purpose (διδασκαλίας χάριν), since it makes things easier to understand just as the diagram does for those who see it in process of construction [*De Cael.* 279b30].

With the exception of Plutarch and Atticus, this interpretation of Plato's *Timaeus* was steadily maintained by virtually all Platonists down to the time of Plotinus. Moreover, according to Atticus, the motivation for this exegesis was the inability of its authors to resist the Aristotelian argument for the eternity of the universe, while, in their pious devotion to the Master, shrinking from ascribing to him a doctrine considered false by Aristotle (Euseb. *PE.* 15.6.6).[1]

---

[1] The following Platonists interpreted Plato's *Timaeus* analytically: Xenocrates, Speusippus, Crantor and his followers, Eudorus of Alexandria, Taurus, Albinus, Apuleius. See A. E. Taylor, *A Commentary on Plato's Timaeus* (Oxford, 1928), pp. 67–69; J. Pépin, *Théologie Cosmique* (Paris, 1964), pp.

It should be noted, however, that there was some disagreement among the Platonists as to the precise formulation of the Platonic theory of cosmogony. Some were willing to assert that according to Plato the world was in reality ἀγένητος but could, for pedagogical reasons, be characterized as γενητός insofar as it is ultimately derived from higher principles (e.g., the One and the Indefinite Dyad, and secondarily, the Ideas and Mathematicals). Others, however, (such as Crantor and his followers) insisted that according to Plato the world was γενητός, though this was not to be understood in a temporal sense. Proclus, for example, attacks Platonists like Xenocrates and Speusippus for asserting that according to Plato the world was γενητός only κατ᾽ ἐπίνοιαν or was feigned to be so σαφηνείας ἕνεκα διδασκαλικῆς, for Timaeus, he insists, infers the existence of the Maker from the premise that the world is γενητός, and if the premise is merely conceptual, the Demiurge must be so too. It would appear that Proclus' objection rests on semantic considerations. In his view the formulations of Xenocrates and Speusippus and their like are misleading and may result in the branding of their ultimate principles (the One and the Indefinite Dyad)[2] as empty abstractions. Proclus, therefore prefers to say

38–43, 86–94; C. Baeumker, "Die Ewigkeit der Welt bei Plato," *Philosophische Monatshefte*, XXIII (1887), 513–529; A. J. Festugière, *Études de Philosophie Grecque* (Paris, 1971), pp. 487–506; G. S. Claghorn, *Aristotle's Criticism of Plato's Timaeus* (The Hague, 1954), pp. 84–98; J. Dillon, *The Middle Platonists* (London, 1977), p. 7. According to the second century Platonist, Severus, although the cosmos had no temporal origin, it is still periodically destroyed and renewed (Proc. *In Plat. Tim.* 1.289. 7–13). See Pépin, *op. cit.*, p. 94; P. Merlan, in *Cambridge History of Later Greek and Early Medieval Philosophy* (Cambridge, 1967), pp. 78–79; Dillon, *op. cit.*, p. 263.

2 Merlan has pointed out that disagreement started early among the Platonists as to whether the two higher principles should have absolutely equal status (Merlan, *Cambridge History*, p. 17). Hermodorus asserted that according to Plato, the Indefinite Dyad or Matter should not be called a first principle, and later Eudorus of Alexandria posits a supranoetic One above the Monad and Dyad. See A. J. Festugière, *La Révélation d'Hermés Trismégiste* (Paris, 1954), IV, 308–310; Merlan, *Cambridge History*, p. 81. On the nature of Speusippus' One, see P. Merlan, *From Platonism to Neoplatonism* (The Hague, 1960), pp. 96–140; H. J. Krämer, *Der Ursprung der Geistmetaphysik* (Amsterdam,

that the world is γενητός, though in the sense that it is ἀεὶ γιγ-νόμενον καὶ γεγενημένον (*In Plat. Tim.* 290.3–25). This semantic distinction is of some importance for our understanding of Philo's position in this matter, for if our thesis that he taught a doctrine of eternal creation be correct, it would strike one as not a little perverse that he should accept Aristotle's literalist interpretation of Plato's creation doctrine in the *Timaeus* in preference to that of Xenocrates and Speusippus (*Aet.* 14–16). He apparently did so, however, in order to substantiate the view that Plato did think that the world was γενητός in the sense that it was the product of a real Demiurgic creativity (cf. *Op.* 171), yet at the same time rejecting Aristotle's temporal understanding of it.[3]

In the light of this debate over the meaning of the *Timaeus'* doctrine of creation, we may now examine Philo's discussion of the eternity of the world in *De Prov.* 1.6–9.[4] After noting that super-

---

1967), pp. 207–218, 351–358; H. Happ, *Hyle* (Berlin, 1971), pp. 208–241; Dillon, *op. cit.*, pp. 12–18; F. Ravaisson-Mollien, "Las Opiniones de Espeusipo acerca de los primeros principios de las cosas examinandas a la luz de los textos aristotelicos," *Revista de Estudios clasicos*, XI (1967), pp. 28–64.

[3] Philo could have rather endorsed the formulation of Crantor and his followers (if we follow Proclus' version, *In Plat. Tim.* 85a, rather than that of Plutarch, *Anim. Procr.* 1.1012D), but he probably preferred not to associate his position with that of the Platonists who coordinated the principle of matter with the One. Moreover, while Eudorus' concept of the One was very close to that of Philo, he not only seems to have employed the ἀγένητος formula which Philo disliked (Plut. ib. 3.1013B), but very likely (under Neopythagorean influence) conceived of the One as emanating both the Monad and the Dyad, a notion which Philo would certainly have rejected (Simplic. *In Phys.* 181, 10 ff., Diels; Alex. Aphr. *In. Met.* 988a 10–11, Hayduck).

[4] See now Aucher's Latin translation from the Armenian reprinted with a French translation, introduction and notes by Mireille Hadas-Lebel (Paris, 1973); P. Wendland, *Philo's Schrift über die Vorsehung* (Berlin, 1892); W. Bousset, *Jüdisch-Christlicher Schulbetrieb in Alexandria und Rom* (Göttingen, 1915), pp. 137 ff.; M. Pohlenz, *Kleine Schriften* (Hildesheim, 1965), pp. 305–383, esp. pp. 313–324; H. Leisegang, "Philo," in PW 20:1, cols. 8–11; S. Lilla, *Clement of Alexandria* (Oxford, 1971), p. 197, n. 2. Bousset finds *Prov.* 1. 7–8 hopelessly contradictory ("Kurz, hier sind vollendete Widersprüche. Und nach allem, was wir von Philos schriftstellerischer Eigenart kennen, tun wir ihm kein Unrecht, wenn wir annehmen, dass er in 7–8 eine Ausführung, in

ficial observation often results in the belief that the world has existed from eternity independent of any creative act (the Aristotelian view), he immediately proceeds to attack the 'sophistic' view[5] "elaborated with drawn-out quibbles," that God did not begin to create the world at a certain moment, but was "eternally applying himself to its creation." The intent of this formulation, says Philo, was to avoid imputing to God a most unbecoming inactivity which would otherwise have characterized his pre-creative state.[6] But in this case, the absurdity of this hypothesis

welcher die platonische Annahme einer vorweltlichen Materie vom Standpunkt der Behauptung der Ewigkeit der Welt aus abgelehnt wurde, gedankenlos und sinnlos in einem Zusammenhang hat stehen lassen, der eine entgegengesetzte Orientierung zeigt." p. 146). I believe, however, that in spite of the stylistic gaucherie of these passages (undoubtedly due to the Armenian translator), it is possible to extract from them a consistent Philonic doctrine. (Wendland, *op. cit.*, p. 184, thought these passages constituted a lost section of Philo's *De Aeternitate Mundi*, and although Bousset was unwilling to go that far, he was inclined to accept Wendland's suggestion that in this section of the *De Providentia* Philo was attempting to fulfill his promise at the end of *Aet.* 150.)

[5] Cf. *Aet.* 14: τινὲς δὲ οἴονται σοφιζόμενοι κατὰ Πλάτωνα γενητὸν λέγεσθαι τὸν κόσυον.

[6] Cf. *Op.* 7: τοῦ δὲ θεοῦ πολλὴν ἀπραξίαν ἀνάγνως κατεψεύσαντο; *Aet.* 83: "Moreover if all things are as they say consumed in the conflagration, what will God be doing during that time? Will he do nothing at all?...But if all things are annihilated, inactivity and dire unemployment (ἀργία καὶ ἀπραξία) will render his life unworthy of the name and what could be more monstrous than this? I shrink from saying, for the very thought is a blasphemy, that quiescence will entail as a consequence the death of God." The same a.gument was employed by the Epicureans. "Moreover I would put to both of you the question," says Velleius the Epicurean, "why did these deities suddenly awake into activity as world-builders after countless ages of slumber? for though the world did not exist, it does not follow that ages (*saecla*) did not exist; ...but from the infinite past there has existed an eternity not measured by limited divisions of time, but of a nature intelligible in terms of extension, since it is inconceivable that there was ever a time when time did not exist. Well then, Balbus, what I ask is, why did your Providence remain idle all through that extent of time of which you speak?" (Cic. *Nat. D.* 1.9.21–22). Cf. Diels, *Dox. Graec.*: 209–301; Lucr. 5.168. A similar argument had already been employed by Parmenides, DK B.8, 9–10: "What need would have made it grow, beginning from non-Being, later or sooner?"

becomes immediately evident; for those who have espoused it in order to remove a minimal accusation against the deity have actually attached to him a maximal one. Their conception of God's creative act consists, in the last analysis, of the bestowal of order and form on a primordial matter which lacked all previous determination. Is this not equivalent, argues Philo, to making matter into a principle of creation alongside of God? While solicitously clearing God of the accusation of temporary inactivity they have thus nonchalantly overlooked the more genuine threat to his sovereign creative power.

Philo now states his own position:

> God is continuously ordering matter by his thought. His thinking is simultaneous with his acting and there never was a time when he did not act, the ideas themselves existing with him from the beginning. For God's will is not posterior to him, but is always with him, for natural motions never give out. Thus ever thinking he creates, and furnishes to sensible things the principle of their existence, so that one always finds these two processes in conjunction [1.7].[7]

At first sight this passage seems baffling. Having concluded his denunciation of those who teach a doctrine of eternal creation on the grounds of their converting the Creator into the mere orderer of a primordial principle, Philo now seems to espouse just such a doctrine in turn. God, in Philo's view, is eternally creating inasmuch as he is ever thinking, and his creativity is constituted by nothing more than the meticulously accurate division of a formless matter through his all-incising Logos (cf. *Her.* 134, 137, 140). The solution, however, is not far to seek, if we focus our attention on some important modifications which Philo has introduced into his own theory of eternal creation. In the mystical monotheism of Philo nothing really exists or acts except God;[8] all else is but a shadow

---

[7] Cf. Spinoza, *Eth.* I.33, sch. 2: "But since in eternity there is no when nor before nor after, it follows from the perfection of God alone that He neither can decree nor could ever have decreed anything else than that which He has decreed, that is to say, God has not existed before His decrees and can never exist without them."

[8] *Det.* 160: "God alone has veritable being. This is why Moses will say of

reality ultimately deriving from the truly Existent. Unlike Plato, who was a pluralist, Philo was thus unwilling to allow even for a self-existing void, and therefore made its pattern an eternal idea within the Divine Mind.[9] In Plato's conception of matter, the self-existing Receptacle is its most stable and permanent constituent: "It must be called always the same, for it never departs at all from its own character" (*Tim.* 50 BC).[10] For Philo, however, not only are the phantasmagoric copies of the ideal four elements indirectly derived from God[11] (whether they are similarly derived for any of the Middle Platonists preceding Philo would depend on whether or not they had anticipated him in making the eternal 'Forms' ideas in the mind of God),[12] but even the virtually non-existent void is but a shadow reflection of an idea in God. Hence what in Philo's view was the crucial defect in the Platonists' doctrine of eternal creation (i.e., the elevation of matter into an

Him as best he may in human speech, 'I am He that is', implying that others lesser than He have not being, as being indeed is, but exist in semblance only, and are conventionally said to exist." Cf. *LA* 2.86; *Cher.* 121; *Her.* 122–124; *Mos.* 1.76. For the theme of man's nothingness and utter passivity in Philo, see D. Winston, "Freedom and Determinism in Philo of Alexandria," *Studia Philonica*, III (1974–75), 47–70.

[9] See D. Winston, "Philo's Theory of Cosmogony," in *Religious Syncretism in Antiquity*, ed. B. Pearson (Missoula, Montana, 1975), pp. 157–171. It was probably for this reason that Philo refused explicitly to attribute any motion to primordial matter (*ibid.*, p. 164, n. 1).

[10] Of Plato's Receptacle, J. B. Skemp writes that "it is more real than the 'images' of the Forms which appear in it." ("Hyle and Hypodoche," in *Aristotle and Plato in the Mid-Fourth Century*, ed. I. Düring and G. E. L. Owen [Göteborg, 1960], p. 207). Cf. Plotinus' concept of matter (ὕλη) as total negativity or absolute evil (*En.* 2.4; 1.8).

[11] See my article cited in n. 9.

[12] See A. N. M. Rich, "The Platonic Ideas as the Thoughts of God," *Mnemosyne*, ser. 4, v. 7, fasc. 1 (1964), 123–133; W. Theiler, *Die Vorbereitung des Neuplatonismus* (Berlin/Zürich, 1964), pp. 1–60; C. J. De Vogel, *Philosophia* (Assen, 1969), I, 372–377; J. H. Loenen, "Albinus' Metaphysics. An Attempt at Rehabilitation," *Mnemosyne*, ser. 4, v. 10 (1950), 44–45; J. Dillon, *The Middle Platonists* (London, 1977), pp. 29, 95.

autonomous albeit passive principle) has carefully been eliminated from his own version of that theory.[13]

Continuing his argument with the Platonists, Philo now confronts them with what he considers to be an inner contradiction in their doctrine. If, says Philo, one refuses to acknowledge the simultaneity of God's thinking and creating, how can one explain the fact that matter which existed from all time was never found in a disordered state? What Philo seems to be arguing is that if one considers matter as an autonomous primordial element, rather than an indirect product of God's thinking, how could it be maintained that it never was in a disordered state? Only if God's thinking is eternally bringing matter into being and simultaneously ordering it can one avoid a primordially formless state of matter. But, continues Philo, if there was a time when matter was disordered, then the origin of the world began when order was imposed upon it, and the Platonists can no longer speak of eternal creation.

Philo's theory of eternal creation can now be stated succinctly. Insofar as God is always thinking the intelligible 'Forms,' he is eternally creating the Intelligible World or Logos, and thereby also indirectly causing its shadow reflection, the sensible world, which he is constantly making to conform as closely as possible to its intelligible counterpart.[14] Corroboration for this interpretation may be found in an oft repeated principle of Philo's theology that God is unchangeable, so that a temporal creation involving as it does a change in God's nature would thus stand in open contradiction to a fundamental assumption of Philo's thought. Nor is it possible to say as St. Thomas later would that God willed freely from eternity that the world should come into existence in time (or have *esse post non-esse*: *Contr. Gent.* 2.31–7; *S.T.* 1.46.1; *De Potent.* 3.17), for Philo has already stated (*Prov.* 1.7) that God's thinking is simultaneous with his acting or creating (cf. *Sacr.* 65; *Mos.*

---

[13] Bousset, *op. cit.*, p. 144, n. 1 (cited in n. 4), suggests that Philo may be referring to Jewish opponents who understood the Aristotelian doctrine of the eternity of the world as teaching its eternal creation through God.

[14] See my article cited in n. 9, p. 170, n. 1.

1.283). In the light of all this we should have to conclude that the many passages in which Philo speaks of creation in temporal terms are not to be taken literally, but only as accommodations to the biblical idiom.[15]

A strangely dissonant note, however, is struck in *Decal.* 58, where it is explicitly stated that "there was a time when the world was not" (ἦν ποτε χρόνος, ὅτε οὐκ ἦν). It may be that in a polemical context in which the target is a form of idolatry (worship of the Universe itself: cf. *Wisd. of Sol.* 13:1–9) dangerously attractive even for a Jew if he belonged to the enlightened Hellenistic class, Philo did not hesitate to use locutions which explicitly negated his precise technical position. Moreover, it is not entirely out of keeping with Philo's usual style of exposition to use the phrase ἦν ποτε χρόνος in a context such as this. For analytical purposes, Philo speaks, for example, of the mind's condition as it would have been, had it no connection with the sense-perceptions transmitted to it by bodily sense-organs. Allegorizing the biblical text concerning the creation of Eve, he naturally describes this state of the mind in temporal terms:

> For there was a time (ἦν γὰρ ποτε χρόνος) when Mind neither had sense-perception, nor held converse with it.... It was but half the perfect soul, lacking the power whereby it is the nature of bodies to be perceived, a mere unhappy section bereft of its mate without the support of the sense-perceiving organs.... God, then, wishing to provide the Mind with perception of material as well as immaterial things, thought to complete the soul by weaving into the part first made the other section, which he called by the general name of "woman" and the proper name of "Eve", thus symbolizing sense [*Cher.* 58–60].

We may conclude, then, that it is unnecessary to take the passage in *Decal.* 58 *au pied de la lettre.*[16]

---

15 See *Op.* 16, 19, and *passim*; *Mut.* 27; *LA* 2.1–2.

16 It should also be noted that according to Philo's own analysis of time (*Op.* 26; *Aet.* 53), it would be absurd to say "there was a time when the world was not," since time and world are for him correlative (cf. Arist. *Phys.* 8.1.251 b11 ff.; Philop. *Aet. M.*, pp. 145–147, Rabe). As to Philo's characterization of God's creative act as one of βούλησις (*Op.* 16), Wolfson comments: "Following

We must now test our interpretation of Philo's creation doctrine by an examination of his theory of miracles to see whether the latter is consistent with the former. One of Philo's favored phrases is πάντα θεῷ δυνατά, a doctrine he never fails to intone as emphatically as he can whenever the opportunity presents itself. According to Philo, God created the heaven only after he had created the earth, so that

> none would suppose that the regular movements of the heavenly bodies are the causes of all things. For he has no need of his heavenly offspring on which he bestowed powers but not independence: for like a charioteer grasping the reins or a pilot the tiller, he guides all things in what direction he pleases as law and right demand, standing in need of no one besides: for all things are possible to God [Op. 46. cf. QG 4.51].

This passage makes it clear that the formula "all things are possible to God" does not include what is not κατὰ νόμον καὶ δίκην, so that God evidently cannot act arbitrarily, i.e., in a way that might be contrary to his own nature. Nor would it be correct to interpret Philo's position (as Wolfson does)[17] in the light of St. Thomas' view which would allow God to act outside the order of nature:

> If we consider the order of things according as it depends on any secondary causes, God can do something outside such order [e.g., produce the effects of secondary causes without them]. For he is not subject to the order of secondary causes, but, on the contrary, this order is subject to him, as proceeding from him, not by a natural necessity, but by the choice of his own will; for he could have created another order of things.

Scripture and Plato, Philo conceives the act of creation as an act of will and design (i.e., not a necessary result of God's nature)" (I:315). This statement is as incorrect for Plato as it is for Philo, for the Demiurge of the *Timaeus* acts in accordance with his unchangeable nature which is good (or more precisely the source of the good), and Philo is here faithfully following his master. Cf. J. Rist, *Eros and Psyche* (Toronto, 1964), p. 76: "for although the *Demiourgos* may be said to will creation, he does not choose it as one of two alternatives. He simply wills it because it is good; being good means doing good, and the *Demiourgos* is thus 'beyond' choice."

[17] H. A. Wolfson, *Philo* (Cambridge, 1948), I, 358.

Moreover,

> God fixed a certain order in things in such a way that at the same
> time he reserved to himself whatever he intended to do otherwise
> than by a particular cause. So when he acts outside this order, he
> does not change [*S.T.* 1.105.6].

Philo, however, gives every indication of explaining God's miraculous acts within the framework of the existing natural order by
simply expanding its parameters. Since our knowledge of the
physical world is extremely limited, as Philo often emphasizes
with a gusto that leads him on occasion to reproduce the Skeptical
tropes (τρόποι or 'modes') designed to bring about suspense of
judgment (ἐποχή),[18] we easily mistake the biblically recorded
miracles for events in contravention of the laws of nature. This is
clearly indicated by Philo when he writes of the Israelites' incre-
dulity concerning the ability of God to rescue them from a
seemingly endless sequence of crises:

> For after experiencing strange events outside the customary without
> number, they should have ceased to be guided by anything that is
> specious and plausible (ὤφειλον ὑπὸ μηδενὸς ἔτι τῶν εὐλόγων καὶ
> πιθανῶν ἄγεσθαι) but should have put their trust in him of whose
> unfailing truthfulness they had received the clearest proofs [*Mos.*
> 1.196].

The speciousness of our perceptions which leads to a narrow-
minded view of what is physically possible is expressed again in
the following passage:

> To think that after witnessing wonders so many and so great,
> impossibilities no doubt as judged by what to outward appearance
> is credible and reasonable (πρὸς μὲν τὰς πιθανὰς καὶ εὐλόγους
> φαντασίας ἀδύνατα πραχθῆναι) but easily accomplished by the

---

18 *Ebr.* 166–205; *Jos.* 125–143. Philo omits two of the ten tropes of Aene-
sidemus as they are stated by Sextus Empiricus (*Pyrrh. Hyp.* 1.36–164) and
D. L. 9.78–89. See H. von Arnim, "Quellenstudien zu Philo von Alexandria,"
Philologische Untersuchungen, XI (1888); C. L. Stough, *Greek Scepticism*
(Berkeley and Los Angeles, 1969), pp. 67–105; E. Bréhier, *Les Idées philoso-
phiques et religieuses de Philon d'Alexandrie* (Paris, 1950), pp. 207–225.

dispensations of God's providence, they not only doubted, but in their incapacity for learning actually disbelieved [*Mos.* 2.261].[19]

Although Philo does not explicitly invoke the physical principles involved in the Stoic theory of *pneuma* in order to explain God's ability to transform the elements at will, he very likely has this doctrine in the back of his mind.[20] Nevertheless, one cannot help but feel that in expanding the natural order to encompass the biblical miracles, Philo has strained it to the breaking point, and has compromised the credibility of his philosophical position. He had, however, before him a striking example of this kind of intellectual legerdemain in the attempt of the Stoics to incorporate divination into their philosophical system. Cicero offers a sharp critique of the Stoic effort to explain the miracles associated with divination:

> Between that divine system of nature whose great and glorious laws pervade all space and regulate all motion what possible connection can there be with — I shall not say the gall of a chicken, whose entrails, some men assert, give very clear indications of the future, but — the liver, heart, and lungs of a sacrificial ox? [*Divinat.* 2.29].

He especially pokes fun at their explanation of how the sacrificer, in his search for favorable signs, is able to choose the proper victim by means of the divine power which pervades the entire universe:

---

[19] See the excellent discussion in Bréhier (cited n. 18), pp. 182–183. Cf. *Mos.* 1.165, where the miracle is called "a mighty work of nature" (μεγαλούργημα τῆς φύσεως). See D. G. Delling, "Wunder, Allegorie, Mythus bei Philo von Alexandreia," *Wissenschaftliche Zeitschrift der Martin Luther Universität Halle-Wittenberg,* VI:5 (1957), 713–740.

[20] For the Stoic theory of *pneuma,* see S. Sambursky, *Physics of the Stoa* (London, 1959), pp. 1–48; D. E. Hahm, *The Origins of Stoic Cosmology* (Columbus, Ohio, 1977), pp. 153–174; and for their own use of it in explaining the miracles of divination, see Cic. *Nat. D.* 3.39.92. (On the complete flexibility of matter, cf. Diels, *Dox. Graec.,* 307, 22. For its use by *Wisd. of Sol.* in order to explain the miracle of the Red Sea, see D. Winston, "The Book of Wisdom's Theory of Cosmogony," *History of Religions,* XI:2 (1971), 193–195; and the same author's commentary on the *Wisd. of Sol.,* Anchor Bible (New York, 1979), pp, 330–332.

But even more absurd is that other pronouncement of theirs which
you adopted: "At the moment of sacrifice a change in the entrails
takes place; something is added or something taken away; for all
things are obedient to the Divine Will." Upon my word, no old
woman is credulous enough now to believe such stuff. Do you
believe that the same bullock, if chosen by one man, will have a
liver without a head, and if chosen by another will have a liver with
a head?...Upon my word, you Stoics surrender the very city of
philosophy while defending its outworks! For, by your insistence on
the truth of soothsaying, you utterly overthrow physiology. There
is a head to the liver and a heart in the entrails, presto! they will
vanish the very second you have sprinkled them with meal and
wine! Aye, some God will snatch them away! Some invisible power
will destroy them or eat them up! Then the creation and destruction
of all things are not due to nature, and there are some things which
spring from nothing or suddenly become nothing. Was any such
statement ever made by any natural philosopher? [*Divinat.* 2.35–7].

In the light of this Stoic caper,[21] it is no longer surprising that
Philo felt free to exhibit the biblical miracles as emphatically as
he did, although he occasionally tried to inject a possible explanation for them which coincided with the normal course of
nature (the plague of darkness, says Philo, may have been a total
eclipse of the sun: *Mos.* 1.123),[22] and attempted to fit the ten
plagues into a neat cosmological pattern. Moreover, just as the
Stoics believed that the miracles of divination were included among
the causes foreordained by Destiny, so Philo must have considered
the biblical miracles as part of the complex patterns of an un-
changing and eternal Logos, in which past, present, and future
are one.[23] If, nevertheless, Philo's exegetical devices are as un-

[21] It may well be that Cicero is utilizing the exaggerated version of an
overzealous defender of the Stoic theory of divination. The Stoic theory was
severely attacked by philosophers like Carneades and Diogenianos. Among
the Stoics themselves, however, only Panaetius seems to have dissented (Cic.
Divinat. 1.6).

[22] For other examples see Wolfson (cited n. 17), I, pp. 350–354. It may be
noted that Philo tells the story of Balaam in *Mos.* 1.269–274 without mentioning
the incident of his speaking ass, and in *Cher.* 32–35 he completely allegorizes
the story. See Delling (cited in n. 19), p. 717.

[23] *Deus* 32. For Philo's concept of time, cf. *Fug.* 57; *Jos.* 146; *LA* 3.25;
Mut. 11; *Sacr.* 76; *Mig.* 139; *Ebr.* 48. See J. Whittaker, *God Time Being* (Oslo,

convincing in this matter as those of the Stoics, we should hasten to point out that his procedure seems to have been to speak to his different audiences on various levels of comprehension, a technique which he projected into the biblical narrative itself.[24] In addressing a general audience, for example, he usually sacrifices philosophical rigor to the larger religious need of preserving the integrity of the biblical tradition in the face of the Greek philosophical challenge without appearing to compromise any essentials

1971); S. Lauer, "Philo's Concept of Time," *Journal of Jewish Studies*, IX (1958), 39–46. For rabbinic views on pre-cosmic time, see E. Urbach, *Ḥazal* (Jerusalem, 1969), pp. 186–187 (Hebrew). The tendency to incorporate the biblical miracles into the original order of nature is also found in rabbinic literature (M. Abot 5.6; Bereshit Rabbah 5.3. See Wolfson, *op. cit.*, I, p. 351, n. 24; Urbach, *op. cit.*, p. 95). Cf. Augustine's doctrine of the *semina* implanted into the cosmos at the time of its creation which produce the miracles (*De Trin.* 3.8; *De Gen. ad Litt.* 6.14; 9.16–18). See R. Grant, *Miracle and Natural Law* (Amsterdam, 1952), pp. 218 ff. Philo, like the rabbis, emphasized the miraculous and truly marvellous character of the natural order itself, in contrast to the unfamiliar events which amaze us with their strange novelty (*Mos.* 1.212–213. Cf. Sifra, Shemini 5.52b, p. 218, Finkelstein; Urbach, *op. cit.*, pp. 92–93). The obverse of the tendency to incorporate the miraculous into the order of nature, was the attempt of the Occasionalists to incorporate the order of nature into the category of the miraculous. A Jewish version of this notion was Naḥmanides' doctrine of 'hidden miracles' (in his comment. to Exod. 6:3), and the astrological version of Abraham b. Ezra. A midway position was the doctrine of Baḥya b. Pakuda and Judah Halevi (*Kuzari*, 109), which blend a hidden natural order within that which is manifest in order to regulate all cosmic events in accordance with the biblical doctrine of divine retribution. Even Maimonides, in his *Treatise on Resurrection*, adopts this doctrine. See G. Scholem, *Ursprung und Anfänge der Kabbala* (Berlin, 1962), pp. 400–401.

24 Cf. *Deus* 53 ff.; *Somn.* 1.237; *Fragments of Philo Judaeus*, ed. J. R. Harris (Cambridge, 1886), p. 8; QG 2.54. Johann Mosheim, in his long note on Philo in his Latin translation of R. Cudworth's *True Intellectual System of the Universe* (1773), had already suggested that there were two systems in Philo, the popular religion on the one hand and the more sublime and recondite on the other. See T. H. Billings, *The Platonism of Philo Judaeus* (Chicago, 1919), pp. 6–7. For Philo's very frequent resort to mystery terminology in order to represent the secret level in his theological doctrines, see S. Lilla, *Clement of Alexandria* (Oxford, 1971), pp. 148–149; V. Nikiprowetzky, *Le Commentaire de l'Écriture chez Philon d'Alexandrie* (Leiden, 1977), pp. 17–28.

on either side. It is the nature of such a pedagogical approach that it renders well-nigh impossible any effort to determine with precision which of the two traditions ultimately has the upper hand when irreconcilable differences between them can no longer be adequately suppressed. In the last analysis, it is the subtle inner flow of Philo's general thought which must guide our interpretation of any particular issue that is obscured by the almost deliberate ambiguity projected by so much of his writing.

CLIO AND THE JEWS:
REFLECTIONS ON JEWISH HISTORIOGRAPHY
IN THE SIXTEENTH CENTURY*

By Yosef Hayim Yerushalmi

The fiftieth anniversary of the American Academy for Jewish Research seems to me a propitious time, not only for celebration, but for pause and reflection. While, happily, research into all corridors and corners of the Jewish past has burgeoned far beyond what the small group that founded the Academy could have anticipated five decades ago, it is curious that a sophisticated history of Jewish historiography, one that would examine its theoretical underpinnings, its methods and goals, remains a desideratum. With but few exceptions there seems to be almost a reticence on the part of Judaic scholars to examine and articulate the latent assumptions of the enterprise in which they are engaged. The lag is especially striking at a time when, partly as a result of the ongoing crisis of the historicist view of the world, the general history of historiography as well as the theory and practice of the historian continue to be subjects of intense and widespread concern reflected in a vast and growing literature. If, as I am persuaded, modern historicism may be even more problematic when viewed within Jewish frameworks, the task of clarification becomes all the more urgent.

The following essay, then, is submitted to this *Festschrift*, not so much in an effort to offer a detailed account of sixteenth-century Jewish historiography per se, as in a spirit of introspection concerning the nature and place of Jewish historiography within the broader context of Jewish experience.

---

* This essay is as lightly expanded version of a Hebrew lecture given by me in June of 1977 to the combined faculties of the Institute of Jewish Studies at the Hebrew University in Jerusalem. While adding some necessary footnotes, I have deliberately eschewed an extensive and cumbersome apparatus, and have thus made no attempt to give a bibliography of existing monographs on sixteenth-century Jewish historiography or on individual historical works.

That the sixteenth century witnessed a noteworthy resurgence
of Jewish historical writing has been, of course, long recognized,
though the phenomenon has yet to be properly analyzed and
evaluated. Within the span of a hundred years no less than ten
important historical works were produced by Jews: Solomon Ibn
Verga's "Scepter of Judah" (*Shebet Yehudah*); Abraham Zacuto's
"Book of Genealogies" (*Sefer Yuḥasin*); Elijah Capsali's "Minor
Order of Elijah" *(Seder Eliyahu Zuta)*, and his Chronicle of Venice
(*Dibrey ha-yamim le-malkhut Veneẕiah*); Samuel Usque's Portu-
guese "Consolation for the Tribulations of Israel" (*Consolaçam
as tribulaçoens de Israel*); Joseph Ha-Kohen's "Vale of Tears"
(*'Emek ha-bakha*) and his "History of the Kings of France and of
the Ottoman Turkish Sultans" (*Dibrey ha-yamim le-malkhey-
Ẕarefat u-malkhey bet Ottoman ha-Togar*); Gedaliah Ibn Yahia's
"Chain of Tradition" (*Shalshelet ha-Kabbalah*); Azariah de'
Rossi's "Light of the Eyes" (*Me'or 'Einayim*); David Gans'
"Sprout of David" (*Ẕemaḥ David*).

These works are of interest, not only for the historical data that
can be extracted from them, nor even for the light they cast on the
age in which they were written. In their ensemble they offer a
valuable key with which to probe certain overarching aspects of
the relation of Jews to historical knowledge generally, both before
and after.

I

Any attempt to come to grips with sixteenth-century Jewish
historiography must entail an assessment of what preceded it.
This is no simple matter, for there are fundamental divisions of
opinion as to whether one can even speak at all of Jewish historiography between Josephus Flavius and modern times. Some would
deny its existence altogether. Others have argued that a ramified
historical literature was created. Such debates often come to grief
over essentially semantic issues. Very much depends upon how
the term "historiography" is defined and conceived. On the whole
it seems to me that the negators have proceeded out of a tacit
modern bias which assumes that the only historiography worthy

of the name must be, if not critical or analytic, at least vaguely secular. Clearly, however, such approaches merely enable one to dismiss almost any medieval historical work, and thus preclude any discussion at the very outset.

At the other pole are those who would broaden the perimeters of historiography to embrace any text that has an historical dimension, or that exhibits any interest whatever in history, with a blithe indifference to its avowed aim or its literary form. Here are two instructive instances of this approach:

To this day Moritz Steinschneider's *Die Geschichtsliteratur der Juden*, published in 1905, serves as the standard bibliographical guide to Jewish historical literature from the close of the Talmudic period to the early nineteenth century. But what is *Geschichtsliteratur*? In his introduction Steinschneider cautioned correctly that history is not to be confused with its raw materials. However, the book itself (several other hands were eventually involved in it) stubbornly defies this principle. It is, in essence, a listing of more than three hundred compositions and texts, most of which cannot properly be subsumed under even the most elastic definition of historiography. A handful of historical works are interspersed among such items as private letters, elegies, penitential prayers, Judah Halevi's *Kuzari*, folk-tales and reports of miracles, communal statutes — it would seem almost as if no literary or documentary genre is absent. Like all the works of the master of Jewish bibliography, this one too is packed with information of importance for a variety of fields. For anyone interested in Jewish historiography, however, Steinschneider's list only serves, by its very nature, to blur the issues.

Some thirty-five years later there appeared in Jerusalem an edition of the "diary" of the famous sixteenth-century messianic adventurer David Reubeni (*Sippur David ha-Reubeni*) prepared by A. Z. Aescoly. This book bears also a preliminary title-page, upon which the following is inscribed: *Historiographical Library of the Palestine Historical and Ethnographical Society, Volume I/II*. For the moment we need not pause to inquire whether Reubeni's so-called diary should be considered a work of historiography or merely an historical source. More germane to our concerns is the general introduction to the projected series, entitled "The Historiographical Library and its Program," written by the historian Ben Zion Dinaburg (Dinur) in the name of the Society.[1] "This historiographical library," he states, "belongs to the literature of ingathering. We want to gather into this library all the historiographical works from biblical times until the beginning of modern Jewish historiography." The formulation is instructive: "From biblical times until..." with no caesura along the way. There is here an obvious hint at continuity, as though somehow no significant interruption had ever occurred in the historiographical creativity of the Jewish people. I do not think I am mistaken in my impression. Coming to the Middle Ages, Dinur writes:

> As for Jewish historiography in the Middle Ages (until the Haskalah period), we are of the opinion that as a matter of priority there is need for a detailed bibliographic-literary survey that will present clear and precise information concerning the entire historiographical legacy which has reached us from this period embracing more than a thousand years. This historiographical legacy is by no means poor even in quantity. The number of historiographical works and fragments from this period may reach into the hundreds.

The claim for a medieval Jewish historiographical legacy of such dimensions must seem astonishing, until we read further and realize what is meant:

> The historical ideas which were active and influential in the course of the generations found expression and manifestation not only in the historiographical literature. They frequently defined themselves with great clarity and fullness in other literary forms, in every age, from the prophetic literature of ancient times to the literature of mysticism and ethics, enlightenment and scholarship, in more recent times.

In short, the plan for a "historiographical library" traversed far beyond the bounds of historiography. The notion was to include not only the recorded historical recollections of the Jewish people, but also its meditations on its place among the nations and on its

---

[1] *Sippur David Ha-Reubeni*, ed., A. Z. Aescoly (Jerusalem, 1940), pp. v-xii.

future destiny, as these expressed themselves in any and all literary forms. The details can be read in the Hebrew original and need not be repeated here. It was, in its way, a grandiose project, never executed. Perhaps it had its own intrinsic virtues. But once again we are confronted with a blatant tendency to stretch the concept of "historiography" to comprise phenomena that, whatever the definition, can hardly be squeezed into such a rubric without bursting it asunder and rendering it meaningless.

Now I am not prepared to offer a fixed definition of historiography, nor do the purposes of this essay require it. In the end, any such definition will prove, if not arbitrary, then either artificial or restrictive. However, if the term is to be used responsibly and not be allowed to turn into a random receptacle, one characteristic should be isolated without which I believe it altogether impossible to understand the phenomenon that the term is meant to represent.

The minimal condition to be satisfied emanates from the very word "historiography" in its literal and etymological meaning — and that is simply, the "writing of history" — in the sense of recording events out of the human past. Whatever its other aims, qualities and contents, a "historiographical" work must be anchored in a recital of concrete events that possess a temporal specificity. Those events need not be political. They may be biographical, social, literary. But they must be there. This precondition, to be sure, does not tell us what historiography is. But at least it helps us to differentiate what is *not* historiography.

Historiography is not to be equated with "ideas of history," nor with an interest in historical processes, nor with attitudes and reactions to historical events, nor with efforts to unveil the "meaning" of history. Though any of these elements may be present in an historiographical work, none of them is a decisive feature. For historiography represents a very specific activity, not to be confused with others. At its source lies an impulse to record events of the past that, for one reason or another, are seen as worthy of remembrance.

By contrast, the quest for meaning in history can be pursued in various ways and through different literary genres that have on intrinsic connection with historiography. Indeed, this is largely how it has been pursued. Interpretations of history, whether explicit or implicit, can be found abundantly in works of philosophy, theology, exegesis, mythology, belles-lettres, often without a single mention of historical events or personalities, and with no attempt to relate to them. The distinction would seem to be elementary, and yet it is consistently ignored. At an international symposium on medieval historiography held some years ago at Harvard, much of the discussion centered around Joachim da Fiore. Yet no matter how one may view the importance of Joachite ideas in the evolution of certain Western conceptions of history, I doubt that the admission of the Calabrian abbot to the agenda helped clarify the topic at hand which, one assumed, concerned the writing of history during the Middle Ages.

The same distinctions apply in the Jewish sphere as well. The prophets of Israel may have held highly articulate views about history, and some of the biblical historians may have absorbed those views and written their chronicles on prophetic assumptions, but the prophets were surely not historians, nor, then as now, were the historians prophets. If we leap momentarily to the sixteenth century and compare, say, Rabbi Judah Loew (Maharal) of Prague with his compatriot David Gans, we may easily agree that Maharal had by far the more profound views on the course and meaning of Jewish history. Nevertheless it is Gans, and not he, who was the historian. Similarly, we can often find important historical data in works belonging to various genres, yet the aim of these works is not at all historiographical, and it is not this which characterizes them. In the biblical commentaries of Isaac Abravanel, for example, as well as in his messianic treatises, there are scattered clusters of historical information whose significance is manifest, but this material remains incidental to the whole. Abravanel himself apparently understood the difference and, as is well known, he began to write a separate historical work to be called "Days of Yore" (*Yemot 'olam*).[2]

---

[2] See Abravanel, *Ma'ayeney ha-yeshu'ah* (Ferrara, 1551), Ma'ayan II, Tomer 3, fol. 21v.

These observations, tentative and incomplete as they are, will suffice to orient us toward the subject at hand.

II

We possess, in all branches of Jewish literary creativity in the Middle Ages, a wealth of thought on the position of the Jewish people in history, of *ideas* of Jewish history, but comparatively little interest in *recording* the mundane historical experiences of the Jews since they went into exile. In light of what has been said thus far, the paradox is only apparent. As to whether a Jewish historiography existed before the sixteenth century — such a sharp formulation of the question can only obscure the real problem, which is of a more subtle order. For two things seem to me equally clear: Historical works were certainly written by medieval Jews, although, taken together, they do not constitute a historiographical phenomenon of the sort that is to be found among other peoples in whose midst Jews lived. *Iggeret Rab Sherira*, *Yosippon*, the Hebrew chronicles of the Crusades, and other known works, are certainly historical compositions, not to be removed arbitrarily from the category of "historiography" because of criteria alien to the times in which they were written. Nevertheless, no historiographical tradition ever emerged out of these, no genre with fixed conventions and continuity. The historical works that were written appeared only sporadically. By and large the distance between them in time and space is significant, the periods of silence long. Only in one well-defined area can one speak at all of a genre, and that is the literature of the so-called "chain of tradition" of the Oral Law (*shalshelet ha-kabbalah*), which dealt with the transmission of rabbinic law and doctrine, and with the luminaries who were its bearers through the ages. Only this type of historiography achieved legitimacy and found a home within Judaism, and here alone can one discover a certain continuity of effort, from the anonymous "Order of Mishnaic and Talmudic Sages" (*Seder tanna'im va-'amora'im*) in the ninth century, to the "Order of the Generations" (*Seder ha-dorot*) of Yehiel Heilprin in the eighteenth. Yet for all the variations they exhibit, and despite their significance as historical sources for us today, most of the many compositions of this type did not come into being out of a desire to write the history of the Jewish people. Their chief impulses lay elsewhere, in response to those heretics and antagonists who denied the validity of the Oral Law, in the practical need to determine points of law according to earlier and later authorities, and in a natural curiosity about the evolution of Jewish jurisprudence. Biographical details concerning the rabbis who were the links in the chain of tradition are generally scanty at best, and historical events are scattered about almost haphazardly. At any rate, if we except the literature of the "chain of tradition" there is no historiographical genre in medieval Judaism, only isolated historical works, but these hardly add up to a "legacy."

What I have sketched here is not a retrospective construct. There were Jews in the Middle Ages who understood that such was the situation. Already Moses Ibn Ezra complained about "indolence" and even "sin" on the part of Jews in the neglect of both the Hebrew language and the writing of history:

> ... and they did not succeed to polish their language, to write their chronicles, and to remember their history and traditions. It would have been fitting that they should not have ignored and despised such matters. Behold...all the other nations have exerted themselves to write their histories, and to excel in them....[3]

This written in the twelfth century, and by a Jew living in the midst of a Muslim culture. At the end of the fifteenth century Solomon Ibn Verga, who grew up in Christian Spain, concludes the third chapter of his *Shebet Yehudah* as follows:

> Thus is it found in the chronicles of the kings of Persia which were brought to the king of Spain, according to the custom of the Christians, for they seek to know the things that happened of old in order to take counsel from them, and this because of their distinction and enlightenment.[4]

---

[3] Moses Ibn Ezra, *Kitab al-Muḥādara wal-Mudhākara*, ed. with Hebrew tr. by A. S. Halkin (Jerusalem, 1975), pp. 50 f.

[4] *Shebet Yehudah*, ed. A. Shohat, int. by Y. Baer (Jerusalem, 1947), p. 21.

Significantly, for Ibn Verga it is a *Christian* custom to read historical chronicles, and here there is a note of envy that is at the same time an implicit criticism of his fellow Jews.

Nor is it possible to agree with those who would find an organic connection between various Jewish historical compositions merely because they happened to be written within a certain span of time. One hears, for instance, about "epochs of historical creativity" in the tenth and twelfth centuries,[5] but such an artificial periodization does not convince. Other than a rough chronological coincidence, it is hard to discover a unifying factor around which to group the recital of the events of the Second Commonwealth in *Yosippon*, the description of the affairs of the Babylonian exilarchate in *Sippur Nathan ha-Babli*, and the history of the Talmudic and Gaonic sages presented in *Iggeret Rab Sherira*, though all three were written in the tenth century. Again, there is no discernible link between Ibn Daud's *Sefer ha-kabbalah*, written against a background of the collapse of Jewish life in Muslim Spain, and the Hebrew Crusade chronicles in Germany, that would justify the suggestion of an "epoch of Jewish historiography" in the twelfth century. At best one may view the Crusade chronicles as a discrete unit, flowing out of a great catastrophe and a common spiritual outlook. Even so, no similar phenomenon is known to us from other times and places in the Middle Ages.

I must emphasize that in what I have outlined thus far, no criticism is intended or implied against the Jews of the past. I do not happen to be among those who would fault medieval Jewry for not writing more history. Quite to the contrary, I can conceive that there may yet arise a future generation that will demand of us why we were so preoccupied, not to say obsessed, with history. The writing of history is far from a natural and ubiquitous human activity to be found in every age and in every culture. If Jews in the Middle Ages wrote relatively little history, that does not point to a flaw or lacuna in their civilization, nor, as has sometimes been

5 See H. H. Ben-Sasson, "Li-megamot ha-kronografiah ha-Yehudit shel yemey ha-benayim," in *Historionim v'askolot historiot* (Jerusalem, 1963), p. 30.

alleged, that they lived "outside history." It merely shows that they did not regard historiography as vital to themselves. There were three highways of religious and intellectual creativity among medieval Jews — Halakhah, philosophy and Kabbalah, each of which offered an all-embracing world-view, and none of which required history in order to be cultivated or validated. These alone led to ultimate truths, to spiritual felicity, and to self-knowledge. In comparison, historical works were at best a form of diversion or, at worst, a waste of time.

It is not that Jews felt the past to be irrelevant to the present. But the relevant past was, for them, the distant, ancient past, the periods of the First and Second Temples. What had happened then had determined what had occurred since, and even provided the explanation for what was now transpiring.

With this in mind we can perhaps better understand why it was that *Yosippon* loomed as the single most important chronicle in the eyes of medieval Jews. Apart from the Bible itself, this was the only available work that offered a detailed account of ancient events in the fateful period whose repercussions were felt to extend to all subsequent generations. When, in the thirteenth century, Judah Mosconi enumerates the many virtues of the book, he writes: "For we can read in it the deeds of our ancestors because of whose sins our city was destroyed...and they ate the sour grapes, but our teeth are set on edge."[6] And when, in the generation of the Spanish and Portuguese exiles, Tam Ibn Yahia sponsored a new edition of *Yosippon* published in Constantinople in 1510, he stated in his introduction:

> And I, in the midst of the exile, wallowing in the blood of the upheavals that are overtaking my people and nation, was roused by my soul and spirit to be among those who have helped to print this book, for this is the one that has laid bare the source of the misfortunes of the House of Judah.[7]

[6] First printed in *Ozar Tob* (supplement to *Magazin für die Wissenschaft des Judenthums*) (Berlin, 1877–78), pp. 17 ff. Reprinted in *Sefer Yosippon*, ed. H. Hominer (Jerusalem, 1965), p. 37.

[7] Reprinted by Hominer, *op. cit.*, p. 41.

Moreover, the book had the good fortune to be accepted as an original work written by Josephus Flavius in the aftermath of the destruction of the Second Temple. Thereby *Yosippon* acquired a halo of authority in the eyes of Jews that was vouchsafed to no other medieval historical work, and that would have been denied it altogether if it had been regarded as the work of a Jew living in southern Italy in the tenth century. Much of the attitude toward *Yosippon* in particular and, by contrast, to historiography in general, is revealed in the following statement by Tam Ibn Yahia:

> Although it is characteristic of historical works to exaggerate things that never existed, to add to them, to invent things that never were, nevertheless this book [*Yosippon*], although it is part of the same genre, is completely distinct from them, and it is the difference between truth and falsehood. For all the words of this book are righteousness and truth, and there is no wrong within it. And the mark of this is that of all the books written after the Holy Scriptures this is [chronologically] the closest to prophecy, having been written before the Mishnah and the Talmud.[8]

In the same manner we begin to understand why, besides the literature of the "chain of tradition," whose very aim necessitated a survey of all the generations of halakhic endeavor in order to argue their unbroken continuity, there is not a single medieval Jewish chronicle that attempts to give a continuous history of what had occurred since the destruction of the Second Temple. The chronological span is generally short, with most compositions confined to contemporary events or those close to the time of the author, usually relating what happened during a persecution. There is little or no attempt to bridge events from one generation to another. More significantly, in most cases there is little search for specific explanations of what had occurred, and in fact the events described are not regarded essentially as novelties. Only in two instances can one detect a full consciousness that something genuinely new has happened and that there is a special importance to the events themselves. In Ibn Daud's *Sefer ha-kabbalah* there is a keen awareness of certain processes as a result of which, in his

---

[8] *Ibid.*, p. 43.

view, spiritual and cultural hegemony among the Jews passed first
from Babylonia to the Iberian Peninsula, and in his own time from
Muslim to Christian Spain. In the Crusade chronicles there is a
palpable sense of the terrifying shift in the relations between Jewry
and Christendom, and an expression of astonished awe at this first
instance of Jewish mass martyrdom on European soil. But Ibn
Daud and the authors of the Crusade chronicles are, in this sense,
exceptional rather than exemplary. On the whole, medieval Jewish
chronicles tend to assimilate events to old and established conceptual frameworks. Persecution and suffering are, after all, the
result of the conditions of exile, and exile itself is the bitter fruit
of ancient sins. It is important to realize that there is also no real
desire to find novelty in passing events. On the contrary, we find a
pronounced tendency to subsume major new events to familiar
archetypes, perhaps because even terrible events are less terrifying
when viewed in patterns rather than in their bewildering specificity.
Thus the new oppressor is Haman and the court-Jew is Mordecai.
Christendom is Edom or Esau, and Islam is Ishmael. Samuel
ha-Nagid is David, and the Andalusian landscape is biblical.
The essential contours of the relationship between Israel and the
Gentiles have been delineated long ago in the Aggadah, and there is
little or no interest in the history of contemporary nations. In
periods of acute messianic tension there may be a spurt of interest
in global events and so, for example, we have texts stemming from
the first century after the rise of Islam as a world power out of
which we can reconstruct minute details of the progress of the
Arab conquests.[9] But there is no historiography here, only a des-
perate apocalyptic equation. The Arab conquests are seen, in
essence, as the wars of Gog and Magog which are to bring an end
to history.

Not that there was a waning in the vitality of Jewish collective

[9] Most of the important apocalyptic texts of this period are assembled in
Y. Eben-Shmuel, *Midreshey ge'ulah*, 2nd ed. (Jerusalem, 1954). Cf. also B.
Lewis, "An Apocalyptic Vision of Islamic History" [analysis and translation
of *Tefilat R. Shimon bar Yohai*], *Bulletin of the School of Oriental and African
Studies*, XIII (1949-51), 308-338.

memory in the Middle Ages, but that it did not express itself or function through historiography. Jewish historical memory had other channels: synagogal poetry (*seliḥot* and *piyyutim*); *Memorbücher*, whose lists of martyrs were kept by the community; special fast-days; "Second Purims." That which was placed into such vessels, that which was transfigured liturgically and ritually, was endowed with a chance for survival and permanence. Ordinary chronicles and historical texts were neglected and forgotten, unless (and here again I refer to the literature of the "chain of tradition") they were of halakhic significance, or were embedded in halakhic or theological works. Most medieval Jewish historical writings went down to oblivion, and they are in our hands today only because they were rediscovered and published by scholars in modern times. Should one desire to know what was the medieval historiographical "legacy" available to Jewish readers after the year 1500, it is only necessary to glance at the development of Hebrew printing. In addition to the ever popular *Yosippon*, only four historical works out of the past were printed in the course of the sixteenth century: *Iggeret Rab Sherira*, *Seder 'Olam Rabba* and *Seder 'Olam Zuta*, and the *Sefer ha-kabbalah* of Ibn Daud[10] (which usually included his brief sketches of the history of the Second Commonwealth and of the Roman emperors). This was, in effect, the entire "historiographical library" that remained in general circulation from all the preceding generations.

Even if we take into consideration everything that had been written, in the final analysis the Jewish historiographical literature of the Middle Ages was sparse enough, and modern attempts to inflate its dimensions only prove how important historiography is to us. Here I must stress once again that if medieval Jews generally did not write history it was not out of lack of talent, nor even for lack of knowledge, but primarily because they felt no need to do so. It just was not sufficiently important to them, for reasons I have

---

[10] Sherira's epistle was first printed with Zacuto's *Yuḥasin* (Constantinople, 1566). The other three works were generally printed together in one volume (Mantua, 1513–14; Venice, 1545; Basel, 1580).

suggested. None of the other explanations usually advanced will suffice. It has been said that sufferings and persecutions numbed the historical creativity of the Jews, that they wrote no history because, lacking a state and political power, they had no history to write about, or that it was because they had neither royal chroniclers nor monks who could devote themselves to historical writing. Such explanations are, however, no more than a form of second-guessing, and they are ultimately self-liquidating. All the aforementioned factors were equally true of the Jewish people in the sixteenth century. Yet in that time a corpus of Jewish historiography was created which surpassed, in scope and quality, all that had come before.

III

Only in the sixteenth century do we encounter, for the first time, a cultural phenomenon within Jewry that can be recognized with little hesitation as genuinely historiographical, though each book that was produced was quite different from the other. As we noted at the outset, ten major works were written. Of their eight authors, five were either exiles from Spain and Portugal or descendants of exiles (Ibn Verga, Zacuto, Usque, Joseph ha-Kohen, Gedaliah Ibn Yahia). One, Elijah Capsali of Crete, was profoundly influenced by Spanish refugees. Only two, Azariah de' Rossi and David Gans, emerge out of a non-Sephardic ambiance (Mantua and Prague, respectively), and their books present special problems. Patently, the primary stimulus to the rise of Jewish historiography in the sixteenth century was the tremendous catastrophe that had overtaken the Jews in the Iberian Peninsula. That is to say, for the first time we encounter a ramified historiographical response to a great historic event. So far as we know, no event in the Middle Ages, not even the Crusades, engendered a comparable literature. In addition to the historical works proper, almost all branches of sixteenth-century Jewish literature are replete with accounts of the Spanish Expulsion of 1492, of the forced conversion that followed in Portugal only five years later, and of the sufferings of the exiles on land and sea. Yet this had hardly been the first expulsion of a European Jewry. The expulsion from France in 1306, while not of the same dimensions, had been no paltry affair. Gersonides had written of the number of French exiles as "twice those who emerged from Egypt."[11] But except for the passage in his commentary on the Pentateuch there are almost no references in fourteenth-century Jewish texts to that great upheaval. The contrast is glaring.

Certainly there must have been more than one reason for this. But above all, there is a highly articulated feeling among the generations following the expulsion from Spain that something unprecedented had taken place. Not only that an abrupt end had come to a great and venerable Jewry, but also something beyond that. Precisely because this expulsion was not the first but, in a sense, the *last*, it was felt to have altered the face of Jewry and of history itself. When Abravanel enumerates the various European expulsions that began from England in 1290, he perceives the expulsion from Spain as the climax and culmination of a process that has shifted the Jewish people, globally, from the West to the East.[12] The larger significance of the Spanish Expulsion is that because of it Western Europe has been emptied of Jews. When Abraham Zacuto compares the expulsions from Spain and Portugal with the earlier French expulsion, he understands the radical difference. Relating that a forebear of his had been among the Jewish refugees from France who had found an immediate haven across the border in Spain, he exclaims: "And from France they came to Spain. But we faced the enemies on one side, and the sea on the other!"[13]

That historical crisis should stimulate historical writing comes as no surprise. To take but one pertinent instance, Hans Baron has shown the nexus between the rise of Italian humanist historiography and the breakdown of the republican system in the Italian

---

[11] Gersonides, *Perush 'al ha-Torah*, on Lev. 26:38.

[12] Abravanel, *Perush nebi'im aharonim*, on Is. 43:6.

[13] Zacuto, *Sefer Yuhasin*, ed. H. Filipowski, int. by A. H. Freimann (Frankfurt a.M., 1924), p. 223.

city-states.[14] The resemblance ends there, however. Except for Azariah de' Rossi, we do not find that the spirit of Italian humanist historiography was absorbed into sixteenth-century Jewish historiography, though some Jewish historians drew information from it. The elements of humanist culture that crop up in the works of Joseph ha-Kohen or Gedaliah Ibn Yahia should not mislead us in this respect, for in the end they remain external trappings. Nor, as is commonly supposed, does the *Shebet Yehudah* of Ibn Verga betray influences of the Italian Renaissance.[15] Recent research has shown that Ibn Verga never came to Italy, but died in Flanders shortly after fleeing from Portugal.[16] If there are external influences in his book they should be sought, as I have long supposed, in the Iberian cultural milieu that was closest to him. But in general the dynamics of Jewish historiography after the Spanish expulsion are imminent to itself and related to what had happened within Jewry. Jews who were "wallowing in the blood of the upheavals" wanted to understand the meaning of those upheavals and, as Ibn Verga put it, "Why this enormous wrath?"

IV

Jewish historiography in the generations following the expulsion from Spain does not only constitute a novum, but was felt as such. The awareness of novelty is expressed most vividly by Joseph ha-Kohen, in an exultant passage that deliberately echoes the biblical Song of Deborah:

> All my people is aware that no author has arisen in Israel comparable to Yosippon the priest, who wrote of the war of the land of Judea and of Jerusalem. The chroniclers ceased in Israel, they

[14] See Hans Baron, *The Crisis of the Early Italian Renaissance*, 2 vols. (Princeton, 1955), especially chs. 1–3.

[15] This view derives from Yitzhak Baer. See his introduction to Shohat's edition of *Shebet Yehudah*, pp. 11, 13 f., as well as his "He'arot ḥadashot le-Sefer Shebet Yehudah," *Tarbiz*, VI (1934–35), 152–179, and *Galut* (Eng. tr.) (New York, 1947), pp. 77 ff.

[16] See M. Benayahu, "Makor 'al megorashey Sefarad be-Portugal ve-ẓetam 'aharey gezerat RaSaV le-Saloniki," *Sefunot*, XI (1971–78), 233–265.

ceased, until I, Joseph, did arise, until I did arise, a chronicler in Israel! And I set my heart to write as a remembrance in a book the bulk of the troubles that have been visited upon us in Gentile lands, from the day that Judah was exiled from its land until the present day.[17]

For all the hyperbole in this passage, it deserves special attention. Joseph ha-Kohen was acquainted with the Jewish historical works of others and drew from them ("I gleaned among the sheaves after the harvesters, whatever my hand could find"). Nonetheless, he considers himself a new creature. Since Yosippon (and let us remember that for him Yosippon was Josephus Flavius of the first century), "the chroniclers ceased in Israel." He states this as something of common knowledge ("all my people knows"), and in terms of the psychology revealed, this testimony is impressive. There is here a consciousness that to write history is something new for Jews, a new beginning after a very long hiatus. Yet if, as he has tacitly admitted, there were historical works in former ages, whence does this feeling arise? What is there about his manner of writing history that enables him to style himself the first Jewish historian since Josephus? Indeed, since we are concerned here not with Joseph ha-Kohen alone, we may well broaden the question. What, in essence, are the novelties within sixteenth-century Jewish historiography as a whole?

To begin with, these works cover a temporal and geographical span far beyond anything that can be found previously. They do not focus merely upon this or that persecution or set of events, but attempt, within the limits of the data available to their authors, a coherent and consecutive survey of many centuries, in an expansive and detailed narration.

A new element is the prominence assigned to postbiblical Jewish history. For the first time we sense a keen interest in the entire course of Jewish history from the destruction of the Second Temple down to the authors' own time. The *Shebet Yehudah* is concerned almost exclusively with events that have occurred since

---

[17] Joseph b. Joshua ha-Kohen, *Sefer dibrey ha-yamim le-malkhey Ẓarefat u-malkhey Bet Ottoman ha-Togar* (ed. Amsterdam, 1733), preface.

the loss of Jewish independence and especially during the Middle Ages. Joseph ha-Kohen begins his *'Emek ha-bakha*: "And it came to pass *after* all the glory had departed from Jerusalem." If he opens his *Dibrey ha-yamim* with "Adam begat Seth," it is only in order to establish the genealogies of the nations, and after half a page he plunges the reader into the seventh century of the Common Era and the rise of Islam. In Usque's Portuguese work there is a clear triple periodization based, not upon the literary history of scholars and sages, but upon the larger rhythms of Jewish history: the periods of the First and the Second Temples, and a third period that comprises "all the tribulations Israel has suffered since the loss of the Second Temple, destroyed by the Romans, until this day." To this third period he devotes as much space as to the other two combined.

This points also to a new attitude toward the history of Jewry in exile. While, by and large, the Jewish historians of the sixteenth century believe, no less than prior generations, that "for our sins were we exiled," and that "the fathers ate sour grapes and the teeth of the sons are set on edge," they do not regard this as a warrant to gloss over the history of those very sons. On the contrary, they lavish their attention upon it. Thus they bestow a new value upon the events that have transpired over the entire course of the Middle Ages. They seem to recognize implicitly that these events too have a meaning for the present and the future which cannot be grasped merely by focusing attention on ancient times, and that they are therefore worth recalling. All this marks a significant change in outlook.

A final novelty is the renewed interest in the history of the nations, especially of the contemporary nations, in which a desire to know various aspects of non-Jewish history combines with an incipient recognition that Jewish destinies are affected by the interplay of relations between certain of the great powers. To these categories belong such books as Capsali's Chronicle of Venice, and large portions of his *Seder Eliyahu Zuta*[18] which are devoted

---

18 See now the recent edition of both the *Seder Eliyahu Zuta* and the Venetian

to the history of the Ottoman Empire. In fact, for all its archaic theological presuppositions, the latter work may properly be regarded as a first attempt to write Jewish history within the framework of general history. From Joseph ha-Kohen we possess not only the chronicle of the kings of France and Turkey, but his Hebrew translations (with insertions of his own) of Francisco López de Gómara's *Historia general de las Indias* (*Ha-India ha-ḥadashah*) and *La conquista de Mexico* (*Sefer Fernando Cortes*).[19] On another level mention should also be made of the various sections dealing with general history in Zacuto's *Sefer Yuḥasin* and Ibn Yahia's *Shalshelet ha-kabbalah*.[20] And of course the entire second part of David Gans' *Ẓemaḥ David*, although, as already indicated, this book arises out of a different cultural setting.

Taken together, the features enumerated thus far are impressive enough, and for that very reason there is no need to inflate their proportions. Jewish historiography in the wake of the Spanish expulsion marks a leap forward when viewed over and against what had preceded it. Within other perspectives its stature tends to diminish. It never reached the level of critical insight to be found in the best of general historical scholarship contemporary with it. Moreover, although ten full-fledged historical works following so closely upon one another mark, for Jews, a period of relatively intense historiographical activity, they do represent but a tiny fraction of the sum of sixteenth-century Jewish literature.

Yet these reservations do not absolve us of our primary duty, which is to evaluate this corpus of historiography within its own context, as one among a gamut of Jewish responses to the trauma of the expulsion from Spain. From this vantage-point the work

chronicle by A. Shmuelevitz, S. Simonsohn and M. Benayahu, 2 vols. (Jerusalem, 1976-77).

[19] Both works are extant in four manuscripts: Paris (Alliance, H81A); Berlin (160); New York (Columbia University, K82); Moscow (Günzberg, 212). All of these also contain his Hebrew version of Joannes Boemius' historical-geographical work *Omnium gentium mores, leges et ritus.*

[20] To these we may also properly add the account of the reign of Suleiman the Magnificent in the Judeo-Spanish *Extremos y grandezas de Constantinople,* written by the sixteenth-century Salonikan rabbi Moses Almosnino.

YERUSHALMI [20]

of the sixteenth-century Jewish historians may properly be seen as a significant attempt, however tentative, to pave the way among Jews toward a concern with the historical dimension of their existence. In itself this phenomenon was laden with potential for future development and, had it continued, who knows where it might not have led. Seen in retrospect, however, we must conclude that it was an attempt that failed.

It was not, essentially, a failure of the historians, though their limitations are obvious in themselves and deserve to be spelled out.

For all their innovations, they could not free themselves from conceptions and modes of thought that had been deeply rooted among Jews for many ages. We have said that events since the destruction of the Second Temple received a new appreciation, and so they did. But in general these events are perceived as important, not because of any causal connection between them, but because the historians seek to find within them hints, configurations, and meanings that lie beyond them. The historical episodes that Usque narrates derive their significance, not from any intrinsic links they might have to one another, but from his conviction that these events are fulfillments of biblical prophecies that predicted what would happen to the Jewish people in exile. By his own time, Usque believed, even the most dire of biblical prophecies had come to pass, and hence redemption was imminent. All that was lacking was that the Portuguese Marranos return openly to Judaism.

Messianic impulses are discernible in both the *'Emek ha-bakha* and *Dibrey ha-yamim* of Joseph ha-Kohen, even though his messianism is generally restrained and often veiled. He himself hints at the messianic framework in a passage repeated in both books, declaring: "The expulsions from France as well as this exceedingly bitter exile [i.e., from Spain] have roused me to compose this book, so that the Children of Israel may know what [the Gentiles] have done to us in their lands, their courts and their castles, *for behold the days approach.*"[21] Behind the "Chronicle

---

[21] *'Emek ha-bakha,* ed. M. Letteris (Krakow, 1895), pp. 102 f.; *Sefer dibrey ha-yamim,* ed. cit., Pt. I, fol. 36v. Cf. also the account of the martyred

of the Kings of France and of the Ottoman Turkish Sultans"
there hovers a veneı able apocalyptic tradition. Although, charac-
teristically, Joseph ha-Kohen does not allow apocalyptic elements
to erupt into the foreground, his book is not a mere exercise in
French and Turkish history, but an attempt to trace the age-old
struggle between Christendom and Islam, whose leading contemporary standard-bearers were perceived by him as France
and the Ottoman Empire. The explicit history remains that of the
French and the Turks; the tradition, however muted — that of
Gog and Magog.

The messianic theme of the *Seder Eliyahu Zuta* is so dominant
as to leave no doubt of Elijah Capsali's intentions. The entire
book is messianic history at its most exubeıant. It is saturated
with biblical messianic language and typologies, and the Turkish
sultans are cast in the redemptive image of Cyrus the Great.

In Ibn Verga's *Shebet Yehudah* there is, by contrast, not a trace
of messianism, and in seveıal respects its boldness and originality
are impressive. Ibn Verga alone transfers the concept of "natural
cause" (*ha-sibbah ha-tib'it*) from the sphere of philosophy and
science to history and, as Yitzhak Baer has shown, it is he who
went farthest in exploring the mundane causes of Jewish histoıical
suffering generally, and of the Spanish expulsion in paıticular.
Still, it remains a fundamental error to consider Ibn Verga, as
some have, to be merely a ıationalist with a precociously secular
conception of Jewish history. The truth is that his use of "natural
cause" by no means precludes or contradicts the notion of divine
providence. A close reading of the book will also reveal to what
extent Ibn Verga was still bound by attitudes that had crystalized
ages ago among the Hispano-Jewish aristocracy and no longer
corresponded to the historical realities of his time.[22]

messianic enthusiast Solomon Molkho in the latter work (Pt. II, fol. 19v),
introduced by the significant phrase: "And a shoot came forth from Portugal
(*va-yeẓe ḥoter mi-Portugal*), Solomon Molkho was his name."

[22] See Y. H. Yerushalmi, *The Lisbon Massacre of 1506 and the Royal Image
in the "Shebet Yehudah"* (Cincinnati, 1976), Supplement No. 1, *Hebrew Union
College Annual.*

All of these features, however regressive they might seem to modern eyes, do not detract from the essential achievements of the historians. A mixture of old and new is to be expected in the initial phases of almost any cultural development. The fate of sixteenth-century Jewish historiography was ultimately determined by an inheritance of a different order — the attitude among Jews toward historical works generally.

We have noted that historiography had never become a legitimate and recognized genre in medieval Judaism. This meant that except for Zacuto and Ibn Yahia, who continued to write within the familiar and accepted mold of the "chain of tradition," the Jewish historians of the sixteenth century found no available slot into which to fit their work. Each, in fact, had to create his own individual forms. But though it made their task more difficult, it is not even this that ultimately defeated them. Something else had passed over from centuries gone by, namely, the relatively low esteem in which historical works of any kind were held by most Jews. Despite their own occasional disclaimers (we shall examine these shortly), it can hardly be doubted that the sixteenth-century historians felt themselves engaged in something that was of high seriousness and purpose. Whether they were taken by the Jewish public as seriously as they deserved, or even correctly understood, is questionable.

Though the reading public of the past is silent almost by definition, there are indirect ways of gauging the attitudes with which our authors had to contend. Most of the historical works under consideration are preceded by introductions filled with apology for the very fact that the writer is dealing with history at all, and offering a host of reasons to justify such a concern. Why was all this necessary? Because the historian knew very well the nature of the audience that awaited him. If even Zacuto, writing within a literary tradition in which distinguished rabbinic scholars of the past had already participated, still feels called upon to declare with a self-deprecatory shrug — "I cannot presume to say that it is a deep science, for because of my sins, as a result of the many persecutions and the want of a livelihood, I have neither strength nor wisdom"[23] — then how much more is there need for special pleading when David Gans presents his detailed chronology of the Gentile nations. These and other apologia go far beyond conventional literary protestations of modesty. Here it is not really the authors' capacities that are at issue, but the value of the enterprise itself. All the introductions sound a common note. It is as though the historian were saying in the same breath: "Dear reader, although both of us know that what I am writing is unimportant, nevertheless it is important...."

A somewhat whimsical but revealing example of another kind can be found in the first edition of the *Dibrey ha-yamim* (Sabbionetta, 1554). We recall the exultant cry of Joseph ha-Kohen in his preface to the work: "The chroniclers ceased, they ceased... until I arose." But in old printed books it is worthwhile to read all the preliminary matter. In this instance, along with the author's introduction, the following verses are inscribed:

> When the author's nephew, Zerahiah Halevi,
> Saw the glory of this book, and the nectar of its honeycombed
> > words,
> The Lord lifted his spirit and he began to speak.
> So he opened his mouth with song and hymn, and declared:
> *Let anyone who delights in a time that was before ours*
> *Take this chronicle and read it when his sleep wanders*, [italics mine]
> For in it he will see the history of the nations,
> And should he merit to witness the end of our exile,
> He will understand the difference between the destiny of the
> > Gentile kings and of our Messiah.

Leaving aside the somewhat curious ending, we may focus upon the lines I have placed in italics. Faint praise this, one might say, in a poem purporting to extol the book. After all, even Bach's "Goldberg Variations," though composed expressly for a case of insomnia, were not intended exclusively for nocturnal performances. Certainly we understand that there is a biblicism lurking behind Zerahiah Halevi's lines (Esther 6:1, "On that night the king's sleep wandered, and he commanded to bring the book of

---

[23] *Yuḥasin*, ed. cit., Author's introduction, p. 1.

records and chronicles...."). But it is also more than a neat turn of
a biblical phrase, and deserves to be taken seriously. Historical
chronicles are to be read "when sleep wanders" (*bi-nedod shenah*),
for otherwise such reading is *bittul Torah*, a waste of time that
could otherwise be devoted to the serious study of sacred texts.
In fact, Zeraḥiah's attitude is by no means unusual. Despite Tam
Ibn Yahia's veneration for *Yosippon*, he is at pains to add in his
introduction to the work that especially "the merchants who are
immersed in temporal successes, and who have not turned to the
Torah in their leisure time, will delight in reading it."[24]

Of all the historical works, Ibn Verga's *Shebet Yehudah* was to
enjoy the widest popularity. I have examined no less than seventeen
different editions printed from the mid-sixteenth century to the
end of the eighteenth, and there may be others. What was at the
heart of this extraordinary success? How was the book read, and
what did its readers see in it? I think one may safely assume that
only isolated readers grasped Ibn Verga's intentions in exploring
the Spanish expulsion and the situation of Jews in Christian
society. There are sufficient indications that what seems central
to us in the book was not what attracted most readers, but rather
other matters. It is interesting, for example, to follow the meta-
morphoses in the texts of the title-pages of the *Shebet Yehudah*,
for these were aimed at focusing the reader's attention on what
were considered the highlights within. Already in the title-page of
the first edition (Adrianople, 1553), published more than four
decades after Solomon Ibn Verga's death, the following description
of the book is given (the words are not of the author, but of the
editor, Joseph Ibn Verga, or the printer):

> This is a book of the generations of Israel, and of the many
> misfortunes that have come upon the Jews in the lands of the

----

[24] *Yosippon*, ed. Hominer, p. 43. Compare, in the seventeenth century,
Joseph Delmedigo's list of recommended readings to the Karaite Zeraḥ ben
Menahem. The historical works, largely those with which we have been dealing,
are endorsed "for cheering the soul when one is sad" (*le-ta'anug ha-nefesh
bi-she'at ha-'iẓabon*). For the text, see S. Assaf, *Mekorot le-toledot ha-ḥinnukh
be-Yisrael* (Tel-Aviv, 1936), I, 101.

nations.... And so it tells of the blood-libel, how many times its falsehood was revealed and made public, and Israel emerged delivered. Similarly, it speaks of religious disputations that were held in the presence of kings, as well as the ceremony of installing the princes [i.e., the exilarchs] in various periods.... Finally, it depicts the structure of the Temple and its inner precincts, the service of the High Priest when he came to his chamber before the Day of Atonement, and the order of the Passover sacrifice, which we shall yet see with our own eyes, as we were promised by our Creator, the lord of compassion.

What is so frustrating about this harbinger of the modern publisher's blurb is the fact that technically each detail is correct, yet the total impression is so far removed from the inner spirit of the book. By the time we come to the third edition, a Yiddish translation printed in Krakow in 1591 "for ordinary householders, men and women" (*far gemayne baale-batim, man un vayber*) we can see from the title-page that the *Shebet Yehudah* has been transmuted perceptually into a standard piece of edifying folk-literature:

> One will find in it marvelous stories of what happened to our fathers in exile, and how many times they underwent martyrdom, the book also specifying in which times and in which countries it all happened, so that a person's heart will be roused to the fear of God. May the Blessed Lord in His infinite mercy and grace continue to keep His people from all evil calamities, and send us the redeemer, Messiah son of David, speedily and in our own days.

More examples could be adduced, but the point remains. The attitude toward historiography among sixteenth-century readers was no different, by and large, from what it had been in prior ages. An historical work was regarded as something pleasant and diverting in moments of leisure, and at best a source of moral uplift. Works concerned with the history of Gentile nations were still described generically as "books of wars" (*sifrey milḥamot*), and in halakhic literature opinions continued divided about whether one is permitted to read them, and when, and in what language.[25]

---

[25] See, for example, Joseph Karo, *Shulḥan ʾArukh*, Oraḥ ḥayyim, no. 307:16, and the gloss of Moses Isserles *ad loc.*

V

Still, one Jewish historical work of the sixteenth century, though
not a chronicle, was received with sufficient seriousness to produce
some very interesting repercussions. I have in mind Azariah de'
Rossi's collection of historical and antiquarian essays, entitled
Me'or 'Einayim and first published in Mantua in 1573–75. Unlike
the other books with which we have been dealing, the *Me'or
'Einayim* has no links to the Spanish expulsion and the spiritual
crisis it provoked. It is rather the fruit of a creative encounter, in
the mind of an Italian rabbi, between Jewish tradition and Italian
Renaissance culture. Unlike so many other books written by
Italian Jews which display a veneer of humanistic learning, here
the humanist spirit has penetrated the very vitals of the work, and
only here do we find the real beginnings of historical criticism.
The *Me'or 'Einayim* remains the most audacious Jewish historical
work of the sixteenth century. Its essential daring lies in Azariah's
reluctance to set up predetermined boundaries between his general
and Jewish knowledge, in his readiness to allow a genuine confrontation between the two spheres, and in his acceptance of the
conclusions that seemed to flow out of it.

For our present purpose the most instructive aspect of the book
lies in what it reveals about the audience and the spiritual climate
of the time. Throughout his writing Azariah shows himself particularly sensitive to public opinion. He writes with utmost care,
and is even prepared to make certain compromises so long as
they do not involve basic principles. Time and again he interrupts
his discussions in order to comment on the objections he anticipates
from his potential readers. Thus, in speaking of various Talmudic
references to the massacre of Alexandrian Jewry:

> Let us now turn back to the city of Alexandria. Our eyes behold
> three different passages concerning it, for the Jerusalem Talmud has
> stated that the evil murderer was Trajan...and the Babylonian
> Talmud in tractate Sukkah said it was Alexander of Macedon,
> while in tractate Gittin it changed its opinion to write that it was
> Hadrian. And if we have now begun to investigate the [historical]
> truth of these matters, that is not because of the thing in itself, for
> what was — was [*mai de-havah havah*], but only because we are

concerned that the words of our sages in relating well-known events should not appear to contradict one another.[26]

Later on, in the same chapter:

At any rate, even were we to admit that some stories reached the ears of the sages with some distortion, and that this is how they related them to us, that in no way diminishes their stature.... And even though this chapter consists mostly of inconsequential investigations [*hakirot shel mah be-khakh*], for it will be said "what was — was, and there is in it no relevance to law or observance," still, the refined soul yearns to know the truth of everything.[27]

And again, in his strictures on the computation of the traditional Jewish era of Creation:

Before we leave this subject it will become clear that the manner in which they, of blessed memory, computed the years was considered a noble science whose worth was known and proclaimed by every enlightened person. However, I can foresee that you will say to yourself, dear reader: "But surely such an investigation is completely farfetched [*hilkheta de-meshiha*, lit: "law for the time of the Messiah"] and even worse, for what have we to do with all this, considering that what was — was, several thousand years ago or more?"[28]

There are many such passages in the *Me'or 'Einayim*, and they demonstrate vividly the reactions that Azariah expected from his readers. He was wary of them on two counts. His overall concern was that they had a low opinion of any historical investigation. "What was — was." This phrase seems to sum up for him the prevalent Jewish mood, and it surfaces so frequently in the book as to be almost a leitmotif. More specifically, however, he sus-

---

[26] *Sefer Me'or 'Einayim*, ed. D. Cassel (Vilna, 1866; reprint, Jerusalem, 1970), I, 182. The phrase *mai de-havah* derives from the Talmud (Yoma, fol. 5v), where the question of the manner in which Aaron and his sons were dressed in their priestly garments is temporarily rejected as being of purely antiquarian interest ("what was — was"). On Azariah's methodology as a whole, see Salo Baron, "La méthode historique d'Azaria de' Rossi," *REJ*, LXXXVI (1928), 151–175; LXXXVII (1929), 43–78.

[27] *Me'or 'Einayim*, I, 189.

[28] *Ibid.*, II, 275.

pected that some of the contents of the book would be construed
as a denigration of the Talmudic sages.

As it turned out, his worries were not in vain. The book was
printed and immediately attacked. In various Italian Jewish
communities it was placed under rabbinic ban.[29] Rumblings were
heard from Prague and from Safed in Palestine.[30] Some rose in
defense of the book. But the question remains — what, in essence,
stirred up the tempest? Azariah was no heretic, but a respected
physician-scholar whose personal piety was not in question.
Mantua was a center of Jewish intellectuals well attuned to the
cultural currents of the time. Indeed, most of the Italian rabbis
who signed the ban were not obscurantists, but men of fairly
broad secular culture.

Could it really have been Azariah's debunking of the rabbinic
legend about the gnat that entered Titus' head through the nose
and finally killed him?[31] Azariah himself relates that there were
Jews who sharply criticized this passage in his book and regarded
what he had done as an insult to the sages. But could the critique
of such an *aggadah* really have seemed like a novelty in the sixteenth century? Did there not already exist long and recognized
traditions within Judaism, whether philosophical or kabbalistic,
which could not accept rabbinic *aggadot* literally, and which
strove to reinterpret them rationally or mystically, at times to the
most radical extremes? In what manner, then, had Azariah de'
Rossi transgressed?

I would suggest that the answer lies, not in the fact of Azariah's
criticism, but in its source, method, and conclusion. Philosophic

---

[29] See David Kaufmann, "Contributions à l'histoire des luttes d'Azaria
de Rossi," *REJ*, XXXIII (1896), 77–87; *idem*, "La défense de lire le Meor
Enayim d'Azaria de Rossi," *REJ*, XXXVIII (1899), 280–281. Cf. S. Z. H. Halb-
erstamm, "Sheloshah ketabim 'al debar Sefer Me'or 'Einayim," in *Tehilah
le-Mosheh* (Leipzig, 1896), Steinschneider Festschrift; Hebrew Section, pp. 1–8.

[30] See the attack of Judah Loew b. Bezalel (Maharal), *Be'er ha-golah* (New
York, 1969), pp. 126–141, and the report of a ban issued by Joseph Karo on
his deathbed, published by Kaufmann in his aforementioned article in *REJ*,
XXXIII.

[31] *Me'or 'Einayim*, I, 214–219.

and kabbalistic critiques and reinterpretations of *aggadah* possessed an age-old legitimacy even though, to be sure, there still
remained Jews in Azariah's time who would not accept even
these.[32] The essential innovation in Azariah's approach lay in his
attempt to evaluate *aggadot*, not within the framework of philosophy or Kabbalah, each a source of truth for its partisans, but by
the use of profane history which few, if any, would accept as a
truth by which the words of the sages might be judged. Worse than
that, Azariah ventured to employ non-Jewish historical sources
for this purpose, drawn from Greek, Roman and Christian writers.
Above all, he did not flinch from the conclusions that emerged
out of the comparison, even when these affected so sensitive an
area as calendar computation. As for Titus' gnat, Azariah would
not reinterpret the legend metaphorically or allegorically, nor did
he spiritualize it in any way in order to salvage it. Citing Roman
and other historians as to the actual date and cause of Titus' death,
he dismissed the story as historically untrue. Such historical
critiques could not yet be tolerated, let alone assimilated, by
Azariah's Jewish contemporaries. On the contrary, it is perhaps
a token of the flexibility of Italian Jewry that the ban upon the
book (it was not pronounced against the author, and only required
that special permission be obtained by those who wanted to read it)
was not always enforced stringently, and there were some who
continued to read it in subsequent generations. Azariah's experi-
ment, however, remained his alone. There were no heirs to his
method.

In a vital sense that is true of sixteenth-century Jewish historiography as a whole. In retrospect we see it as a sudden flowering,
and an equally abrupt withering. It produces no real continuity
and has no parallel for the next two hundred years. At the end of
the sixteenth century those who still sought the meaning of Jewish

---

[32] A striking instance in the sixteenth century, though perhaps an isolated
one, of the most extreme antagonism to non-literal interpretation of aggadah,
is provided by the Safed Mishnaic scholar Joseph Ashkenazi. See G. Scholem,
"Yediot ḥadashot 'al R. Yosef Ashkenazi, ha-Tanna mi-Ẓefat," *Tarbiz*,
XXVIII (1959), 59–89, 201–233.

historical suffering and of the length of exile found it in the
Kabbalah of Isaac Luria and his disciples, and it is surely more
than coincidence that a people that did not yet dream of defining
itself in historical categories should find the key to its history in
an awesome metahistorical myth.

I do not mean by this to imply in any way that sixteenth-century
historiography and Lurianic Kabbalah stood in a consciously
competitive relationship in which the latter was "victorious."
Though both were ultimately related to the Spanish expulsion,
each represented a separate response with its own inner dynamics.
If I juxtapose the two, it is not in order to suggest an organic
lateral relationship, but because of what the juxtaposition reveals
about the mentality of Jews. That the historiographical effort
proved abortive, while the Lurianic myth permeated ever-
widening circles in Jewry, seems to me a datum of no small consequence for an understanding of important facets of that mentality. Whatever Lurianic Kabbalah may have meant to Jews
(and Gershom Scholem has unveiled for us both its conceptual
audacity and overwhelming pathos), its rapid reception by the
Jewish world is significant in itself. Clearly, the bulk of Jewry was
unprepared to tolerate history in imminent terms. It is as though,
with the culminating tragedy of the expulsion from Spain, Jewish
history had become opaque, and could not yield a satisfactory
meaning even when, as among most of the historians, it was
viewed religiously. Patently, however, Jews were spiritually and
psychologically prepared for that which Lurianic Kabbalah
offered them: a mythic interpretation of history that lay beyond
history, and endowed the individual with the power to participate
actively in hastening its messianic liquidation.

For us, both the Jewish historiography and the Kabbalah of the
sixteenth century have become "history." Not only are we equi-
distant from both; we also study both — historically. But if we
style ourselves historians and do not aspire to be kabbalists, that
should not indulge us in the illusion that we have salvaged the
one over the other.

There is no continuum between sixteenth-century Jewish

historiography and Jewish historical scholarship as we know it and practice it in modern times. The rupture has been complete and decisive. To the degree that we have become historians (and there is no Jewish scholarly discipline today that is not historical), our roots lie in other soil. The fact that, in 1794, the *Me'or 'Einayim* was republished by the Maskilim in Berlin should not mislead us in this respect. At that time the *Historisches Journal* had already appeared in Göttingen for more than two decades, Barthold Niehbur was eighteen years old, and Ranke would be born a year later. We are not the heirs of Azariah de' Rossi, but of these men and others, and the mode whereby we came into this inheritance has implications of its own. If the historical consciousness of the modern West is the result of gradual and coherent developments within European culture, Jews absorbed it abruptly when they plunged into that culture in the nineteenth century. The quest for Jewish history inaugurated by *Wissenschaft des Judentums* emanated from the convergence of a religious collapse from within and assimilation from without.[33] These observations involve neither judgment nor regret, both irrelevant in face of what seems, in retrospect, to have been inevitable.[34] In the measure that we have become modern Western men and women, the historical outlook is now part of our innermost selves.

As a result, Jewish scholars since the nineteenth century have been building, at an ever-accelerating rate, a vast edifice of historical research. Whether, despite what has been achieved, one can say even now that historiography has found a home within Jewry

[33] The change can be seen within the span of a generation. Compare, for example, the discussion of the uses of history in *Me'assef*, I (1784), 7–28, where the function of history is still perceived as ancillary to traditional religious concerns, and Immanuel Wolf's famous manifesto of 1822 "On the Concept of a Science of Judaism" (Eng. tr. by L. Kochan in *Leo Baeck Institute Yearbook*, II [1957], 194–204), in which historical studies are assigned the central role of clarifying "the fundamental idea of Judaism," and "the scientific [i.e. historico-critical] attitude" is hailed as "the characteristic of our time."

[34] I refer here only to the absorption by Jews of the historical spirit and method. The specific deficiencies or biases of nineteenth-century *Wissenschaft* are a separate matter, and need not detain us here.

at large is another matter. Whether contemporary Jewry, having lived through its own unparalleled cataclysm, looks to history for meaning, or awaits a new myth, will also bear discussion. These and other queries arise, unsummoned, "when sleep wanders," even though one knows that the work will continue in the morning.

HEBREW SECTION

ספר היובל

של

האקדמיה האמריקנית למדעי היהדות

ספר היובל

של

האקדמיה האמריקנית למדעי היהדות

תרפ״ח—תרפ״ט/תשל״ט—תש״ם

חלק עברי

העורכים

שלום בארון ויצחק ברזילי

ירושלים, תש״ם

האקדמיה האמריקנית למדעי היהדות

מספר הכרטיס בקטלוג של ספריית הקונגרס : 21001־30

הוצא לאור בסיוע
קרב הרב יהודה לייב ואשתו חנה מנוחה אפשטיין
והמוסד לזכר אלכסנדר קוהוט

נדפס בישראל
בדפוס ״מרכז״, ירושלים

פתיחה

את ראשיתה של האקדמיה האמריקנית למדעי היהדות יש לראות ב־15 ליוני
1920, כאשר קבוצת מלומדים יהודיים בארה״ב (דוד ש. בלונדהיים, ישראל
דווידסון, גוטהרד דייטש, ישראל פרידלנדר, לוי גינזברג, יצחק הוסיק, יעקב
בצלאל לאוטרבך, צבי מלטר, מכס ל. מרגוליס, אלכסנדר מרכס, דוד ניימרק,
צבי א. וולפסון ושלמה צייטלין) התחילה מתכנסת מזמן לזמן באורח לא רשמי,
בראשותו של פרופ׳ ל. גינזברג, כדי להחליף ביניהם דעות בעניני חכמת ישראל.
ב־1924 נצטרפו לחוג זה בן־ציון הלפר ויעקב מן. פרוטוכולים מפורטים של
פגישות אלו לא נרשמו כנראה, וכן לא נשתמרו כל תעודות אחרות.

ב־1928 הוחלט לתת לכינוסים בלתי־רשמיים אלה צורה אירגונית ברורה.
בהעדרו של פרופ׳ ל. גינזברג, ששימש אז כפרופ׳־אורח בירושלים, מילא את
מקומו פרופ׳ מרכס כנשיא־בפועל. יחד עם פרופ׳ בלונדהיים, מזכיר האירגון,
הצליח, ב־20 לדצמבר 1929, להשיג צ׳רטר בשביל האקדמיה. מכיוון שהפרופי־
סורים מרכס ובלונדהיים שימשו אז כעמיתים באקדמיה האמריקנית לחקר
ימי־הביניים, לקחו להם את צורת האירגון של מוסד זה כדוגמה לאקדמיה.
ב־1928 הענק התואר "עמית" לכל אחד מקבוצת המייסדים הראשונים, וכן
הענק תואר זה באותה שנה לפרופיסורים שלום בארון ואליעזר פינקלשטיין.

הכנס הפומבי הראשון של האקדמיה התקיים ב־27 לדצמבר 1927, ובו
הרצה פרופ׳ מרכס על תפקידי האקדמיה. הוא ציין במיוחד את תרומותיהן
המדעיות החשובות של הוותיקות והידיעות שבאקדמיות אירופה וקרא לחכמי
ישראל בארה״ב לצאת בעקבותיהן. באותו כנס נידונו גם שלוש הרצאות שהרצו
הפרופיסורים מרגוליס, וולפסון ובארון. ב־1930 הופיע הכרך הראשון של
הרצאות ודיונים ("פרוסידינגס"), שנוסף על הרצאתו של מרכס ומחקרו של
בארון, הכיל גם מחקרים מאת ישראל דווידסון, אליעזר פינקלשטיין ויצחק
הוסיק.

עתה, חמישים שנה אחרי התחלות צנועות אלו, אנו שמחים להגיש לקהל
החכמים ולכל שוחרי תורה ודעת שבארצות־הברית, ישראל ושאר ארצות העולם
ספר יובל זה על שני מדוריו, האנגלי והעברי. בגלל אפיו החגיגי המיוחד של
הספר הוגבלה ההשתתפות בו לעמיתים בלבד, שהם הם בעיקר שנשאו תמיד
בעולה של עבודת האקדמיה. זכותם היא עתה להיות גאים בהשגי האקדמיה
בעבר ולקוות שעוד תשגה ותאדיר בעתיד.

ה ע ו ר כ י ם

לוח העניינים

TABLE OF CONTENTS

HEBREW SECTION

TABLE OF CONTENTS

ENGLISH SECTION

* deceased

מדרכי הקודיפיקציה – על ס׳ הטורים
לר׳ יעקב ברבי אשר

מאת אפרים א׳ אורבך

לפני למעלה ממאה שנה כתב ההיסטוריון הגדול – גדול בתפיסתו וגדול
בטעיותיו – צבי גרץ דברי הערכה על ס׳ הטורים, וזו לשונו:

הקודקס הדתי של ר׳ יעקב עשוי לשמש קנה מידה, כדי להכיר עד כמה
שהיהדות הרשמית ירדה מאז זמנו של הרמב״ם. בס׳ החוקים של הרמב״ם
שולט הרעיון: כל מצוה שבפולחן אף המוזרה ביותר – טובה או רעה –
נקשרת עם עצם מהותה של הדת ומתוארת כנובעת ממנה ובמידה מסוימת
כמסקנתה. בקודקס של ר׳ יעקב קיים לעומת זאת בדרך כלל ויתור על
המחשבה. הדקדקנות הדתית כפי שמצאה את משכנה בקהלות אשכנז
יושבת כאן כמחוקקת ומטילה חומרות וסגופים... בקביעת הלכות מחייבות
שמר הרמב״ם על זיקתו לתלמוד ורק לעתים רחוקות הכניס מהוראותיהם
של הגאונים... לעומת זאת הכניס בנו של ר׳ אשר לס׳ החוקים שלו את
כל מה שהשמיע אי־פעם ואי־שם חסיד נוטה להפלגה אם מתוך יראת
הוראה ואם מתוך פרשנות למדנית... לפיכך רבים במספרם היסודות
המחייבים הנובעים מרבנים על אלה המשתמעים מהתלמוד עצמו. ניתן
לומר שבידיו היתה היהדות התלמודית ליהדות רבנית... וכמו בתוכן כך
גם בצורה נבדל הקודקס של ר׳ יעקב מזה של הרמב״ם. במידה שהוא
הולך בעקבותיו מורגש גם בו סדור שטתי; לעומת זאת בחלקים
העצמאיים נחפש לשוא את הסדר המאיר והמחבר, כבחוליות של שר־
שרת, של הרמב״ם. גם התאור והסגנון אין להם אותה בהירות ואותו דיוק
של לשון הרמב״ם. עם זאת זכה הקודקס הדתי – של ר׳ יעקב – להכרה
כללית.

עד כאן דברי גרץ.[1] שנה לאחר שנכתבו דברים אלה הופיע במונטסשריפט
(כרך י״ג, 1864). מאמר של בוכהולץ בשם ״סקירה היסטורית על קודיפיקציות

---

[1] *Geschichte der Juden* VII (,לייפציג, 1894), 299–300. תרגומו של שפ״ר, דברי ימי
ישראל, חלק ה׳, עמ׳ 280, אינו אלא פרפרזה חיוורת.

השונות של חומר ההלכה.״ [2] בדבריו על ס׳ הטורים נאמר: אם מתבוננים למדת
העצמאות שבה סכם המחבר נושאי הלכות חדשים והקנה להם שלמות, אם
שוקלים בנוסף לזה את הקשר הפנימי ההגיוני שבכל פרק ופרק ואת הצרוף
הרצוף של החומר אשר עדיין לא היה קיים כלל בימי הרמב״ם, הרי החיבור
מופיע כיצירה עצמאית של בעל שאר רוח ברוך כשרונות. ר׳ זכריה פרנקל,
עורך המונטסשריפט, הוסיף הערה שבה נאמר: ״אנו מצטרפים לדעתו של
המחבר וחייבים לציין מתוך צער את תאורו של ד״ר גרץ כבלתי נכון.״ דעה
זו נתקבלה על דעת א״ה וייס, שלא הוסיף מדיליה מאומה אלא כמה דברים
נמלצים. אמנם לא היתה כוונתו של ר׳ יעקב לחבר ״ספר חקים להכריע
ההלכה אשר תהיה חק לא לשנות... רק זאת היתה מחשבתו לקבץ באמונה
הדינים לפי התלמוד ולפי דעות גדולי הפוסקים.״ אבל יחד עם זה ״כל משכיל
על הדבר לא יכחיש כי נתן רבינו יעקב לספרו צורה מדעית ואין בכל אשכנז
וצרפת ממין הזה.״ [3] הצד השוה שבכל הדברים הנ״ל שהם דברי הערכה
הנובעים במדה זו או אחרת מתוך התרשמות ומתוך מגמות מסויימות, שאין
צורך להאריך בפרושן. דיון מפורט ראשון על ספר הטורים נמצא במונוגרפיה
על משפחת הרא״ש [4] של אברהם חיים פריימן זק״ל, שחברה בהיותו בן 20.
הוא עמד על גישתו של ר׳ יעקב, כפי שבאה לידי ביטוי בעדויותיו הוא עצמו
בהקדמות לחלקים השונים של הטור, על מקורותיו ועל בדיקה של גוף החבור,
שעליה בסס את דבריו, על יחסו של ר׳ יעקב לקודמיו וכן על דרכו בהכרעות
בין דעות חולקות ועל שיטתו בסדורן של הסטיות ודרך הצגתן. השיגו הגדול
של בעל הטורים הוא לדעתו בהשתלטותו על החומר הרב שעמד לרשותו,
בכושר הבחירה מתוך שפע הדעות והמקורות ובכל זאת בהצלחתו ליחשב,
כדברי מרן ר׳ יוסף קרו, כ״כולל רוב דעות הפוסקים.״ במקום שגילו את
חולשתו של החבור, דוקא בו מצא פריימן את שבחו. אמנם לא עלה בידיו של
ר׳ יעקב בן הרא״ש לחבר חיבור בעל סדור מופתי וסגנון אחיד ומופלא כמו
ה״משנה תורה״ של הרמב״ם, אבל מגמתו לא היתה יצירה ספרותית מופתית
אלא חיבור ספר פסקים שישמש צרכים מסויימים, שאותם כבר לא מלא חיבורו
של הרמב״ם; ומבחינה זאת יש לראות בספריו התקדמות בתהליך הקודי־
פיקציה. לסכום דומה הגיע מנחם אלון בתאור דרכו של ר׳ יעקב בר׳ אשר

Dr. P. Bucholz, "Historischer Überblick über die mannigfachen Codifica- [2]
tionen des Halachastoffes von ihren ersten Anfängen bis zu ihrem letzten Ab-
schlusse", *Monatschrift für Geschichte und Wissenschaft des Judentums*, XIII
(1864), 201–217, 241–259.

[3] דור דור ודורשיו (וילנה תרנ״ג; ת״א, תשכ״ד), חלק ה׳, עמ׳ 121.
"Die Ascheriden (1267–1391)," *Jahrbuch der Jüdischen Literarischen Ge-* [4]
sellschaft (Frankfurt a. M., 1920), pp. 170 ff.

בפרק על ספרות הפוסקים שבספרו "המשפט העברי",[5] תוך השוואה עם דרכי הקודיפיקציה שקדמו לו ועם דרכו של ר׳ יוסף קרו אחריו.

השאלה שבדעתנו להעלות היא, האם השינוי הבולט שבסדור ספר הטורים ביחס לקודמיו אין גם לראותו על רקע הזמן והסביבה שבה חי ויצר ר׳ יעקב? מכאן גם תוצאה לשאלה אחרת כללית יותר: באיזו מידה פועלים בכל מפעלי קודיפיקציה אותם גורמים ואותן תופעות? שאלות אלו אינן באות כדי להעמיד את דיוננו על השפעות, אלא להבליט את המשותף שבתהליכי קודיפיקציה שונים ויחד עם זה להבין את המיוחד שבכל אחד מהם. ר׳ יעקב פעל במחיצת אביו הרא"ש וידע את השאלות שעמדו על הפרק, שהובאו בפני אביו, בתוכן שאלות שבאו מ"הגדולים ההולכים בחצר המלך", מהסוג "אם יש צד שיוכל אדם להנחיל נכסיו לבנו הגדול ובנו הגדול לבנו הגדול וכן עד סוף כל הדורות כמשפט המלוכה שלא יהא זכות לשאר היורשין."[6] "משפט המלוכה" כאן אינו מליצה בעלמא, אלא תואם הוא בדיוק את המציאות של סוף ימיו של הרא"ש. לפי החוקים הספרדיים המקומיים נאסרה דוקא העדפת אחד הבנים על האחרים. אבל הזכות להעמדת "מאיורטים" נתנה בראשונה לאצילים ע"י המלך יעקב השני בארגוניה ב־1302 ובשנת 1311 הורחבה זכות זו לכלל האזרחים.[7] גם יהודים, מהגדולים ההולכים בחצר המלך, רצו ליהנות ממנה. ר׳ יעקב הביא בהלכות נחלות שבחו"מ, סי׳ רפ"ב, את לשון השאלה ואת תשובת אביו האומרת "ללכת בחוקי הגויים להעביר הנחלה מכל זרעו ולהעמידה ביד בנו הגדול, אסור לכל בן ברית להעלות דבר זה על לבו". בשאלות אחרות מדובר על "מנהג כתוב ומקויים בכח כתבי הרבנים מטעם המלך".[8] התקופה שבה חי ופעל ר׳ יעקב היא תקופה של נסיונות חוזרים ונשנים להחדרת המשפט הרומי, כפי שהוא מצוי ב־Corpus iuris civilis בחלק ה־Digesta,

---

[5] המשפט העברי, תולדותיו, מקורותיו, עקרונותיו (ירושלים, תשל"ג), חלק ג׳, עמ׳ 1058 ואילך, וגם עמ׳ 1114. חיים טשרנוביץ (רב צעיר), תולדות הפוסקים, חלק ב׳ (ניו-יורק, תש"ז), עמ׳ 199 ואילך, התעלם שלא בטובתו מדברי פריימן. הוא מונה את הטור בחסרונות בסדור ההלכות וטוען, שאפשר היה לבחור בסדור אחר, אבל בכל זאת כותב אף הוא בעמ׳ 219: "עלינו להודות שהוא ספר למוד טוב מצד סדורו הפורמלי," ובעמ׳ 219: "נסדר כל זה במערכה שלמה והוא עולה על כל הפוסקים שקדמוהו מצד המעשיות והשלמות שבו."

[6] ראה ספר שאלות ותשובות להרב רבינו אשר ז"ל, כלל פ"ד, א׳; וראה י. בער, תולדות היהודים בספרד הנוצרית, מהדורה שנייה (תל-אביב, 1965), עמ׳ 186.

[7] ראה Eduard Gans, Das Erbrecht in Weltgeschichtlicher Entwicklung (Stuttgart, 1829), Band III, 437

[8] ראה מאמרי, "שו"ת הרא"ש בכתבי יד ובדפוסים," שנתון המשפט העברי, כרך ב׳ (ירושלים, תשל"ה), מעמ׳ 15 ואילך.

לשיטות המשפטיות הלוקליות, כדי להביא לידי אחודם של ה־Fueros
המקומיים. המחצית השניה של המאה הי"ג היא זמן פעילות גדולה בתחום
הקודיפיקציה. Alfonso el Sabio [החכם] (1252–1284) המשיך במפעל שהחל
בו אביו. בשנת 1255 הושלם ה־Fuero Real בארבעה ספרים. הראשון דן
בשאלות דת; השני בסדרי משפט וראיות; השלישי בדיני משפחה, ירושה
וחיובים, והרביעי בענשים והוספות. חבור זה, עדיין שולט בו היסוד המשפטי
הגותי, אלא שיש בו אחוד של ספרי חוקים מקומיים. קודקס זה שמש רק מעין
הכנה למפעל גדול יותר, שהושלם ב־1265. שמו המקורי של הקודקס היה
Libro de las Leyes, Fuero de las leyes. היו בו שבעה חלקים ועל שמם
הוא נקרא מאז ראשית המאה הי"ד Siete Partidas. יש בו קומפילציה של
המשפט הרומי, המשפט הקנוני והמשפט המקומי, ומשום השלמת קליטתו של
המשפט הרומי במשפט הספרדי. יהא חלקו של המלך בחבורים של Partidas
מה שיהא, ברור שהסמכות המלכותית עמדה מאחורי המפעל. בהקדמה
(Prologo I, 5) מוגדרת מטרת החבור כשואפת בראש וראשונה להגשמת
רעיונו של אבי המלך Fernando el Santo; שנית ליצירת קו מנחה בשביל
המלכים הבאים שיקל עליהם את תפקידם, ושלישית להפצת דעת המצב
התחוקתי והמשפטי בין בני העם שלא ישגו אלא יאהבו את אדוניהם
וישמעו להם. שבעת ה־Partidas מחולקים ל־tituli, הלכות, ואלה
לסימנים. החלק הראשון כולל את כל הנוגע לעניני האמונה הקתולית;
החלק השני כולל את המשפט הצבורי: זכויות הקיסר, המלכים, השרים
הפקידים וכו'; החלק השלישי — את הפרוצדורה המשפטית, דיינים, ראיות,
חזקה וקנין; החלק הרביעי — דיני אישות; החלק החמישי, דיני חיובים,
כולל דיני מקח וממכר ומשפט ימי; החלק הששי — דיני ירושה ואפו־
טרופסות, וההלק השביעי דיני עונשים.

בפרולוג קבע המלך במפורש שמכאן ואילך ישמשו ה־Siete Partidas
כספר חוקים בעל תוקף בלעדי. והנה עמדו החוקרים על התופעה המתמיהה
שעוד בימי אלפונסו עצמו יצאו ה־Siete Partidas מכלל שימוש, או,
יותר נכון, לא הגיעו לכלל זה. קליטת חלקים מהמשפט הרומי עוררה התנגדות
מצדם של כל אלה שחששו לאבוד פריבילגיות קיימות או לקפוח זכויות מחמת
שנויים מחוקים קודמים. ב־1272 השיגה האצולה מאת המלך אלפונסו הכרה
מחודשת ב־Fuero Viejo. אלפונסו שאף להשיג את כתב הקיסרות ורצה
להבטיח לעצמו את תמיכת האפיפיור. לפיכך הועניקו לכנסיה זכויות מרחיקות
לכת. משהתברר למלך שאפסו סיכוייו להשיג את המבוקש פחת ענינו
בהשלטת "שבעת החלקים" למעשה. החבור תפס מקום בהוראה האוניברסיט־
אית, אלא שלא הוכר כספר חוקים רק כעבור כמעט תשעים שנה, וזה גם
כן רק תוך כדי פשרה. ב־Ordenamiento de Alcala משנת 1348, כשלוש

שנים לאחר פטירתו של בעל הטורים, נקבע, שעל ידו ישארו בתוקפם
ה־Fueros, אבל במידה שאין בהם תשובה לשאלות ישמשו ה־Partidas
מקור השלמה.[9]

סקירה קצרה זו על דרכי הקודיפיקציה המשפטית בספרד סמוך לזמנו של
בעל הטורים ובזמנו תסייע בידינו לעמוד על קיום משותפים לכל מפעל
קודיפיקטורי, ומה שבעיני חשוב יותר על המיוחד שבס׳ הטורים.

ר׳ יעקב הקדים הקדמה לכל ספר. הקדמות אלו דומות בחלקן הראשון לא רק
זו לזו אלא להקדמות המצויות בכל קודקס אחר. ההקדמה פותחת בדברי שבח
לאלהים ומצורפת אליה תלונה על המצב הבלתי נסבל בתחום ידיעת החוקים.
כך, למשל, פותחת התוספתא במסכת עדויות: "משנכנסו חכמים בכרם ביבנה
אמרו עתידה שעה שיהא אדם מבקש דבר מדברי תורה ואינו מוצא מדברי
סופרים ואינו מוצא... שלא יהא דבר מדברי תורה דומה לחבירו אמרו נתחיל
מהלל ומשמאי" וכו׳. והרמב"ם בהקדמתו למשנה תורה כותב בסגנון שלו
דברים דומים: "ובזמן הזה תכפו הצרות יתירות... ואבדה חכמת חכמינו...
לפיכך אותם הפירושים וההלכות והתשובות שחברו הגאונים... נתקשו בימינו
ואין מבין ענייניהם כראוי אלא מעט במספר ואין צריך לומר התלמוד
עצמו...".

וכן כותב ר׳ יעקב בהקדמתו לספר "אורח חיים": "ונסתמו מעינות חכמתנו
ונשתבשו הסברות וגדלו המחלוקות ורבו הדעות ולא נשארה הלכה פסוקה
שאין בה דעות שונות...". מצב זה הוא בא לתקן: "וקראתי ספר זה אורח חיים
כי הוא יסיר ממוקשי מות..." על הדרך שהוא נוקט בה, הוא אומר: "ואין
ברצוני להאריך בראיות אלא לכתוב דברים פסוקים ובמקום שיש דעות שונות
אכתבם ואכתוב אחרי כן מסקנת אדוני אבי הרא"ש ז"ל." הוא מונה ומפרט
עניינם של ג׳ החלקים שבספר זה ומוסיף: "וראיתי עוד לעשות סמנים לכלול
כל ענין וענין במלות קצרות ולכתבם בתחלת הספר במספר למען היות
נקל לבקש כל ענין לענין." ההקדמות הנפרדות לכל חלק של הטורים
מצביעות על כך שר׳ יעקב לא כתב את חיבורו בחדא מחתא, אבל אין גם סביר
להניח שלא תכנן את המבנה של ספרו כחיבור כולל. כפי שנראה, קרוב לומר

[9] תאור זה מבוסס בעיקרו על ספרו של Fr. W. von Reichhaupt, *Geschichte der*
spanischen Gesetzesquellen (Heidelberg, 1923), 98–131; תאור דומה נמצא כבר
בספרו הנ"ל של אדוארד גנז, אלא שהוא בקרתי ביותר ביחס ל־Siete Partidas.
ר׳ שם, עמ׳ 426. אין לנו כאן ענין בשאלת ההשפעה של המשפט העברי ב־Partidas;
זו מצויה בו יותר מאשר ב־Fueros האחרים. חדרו לתוכם מלים עבריות כגון fijos
manzeres –ממזר, ראה Reichhaupt, שם, עמ׳ 167, עפ"י F. Fernandez Y. Gonzalez,
Institucione juridicas del pueblo de Israel en los differentes Estudos de la Pen-
insual ibérica (1881).

שבשבעת סדורם של החלקים הראשונים צפה מראש את בעית סדורם של החלקים האחרונים, הגם שלא פרש. הוא העדיף לכונן את הבניין כולו ולתארו כשעמד כבר על מכונו מאשר להודיע מראש על התכנית. בהקדמה ל״יורה דעה״ כותב ר׳ יעקב: ״ואחברה ספר בענייני איסור והיתר ושאר כל הדברים הצריכים לזמן הזה״, ובהקדמה ל״אבן העזר״: ״מצוות רבות נצטוו בעניין חיבור האדם עם אשתו כל ימי היותם עד הפרדם, ועוד תקנות רבות נתקנו בהן אחרי כן ואמרתי לחבר בהן ספר.״ בהקדמה ל״חושן משפט״ הרחיב את היריעה, ואחרי תאור בתי הדין בימי הבית הוא המשיך:

ובראותי אני יעקב בן הר״ר אשר זצ״ל כי בעונותינו חרב מקדשנו ובטלו כל אלה — אין לשכה ואין סנהדרין ולא בירה ולא פרהדרין אין לא מלך ולא שרים... לא שופטים ולא שוטרים... צלמות ולא סדרים, השופטים נשפטים השוטרים בשטרים, העוצרים נעצרים, העוזרים נעזרים... איש הישר בעיניו יעשה ומי יאמר לו מה תעשה... יש אשר ידרוש את דבר המשפט ולא ישכון עליו ענן אורו כי קט מהשיגו שכלו, ויש אשר ישכן עליו ענן ואורו אבל הוא ברצותו יחשוך מאורו כי יראה מדת הדין מתוחה כנגדו יאמר משפט אבחרה לי כדבר אחד מהמחברים ובהם אדברה ויריוח לי ומקלי יגיד לי, על כן עוררתי ועלתה במחשבתי לחבר ספר במשפטי הדינים על דרך פסקי אדוני אבי הרב ר׳ אשר זצ״ל אשר הם בנויים על יסוד הרב הגדול רבינו יצחק אלפסי אשר סילת ובירר התלמוד [בנפה] ברורה 10 ויוציא לאור כל תעלומה ובמעט מקומות אשר אין דעתו משוה עם דעת שאר המחברים כמו הרב רבינו משה בר מימון ז״ל וזולתו אני כותב דעתם ודעת מורי אבי הרא״ש ז״ל והסכמתו למען אשר ירוץ הקורא בו ויעש ככל אשר ימצא במקום ההוא ולא יסור ממנו ימין ושמאל וקראתיו חשן המשפט ואתן אל חשן המשפט את האורים ואת התומים יען כי הוא נדרש לכל שואל... ובו נשלמו ארבע[ה] הטורים אשר חצבתי בעזרת שוכן מרומים... הטור האחד אורח חיים שם נתתי את הברכות ואת התפילות והלכות שבת ומועד ומשפטיהן וקראתיו אורח חיים כי ממנו תוצאות חיים. והטור השני יורה דעה הוא ההולך קדמת איסור להורות את בני ישראל את המותר ואת האסור וקראתיו יורה דעה כי הוא יורה דיעה ויבין שמועה והטור השלישי אבן העזר שם עשיתי לאדם עזר כנגדו גם בשלחה גרש איך יגרשנה מנגדו וקראתיו אבן העזר יען כי הוא להועיל גם לעזר.

---

10 בדפוסים ״בנפה ברורה,״ בכ״י בריט׳ מוזיאום 27137, שנכתב לפי הקולופון ע״י ״יהודה בר׳ יוסף בשנת ק״כ (1360) — פחות מעשרים שנה לאחר פטירת המחבר — חסרה המלה ״בנפה״. הסופר התקשה כנראה בקריאתה והשאיר מקום ריק.

כאן מופיע לראשונה השם ארבעה טורים. בהקדמה זו שנכתבה לאחר השלמת
הטור הרביעי ישנה הערכה עצמית של המחבר המשקיף על מלאכתו הגדולה.
כאן הנימה שונה מאשר בהקדמה לאורח חיים. שם הוא הציג את עצמו
"כתלמיד הלומד על פי המלמד וכותב דבריו להתלמד".

בהקדמה זו נשארו עוד כמה דברים הטעונים הבהרה ושיש בהם להוסיף
להבנת המוטיביציה ודרכו של בעל הטורים. הקובלנה שלו על הקושי בקביעת
הלכה אינה חורגת ממה שמצאנו בדברי התוספתא ובדברי הרמב"ם והיא גם
הקובלנה המצויה אצל קודיפיקטורים אחרים החל מיוסטיניאנוס. במכתבו
לטריבוניאנוס, שבו הוא מטיל עליו את התפקיד של אסוף ה-Digesta,
כותב הקיסר: "אבל אנחנו מצאנו שכל המסורת המשפטית מאז יסודה של
רומא ומזמנו של רומולוס נתבלבלה (ita esse confusum) ונתרחבה עד
לבלי גבול ואין בעל טבע אנושי המסוגל להגיע לכלל מסקנה (et nullius
humanae naturae capacitate concludatur)". לפיכך הוא מצוה לאסוף
את כל מה שנכתב ונמסר, לנפות ולברר ולהגיע לכלל הלכה פסוקה בשפה
מובנת לכל. את החומר הנאסף צוה לחלק לחמשים ספרים ולהכתירם בשמות
מתאימים, והוא גם קבע את שם החיבור Digesta או Pandektai. כשהוא
מודיע כעבור שלוש שנים [11] לסינט על תוצאות הפעולה הוא מדגיש שמתוך
יחס של כבוד לקדמונים לא הרשה להשכיח את שמותיהם של מורי ההוראה,
ועל יד כל דין נרשם שמו של חכם המשפט שהביאו. דברים דומים מצאנו
בפרולוג ל-Fuero Real ויש למצוא כמותם בפרולוגים אחרים. ודאי שדמיון
זה אין עדיין להביאנו למסקנה של שימוש ב-Digesta, או אפילו של ידיעה
ושמיעה על קיומם. אף ספק בעיני אם תופעה מדהימה יותר, שמיד נעמוד עליה,
יש בה כדי לשמש כהוכחה למסקנה מעין זו. בסדורן של ההלכות שב"חושן
משפט" קיים הבדל בולט בין סדורו של ר' יעקב ובין הסדר שבו נקט הרמב"ם.
במשנה תורה הסדר הוא: ספר י"א, נזיקין, ובו הלכות נזק ממון, גנבה, גזלה
ואבדה, חובל ומזיק ורוצח. ספר י"ב, קנין, ובו הלכות מכירה, זכיה ומתנה,
שכנים, שלוחים ושותפים ועבדים. ספר י"ג, משפטים, ובו הלכות שכירות,
שאלה ופקדון, מלוה ולוה, טוען ונטען ונחלות, וספר י"ד, שופטים, ובו הלכות
סנהדרין, עדות, ממרים, אבל ומלכים. לעומת זאת פותח טור חושן משפט
בהלכות דיינים, עדים, שטרות, מלוה ולוה, טוען ונטען, חזקות, שותפים,
קניין, מכירה, מתנה, אבדה ומציאה, נחלות, פקדון. גנבה, נזיקין, חובל בחברו
וחייבי מיתות בית דין. סדר זה תואם בהרבה את הסדר שב-Digesta.

---

[11] על השאלה היאך נתאפשר תוך ג' שנים לבדוק את החומר הרב – אלפים
חיבורים – ולצמצמו לכדי 5 אחוזים, ראה M. Kaser, *Röm. Rechtsgeschichte*
(Göttingen, 1967), pp. 249–50. ואולי אפשר להקיש מדרך עבודתו של ר' יעקב,
בהכנת קצור פסקי הרא"ש, על דרך עבודתם של היוריסטים של יוסטיניאנום.

בראשו עומד הספר de iustitia et iure ואחריו de iurisdictione ורק בספר
ה־47 נדונים הלכות גנבה, de furtis, ולאחר מכן בסימן י׳ de iniuriis et
famosis libellis התואמים את הלכות נזיקין והלכות מוסר הבאים בחושן
משפט אחרי הלכות גנבה. יש גם התאמה בשמותיהן ובמקומם של סימנים יחידים.
סימן י״א בחו״מ הוא ״כיצד הזמנה לדין ועל פי מי״ ובו נדון דינו של
המסרב. הטיטולוס הרביעי בספר השני של ה־Digesta הוא in ius vocando
ובהמשך לכך על המסרב להעניות להזמנת בית הדין. הרמב״ם קבע את מקומם
של דיני הפקר בספר הפלאה, בהלכות נדרים, פ״ב, ומסר את טעמו בזה
הלשון: ״ההפקר אף על פי שאינו נדר הריהו כנדר.״ לעומת זאת מצאו הלכות
הפקר את מקומן בחו״מ סמוך להלכות אבדה ומציאה ואלה הן המשך של
הלכות מתנה. ב־Digesta בא הפרק pro derelicto בספר ה־41, אחר הפרק
pro donato. אפשר להביא עוד דוגמאות מסוג זה, אבל כנגדן עומדות
דוגמאות אחרות שאין סדרן תואם את ה־Digesta. די להצביע על עצם
הפרדת הלכות אישות, קידושין, כתובות וגיטין כחלק כאבן העזר, קביעת מקומם
של דיני רבית ביורה דעה, בעוד שב־Digesta דינים אלה משולבים במסגרת
פורמלית מסוימת. ברם סטיות אלה אין בהן לכשעצמן להוציא מכלל אפשרות
ידיעה מצדו של ר׳ יעקב בסדרים של ספרי משפט שבסביבה, שכן בעניינים
רבים ובחלקים גדולים היה סדרם של דיני הטור כסדרם של ה־Digesta.
ב־Partidas כולל החלק האחרון דיני עונשין ודרכי בצועם, כמו בטור.

אמנם בדפוסי הטור ברשימת הסמנים (הם מופיעים יחד עם חידושי מהר״י
קארו בסוף הספר) רשום סימן תכ״ד ״חובל אביו ואמו,״ סי׳ תכ״ו: ״רואה
חברו טובע בנהר חיב להצילו״, וסי׳ תכ״ה חסר ברשימה. אבל בכתבי יד [12]
ובדפוסים ראשונים נמצא סי׳ תכ״ה, והוא: ״דיני נפשות דנידונין בזמן הזה״.
וגוף הסימן הושמט רובו ככולו. הוא נגמר בתשובת גאון המסתיימת במלים
״לעשות גדר לדבר שיש בו צורך רבים קנסינן לפי צורך השעה״. אבל בכתבי
יד ובדפוסים ראשונים ממשיך: ״אע״ג שאין דנין האידנא דיני נפשות בד״א
דיני נפשות שצריכין ב״ד ועדים אבל הנהרגין בלא ב״ד נהרגין גם עתה״,
והוא מנסח דיני׳ רודף, הבא במחתרת וכל אלה שקנאין פוגעין בו כנהוגים
בזמננו, ולאחר שהביא את דברי הרמב״ם [13] ״היה יכול להצילו באחד מאבריו
ולא עשה אלא הרגו הרי זה שופך דם ו חייב מיתה אבל אין ב״ד ממיתין אותו,״
מוסיף הטור: ״ואיני יודע כיון שחייב מיתה למה אין בית דין ממיתין אותו.״
דין זה תואם את ההתפתחות שחלה בגישתו של הרא״ש ביחסו ל״מנהג בארץ
ספרד״ להעניש בעונש מות. אמנם תחלה כתב ״והנחתי להם כמנהגיהם אבל

[12] בכ״י מנטובה 31, חלוקת הסמנים שונה במקצת והסימן שלפני האחרון הוא המספר
תכ״ט.
[13] הל׳ רוצח, פ״א, הי״ג, ור׳ בכ״מ ובמל״מ, שם.

מעולם לא הסכמתי עמהם על איבוד נפש.״ אבל במשך הזמן הסכים ובתשובות
שלא היו ידועות עד לפני זמן אף נקט יוזמה בנדון. ר׳ יעקב בר אשר בעצמו
חתם כשני על תשובה המסתיימת במלים: ״הלכך מכל אלו הטעמים יראה שיש
לאיש הזה משפט מות וכל המליץ עליו ומדבר בזכותו אסור לספר הימנו וכל
המשתדל בהריגתו הרי זה מבער עושי רשעה.״ כשם שהצנזורה הפנימית
בערה את ס׳ הטורים כך גם העלימה תשובות מסוג זה, שבחלקן נשמרו רק
בכתבי יד.[14]

דיני המלכות ומעמדם של הערכאות של המלכות היו לר׳ יעקב כפי
שמוכח מחו״מ סי׳ ס״ח הכולל ״הלכות שטרות הנעשים בערכאות של גויים״,
שבו מובאים כרגיל בשפע דברי הרא״ש והמסתיים בהבאת דברי הרמב״ן.
חתימתו של הסימן חשובה במיוחד:

> דלא עדיפי בערכאות מבסופרי ישראל שאין דינין של מלכים אלא
> להכשיר שטרות שלהן ולעשות סופר שלהם נאמן כמאה עדים שלנו, אבל
> לעניין דרכי הקנאה לא עדיפי משטרות שלנו שאף הגוים במקומות הרבה
> בדינין חלוקין דנין אותם וכשחסר להם דרך מהנימוסים שלהם לפי דעתו
> של דיין פוסלין אותו, זה בורר לו דין וניםוס אחד וזה בורר לו דין
> וניםוס אחר כפי מחלוקת חכמיהם ומנהג מקומותיהם שאין המלכים
> מקפידים אלא בהכשר שטרות שלהם.

בהביאו את תשובת הרמב״ן כלשונה,[15] ללא תוספת הערה, רומז בעל הטורים
לכך שהמצב לא נשתנה עד לימיו ותאור זה תואם לחלוטין את מה שלמדנו על
שליטתם של Fueros המקומיים, למרות הנסיונות הקודופיקטוריים מצד
המלך.[16] הידיעה על המניעים הקודיפיקטוריים הכלליים מסייעת בידינו להבין
את דברי ר׳ יעקב על המניעים שהביאוהו לחבר את ספרו. הוא בא לתקן את
המצב של ״איש הישר בעיניו יעשה ומי יאמר לו מה תעשה.״ מצב זה מתגלה
בשנים: באותם אנשים אשר דורשים את דבר המשפט, אבל שכלם קצר
מהשיגו, אבל גם באלה ״אשר ישכן עליו ענן אורו, אבל ברצונו יחשיך מאורו
כי יראה מדת הדין מתוחה כנגדו ואמר משפט אבחרה לי בדבר מהמחברים
ובהם אדברה וירוח ומקלי יגיד לי.״ כמה פירושים נאמרו בדברים נמלצים
אלה,[17] בהבאת הפסוק מהושע (ד׳:י״ב) רומז ר׳ יעקב לכאורה לפרושו של רב

[14] ר׳ מ״ש ״שאלות ותשובות הרא״ש בכ״י ובדפוסים,״ שנתון המשפט העברי, ב׳,
עמ׳ 78, הע׳ 16.
[15] התשובה נשלחה לר׳ שמואל הסרדי, ר׳ ס׳ התרומות, שער ס״ז, ח״ד ה׳, וראה
ש. אסף, ספרן של ראשונים (ירושלים, תרצ״ה), עמ׳ 103.
[16] על ה־Fueros Municipales, ר׳ בספרו של רייכהאופט, עמ׳ 73 והלאה.
[17] ראה מ. אלון, עמ׳ 1062, שפירש על בעל הדין, ר׳ שם עמ׳ 179. המרכאות על מקלו,

יוסף (פסחים נ״ב, ע״ב): ״כל המיקל לו יגיד לו״; אבל נראה לי שצדק פריימן
בדעתו שאין ר' יעקב מתכוין למיקל כנגוד למחמיר, אלא לבוחר לו את הדרך
הקלה, דהיינו לנהוג בדרך קבע כאחד המחברים ולפסוק כמותו. ונראה שיש
מקום להשערה, שאולי הדברים מכוונים נגד ההסכמות שהתפשטו בקהלות
שונות לפסוק בכל ענין כרמב״ם. עניין זה עשוי היה לעורר במרוצת הזמן
שאלות, במקרים שהכרעת הרמב״ם עמדה נגד ההלכה הרווחת במקומות אלה
לפני ההסכמה. ברור שהסכמות אלו באו מתוך אותה מגמה של נוחיות, למנוע
את הצורך להכריע, אבל כשם שלא עלה בידי Fuero Real לדחוק את
Fueros המקומיים והקודמים כך לא היה בהסכמות לפסוק כרמב״ם, על
הכרעותיו החד־משמעיות, משום פתרון. אמנם ר' יעקב חבר את ספרו על פי
ספר הפסקים של אביו, הרא״ש, אבל במקומות שאין דעתו כדעת הרמב״ם
וזולתו הביא את דעותיהם, כשם שהוא מביא את תקנות הנישואין של קהל
טוליטולא יחד עם התשובות שהשיב עליהן אביו הרא״ש. גם בתחום זה
הוכשרה מלאכתו של ר' יעקב על ידי אביו הרא״ש. חו״מ סי' ס״א נושא את
הכותרת ״שאלות לאדוני אבי הרא״ש ז״ל״ וכולו אינו אלא תמצית תשובות
הרא״ש, ונביא דוגמא אחת מתקנות הקהלות בדיני שטרות:

ששאלת מלוה שירד בעצמו לנכסי לוה בלא רשות בית דין, ומכר מנכסיו
עד כדי חובו, מחמת שרגילין לכתוב בשטרי חובות שיש רשות למלוה
למכור בחובו כל מה שימצא ללוה בין בפניו בין שלא בפניו בלא רשות
בית דין ובלא שומא והכרזה בין בשוויו בין בפחות. תשובה, אמת היא כי
מה שנהגו הסופרים לכתוב בשטרות שיש לנהוג על פי מה שנהגו לכתוב.
ומיהו בנדון זה נ״ל דלאו כל כמיניה דמלוה לירד לנכסי לוה אלא בכח
בית דין. וכיוצא בזה דנתי כבר בכאן על מה שנוהגין לכתוב בשטרות בין
בדיני ישראל בין בדיני אומות העולם ואמרתי חלילה וחס שיהיה רשות
למלוה לתבוע ללוה בדיני אומות העולם, דאפילו אם המלוה והלוה
עומדים לפנינו ואומר הלוה למלוה אם תרצה תתבעני בדיני האומות
מחיינן למלוה ואמרינן ליה שלא יתבענו אלא בדיני ישראל, ואי לא ציית
משמתינן ליה. והא דאיכתיב בין בדיני אומות העולם, יש לפרשו שלא
לעקור דברי תורה, כגון אם גברא אלמא דאין כח בדייני ישראל לכופו,
אז יש לו רשות להביאו לדייני אומות העולם שלא יפסיד ממונו. וכן
בנדון זה אע״פ שכותבין בשטרות שיש רשות למלוה לירד לנכסי לוה אין

────────────

שם הע' 178, אינם בכ״י ובדפוסים ראשונים. כל הקשר הדברים מראה שהמדובר במורי
הוראה.

¹⁸ חו״מ, סי' ס״א, סעיף ט' והלאה; והשוה שו״ת הרא״ש, כלל ס״ח סי' י״ג. ר' יעקב
נהג כלפי התשובות כשם שנהג בקיצור פסקי אביו.

לעבור על דברי תורה, דתנן המלוה את חברו לא ימשכננו אלא בבית
דין... ויש לפרש הלשון בעניין שלא יהא בו עברה.

פרשנות זו מבטלת למעשה את ההודעה שבראש התשובה ש״כל מה שנהגו
הסופרים לכתוב... יש לנהג ע״פ מה שנהגו.״ הבאת לשון הרא״ש בתשובותיו
במקום נוסחה פסקים באה להקנות לדברים סמכות מיוחדת.

בעניינים אחרים מנסה ר׳ יעקב בעצמו למצוא טעם למנהג ספרד גם
כשאינו תו.אם את ההלכה.[19] בספרו המציא ר׳ יעקב בן אשר ספר פסקים לדיין
ולמורה ההוראה שעל פיו הוא יכול להכריע לא רק במקום שהפסיקה היא חד
משמעית אלא גם כשישנן דעות שונות. הוא יכול למצוא אותן מנוסחות
ולהפעיל את כח שפוטו תוך התחשבות בגורמים שונים ״בדבר הצריך לעולם״.
כמו שראינו, זו היתה הדרך שבה נאלצו ללכת גם קודיפיקטורים שמאחוריהם
עמדו כוח של שלטון וסמכות של מלכות. לכך התכון בדבריו: ״ויעשה ככל
אשר ימצא במקום ההוא ולא יסור ממנו ימין ושמאל.״ ברצותו לתת ספר
פסקים כולל ומקיף ידע גם את הצמצום ונשמר מלעשותו לאוסף קזו-
איסטי. גם מתשובות אביו לשאלות שונות הכניס בעיקר מה שנראה לו כבעל
חשיבות עקרונית, והשמיט מקרים, שאמנם נתנה בהם הכרעה, אבל נראו
כיוצאי דופן. הוא נזהר מסטיות מגוף הנושא ואינו פורץ את גדרו של ברור
ההלכה ע״י הרחבה של שקלא וטריא. מבחינות אלה הוא נבדל לטובה לא רק
מספרי הלכה כמו הראבי״ה, האור זרוע וס׳ התרומה אלא גם מה-
Decretum Gratiani שהיה במשך הזמן ל-Corpus iuris canonici על
החלוקה שלו ל-causae ול-quaestiones ועל הסטיות המרובות שבו מהנושא
העיקרי.[20] מגמתו השניה היתה ליצור ספר לימוד של ההלכה אשר ירוץ
הקורא בו. סגנונו השוטף והמלבב, הגדרותיו, המעבר הנוח והרצוף מעניין
לעניין עשו את שלהם. דרך הרצאתו דומה לזו של אביו ושל חכמי אשכנז
וצרפת, אבל הוא מושפע בהרבה מניסוחיו של הרמב״ם גם במקומות שלא

---

[19] באבן העזר, סי׳ ס״ה, כותב הטור: ״צריך לעשות שום דבר זכר לאבלות
בירושלים... ואמר רב זה אפר מקלה שבראש חתנים, וכן נוהגין באשכנז בשעת ברכה
לתת אפר בראשו במקום תפלין... ובספרד נוהגין ליתן בראש עטרה עשויה מעלה זית,
לפי שהזית מר זכר לאבלות ירושלים.״ באו״ח הלכ׳ ט״ב, סי׳ תק״ס, עדין לא הביא את
ענין עטרה של זית אלא את הרמב״ם שפסק כשמואל, שעטרות של חתנים אף של ורד
והדס אסורות והוסיף: ״ואיני יודע למה דהא קי״ל כרב באיסורי ורב התיר של ורד
והדס.״ אבל יש שגם יצא בדברים חריפים נגד מנהג ספרד, ר׳ או״ח, סי׳ תקפ״ה.

[20] בתוך הפרקים המוקדשים לדיני אישות מצא את מקומו דרך אגב ה-Tractatus
de poenitentia. ראה W. M. Plöchl, Geschichte des Kirchenrechts (1955), II, pp.
413 ff. גרטינוס לא העתיק ממקורות ראשונים אלא מתוך קבצים קודמים של המשפט
הכנסיתי. ראה H.E. Feine, Kirchliche Rechtsgeschichte (Weimar, 1954), pp. 245 ff.

נזכר שמו. כך, למשל, בחו״מ סי׳ שנ״ו אנו קוראים: "אסור לקנות מן
הגנב שום דבר והקונה ממנו עון גדול הוא, שמחזיק ידי עוברי עבירה שגורם
לו לגנוב פעם אחרת שאם לא ימצא קונה לא היה גונב." זו ממש כמעט
לשון הרמב״ם בשנויים קלים, שמן הראוי לשים לב להם: "אסור לקנות מן
הגנב החפץ שגנב ועון גדול הוא שהרי מחזיק ידי עוברי עבירה וגורם לו
לגנוב גנבות אחרות, שאם לא ימצא לוקח אינו גונב וע״ז נאמר חולק עם
גנב שונא נפשו." (הל׳ גנבה, פ״ה, ה״א).21 לעומת זאת הננו מוצאים בטור
פתיחות של הלכות, שנראות כאלו מידי הרמב״ם יצאו, אבל באמת אינן
ברמב״ם. אביא דוגמא. ספר נזיקין פותח ברמב״ם בהלכות נזקי ממון, ואלו
מנוסחות ללא הקדמה: "כל נפש חיה שהיא ברשותו של אדם שהזיקה
הבעלים חייבין לשלם שהרי ממונם הזיק שנ׳ כי יגוף שור איש את שור
רעהו..." לעומת זאת בחו״מ סי׳ שע״ח מתחיל הלכות נזיקין: "כשם
שאסור לגנוב ולגזול ממון חברו כך אסור להזיק ממון שלו אפילו אם אינו
נהנה כיון שמזיקו בין במזיד בין בשוגג חייב לשלם...". עד סי׳ שפ״ט נדונים
נזקים שאדם עושה או גורם לממון חברו; סי׳ שפ״ט מתחיל בהלכות נזקי
ממון: "כשם שאסור לאדם שיזיק את חברו ואם הזיק חייב לשלם כך צריך
לשמור ממונו שלא יזיק..."

ר׳ יעקב התחיל בכתיבת חיבורו לאחר פטירת אביו, שכן באו״ח סי׳ ק״ב הוא
כותב על סברא של אביו: "אע״פ שיש להשיב מ״מ אין משיבין את הארי אחר
מותו..." הרא״ש נפטר בשנת ה׳ אלפים פ״ז (1327). מאו״ח סי׳ ס״ז ניתן
להסיק שחלק זה של החיבור נכתב בין שנת פ״ט (1329) לשנת צ״ו (1336), כי
הוא מציין שנת פ״ט כשנה האחרונה לשמטה.22 אם מביאים בחשבון את
התקופה הקצרה שבה נכתב החיבור ואת עבודת ההכנה שקדמה לו, כפי שאנו
מכירים אותה מקיצור פסקי הרא״ש שנתחבר על ידי ר׳ יעקב, הרי לא נראה
שסוף המעשה לא היה במחשבה תחלה. קשה להניח שבשעת סדורם של נושאי
הלכה מסויימים ב״יורה דעה" לא חשב על "חושן המשפט." הדבר יוכהר ע״י
השוואה עם סדורו של הרמב״ם. הרדב״ז יצא למצוא הסבר לסדורם של
הפרקים ב״הלכות ממרים" ב״יד החזקה," וזה לשונו: "פרק א׳—ד׳ ביאר
דברי המופלא הממרה על ב״ד הגדול והקדימן למעלתן. פ״ה ביאר בו דיני

21 נציין שנוסח דומה נמצא ב‏‎-Digesta בשם מרקיאנום: Pessimum genus est
receptatorum sine quibus nemo latere dia potest.

22 ר׳ פריימן, במאמרו הנ״ל, עמ׳ 20. להערכת ס׳ הטורים; ר׳ חיים מיכל, אור החיים
(פראנקפורט, תרנ״א), עמ׳ 489; פריימן שם, עמ׳ 191 ואילך; ומ. אלון בספרו הנ״ל, עמ׳
1079, ולמובא שם בהע׳ 274 משו״ת המהר״י מינץ סי׳ ט״ו, ר׳ בדברי הרמ״א, ד״מ, יו״ד
ל״ה, סעיף י״ג שהביא רק את התחלת דבריו של מהר״י מינץ: "א״כ ראוי לפסוק כדעת
הטור עכ״ל."

המימרה על אביו, וסמוך לו פ״ו בכבוד ומורא האב, והוא מעניין הפרק הקודם
לו. פ״ז באר בו דיני בן סורר ומורה והיה ראוי למיעוט מציאותו עד שיש מי
שאמר לא היה ולא עתיד להיות; ולמה נכתב, דרוש וקבל שכר, וסדר זה נכון
וברור.״ ואחר הלכות ממרים באות הלכות אבל, והרמב״ם בעצמו נאלץ
להצדיק סדר זה בדברים שנראים לא יותר ברורים מאלה של הרדב״ז: ״ואין
אדם מתאבל על הרוגי בית דין ולפי זה כללתי הלכות אלו בספר זה, שהן מעין
קבורה ביום מיתה שהיא מצות עשה.״ הלכות גרים נמצאות ב״יד החזקה״
במסגרת הלכות איסורי ביאה (פי״ג–י״ד) והלכות ספירת העומר בהלכות
תמידין ומוספין. שונה הוא סדרן של הלכות אלו בספר הטורים, ולא רק משום
שצומצם להלכות הנוהגות בזמננו. הלכות ספירת העומר, למשל, מצויות בטור
״אורח חיים״ בסימן תפ״ט שכותרתו היא: ״סדר תפלה ליל שני של פסח
וספירת העומר.״ הלכות כיבוד אב ואם והלכות גרים מצאו את מקומן כפרקים
נפרדים בטור ״יורה דעה.״ שם גם קבע את מקומן של ״הלכות רבית״ (סי׳
קנ״ט–קע״ח), בסמוך להלכות ע״ז וחוקות הגויים, שכך הוא פותח אותן בעניין
שהיה אקטואלי ביותר, וזה לשונו: ״דבר תורה מותר להלוות לגוי ברבית,
דטעמא דרבית דכתיב וחי אחיך עמך, וגויים לא היו מצווין להחיותו וחכמים
אסרוהו משום גזירה שמא ילמוד ממעשיו ובכדי חיי שרי וכו׳.״

סדורו הקודיפיקטורי של ר׳ יעקב נתקבל מהר. גדול הוא מספר כתבי היד
שנכתבו במאה הארבע עשרה והחמש עשרה ושישרדו.[23] ומאז שנדפס לראשונה
כספר העברי השני ב־Piove di Sacco בשנת רל״ה (1475) נדפס עד ר״ס
(1500) עוד תשע פעמים בספרד, פורטוגל ואיטליה. התפשטות מהירה זו
גררה אחריה שבושים, השמטות והוספות, ולא רק בדפוסים מאוחרים. המדפים
של דפוס אויגשפורג קובל כבר בשנת ש״י (1550) ״כי הנה הקדומים כולם
נמצאו בעלי מומים... ובפרט שני החלקים האחרונים עלו כולם קמשונים.״
הדפוס הזה הוגה לפי ספר מוגה בדקדוק רב ע״י ״הגאון מה״ר אברהם מפראג
מאיר דורנו״. הכוונה לאביו של בעל השל״ה. ואמנם תוקנו והוגהו בדפוס זה
דברים באו״ח סי׳ תרצ״ז: ״וכן חתן לא ילך לבית הכנסת אלא יקרא בבית
וא״א הרא״ש ז״ל כתב כדברי הרמב״ם ז״ל.״ כ״ה בדפ׳ שונצינו ר״ס, פאנו
רע״ו, ובדפוס ויניציה רפ״ב, אבל בדפ׳ אוגשפורג הוגה: ״כדברי מהר״ם,״

---

[23] הם נכתבו בארצות שונות גם מחוץ לספרד ולאשכנז. כ״י וטיקן 153, הכולל את טור
יורה דעה, נשלם בחודש תשרי בי״ב ימים בשנת ק׳ ו׳ מ׳ (1386) קרא לפרט היצירה
בירושלים. בו׳ לחודש אייר שנת קס״א (1401) נסתיימה כתיבתו של כ״י מינכן 118,
הכולל את חשן המשפט. אחד מבעליו הנכרים רשם בסופו totum hebraeorum
corpus scriptum. רבים כתבי היד ללא קולופונים. סך הכל של כתבי היד, שלמים
וחלקיים, הרשומים במכון לתצלומי כ״י, מגיע ל־140.

24. ואמנם בדפוס רמ״ה ובכ״י כתוב: "כדברי הר״מ מרוטנבורק זצ״ל". ברור שלא תמיד הדפוס המוקדם הוא המשובח, וכלל זה כחו יפה לגבי כתבי יד. הגיעו לידינו כתבי יד אחדים כתובים כתיבה מהודרת וגם מאוירים. הם נכתבו כנראה בשביל בעלי בתים עשירים. בכ״י אוקספורד 1860 — כ״י מהודר מהמאה הארבע עשרה — הכולל טור אורח חיים ויו״ד נמצאים איורים יפים של דמויות בני אדם, מהן לא צנועות ביותר. והנה סי׳ קמ״א שבכל הדפוסים מסתיים במלים: "והא דאסרינן בצורת אדם ודרקון דוקא בצורה שלמה בכל אברים, אבל צורת ראש או גוף בלא ראש אין בה שום איסור לא במוצאו ולא בעושה." אבל האיורים שבכ״י הן צורות שלמות שיש בהן גם גוף וגם ראש, ואמנם כל הסיום לא הועתק ע״י הסופר של כ״י זה.25 ההשמטות וההוספות שבכ״י ובדפוסים יוצאות ללמד לא רק על הטור אלא פעמים רבות אף על דעות המשמיטים והמוסיפים.

ראוי ספר זה שקבע את דמות ההלכה לדורות — שכן מבחינת סדורה וחלוקתה החזיקו בדרכו כל הבאים אחריו החל מר״י קרו בש״ע ובעל הלבושים וכלה ב״ערוך השולחן" — שיופיע במהדורה מבוססת על כתבי היד המשובחים תוך תשומת לב לכל הנוסחאות.

---

24 ואפשר להרבות בדוגמאות של נוסחאות שונות שלא ניסו לתקנן. באה״ע סי׳ קי״ח, סעיף צ״ג, נאמר בדפוסים שלפנינו: "עדות על תלמיד אחד שמת והתיר א״א הרא״ש ז״ל את אשתו ואת גיסתו." אבל בדפוס אוגשפורג "זה נוסחו," כלומר נוסח העדות, וכ״ה בכ״י בודל. 712, הכולל בחלק הראשון טור חו״מ עד דף 283 ומכאן אילך אה״ע: "...את אשתו וזה נוסחו." וכן גם בדפוס קניגסברג, תרכ״א-תרכ״ד. מציין אני עובדא זו כי הנסיון היחיד לפרסם תיקונים בספר הטור (חיפה תשל״א) של הרב דוד כהן נעשה על פיו בלבד.

25 מענין ביותר מבחינת איוריו הוא כ״י מיכאל 127. איורים פריבוליים מצויים גם בטופס של ס׳ הטורים משנת רפ״ב שבבית הספרים הלאומי.

על השמטת סופרים בטור אבן העזר עמד כבר התשב״ץ, ח״ג, סי׳ פ״ו.

אחד-העם (אשר-הירש גינצברג): קווי-יסוד לדמותו ותורתו
(חמישים שנה למותו, בכ״ח טבת, תרפ״ז)

מאת יצחק ברזילי

פרקי חיים

בן שבעים שנה וארבעה וחצי חדשים היה אחד-העם במותו (18.8.1856—
2.1.1927), ורעות, מלאות סבל וחולי, היו שנות חייו האחרונות. קצרה יחסית,
לא יותר משמונה דור אחד, היתה תקופת פעילותו הספרותית. קרוב לבן שלו-
שים ושלוש היה כשנתפרסם ב״המליץ״ מאמרו הראשון, ״לא זה הדרך״
(גליון 53, י״ב אדר, תרמ״ט — ה-3 במרץ 1889), ובן חמישים ואחת כמעט
כשהגיע ללונדון בסוף 1907 ומעיין יצירתו החל מדלדל והולך עד שחרב כמעט
לאחר שנים מועטות. אולם במשך תקופה קצרה זו הפך לאישיות מרכזית של
הדור וזכה להשפעה שאך מעטים זכו לה. אין ספק, שתים היו הסיבות לכך:
אישיותו ותורתו. אך בטרם נעמוד על אלה, נסקור בקצרה את פרשת חייו.

ארבעה פרקים היו בהם[1] ושונים היו זה מזה גם במקומות בהם ישב וגם
בפעולות בהן עסק. עד גיל שתים-עשרה ישב בעיירת מולדתו, סקווירא
שבאוקראינה, ולאחר מכן, במשך שמונה-עשרה שנה (בהפסקות קצרות),
בכפר גאפטשיצא, שאביו החזיק בחכירה, על יד העיר פוהרביטש.[2] במכלול
חייו מהווֹת שנים אלה תקופת הכנה לקראת פעולותו בעתיד. היו אלה שנות
התמדה ושקידה בלימודים שכמותן מצויות היו אך בדורות העבר. ראשיתן
בש״ס ופוסקים, והמשכן בספרות המוסר והמחשבה שלנו מימי-הביניים,
במקרא, דקדוק וספרות ההשכלה, וסופן בלשונות אירופה, חכמת ישראל
וספרות המחשבה הכללית של המאה השמונה-עשרה והתשע-עשרה.[3] אכן, היה
אחד-העם אחד היהודים המלומדים והמשכילים ביותר שבדורו. חוץ מהעברית

---

[1] אהה״ע בעצמו חילק את חייו לחמש תקופות. את תקופת חייו הראשונה, לפני בואו
לאודיסה, הוא חילק לשני פרקים: זה של ימי ילדותו בסקווירא, וזה של ימי נעורין
ושנות העשרים של חייו כשישב בכפר. ראה ״פרקי זכרונות״, כל כתבי אחד העם
(ירושלים, תש״ז), עמ' תצ״ו.

[2] בתרמ״ד ישב באודיסה רק ״ירחים אחדים״ והוכרח לשוב לכפר. רק בסיון תרמ״ו
התיישב בה ישיבת קבע. אגרות אחד העם ב-6 כרכים, הוצ' יבנה ומוריה
(ירושלים-ברלין, תרפ״ג-תרפ״ה), כרך ה', עמ' 296.

[3] כל כתבי, עמ' תס״ו והלאה; אגרות א', 143; ב', 250—251; ג', 134; ד', 220; ה',
188—187, 267—266, 298—296.

הצלולה והמדוייקת שלו הוא כתב גם רוסית באופן חופשי[4]. בראשית 1909,
כשכתיבתו העברית פחתה, נפוצה השמועה שהוא עומד בכלל לעזוב את
הספרות העברית ולעבור לרוסית[5]. אף ידיעתו בגרמנית היתה כמעט שלמה.
הוא רצה לתרגם בעצמו לגרמנית את מאמר־התשובה שלו על הביקורת שכתב
נורדוי נגד מאמרו על "אלטנײלנד" להרצל[6]. הוא לא הגיע אמנם ליכולת
כתיבה בצרפתית[7], אבל הוא הירבה לקרוא בלשון זו[8] והבנתו בה היתה כה רבה
עד שידע להעריך את "רעיונותיו המבריקים" וסגננונו "הנפלא" של רנן[9].
ובנוגע לאנגלית — ידיעתו בה קדמה בהרבה שנים את התישבותו בלונדון
בסוף 1907[10], כאשר ד״ר ז. שכטר הציע לו שיקבל עליו את הנהלת
"דרופסי קולג׳" שעמד להיפתח אז, השיב לו אחד־העם בין היתר: "לשון
אנגלית לא זרה לי. הנני חושב כי שנה אחת באמריקה היתה דיה לי להכשירני
לקריאת שיעורים והרצאות בלשון הזאת."[11] אחד־העם ידע כנראה לפענח גם
טכסט לטיני, ואף היוונית לא היתה לגמרי זרה לו[12].

פחות ידועה היא "למדנותו," ואחת הסיבות לכך היא בלא־ספק בסגננונו
העברי המנופה והבהיר. אחה״ע היה בין הראשונים בפובליציסטיקה העברית
שהשתמש בלשון שימוש של כלי גרידא ולא כמטרה לעצמה. על ידי כך הוא
ניתק את הפרוזה שלנו ממסורת המליצה הארוכה של הסגנון הרבני והמשכילי
כאחד, מסורת של שיבוצי מקראות ומאמרי חז״ל. רק במאמרים כ"שלטון
השכל" ו"על שתי הסעיפים" מתגלית מקצת מדעת היהדות הרחבה שנשא

[4] כל כתבי, "נשכחות," עמ' שצ״ה והלאה; השלח כ' (ינואר–יוני, 1909), עמ' 304.

[5] השלח כ', עמ' 187, ותגובת אחה״ע ב"מכתב אל העורך", שם, עמ' 304.

[6] כל כתבי, עמ' ש״כ; אגרות, ג', עמ' 103.

[7] אגרות, ה', עמ' 266.

[8] כל כתבי, ט״ז, הערה 2; ס״ב, הערה 1; ס״ד, הערות 1, 2; ס״ז, הערות; ס״ח,
הערה 1; וצ״ט, רפ״ג, ש״א.

[9] אגרות, ה', עמ' 221.

[10] ב"פרקי זכרונות" הוא כותב, שלאחר שהגיע לאודיסה בפעם הראשונה בתרמ״ד,
"התחילו לי חיים חדשים. מצד אחד נפתחו לי מקורות חדשים להשלמת השכלתי ולא
הרגשתי עוד מחסור בספרים. גם בלמודי הלשונות צרפתית ואנגלית עסקתי והצלחתי
בזמן קצר להשיג מבוקשי העיקרי: להבין בספרים הכתובים בהם," כל כתבי, עמ'
תס״ח. בקיץ תרנ״ג, לאחר ביקורו השני בארץ, שהה איזה חודשים בפריז ובלונדון.
אחת המטרות של ישיבתו בלונדון היתה "ללמוד אנגלית כראוי, כי מאוד אחפוץ להגיע
בה עד מדרגת סופר כל שהוא", שם, עמ' תע״ב. בזמן אותו ביקור רכש לו אנציקלו־
פדיה של הספרות האנגלית, שם, עמ' תע״ג.

[11] אגרות, ג', עמ' 235–237; ראה גם שם, 205, 207; ד', עמ' 189.

[12] "פרקי זכרונות", כל כתבי, עמ' תס״ז, תצ״ה; אגרות, ה', עמ' 181–182, 276–277.

בתוכו, ואף זה בצורה צנועה ומאופקת.[13] אך מרשימותיו האוטוביאוגרפיות
נמצאנו למדים שבעודינו נער בן שש עשרה — שבע עשרה סיים את הש״ס,
רכש לו בקיאות בשו״ת [בעיקר בענייני גיטין] ובמשך מספר שנים היה כותב
״הערות על רוב הש״ס והש״ע והרמב״ם.״ [14] לימים הוא קרא את גייגר וגרץ,
מונק, רנן, שירר, נלדקה, לצרוס ושטיינטל בחכמת ישראל, ואת לוק, יום,
מיל, הרברט ספנסר וסדג׳וויק בהגותה של אנגליה. הוא קרא גם בשקספיר,
שילר, ניטשה, מטרלינק, גיאורג ברנדס ובאחרים.[15]

התקופה השנייה והחשובה בחייו היא תקופת אודיסה (1907—1886), שנמשכה
למעלה מעשרים ואחת שנה, מאמצע שנת 1886 עד שילהי 1907, כלומר, משנות
חיבת ציון הראשונות, דרך ימי הציונות של הרצל ועד שנים אחדות אחרי
מותו. אודיסה מאותן השנים היתה המרכז החשוב ביותר של יהדות אירופה
המזרחית, הן מבחינת הפעילות הציבורית והן מבחינת הפעילות הספרותית.
כאן ישבו מנדלי, פינסקר, לילינבלום, רבניצקי, ז. אפשטיין, לוינסקי,
דובנוב, בן עמי, ומאוחר יותר אף ״רב צעיר״, ביאליק, קלוזנר ואחרים.[16]
שנים אלה היו הפוריות בעבודתו הספרותית. כל המאמרים שהוכנסו אחר כך
לשלושת הכרכים הראשונים של על פרשת דרכים, ואף חלק ניכר מכרך
ד׳, נכתבו כאן.

התקופה השלישית בחייו היא תקופת לונדון, שנמשכה ארבע-עשרה שנים,
מסוף 1907 עד סוף 1921. תקופת שפל וירידה היא. בבואו לכאן הרגיש אחה״ע
שזקן מדי היה כדי להסתגל לסביבה החדשה ולהכות בה שורש. כזר הרגיש,[17]
והמחשבה על התיישבות בארץ עלתה בליבו לעתים תכופות.[18] רוב ימיו עברו
עליו ב״סיטי״, בעסקי חברת ויסוצקי, ולפעולה ספרותית אינטנסיבית לא
הגיע עוד. אמנם הוא המשיך לכתוב, ומאמרים כמו ״על שתי הסעיפים״
(תר״ע) ו״סך הכל״ (תרע״ב) היכו גלים בשעתם ועוררו רעש בציבור היהודי,
אולם פריוונו הספרותי הלך וירד, מחלותיו תכפו, והוא הוכרח לעתים יותר
ויותר קרובות לקחת לו חופשות של מנוחה והבראה ביבשת. לבסוף, משנת
1915 בערך, הכתיבה כמעט שנאסרה עליו.

[13] ראה גם את דעתו ״המקצועית״ על ״קיצור התלמוד״ להרב טשרנוביץ, אגרות, ו׳,
עמ׳ 13—12, וכן שם, א׳, עמ׳ 212, 243.

[14] אגרות, ה׳, עמ׳ 297; שם, א׳, 212; ו׳, 13—12.

[15] כל כתבי, עמ׳ ס״ב, ס״ד, ס״ז, צ״ט, קנ״ו, קס״ב, קס״ד, קע״ט, רס״ט, ש״א ועוד;
אגרות, א׳, עמ׳ 34, 39, 97; ב׳, 17—16, 47; ג׳, 97; ה׳, 221 ועוד.

[16] ראה ב. שוחטמן, ״אודיסה״, הרב י. ל. הכהן פישמן (עורך), ערים ואמהות
בישראל, חלק שני (ירושלים, תש״ח), עמ׳ 108—58. ראה בעיקר מעמ׳ 84 והלאה.

[17] אגרות, ג׳, עמ׳ 290, 293; ד׳, עמ׳ 1, 10, 294.

[18] שם, ד׳, עמ׳ 85, 289; ה׳, עמ׳ 10, 16, 188, 281; ו׳, עמ׳ 36, 59, 61.

התקופה האחרונה והקצרה בחייו היא זו של ארץ ישראל, או, ביתר דיוק,
של תל-אביב, אליה הגיע בראשית 1922 ובה שבק חיים לכל חי אחרי חמש
שנים, בראשית 1927. חולה רציני היה כבר אז, סובל מהסתיידות העורקים
ומקשיי נשימה,[19] ואף הספיק בשנים ההן לסדר ולהביא לדפוס את ששת
הכרכים של אגרותיו עם ״המילואים״, שלא הוכנסו להוצאות הראשונות של
על פרשת דרכים.

אישיותו

בשירו ההגותי-סמלי, ״האדם אינו אלא״ העלה ש. טשרניחובסקי מעין
פילוסופיה דטרמיניסטית בנוגע לזיקה שבין נוף ילדות וגורל אדם עלי
אדמות:[20] שחיי האדם אינם אלא תהליך התממשות של אותות וסמלים שנוף
הילדות חרת בנפשו בעודו ילד; פרשת התרשמויות ראשוניות הלובשת עור
וגידים ״תוך מלחמת הקיום.״ ייתכן שאמת-מה בתורה זו לגבי דרך חייו
ויצירתו של המשורר, אולם אין היא תופסת לגבי אחה״ע. ואף אם נאמר
שאמת-מה בה בה גם לגביו, שונה המובן של מרכיביה ושונה היחס שביניהם. לא
נוף טבע הוא שהיה לו השפעה כלשהי עליו, אלא נוף אדם ותרבות.[21] נוף
דעות וספרים הוא שנחרת בנפשו (ואף זה בתקופת חיים יותר מאוחרת),
ומסיבות חייו הן שטילטלוהו למקור מחצבתם של אלו. כוונתנו, כמובן,
לעקירתו מנוף מולדתו הרוסי והתיישבותו באנגליה לתקופה של ארבע-עשרה
שנה. בוודאי, אין לראות במעבר זה אלא מקרה, אולם אם אנו מעלים על
ליבנו את ההשפעה שהשפיעו עליו הוגים כיום, מיל וספנסר בפרשת הדת
ותורת ההתפתחות, הרי שהיקלעותו למקורה של זו מתמלאת כמעט משמעות
סמלית.

לא זה בלבד שקירבת-רוח הרגיש לכמה וכמה מגדולי מחשבתה של אנגליה,
אלא אף במזגו קרוב היה לטיפוס האנגלי. אדם מסתייג ומאופק היה, שמרני
וזהיר, נרתע מקיצוניות ומאמין בצמיחה איטית ובהתפתחות הדרגתית. רגיש
ומתרגש היה, אך ידע לשמור על קור רוחו ולהסתיר ברבים את רגשותיו.[22]
ועוד עובדה טיפוסית היתה לחייו והשפעה מכרעת היתה לה על דעותיו

---

[19] שם, ר׳, עמ׳ 52, 61, 63.

[20] ש. טשרניחובסקי, שירים, הוצ׳ שוקן (ירושלים ותל-אביב, תש״ה), עמ׳ 466–469.

[21] ב״פרקי זכרונות״ הוא כותב: ״אף על פי שגרתי בכפר כל מיטב שנות נעורי, לא
למדתי שם לאהוב את הטבע... אני הייתי טרוד בלמודים וספרים, ולא שמתי לב אל
הדר הטבע״, כל כתבי, עמ׳ תפ״ג–תפ״ד.

[22] לדובנוב כתב: ״הלא ידעת שאינני מסוגל להביע רגשותי ׳בקול רם׳. רבים חושבים
שאני בכלל אינני מוכשר לבוא לידי התרגשות. זה לא אמת. אבל יש בתכונת נפשי איזה
דבר המונע אותי נגד רצוני לגלות רגשות לבי באיזו צורה ׳חיצונית׳ ״, אגרות, ה׳, עמ׳
273. ראה גם שם, עמ׳ 73–74; ד׳, עמ׳ 167.

ופעולתו. בעל תורת "המרכז הרוחני" שלנו — איש מעשה ועסקים היה רוב
ימיו. רק במשך שש שנים בלבד, מסוף 1896 עד סוף 1902, שנות עריכתו את
"השלח", היה לאיש ספרות מקצועי שעל הספרות היתה פרנסתו, ואילו במשך
יתר שנות חייו — בעולם המעשה עברו ימיו, ובספרות עסק רק בשעות הפנאי
המועטות שנשארו לו. וקשה שלא לתמוה ולתהות על ההשגים האינטלק־
טואליים שאחה"ע יכול היה להגיע אליהם אילו לא היה צריך לשלם מחיר כה
יקר בעבודה ובזמן בעד חירותו הכלכלית. לפחות הוא בעצמו ראה בדרך חייו
זו משום תקלה ומכשול לעבודתי הספרותית [23] ומשום תעודת עניות לספרות
העברית של ימיו. בסוף 1902, כשהחליט לעזוב את עריכת "השלח" ולקבל את
המשרה שהוצעה לו בחברת ויסוצקי, הוא כתב במרירות:

לא הגדתי לכם אף אחת ממאה מכל אשר בלבי... מכל אשר ירגיש סופר
דברי ימינו בעתיד... בבואו לספר לקוראיו, כי בדורנו זה, שכל כך
הרבה להתפאר ב׳תחיתו׳, הוכרח אחד מראשי הסופרים הלאומיים, שעמד
שש שנים בראש מכה"ע היחידי שהיה ראוי לשם ׳ספרות׳, לפשוט מעליו
׳חלוקא דרבנן׳ ולהיות פקיד בבית מסחר בשביל להנצל מלחם של בזיון
ושנוררות.[24]

למרות דברים מפורשים אלה מפי בעה"ד בעצמו, ספק הוא אם שינוי בתנאי
חייו הכלכליים היה משפיע במידה ניכרת על תרומתו ההגותית. נראה לנו
שבעצם מיצה אחה"ע את עצמו ונתן מה שהיה בידו לתת. אמנם הוא בעצמו
הרגיש שכמה צדדים בתורתו, בעיקר דעתו על המוסר כעיקרה של היהדות
וכנקודת־מוקד בתפיסת הלאומיות שלו, יש מקום לערער עליהם, ובמשך
שנים רבות חלם על התעמקות בפרשה זו, על מנת לחבר ספר מקיף וממצה
עליה, אולם לידי מעשה הוא לא הגיע. "זה כשנתיים", הוא כותב לי. קלוזנר
ב־1904, "אני חולם על דבר חבור ספר על נושא אחד כללי שיברר מהותה של
היהדות הלאומית ודרך התפתחותה, וממילא יהיה כעין תשובה על שאלת
קיומה של היהדות" (שעורר אז ש. י. הורוויץ).[25] כשנתיים אחר כך הוא חוזר
על אותו רעיון במכתב לז. שכטר:

הענף היותר קרוב ללבי מענפי חכמת היהדות הוא מוסר היהדות, לא
במובן הדוגמטי, אלא בדרך התפתחותו ההיסטורית. ואחד מחלומותי
היותר יפים, שעדיין לא אבדה תקוותי לראותו הולך ומתקיים, הוא
לכתוב ספר על הנושא הזה או חלק ממנו.[26]

[23] שם, ד׳, עמ׳ 137, 256—255.
[24] שם, ג׳, עמ׳ 90.   [25] שם, שם, עמ׳ 192.
[26] שם, שם, עמ׳ 237—236; ראה גם ק. סילמן, "שיחה עם אחד העם", הפועל הצעיר,
גל׳ 4—3, עמ׳ 24—23.

אין זאת אלא שהרצון לחבר ספר כזה, הוא שהניעהו להענות להזמנתו של
כורש אדלר ב־1912 לבוא ל״דרופסי קולג׳ " לשורת הרצאות על המוסר
היהודי. קווה קיווה שהתחייבות זו תאלצהו ותדרבנהו לעסוק בנושא באופן
אינטנסיבי. אולם משהתקרב מועד ההרצאות המוסכם, הוא חזר בו. הוא הגיע
לכלל מסקנה, כתב אז לד״ר י. פרידלנדר, שעוד הרבה צדדים בנושא דורשים
עיון מעמיק יותר, מה שעלול לקחת עבודה של שנים.27 מכאן ואילך שוב לא
היה בטוח אם אי־פעם יגשים חלומו זה. לזלמן אפשטיין, שהתאונן לפניו על
ש״כשרונו לא הביא את הפרי שיכול היה להביא," הוא השיב:

גם אני מרגיש כזאת בנוגע לעצמי, ותמה אני אם יש אדם מישראל שיוכל
להיות שבע־רצון מעבודת חייו, כשעושה חשבונו עם נפשו בטרם ירד
המסך. במצבנו הנורא אי אפשר שימצא לנו שדה־עבודה רחב־ידיים
למדי ותנאי־עבודה נאותים למדי בשביל שנוכל להוציא מן הכח אל
הפועל כל מה שהכשירנו לו הטבע בצאתנו לאויר העולם.28

אם במכתב זה עוד תלה אחה״ע את קולר אי־הגשמת תכניתו בתנאים
חיצוניים, הרי במכתב לדובנוב, כעבור למעלה משנה, הוא הוסיף על אלה אף
גורמים אישיים־סוביקטיביים: "אפשר ג״כ, שאני בעצמי לפי תכונת רוחי
ואופן חנוכי ועבודתי הקודמת — איני מסוגל לעבודה כזו, הדורשת הצטמצמות
כל הכוחות הרוחניים בנקודה אחת במשך שנים רבות." 29 ברור, איפוא, שלא
גורמים אוביקטיביים בלבד הם שמנעו ממנו לעשות יותר משעשה, ובעיקר
בנושא שהיה קרוב לליבו כל חייו, אלא מעצורים מסוג אחר. הוגה דעות
מעמיק, בעל מחשבה צלולה וכוח ניתוח, היה אחה״ע, אולם לא חוקר שיטתי.
מחשבתו נצמדה תמיד לבעייה אקטואלית, מוגבלת ומוגדרת, ובמסגרתה היה
בכוחו להעמיק ולחדש. אולם להינתק מבעיות השעה ולהלין עצמו באוהלה של
תורה לשמה, על מנת לחקור ענין לאשורו ולבססו ביסוס מדעי — לזה בוודאי
לא היתה לו לא נטייה ולא סבלנות.30 במקרה דנן, בוודאי שנוספה עוד סיבה
לרפות את ידיו, והיא, הקושי שבעצם הנושא בו בחר — המוסר היהודי. שתי
מטרות הציב לו אחה״ע בפרשה זו: ראשית, להפריד בין המוסר היהודי והדת
היהודית ולהעמיד המוסר על גורמים אוטונומיים־אימננטיים, ושנית, לקשרו

27 אגרות, ה׳, עמ׳ 61.
28 שם, שם, עמ׳ 39.
29 שם, שם, עמ׳ 180.
30 שם, ד׳, עמ׳ 26; ה׳, עמ׳ 111. וראה דר׳ נח ח. רוזנבלום, "אחד העם והידע
ההיסטורי", ספר היובל לכבוד שלום בארון, III (ירושלים, תשל״ה), של״א־
שנ״ב, בעיקר ״ב״.

קשר אינטגרלי עם הלאומיות היהודית ולהוכיח תוקפו וחיובו לגבי המאמינים
בה — משימות קשות בלי ספק ואולי אף בלתי אפשריות.

תהא דעתנו בדבר השפעת פעילותו המסחרית של אחה״ע על פריונו הספ־
רותי מה שתהא, אין ספק שפעילות זו הטביעה את חותמתה על טיבה ורוחה של
יצירתו. קיים קשר ישיר בינה ובין הריאליזם החריף המציין מאמרים כ״לא זה
הדרך״, ״אמת מארץ ישראל״, ״בתי הספר ביפו״, ״היישוב ואפוטרופסיו״,
״הציונות המדינית״, ״סך הכל״ ורבים אחרים. כבעל חשבון, היודע ענייני
תקציבים ומאזנים, וכבעל עין חדה ומוח מנתח היודע להסתכל בפרטים,
לצרפם לכללים ולהסיק מהם המסקנות ההגיוניות, הוא מופיע במאמרים
אלה.[31] אכן, אין זה מקרה שהוא נשלח כמה פעמים לארץ ישראל על ידי
״הועד האודסאי״, כדי לעמוד מקרוב על מצב היישוב. כי אמנם לא היה אדם
מתאים ממנו לתפקיד זה של בוחן ובודק. כשהשעה היתה צריכה לכך היה
בכוחו לרכוש לו בזמן קצר מומחיות וידע בענייני פלחה וכרמים, ייצור
ושיווק, קניית קרקעות ובעיות עבודה וחינוך. ואמנם לא רחוקים היו עניינים
אלה מניסיונות חייו הקודמים. אפילו בנעוריו, כשישב בבית אביו על התורה
והעבודה, ״הייתי משתתף בענייני מסחרנו פחות או יותר, ביחוד בימי הקיץ
כשהיה אבי יוצא לחו״ל להתרפא.״ ומה היו הדברים שעסק בהם? ״עבודת
האדמה בכפר, בית משרפות יי״ש, עסקי יערות, פיטום שוורים ועוד דברים
שהיו קשורים בהנהלת עסקי הכפר.״[32] יתרה מזה: ריאליזם זה אופייני הנהו
לא רק למאמריו בענייני מעשה, אלא גם לאספקטים ״הרוחניים״ של יצירתו:
לדעותיו על הדת, המוסר, ההיסטוריה, הספרות העברית ובעיות ההווה.
רוחניותו ״ארצית״ היא תמיד, פרגמטית, ואינה חורגת מהגבולות האימננטיים
של המציאות האנושית הקיומית.

אילו היה אחה״ע רק זה, מסתכל צלול־דעת ורואה נכוחות, העומד על
משמר השכל הישר וההערכה המפוכחת, ומזהיר נגד כל אשליות שבדימיון
והליכה בגדולות, בודאי ובודאי שלכבוד ולהוקרה היה ראוי, אולם ספק הוא
אם היה זוכה להשפעה רבה. אין השפעה על דור שלם יכולה להיות אך פרי
כוחות מרסנים שבציגון הרוחות ובקיצוץ הכנפיים. אמנם ריאליסט היה וצמוד
לקיים ומציאותי, אולם יחד עם זה גדול־אמונה היה ביחוד האומה, בכוחות
היצירה הטמונים בה ובעתיד שעוד שעוד נכון לה. רק מיזוגם של השנים, של

---

[31] ב־1899 הוא כתב לא. גוטמן בניקולאיב: ״רוב שנותי גדלתי בין הסוחרים ולא אוכל
עד היום להשתחרר מן הפדנטיסמוס בעניני כספים שסגלתי לי בחברתם״, אגרות, ב׳,
עמ׳ 16. ברוח דומה הוא כתב לא. קפלן מחברת ״אחיאסף״ בורשה: ״לא מבית המדרש
יצאתי להיות רידקטור בישראל, ולהנם תחשוב שלא אדע את ההבדל בין חתימת
פנקסים ובין בילנס חודשי... היו לי עסקים יותר גדולים וסבוכים״, שם, א׳, עמ׳ 107.
[32] ״פרקי זכרונות״, כל כתבי, עמ׳ תצ״ה.

ריאליזם מזה ואמונה לוהטת מזה, הוא שעשהו לדבר הדור. מעשיותו נרתמה
לחזונו, וחזונו — לא ניתק מעולם מקרקע המציאות ומגבלותיה.

אישיות מרכזית היה אחה״ע בדורו. לא עבר אלא זמן קצר מאז באו
לאודסה ב־1884 והוא נבחר לוועד חובבי ציון שבעיר ונעשה מראשי המדברים
בו.[33] עם ייסוד ״בני משה״ (תרמ״ט), בעיקבות ״לא זה הדרך״, היה הוא להם
לפה ולמנהיג.[34] באמצע שנות התשעים, כשהוחלט על הוצאת ״השלח״, שוב
נתלו העיניים בו כעורך. בתור עורך היה אחה״ע לדבר הדור ותחת ידו היה
״השלח״ לבמה הספרותית החשובה של הזמן. הוא חינך את קהל הסופרים
והקוראים כאחת לאחריות ספרותית וציבורית, לטעם טוב ולכתיבה עניינית,
בהירה וסדירה. די לדפדף באיגרותיו מאותן השנים כדי לעמוד על קשריו
הרחבים. הוא קרב לעברית את הידועים שבחכמי הזמן: את דוד קויפמאן, דוד
כהנא, מאיר איש־שלום, ש. קרויס, ברנפלד, מלטר, ניימרק ואחרים. הוא
עמד בקשרים עם מנדלי, לילינבלום, רבניצקי, לוינסקי, פרישמן, ברדי־
צבסקי, דרויאנוב, ברייניון, אהרנפרייז, פיארברג, רב צעיר, קלויזנר
ואחרים מרוסיה ופולין, ועם ש. בן ציון, א. ז. רבינוביץ, מ. סמילנסקי, יהושע
ברזילי, ד. ילין ואחרים מהארץ.

ללא משוא־פנים היה, וכשם שידע לקרב, ידע גם לרחק. הוא לא גרס תחילה
את כתיבתו האימפרסיוניסטית של הלל צייטלין,[35] כשם שלא היה מרוצה
מכתיבתו חסרת הסדר והדיוק של שאול פנחס רבינוביץ.[36] הוא תבע בהירות
ופשטות, ולא היה דבר שהרתיעו יותר מאשר עירפול דברים וגיבובם. בעיקר
הוא לא היה יכול להגיע לעמק השווה עם מיכה יוסף ברדיצבסקי. שונים היו
השניים לא רק בהשקפותיהם על בעיות הדור ובגישתם לספרות, אלא גם במזגם
ובסיגנונם. שקול ומתון, שואף לסדר ולבהירות היה אחה״ע, ואילו ברדי־
צבסקי — אימפולסיבי היה, קצר־נשימה, מבריק ומזדרק מעניין לעניין.
הגיונותיו ודעותיו, פרי הברקות אינטואיטיביות היו ופחות פרי שיקול הגיוני
מדייק ומנתח. הוא גם היה חסר סבלנות בכל הנוגע לסגנון, למבנה, לסדר
ורציפות. מה הפלא שאחה״ע החזיר לו כמה וכמה מסיפוריו ורשימותיו.[37]
אולם לא בברדיצבסקי בלבד נהג כך. במידת הדין, ולא תמיד במידת הערכה
ספרותית נכונה, הוא נקט גם כלפי פרישמן,[38] ביאליק,[39] טשרניחובסקי,[40]

[33] כל כתבי, עמ׳ תס״ח.
[34] שם, עמ׳ תל״ז.
[35] אגרות, א׳, עמ׳ 68—67; ב׳, עמ׳ 26.
[36] שם, ב׳, עמ׳ 23, 44, 240—239.
[37] שם, א׳, עמ׳ 146, 179, 180, 181, 185, 246—245, 250; ב׳, עמ׳ 228.
[38] שם, א׳, עמ׳ 40, 45; ב׳, עמ׳ 184.
[39] שם, ב׳, עמ׳ 57.
[40] שם, שם, עמ׳ 264—263.

ברנר,[41] ברייניו,[42] קלויזנר,[43] הורודצקי,[44] ואחרים. על ידי כך הוא הרגיז
פעמים, ושלא בכוונה, אף העליב, אך יחד עם זה הוא העלה את רמת הספרות
ותרם לשיפור הטעם, הסגנון וההיגיון בה.

איש ציבור מובהק היה במשך כל חייו ועוקב בעניין ומסירות אחרי כל
המתרחש בעולם היהודי. אין לך כמעט גליון של "השלח" בעריכתו, בו לא
הוקדש מקום רב למאורעות ותופעות מכל העולם היהודי של הזמן. הוא בעצמו
היה משתתף בוועידות ובאסיפות של ציוני רוסיה, נוסע לקונגרסים הציוניים
וכן שימש כחבר משלחת מטעם חובבי ציון ל"נדיב" בדבר שיחרור המושבות
מהאפוטרופסות שלו. ארבע פעמים הוא ביקר בארץ, לפני שהתיישב בה
ישיבת קבע. אפילו בתקופת לונדון, כשרחוק היה ממרכזי הפעילות היהודית
וכוחותיו הלכו ותשו, הוא לקח עוד חבל פעיל בעבודות ההכנה לייסוד הטכניון
בחיפה, ויחד עם שמריהו לוין נלחם על העברית כלשון ההוראה בו לעתיד,
ומשגברה בשנות מלחמת העולם הראשונה הפעילות המדינית בלונדון, שותף
אף הוא בה לעתים קרובות על ידי ח. וויצמן, צ׳לנוב וסוקולוב.

המבקר

בעמדת מבקר תפס מראשית דרכו, ובה החזיק עד סוף פעולתו הספרותית.
כשפירסם בניסן תרע"ב את ה"סך הכל" שלו, ובו דעותיו המסתייגות בנוגע
להיקף ההתיישבות היהודית העתידה בארץ וספקותיו בנוגע לאפשרות עלייתו
של מעמד איכרים ופועלים חקלאים יהודים בה,[45] וגל של התנפלויות נשפך
עליו,[46] כה כתב למשה סמילנסקי:

> איש מלחמה אני זה עשרים וארבע שנה ואיני זוכר אף מקרה אחד שיצא
> מי מן הסופרים לעמוד לימיני בעת שהתנפלו עלי מכל עברים. כך היה
> אחרי ׳אמת מארץ ישראל׳, כך היה בימי מלחמתי עם הציונות של הרצל
> וכו׳ וכו׳. תמיד הייתי יחיד נגד הרבים, ולא נפל לבי ולא נחלשה דעתי.[47]

במלים קצרות אלה סיכם אחה"ע בעצמו את דרכו בספרות זמנו, שבבחינת
עמידה ארוכה אחת בשער היתה. אם את חובבי ציון הוא ביקר על מעשיהם

[41] שם, שם, עמ׳ 91.
[42] שם, שם, עמ׳ 257.
[43] שם, שם, עמ׳ 230 ; ג׳, עמ׳ 32.
[44] שם, ב׳, עמ׳ 12—11, 26.
[45] כל כתבי, עמ׳ תכ"א—ת"ל.
[46] ראה, למשל, את תגובתו החריפה של יוסף אהרונוביץ "על ה׳סך הכל׳", הפועל
הצעיר, 5, גל׳ 16, עמ׳ 6—3.
[47] אגרות, ה׳, עמ׳ 2.

הנחפזים שללא הכנה אירגונית היו וללא חריש לבבות עמוק, שמן ההכרח היו לדעתו שיקדמו להם, הוא ביקר את הציונים המדיניים על הפומביות הקולנית שלהם, על התיימרותם ב״מעשים גדולים״ תוך הזנחת ״יום הקטנות״ ועניני רוח ותרבות, אך מעל לכל — על היות התעוררותם פרי גורמים שליליים בעיקר ומנהיגיהם יהודים מערביים ללא דעת יהודית וללא שרשים בתרבות האומה. כמובן, אין זה הכל. רחב היה היקפה של ביקורת זו והיא כללה את כל חזיונות הדור ודורות העבר הקרוב. היא עשתה את חשבונה עם ההשכלה ובנות־לווייתה: חכמת ישראל, תנועת הריפורמה וההתבוללות המערבית על צורותיה השונות, כשם שהיא לא העלימה גם את עינה מהלאומיות בנוסח ״האוטונומיזם״ של דובנוב וה״בונד״ ומכל תופעה אחרת שהיתה לה איזו שהיא נגיעה בגורל ישראל.

לכאורה ביקורת דיסקורסיבית היתה זו, נאחזת באקראי בעניינים מעניינים שונים, ובטרם הגיעה למיצויו של האחד וכבר היא אצה וניטפלת לעניין אחר. כך, כנראה, חש לא פעם אחה״ע בעצמו. מכאן חוסר הסיפוק שהרגיש לפעמים בעבודתו וחלומו על חיבור מקיף ושלם שיברר וימצה באופן שיטתי את עיקריה של הלאומיות היהודית ויעמידה על בסיס עיוני רחב, ולא היא. המעיין בכלל מאמריו, מזמניהם השונים ועל נושאיהם הרבים, מסתבר לו, שלא עניינים נפרדים לפניו אלא פרקים של מסכת אחת, בבחינת ענפי אילן אחד שששרש אחד להם ומקרקע אחת הם יונקים. לא ידע, כנראה, אחה״ע בעצמו שאכן הוא כתב את הספר שחלם עליו. אלא מה? הוא בעצמו לא היה, כנראה, לגמרי משוכנע באמיתו ולא היה מרוצה מביסוסו העיוני.

הכינויים ״מבקר״ ו״ביקורת״ ביחס לאחה״ע והגותו, סכנה של סילוף בהם שבהמהמעטת דמות וערך, הן לגבי האיש והן לגבי משנתו. ביודעים או בלא־יודעים נלווים הם בליבנו למושגים של חוסר מקוריות ויניקה מרשויות זרות. אך תהא דעתנו על מחשבתו מה שתהא, מקורית היא בעיקרה ומרעננת בחדירתה ובראשוניות הסתכלותה. יתר על כן, אופיה הביקורתי אך מטודי הינהו ולא מהותי. היא נזקקת לנושאי ביקורתה לא לשם עצמם, אלא לשם בירור וליבון תורתה היא. בבחינת פינוי חלקת קרקע היא שהעלאתה קוצים וצמחי בר, ומן ההכרח להבר אותה כדי להזריעה בזרע בריא נושא פרי. בקיצור, ביקורת בונה היא, שמתוך התמודדותה בהשקפות הנוגדות אותה, היא מבהירה ומעמיקה את תורתה היא.

תורה זו אינה אלא תורת הלאומיות היהודית, או, ביתר דיוק, הלאומיות הציונית, שאחה״ע היה גדול מנסחיה ומטיפיה. העיון במהות היהדות שתורה זו הזקיקתו לו, לא חדש היה ולא הוא שפתח בו. מרכזי הוא במחשבה היהודית מכל הדורות, אלא שבכל ניסוחיה הקודמים העמדה מהות זו תמיד על הדת היהודית, על אותו קשר מופלא שבין הקב״ה, ישראל ואורייתא. אפילו

בניסוחיה המשכיליים מהמאה התשע-עשרה, היא לא הוצאה ממסגרת זו.
אופיה "השמיימי" של היהדות נשתמר כולו במשנתו של שד"ל, בה העמדה זו
על מוסר החמלה ועל שכר ועונש ובחירת ישראל.[48] רנ"ק הכניס אמנם
למשנתו את עיקרון ההתפתחות ההיסטורית [49] ועל ידי כך הוא פתח פתח
לגישה ביקורתית הן לגבי המקרא והן לגבי תורה שבעל פה,[50] אולם אף הוא
לא סטה מאמונת היסוד, והיא, שייחוד האומה ייחוד דתי הוא ועיקרו בדביקות
האומה ברוחני המוחלט, ובה — בדביקות זו — גם הערובה לנצחיותה.[51] אפילו
פרץ סמולנסקין, שבלא ספק היה בין חלוצי הלאומיות החילונית בספרות
העברית החדשה, לא היה יכול להעלות על דעתו לאומיות יהודית שתהא
מנותקת לגמרי מהמסורת, ואף הוא חייב את שמירתן של כמה וכמה מצוות-
יסוד כחלק מההזדהות הלאומית.[52]

פרשת הדת: בין חירות עיונית וחובת אהבה וכבוד

אחה"ע היה הראשון שהעלה תורה של לאומיות יהודית המנותקת ניתוק גמור
מהדת. לפחות מבחינת המציאות ההיסטורית של ימיו ניסוחה היה יותר פרו-
גנוסטי מאשר משקף מצב דברים ריאלי. רובו המכריע של עמנו במזרח
אירופה עדיין היה שומר מסורת [53] כשהוא הכריז שתקופת שלטון הדת בחיי
האומה מתקרבת לקיצה ושמעתה ואילך אין לפניה דרך אחרת, כדי להבטיח
את המשך קיומה, אלא על ידי הגשמת הלאומיות הציונית.[54]

לאומיות זו, טוען אחה"ע, לא חדשה היא בעצם, אלא בבחינת "רעיון
מאוחר" היא, שבמשך דורות היה גנוז בתודעת האומה וכבר חשבוהו לדבר
"שעבר זמנו בפועל", והנה באו מסיבות החיים והחיוהו ב"תמונתו החדשה"
של חיבת ציון.[55] שרשים עתיקים לה בהוויית העם הקדומה, כאשר "חפץ
הקיום הלאומי חי בקירבו חיים בריאים וטבעיים, והעם הלך אחריו אל כל

---

[48] ראה "יסודי התורה" במחקרי היהדות, כרך 1, חלק 1 (ורשה, תרע"ג), עמ' 48–
9; ראה גם "מהות היהדות" בשמואל דוד לוצאטו, כתבים, ההדיר וצירף מבוא
והערות מנחם עמנואל הרטום, ספרית דורות, מס' 47 (ירושלים, 1976), עמ' 56–47.
[49] ראה "הקדמת רבי נחמן קרוכמאל ל"שערי אמונה צרופה" במורה נבוכי הזמן
(ברלין, תרפ"ד), עמ' ו–ז'.
[50] שם, שערים י"א–י"ד.
[51] שם, שער ז' וראשית שער ח'.
[52] ראה "עת לטעת", פרץ... סמולנסקין, מאמרים, כרך 2 (ירושלים, תרפ"ה), עמ'
30; "עת לעשות", שם, כרך 1, עמ' 174–173.
[53] ראה "תורה מציון", כל כתבי אחד העם, עמ' ת"ז.
[54] שם, עמ' כ"ב, פ"ט, קל"ז-קל"ח, ת"ב–ת"ג ועוד.
[55] "מוקדם ומאוחר בחיים", שם, ע' פ'.

אשר נחהו ולא התחכם יותר.״ 56 ראיה לקיומו של רגש זה מקדמת דנא הוא
מוצא באופי הקיבוצי של תורת משה, שתכלית כל מצוותיה וחוקיה היתה
״הצלחת כלל האומה בארץ נחלתה, ואל אושר האיש הפרטי לא תשים לב. כל
איש ישראל הוא בעיניה רק אבר אחד מעם ישראל, והטוב אשר ישיג את
הכלל הוא השכר למעשי הפרט.״ 57 יתרה מזה, רגש זה, או ״חפץ הקיום,״ כפי
שמכנהו אחה״ע — בו בעצם אף שורש הדת, והוא הוא שכיוון את התפתחותה
משלביה הפרימיטיביים-אליליים עד לדרגתה העליונה, זו של המונותיאיזם.
בעיקבות ״דוד יום ותלמידיו״ מלמדנו אחה״ע שמקור הדת אינו בדעת,
בהסתכלות בפלאי העולם, אלא ברגשות ״הבהלה והפחד״ של האדם מפני
רעות הטבע והחברה כאחת. מפחד ״תהפוכות הטבע ומחיות רעות״ הגיע האדם
״לרעיון הגדול כי יש אדונים לכל חזיונות הטבע, אדונים שאפשר לפייסם
בדברים ולכפר פניהם במנחה;״ ומפחד הרעות שבין איש לרעהו הוא הגיע
לרעיון של ״אלוהי משפחה מיוחדים,״ שבתהליך ההתפתחות ההיסטורית הפכו
לאלוהי השבט, ובדרגה יותר גבוהה — לאל הלאומי. 58

כוחות אלה פעלו גם בהוויית ישראל הקדומה. עובדי עבודה זרה היו
אבותינו, עובדים לאלילי הטבע והשבט, ורק הסכנה הלאומית בימי הפלשתים
היא שהעלתה בליבם את האל הלאומי. 59 בדומה לכך היתה ההאבקות שבין
המעצמות הגדולות בתקופת המלכים, כאשר ארץ ישראל היתה מרמס
לצבאותיהן, סיבה לעליית המונותיאיזם. תחילה דימדם הרעיון בליבות
יחידים, ורק בעיקבות החורבן וגלות בבל נוצרו התנאים הנאותים להתפשטותו
בקרב כל שכבות האומה. הרגש הלאומי שגבר אז והגיע למדרגה גבוהה, לא
יכול היה להשלים עם העובדה שאלוהי בבל הם שניצחו את אלוהי ישראל,
ובגין התגברות רגש זה ניקלטה אז בלבבות האמונה שאלוהי ישראל הוא גם
אלוהי העולם, וכשם שהעלה את בבל הוא עוד ישפילנה, וכשם שהגלה את
העם הוא עוד יגאלנו. אמנם אין אחה״ע אומר במפורש שהלאומיות היא
שהולידה את המונותיאיזם, אבל היא שעזרה להתפשטותו בעם. בשעת שפל
לו, חיפש העם עידוד ומיפלט בדת, ואכן, הצילה הדת את הלאומיות, אולם
מחיר גבוה שילמה הלאומיות בעד הצלה זו, וכמעט בנפשה היה הדבר:

הרעיון הדתי הגדול אשר התעורר לתחיה בעמנו אחר החורבן הראשון,
מתחילה רק כיסוד וחיזוק אל התקוה הלאומית, התפתח והתחזק אחרי כן

56 ״חשבון הנפש״, שם, עמ׳ ס״ג.
57 ״לא זה הדרך״, שם, עמ׳ י״ב.
58 השווה: David Hume, "The Natural History of Religion," section II, VI, IX;
idem, "Dialogues Concerning Natural Religion," Pt. X in *Hume Selections*
by Charles W. Hendel (Scribner, 1927).
59 ״מוקדם ומאוחר בחיים״, כל כתבי, עמ׳ ע״ט.

בימי הבית השני, עד שמילא לב העם והתרומם על כל אשר בו וגם על
הרעיון הלאומי, אשר ממקורו שאב לפנים כוח וחיים. כל החפצים
האחרים נסוגו אחור מפני הדתיים, והעם לא שאל ולא ביקש עוד כמעט
מאומה, כי אם לעבוד את ה׳ במנוחה ושלום.[60]

אמנם הרגש הלאומי עוד המשיך לחיות, ועדות לכך מלחמות החשמונאים
והמדינה שהקימו, המלחמה הגדולה ברומא ומרד בר כוכבא, והתנועות
המשיחיות של הדורות הבאים. אולם אופיו הראשוני ניטל ממנו, והוא ביתק
והלך מארציותו ונתקשר יותר ויותר לאמונות ותקוות שלא מעלמא הדין.[61]
אין ספק, תורה זו על מקור הדת והתפתחותה, הרסנית ושלילית הינה
מבחינת המסורת, שכן מערטלת היא את הדת מאופיה הטרנסצנדנטי ומעמידה
אותה על גורמים היסטוריים-ביאולוגיים גרידא. אולם בעצם אין אחה״ע
ניזקק לה לשם עצמה ואין הוא אפילו מרחיב הדיבור עליה — אלא כדי
להבליט את הקשר הישיר שבין התפשטות המונותיאיזם והלאומיות; שהאח־
רונה היא שהסבה את הראשונה. במכתב לדובנוב מינואר 1911, הוא כותב:

הנני מחפש זה כבר בספרים המדברים על תקופה זו (ימי גלות בבל)
בשביל לראות, אולי הגיע מי לברר ולפרסם אותה ההשקפה שאני אך
רמזתי עליה במקום הנזכר (׳מוקדם ומאוחר בחיים׳) ושלפי דעתי אמיתית
היא וחשובה לנו ביחוד. שהרי לפי המוסכם, תקופת בבל, ישעיה השני,
היא שהניחה יסוד לאוניברסליסמוס, בניגוד ללאומיות היהודית הצרה,
וע״כ נתפשט אז רעיון ׳אל עולם׳ וכו׳, בעוד שלפי השקפתי, רעיון
האחדות יצא — ויכול היה לצאת — מגבול החזון הנבואי להיות לאמונת
העם כולו רק על ידי הלאומיות (ההדגשה שלו). עד עתה לא ראיתי
מי שעמד על זה, והרמז הקצר במאמרי הנ״ל לא זכה שישימו לו לב
ויפתחו את הרעיון לפרטיו.[62]

ברור, אסמכתא היסטורית קדומה חיפש אחה״ע להשקפתו בדבר פרימט
הלאומיות בתולדותינו. ״להוכיח״ רצה שהיתה תקופה בדברי ימי העם
כשקיומו טבעי היה כקיומם של עמים אחרים, ורצון השמירה על קיום זה הוא
שהסב את עליית הדת והתפתחותה. אם היה ברעיונות אלה משום אתגר, הוא

---

[60] שם, שם, עמ׳ פ.

[61] שם, שם, עמ׳ ס״ג, פ׳.

[62] אגרות, ד׳, עמ׳ 199. ראה גם את מכתבו לי. קלויזנר ממאי 1909, בו הוא מודה לו
על ח״א מ״היסטוריא ישראלית״ ששלח לו, וכותב בין היתר: ״נעים היה לי לראות ג״כ
שקבלת את השקפתי ע״ד הסבה הלאומית (הדגשה שלו, י. ב.) להתפשטות המונו־
תיאיזם בישראל בתקופת גלות בבל (במאמרי ״מוקדם ומאוחר בחיים״), שם, שם, עמ׳
82.

לא היה מכוון נגד יהודים שומרי דת ומסורת, אלא נגד ממעטי דמותה של
הלאומיות היהודית בשם אוניברסליזם תעודתי, שפשטו ביהדות מרכז אירופה
ומערבה מימות תלמידי מנדלסון ובמשך כל המאה התשע־עשרה. כלפיהם
מכוונת היתה הדגשתו, שאוניברסליזם זה, לא זה בלבד שלא בא בכוונה תחילה
לסלק את הלאומיות היהודית "הצרה", אלא, להיפך, הלאומיות היא שהעלאתה
אותו מעיקרו לשם חיזוקה וקיומה היא.

אולם לא הסתפק אחה״ע בכך. מכיוון שנתפס לתורת ההתפתחות ולגישה
רציונליסטית בכלל, הוא עשה אותן יסוד אף להשקפתו על אמונות יסוד
אחרות שביהדות המסורת. כשם שהעמיד את מקור מושג האל על גורמים
ביאולוגיים, והם, פחדי האדם במלחמתו עם רעות הטבע והחברה, כן העמיד אף
את האמונה בהשארת הנפש והעולם הבא על גורמים אלה. אמונה זו לא היתה
לדידו אלא ילידת דימיון הזיקנה ש״אין לה הכח והכישרון להתנחם ב״הבל
הבלים׳ ולמות במנוחה." 63 והוא דינה של הנבואה, שאף אותה הוא ניתק
ממקורה הטרנסצנדנטי. מיוחדת היא אמנם לישראל, אך כל מקור אחר אין לה
אלא רגישותה המוסרית של האומה ומצפון הנביא. אף משה, "אדון הנביאים,"
דמותו — פרי רוח האומה היא, ואין בכך כדי להעלות או להוריד אם אישיות
היסטורית היה או אך יציר דימיון העם.64 ברור גם מכאן שההתגלות — אבן
הפינה של בנין האמונה הישראלית — כל מקום לא נשאר לה במסגרת השקפה
רציונליסטית זו.

אך מ״עז״ זה של תורת ההתפתחות ניסה אחה״ע להוציא גם שמץ של
"מתוק," והוא, יחס פרגמטי חיובי כלפי המסורת, ובכך ייחודו בספרות הדור.
תורת ההתפתחות, כתב, מלמדת אותנו שתרבות האדם, החמרית והרוחנית,
משועבדת לחוקיות נצחית של השתנות בלתי פוסקת, לה משתעבדת כל מלכות
הדומם, הצומח והחי. הסביבה הטבעית והמסיבות ההיסטוריות המשתנות ללא־
הרף מעבירות מן העולם את תרבות העבר ומעלות עולמות חדשים עם מוסדות
וערכים חדשים. אין לנו אלא לקבל דעה זו, הוא כותב, ובידינו כלל־התנהגות
בטוח כלפי תרבות העבר שלנו. אם נבין שתרבות אבותינו פרי זמנם היתה
ופרי התנאים המיוחדים בהם חיו, כשם שתרבותנו אנו היא פרי תנאי הזמן
שלנו, לא תהיה עוד כל עילה בידינו להלחם בתרבות זו ולהשפיל על ידי כך
את זכר אבותינו ודרכי חייהם. "דור דור וצרכיו, דור דור ואמיתותיו: כבודם
של הראשונים במקומו מונח. הם חשבו את מחשבותיהם ועשו מעשיהם כראוי
להם לפי מצבם בדורותם, ואף אנו כן, לפי מצב רוחנו וחיינו עכשיו."
מחוייבים אנו בכבוד האבות, מפני שהם חלק מעצמותנו, אולם איננו מחוייבים
להמשיך בדרכיהם ולחיות במסגרות שהם יצרו. 65

63 "עבר ועתיד", כל כתבי, עמ' פ״א.
64 "משה", שם, עמ' שמ״ב והלאה.
65 "נחלת אבות", שם, עמ' רע״א–רע״ג.

הפרדה זו בין חובת "הכבוד" כלפי תרבות העבר מזה וההשתחררות הגמורה
מכוחה הנורמטיבי והמווסת מזה, היא היא למעשה עיקר תורתו של אחה"ע
בפרשת הדת, והיא היא המייחדת אותו בקרב רוב סופרי הדור ומשורריו.
להלכה לפחות ומבחינה עיונית אין כל הבדל בינו וסופרים קיצוניים כברדי־
צבסקי, ברנר ואחרים. רציונליסטים הינם כולם ורואים את עצמם פטורים
מחובות היהדות הדתית. אולם למעשה ומבחינת היחס הסוביקטיבי למסורת
קיים הבדל ניכר ביניהם. אחה"ע מדגיש שעל הקרקע ההיסטורית של האומה
הוא עומד,[66] ואילו הם מכריזים על אנטי־היסטוריותם. הוא מטיף להמשך
ולמיזוג של הווה בעבר, ואילו הם קוראים למרד, לניתוק ולהתחלה שתהא
חדשה כולה.[67] מבחינת היחס למסורת, היו רק שנים בין סופרי הדור שקרובים
היו לדעתו, והם, ביאליק ופייארבררג.

והנה צרור עובדות להסמיך בו דעה זו על יחסו הכפול של אחה"ע כלפי
המסורת, יחס של שחרור גמור ממנה מזה ושל כבוד ואהבה לה מזה. ידוע,
למשל, שבחייו האישיים לא הקפיד אחה"ע על שמירת שבת,[68] אולם הוא הגן
על ערכה ותוקפה הציבוריים, ובעצם לא שונה היתה דעתו על חשיבותה
הלאומית מזו של ר' יהודה הלוי דורות רבים לפניו. וכה כתב בתרנ"ז:

מי שמרגיש בלבו קשר אמתי עם חיי האומה בכל הדורות הוא לא יוכל
בשום אופן... לצייר לו מציאות עם ישראל בלי 'שבת מלכתא'. אפשר
לאמר בלי שום הפרזה, כי יותר משישראל שמרו על השבת שמרה השבת
אותם, ולולא היא שהחזירה להם 'נשמתם' וחדשה את חיי רוחם בכל
שבוע, היו התלאות של 'ימי המעשה' מושכות אותם יותר ויותר כלפי
מטה, עד שהיו יורדים לבסוף לדיוטא התחתונה של 'חמריות' ושפלות
מוסרית ושכלית. ועל כן בוודאי אין צורך להיות ציוני בשביל להרגיש

---

[66] אגרות, ה', עמ' 172.

[67] "עבר ועתיד", "תורה מציון" ועוד, כל כתבי, עמ' פ"א–פ"ג, ת"ו והלאה. מיכה
יוסף ברדיצ'בסקי, "שינוי ערכין", כל מאמרי מיכה יוסף בן־גוריון (ברדי־
צבסקי) (תל־אביב, תשי"ב), עמ' כ"ז והלאה. ראה ביחוד: "סתירה ובנין", "זקנה
ובחרות", "עבר והוה", "לשאלת העבר" ועוד. י. ח. ברנר, "מכאן ומכאן", כל כתבי
ברנר, כרך 1 (ישראל, תשט"ז), עמ' 325 (טור משמאל), עמ' 325 (טור מימין), עמ' 330
ועוד.

[68] במכתב מאפריל, 1916, לדר' ש. דייכס מלונדון, הוא מודה שלפעמים הוא עושה את
שבתו חול. ומדוע?

מפני שכל ימי הייתי אומר לעצמי... עשה מה שתעשה, בין בחול בין בשבת,
אך אל תעשה את תורתך חול ומדרס לפרנסים בורים. בעולם הבא אפשר
שאקבל ענשי על זה, אבל בעולם הזה אני שמח בחלקי ואיני מתחרט על
שבחרתי בפרנסה שיש בה לפעמים חלול שבת, ונצלתי על ידי כך מעבודת
הצבור, שיש בה חלול כבוד התורה, אגרות, ה', עמ' 255.

כל הדר הקדושה ההיסטורית החופפת על ׳מתנה טובה׳ זו ולהתקומם בכל
עוז נגד כל הנוגע בה.[69]

מה הפלא שהוא נרתע ונעלב מדברי נורדוי בעניין השבת. בתשובה על שאלה
מהפסגה בדבר יחסו לשבת, כתב נורדוי שמבחינה אישית אין שאלה זו
"במציאות כלל" לגביו ושהוא שובת בזמן שאפשר לו ואינו מקשר כל כוונה
דתית בשביתה זו.[70] בדברים אלה, כותב אחה"ע, הוא הרגיש "כאילו רוח
צפונית קרה באה אל ליבו והשליכה קרח על ההרגשות היותר קדושים."[71]
יותר חריפה, זועמת וסרקסטית היתה תגובתו על דברי סולומון ריינך,[72]
ממנהיגי יהדות צרפת וכי"ח בשילהי המאה הקודמת ובראשית המאה שלנו.
בשורה של שלושה מאמרים ב"אוניברס איזראליט" יצא המלומד והמנהיג
הצרפתי ללמד את אחיו "הנחשלים" ממזרח אירופה פרק בהלכות נהג תרבותי
מודרני. מגובהי המחקר החדש הודיע להם על "הגילוי" המדעי, ששורשם של
מוסדות כשבת וכשרות הוא "באמונות ובהרגשות הגסות של האדם הקדמוני,"
ומשום כך עליהם לבטלם כדי להפיל את החומה המפרידה ביניהם והחברה
האירופית התרבותית.[73] אילו היה ריינך, כותב אחה"ע, סתם "מלומד" השולח
את דברו ממרום האולימפוס להמון הלא־יודעים, לא היה בכלל שם לב
לדבריו. "זהו חזיון שכבר הורגלנו בו." אבל ריינך פרנס הציבור הוא, "אחד
מראשי חברת ייק"א וכי"ח," שנתמנה לדאוג לכלל ישראל. ואם אדם כזה
"מתפאר בפומבי, שכבר נבדל מקהל אחיו במנהגי ביתו ומאכל שולחנו," הרי
זו "עזות שאין למעלה ממנה" המראה "שכבר נתרוקן ליבם (של אנשים
כמוהו) מכל רגש יהודי אמיתי."[74]
בשיקול דעת וברצינות, וללא שמץ של התרגשות, יצא אחה"ע נגד יהודי
מערבי אחר, קלוד מונטפיורי,[75] שבשני כרכים עבי־כרס לימד סנגוריה על
"הברית החדשה" וטען "שהיא צריכה להחשב כחלק מהיהדות — החלק היותר
נאה, וישוע הנוצרי צריך להחשב כנביא בישראל — הנביא היותר גדול."[76]

[69] "שבת וציונות", כל כתבי, עמ׳ רפ"ו; הכוזרי, מאמר שלישי, סי׳ ה׳, ו׳.
[70] הפסגה, שבועון, יו"ל ע"י מ. שור, כרך ה׳ (שיקגו, 1898), גל׳ 23. ראה גם גל׳ 17.
[71] כל כתבי, עמ׳ רפ"ו.
[72] ראה עליו ב־ *Encyclopedia Judaica*, XIV (Jerusalem, 1972), p. 56
[73] ראה S. Reinach, "L'Emancipation Interieure du Judaisme," *L'Univers.*
Israelite, 56 année, no. 6 (26 Octobre, 1900), pp. 171–175; no. 8 (9 Nov),
pp. 229–231; no. 12 (7 Dec.), pp. 361–365.
[74] "גואל חדש", כל כתבי, עמ׳ ש"ב.
[75] ראה עליו ב־ *EJ*, XXI, pp. 268–269
[76] *The Synoptic Gospels*, edited with an Introduction and a Commentary by
C. G. Montefiore in two volumes (London, 1909, 2nd ed., London, 1927).

אחה״ע הגיב במאמרו ״על שתי הסעפים״, שהוא מהמצויינים שבמאמריו
לעומק ולחריפות. בו הבליט את ההבדלים היסודיים שבין היהדות והנצרות
וסיים:

כל יהודי אמיתי בין שהוא ׳אורתודוכס׳ או ׳ליברלי׳, מרגיש בעמקי
לבו, שיש ברוח עמנו איזה דבר מיוחד... אשר הטהו מן הדרך הסלולה
לשאר העמים והביאהו לברוא את היהדות על אותם היסודות שבשבילם
הוא נתון עמה עד היום ב׳קרן זוית׳, מבלתי יכולת לותר עליהם. מי שיש
בלבו הרגשה זו — ישאר בפנים. ומי שאבדה לו כבר הרגשה זו — יצא.
לפשרה אין כאן מקום.[77]

כפי שראינו לעיל קיבל אחה״ע את דעתם של חכמי המערב בנוגע להת-
פתחות האמונה הישראלית, בעיקר מושג האלוהים. אולם בתור עורך ״השלח״
היה מסרב לתת מקום בו לדעות ביקורתיות, בייחוד אם היה בהן כדי לפגוע
באחדות התורה. לש. ברנפלד, ששלח לו מאמר מסוג זה, הוא כתב:

אמנם הנני מרשה לעצמי ליתן מקום לפעמים להשקפות חפשיות ע״ד
בקרת המקרא, אבל רק בדרך אגב. אולם לקבוע פרקים שלמים ב׳השלח׳,
שכל עיקר נושאם [78] יהיה לבטל אחדות התורה [79] ולהציע השקפות
הבקרת החדשה, איני מוצא לאפשר. אילו היו באמת הדברים מבוררים
כבר כל צרכם על יסודות מדעיים שאין אחריהם כלום, לא הייתי מקפיד
על זה, אבל הרי אנו יודעים, כמה מן הספק יש בכל זה ומה רחב כאן
המקום להשערות סוביקטיביות, ובשביל השערות כאלה איני רואה צורך
להדאיב לבות המאמינים ולפגוע ברגש היותר קרוב להם.[80]

ועוד עובדה באותו עניין. בשנים שקדמו למלחמת העולם הראשונה,
כשתוכנית ייסוד הטכניון בחיפה עלתה על הפרק וחברת ״עזרה״ הגרמנית,
שנעשתה שותפה עיקרית במפעל, תבעה להכניס למצע האידיאולוגי של
המוסד סעיף שיבטיח את שמירת הדת בו, כה כתב אחה״ע לשמריהו לוין,
שיחד אתו שימש כחבר הקורטוריום:

סוף סוף כולנו מתייחסים באהבה וכבוד להדת... אנו לאומיים העומדים
על בסיס ההיסטוריה ולא לאומיים של ז׳רגון כבעלי ׳הבונד׳. אנו, אם
מאמינים או כופרים, לא נוכל להעביר בקולמוס על היסוד הדתי ולראאותו

[77] כל כתבי, עמ׳ שע״ז; ראה גם אגרות, ד׳, עמ׳ 137, 146, 152, 160.
[78] הדגשה שלו.
[79] הדגשה שלו.
[80] אגרות, ג׳, עמ׳ 52.

כאילו אינו. ואם מתיחסים אנו באהבה וכבוד אל לאומיותנו, הרי גם הדת
בכלל, אלא שאנו רואים בה לא ׳חזות הכל׳, כי אם חלק [81] מרוח העם
ההולך ומתפתח ביחד עם החיים.[82]

בעיקר לא היה יכול אחה״ע להשלים עם הכיוון האינדיבידואליסטי, האנטי-
דתי והאנטי-היסטורי שהשתלט בספרות העברית של דורו, ובייחוד בשירה.
לדעתו נוגד היה כיוון זה את האופי ״הקיבוצי״ של היהדות, שהעדיפה את
הציבור על היחיד,[83] וכן עומד היה בסתירה לדעתו הוא בדבר אחדותה של
תרבות ישראל מכל הדורות ויחס הכבוד המתחייב מזה לגבי כל שלביה.[84] מה
הפלא שהוא דחה כמה וכמה מיצירות מ. י. ברדיצבסקי ששלח לו על מנת
להדפיסן ב״השלח״. כך, למשל, הוא סרב להדפיס את ״סתירה ובנין״ שלו,
וטעמו עמו: ״הבא ודורש בפומבי לסתר את היהדות ההיסטורית עד היסוד —
מחויב הוא לתמך דבריו בראיות חזקות לקוחות מן החיים וההיסטוריה... ואין לו
רשות להשתמש במשפטים כוללים.״[85]

מטעם לא לגמרי ברור ומתוך הערכה אמנותית בלתי נכונה הוא החזיר
לקלוזנר את שירו הנפלא של טשרניחובסקי, ״מתוך עב הענן״,[86] ולא היה
מרוצה גם ממאמרו של קלוזנר על טשרניחובסקי.[87] דעותיו של המשורר
״מסוכנות״ היו בעיניו: ״רוח השירה הנסוכה על דעות כאלה מוסיפה עוד על
סכנתן והפסדן, כמיני מתיקה שמערבבים בסם המות לזבובים.״[88]

את מורת רוחו החריפה ביותר עוררה בו שירת ש.[89] הוא הביע את זה במכתב
לרבניצקי:

אין דעתי נוחה מיצירתו מפני שה׳מלאכותיות׳ שבה מרובה על הטבעיות
של כשרון אמתי... פרסומו הגדול אני מיחס בעיקרו לזה שנעשה
׳בוגוטבורץ׳ [90] והראה גבורה נפלאה בהטחת דברים כלפי ׳היושב בשמים׳
ושותק. לפי שביעמינו, אם רוצה אדם להתפרסם ולהתחבב על קהל הנערים
אין לו דרך יותר ישרה למטרתו מחלול הקודש, בין קדש דתי, מוסרי

---

[81] הדגשה שלו.

[82] אגרות, ד׳, עמ׳ 13; ראה גם שם, עמ׳ 7, 14.

[83] ״לא זה הדרך״, כל כתבי, עמ׳ י״ב, טור משמאל.

[84] ״תחית הרוח״, שם, עמ׳ קע״ה-קע״ו; אגרות, ה׳, עמ׳ 172.

[85] אגרות, א׳, עמ׳ 98; כל כתבי מ. י. ברדיצבסקי (תשי״ב), עמ׳ כ״ט-ל׳.

[86] אגרות, ב׳, עמ׳ 263—264.

[87] הכוונה לדבריו הנלהבים של קלוזנר על ״חזיונות ומנגינות״, חלק ב׳, שהופיע
בהוצ׳ ״תושיה״ (ורשה, תרס״א). ראה השלח, 8[2] (1901), עמ׳ 368—354.

[88] אגרות, ב׳, עמ׳ 262.

[89] שניאור כנראה.

[90] ״נלחם בהקב״ה״.

או לאומי — הכל הוא סימן ל׳פרוגרס׳, וכל מי שעושה זאת בסגנון יותר
גס ומכוער הרי הוא גדול מחברו. (כבר הגיע הזמן שידעו) גם אצלנו
להבחין בין מחשבה חפשית ובין היסטריא של אפיקורסות.[91]

להשלמת התמונה מן הראוי להעיר בהקשר זה על ״מקרה״ ברנר בהפועל
הצעיר, שבשעתו הפך למעין ״סערה בצלוחית של מים.״ כידוע לא היה
ברנר בין הזהירים ביותר בעטם, ולפעמים כתב דברי קיטרוג נגד עם ישראל
ותרבותו שמעמטים כמוהם לבוז עצמי ולהלקאה עצמית.[92] באחת מרשימותיו
בהפועל הצעיר מ־1910 נפלט מעטו מאטו המשפט, שאבותינו בדורות העבר ״היו
מתרפסים לפני איזה אב שבשמים.״[93] דברים אלה זיעזעו כל כך את אחה״ע
עד שהחליט לפרסם ״מכתב גלוי״ ב״הצפירה״ ולבקש מווער חובבי ציון
שיפסיק את תמיכתו ב״הפועל הצעיר״.[94] ״האמנם לא תרגישו״, כתב
ללדז׳ינסקי באודיסה, ״כמה מן העלבון יש בחוצפה כזו ביחס לאותה האמונה
שמסרו בני עמנו את נפשם עליה במשך אלפי שנה?״[95] באותו ענין הוא כתב
גם לדרויאנוב בוילנה:

בתור חבר לחברת התמיכה הנני מוחה בכל תוקף על שהוער נותן יכולת
לבחורים שלא שמשו כל צרכם להדפיס דברים כאלה. אם רוצים הם
להראות גבורה של שטות בחוצפה כלפי שמיא, יעשו זאת על חשבונם
ועל אחריותם, אבל אם הדבר נעשה על חשבון הצבור, הרי כולנו
אחראים לו... כמדומה לי, שעדיין כבוד ׳אבינו שבשמים׳ חביב על רוב
היהודים לא פחות מכבודו של הרצל, ומה צריך היהודי להרגיש כשהוא
קורא במכ״ע היוצא בא״י בעזרת הועד, שאבותינו היו מתרפסים לפני
׳איזה אב שבשמים׳?[96]

ולא נחה דעתו עד שכתב את מאמרו המצוין ״תורה מציון״ (תרע״א), בו
הבהיר את מובנו של יחס לאומי הוגן כלפי ערכי הדת והמסורת של האומה

[91] אגרות, ה׳, עמ׳ 126; ראה גם שם, 51. דעה זו השפיעה כנראה גם על הערכת
שניאור על ידי צמח, ראה ש. צמח, עירובין (דביר, תשכ״ד), עמ׳ 62—51.
[92] ראה, למשל, ״מעבר לגבולין״, פ׳ ט״ו; ״מכאן ומכאן״, כל כתבי י. ח. ברנר,
כרך א׳ (ישראל, תשט״ז), עמ׳ 216, 326—325, 330, 345, 346.
[93] הפועל הצעיר, 4, גל׳ 3, עמ׳ 6, הטור משמאל.
[94] על התגובה של סופרי הארץ להפסקת העזרה, ראה ״מאסיפת הסופרים״, שם, גל׳
10—9, עמ׳ 23—21; א. ד. גורדון, ״מכתב גלוי לחברי הפועלים״, שם, גל׳ 11; י. ח. ברנר,
״לברור הענין״, שם, גל׳ 12, עמ׳ 13—17, ועוד. ראה גם ״איש עברי״ (קלוזנר), ״חירות
ואפיקורסות״, השלח, 24 (ינואר, 1911), עמ׳ 91—88.
[95] אגרות, ד׳, עמ׳ 181.
[96] שם, עמ׳ 184, 206, 248—247.

ולימד את ״הצעירים המתמרדים״ לקח בדרכי מחשבה הגיונית ובאחריות
ציבורית־לאומית.[97]

מעניין לבסוף להעיר — ואילו אך בקצרה — על יחסו של אחה״ע לריפורמה.
אין הוא פוסל אותה לגמרי, אבל אין הוא גם מתייחס אליה בחיוב. במסגרת
ההיסטורית של המאה ה־19 הוא רואה בה ״חיקוי של התחרות״ ולא ״חיקוי של
התבוללות;״[98] אולם כשהיא לעצמה, מופרכת היא בעיניו. מבוססת היא,
לדעתו, על ההפרדה המלאכותית שבין תוכנה הפנימי של הדת לבין קליפתה
החיצונית, כלומר, המצוות בהן היא נתגלמה או הלשון בה נתלבשה. שאיפת
הריפורמה לשמור על ״התוך״ בלבד תוך סילוק הקליפה הריהי בסתירה
לאופיים המיוחד של דברי קודש, שבם ״המטרה מקדשת את האמצעים קדושה
לעצמם״ וכל ניסיון להפריד ביניהם מן ההכרח שיביא להרס הכל.[99] ובניסוח
שונה :

כל האומר לתקן את הדת הרי הוא בעיני כאילו אומר לקרר את האש,
כלומר, שני הפכים בנושא אחד. הדת היא דת כל זמן שבעליה מאמינים
במקורה האלהי, בעוד שרעיון התיקון יוכל לעלות על הלב רק אחר
שאבדה אמונה זו, והשכל האנושי לא יירא עוד מגשת אל הקודש
ומלראות בו מגרעות הדורשות תקון בידי אדם.[100]

אין זאת אלא שדחה אחה״ע את התיקון המלאכותי בידי אדם מפני שהאמין
בתיקון טבעי בידי הזמן המשנה ומחליף את הכל, לרבות הדת.[101] ואולי לא
היתה עמדתו זו אלא תגובה טבעית של בן יהדות אירופה המזרחית, ״הלמ־
דנית,״ על תורת המערב, ״העם־ארצית.״

הערות אחדות על קיטרוגו של ברוך קורצווייל נגד אחה״ע

אין ספק, אדם חילוני וחפשי בדעות היה אחה״ע, אולם עמוקים היו שרשיו
ביהדות המסורת ורבה היתה אהבתו לה והכבוד שרחש לה. ״מי שאינו חש
בנפשו שום קירבת רוח לאותו העולם העליון״ — כתב בקשר עם פרשת
ברנר — ״שבו השקיעו אבותינו את מוחם ולבם בכל הדורות וממנו שאבו את
כוחם המוסרי — יכול להיות אדם כשר, אבל יהודי לאומי איננו,[102] אף
אם הוא ׳דר בארץ ישראל ומדבר בלשון הקודש׳.״[103]

[97] כל כתבי, עמ׳ ת״ו–ת״ט.
[98] ״חקוי והתבוללות״, שם, עמ׳ פ״ט.
[99] ״בין קודש לחול״, שם, עמ׳ ע״ג–ע״ד.
[100] הדגשה שלו.
[101] ״דברי שלום״, כל כתבי, עמ׳ נ״ח–נ״ט.
[102] הדגשה שלו.
[103] ״תורה מציון״, כל כתבי, עמ׳ ת״ח.

אין זאת אלא שיחס כפול זה של אחה״ע כלפי המסורת היהודית נעלם מברוך
קורצווייל ז״ל, או שבכוונה התעלם ממנו; אחרת לא היה משתער עליו בשצף
קצף כזה ולא היה נתפס לדרכי זלזול והשפלה ומסלף את דמותו ודמות הדור
כולו. הביקורת שמתח קורצווייל על אחה״ע ותורתו 104 אמוציונלית היא
וכולה אינה אלא זעקת שבר על חותם הליגליות כביכול שהטביע אחה״ע
בסקולריזם המודרני בקרב מחנה הלאומיים. מלאה מרירות היא על כפירתו
באל טרנסצנדנטי ובמקורה השמימי של הנבואה, על התעלמותו מן היסוד
האמונתי־דתי ברמב״ם, על העמדתו את היהדות על המוסר בלבד, ובכלל על
לכתו שולל אחרי תורת ההתפתחות של חכמי המערב. אילו היה קורצווייל
מסתפק באלה, לא היה מקום לפולמוס דברים נגדו, ודבריו היו מתקבלים
כטיפוסיים לדרכי מחשבתו של איש האמונה, שנחרד כולו מההשקפה
הרציונליסטית־חילונית, שאחה״ע היה אחד מנציגיה החשובים בספרותנו.
אולם לא הסתפק קורצווייל בכך, ומתוך רצון למוטט את בנינו העיוני של
אחה״ע הוא מיעט בכוונה את דמותו וכפר בחשיבותו ההגותית וההיסטורית.
נעלה אך נקודות אחדות מביקורת זו וננסה להשיב עליהן.

טוען קורצווייל נגד אחה״ע שבכלל לא היה פילוסוף, ולראיה לו הוא מביא
תנאים דמסייעים, את פרנץ רוזנצווייג, הרב ברייער, יוליוס גוטמן
וח. י. רות 105 — עדים הרחוקים כולם מרחק רב מעולמו של אחה״ע ומתחום
השפעתו. וניתן לשאול: עדים אלה — לשם מה הם? וכי התיימר אחה״ע מעולם
להתעטף באצטלא זו של פילוסוף? גלויות הוא כותב:

מן הספרות הכללית נתחבבו עלי ספרי האנגלים. ביחוד הפילוסופים לוק,
יום ודומיהם. את הצרפתים קראתי אך מעט, כי לא אהבתי את הסגנון
המליצי שלהם. באשכנזית אהבתי את ספרי ההשכלה שלהם, כהרדר
וכדומה לו. את המעמיקים ביותר (קנט, הגל וכו') לא אהבתי ביותר ולא
עסקתי בהם הרבה... מן הספרות העברית חבבתי בעיקר את הספרות
הפילוסופית מן הרמב״ם עד הרנ״ק, ובהם הגיתי יומם ולילה עד שנפתחו
לפני שערי הספרות הכללית.106

אף כעורך ״השלח״ היה חוזר ומדגיש שאין הוא מעוניין בדברי חכמה ומחקר
המיועדים ליחידים, אלא בדברים של טעם בשביל הציבור המשכיל.107 דווקא
מפני שלא היה פילוסוף ״מקצועי,״ עוסק ב״עיוניות״ לשמה, אלא אדם שכולו

104 ספרותנו החדשה — המשך או מהפכה? (הוצ' שוקן, ירושלים ותל־אביב,
תשכ״ה), עמ' 224—190.
105 שם, עמ' 194—193.
106 ״פרקי זכרונות״, כל כתבי, עמ' תצ״ה.
107 אגרות, א', עמ' 58—57; ב', עמ' 241, ועוד.

משולב ומעורה בחיי בני עמו ועומד בשתי רגליו על קרקע המציאות, בהיר
שכל ובעל סברה, לקח הלבבות והשפיע.

צדק קורצווייל בטענתו שאחה״ע הושפע בכו״כ מיסודות הגותם על הדת
והמוסר מחכמי המערב, ודעתו על המוסר כעיקר היהדות — תורה ישנה היתה
בבית מדרשם של הליברלים היהודים במשך כל המאה ה־19.[108] אולם אף
בכך — אך אל דלת פתוחה הוא מתפרץ, שכן אחה״ע בעצמו הצביע על יום,
מיל, ספנסר, סדג׳וויק ואחרים כעל המקורות לכו״כ מדעותיו הכלליות.[109]
מאידך, כל הדן במישרים לא יכחיש את השימוש המקורי והעמוק שהוא עשה
ברעיונות אלה לשם ביסוס משנתו הלאומית.

אפילו סגנונו הצלול של אחה״ע ואווירת השלווה האופפת את הפרוזה שלו
מטרידים את קורצווייל הסוער והמשתער. אין הוא יכול להרגע, כיצד אפשר
לכתוב מתוך שלוות־נפש כזו דברי כפירה כאלה שיש בהם משום ״דסטרוקציה
טוטלית של הבסיס האמונתי־הדתי.״ ולא נחה דעתו עד שהכתיר דרך כתיבה זו
בתואר האינקביזיציוני של ״דמוניות,״[110] תואר שריח של ערמומיות והונאה־
מדעת עולים ממנו. אולם כל המצוי אצל אחה״ע יודע כמה אין תואר זה הולם
את האופי הגלוי והמוסרי של יצירתו. גלויות הוא כותב ל״אחד הרבנים״:
״בטלית צבועה לא נתעטפתי מעולם,״[111] ואפילו הבר־פלוגתא הגדול שלו,
מ. י. ברדיצ׳בסקי, הודה: ״בישרו המדעי של אחד העם אין להטיל ספק.״[112]

תיתי לי לקורצווייל שהעלה על נס את כוח החזון והאינטואיציה של הרצל,
אולם דבריו לגבי אחה״ע, שהוא ״הוליך שולל את בני דורו... לדרך התלישות
לגבי בעיות זמנו,״[113] ללא כל אחיזה ואמת הם. די להזכיר אך אחדות
מדעותיו על בעיות יסוד כמו שנאת ישראל, שתתמיד, לדעתו, אפילו
כש״ההומניות תתפשט ותתקף באמת את כל בני האדם;״[114] על הערבים,
שהתנגדותם למפעל היהודי בארץ תגבר ותלך בד בבד עם התקדמות הציביל־
זציה בה;[115] על האוטונומיזם של דובנוב, שללא כל סיכוי של הצלחה הוא,[116]
על אמריקה שעתידה היא להיות מרכז היהדות[117] ועל ענינים רבים אחרים,
כדי להיווכח כמה מעורה במציאות זמנו היה ומה שרירותיים וללא יסוד הם

[108] ספרותנו החדשה, עמ׳ 198—197.
[109] ראה שמות חכמים אלה ב״רשימה״, בסוף כל כתבי אחד העם, תקמ״ט.
[110] ספרותנו החדשה, עמ׳ 213.
[111] ״דברי שלום״, כל כתבי, עמ׳ נ״ז.
[112] כל מאמרי מי״ב, עמ׳ ק״א, טור מימין.
[113] ספרותנו החדשה, עמ׳ 219—218.
[114] ״שתי רשויות״, כל כתבי, עמ׳ פ״ו.
[115] ״אמת מארץ ישראל״, שם, עמ׳ כ״ד, כ״ט.
[116] ״שלוש מדרגות״, ״שלילת הגולה״, שם, עמ׳ קנ״ב—קנ״ג, ת״א.
[117] אגרות, ב׳, עמ׳ 147, ועוד.

דברי המבקר. אפילו עתה קשה להכריע, מי קרבנו להגשמת החזון של מדינת
ישראל יותר, תלמידי הרצל או תלמידי אחה״ע, ואם לא היתה זו אותה תפיסה
שלו לגבי דרך התחייה כתהליך של צמיחה וגידול איטיים, שהכריעה במידה
רבה את גורלו של היישוב אפילו בזירה המדינית.

מוזרה היא טענה אחרת של קורצווייל, והיא, שהרצל השאיר פתח פתוח
לכל האפשרויות הדתיות ואילו ״אחה״ע הפקיע כל שייר של אמונה ובמקומה
הנציח את השאננות המשכילית בת צביון המוני־ליברלי.״ [118] וקשה שלא
לשאול: וכי פוסק בענייני דת היה הרצל ולדברו בשטח זה ייחל העם? ובנוגע
לאחה״ע: וכי בחלל ריק עלתה הלאומיות היהודית, ללא השפעת הרציונליזם
המערבי מזה והזרמים הסוציאליסטיים־מהפכניים שברוסיה על אופים האנטי־
דתי מזה, ורק הרב־מג אחה״ע הוא שעמד על עמו ובמטה קסמו הדימוני הכניס
ללבו את כל האפיקורסות השטנית? אין ספק, השפע השפיעה הפובליציסטיקה
שלו, אולם לא בה בלבד אפשר לתלות את קולר האופי הסקולרי של התנועה
הלאומית. אופי זה היה פרי התפתחות ארוכה, שאף אחה״ע בעצמו אך אחד
מפירותיה היה. יתרה מזה: למרות גישתו הרציונליסטית וההתפתחותית
לתרבות העבר, לא ניסה אחה״ע מעולם לחזות מראש מה תהיה דמותו הרוחנית
של היישוב בעתיד. הוא האמין באמונה שלמה בכוח היצירה של האומה,
אולם הוא גם שכתב: ״באיזו צורה יתגלה כח היצירה בעתיד, אי אפשר לחזות
מראש.״ [119]

מופרז הוא גם הניגוד העמוק, כביכול, שהעלה קורצווייל בין הזיקה לנושא
הדתי ו״עוצמת חזון האבדן שבנשמת המשורר״ ח. נ. ביאליק מזה לבין הפתרון
ללא־אל וה״בינוניות השאננה״ שבפובליציטיקה האחד־העמית מזה. [120] אילו
היה קורצווייל שופט בכוחות, ללא משוא פנים ופתוס קדוש, היה מגלה שדוקא
בפרשת הדת מרובה הקירבה שבין השניים מהמרחק שביניהם. אכן הפתוס של
״ואם יש את נפשך לדעת״ מהדהד במאמרים כ״הציונות והשבת״, ״גואל
חדש״ ובעיקר ״תורת ארץ ישראל״, כשם שמאידך גיסא מורגשת השפעת
אחה״ע העמוקה בשירים כ״על סף בית המדרש,״ ״אכן חציר העם,״ ״מתי
מדבר האחרונים.״ ״אכן גם זה מוסר אלהים״ ובכמה וכמה ממאמרי ביאליק
בענין כינוס היצירה העברית. היוצא לחפש גילויי אפיקורסות בספרותנו
ימצא למכביר אף בשירת ביאליק. אלא מה? מלווים הם בה תמיד בביטויי
מאבק וכאב, צער ויאוש על עולם שהיה ואינו עוד, ועל חיים שנתרוקנו
מתוכן מפני האמונה שנתמוטטה ואבדה — רגשות וביטויים שאינם נראים

[118] ספרותנו החדשה, עמ׳ 219.
[119] אגרות, ה׳, עמ׳ 30.
[120] ספרותנו החדשה, עמ׳ 221.

לעיין ואינם כה מורגשים במאמרי אחה״ע. אולם הבדל זה אינו מהותי, אלא
פרי מזגיהם השונים ודרכי יצירתם השונות, דרך השירה מזה והמסה מזה.

ולבסוף, טענת קורצווייל שפתרונו של אחה״ע לא בא בגדר פתרון היה [121] —
אך חלק מן האמת בה ולא כולה. בוודאי שלא פתרון לדורות ולכלל האומה
היה — וכי מצויים פתרונות כאלה? — אולם פתרון לדור, במסיבות היסטוריות
מיוחדות, ולחלק ניכר באומה, החלק הפעיל והמודע ביותר לגורלה, בוודאי
שהיה, ואכן פתרון זה הוא שהעלה כוחות יצירה ופעילות, שאת תוצאותיהן
אנו מרגישים עד עתה.

קווי־יסוד של השקפתו הלאומית

כאמור, עיקר חשיבותו של אחה״ע הוא בתרומה שהוא תרם לביסוסה העיוני
של הלאומיות הציונית, ומן הדין שנעמוד על קווייה הכלליים של תורתו זו.
בראש וראשונה אופטימית היא וחדורה באמונה עמוקה באמיתה ובדרכה.
אמיתה ברורה לפניה, והיא, שאין פתרון אחר לבעיית המשך קיומו של עם
ישראל בזמן החדש אלא על ידי הקמת "מרכז רוחני" בארץ ישראל שממנו
תצא השפעה על יהדות העולם כולה להחיותה ולחזקה. אף דרכה נהירה לה,
והיא, דרך החינוך ההדרגתי של האומה וההתקדמות הזהירה והאיטית. מסתפקת
במועט היא כביכול, אולם בקצה הדרך רומז אף לה חלום מדינה יהודית.[122]
מתוך חכמה שלאחר־מעשה אפשר לטעון נגד תורה זו שחסרת דמיון
היתה ומתעלמת מלחיצת המציאות היהודית לפתרון מהיר ובעל תנופה.
אולם מידת זהירות זו שלה, טעם זקנים היה בה, זקנים למודי נסיון היסטו־
רי שבאכזבות משיחיות חוזרות ונשנות, ופרי הרגשת אחריות עמוקה כלפי
עתיד האומה. מאלפים בנידון זה הם דברי י. א. לובצקי,[123] מחסידי אחה״ע,
שכשנתיים אחרי הופעת הרצל כתב:

אנחנו היהודים הלאומיים... אנחנו נראה בהציונות המערבית, הפוליטית,
התחדשות אחת מאלו התקוות הרבות שהביאו מגפה במחננו ורעל בעור־

---

[121] שם, עמ׳ 200—199.
[122] בתרנ״ח כתב:

...ואז כאשר הקולטורא הלאומית בארץ ישראל תגיע למדרגה כזו, נוכל
לבטוח בה כי היא עצמה תקים אנשים מבניה (הדגשה שלו) שיהיו מוכשרים
להשתמש בשעת הכושר בשביל ליסד שם גם ׳מדינה׳ – לא רק מדינת יהודים,
כי אם מדינה יהודית באמת.

"מדינת היהודים וצרת היהודים", כל כתבי, עמ׳ קל״ח. ב־1914 הוא כתב
לאיינשטטדט־ברזילי: "אין אני חושב כלל לנמנע שתכלכל ארץ ישראל ברבות הימים
הרבה מיליונים בני אדם", אגרות, ה׳, עמ׳ 171.

[123] ראה עליו ג. קרסל, לקסיקון הספרות העברית בדורות האחרונים
(ישראל, 1967), כרך שני, עמ׳ 176.

קינו... אלו התקוות שהרבו בנו שמות יותר מאויבינו בנפש... ומה יהיה
אם לא תצלח? היא תביא סוף יאוש וריקנות נוראה בחיינו... נחוץ
לעבוד... לעשות... מבלי לחשוב על אודות המטרה הרחוקה בעתיד. נחוץ
ליסד קולוניות... בתי ספר, להפיץ דעת... להוציא ספרים... אבל מה
יהיה אחרי כן? על אודות תכלית כל המעשים האלה לא חפץ שום איש
לחשוב...[124]

אופטימית היתה לאומיות זו גם מבחינת הערכתה את הפוטנציאל היצירתי
של האומה. קבל מתייאשים וראי שחורות היא הכריזה שעוד לא נס ליחה ולא
פג טעמה של האומה, וככוחה אז כן כוחה עתה להתחדש וליצור. לא התנ״ך
בלבד בחזקת יצירה הוא, אלא אף התלמוד, השלחן ערוך והחסידות. אף חכמת
ישראל וההרפורמה מעידים על כוחות יצירה התוססים עוד באומה. אלא מה?
בתנאי ההווה ובעקב השפעתה הגדלה וההולכת של התרבות החילונית על הנוער
היהודי, מפסידה האומה את טובי בניה לתרבויות הזרות. אכן, זכותו של
אחה״ע היא וזכות תלמידיו, ביאליק ופייארברג בעיקר, שהזעיקו את הדור על
סכנת הכירסום והסחף הנשקפת לאנרגיה הרוחנית של האומה כתוצאה של
זרימת־חוץ זו של מיטב כוחה ואונה. מבחינה זו ניתן להגדיר את הלאומיות
האחד־העמית כביטוי לכמיהת האומה למסגרת של חיים טבעיים בה תוכל
לשמור על כוחות הרוח שלה וליצור בתנאים של חירות.[125]

תכונתה האחרת של לאומיות זו היא אופיה הטוטאלי. טוטאלית היא
מבחינת המטרה שהיא מציבה לעצמה ומבחינת התשתית של תרבות העבר
שעליה היא שואפת להקים את בנין העתיד שלה. אמנם אין היא מאמינה עוד
בקיבוץ גלויות ובחיסולה של גלות,[126] אולם המרכז הרוחני שלו היא מטיפה –
מטרתו אינה לעצמו אלא לכלל האומה. בתנאי ההווה, תנאים של אבדן כוחה
המאחד של הדת והתגברות השפעתן של התרבויות הלאומיות, רואה היא
במרכז "טבעי" כזה משום ערוי דם הכרחי, לו בזקקת יהדות התפוצה, כדי
לשמור על אחדותה ולהמשיך בקיומה ההיסטורי. טוטאלית היא גם מבחינת
ההזדהות עם תרבות העבר שהיא מטיפה לה. שלמה היא וללא העדפה של דור
על דור, יצירה על יצירה. בנידון זה נוגדת היתה את הילכי הרוח האנטי־
היסטוריים שהשתררו בספרות העברית של הזמן.

[124] "הציונות ומתנגדיה", השלח, 4 (1898), עמ' 381–377; ראה גם אגרות, ב', עמ' 60–
59; ג', עמ' 210.

[125] "תחית הרוח", כל כתבי, עמ' קע״ה–קע״ח; ח. נ. ביאליק, "על סף בית
המדרש", "אכן גם זה מוסר אלהים"; פייארברג, "לאן?", הוצ' ספרית דביר לעם, עמ'
137.

[126] "הציונות המדינית", כל כתבי, עמ' קל״ו והלאה; "הגיעה השעה", שם, עמ'
ש״פ–שפ״א; "מלים ומושגים", שם, עמ' שצ״ב–שצ״ד.

ועוד תכונה יסודית טיפוסית הינה ללאומיות זו, והיא, אופיה האינטגרלי
המובהק. אין היא מסתפקת בתביעה של ״מעשים״ לאומיים, ואפילו לא
בלימוד הלשון העברית ודעת קורות האומה ותרבותה, אלא מחפשת היא
דרכים כיצד לעצב את חייו ואישיותו של היהודי הלאומי: להחדיר את האיד-
אל הלאומי ״אל עמקי לבבו ולקשרו עם כל רגשותיו ונטיותיו, באופן שירגיש
האדם את מציאותו בכל עת, בקביעות ולא באקראי, וימצא בו מורה דרך בכל
עניני החיים.״ [127]

שתי דרכים, סבר אחה״ע, מוליכות למטרה זו: דרך הדעת ודרך ״המוסר
הלאומי,״ ומבחינת ספיקות הרוח — דרך השכל והרגש. יהודי תלמיד חכם
ובעל מידות זה לא יכול היה להעלות בדעתו לאומיות יהודית שלא תהא
מושרשת בשתי המסורות העתיקות של האומה, מסורת החכמה מזה והמוסר
מזה. מעל לכל שאף להפיץ דעת יהודית, ומשוכנע היה שרק בה הערובה
לחיזוקן ולהעמקתן של הרגש הלאומי.[128] לשם כך הגה את הרעיון של ״אוצר
היהדות בלשון העברית,״ כלומר, אנציקלופדיה יהודית בעברית. לא לחוג צר
של אנשי מחקר שהמדע יהא להם עיקר נתכוון, אלא לעם כולו, ובעיקר ל״בני
הנעורים,״ כדי לעזור להם לרכוש ״השקפה רחבה ומושכלת בפרקים שונים
מחיי עמנו ופעולותיו והלך רוחו, אשר תביאם סוף סוף להוקירו ולאהבו אהבה
בדעת;״ ובנוסחא שונה במקצת: ״עיקר מגמתנו הוא להפיץ ידיעת היהדות בקרב
העם, בשביל לחזק את הקשר בינה ובינו.״ [129] מטרה זו, חיזוק הרגש הלאומי
על ידי הדעת, היא שהיתה גם נר לרגליו בעריכת ״השלח,״ בה עסק במשך
שש שנים (1897—1902). כצנור דעת ל״כלל העם״ ראה אותו ולא כ״בית מדרש
לחכמים;״ ולא דעת סתם, אלא זו שיש בה כדי להפיץ אור על ״עצמותנו
הלאומית ההיסטורית״ וכדי לתרום ״לדעת את עצמנו, להבין את חיינו
ולכונן עתידותינו בתבונה.״ [130] סיומו של משפט אחרון זה, המגדיר את
מטרת דעת העבר כאמצעי לכינון העתיד, מעמידנו על האופי הרנסנסי הברור
של מחשבת אחה״ע בפרשה זו. בדומה לרנסנס האירופי, שתחלה השקיע עצמו
בהחייאת התרבות הקלסית ועמד על שכם ״העתיקים,״ ורק אחר כך על רגליו
הוא עמד והזדרך לקראת העתיד, ראה גם אחה״ע את הרנסנס שלנו כמצריך
תחלה שקיעה בעבר כתנאי לבנין העתיד. לפנינו כאן גם ניסוח ראשון של

[127] ״המוסר הלאומי״, שם, עמ׳ ק״ס.
[128] ברעיון זה הקדים פרץ סמולנסקין את אחה״ע. ראה פרץ סמולנסקין, ״עם עולם״,
מאמרים, 157—162; ״עת לטעת״, שם, II, 290—286.
[129] ״על דבר אוצר היהדות בלשון העברית״, כל כתבי, עמ׳ ק״ו, טור משמאל; עמ׳
ק״ט, טור מימין.
[130] ״תעודת השלח״, שם, עמ׳ קכ״ו-קכ״ז.

רעיון "הכינוס," שפותח כעבור שנים אחדות ביתר פירוט והרחבה על ידי
ביאליק.[131]

הדרך השנייה להפצת הלאומיות ולהחדרתה בעם היא על ידי "המוסר
הלאומי." האמן האמין אחה"ע,

כי למרות המצא איזו כללים מוסריים המקובלים ומוסכמים לכל עמי
הקולטורא, יש בכל זאת לכל עם ועם מוסר מיוחד, בהסכם לתכונת רוחו
הלאומי ומהלך חייו ההיסטוריים... תכונתו וצרכיו של כל עם, מצבו
הגשמי והרוחני, המאורעות שעברו עליו בזמנים שונים — כל אלה
נותנים צורה מיוחדת ליחוסו אל חזיונות החיים, וממילא גם להשקפותיו
המוסריות ואופן הגשמתן למעשה... ואם כך הדבר גם בכל שאר האומות
הנאורות... קל וחומר עם ישראל, שמראשית היותו הוא 'עם לבדד
ישכון', מובדל מכל העמים בחייו ההיסטוריים לשעבר ובמצבו וצרכיו
בהוה.[132]

יתר על כן, לא זה בלבד שמוסר מיוחד לו לעם ישראל, אלא שהוא הוא עיקר
מהותו ובו מצאה רוחו את ביטוייה הנאמן והעליון. "אישיותה העצמית של
האומה כולה (היא) אישיות מוסרית שנתלבשה על ידי סבות היסטוריות שונות
בצורה דתית."[133] רעיון זה מרכזי במחשבתו והוא חוזר עליו במסגרות
ובמסיבות שונות. עם ישראל הוא עם הנבואה, "כאילו היתה תכונה עצמית לו,
הטבועה ברוחו הלאומי." ועיקרה של הנבואה "ממשלת הצדק המוחלט בכל
הבריאה כולה."[134] אף משה רבנו, "טופסה האידאלי של הנבואה היש־
ראלית" — הצדק המוחלט שלט בנפשו ואותו הוא רצה להשליט בעולם.[135] אם
אפשר לדבר על "אדם עליון" ביהדות, דמותו מוסרית היא ביסודה ומנוגדת
תכלית הניגוד לדמות שהעלה ניטשה.[136]

מכיוון שכך, מגיע אחה"ע למסקנה שעל התנועה הלאומית "לדרוש מכל
נושאי דגל הלאומיות, כי ישימו אל לבם לדעת את המוסר הלאומי האמתי וישתד־
לו להתאים עמו את חייהם."[137] אמנם לעת עתה הוא מכוון דרישתו זו רק

[131] ראה בעיקר "הספר העברי", כל כתבי ח. נ. ביאליק, מהדורה שמינית, הוצ'
דביר (תל־אביב, תש"ז), עמ' קצ"ד־ר"א.
[132] "המוסר הלאומי", כל כתבי, עמ' קס"ב.
[133] "הערת העורך", השלח, 5 (1899), עמ' 104.
[134] "כהן ונביא", כל כתבי, עמ' צ"א.
[135] "משה", שם, עמ' שמ"ב־שמ"ז.
[136] "שינוי ערכין", שם, עמ' קנ"ה; ראה גם "חיקוי והתבוללות", שם, עמ' פ"ח; "על
שתי הסעיפים", שם, עמ' שע"ג ואילך.
[137] "המוסר הלאומי", שם, עמ' קס"ב, הטור משמאל.

״למשכילים שבנו שהם צריכים להבין ערכה תחלה ולהתיצב בראשה,״ אולם
הוא מקווה ש״מהם תצא ותתפשט גם בקרב העם.״ [138]

לפנינו, איפוא, כאן כמה וכמה מגופי תורתו: א) העמדת מהות היהדות על
המוסר ולא על הדת, ב) הפקעת המוסר מרשות הדת, ו-ג) שילובו האינטגרלי
של המוסר במושג הלאומיות היהודית. כל השלשה — עוררים קמו עליהם גם
בחייו וגם לאחר מותו. [139] ידועים הדברים ולא נעמוד עליהם כאן. דיינו אם
נעיר, שתורה זו המקשרת לאומיות ומוסר ומטילה את חובת המוסר על
המאמינים הלאומיים, לא יכלה לעלות אלא על לבו של אדם ששרשיו ומעינות

[138] שם, עמ׳ קס״ד.
[139] ברדיצבסקי, למשל, טען נגד עצם המושג של מוסר יהודי אחיד:
כשאני לעצמי, אין אני יודע, אם זה היה המוסר הלאומי שלנו, שעורר אותנו
בימי קדם לכבוש לנו את הארץ בזרוע, או זהו המוסר הלאומי, שבא בלבנו
בערוב שמשנו... הדבר מוטל בספק, אם ביכנה ובנותיה ניתן המוסר הלאומי,
או חי בין אלה שנשארו בתוך חומת ירושלים ונפלו על חרבם. ...אין אנו
יודעים אם או אל קנא ונוקם הוא אלהי ישראל או זהו אלהי העברים, שאל רחום
וחנון הוא. ...ענין המוסר הלאומי הוא רק עיקר בדוי מן הלב, עיקר כשאר
העיקרים הדתיים, שהולכים ובאים, הולכים ובאים.
״תרבות ומוסר״, כל כתבי מ. י. ברדיצבסקי, עמ׳ ל״ח; ראה גם שם, ״אנו והם״,
עמ׳ מ״ז–מ״ח; ״המוסר הלאומי״, עמ׳ ק״ו ואילך; ״המוסר והדת״, עמ׳ ק״ז-ק״ח, ועוד.
דוד ניימרק הודה אמנם ב״ערכו הנשגב של האידאל המוסרי״ ביהדות, אבל טען נגד
אחה״ע ש״אישיותה העצמית של האומה בכללה אישיות דתית היא״, ואין להפריד בין
הלאומיות והדת:
יהדות דתית בלי יהדות לאומית היא פורחת היא באויר, כמחשבה בלי מוח ההוגה
אותה. ובאותה מידה עצמה, ואולי עוד במידה יותר מרובה, יכולים אנו
לאמור להציונות שאינה אלא לאומית, כי יהדות לאומית בלי יהדות דתית,
׳מוזמוזה׳ היא, כמוח שנתרוקן מכל מחשבה. אחת היא מה אנו ממיתים, את
הגוף או את הנשמה. ברייה חיה צריכה לגוף ונשמה בבת אחת!
״הציונות והעם״, השלח, כרך 5 (1899), עמ׳ 103; ראה גם ״מוסר היהדות״, שם, כרך 6
(1899), עמ׳ 71.

יותר מקיפה וחודרת היתה בביקורתו של יחזקאל קויפמן על תורת הלאומיות של
אחה״ע. לא נזדקק כאן לכולה, אלא לנקודה זו בלבד, והיא, שילוב המוסר בלאומיות:
אחד העם הניח ליסוד מוסד, שהלאומיות אינה מחייבת את האדם להאמין
באמונות הדתיות של אבותיו. אבל דמה עם זה, שהיא מחייבת חובת אמונה
ברשויות תרבות אחרות, ביחוד – ברשות המוסר הלאומי. אבל באמת אין שום
מושכל להבחנה זו. מה שנכון ביחס לדת, נכון הוא ביחס לכל מיני אמונות
ודעות: ההערכה הלאומית אינה תלויה בהן... אנכרוניזמוס היא הדרישה
שדרש אחה״ע מצעירי דורו, שיסגלו את דעותיהם לדעות היהדות וישישתדלו
לחדש את היהדות על ידי הרכבת דעות חדשות בישנות.
יחזקאל קויפמן, גולה ונכר, כרך 2, הוצ׳ דביר, הדפסה שניה (תל-אביב, תשכ״א),
מע׳ 348 ואילך. המובאות דלעיל הן מע׳ 377, 378; ראה גם י. קויפמן, ״תורת אחד העם״,
בין נתיבות (חיפה, תשי״ב), עמ׳ 133–86.

רוחו ביהדות הדתית־הנורמטיבית היו. זה יתברר לנו ביהוד אם נעלה על
לבנו שמה שאהה״ע מתכוון לו ב״מוסר״ אינם איזה עיקרים רציונליים
מופשטים, בבחינת פילוסופיה של מוסר, אלא כללי מעשה שבכוחם להנחות
וללוות את היחיד בפרטי חייו ובמצביהם השונים. כך, למשל, החשיב אהה״ע
את מוסר היהדות (Ethik des Judentums) של מוריץ לצרוס (1898)
והמליץ לא פעם על הצורך לתרגמו לעברית; [140] אולם לא ספר כזה, כתב,
יכול לספק את צרכי היהודי הלאומי,

> כי לבו (של החכם הזה) רק אל יסודי המוסר הכלליים, ולא הכניס עצמו
> בפרטי [141] שאלות החיים המעשיים... ואנחנו הן לא לזה אנו צריכים, כי
> אם לדעת ידיעה אמתית ופרטית, מה הן החובות שהמוסר הלאומי האמתי,
> בלי כל תערובת זרה, מטיל עלינו ביחסנו לעצמנו ולזולתנו.[142]

אין זאת אלא שלמעין ״שלחן ערוך״ חדש יצא לבו שילמד ״כיצד לחיות
כיהודי לאומי, בנפשו פנימה, בביתו, בשוק החיים״.[143] כה עמוקה היתה
אמונתו של אהה״ע בלאומיות הציונית עד שחשב כי די כוח בה לההפך למקור
חובות ומצוות שהיהודי הלאומי ישתעבד להן מרצון ויסדיר כל חייו על פיהן,
כשם שהיה נוהג היהודי הדתי לגבי המצוות והחיובים הטרנסצנדנטיים. ברור,
כדת חדשה היתה הלאומיות החילונית בשבילו ודרכי השפעה ותוקף דתיים
שאף למצוא לה.

בשם החירות

כעולם צלול ורגוע, ללא עבים להקדירו וללא סערות להסעירו, הוא רושמה
של הפרוזה האחד־העמית. מכאן מידת השכנוע בה היא פועלת על הקורא
והאשלייה שהיא יוצרת בו שאמיתה אמת אוביקטיבית היא, פרי שיקול עיוני
טהור וללא שמץ של זעזועי נפש, היסוסים ונטיות אישיות. אולם רושם זה
מוטעה הינהו. אמנם, רובה ככולה דברי הגיון ומחשבה הם, אולם טבועים אלה
בחותם אישיותו ונטיות רוחו המיוחדות. זיקה זו שבין האיש ותורתו מורגשת
ביחוד במוטיב החירות המחדיר את יצירתו כולה ובבחינת רוחה ונשמתה הוא.
פרט לפרץ סמולנסקין איני יודע יהודי אחר, מבין גדולינו במזרח ובמערב
במשך המאה התשע־עשרה, שנשא את יהדותו בגאווה ובחירות כמוהו. בעינו
החדה וברגישותו הרבה לכבוד האדם והיהודי היה תר אחרי כל גילויי
שיעבוד — שיעבוד הנפש בעיקר — וללא חת היה מערה את שורשם ומוקיעם

[140] אגרות, ב׳, עמ׳ 79; ג׳, עמ׳ 31, 97.
[141] הדגשה שלו.
[142] ״המוסר הלאומי״, כל כתבי, עמ׳ קס״ג–קס״ד.
[143] שם, עמ׳ קס״ד, טור משמאל.

ברבים. עוד בראשית דרכו הראה מה יקר היה המחיר ששילמו יהודי צרפת
בעד שוויונם האזרחי מאז ימי המהפכה עד ימיו. מחיר של סילוף־מדעת של
מהותם והתכחשות לעצמם. את היהדות צימקו ורוקנוה מכל תוכן יהודי חי,
אולם לחלק אינטגרלי מהחברה הצרפתית לא היו; ואחרי מאה שנות "שוויון"
עדיין מוקפים הם בים של שנאה וחוששים לגלות ברבים שמץ מהרגשתם
היהודית, שמא פסול יראו בכך לפטריוטיותם.144 מן הראוי לדפדף בכרכי
"המגיד," "המליץ," ו"הכרמל" משנות הששים, כדי לראות מה רבה היתה
יראת הכבוד בה עמדה יהדות מזרח אירופה לפני אחיה הנאורים שבמערב,145
ואילו עתה, אחרי שנות דור אחד בלבד, לא זה בלבד שסר הודה וזיווה של
יהדות זו בעיני נציגיה הגאה של יהדות המזרח, אלא כראויה לרחמים נראתה
לו. נתחלפו היוצרות: לא היא שתציל עוד את יהודי מזרח אירופה המדוכאים,
אלא, להיפך, הם הם שישחררוה מה"עבדות בתוך חירות" שלה וימלאוה
בחיים יהודיים חדשים.146

כאדם חפשי, ללא רגשות פחד ונחיתות, וכדברו הגאה של הקיבוץ היהודי
הגדול שבמזרח אירופה, מופיע אחה"ע במאמריו. אפילו עשרות מיליוני
הפרנקים שהזיל "הנדיב הידוע" מכיסו לטובת המושבות הראשונות בארץ, לא
היה בהם עוד כדי להטיל מורא עליו ולהשתיקו, משהרגיש שהמחיר ששילמו
בני המושבות בעד השקעה זו ממש בנפשם היה, בחירותם ובכבוד האדם
שלהם. חשבון נוקב עשה אחה"ע של משק אפוטרופסי זה והמסקנה שאליה
הגיע היתה שמרובה הפסדו על שכרו. אפוטרופסות זו היא שהחריבה, לדעתו,
את "האהבה והכשרון לעבודה, את הרצון והאנרגיה, את האידאליסמוס
הלאומי ורגש הכבוד האנושי; לא השאיר אחריו בלתי אם לב מר ורוח נכאה,
יאוש וקצף אין אונים."147 מכיוון שכך, אין הוא רואה כל דרך אחרת להציל
את הישוב, אלא אם יחזירו לו את חירותו ויתנו לו לעמוד על רגליו.

החיים — כתב — הם מלחמה תמידית בין חפץ הקיום שבלב האדם ובין
תנאי הקיום שמחוצה לו. במלחמה התמידית הזאת יתפתחו כוחות האדם
עד שיכשר להסתגל לתנאי קיומו או לשנותם לפי צרכו, ומי שאינו
מוכשר לא לזה ולא לזה הוא המנוצח.148

144 "עבדות בתוך חירות", שם, עמ' ס"ט ואילך.
145 עוד בראשית שנות ה־70 הרבה פ. סמולנסקין בשבחיה של כי"ח הפריזיות וראה בה
ובפעולותיה ברכה לכלל ישראל; ראה "עם עולם," מאמרים, כרך 1, עמ' 52–38;
ראה גם קבורת חמור, פרק ג', מהד' דוד ויינפלד, ספרית "דורות", עמ' 68.
146 "גואל חדש", כל כתבי, עמ' ש"ב–ש"ג.
147 "הישוב ואפוטרופסיו", שם, עמ' רי"ח.
148 שם, שם, עמ' רי"ב.

בשם החירות וכבוד היהודי מתח גם אחה״ע את ביקורתו החריפה על ״אלט־
ניילנד״ להרצל. האופי הקוסמופוליטי של חברת ״אלטניילנד,״ הליברליזם
המופרז בה והרצון הגלוי מצד יהודיה להתרצות לשכניהם הנוצרים — בכל
אלה ראה סימנים ברורים של הפסיכיקה העבדותית של יהודי המערב:

הסבלנות (של ׳אלטניילנד׳) אינה הולכת קוממיות, אלא זוחלת ומת־
רפסת; כי הסבלנות של בני־חורין אמיתיים אינה צעקנית ואין דרכה
להתראות ולהתהדר לפני הכל... (היא) אינה אלא התבטלות לפני ׳האדון
מאתמול׳ והשתדלות גלויה להראות לו על כל צעד, שהננו מוכנים
ומזומנים לפנות לו מקום בראש, למשכו בכנף בגדו לפני ולפנים של
חיינו הלאומיים והחברתיים, גם במקום שאין לו עם החיים האלה שום
קשר פנימי... לזו קוראים סבלנות רק עבדים משוחררים, שעדיין צלצול
השלשלאות באזנם ורוחם עודנו חציו עבד, אבל בני חורין אמתיים יקראו
לזו לא ׳סבלנות׳ כי אם ׳התרפסות שפלה׳ ויביטו על המראה לא בכבוד
וחבה, כי אם בגועל נפש.[149]

ומשרבו המחאות על דברים חריפים אלה מצד נאמני הרצל, כה הגיב אחה״ע
במכתב למ. לוין באודיסה:

אם יש עוד בקרבנו אנשים הראויים לשם זה צריכים הם להתאחד יחדו,
בשביל להרים דגל חדש מחודש: דגל החרות הפנימית,[150] דגל הכבוד
האנושי. הנסיון הראה, שגם הציונות, לצערנו, יכולה לדור בכפיפה אחת
עם שפלות רוחנו הרגילה, עם כריעה והשתחויה לפני כל מה שריח
׳גויות׳ נודף ממנו.[151]

ברוח זו הגיב גם אחה״ע על ״מאורע״ ביהדות אמריקה דאז, או, ביתר דיוק,
בקרב היהדות הריפורמית שלה. בקיץ 1907 גורשו מבית המדרש שבסינסינטי
מורים אחדים, בשביל שחשדו בם, שמחנכים את התלמידים ברוח הלאומית
העברית.[152] בלעג גלוי כתב אז אחה״ע:

נמצאו בין כתלי בית מדרשם אנשים הכופרים בעיקר הגדול של תעודת
ישראל בגולה להיות לאור גויים ולהורות לכל העולם דרכי צדק של
היהדות, ותחת זה מעוררים האנשים האלה בפומבי שאלות לאומיות,
כאילו היהודים הם עוד עם מיוחד ולא כנסיה של ׳בני הנביאים׳, נושאי

[149] ״החטא ועונשו״, שם, עמ׳ שכ״א.
[150] הדגשה שלו.
[151] אגרות, ג׳, עמ׳ 121.
[152] ״סימן השאלה״, כל כתבי, עמ׳ שצ״ט, טור מימין.

דגל הצדק בין העמים. ולא נחה דעתם של ׳בני הנביאים׳ עד שהוציאו את
המורים הלאומיים מתוך קהלם.[153]

באותו זמן, הוא ממשיך לספר על יסוד מאמר בעתונות האנגלית, החלה
"להתפשט באמריקה מחלה מוסרית, המגלה את החיה הרעה שבאדם... והיא,
שנאה... בני יפן וסין. ובשם "הקולטורא הלבנה" עושים בני אמריקא מעשי
שוד ורצח לעיני השמש ולא יתבוששו." ותמה הוא שואל: אם כה רגישים הם
"בני הנביאים" לתעודת הצדק העולמי שלהם,

למי נאה היה למחות עתה נגד עלבון הצדק והשפלת ערכה של האנושיות,
אם לא להם, למגיני היהדות ותעודתה באמריקא? וכי יש לך שעת הכושר
יותר מזו להראות באמת לכל העולם כי תעודתנו בין הגויים לא מליצה
ריקה היא ?

אבל "בני הנביאים" של סינסינטי הסתתרו עם תעודתם בבית־מדרשם ושתקו.
ואם ישאל השואל, "מדוע"? מדוע לא נהגו כנביאים מקדם, שנלחמו ללא
מורא לאמת ולצדק — תשובתו של אחה״ע ברורה היא: הסיבה היא בהבדל
שבין מצבם ומצב הנביאים. הנביאים "ישבו בתוך עמם ובארצם הלאומית...
ולא יראו לעמוד לימין העשוקים בכל עת ובכל מקום," ואילו הם בגלות הינם
ואינם מעיזים "לפתוח פה נגד הבעלים." [154] מסקנתו ברורה: אם אכן תעודה
לנו, היא המחייבת אותנו לשוב לארץ, כי רק בה נוכל לפעול בתנאי חירות.

אין כדוגמאות דלעיל כדי להעמיד אותנו על השינוי העמוק שנתחולל במשך
דור אחד בלבד במנטליות של יהדות אירופה המזרחית. במקובץ ניתן לראות
בהן, ובדוגמאות רבות אחרות מסוגן, משום הכרזת מלחמה ממש על דרכה
ההיסטורית של יהדות המערב במשך המאה התשע־עשרה. עדות הן גם
להרגשת הביטחון העצמי וההתעצמות הפנימית שעלו וגאו ביהדות זו, למו־
דעותה לכוחה המכריע ביהדות העולם ולמעיינות האנרגיה שתססו בה ותבעו
את הזרמתם לערוצי חיים ויצירה לאומיים.[155]

אחה״ע לא העלים גם את עינו מתופעות של "עבדות רוחנית" בין יהודי
מזרח אירופה. ב־1905, כאשר נתעוררה לשעה קלה התקווה בין יהודי רוסיה
שתקופה חדשה מפציעה ועולה בחייהם, בעקב הזעזועים המהפכניים שפקדו

---

[153] שם, שם.

[154] שם, שם, טור משמאל.

[155] כידוע, הקדים פ. סמולנסקין את אחה״ע בביקורת שהוא מתח על אספקטים שונים
של תרבות יהודי המערב במאות ה־18 וה־19 : על משה מנדלסון והשכלת ברלין,
הריפורמה, פעולות כי״ח ועוד. ראה בעיקר "עם עולם", "עת לטעת", "שאלת היהודים
שאלת חיים", מאמר שני; התועה בדרכי החיים, חלק ד׳, מכתבים י׳, י״ב; פרק
כ״א ועוד.

את המדינה וכינוס ה״דומה״, היה הוא בין היחידים שטען כי חובתם הראשו־
נית של יהודי רוסיה היא לעצמם ולא לציבור הרחב. הם המקופחים והמעוולים
ביותר בחברה הרוסית ועליהם לרכז את מאמציהם בביטול ״מצבם המיוחד,
מבלי להמתין עד שיבוא זה מאליו, כתולדה ׳הגיונית׳ מתוך ׳האושר הכללי׳,
לעתיד לבוא״. אולם דעתו דעת מיעוט היתה ונצחו הרבים, שהיו בעד שיתוף
מלא עם ״הכוחות הפרוגרסיביים״ לשם העברת השיעבוד הכללי ולא בעד
הבלטת העניין היהודי המיוחד. ״החזיון הזה״ — כתב אז — ״מעיד עלינו בני
הגלות, שרגש הכבוד האנושי פגום בלבנו ואין אנו מוכשרים להרגיש חרפתנו
כבני אדם בריאים.״ [156] ומשהצביעו ״הפרוגרסיסטים״ על כך ש״בחורי
ישראל יוצאים ליהרג על ׳האשר הכללי׳ ועומדים בשורה הראשונה של מחנה
׳הפרוגרס׳... וכי אפשר לבעלי נפש פגומה להראות גבורה כזו?,״ השיב להם
אחה״ע, שאכן אפשר ואפשר הדבר, וגבורת צעירי ישראל המוסרים נפשם
למען המהפכה אינה אלא גבורת עבד:

דרכו של עבד לרוץ עם מרכבת האדון, אחת היא אם אחר המרכבה או
לפניה. ומוכשר הוא העבד למעשי גבורה ומסירת נפש לטובתו והנאתו
של האדון,[157] שלא על מנת לקבל פרס לעצמו, אלא רק משום
שהמעשה רצוי לאדונו...[158] ישנה פסיכולוגיא מיוחדת של מעמד
העבדות, פסיכולוגיא היורדת עד תהומה של נפש ועוברת בירושה מדור
לדור עד שקשה להפטר ממנה אפילו בשנוי מצב. חזיון זה, שבולט ביותר
בחיי היהדות המערבית, נראה כבר גם בקרבנו בארץ הזאת. את החירות
החיצונית אמנם לא השגנו עוד, אבל חיינו הפנימיים ורגשות רוחנו הלא
נשתנו הרבה מאד מימי ׳המשכילים׳ של אמצע המאה שעברה ועד עתה,
ואך דבר אחד עומד קיים בלי שנוי: ׳גבורי החירות׳ שבימינו, כ׳גבורי
ההשכלה׳ לשעבר, בכל היותם מוכנים למסור את נפשם על ׳האידאל׳, אי
אפשר להם בלי ׳אדון׳ מן החוק, שאליו נושאים עיניהם ועל מזבחו
מביאים קרבנותיהם. ההבדל אינו אלא זה: שבדור ההשכלה היה ׳האדון׳
לבוש בגדי שרד ועובד עבודת הממשלה, ועתה הוא לבוש מעיל גס ועובד
בבתי־חרושת. אדון באדון נתחלף, אבל העבד נשאר כשהיה.[159]

עד כמה שידוע לי היה ברנר בספרות העברית של הזמן שבסיפוריו
״בחורף״ (1903) ו״מסביב לנקודה״ (1904) הקדים את אחה״ע בהצצה מפוכחת

[156] ״נשכחות״, כל כתבי, עמ׳ שצ״ה.
[157] הדגשה שלו.
[158] ״נשכחות״, כל כתבי, עמ׳ שצ״ו, טור מימין.
[159] שם, שם, טור משמאל; ראה גם אגרות, ג׳, עמ׳ 213.

וחודרת זו לתוך נפשו של הנוער היהודי המהפכני ברוסיה.[160] אין זאת אלא
ששניהם הגיעו — כל אחד על פי דרכו — לאותה מסקנה מתוך אותה תכונה
שבנפשם, והיא, אהבת האמת והנאמנות לעצמם.

תגובה דומה הגיב אחה״ע מספר שנים קודם לכן (סוף 1902), ואף היא קשורה
בבעייתיה של יהדות רוסיה. היו אלה השנים האפלות של ימי ניקולאי השני,
כאשר עניבת החנק הכלכלי והתרבותי נתהדקה והלכה מסביב לצווארה של
יהדות זו. הכניסה לבתי־הספר התיכונים והגבוהים נעשתה יותר ויותר
מוגבלת וקשה; אולם מספר צעירי ישראל המתדפקים על שעריהם גדל
והלך.[161] אך נמצא בקרב יהודי רוסיה מי שטען שהיהודים מגזימים בקובל־
נותיהם על גורלם ושמצבם התרבותי טוב בעצם מזה של העמים אשר בקרבם
הם יושבים.

זהו מהלך המחשבות של העבדים — הגיב אחה״ע — שאין להם אידאל
יותר גדול מהדמות לאדוניהם [162] בכל הדברים! ׳האדון׳ הוא להם קנה־
המידה, שבו הם מודדים את עצמם וערכם הפנימי. ואם מוצאים הם,
שכבר הגיעו למדה זו ואין להם להתבייש בפני אדונם, ישמחו בחלקם ולא
יעיזו לבקש יותר. אבל אדם בן־חורין מודד את נפשו ומצבו לא במדתם
של אחרים, אלא בזו של עצמו. האי״דאל שלו הוא — לא להגיע למדרגתם
של אנשים הסובבים אותו, אלא להגיע לאותה המדרגה שכחות נפשו
מכשירים אותו להשיגה... כמה מטמטום הלב וכחות הרגש צריך שיהיה
באדם בשביל שלא להבין את הצער הפנימי הגדול, בהיות הנפש מרגשת
בקרבה כחות מרובים המבקשים להם מוצא — ואין.[163]

ולבסוף — תגובה על סוג שיעבוד אחר ומאזור אחר. כידוע, היה אחה״ע
חסיד ה״חיקוי של התחרות״ אך היה נרתע מה״חיקוי של התבטלות״. מה הפלא
שהוא נזדעזע, כשגילה ב״הצבי״ של בן יהודה מירושלים סיפור מתורגם
מצרפתית, שהיה מתובל ב״זמה הצרפתית״ כשהיא ״מוטעמת ומפורשת בכל
דקדוקיה״:

הרוח הלאומי הזה שאנו מתגנדרים בו — כתב — הרי מימות משה ועד
עתה שונא זמה הוא, ומה הוא איפוא ניבול פה זה בלשוננו הלאומית,
במכ״ע לאומי שבלאומיים — אם לא עוד הפעם ׳התבטלות הישות׳ מפני

[160] השווה ״בחורף״, כל כתבי י. ח. ברנר, כרך 1 (ישראל, תשט״ז), עמ׳ 32, טור
משמאל; ״מסביב לנקודה״, שם, פרקים י׳, י״א, י״ב ועוד.
[161] S. M. Dubnow, *History of the Jews in Russia and Poland*, III (JPS, 1920),
pp. 26 ff.
[162] הדגשה של אחה״ע.
[163] ״תחית הרוח״, כל כתבי, עמ׳ קפ״ג–קפ״ד.

רוח זר, צרפתי, שבא לארץ והטיל זוהמא בלבבות? והרי מכאן ראיה,
שגם בארץ אבותינו עבדים אנחנו ברוח, ובשפלותנו בעיני עצמנו אנו
מזקים גם פה את הרע, ואין רוחנו הלאומי יכול לעמוד בפני אויביו
התקיפים ממנו.[164]

התביעה למחשבה ולפעולה מתוך חירות היא גם המונחת ליסוד דעותיו של
אחה״ע על חכמת ישראל, הריפורמה ויידיש. הוא העריך את פעלה של חכמת
ישראל במערב, שמתוך עיסוקה בעבר האומה היא עוזרת לבנות את ״האני״
הלאומי השלם,[165] אולם הוא מצא אותה משועבדת ל״זרים,״ לאמנסיפציה
במקרהו של ל. צונץ ולריפורמה במקרהו של א. גייגר.

(צונץ) ראה בה אמצעי להפוך לב העמים לטובה עלינו ולהשיג את
האידאל היותר גדול של הימים ההם — שווי הזכויות. וגייגר העמיק
לחקור ב׳חכמת ישראל׳ בשביל למצא בה יסוד וסמך להאידאל הגדול
שלו — להרפורמציא הדתית, שהיתה גם היא בעיקרה אמצעי להשגת שווי
הזכויות. ואף ר׳ זכריה פראנקל, שהיה קרוב לרוח העברי יותר מהם, לא
נמנע מלגלות דעתו ברבים בשנות הששים... כי אחר אשר בטלו אז
ההגבלות האחרונות של זכויות היהודים בפרוסיא, הנה בטלו גם החיים
הלאומיים של היהודים שם, וכל כחותיהם צריכים להיות שקועים
ונבלעים בחיי העם אשר בקרבו הם יושבים.[166]

היא היתה ״משועבדת״ בעיניו אף במובן אחר. רובה היה ברשותם של
שאינם בני־ברית ודעותיהם הן שהיו שליטות בה ואף מקובלות על חכמי
ישראל. כך, למשל, קיבלו חכמי ישראל את הנחת החוקרים הנוצרים שבמקרה
של סתירה בין מקורות התלמוד והמדרש מזה לבין המקורות הנכרים מזה,
הבכורה ניתנה לאחרונים על הראשונים.[167] והוא הדין בנוגע לפלפול התל־
מודי: ״בלי בקורת ובחינה מדעית נתפשטה גם בקרבנו השקפת הנכרים על
הפלפול התלמודי, כי מתנגד הוא להההגיון האמתי ולהשכל הבריא,״ ולא העלו
כלל על דעתם ״כי ההגיון התלמודי צריך למוד ויש לו על מה שיסמוך וכי
ההבדל שבינו ובין ההגיון של היונים אינו מקרי בלבד ואינו מעיד על חסרון

---

[164] ״חיקוי של התבטלות״, שם, עמ׳ ר״ע־רע״א. לצערי לא השגתי את ״הצבי״ בניו־
יורק ולא יכולתי לזהות את הסיפור.

[165] ״עבר ועתיד״, כל כתבי, עמ׳ פ״ב.

[166] ״תחית הרוח״, שם, עמ׳ קע״ח.

[167] ענין זה היה סלע למחלוקת בין שי״ר ומרכוס יוסט בסוף שנות ה־30 וראשית שנות
ה־40 של המאה הי״ט. ראה כרם חמד, 7 (פראג, 1843), מכתב ח׳, עמ׳ 152־138; ראה
גם Isaac Barzilay, *Shlomo Yehudah Rappaport (Shir)* (Massada, 1969), pp.
106 ff.

ידיעה מצד חכמי ישראל, אלא מקורו בהבדל יותר פנימי ועצמי שבין רוח
ישראל ורוח היונים בכלל.״ [168]

אחה״ע חלק על מוסכמה אחרת של החוקרים הנוצרים, ובעקבותיהם גם של
רבים מחכמי ישראל, והיא, ״ההבדל היסודי והפנימי שבין תורת הנביאים
לבין ׳היהדות׳ המעשית שנולדה בימי בית שני וקבלה צורתה האחרונה
בדורות שלפני החורבן.״ [169] יודע הוא אמנם שרב המרחק בין עולם המקרא
מזה לבין עולם התלמוד ושלחן ערוך מזה; בכל זאת חושב הוא ש״רוח אחד״
בראם וחותם אחד טבוע בצורתם. [170] הקיצוניות המוסרית של הנביאים היא
שנתלבשה בקיצוניות מעשית ביצירות המאוחרות. [171] משום כך הוא תובע
להפקיע את חכמת ישראל מרשות בעלותה הזרה ולא רק להשיבה לבעליה
האמיתיים אלא גם לדרכי חקירה שיעמידוה על המיוחד שבה.

את הביטוי הבולט של הפסיכיקה של ״עבדות בתוך חירות״ מצא אחה״ע
ברעיון התעודה, בסיסה העיוני של יהדות הריפורמה. רעיון זה, שעם ישראל
אינו עם עוד אלא כנסיה דתית בלבד, המחוייבת להמשיך ולהתקיים כדי
״לדעת את אלהים ולהביא את האחרים לידי ידיעה זו,״ לא היה לדעתו אלא
״דברי שעשועים״ שבדו מלבם יהודי המערב כדי לזכות בשויון האזרחי מזה
ולהשאר במסגרת היהדות מזה. אם רעיון כזה — הוא כתב — יכול היה עוד
להתלבש באצטלא של ״מדעיות״ במחצית הראשונה של המאה הי״ט,
כשהאמונה ב״תכליות״ עוד היתה מקובלת, אין הוא אלא אנכרוניזם עתה,
בסוף המאה, שני דורות אחרי שדרוין עמד וביטל כל ״תעודה או תכלית אף
במקום שהיא נראית ביותר לכל עין פשוטה.״ ואם בכל זאת ממשיכים יהודי
המערב להחזיק ברעיון, אין זאת אלא שכהסוואה הוא משמש להם להסתיר
מאחוריו את הרגש היהודי שעדיין חי ומפעם בלבם. [172]

ולסיום — פרשת היידיש, שיחסו כלפיה ינק אף הוא במידה רבה מהרגשת
החירות והגאווה היהודית שלו. סוף המאה ה־י״ט וראשית המאה שלנו היו
תקופת נצחונות גדולים ליידיש. יצירות מנדלי, שלום עליכם ופרץ הוסיפו לה
מימד ספרותי על המימד העממי, כלשון הדיבור של המוני האומה במזרח
אירופה. [173] אולם היתה זו ההכרזה של ועידת צ׳רנוביץ (1908) על יידיש

---

[168] ״תחית הרוח״, כל כתבי, עמ׳ קע״ח.

[169] שם, שם, עמ׳ קע״ה.

[170] הדגשה שלו.

[171] ״תחית הרוח״, כל כתבי, עמ׳ קע״ו.

[172] ״עבדות בתוך חירות״, שם, עמ׳ ס״ח; ״כהן ונביא״, שם, עמ׳ צ׳–צ״ב; ״שינוי
הערכין״, שם, עמ׳ קנ״ו–קנ״ז. השווה שד״ל, מחקרי היהדות, כרך 1, חלק 2 (ורשה,
תרע״ג), עמ׳ 29–24, הערה על תורת התעודה של ד״ר לודוויג פילפסון.

[173] ראה "Yiddish Literature" in EJ, XVI, pp. 810–815

"כלשון לאומית" 174 והמלחמה שקנאיה פתחו נגד העברית 175 שעוררו את
מורת רוחו של אחה״ע. הוא לא התנגד, כמובן, ליידיש כלשון דיבור ואף לא
כלשון ספרות, אולם התורה בדבר "לאומיותה," שהטיפוה אנשי "הבונד"
בעיקר, חסרת־שחר היתה בעיניו:

חזון כזה לא היה עוד בעולם, שיחשוב עם ללשונו הלאומית איזו לשון
זרה אשר דבקה בו באיזו ארץ נכריה, לאחר שעברו עליו תקופות היס־
טוריות ארוכות שבהן לא ידע את הלשון הזאת. 176

כל התנועה האידישיסטית היתה בעיניו בבחינת התמרדות של עמי הארץ,
המוכנים לוותר על הירושה התרבותית של האומה ולהתחיל מן ההווה, כדרכם
של העמים בעלי התרבות הנמוכה ביותר. בתגובה על ועידת צ׳רנוביץ הוא
כתב:

שתי מרידות של עמי הארץ יודעת ההיסטוריא שלנו, ושתיהן לא היו
אולי מצליחות כל כך אלמלא הרעישו עליהן את העולם, ואולם הללו
יצאו לפחות בדגלים מוסריים חשובים, ובראשון ישוע הנוצרי והבעל שם
טוב, אבל זו שדגלה ז׳רגון אשכנזי ונושא הדגל ש. א...177... שובו למנו־
חתכם אחים! כל רע לא יאונה. 178

בדאגה וברציניות יותר גדולות הוא כתב באותו ענין כמה זמן אחר כך (1909)
לש. דובנוב:

אם אחר היסטוריא של אלפי שנים יתחיל עמנו לפתח את הקולטורא שלו
מ׳בראשית׳, ליצור לו שפה ספרותית חדשה עם ׳ערכים ספרותיים
וקולטוריים׳ שיהיו מעין חקוי של קולטורות זרות, כמו שעושים
הליטאים, הרוסים וכו׳ — איני רואה שום טעם ושום צורך בקיום לאומי
שפל כזה, ומוטב שנסגור את ספר ההיסטוריא שלנו משנוסיף בו עלים
ריקים כאלה. 179

וכן כתב באותו ענין לרבניצקי:

אין אתם רוצים להבין שכל עצם קיומנו בגלות אפשרי הוא רק בהיותנו

174 ראה "Czernowitz Yiddish Language Conference," ibid., V, pp. 1211–1212
175 אגרות, ד׳, עמ׳ 187.
176 "תחית הרוח", כל כתבי, עמ׳ קע״ט; אגרות, ג׳, עמ׳ 241; ד׳, עמ׳ 124.
177 הנני משער שהכוונה לשלום אש.
178 אגרות, ד׳, עמ׳ 45.
179 שם, שם, עמ׳ 101.

מרגישים את עצמנו כ׳אריסטוקרטיא היסטורית׳,[180] ובשעה שתתחדל
הרגשה זו ונהיה בעיניו כשאר האומות הקטנות, בלי ערך קולטורי
היסטורי, רק עם לשון חדשה ולאומיות חדשה ׳דימוקרטית׳ — אז נהיה
באמת האומה היותר שפלה בעולם.[181]

בשביל יהודי שרשי כאהה״ע, שעמד על הקרקע ההיסטורית של האומה ותבע
נאמנות ומודעות לכלל תרבותה, לא היתה ״לאומיות דמוקרטית״ זו, על אופיה
האנטי־דתי והאנטי־היסטורי המובהק, אלא השפלה עצמית והתכחשות לרוחה
האריסטוקרטי של תרבות עם עתיקה.

מאז ועד עתה: הערות סיכום וסיום

שני דורות מאז מותו של אהה״ע ושלשה דורות בערך מאז כתב את רוב
מאמריו הינם תקופה ארוכה וקצרה כאחת. ארוכה — מבחינת הבעיות והעניי־
נים שהוא עסק בהם ואשר בינתיים הגיעו לקצה מסלולם ההיסטורי ועל
פתרונם באו, לחיוב או לשלילה; וקצרה — מבחינת העניינים שהינם עדיין
חלק מהמציאות ״הפרובלמטית״ שלנו ומשפטם הסופי טרם נחרץ. מבחינה זו,
אין הערכת אהה״ע כיום יכולה להיות עוד שלמה אלא חלקית בלבד. מה
שמקשה עוד יותר על הערכה זו הוא השינוי הטרגי והפתאומי־כמעט שנתחולל
בגורל יהדות אירופה בשנים המועטות המפרידות בין דורו והדור שלאחריו.
אילו אף היה אהה״ע היסטוריון — מה שלא היה — שאוזנו קשובה לדופקם של
התהליכים ההיסטוריים, ספק הוא אם היה יכול לחזות מראש את הגורל החרוץ
שצפוי היה לאותה גולה, שבהמשך קיומה הוא היה כה משוכנע ולעתידה הוא
כה דאג. סוף סוף אפילו גדולי ההיסטוריונים שלנו מהדורות האחרונים,
שהאריכו ימים אחריו ושקרובים היו ממנו קרבת זמן לאותה תקופה — שמץ
דבר לא גונב אף אליהם מאותה טרגדיה נוראה שארבה לנו מאחורי הפרגוד.
מפוכח אמנם היה אהה״ע בדעתו בנוגע לעתידה של האומה בגולה ולא האמין
שאפילו התפשטות ההומניזם תעקור את השנאה אליה;[182] אולם שנחשול
שנאה כנאציזם יציף את אירופה כולה וימחק את צלם האלהים מעליה — את
זה לא העלה כלל על דעתו. במסגרת תורת ההתפתחות שלו, על הדינמיקה
ה״כמעט סטטית״ שלה, לא היה מקום להתפרצות שטנית כזו של החיה
שבאדם.

אולם אם מסיחים אנו את דעתנו מקטקליזם איום זה ומנסים להעריך את

---

[180] הדגשה שלו.

[181] שם, שם, עמ׳ 131; ראה גם ״תחית הרוח״, ״ריב לשונות״, כל כתבי, עמ׳ קע״ט,
ת״ג–ת״ו ועוד.

[182] ״שתי רשויות״, כל כתבי, עמ׳ פ״ה, פ״ו.

מחשבותיו ודעותיו במסגרת המציאות "הנורמלית", שאף היא המשיכה לפעול
בקורות הדורות האחרונים שלנו — אין ספק שרובן ככולן במבחן הזמן עמדו
והמציאות ההיסטורית הוכיחה את יושר שכלו והסתכלותו הריאליסטית. והנה
דוגמאות אחדות בלבד. נכוחות, למשל, הוא ראה את הבעיה הערבית, וראשון
לרואיה היה. עוד לפני שמונים ושבע שנה העיר ב"אמת מארץ ישראל"
(תרנ"א), אחד ממאמריו הראשונים, שאשלייה היא לחשוב כי הארץ היא
בלתי-מיושבת והיושבים בה פראי אדם, ומשום כך נוכל לרכוש בה אדמות
כרצוננו ולהתיישב בכל מקום שנרצה. האמת שונה היא: את האדמה הטובה
מעבדים הערבים בעצמם, ורק "שדות חול או הרי אבן" הם משאירים בלתי-
מעובדים. ואשר ליחסם להתיישבות היהודית:

רואים ומבינים הערביים את מעשינו וחפצנו בארץ, אבל הם מחשים
ועושים עצמם כלא-יודעים, לפי שאינם רואים במעשינו עתה שום סכנה
לעתידותיהם, והם משתדלים לנצל גם אותנו, להוציא תועלת מן האורחים
החדשים בהיות בהיות לאל ידם... ואולם, אם תבוא עת אשר חיי בני עמנו בא"י
יתפתחו כל כך, עד שידחקו מעט או הרבה רגלי עם הארץ, אז לא על
נקלה יניח זה את מקומו... קול תרועת הלוקומוטיב יביא בלי ספק
שינויים גדולים במצב הארץ ויושביה, והעבודה תכבד עלינו עוד
יותר.[183]

לא ארכו הימים ובעשיריה הראשונה והשנייה למאתנו נעשו מודעים לבעייה
זו גם א. ד. גורדון, י. ח. ברנר, ד. בן גוריון ואחרים מבני העלייה השנייה,[184]
אולם זכות ראשון שמורה אך לו.

אחה"ע ראה גם מראש את הגורל הצפוי לתורת האוטונומיזם של דובנוב. לא
הספיקה הדיו להתייבש על הסעיפים על דבר זכויות המיעוטים שבחוזה ורסיי
וכבר החלו לקצץ בהם, ובשנות השלושים כבר היו בטלים ומבוטלים ברוב
המדינות החדשות שחתמו עליהם. לא זה בלבד שהוא צדק בנוגע ליחס השלי-
לי, שהוא צפה מראש מצד הממשלות הנוגעות בדבר, כלפי אוטונומיה יהודית
במדינותיהן הסוברניות,[185] אלא אף בנוגע לאי-רצונם וחוסר-יכולתם של
היהודים עצמם לפתח אוטונומיה חילונית כזו.[186]

[183] כל כתבי, עמ' י"ד; ראה גם, שם, עמ' כ"ט; אגרות, ד', עמ' 37, 170, 175, 241—
242, 289; ה', עמ' 113.
[184] ראה כתבי א. ד. גורדון: האומה והעבודה (ירושלים, 1952), עמ' 96, 203,
245—243; כל כתבי י. ח. ברנר, 1, עמ' 177, 212, 336, 339, 389; ופסי (זאב
סמילנסקי), "מן הדמיון אל המציאות", העולם (1908), גל' 34, 35, 36, 37, 38; דוד בן
גוריון, אנחנו ושכנינו (תל-אביב, תרצ"א).
[185] "שלוש מדרגות", כל כתבי, עמ' קנ"ב-קנ"ג.
[186] "שלילת הגלות", שם, עמ' ת"א. ראה גם Oscar Janowski, *Nationalities and*

לצערנו הרב נתאמתה גם נבואתו רואת־השחורות של אחה״ע בנוגע לייידיש.
הקיבוץ היהודי במזרח אירופה עוד מנה מיליונים של דוברי יידיש ועוד פרחו
בקרבו ספרות יידית ועתונות ותיאטרון יידיים כשהוא הוציא את משפטו
שפריחה זו בבחינת קקיון יונה היא, וחרוצים ימיה לא רק בקיבוץ העולה של
יהדות ארצות הברית, אלא אף במקום חיותה, ברוסיה־פולין.[187] בוודאי, לולא
השואה לא היה כליון חרוץ כזה יורד על לשון ותרבות יידיש בפתאומיות
ואכזריות כאלה, אולם ספק הוא, אם אפילו אז היה התהליך ההיסטורי משתנה
ביסודו.

מעינו הבוחנת והחדה לא נעלמה גם תופעה אחרת, והיא, קיומה הארעי
גרידא של הספרות העברית בגולה. עוד בראשית המאה שלנו, כשרוב הסופ־
רים העברים ישבו באודיסה, ורשה, וילנה או ברלין, ואילו מספר הסופרים
והקוראים העברים בארץ עדיין קטן היה, הוא כבר הגיע למסקנה ״שכשם
שאין הרוח העברי יכול להתפתח די צרכו בלי מרכז חפשי ׳במקום חיותו׳, כן
לא יוכלו גם לבושי הרוח: הלשון והספרות.״[188] תנועת החופש ברוסיה של
שנת 1905, ״שמשכה אחריה כמעט כל משכילי עמנו שם, ועבודתנו הלאומית
והספרות העברית נתדלדלו אז עי״ז מאד,״[189] העמידתו על רפיון יסודה של
תחיית לשון וספרות זו בסביבה הזרה והביאתו למסקנה ש״כל עמלנו לעוררן
לתחיה בארץ נכריה לא יועיל אלא לשעה, עד שזיק יצא מתחת הפטיש של
החיים הנכרים הסובבים אותנו, ויחריב בזמן קצר מה שבנינו שנים רבות
בשארית כוחנו.״[190] וכך, כבר ב־1906, עת רק החל להתלקט בארץ קומץ
הסופרים של ימי העליה השנייה, ועוד בטרם נוסד בה ״הפועל הצעיר״ ובטרם
עוד נצטרפו למנין החדש סופרים כברנר, עגנון, שמעוני ואחרים, וכבר
השמיע אחה״ע את דעתו הברורה ״שקודם כל ויותר מכל נחוץ לנו מרכז
ספרות בא״י,״ ורק שם יכולה להיות תקומה לה.[191] אמנם המשיכה עוד
הספרות העברית זמן־מה את קיומה הספרדי במזרח אירופה, אולם לא עברו

National Minorities (New York, 1945), chap. VII; "Poland" in *EJ*, XIII, p.
739; א. הרטגלאס, ״מלחמות יהודי פולין על זכויותיהם האזרחיות והלאומיות״, בית
ישראל בפולין, ערך י. היילפרין, א׳ (ירושלים, תש״ח), עמ׳ 151–128. בנוגע לרוסיה
הסוביטית וכשלון ״התרבות היהודית הפרולטרית״, ראה "Russia" ב־*EJ*, כרך 14,
בעיקר עמ׳ 468–464; Salo W. Baron, *The Russian Jew Under the Tsars and Soviets*
(New York, 1964), pp. 225, 228, 268–273.

[187] ״תחית הרוח״, כל כתבי, עמ׳ קע״ט–ק״פ; ״ריב לשונות״, שם, עמ׳ ת״ג–ת״ו;
ראה גם אגרות, ד׳, עמ׳ 135.

[188] ״הגיעה השעה״, כל כתבי, עמ׳ שע״ט, טור מימין.

[189] שם, שם, בהערה, טור משמאל.

[190] שם, שם, עמ׳ שע״ט.

[191] אגרות, ג׳, עמ׳ 269; ד׳, עמ׳ 10, 57, 113.

אלא ימי דור אחד ובראשית שנות השלושים כבר היה היישוב הקטן בארץ
שומר ״הגחלת האחרונה״ ואין מלבדו.

בין קטרוגיו של קורצווייל נגד אחה״ע היה גם הקטרוג שהוא התעלם ״מן
התנועות הסוציאליסטיות והבעיות הסוציאליות בכלל.״ [192] האמת היא שהוא
לא ״התעלם,״ אבל לבו לא נתחמם בו מעולם למגמות ה״פרולטריזציה״ ו״דת
העבודה״ שעלו בימי העליה השנייה. הוא לא האמין בפרולטריון יהודי חקלאי
שיעלה בארץ ואפילו לא במעמד ניכר של אכרים יהודים יושבי כפר, על פי
הדוגמא של הארצות האגרריות שבמזרח אירופה. לעומת זה הוא האמין,

[ש]יכול היהודי להיות ׳פרמר׳ חרוץ, ׳בעל בית׳ כפרי, מעין בועז
בשעתו, המתפרנס מעבודת האדמה ובקי בה ושקוע בה... אבל יחד עם זה
שואף הוא גם לחיות חיי אדם בן תרבות, ליהנות מפרי הקולטורא של
זמננו הנאת הגוף והנפש, ואין האדמה סופגת לתוכה את כל ישותו. הטופס
היפה הזה הולך ונברא לעינינו בא״י ובמשך הזמן יגיע בודאי למדרגה
של שלימות בלתי מצויה. [193]

לאור המציאות ההיסטורית של היישוב בארץ בתקופה שקדמה לייסוד המדינה,
כשמגמות הפרודוקטיביזציה לשם יצירת יהודי חדש וחברה יהודית חדשה היו
בבחינת השאור בעיסתו של מפעל התחייה והגיעו להשגים ריאליים חשובים,
ניתן היה אולי לבקר את אחה״ע על שמרנותו ואי־רגישותו הסוציאלית. אולם
במסגרת ההיסטורית הרחבה יותר, זו של שלשת־ארבעת הדורות האחרונים,
ובעיקר לאור המציאות הישראלית של שלושים השנים מאז ייסוד המדינה,
ניטל עוקצה של ביקורת זו. מסתבר שתפיסתו ״הבעל־הביתית״ והפרוזאית
כביכול של טיפוס היהודי החדש שציפה כי יעלה בארץ היתה יותר חודרת
ומרחיקת ראות מזו של משוררינו וחולמי חלום חברה חדשה בארץ.

אולם חשיבותו של אחה״ע לא היתה ברוח ״הנבואה״ שבו. לכל היותר ניתן
לייחס ראיית עתיד חודרת זו לכוח הניתוח הריאליסטי שלו, ואילו השפעתו
על בני דורו והדור שלאחריו — פרי גורמים אחרים היתה. בראש וראשונה
היא נבעה מן העובדה שתורתו הלאומית, למרות אופיה החילוני המובהק, גברו
בה יסודות ״ההמשך״ על יסודות הניתוק, ובעצם היא נשארה נאמנה אם לא
לתורה במובנה ההלכתי הרי במובנה הרוחני, כפי שתפס אותה פ. סמולנס־
קין. [194] לכאורה דרוויניסט היה וכופר בתכליות ותעודות לאומיות, אולם
אמונתו בייחוד האומה ובייעודה מזדעקת ממש ועולה מכל יצירתו. שיבת ציון

[192] ספרותנו החדשה – המשך או מהפכה? עמ׳ 218
[193] ״סך הכל״, כל כתבי, עמ׳ תכ״ב.
[194] ״עם עולם״, מאמרים, 1, עמ׳ 72–71, 95–94, 157 ואילך, 189–180; ״עת לטעת״,
שם, 2, מעמ׳ 24 והלאה, ועוד.

שלו — ארצית טהורה היא כביכול, אולם שקויה אף היא בבסמו של החלום על
ממלכת כהנים ובני־נביאים כי תעלה עוד. מבחינה עיונית צדקו בוודאי
מבקריו בביקורת שמתחו על הזיווג שבין לאומיות ומוסר במשנתו, אולם אף
בכך — על הקרקע ההיסטורי של תרבות האומה הוא עמד. בין אם אמיתית
התורה או לא, עצם התביעה לזיווג כזה והצפייה שציפה כי בתנאי חירות עוד
ישוב ויתגלה גאון האומה בשדה המוסר — אי אפשר היה שלא ייהפכו לגורם
מעצב חשוב בכל מפעל התחייה. מדעת או שלא מדעת, במישרין או בעקיפין,
בתוספת נופך של סוציאליזם או כשהיא בפני עצמה, השפע השפיעה התורה
על בני הדור.

ועוד רעיון שבעל השפעה היה בתקופת התחייה — בבית מדרשו של אחה״ע
היתה לידתו, והוא רעיון ההגשמה העצמית. אמנם לבש הרעיון צורה חדשה
ועמוקה יותר במשנותיהם של א. ד. גורדון וי. ח. ברנר והבאים אחריהם, אולם
בגרעינו הראשוני, כתביעה המכוונת כלפי היחיד בישראל שיקום ויעשה למען
העם והארץ, ממנו בא לראשונה. עוד בתר״ן הוא כתב:

כל רעיון, בין דתי בין מוסרי או חברתי, לא יקום ולא יהיה בלעדי חבר
׳כהנים׳ אשר יקדישו לו חייהם ויעבדוהו בכל נפשם ובכל מאדם... ובכל
מקום סכנה יהיו הם הראשונים למסור נפשם עליו. הרעיון החדש הוא
דרך לא עבר בה איש, וכל דרך כזו בחזקת סכנה עומדת. לא מאת המון
העם, החפץ חיים, נוכל לדרוש איפוא, ולא עליו נוכל לסמוך, כי יכבוש
דרך לפני הרעיון בחרף נפש. זאת יעשו הכהנים, אשר להם הכוח והעוז
המוסרי הדרוש לזה, והעם יבוא אחרי כן, בהיות כבר הדרך כבושה
וסלולה לפניו... אלה מהם שהיכולת בידם לעלות לארץ, יעלו ויאחזו בה,
והיו ליתר העולים למורי דרך, למלאכי שלום, ונתנו מרוחם עליהם,
בהיותם למופת בקרבם לעבודה, לסבלנות, לאהבה, לאחדות.[195]

את חשיבות אחה״ע יש להעריך משתי נקודות ראות, מזו של דורו ומזו של
יהדות המאה התשע־עשרה כולה. בתקופת כשלון לחיבת־ציון הוא הופיע,
ותורתו היא שחיזקה את רוח בני הדור אף לאחר כשלון נסיונותיו של הרצל.
היא היא שלימדה סבלנות ואורך־רוח וחיסנה נגד הייאוש שבאכזבות זמניות.
דווקא על ידי כך שהדגישה את חשיבות חריש הלבבות העמוק כתנאי לגאולה,
היא יצרה מסגרות פעילות רבות שהיו פחות תלויות בהצלחות או בכשלונות
ארעי. וכך כתב עליו קלויזנר בשילהי 1897:

הרעיונות החדשים של אחד הסופרים (אחה״ע, י. ב.), שנתפרסמו בשנים
האחרונות והביאו לידי ההכרה הברורה, כי העיקר הוא התפתחות לבו

<hr>

[195] "הכהנים והעם", כל כתבי, עמ׳ י״ט.

המאובן של עמנו — השיבו לצעירינו את אמונתם, כי הרבה הרבה אפשר
להם לפעול ולעשות לטובת היהדות והתפתחותה, לטובת הארץ, הספרות
והשפה. כל אחד מישראל לפי כחו, תכונתו וכשרונותיו, יכול להשתתף
בעבודת העם, יכול להביא תועלת להשגת המטרה הרצויה באיזה מקצוע
מעשי, חברותי או ספרותי: לבנין עדי עד נחוצים גם אבנים, גם טיח, גם
גודרים וגם בנאים אומנים. הכרה כזאת המתפשטת, לשמחתנו, יותר
ויותר בקרב כל המפלגות, היא היא היסוד לכל המעשים הרבים והטובים,
הנעשים כעת בחיינו ובספרותנו, ואשר תוצאותיהם תוכלנה להיות
גדולות וכבירות באמת, אם רק האמונה בכחו של רעיון רם ונשא תגדל
ותחזק בין כל מפלגותינו, עד ששום רוח מצויה, המנשבת מזמן לזמן
בחלל העולם האירופי ולעומת שבאה כן תלך, לא תזיז אותה עוד
ממקומה.196

אם נסתכל בו במסגרת תולדות המפעל הלאומי כולו ולא רק במסגרת הצרה
של ימי הרצל, יינטל גם עוקצו של העימות שבינו לבין הרצל. בעצם, לא
מנוגדות היו תורותיהם, אלא משלימות זו את זו. הקדימה אמנם תורת אהה"ע
את תורת הרצל, אך אילו נשארה בעלת שלטון יחיד בצבור היהודי, ספק הוא
אם התנועה הלאומית היתה אי־פעם מגיעה לממדים של תנועת עם. מאידך,
לולא פעולת אהה"ע, מי יודע אם היה המשך לחזון הרצל לאחר כשלונותיו
המדיניים. הרצל הופיע בשעת חולשה לאחד־העמיות, ותורת אהה"ע היא
שיצרה מסגרות להמשך פעולה בשנות השפל להרצליאניות.

במסגרת תולדות ישראל של המאה ה־19 כולה, תורת אהה"ע הריהי בבחינת
הצטללות תודעתה העצמית של האומה, מעין אור־פתאום שעלה בה והאיר גם
את דרך עברה הקרוב וגם את דרך העתיד שלפניה. אמנם לא פתאומי היה
האור, וכבר הפציע ועלה לפני כן בלבותיהם של משה הס, דוד גורדון, פרץ
סמולנסקין ובלבותיהם של בני זמנו פינסקר ומשה לייב ליליינבלום. אולם הוא
העמיק ראות מהם. יותר ממישהו לפניו הוא העמידנו על אופיה העקר והשלילי
של מאה זו בקורותינו. הוא הוא שירד לעומקה של הפסיכיקה של ההשכלה,
הריפורמה, חכמת ישראל המערבית, האוטונומיזם הדובנובי והלאומיות
היידישיסטית, ובניסוחים קלסיים ממש הבהיר שדרכן לא דרך היא, שכולן לא
על הקרקע ההיסטורית של האומה עלו והמטרות שהציבו לעצמן ילידות חוץ
היו או פרי מסיבות מקומיות וזמניות גרידא. מטבעות לשון והגות כ"חיקוי של
התחרות" ו"חיקוי של התבטלות", "עבדות בתוך חירות", "אני לאומי", "אדם
באהל", "מוסר לאומי", "מרכז רוחני", "חצי נחמה" ורבים אחרים כמוהם,
כאבוקות אור היו שהאירו תופעות־יסוד וגושי־מציאות מרכזיים שבהווייה

<hr>
196 "יסוד התנועה החדשה", השלח, 2 (1887), עמ' 549.

העבר וההווה שלנו ומחיצות הערכה הקימו בין הטוב והרע, הרצוי והמזיק לנו.
ניסוחים קולעים אלה נחרתו בלבבות והפכו סיסמאות לדור.

האם עמדה תורתו העיקרית, זו של "המרכז הרוחני", במבחן הזמן? כאמור,
מהלומת המוות שניחתה על ראשה של יהדות אירופה המזרחית חיסלה אמנם
אבר יסודי בנוסחת הפתרון האחד־העמית, אולם עלייתה הגדולה של יהדות
ארצות הברית והתרחבותם של היישובים היהודיים במערב אירופה ובאמריקה
הדרומית ממשיכים אף עתה להשאיל לה מובן ותוקף, ושאלת יעילותה של
הנוסחא בעינה עומדת. מעל לכל הוכיח הזמן את אמת נבואתו בנוגע למרכז
עצמו. התפרצות כוחות והתפרחות כשרונות כאלה שעדים אנו להן במדינת
ישראל בדור הראשון לקיומה החפשי — כמעט ללא תקדים הן בקורותינו או
בקורות איזו שהיא אומה אחרת. שרבה גם ההשפעה הזורמת מהמרכז
לתפוצה — אף בזה לית מאן דפליג. מה צורה תלבש השפעה זו בעתיד,
כשהמדינה תגיע אולי למי־מנוחות והדאגה לקיומה תפסיק לשמש גורם מקשר
ומאחד בינה ולתפוצה, ואם די כוח יהא בה, בהשפעה זו, כדי לפעול נגד
הכירסום והסחף המאיימים על קיבוצי ישראל בתפוצה מצד הסביבה והתרבות
החילוניות — מי חכם וידע? אך יהא הפתרון הצפון בחיק העתיד מה שיהא, אין
ספק שבמידה שננסה להתמודד עם עתיד זה, לעצבו ולכוונו, הדרך שהנא
מוכרחים ללכת בה לא תהא אחרת מזו שהורה לנו אחד העם לפני שלשה
דורות ויותר, והיא, חנוך האומה על ידי הפצת דעת קורותיה ותרבותה,
והחדרתה בתודעת ייחודה וגורלה המופלא בקורות האדם.

תוך כדי עיונים במסכת אבות דר' נתן

מאת יהודה גולדין

א

שנינו במשנה סוכה ד', ח': "ההלל והשמחה שמונה, כיצד? מלמד שחייב[1]
אדם בהלל ובשמחה" וכו'. וכן בכ"י קופמן ובכ"י פריז ופרמא, וכן בדפוס
נאפולי ובמתניתא דתלמודא דבני מערבא הוצ' לו. לפנינו משנה מקוצרת,
מעיר הרי"ן אפשטיין. מעניין, אע"פ שישנן עוד משניות שלמות, מקוצרות,
וקטועות,[2] אין "כיצד — מלמד ש..." חוזר בהן. "כיצד", "שהוא משמש
כרגיל לפרש הלכה שקדמה לו",[3] מופיע בלבדו בכל הספרות המדרשית —
התלמודית; אף "מלמד" בלבד ובלי "כיצד" וכהתחלת תשובה,[4] שכיח. ברם
זיווג זה של "כיצד" ו"מלמד ש..." מיד אחריו, כמעט ואינו מצוי במקורות
הקלסיים. בדקתי ענין זה בעזרת הקונקורדנציות של ר' ח. י. קאסאווסקי ז"ל
ושל ר' בנימין בנו יבלח"א, ואף אם יתכן שנעלמו ממני דוגמאות אחדות,
המסקנה שהגעתי אליה בעינה עומדת, והיא, שכרגיל אין חז"ל מעדיפים מטבע
זה, של "כיצד מלמד ש..." על ניסוחים אחרים הרווחים בספרות.

מאידך גיסא, נוסח זה של שאלה ופתיחה לתשובה שבצדה מופיע באבות דר'
נתן נוסחא א', לא פעם ולא שתים אלא פעמים רבות, במספר רב של סעיפים
הבאים לפרש מימרא מהמשנה אבות (וג' פעמים אף מימרא לא מפרקי אבות,
דף י"ג עמוד א'; והשווה את הנוסח בתוספתא סנהדרין ח', ו' ובירושלמי סוף
פרק אחד דיני ממונות ובבבלי ל"ח, א'). המדובר כאן הוא בנוסחא א', ולא
בנוסחא ב' (אלא שכאן תמצא "מלמד" לבדו, למשל: ג' עמ' ב', י"א עמ' ב',
כ"ד עמ' א', כ"ה עמ' א'), שכן בנוסחא ב' חסר הצרוף הזה לגמרי. הוה אומר
ששתי הנוסחאות לא מבית מדרש אחד או מעריכה אחת יצאו; לא זה שעיצב

---

[1] על "כיצד — מלמד ש..." במשנה זו, עיין הרי"ן אפשטיין, מבוא לנוסח המשנה,
(ירושלים, תש"ח), 1038, ור"ח אלבק, משנה סוכה, 477.

[2] על משניות קטועות ומקוצרות עיין הרי"ן אפשטיין, 38—1037.

[3] הרי"ן אפשטיין, 1032. ועיין עוד ר"א הפרופ' גולדברג, פירוש למשנה מסכת
שבת (ירושלים, תשל"ו), 219.

[4] על "מלמד", ראה גם ר' בנימין זאב בכר, ערכי מדרש (תל־אביב, תרפ"ג), 66,
214.

את א׳ עיבד את ב׳ — וזה מסייע לטענתו ולהוכחותיו של הפרופ׳ אליעזר
אריה פינקלשטין עוד לפני כארבעים שנה במאמרו על שתי הנוסחאות של
אדר״ן.[5] והפעם אולי מותר להוסיף, שבבית המדרש בו נוצרה נוסחא א׳ שמש
"כיצד מלמד ש..." שיגרה אקדמית טכנית. כשם שבבמדרשי ר׳ ישמעאל
מובאים, למשל, פעמים רבות פרושים בנוסח "למה נאמר? לפי ש...", כן
באדר״ן נוסחא א׳ משמש "כיצד — מלמד ש..." סגנון קבוע ומקובל בתורת
הפרשנות וההסבר של בית מדרש מיוחד. ולא נוסחה זאת בלבד מופיעה כאן,
להוציא את כל האחרות. יש ויש שמופיע גם "כיצד" לחוד, וכן גם "מלמד
ש..." בלי "כיצד", לרבות צורות אחרות של פתיחה לפירוש, הידועות לנו
מהמקורות בכלל. אולם "כיצד — מלמד ש..." תופש באדר״ן א׳ חלק חשוב
מהפתיחות לפירושי הטקסט, מה שאינו מצוי בטקסטים אחרים.

כהוכחה לדברי הנני מצרף כאן את הרשימה דלהלן המבליטה מה חביב היה
הסגנון של "כיצד — מלמד ש..." לעורכים או לעורך של אדר״ן נוסחא א׳
(הכל ע״פ הוצאת רש״ז שכטר ז״ל):

א׳ (עמוד) ב׳ — "הוו מתונין בדין, כיצד, מלמד שיהא...

שם, למטה — "ד״א הוו מתונים בדין, כיצד, מלמד שיהא...

י״ג, א׳ — "בקול, כיצד, מלמד ששינה הקב״ה...

שם — "בנעימה, כיצד, מלמד ששינה הקב״ה...

שם — "במראה, כיצד, מלמד ששינה הקב״ה...

י״ד, א׳ — "ביתך בית ועד לחכמים, כיצד, מלמד שיהיה ביתו...

י״ז, א׳ — "פתוח לרוחה, כיצד, מלמד שיהא ביתו...

י״ח, א׳ — "עשה לך רב, כיצד, מלמד שיעשה לו את רבו...

י״ח, ב׳ — "וקנה לך חבר, כיצד, מלמד שיקנה אדם...

כ״א, ב׳ — "מן הפורענות, כיצד, מלמד שיהא לבו של אדם...

כ״ב, א׳ — "כעורכי הדיינין, כיצד, מלמד שאם באת לבית המדרש...

כ״ב, ב׳ — "אהוב את המלאכה, כיצד, מלמד שיהא אדם...

כ״ג, ב׳ — "ושנא את הרבנות, כיצד, מלמד שלא יניח אדם...

שם — "ואל תתודע לרשות, כיצד, מלמד שלא יצא לו לאדם שם...

כ״ד, א׳ — "ד״א (השני!) אל תתודע לרשות, כיצד, מלמד שלא יכוין
אדם...

כ״ד, ב׳ — "אוהב שלום, כיצד, מלמד שיהא אדם...

כ״ו, א׳ — "רודף שלום, כיצד, מלמד שיהא אדם...

כ״ו, ב׳ — "אוהב את הבריות, כיצד, מלמד שיהא אדם...

כ״ז, א׳ — "ומקרבן לתורה, כיצד, מלמד שיהא אדם...

כ״ח, ב׳ — ״נגד שמא ואבד שמיה, כיצד, מלמד שלא יוציא (!) לו
לאדם...

שם — ״ודלא מוסיף יסיד, כיצד, מלמד שאם שנה אדם...

שם — ״עשה תורתך קבע, כיצד, מלמד שאם שמע אדם...

כ״ט, א׳ — ״אמור מעט ועשה הרבה, כיצד, מלמד שהצדיקים אומרים...

שם — ״בסבר פנים יפות, כיצד, מלמד שאם נתן אדם...

ל׳, ב׳ — ״כבוד חברך חביב עליך כשלך, כיצד, מלמד שכשם שרואה...

שם — ״ואל תהא נוח לכעוס, כיצד, מלמד שיהא עניו...

ל״א, ב׳ — ״עין הרע, כיצד, מלמד שכשם שאדם...

ל״ב, ב׳ — ״ושנאת הבריות, כיצד, מלמד שלא יכוין אדם...

ל״ג, א׳ — ״כיצד, מלמד כשם שאדם...

(האם טעות הדפוס כאן, ועלינו לקרא ״מלמד שכשם שאדם״ וכו׳?)

ל״ז, א׳ — ״שינה של שחרית, כיצד, מלמד שלא יתכוין אדם...

שם — ״ויין של צהרים, כיצד, מלמד שלא יתכוין אדם...

ל״ז, ב׳ — ״ושיחת הילדים, כיצד, מלמד שלא יתכוין אדם...

שם — ״בתי כנסיות של עמי הארץ, כיצד, מלמד שלא יתכוין אדם...״

בסך הכל שלש ושלושים פעם. גם ה״הוספה ב׳ לנוסחא א׳״ בהוצאת רש״ז
שכטר, 150—166, על אף השינויים וההוספות שחלו בה, יסודה בנוסחא א׳.
בהוספה זו מופיע ״כיצד — מלמד ש...״ מספר פעמים, למשל, בעמ׳ 151, 157,
163, ו־166 (חמש פעמים בעמוד האחרון בלבד). ואם כן, שימוש זה לא ארעי
הוא אלא בבחינת מטבע לשון אקדמית שנוצרה בכוונה בבית מדרש מסוים
משום איזה שהוא טעם פדגוגי.

ב

יוסף בן יוחנן אומר: ״ויהיו עניים בני ביתך״. מה זאת אומרת? לפי נוסחא א׳
של אדר״ן ״ויהיו עניים בני ביתך״ פירושו ״ולא בני ביתך ממש, אלא שיהיו
עניים משיחין מה שאוכלים ושותים בתוך ביתך כדרך שהיו עניים משיחין מה
שאוכלין ושותין בתוך ביתו של איוב״ וכו׳. לפי נוסחא ב׳ של אדר״ן פירוש
הדברים ״ויהיו עניים בני ביתך״ הוא ״לא עני ממש, אלא מי שהוא ענו ואשתו
ענוה ובניו ובני ביתו ענוים, אף הכלבים שלו אינן מזיקין״ וכו׳.

שני הפירושים אינם זהים. נוסחא א׳ באה להסביר שבני ביתך אינם בני
ביתך ממש, והמדובר הוא בעניים דעלמא. נוסחא ב׳ מדגישה שעני במאמר זה,
משמעו ענו. מכל מקום, לא רב הוא המרחק בין שתי הנוסחאות. נוסחא א׳
(בפרק השלם) מגישה לפנינו בעצם שני הסברים: (א) ״בני ביתך״, לאו דווקא
בני ביתך הם, אלא אזהרה לקבל את העניים בעין טובה, כעין קבלתך את בני

ביתך במאכל ובמשתה. ונוסחא זו ממשיכה בתיאור הנהגתם המעולה של איוב
ושל אברהם כלפי עניים ואורחים. (ב) אחרי זה מוסיף הפרק ללמדנו שחייבים
אנחנו ללמד את בני ביתנו ענוה. גם לנוסחא ב׳ שני פירושים: (א) שעל בני
ביתנו להיות ענוים, ו־(ב) שלפנינו מספר רעיונות ואמרות על עניים מרודים.
סוף דבר, מה שנראה היה ברגע ראשון כפירושים שונים מפני שאינם זהים
לגמרי, נראה לבסוף כשתי נוסחאות שיצאו מתוך השקפה מוסרית כללית אחת.
שתיהן עוסקות גם בעניות וגם בענוה.[1]

אולם, מהו הגורם לפירושים שונים אלו בכלל, שהאחד מדגיש לא בני ביתך
ממש והאחר לא עני ממש?

דומה אני שגם נוסחא א׳ וגם נוסחא ב׳ באות להעיר שהמשפט ״ויהיו עניים
בני ביתך״ לא קללה הוא. אחרת אולי אפשר להבין את המשפט כאילו רצה
יוסף בן יוחנן לקלל את בעל הבית, כדברי הצועק מתוך רוגז, מי יתן והיו בני
ביתך עניים! [אמנם אפשר הוא (אע״פ שאין זה נראה בעיני כלל וכלל),
שיוסף בן יוחנן התנגד לגמרי להכנסת אורחים ולעזרת עניים, כאילו הוא
מזהיר, אם יהיה ביתך פתוח לרוחה אזי בעתיד ישארו כל בני ביתך (כולל
אנשי משפחתך — עיין, למשל, נוסחא א׳, דף י״ז, ב׳) עניים מרודים.[2]
ואדר״ן הופך את כל המאמר לטובה ולחסד. ולא על הסבר — בדוחק זה רצוני
להתעכב כאן, אלא להדגיש שאכן, דברי יוסף בן יוחנן דו־משמעיים הם]. על
כן מורה נוסחא א׳ שלא על בני ביתך ממש נאמר שיהיו עניים, ונוסחא ב׳
מסבירה, שכאשר נאמר ״ויהיו עניים בני ביתך״ לא לעניות מתכוון בעל
המאמר במשנה, אלא לענוות, שענוים יהיו בני ביתך.

ג

קרוב לודאי שאין לך תרבות, עתיקה או בת ימינו, שאינה עושה שימוש מיוחד
במספרים מסוימים. יתכן שתופעה זו נעוצה במשהו פסיכולוגי או מיסטי, או
בשניהם יחד. לא כאן המקום להפוך ולהַפך בנושא הזה כמו שדרוש, אבל ברור
ש(בפרקי אבות) ובאדר״ן נמסרים מאמרים שבהם מספר מסוים — למשל,
עשרה או שבעה או ארבעה או שלשה ועוד — מקיף עניים שיש קשר ביניהם,

[1] שיטה אחרת לרא״א פינקלשטין, מבוא למסכתות אבות ואבות דר׳ נתן (ניו־
יורק, תשי״א), עמ׳ ל״א ול״ב. ועל ״בני ביתך״ עיין רע״צ הפרופסור מלמד בלשוננו,
כ׳, תשט״ז, עמ׳ 11—110; והשווה דעתו של W. F. Albright, *BASOR*, 163 (October,
1961), 47, and nn. 54—56. על ״מטיבים לבן ביתו של בשר ודם״, עיין ספרי בהעלתך
ע״ח, עמ׳ 76. ועל בני ביתו=אשתו, עיין הגר״ש הפרופסור ליברמן, תוספתא כפשוטה,
פסחים, 627, שורות 49—48. ועתה עיין עוד מ׳ סוקולוף, I (1978) 82, *Maarav*.

[2] על ״עניים מרודים״, ראה את דבריו של רא״ש הפרופסור רוונטל ב־ *Israel
Exploration Journal*, XXIII (1973), p. 75.

ולפעמים ענינים שהקשר ביניהם רופף. כך למשל, פותחת שורה של מאמרים
ב״שבעה בריות זו למעלה מזו״... ומכאן והלאה יסופר על שבעה פרושים,
שבעה דברים שרובן קשה ומיעוטן יפה, שבעה דברים שבהם ברא הקב״ה את
עולמו... שבעה מדות שדרש הלל לפני בני בתירה, ועוד. (ועל מספר שלש,
עיין הרע״ב למשנה שקלים ג׳, ג׳, ד״ה שלש פעמים). ומכיוון שהעיקר
במאמרים אלה הוא הצהרת המספר, אין תימה שלפעמים מתוספים או נגרעים
פרטים מעצם הענין (עיין למשל באדר״ן נוסחא א׳, נ״א עמ׳ א׳, הסעיף
"אחת עשרה היא כתיב ביר״ד בתורה; עמ׳ ב׳, "עשר מעלות נסתלקה שכינה";
נ״ב עמ׳ א׳ "עשרה נסים נעשו לאבותינו בירושלים"). ואין הכרח להחליט
תמיד שהטקסט טעון תיקון. אף כשהטקסט בסדר, ברי שיש לפנינו מספר
עגול, שהעורכים הקדמונים אספו את החומר שירשו וסידרו אותו ע״פ המס־
פרים העגולים שהיו קיימים בזמנם. ואין מן הנמנע אפילו שגם מלכתחילה בא
המאמר צמוד למספר.

נוסף על המספרים שכבר הזכרנו לעיל, וגם אחרים, מופיע באדר״ן (נוסחא
א׳, ג׳ עמ׳ א׳) המספר כ״ב. על בנימין הצדיק שקיים אלמנה ושבעה (!) בנים,
מסופר שמלאכי השרת בקשו רחמים עליו לפני הקב״ה. תפילתם נענתה
ולבנימין נוספו כ״ב שנה על שנותיו. בן עשרים ושתים שנה (בן כ״ח על פי
נוסחא ב׳ ופרקי דר׳ אליעזר) היה ר׳ אליעזר בן הורקנוס עת שהתחיל ללמוד
תורה. קודם שישרפו קנאים את כל מה שצבר כלבא שבוע (נוסחא א׳, ט״ז, ב׳)
מצא שיש לו מזון עשרים ושתים שנה סעודה לכל אחד ואחד בירושלים
(בנוסחא ב׳, "מזון ג׳ שנים לכל אחד ואחד שבירושלים"). אולי ראו הקדמו־
נים הקבלה בין המספר כ״ב ומספר אותיות האלף־בית.* אך יהא מקור המספר
מה שיהא, הרוצה בדוגמאות נוספות לשימוש במספר כ״ב כמספר עגול, יעיין
בכרך המפתחות (שהכין המנוח פרופ׳ בועז כהן ז״ל) לאוצר היקר של הגר״ל
הפרופ׳ גינצבורג ז״ל, Legends of the Jews, VII, 483f.

עוד מספר שכדאי לעמוד עליו הוא המספר ארבע מאות. באדר״ן נוסחא א׳
הוא מופיע פעמיים: "מעשה בשני בני אדם... (ש)המרו זה את זה וזה את זה
בארבע מאות זוז" וכו׳ (ל׳ עמ׳ ב׳) (ובנוסחא ב׳ ל״א עמ׳ א׳, הסיפור
מסתיים: "מוטב לך שתפסיד ארבע מאות דינר על ארבע מאות דינר" וכו׳).
אולם לפני זה, בפרק ג׳, ח׳ עמ׳ א׳, מובא בנוסחא א׳ מעשה בר׳ עקיבא
שחייב לאדם אחד לשלם ארבע מאות זוז לאשה שביזה אותה. סיפור המעשה
ידוע כבר ממשנת בבא קמא ח׳, ו׳. והמספר ארבע מאות נראה בעיני כמספר
עגול שפירושו סכום עצום, כאילו בחר המְסַפֵּר בלשון גוזמא והפלגה. אין

---

* ועתה ראיתי את הערת הגר״ל גינצבורג באוצרו, v 107, הערה 98. (ועיין גם
בראשית רבא, א׳, י״ז, 12.) על ד׳ מאות, vi 326, הערה 53.

זאת אומרת שהמשמעות של ארבע מאות היא תמיד רק מליצית. כך, למשל,
אם המשנה (כתובות א׳, ה׳) מעידה שב״ד שלכהנים היו גובין לבתולה ארבע
מאות זוז, ולא מחו בידם חכמים, אין טעם מספיק להכחיש עדות זו — ומה גם
שרב יהודה אמר בשמו של שמואל (בבלי י״ב, ב׳) שלא בית דין של כהנים
בלבד נהגו כך, אלא אף משפחות המיוחסות בישראל, אם רצו, עושות כן.
ואולי איפכא, אפשר שמה שמעיד רב יהודה בשמו של שמואל מוכיח להפך,
שסכום קצוב לאו דווקא, אלא ״ארבע מאות״ מובנו כמות גדולה עד מאד אצל
העשירים והמיוחסים.

והוא הדין אף בספור על ר׳ עקיבא. נכון שקודם שמוסרת המשנה את
המעשה על ר׳ עקיבא, היא פוסקת ״פרע ראש האשה בשוק, נותן ארבע מאות
זוז״. אולם זהו המבנה של משניות, שמראש מזכירות את ההלכה ואחר כך
מביאות את ספור המעשה שממנו מתפחתת ההלכה. לכל הפחות באדר״ן ניכרת
חשיבותו הגדולה של ר׳ עקיבא. כאן אנו קוראים ״מעשה באדם אחד שעבר
על דברי רבי עקיבא״ (ח׳ עמ׳ א׳). הוא הוא שהוציא את המשפט על אותו
אדם גס. יש לומר שהכוונה היא כי קנס עצום קָנַס ר׳ עקיבא את הַמְבַזֶה אשה
(ואפילו ״בזויה״ — ראה אדר״ן) ללמדו גם דרך ארץ וגם חומרת ההלכה
ביחסים שבין אדם לחברו.[1]

ברור איפוא שאין כוונתנו לומר שלעולם אין מובן מדייק למספר ״ארבע
מאות״. אך ראוי גם לציין שבחכמה מאמרים ומסורות ואגדות אנו נתקלים
במספר זה כמליצה בלבד. נציין רק שתים: ״ארבע מאות בתי כנסיות היו
בכרך ביתר ובכל אחת ואחת היו בה ארבע מאות מלמדי תינוקות, וכל אחד
ואחד היו לפניו ארבע מאות תינוקות של בית רבן״ (גיטין נ״ח, א׳). כמו כן
מה שמסופר על אותה כמין חוה נאה ומפורסמת שהיתה נוטלת ארבע מאות
זהובים בשכרה וכו׳ (ספרי שלח, פיסקא קט״ו, 29—128). ועוד דוגמאות ב־
Legends of the Jews, VII, 169.

השימוש התכוף במס׳ ארבע מאות ידוע לכל הולכי לבית המדרש, אולם, מה
סיבתו? מדוע נתייחד מס׳ זה כביטוי של הגזמה? לדעתי, הסיבה לכך היא
שמספר זה מופיע פעמים בספר בראשית (חוץ מ״ארבע מאות שנה״ בט״ו,
י״ג, ושמא אף כאן רמז לתקופה ארוכה מאד): ״ארבע מאות שקל כסף״

---

[1] ואע״פ שבתלמוד נושאים ונותנים בשאלת נתינת זמן, וגם (למשל ברמב״ם, פירוש
המשנה) גומרין ש״אין הלכה כר׳ עקיבא בהשוותו כל אדם״ (בתרגומו של הרב יוסף
קאפח), אין חולק כנראה על עצם סכום הקנס שחייב ר׳ עקיבא לאותו אדם לשלם.
וענין קרוב לעניננו ראה באותצ״ג על מסכת בבא קמא, תשובות, עמ׳ 67. עיין גם
בדבריו של ג. אלון ז״ל, תולדות היהודים בא״י בתקופת המשנה והתלמוד
(ישראל, תשי״ט), I f, 135. אגב, אף פריעת הראש ע״י האשה בפני בעלה נראית
כפריצות (?), עיין אדר״ן, נוסחא ב׳, י״ח עמ׳ א׳.

שָׁקַל אברהם לעפרון (בראשית כ״ג, ט״ו, ט״ז), "ואַרבע מאות אִיש" שהיו
במחנה של עשו (ל״ב, ז'). כפי שהעירו רבים על המשא והמתן בין אברהם
ועפרון, קיחת מערת המכפלה עלתה לאברהם ביוקר; אל עשו נלוו אנשי זרוע
לא מעטים.

סח לי פעם עמיתי לשעבר Professor Frederick A. Pottle שאולי ארבע
מאות כגוזמא משקף את עֵרכה המספרי של האות "ת", האות האחרונה באלף־
בית; כשם שהיא האות שאין למעלה הימנה, כך 400 הוא הסכום הגדול ביותר.
לכאורה פתרון נאה, אך קשה, כי לדעת המומחים לא השתמשו באותיות הא״ב
לשם מספרים קודם לתקופת ההלניזמוס,[2] ואם כן אין לפרש את המספרים
במקרא על פי שיטה זו. מאידך, מי יערוב לנו שבתקופת חז״ל, כאשר בדקו
ומנו כל ביטוי ותיבה שבמקרא, לא רחפו לנגד עיניהם גם ערכי המספר של
אותיות האלף־בית השונות?*

[2] עיין עמ' 32 והערה 21 בספרו של הפרופ' ח.א. גינזברג, (Studies in Koheleth, New
York, 1950). וכן בספרו של הגר״ש ליברמן, Hellenism in Jewish Palestine (New
York, 1962), 73, n. 11.

* [לאחר ששלחתי דפים אלה לעורך, העיר לי ר״ד הפרופסור הלבני שמ״א
שאצקעס, ספר המפתח (ניו־יורק, 1929), ח' ע״ב וט' ע״א, כבר עמד על המס' 400
כגוזמא ואף רמז ללקיחת שדה עפרון. אך הפרוש שונה מפירושי; ושמשלם פישל בעהר,
דברי משלם (פרנקפורט ענ״מ, תרפ״ו), עמ' מ״ה–מ״ז, פירש את מס' עשרים ושנים
כ״רק גוזמא בעלמא"; והוא מונה שם ט״ז מקומות שבהם מופיע השימוש המוגזם הזה].

ספקי דגברי

מאת דוד הלבני

שני צדדים למטבע, אך בזכרונו של המשתמש נחקק לרוב רק צד אחד של
המטבע, והוא המושך אותו ביפיו והאהוב עליו בתכנו. בד בבד עם העידוד
של "כל האומר הלכה בשם אומרו, מביא גאולה לעולם" והחשבת הדייקנות
ב"אמרי לה ר' אחאי, ואמרי לה ר' אחא", למשל, נמצא בתלמוד גם "ההוא
מרבנן", "ואמרי לה כדי". אולם צד זה של מטבע המסירה לא נחקק כדי צרכו
בזכרונו של הלומד. מטרת המאמר הזה לפתוח בדיון עליו ולהגיש לפני הלומדים
את הצד השני של המטבע.

*

שנינו בגמרא חולין י"ח, ב': ר' זירא אכל מוגרמת דרב ושמואל (מבהמה
שהגרגרת שלה נשחטה לא בטבעת העליונה שלצד הראש אלא בשאר
הטבעות). אמרי ליה (1) לאו מאתריה דרב ושמואל את (ולרב ושמואל אין
שאר הטבעות מקום שחיטה)? אמר להו מאן אמרה (שלרב ושמואל אין שאר
הטבעות מקום שחיטה). יוסף בר חייא (סתם רב יוסף). יוסף בר חייא מכולי
עלמא גמיר (ואין לסמוך על מסירתו). שמע רב יוסף איקפיד, אמר אנא מכולי
עלמא גמירנא. אנא מרב יהודה גמירנא דאפילו ספקי דגברי גריס (אם היה לו
ספק ממי שמע את ההלכה, היה אומר ספק מר' פלוני זה או מר' פלוני זה),
דאמר רב יהודה אמר ר' ירמיה בר אבא ספק משמיה דרב ספק משמיה
דשמואל שלשה מתירין את הבכור במקום שאין מומחה.

רב יוסף משבח את דייקנותו של רב יהודה [2] במסירת בעלי השמועות, שאם
היה לו ספק מי הוא בעל השמועה לא היה מעלים את הדבר אלא היה אומר
"ספק משמיה דר"פ ספק משמיה דר"פ".

---

[1] חבריו או תלמידיו בני הישיבה? ראה מ"ש להלן ביחס ל"רבנן".

[2] רש"י ד"ה דאפילו, מניח שגם הדיבור "ספק משמיה דרב ספק משמיה דשמואל"
נאמר על ידי ר' ירמיה בר אבא. ואולי דייק כאן מן הלשון "אפילו ספקי דגברי גריס",
אפילו את הספק של האחרים היה מוסר. אבל מזה שרב יוסף שיבח את רב יהודה ולא
את ר' ירמיה בר אבא, ומה גם שבע"ז ט"ז, ב' רב יהודה הוא זה שאמר "ולא ידענא אי
מרב אי משמואל", נראה שדיבור זה מרב יהודה הוא, ששכח אם ר' ירמיה בר אבא אמר
כן בשם רב או בשם שמואל. והשווה גם רש"י בכורות ל"ז, א', ד"ה תפשוט: דהך
קמייתא דאמר רב יהודה לעיל ספק משמיה דרב ספק משמיה דשמואל.

כיוצא בו משבח ר׳ זירא את ר׳ חייא בר אבא בברכות ל״ג, ב׳ ורב ספרא
את רב הונא בריה דרב איקא בפסחים נ״ב, ב׳, והם מעלים על הנס את
דייקנותו של רחבא באמרם: "דדייק וגמיר שמעתא מפומא דמרא שפיר
כרחבא דפומבדיתא דאמר רחבא אמר רבי יהודה הר הבית סטיו כפול היה,
סטיו לפנים מסטיו".

במה מתבטאת דייקנותו של רחבא במימרה זו בשם רב יהודה, "הר הבית
סטיו כפול היה וכו׳ ", עד שר׳ זירא ורב ספרא ראו בה דוגמא להשוות אליה את
הדייקנות של שאר האמוראים, לא ברור. אמנם נוטים אנו לקבל את פירוש ר׳
חננאל ורש״י פסחים שם (ואילו בברכות שם הוא דוחה אותו), כפי שפירש
אותו ר׳ רפאל נטע רבינוביץ בדקדוקי סופרים, ביצה י״א, ב׳ אות א׳, שרחבא
היה מסופק אם שמע את המימרה "הר הבית וכו׳ " מרבי יהודה נשיאה או מרב
יהודה (בר יחזקאל). וכדי להביע ספק זה, קרא רחבא את הרי״ש של רבי
בקמץ (ולא בפתח, כרגיל. בימי הביניים הוסיפו אות אל״ף אחרי הרי״ש,
ראבי, כדרכם לשים אל״ף במקום קמץ) להעיר את אזן השומעים שספק בידו
איזה ר׳ יהודה הוא. הערוך תמה על זה: "אילו היה אומר רבי (בקמץ) לא היה
אומר לא רב ולא רבי ואינה מלה כלל". כלומר, איך ינחש השומע כשישמע
מלה זרה זו של רבי בקמץ שהיא באה להודיע שאינו ידוע אם בעל המימרה
הוא ר׳ יהודה או רב יהודה? אך גם בעל הערוך אומר שלפירוש זה "מצאנו
סיוע" בגמרות הנ״ל. היינו, שאין לפרש בדרך אחרת את הגמרות שם. ועלינו
ע״כ לומר שקריאה "זרה" היתה ידועה כסימן שהמילה מפוקפקת היא (מעין
נקודות על אותיות בכת״י שסימן הן למחיקה). וכאן יישער השומע שהפקפוק
הוא אם הכוונה היא לרבי יהודה, או לרב יהודה.

נמצא שגם רחבא, כמו רב יהודה רבו,[3] היה ידוע כמוסר נאמן שהיה גורס
אפילו ספיקי דגברי.

מן השבח ששיבחו את רב יהודה ורחבא על שהיו גורסים ספיקי דגברי, יוצא
שאחרים לא היו עושים כמוהם ולא היו גורסים ספיקי דגברי. נוהג זה של
אחרים מתאשר בעקיפין על ידי זה שבין מאות הפעמים שנאמר בש״ס "לא
ידענא" וכדומה, לא מצינו ספיקי דגברי. הספק הוא תמיד בתוכן ולא בזיהוי
האומר.[4] מלבד בע״ז ט״ז, ב׳, וגם שם הוא בשם רב יהודה: "גמירו מינאי הא

[3] ראה דקדוקי סופרים שם וערוך השלם ערך "רב". והשווה גם תוס׳ חולין סב, א׳
ד״ה אמר.

[4] מ״ש בירושלמי, מעשר שני ב׳, א׳ (נ״ג, ג׳), ביצה ה׳, ד׳ (ס״ג, ב׳): "דתמן אמרין בשם
רב חסדא ולא ידעינן אי מן שמועה אי מן מתניתא", וכן מ״ש בירושלמי יבמות א׳, א׳ (ו׳,
א׳): "א״ר מנא שמעית בשם שמואל וכו׳ ולית אנא ידע מן מה שמעית" (ולהלן שם
[ודמאי א׳, ג׳ (כ״ב, רע״ב)] ומקבילה. וראה גם שם ח׳, ב׳ (ט׳, סע״א]: א״ל ר׳ מנא מנן
שמע ר׳ הדא מילתה? א״ל מן ר׳ בא), אין ענין לעניננו. ועיין מ״ש להלן הע׳ 31.

מלתא דמגברא רבה שמיע לי ולא ידענא אי מרב אי משמואל". המימרה בנדה
י', ב': עולא א"ר יוחנן משום ר"ש בן יהוצדק וכו' המסיימת "ולא ידענא אי
דידיה אי דרביה", הוא מקרה אחר. עולא לא היה בטוח אם המלים האחרונות
במימרה שר' יוחנן מסר בשם ר"ש בן יהוצדק, "כתמה גמי טהור", הן עדיין
דברי ר"ש בן יהוצדק או הן כבר דברי ר' יוחנן שהוסיף אותן לדברי ר"ש בן
יהוצדק. וכן מה שנאמר בברכות כ"ח, א' "משום דמספקא ליה בר' יהושע בן
לוי", אין הפירוש שר' זירא לא ידע ממי שמע את ההלכה, מר' יוחנן או מר'
יהושע בן לוי (ספקי דגברי), אלא כמ"ש רש"י שם, שמקודם חשב שר'
יהושע בן לוי אמרה: (ועכשיו הוא יודע שר' יוחנן אמרה).

רוב האמוראים לא מסרו לדורות את ספקותיהם כשלא ידעו את שם האומר.
(עלי להעיר שרב יהודה היה כל כך קרוב לרבותיו רב ושמואל עד שאפילו
כשאינו מזכיר את שמותיהם הניחו שמן הסתם שמע את ההלכה מהם.[5] כמו,
למשל, ביבמות י"ח, א': א"ל אביי לרב יוסף הא דרב יהודה דשמואל הוא וכו'
דאי דרב קשיא דרב אדרב וכו'.[6] וכן להפך: ההלכה נאמרה סתם בשם רב או
שמואל ומן ההמשך יוצא שרב יהודה אמרה בשם רב או שמואל. כמו בחולין
מ"ג, ב': רב אמר במשהו וכו' כי אתא רמי בר יחזקאל אמר לא תציתו להו
להני כללי דכייל יהודה אחי משמיה דרב הכי אמר רב וכו' וכתובות
ס', א': שמואל אמר שלשים יום וכו' כי אתא רמי בר יחזקאל אמר לא
תציתינהו להני כללי דכייל יהודה אחי משמיה דשמואל הכי אמר שמואל
וכו'.[7] וכן אנו מוצאים תכופות שבגירסה אחת כתוב אמר רב או אמר שמואל
ובגירסה אחת כתוב אמר רב יהודה אמר רב או אמר רב יהודה אמר שמואל.
מזה שרב יהודה גרס ספקי דגברי ביחס לרב ושמואל, אין להסיק איפוא
שהיה גורס ספקי דגברי גם ביחס לשאר אמוראים.)

נשאלת השאלה: אלה האמוראים שלא היו גורסים ספקי דגברי, מה היו הם
עושים כשהיה להם ספקי דגברי; כשלא ידעו מי הוא בעל השמועה, ר' פלוני
זה או ר' פלוני זה? (בין אלפי השמועות שמסרו בוודאי היו גם כאלה שלא
ידעו מי הוא בעל השמועה). האם מסרו את השמועה סתם (באורח אנונימי)? או
כשהיתה להם שמועה שמחברה בלתי נודע העלימו את הדבר ומסרו אותה

---

[5] ראה יבמות צ"ו, סע"ב: "אף ר' אלעזר תלמידך יושב ודורש סתם והכל יודעים כי
שלך הוא" וירושלמי ברכות ב', ו' (ד', ב') ומקבילה: "כ"ע יודעין דר' מאיר תלמידו
דר' עקיבא וכו' ". וראה גם קרבן העדה ר"ה ד', ד': "אמר לון דכוותכן דאית לכן
רברבין סגין וכו' ".

[6] ר' עקיבא איגר בגיליון הש"ס, שם, מציין עוד שלושה מקומות: עירובין ז', א' ; פ"ה,
א'; כתובות י"ב, ב'. משום מה השמיט את ב"ב י"ג, א'.

[7] בחולין, שם (מ"ד, א'), אומר רש"י: "סתם שמעתתיה דרב בדרי בתראה, רב יהודה
הוה אמר להו בבי מדרשא". ולפי הגמרא כתובות הנ"ל, יש להוסיף סתם שמעתתיה
דרב "ושמואל" וכו'.

בשמותיהם הם? שאלה זו יש לשאול גם כשלא ידעו כלל מי הוא בעל
השמועה, האם מסרו אותה סתם או בשמותיהם הם?

דעתנו היא שהיו מוסרים אותה בשמותיהם הם והשומע יכול היה לטעות
ולחשוב שמהם היא. לכן נשתבחו רב יהודה ורחבא על שלא נתנו מקום לטעות
ולא היו מוסרים אותה בשמותיהם הם אלא הזכירו בפירוש "ספק משמיה דר'
פלוני ספק משמיה דר' פלוני". שכן אם האחרים היו מוסרים את השמועה סתם
לסימן שמחברה בלתי נודע והשומעים הבינו כן, כי אז גם אחרים היו ראויים
לשבח כרב יהודה ורחבא. אלא אם כן נאמר ששיבחו את רב יהודה ורחבא על
שהזכירו את השמות המפוקפקים והקילו על ידי כך את הזיהוי, בעוד שאחרים
לא הזכירו שמות כלל והכבידו על ידי כך את הזיהוי. אך לא מסתבר כן. יש
בשבח ששיבחו את רב יהודה ורחבא מעין ריח של תוכחה כלפי שאר האמו־
ראים על שאינם עושים כן. ולוא היה זה רק ענין של הקלת זיהוי או הכבדתו,
מה לתוכחה לכאן? אבל אם העלימו את העובדא ששמועה זו קדומה להם
ומסרו אותה בשמותיהם הם והטעו את אלה בין השומעים שאינם יודעים
ספקי דגברי נמסר בשם המוסר האחרון, אז יש מקום לתוכחה. ומי שמונע את
הטעות הזאת (כמו רב יהודה ורחבא) ראוי לשבח.

חוץ מזה, רובא דרובא של הסתמות בגמרא הם שקלא וטריא, בניגוד להלכה
פסוקה (אפודיקטיבית) שאין בה לא מן הויכוח ולא מן הנימוק. יוצאים מן הכלל
הם מקומות כמו בפסחים ט', ב': תשע ציבורין של מצה ואחד של חמץ וכו',
סוכה ג', ס"ע"ב: היתה גבוה מעשרים אמה וכו', יבמות ל"ז, ב': ספק ויבם
שבאו לחלוק בנכסי מתנא וכו' ועוד מקומות אחדים. בפסחים שם מוסיף רש"י:
"פסקי הלכות הן", ובסוכה שם הוא מוסיף: "פיסקי שמועות של כל בני
הישיבה שהיו בימי מדרשו של רב אשר שסידרו את הגמרא". רש"י הרגיש
שאין מדרכו של הסתם להיות אפודיקטיבי, למסור הלכות קצובות. וכדי שלא
נטעה ונחשוב שגם שם איך שהוא שקלא וטריא היא, מדגיש רש"י "פסקי
הלכות הן", "פיסקי שמועות של כל בני הישיבה וכו'". וראה גיטין נ"ב א':
"משוך פירי מיתמן וכו'. סבור מינה (בני הישיבה) וכו' אמר להו רב שישא וכו'.[7א]

ולוא היו מוסרים ספקי דגברי כסתמות, כי אז צריכות היו להיות הרבה
הלכות פסוקות בין הסתמות. המקרים שהזכרנו לעיל של ספקי דגברי הם
כולם הלכות פסוקות. ומכוון שאין הרבה הלכות פסוקות בין הסתמות, נראה
כשלא ידעו מי הוא המחבר של השמועה לא היו מוסרים אותה סתם אלא בשם
מי שהביא אותה לביהמ"ד.[8]

[7א] וראה גם ב"מ ק"ח א': השתא דאמרת צריך למיקנא וכו' סבור מינה (בני הישיבה)
א"ל מר קששישא וכו' מתנא לית ביה משום דינא דבר מצרא אמר אמימר וכו'.
[8] ראה תוס' עירובין ל"ח, רע"ב ד"ה אמר וירושלמי ע"ז ד', סהל"א (מ"ג, ד'): ולא ר'
חייא רבה תניתה? אלא מן דשמעת מיניהו חזק וקבעה.

אלה הן ראיות עקיפות, אבל יש גם ראיות ישירות לכך. שלש פעמים נמצאת
בש״ס השאלה, ״גמרא או סברא״? (עירובין ס׳, א׳; יבמות כ״ה, ב׳; ב״ב
ע״ז, א׳). בב״ב, שם, נאמר: אמימר אמר (הלכה פסוקה) הלכתא אותיות נקנות
במסירה. ורב אשי שאל אותו: ״גמרא או סברא?״ כלומר, הלכה זו קבלה היא
בידך מרבותיך או אתה חידשת אותה מדעתך? ברם, אם קבלה היא מרבותיו
אמימר היה אומר ששמע אותה מרבותיו ולא היה מוסר אותה בשמו הוא. אלא
ודאי ידע רב אשי שרוב האמוראים נוהגים למסור הלכה שמחברה לא נודע,
בשמותיהם הם ומשום כך שאל את אמימר אם גם הלכה זו היא מסוג זה או
שהוא, אמימר, חידש אותה מדעתו (כלומר, הכריע כן מדעתו).

עכשיו שאנו מודעים לתופעה זו — שרוב האמוראים (מלבד רב יהודה
ורחבא), כשמםוספקים היו מי הוא האומר, היו מוסרים את ההלכה בלא אומר,
בשמותיהם הם — אפשר למצוא דוגמתה מכללא בעוד מקומות בש״ס, כמו,
למשל, פסחים ל״ב, ב׳. שם רב נחמן בר יצחק שואל את ר׳ חייא בר אבין
לפרש לו ברייתא. ר׳ חייא בר אבין פירש לו. פירוש זה מצא חן בעיני רב
נחמן בר יצחק והוא מביע לו את תודתו באמרו: ״תנוח דעתך שהנחת את
דעתי״. ר׳ חייא בר אבין, במקום שיעריך את תודתו של רב נחמן בר יצחק,
מתקיף אותו ואומר לו: ״מאי ניחותא, דרבה ורב ששת שדו ביה נרגא״.

ברם אם רבה ורב ששת שדו ביה נרגא (לא היו בטוחים בנכונותו של
הפירוש) אז כבר הם פירשו כן (או, יותר נכון, כבר מקודם להם פירשו כן
והם פיקפקו בפירוש) אם כן, כשפירש ר׳ חייא בר אבין את הברייתא לרב
נחמן בר יצחק, למה לא מסר כן? למה לא אמר דבר בשם אומרו? משום שלא
היה ידוע מי היה המחבר של פירוש זה, וכשאין יודעים מי הוא המחבר
מביאים אותו בשם המוסר האחרון. וכשלא ידעו את המוסר האחרון, אם היא
הלכה שאינה שנויה במחלוקת וסתמית היא בלא שם[א8] מביאים אותה
כ״אתמר״[ב8] או כ״דאמר מר״ ״האמר מר״, ״ואמר מר״, ״והאמר מר״.[ג8] או

[א8] אמנם מצינו ״אתמר״ גם לפני דעה אחת ובשם, כמו בפסחים פ׳, רע״ב: אתמר היו
שלישיתן זבין וכו׳ אמר ר׳ מני בר פטיש וכו׳, ומנחות ל״ד, רע״א: אתמר לול פתוח מן
הבית לעליה אמר רב הונא וכו׳. ואולי גם שם נאמר ״אתמר״ משום שלא ידעו מי הביא
את דבריו ר׳ מני בר פטיש ורב הונא לביהמ״ד, מי היה המוסר האחרון. וכן כשאתמר
בא לפני ברייתא (ראה הערה הבאה), יש לומר שלא ידעו מי הביא את הברייתא
לביהמ״ד. וראה גם יבמות מ״ג, א׳: אתמר דרב ושמואל דאמרי תרוייהו וכו׳. ש״אתמר״
בא תמיד לפני מחלוקת, פשוט לא נכון.

[ב8] ראה המקומות המצויינים במקורות ומסורות, יומא — חגיגה, מבוא עמ׳ 12
(נשמט משם ב״ק קט״ו, א׳: אתמר גנב ופרע בחובו וכו׳ עשו בו תקנת השוק). אלא
שעכשיו איני חושב שהלכות אלה נלקחו מברייתות. תקנת השוק, ב״ק שם, אינה ברייתא
חולקים בה לעיל שם רב ושמואל. וכן הלשון הארמית בחולין ק״י, א׳: אתמר כבדא

כהלכה סתמית, כמו, למשל, גיטין מ״ב, א׳: נגחו שור יום של רבו — לרבו וכו׳.[ד8]

ואם היא הלכה השנויה במחלוקת, אם המחלוקת היא רק בדין, מביאים את שתי הדעות בשם ״איכא דאמרי״. (כמו למשל שבת קנ״ג, א׳: ״איבעיא להו חרש וקטן מאי וכו׳ איכא דאמרי לחרש יהיב להו. איכא דאמרי לקטן יהיב להו״. ועוד ועוד). ואם המחלוקת היא גם בדעת ר״פ, מביאים את הדעה הראשונה סתם בשמו ואת הדעה השניה בשם איכא דאמרי בשמו. ״אמר ר״פ וכו׳ איכא דאמרי (או ואיכא דאמרי) אמר ר״פ וכו׳ ״.[ה8] אבל מצינו גם (שבת ק״ג, ב׳; ב״מ מ״ב, א׳; נדה י״ד, א׳ ועוד) אמר ר״פ וכו׳ ואיכא דאמרי (סתם בלא שם). וכו׳.

*

והנה נוהג זה לא לגרום ספקי דגברי אפשרי רק כשאין דיאלוג (דו שיח) במימרה. אבל כשיש דיאלוג או איזו פעולה משותפת אחרת במימרה ואין יודעים את שם אחד המשתתפים, אין להעלים את הספק וליחס את הדיאלוג לזמנו של המוסר האחרון. כשהאמורא המשתתף בדיאלוג חי לפני זמנו של המוסר האחרון, בוודאי שאין לייחס לו, אלא אפילו אם חי בזמנו של המוסר האחרון אין לייחס לו דיאלוג שלא נתקיים. במקרה כזה משתמשים בביטוי ״ההוא מרבנן״. הפעולה המשותפת מכריחה את המוסר למסור לדורות שאכן יש ספקי דגברי (והספקי דגברי מתבטא ב״ההוא מרבנן״).

ראוי להוסיף ש״ההוא מרבנן״ הוא אמורא ממש ובזה הוא שונה מבעלי

עילוי בשרא וכו׳ מראה שאינה ברייתא. ועוד. הם מקרים כשלא ידעו לא את מחברם ולא את מוסרם.

[ג8] ביניהם יש גם כאלה שאנו יודעים מי אמרם. אלא אפילו כשאנו יודעים מי אמרם על סמך גמרא אחרת, יתכן שמי שאמר ״אמר מר״ לא הכיר את הגמרא ההיא.

[ד8] הגמרא שם קוראת להלכה זו ״מימרא״. אמנם לא משום שסתמית היא אלא כמ״ש רש״י — וראיה לדבריו מב״ב מ״ח, סע״א וכמ״ש הרשב״ם שם — משום שאינה לא משנה ולא ברייתא (ואמורא יכול לחלוק עליה). ואפשר שבעל ה״אי בעית אימא״ הראשון שם ניסה להשלים את דברי האמורא עם ההלכה הסתמית, חשב שהלכה סתמית (ובמיוחד כשהיא בעברית) מן הסתם ברייתא היא (בלא ציון. כידוע נמצאות גם בבבלי ברייתות בלא ציון של ת״ר, תניא וכדומה. ראה מבואות לספרות התנאים עמ׳ 255 ויש להוסיף). ועיין גם רש״י סנהדרין נ׳, ב׳ ד״ה מרגלא, בגמרא שם: מאי ר״ש וכו׳ ותוספתא שם י״ב, ב׳. האם יש להוכיח מזה שהציונים לברייתות נכנסו לגמרא לאחר שכבר היתה מסודרת ולפעמים שכחו המכניסים להכניסם? על זה אדון, אי״ה, במקום אחר.

[ה8] המכוון הוא בעיקר להלכות קצרות. אבל כשיש בהן שקלא וטריא ובמיוחד כשהשקלא וטריא ממושכת היא אז הענין קשור כבר בעריכת התלמוד והוא הרבה יותר מסובך.

"איבעיא להו", "בעו מיניה", "סברוה", "מיתיבי"‎[9], "מיתיבי"‎[9א] "תלמיד", או
"תלמידי" שהם, כנראה, "בני ישיבה שטרם הגיעו לדרגה שדבריהם יצוטטו
בבית המדרש בשם אומרם"‎[10]. כך מוכח מן הזיהוי המאוחר שאנו מוצאים
לפעמים בגמרא אחרי "ההוא מרבנן", כמו "ההוא מרבנן ור' יעקב שמיה"
(רגיל ביותר‎[11]), "רב טבות שמיה ואמרי לה רב טביומי שמיה"‎[12], "רב טבות
שמיה ואמרי לה רב שמואל בר זוטרא שמיה"‎[13], "רב חלקיה בריה דרב אויא
שמיה"‎[14] ורב תחליפא בר מערבא שמיה"‎[15].

וכן שונה "ההוא מרבנן" מ"רבנן" (לא רק בזה שזה יחיד וזה רבים). הביטוי
"רבנן" נמצא הרבה פעמים בש"ס וכולל סוגים שונים (רבנן בניגוד לדאו־
רייתא, רבנן החולקים על דעת יחיד, סתם חכמים ועוד‎[16] שמוצאם מתקופות
שונות. אך גם הסוג הקרוב ביותר ל"ההוא מרבנן", כשהרבנן משתתפים
בדיאלוג או בפעולה משותפת אחרת, שונה הוא ממנו בזה שאין אחריו זיהוי
והרבנן אינם אמוראים ממש אלא תלמידי בני ישיבה‎[16א] שלא זכו ששמותיהם
ייזכרו בביהמ"ד.‎[17] אבל אחרי "צורבא מדרבנן" יש לפעמים זיהוי (שבת

[9] על "חבורה", ראה רש"י פסחים ס"ד א', ד"ה "מפי חבורה". "שאיל בי מדרשא,
אמרי, ואמרי ופשטיה וכו'" גם הם, כנראה, מבני הישיבה הם. אבל ראה ע"ז ל"ג א'.

[9א] אלא שתכופות מתחלפת "ת"ש" ב"מיתיבי". ראה, למשל, ר"ח פסחים ב', ב'.

[10] ראה סדר תנאים ואמוראים סי' עא, ספר כריתות, לשון לימודים, ח"ה, שער ג', סי'
עו; הליכות עולם, ש"ב פ"א ומ"ש אנו ב"מקורות ומסורות", יומא–חגיגה, מבוא ע' 11,
הע' 21. וראה גם שארית יוסף (הוצ' ר"י ליינער), עמ' 53, נתיב הפירוש, ראש הדרך
השלישי: ולפ"ז נאמר דתרי סתמא דגמרא נינהו חדא מבני הישיבה וחדא מרב אשי וכו'.

[11] שבת קל"ד, ב'; עירובין פ', א'; סוטה מ"ו, א'; קידושין י"ג, א'; נ"ה, א'; ב"ק צ"ד.
ב' (ב"מ ל"ג, א'); ע"ז כ"ח, ב'; ע"ה, ב'; חולין ע"ו, א'.

[12] סנהדרין צ"ז, א'.

[13] ב"מ מ"ט, א'.   [14] ב"מ צ"ו, ב'.

[15] מו"ק כ"ז, א' (נדרים נ"ו, ב'; סנהדרין כ', א').

[16] ראה זאב בכר "Tradition und Tradenten", עמ' 559 ואילך. בקשר ל"רבנן
באגדתא", ראה את מחברתו של ז. בכר, "Rabbanan" (שטרסבורג, 1914), 11 במבוא,
שם, עמ' 1/, הוא קורא להם "Halbanonymen" (אנונימים במקצת).

[16א] ואין לערבב אותם בבעלי הסתמות. "רבנן" אלה פעלו בכל תקופות הגמרא ואילו
הסתמאים – בעיקר לאחר פטירת רב אשי, ("סוף הוראה"). "רבנן" אלה הם בבחינת
תלמידים, ואילו הסתמאים בבחינת עורכים. מאידך גיסא, אין לערבב אותם ב"תרביצא"
(מנחות פב, ב ורש"י, שם: בבית המדרש שמרביצים בו התורה). עליהם אומר רב האי
גאון, תשובות גאונים קדמונים, סי' עח, "שלא היו בקיאין". ובזבחים קד א, ד"ה והעור
אומר רש"י: "דתלמידי תרביצאי היא וטעו במה ששנינו במשנתנו". הם ישבו בחצר,
לא נכנסו לבית המדרש ולא הגיעו לדרגת "רבנן". ראה מ"ש ר' יצחק הלוי בדורות
הראשונים, ח"ג, עמ' 227 ואילך, ולפניו קצת מהדברים נאמרו ע"י ר"נ בריל בשנתון
שלו, ח"ב (1876) עמ' 1–80.

[17] ביד מלאכי סי' תר: "ולי המך נראה דשם רבנן נאמר על הרוב על התלמידים

קל״ט, ב׳; חולין נ״א, א׳ [ראה דק״ט שם]; נדה ל״ג, ב׳) והוא כמו ״ההוא
מרבנן״ אמורא ממש.

במקומות מעטים אנו מוצאים בש״ס ״ההוא סבא״. גם הוא בא לרוב אחרי
״א״ל [18] וגם הוא, כמו ״ההוא מרבנן״, אמורא ממש הוא. אע״פ שאין זיהוי
אחריו, אין להבדיל בינו ובין ״משום זקן אחד״ [19] שיש זיהוי אחריו. [20]

״חברייא״ שנמצא פעמים אחדות בבבלי יכול להיות בני ישיבה, כמו בחולין
י״ד, א׳: ״ונסבין חברייא למימר ר׳ יהודה היא וכו׳ ״, או אמורא ממש כמו
ל״ד, א׳ שם: ״אמר עולא חברייא אמרין וכו׳ ומנו רבה בר בר חנה״.

״מאן דהו״ שנזכר שלש פעמים בש״ס (ביצה כ״ז, א׳; מו״ק כ״ב, ב׳; וחולין
נ׳, א׳), מרש״י שם משמע שלא היה אמורא ממש. כך הוא אומר בביצה: ״אחד
מן התלמידים מי שהוא לא נודע שמו״. [21] ובחולין הוא אומר: ״אחד מן התלמי־
דים ולא היו זכורין אלו שסידרו הגמרא מי היה״ (מחלק שני של דיבורו נראה
כאילו רש״י חשב אותו לספקי דגברי). אבל הרש״ש בהגהותיו שם לביצה
מפרש ״מאן דהו״, אחד מן האמוראים שנזכרו מקודם, ר׳ ירמיה ואיתימא ר׳

בני הישיבה וכמו שפירש״י בפ״ד דברכות כ״ח א׳ ושם מ״ז ב׳ ונ״ט א׳ ובבבתרא ר״ב
א׳ ״. וראה גם רש״י עירובין נ״ג, ב׳ ד״ה צפון ומגילה ט״ז, א׳ ד״ה לרבנן — תלמידיו.

אבל יש גם מקרים מעטים בבבלי שהרבנן אינם תלמידים אלא חברים, עמיתים של
האמורא. ראה, למשל, כתובות ק״ד, א׳: ההוא יומא דנח נפשיה דרבי גזרו רבנן
תעניתא וכו׳. אמרו ליה רבנן לבר קפרא זיל עיין וכו׳, קידושין לב, א ע״ז ע״ה, ב׳:
אורו ליה רבנן לר׳ ירמיה וכו׳, חולין י״ח, א׳: איקלעו מר זוטרא ורב אשי לגביה. אמר
להו עיינו רבנן במלתא דתלו ביה טפלא ועוד. לפעמים רבנן הם גם רבותיו של אמורא.
ראה כתובות י״ז, א׳: כי סמכי רבנן לר׳ זירא וכו׳ ולר׳ אסי וכו׳. אבל בכת״י מינכן
ליתא המלה ״כרבנן״. בעירובין ס״ה, ב׳ אחרי תרי גברי רברבין, ואין להגביל את
״רבנן״ ל־״חבורת חכמים היושבים בישיבת הכלה או חבורת החכמים של ישיבת הכלה
הרשמית בהזדמנות אחרת, כגון בשעה שבתות הרגילי של ראש הגולה״ (״שלטון רשות
הגולה והישיבות״ לרי״ש צורי, עמ׳ 49 ואילך).

[18] אבל ראה גם ברכות ה׳, ב׳, מכות י״ט, ב׳.

[19] השווה בבלי סוטה מ״ה, א׳: אמר אביי הריני כבן עזאי בשוקי דטבריה. א״ל ״ההוא
מרבנן״ לאביי שני חללים זה ע״ג זה וכו׳ עם הירושלמי פיאה ו׳, ג׳ (י״ט, ג׳): רב כד נחית
לתמן אמר אנא הוא בן עזאי דהכא. אתא ״חד סב״ שאל ליה שני הרוגים זה ע״ג זה וכו׳.

[20] אותה השאלה, אמנם קצת בהקשר אחר, הושבה בפסחים ט״ו, ב׳ על ידי ״ההוא סבא״
ובכ׳, ב׳ על ידי אביי. האם יש להוכיח משם שאביי הוא ההוא סבא? מסופקני מאוד.
ובמיוחד כשהשאלה נשאלה על ידי ר׳ ירמיה והסבא השיב לו פנים אל פנים, ״א״ל״,
ור׳ ירמיה, כנראה, לא היה כבר בבבל בבגרותו של אביי. דברי הדק״ס עירובין כ״ז,
א׳, אות ז׳ תמוהים. והשווה תוס׳ חולין ו׳, רע״א וב־״יבין שמועה״ להליכות עולם ראש
השער השני.

[21] וכן בחידושי המאירי שם: מי שהוא ולא נודע מי היה.

זירא [22] ובחולין ר׳ זירא ״או ר׳ אבא המוזכרים לעיל״. ״מאן דהו״ היינו או
זה או זה. לפיו, ״מאן דהוא״ אמורא ממש הוא.[23]

*

לעיל קראנו לזיהוי ״ור׳ פלוני שמיה״ זיהוי מאוחר. מי שאמר ״ההוא
מרבנן״ לא אמר ״ור׳ פלוני שמיה״. שכן אם אָמְרו וידע את שמו של האמורא,
למה סתם מקודם ואמר ההוא מרבנן. אלא ודאי אחר הוא ומאוחר. בראשונה
לא ידעו את שמו ואח״כ זיהו אותו. אך הניסוח הראשון (הסתום, ההוא מרבנן)
לא זז ממקומו. וכיוצא בו אמרנו [24] ביחס למה שנמצא כמה פעמים בש״ס
״ומנו ר׳ פלוני״ — גם הוא זיהוי מאוחר [25] וכמו אצל ״ור״פ שמיה״, הניסוח
הסתמי הקודם נשאר גם לאחר הזיהוי. ואם יש לך ספק בדבר צא ובדוק מ״ש
בשבת קנ״ו, א׳; חולין צ״ג, א׳; רב הונא בר חייא אמר ללוי בנו: הכי אמר
אבוה דאמך משמיה דרב ״ומנו ר׳ ירמיה בר אבא״ וכו׳. ללוי נכדו של ר׳
ירמיה בר אבא לא היה צורך לזהות את שמו של הסבא שלו. הזיהוי ע״כ ממי
שהוא אחר מאוחר לו.

על פי זה פירשנו שם גם מ״ש במגילה כ״ג, א׳ (וראה גם סנהדרין י״ד, א׳;
שבועות ט״ז, ב׳): ״פליגי בה ר׳ יצחק בר נחמני וחד דעימיה ומנו ר׳ שמעון
בן פזי, ואמרי לה ר׳ שמעון בן פזי וחד דעימיה ומנו ר׳ יצחק בר נחמני״. מה
ההבדל בין שני לשונות אלה, בין ר׳ יצחק בר נחמני וחד דעימיה ומנו ר׳ שמעון
בן פזי ובין ר׳ שמעון בן פזי וחד דעימיה ומנו ר׳ יצחק בר נחמני? לשניהם
המחלוקת היא בין ר׳ יצחק בר נחמני ובין ר׳ שמעון בן פזי?
השערתנו היא שמקודם נמסרו שני הלשונות בלא הזיהוי, היינו, בלשון אחד

[22] ואין זה ספקי דגברי אלא שני נוסחאות וכל נוסח בטוח שהצדק אתו. וכיוצא בו
אמרי לה וכו׳ ואמרי לה וכו׳ וכדומה. ולא כתבתי את זה אלא מפני שראיתי מ״ש ר׳
ראובן מרגליות, ב״שם עולם״, (מוסד הרב קוק, ירושלים, תשכ״ב) עמ׳ ט״ו.

[23] כשאמרו ״רבותינו״ ידעו למי מתכוונים, אלא שלפעמים שכחו אח״כ. ראה כתובות
ב׳, ב׳ ומקבילות: ״מאן רבותינו? אמר רב יהודה אמר שמואל בי דינא דשרו משחא״
(במקבילה בירושלמי תרומות י׳, ו׳ (מ״ז, ב׳) ליתא הזיהוי) סנהדרין י״ז, ב׳: רבותינו
שבבבל, רב ושמואל, רבותינו שבא״י ר׳ אבא. ראה גם הע׳ 25.

[24] מקורות ומסורות יומא – חגיגה, מגילה עמ׳ תק״ב.

[25] שבת קמ״ו, ב׳ יכול היה לומר ״ומשום כבוד רבותינו, רב כהנא ורב אשי, לא ישב״.
עכשיו שאומר ומשום כבוד רבותינו לא ישב עליו ״ומנו״ רב כהנא ורב אשי, משמע
שה״ומנו״ וכו׳ מאוחר הוא. ועיין גם דק״ס ב״ב ע״ה, א׳ אות ל׳. אגב, ל״רבותינו״ שם יש
מובן של חברינו. עיין רש״י שם ותוס׳ ב״ב ל״ד, א׳, ועוד. ובמסכת כלה, הוצ׳ ר״מ היגר,
עמ׳ 193: ״קרי להו רבותיו וקרי להו חבריו. כיון דחזו דקא גבר עליהו קרי להו
חבריו״. וראה גם ברכות כ״ב, א׳: א״ל רב הונא לרבנן ״רבותינו״ מפני מה אתם מזל־
זלים בטכילה זו. ושם ל״ח, ב׳: ״ורבותינו״ היורדין מא״י ומנו עולא וכו׳ ״וחברינו״
היורדין מא״י ומנו עולא וכו׳ (ובדק״ס שם אות ז׳). ולהיפוך בר״ה ל״א, ב׳: אי ס״ד
דר״י בן זכאי, חברו דר״א מי הוה רבו הוה וכו׳. ועיין גם יד מלאכי, סי׳ רלה.

היה: "פליגי בה ר׳ יצחק בר נחמני וחד דעימיה" ובלשון אחד היה: "פליגי בה
ר׳ שמעון בן פזי וחד דעימיה" וחשבו שיש מחלוקת בין הלשונות. אח״כ זיהו
את "וחד דעימיה" של לשון ראשון בר׳ שמעון בן פזי ו"החד דעימיה" של
לשון שני בר׳ יצחק בר נחמני באופן שאין מחלוקת בין הלשונות ולא היה להם
לומר יותר "ואמרי לה". אלא כמו שאמרנו, הזיהוי המאוחר לא שינה את
הניסוח הקודם.

וגדולה מזה אנו מוצאים בפסחים ג׳, ב׳: "הני תרי תלמידי דהוו יתבי קמיה
דהלל וחד מינייהו ר׳ יוחנן בן זכאי. ואמרי לה קמיה דרבי וחד מינייהו ר׳
יוחנן. חד אמר מפני מה בוצרין בטהרה ואין מוסקין בטהרה וחד אמר מפני מה
בוצרין בטהרה ומוסקין בטומאה. אמר מובטח אני בזה שמורה הוראה בישראל.
ולא היה ימים מועטים עד שהורה הוראה בישראל".

הראשונים חולקים איזה משני התלמידים הורה הוראה בישראל, זה
שהשתמש בלשון נקייה ואמר "ואין מוסקין בטהרה" או זה שהשתמש בלשון
קצרה ואמר "ומוסקין בטומאה". אך יהא הפירוש מה שיהא, ברור שר׳ יוחנן
בן זכאי, או ר׳ יוחנן, היה זה התלמיד שהורה הוראה בישראל, וכל אחד מן
הראשונים, לפי שיטתו הוא, יכול היה לזהות את בעל המימרה שעליו ניבא
הלל או רבי שיורה הוראה בישראל כר׳ יוחנן בן זכאי או ר׳ יוחנן. כך הוא
באמת ברי״ף (אלא שהוא מכריע כלשון שני [26]): "ולא היה ימים מועטים עד
שהורה הוראה בישראל ומנו ר׳ יוחנן". ולמה נאמר בגמרא "חד אמר וכו׳ וחד
אמר וכו׳" כאילו יש ספק בדבר? משום שבמקור לא היה "וחד מינייהו ר׳
יוחנן בן זכאי" או "וחד מינייהו ר׳ יוחנן", ואז באמת לא ידעו מי הוא בעל
המימרה שעליו ניבא שיורה הוראה בישראל. אח״כ כשזיהו והוסיפו "וחד
מינייהו ר׳ יוחנן בן זכאי", "וחד מינייהו ר׳ יוחנן", וידעו כבר מי הוא בעל
המימרה שעליו ניבא שיורה הוראה בישראל, הניסוח הקודם בצורת "חד אמר
וכו׳ " לא זז ממקומו.

*

לפי האמור, אין לומר כמ״ש במקום אחר [27] ש"ואמרי לה כדי" היינו
שנשתמכח שם אומרה (כשלא ידעו מי אומרה, מסרו אותה בשם המוסר האחרון)
אלא "כדי" היינו סתם. ז״א, שמוצאו מתקופת הסתמאים שחיו אחרי פטירתם
של רבינא ורב אשי (אחרי "סוף הוראה"). [28] "ואמרי לה כדי" בא תמיד אחרי
"אמר ר״פ" והניגוד הוא שלשון ראשון, הבא אחריו נאמר על ידי אחד

[26] כאיזה לשון פוסקים, כראשון או כשני? בזה חולקים הראשונים ואף הגאונים, הביא
אותם בחלקם ר״ח אלבק במבוא לתלמודים עמ׳ 544 הע׳ 35. מן הרי״ף כאן אנו רואים
שהכריע כלשון שני גם בענין היסטורי.
[27] מקורות ומסורות, יומא – חגיגה, מבוא עמ׳ 8 הע׳ 13.
[28] ראה שם במבוא בו טיפלנו בענין הסתמות באריכות.

האמוראים וללשון שני על ידי אחד הסתמאים.[29] וראיה מראש נדרים ונזיר
בנזיר נאמר "אמר רבא ואמרי לה כדי", ובנדרים נאמר סתם. ה"כדי" של
נזיר הוא הסתם של נדרים.

זה מסביר גם כן למה נמצא בש"ס רק עשר פעמים "ואמרי לה כדי". במשך
מאתים שנה של תקופת האמוראים, בוודאי שנשתכח שם בעל השמועה יותר
מעשר פעמים. וכן, למה לא נמצאות בין ה"ואמרי לה כדי" הלכות פסוקות.
בין המימרות שנשתכחה שם אומרן בוודאי היו גם הלכות פסוקות. ועוד, ככל
שהדבר קדום יותר, הוא עלול להשתכח יותר. וצריכים היו להיות יותר ספקות
בשם האומר ביחס לאמוראים ראשונים מאשר ביחס לאמוראים אמצעיים
ואחרונים. ואינו כן. חציו של ה"ואמרי לה כדי" בא אחרי אמר רבא ואילו
אחרי אמורא ראשון כמעט ואינו נמצא (מלבד בהוריות ח', סע"א, ושם הוא
ליתא בדפוסים ראשונים).

אבל אם "ואמרי לה כדי" סתם הוא,[29א] ומתקופת הסתמאים מוצאו, אין
להתפלא על כל זה. תקופת הסתמאים תקופה קצרה היתה ולא נתחדשו בה
הרבה הלכות פסוקות.[30] בין אמורא ראשון וסתם אין מקום לספיקות רבים.
מרחק גדול בזמן מפריד ביניהם. אבל בין אמורא אמצעי, ובמיוחד בין אמורא
אחרון, ובין הסתם הקרובים בזמן עלולים להיות ספיקות. לכן מצינו "ואמרי
לה כדי" רק ביחס להם.

*

למרות השבח ששיבחו את רב יהודה ורחבא על שמסרו ספקי דגברי, נראה
שגם הם לא היו עקביים; אחרת היינו מוצאים בין מאות המימרות של רב
יהודה בשם רב ושמואל (והמימרות בשם אמוראים אחרים) יותר משני מקרים
של ספקי דגברי (ואפילו מרחבא שמספר מימרותיו הוא הרבה פחות, צריך
היה להיות יותר ממקרה אחד של ספקי דגברי). מאידך גיסא, נראה שהם לא
היו יחידים בדבר. אמוראים כמו ר' ינאי (גיטין פ"ב, ב'; חולין נ', א') ור'
בורים (שמו המדויק לא בטוח, גירסות שונות בברכות נ"ה, ב'; ב"ק פ"א, א';
פ"ב, א'; חולין צ"ח, א') שמסרו "משום זקן אחד", גם הם דייקו למסור ספקי
דגברי. ר' זירא משבח את ר' חייא בר אבא (ברכות ל"ח, ב') באותו לשון
("דדייק וגמיר שמעתה מר' יוחנן") שרב ספרא שיבח את רב הונא בר איקא

---

[29] "כדי" שם חכם, אינו בא בחשבון. ראה סדר הדורות, הוצ' ר"נ משכיל לאיתן, ראש
אות כ'.

[29א] ראה באר שבע הוריות שם כשם "ואית דאמרי".

[30] דברי רב שרירא גאון, הוצ' רב"מ לוין, עמ' 69: "אע"ג שהוראה לא הוה, הוה איכא
פירושי וסבארי קרובים להוראה" תואמים יותר את תקופת הסתמאים. הנני מקוה לדון
בנושא זה במקום אחר באריכות. לע"ע ראה מקורות ומסורות עירובין (עם שבת
ופסחים), העומד להופיע בקרוב, ל"ב, ב'.

ודימה אותו לרחבא. נראה שגם ר׳ חייא בר אבא היה נוהג למסור ספיקי דגברי
(אגב, ר׳ זירא היה קפדן בדייקנות המסירה. מלבד ביקורתו על רב יוסף על
ש״מכולי עלמא גמיר״ ושבחו את ר׳ חייא בר אבא, הוא גם שאל (ירושלמי
שבת א׳, ב׳ (ג׳, א׳) ומקבילה) לר׳ יסא: ״חכים רבי לבר פדייה דאת אמר
שמועתא משמיה״ ולר׳ אבא בר זבדא שאל: ״חכים רבי לרב דאת אמר
שמועתא משמיה״, ושאל (עירובין מ״ו, א׳; יבמות ס׳, ב׳; גיטין ל״ט, ב׳ 30א)
לר׳ יעקב בר אידי ולר׳ חייא בר אבא ״בפירוש שמיע לך או מכללא שמיע
לך״. הוא גם מצטט את הספקי דגברי של ר׳ יהודה בע״ז ט״ז, ב׳.31 הדיבור
הנמצא כמה פעמים בירושלמי ״והוה ר׳ זירא מסתכל ביה״ 32 גם כן קשור
כנראה בענין נאמנות המסירה. הסתכל בו לדעת אם אכן מסירתו נאמנה היא.
ראה ירושלמי מגילה, שם: ״א״ל מה אתה מסתכל בי. אנא אמר שמועה ואת
אמר מן דעה״ [סברא]. לא לחנם אומר הירושלמי, שבת, שם: ״ואיש אמונים
כי ימצא, זה ר׳ זעירא״. ופירש בעל קרבן העדה: שאינו אומר שמועה בשם
אדם אלא אם כן נתאמת לו ממי שיצאו הדברים. ואולי גם הוא מסר ספיקי
דגברי.

בקשר לזה יש להוסיף מה שמצינו הרבה פעמים בש״ס, כשאמורא (או תנא)
מוסר מעשה שהיה בתקופה קדומה לו, כמו, למשל, רב יהודה אמר רב
(כתובות פ״ב, ב׳) מוסר על הכתובה שתיקן שמעון בן שטח. מניין לו עובדא
זו? וודאי שמע אותה ממי שהוא (ואותו מי שהוא שמע אותה ממי שהוא אחר,
וכך עד זמנו של שמעון בן שטח). למה אינו מזכיר את שמו של המי
שהוא? 32א האם גם זה מקרה של ספיקי דגברי, שלא ידעו מי אומרה, לכן
מסרו אותה בשם המוסר האחרון? האם זו היא התשובה גם לשאלה המטרידה
של ״תניא נמי הכי״, כשאמורא מוסר מימרה הנמצאת מלה במלה ובאותו
הסדר בברייתא? (״תניא כוותיה״ אינה תמיד מלה במלה). המימרה של רחבא

30א אבל בסוף העמוד שם מסר ר׳ זירא, לפי ר׳ חייא בר אבין, הלכה בשם רב נחמן
מכללא שלא לנכון (״ולא היא וכו׳״). אלא שבכת״י אוקספורד ליתא שם ״אמר ר׳
זירא״.

31 וראה גם ירושלמי שבת ב׳, סהל״א (ד׳, ד׳): א״ר זעירא ומה הוה טיביה (של יונתן בן
עכמא, הזה דאת אמרו הלכה משמיה – פני משה) א״ל אדם גדול הוה ובקי במשנתנו
וכו׳; נדה מ״ח, א׳: אזכה ואיסק ואגמר לשמעתא מפומיה דמרא וכו׳ ומ״ש לעיל בקשר
ל״מאן דהוא״ בשם הרש״ש.

32 מגילה ג׳, ה׳ (ע״ד, רע״ב), ד׳, א׳ (ע״ה, א׳), כתובות ה׳, ו׳ (ל׳, א׳) גיטין א׳, א׳ (מ״ג,
ג׳) ב׳, א׳ (מ״ד, א׳). ועיין גם ברכות ו׳ א׳ (י׳, א׳): והוה ר׳ חייא בר ווא מסתכל ביה
וכו׳ כלאים א׳, א׳ (כ״ו, ד׳): ר׳ יעקב בר זבדי וכו׳ א״ל מה את מסתכל וכו׳, מע״ש, ד׳,
ד׳ (נה׳, א׳), והוה ר׳ לעזר מסתכל ביה וכו׳.

32א אין זה ענין של שלשול של שמועות שמדובר עליו בנזיר נ״ו, ב׳ וירושלמי שבת א׳, ב׳
(נ׳, א׳) ומקבילה.

שר׳ זירא ורב ספרא שיבחו אותה כל כך על מסירתה המדוייקת וכן המימרה
של רב יהודה אמר רב בכתובות שם, נמצאות בברייתא והן בין המימרות
שהגמרא אומרת עליהן תניא נמי הכי. השאלה היא ממה נפשך: אם לא ידעו
את הברייתא, איך התכוונו מעצמם לאותן המלים ולאותו הסדר? ואם ידעו את
הברייתא, למה לא הזכירו אותה? אולי שמעו את הברייתא אלא ששכחו ממי
שמעו אותה (לומר סתם ברייתא, לא היה מספיק). לכן דנו אותה כדין ספקי
דגברי של מימרות ומסרו אותה בשמותיהם הם. מכיוון שעל מימרות ״רב
יהודה אמר רב״ או ״אמר שמואל״ נאמר יותר ״תניא נמי הכי״ מכל מימרת
אמורא אחר, הרי ראיה לדברנו הנ״ל שגם רב יהודה לא היה עיקבי ולא תמיד
מסר ספקי דגברי.

כל זה השערה גרידא והדבר צריך עיון גדול ולא באתי אלא להעיר.

*

בעיסוקנו כאן בפרשת ספקי דגברי, עסקנו בעיקר בתלמוד בבלי. מלבד
מובאות אחדות מתלמוד ירושלמי, כמעט ולא נגענו בו. וכן לא נגענו במשנה,
ואין בדעתנו לטפל בהם כאן בפרוטרוט, אלא להעיר על גודל ההבדל בין
הגמרא והמשנה ביחס לשאלתנו ועל שינויים שבין הבבלי והירושלמי בעניינינו.
במשנה, השמות של בעלי השמועות אינם רק מקור לדעת מי אומרן אלא הם
משמשים גם קנה מדה למדוד על ידו את מידת הסמכות של המימרות. אם
המימרה באה בשם אומרה, אז היא נחשבת כדעת יחיד ואין הלכה כמותה. ואם
היא באה בלא שם אומרה — כדעת חכמים עם מחלוקת בצדה והדעה שכנגד
מובאה בשם אומרה, או כסתם משנה בלא מחלוקת כלל — אז הלכה כמותה (אך
גם שם יש דרגות. תוקפה של סתם משנה עולה על זו של דעת חכמים. סומכים
על דעת חכמים בהתאם לכלל ״יחיד ורבים הלכה כרבים״ שיש לו הרבה
יוצאים מן הכלל. ואילו על סתם משנה סומכים בהתאם לכלל שנתן ר׳ יוחנן:
״הלכה כסתם משנה״, שמעטים הם היוצאים מן הכלל. אע״פ שהגמרא אומרת
עליו ״אמוראי נינהו ואליבא דר׳ יוחנן״,[32]ב שיש מי שחולק בשם ר׳ יוחנן על
כלל זה, ולפעמים היא גם אומרת על סתם משנה ״יחידאה היא״ ואין סומכין
עליה, מכל מקום מרובים הם המקרים שהההלכה היא כסתם משנה מאשר הלכה
כדעת חכמים). ואם המימרות באות בשם אומרן ויחידים חולקים בהן, נשארים
בידינו כללים איך לפסוק את ההלכה. ״הלכה כר׳ עקיבא מחבריו״, ״ר׳ מאיר
ור׳ יהודה הלכה כר׳ יהודה״, ״ר׳ יוסי נימוקו עמו״ ועוד.[33] ואף כשאין הלכה
כמותם נראה שייחסו סמכויות שונות לשמות שונים. מסדר המשנה מסר
לפעמים את המימרה בשם סמכות גדולה אע״פ שבעל סמכות קטנה אמרה
מקודם. ראה, למשל, משנה מקואות ו׳, ה׳: ר׳ יהודה אומר בגדול וכו׳.

[32]ב רשומים באוצר לשון התלמוד, כרך ה׳ עמ׳ 2439 והשמיט את יבמות ט״ז, ב׳.
[33] ראה עירובין מ״ו, ב׳ וירושלמי תרומות ג׳, א׳ (מ״ג, א׳).

השמיט את "משום ב"ש" שבתוספתא (שם ה', ב'), כדי להעניק סמכות נוספת
לדעה זו של ר' יהודה, אע"פ שהיא דעת יחיד שאין הלכה כמותה.33א

בקיצור, מסדר המשנה לפעמים — ודווקא כשההלכה היתה סמכותית ביותר —
לא הזכיר כלל את שם האומר אלא הביא אותה כסתם או כדעת חכמים. ואף
כשהזכיר את שם האומר לא תמיד הזכיר את שם האומר הראשון (והשמיט
תכופות ב"אמר ר"פ משום ר' פלוני" את "ר"פ משום").34 בעיני מסדר
המשנה היה יותר חשוב לדעת איך לפסוק את ההלכה מלדעת מי אומרה.

וניתן לשער כשהיתה לו מימרה עם ספקי דגברי, אם הלכה כמותה, הביא
אותה כסתם או כדעת חכמים. ואם "העיד" התאים (המובן הטכני של "העיד"
טרם נתברר), הביא אותה כ"העיד ר' פלוני"34א בשם המוסר האחרון. ואם הלכה
עתיקה היא, ציטט אותה כ"אמרו" או כ"אמרו חכמים".35 ואם היתה לו מימרה
עם ספקי דגברי שאין הלכה כמותה, מסופקני מאד אם מסדר המשנה היה
מביא אותה כלל.36 המשנה בחרנית היא 37 והשאירה הרבה בחוץ (ברייתא),

33א השווה ר"ש שם. ועיין גם תענית ב', ב': ר' יהודה "משום ר' יהושע" ומשנה א' ב':
ר' יהודה אומר וכו' (וגבורת ארי שם ד"ה תרי): תוספתא זבחים ח', י"ז: ר' יהודה אומר
"משום ר"ג" ובמשנה שם ח', ו: ר' יהודה אומר וכו' (ועיין גמרא שם מט, רע"א): משנה
כלים ח', ט' ותוספתא שם ב"ק ו', ז' (שם אמנם נראה שביחס לר"ג הכריע מסדר
המשנגה כר' יוסי וביחס להלכה כר"מ). והשוה גם תוספתא מקואות ו', י"ט: ר' יוסי
אומר "משום ר' ישמעאל" ומשנה שם ט', ו': ר' יוסי אומר וכו' (ועיין רש"י שבת קי"ד,
א' ד"ה ר' יוסי): מכילתא מסכתא דנזיקין ספרי"ד: רשב"א אומר "משום ר"מ" ותוספתא
ב"ק ט' ט' (ומקבילות): היה רשב"א אומר וכו'.
34 את זה אפשר לראות בנקל כשמדמים את "משום ר"פ" שבתוספתא (אוצר לשון
התוספתא כרך ו' ערך שם עמ' 477 ואילך) עם הציטטות המקבילות במשנה. ועיין גם
בבלי נזיר נ"ו, ב'.
34א "העיד" כולל גם כשר"פ חידש את ההלכה וגם כשמוסר מה ששמע מאחרים. ראה,
למשל, עדיות ב', א'–ב': "ר' חנינא סגן הכהנים העיד ארבעה דברים; מימיהם של
כהנים וכו' (מה ששמע מפי אחרים), "מימי לא ראיתי וכו'" (עדות עצמו). וכן שם ה',
ו'–ז': "עקביה בן מהללאל העיד ארבעה דברים וכו' אני שמעתי מפי המרובים וכו'".
אע"פ ששמע מפי אחרים, נאמר עליו "העיד עקביה בן מהללאל".
35 למלים "אמרו חכמים" אם הן באות בניגוד לתורה, כמו, למשל, חולין ג', ו':
ו"סימני העוף לא נאמרו (בתורה). אבל אמרו חכמים כל עוף הדורס טמא" או כריתות
ו', ט': "מלמד ששניהם שקולים. אבל אמרו חכמים האב קודם לאם בכל מקום" — יש
להן, כנראה, פחות סמכות מאשר למלה "אמרו" בלבד, מעין ההבדל שבין סתם ודעם
חכמים. ראה משנה אבות א', י': "באשתו אמרו (במשנה עתיקה) ק"ו באשת חברו. מכאן
אמרו חכמים (אח"כ) וכו'". ראה תוספות יו"ט שם.
36 "ויש אמרו" או "ויש שאמרו" אינו מציין ספקי דגברי. ידעו מי אמרה אלא שקוראים
לו י"א. ראה סוף הוריות: אסקו לר' מאיר אחרים ולר' נתן יש אומרים. ואכמ"ל. וראה
גם עירובין י"ג, א': כל מקום שאתה מוצא משום ר' ישמעאל אמר תלמיד אחד (עדיין
תלמיד היה?) לפני ר' עקיבא, אינו אלא ר' מאיר וכו'.
37 עיין ברכות כ"ז, א' ומקבילות: ותנן בבחירתא כוותיה.

ומימרה שאין הלכה כמותה ושם אומרה מסופק לא הוכנסה כלל לתוך
המשנה.[38]

*

ואשר לירושלמי, שונה הוא מן הבבלי בזה שהסתם שלו יותר אפודיקטיבי
ופחות ויכוחי מזה של הבבלי. כך שהראיה שלנו לעיל ששאר אמוראים (מלבד
רב יהודה ורחבא) שלא גרסו ספקי דגברי, כשלא ידעו מי אמר את ההלכה לא
שנו אותה "כסתם" משום שאז צריכות היו להיות יותר הלכות פסוקות (אפו־
דיקטיביות) בין הסתמות — נכונה יותר ביחס לבבלי מאשר לירושלמי.

שינוי יותר חשוב הוא שבבבלי לא נמצא סתם במובן אנונימי אלא ביחס
למשנה, "סתם משנה", והכוונה היא למשנה בלא שם אומרה. ואילו בירושלמי
נאמר בערך עשרים פעם על אמורא ש"אמר לה סתם" והכוונה היא למה
שנקרא בבבלי [39] "בלא גברי" (אמורא זה שנה אותה בניגוד לאמורא
אחר ששנאה אותה בשם אמורא קדום) כמו, למשל, כלאים ז׳, ו׳ (ל״א, ו׳): "ר׳
יוסה אמר לה סתם (בשמו) ר׳ חנינא מטי בה בשם ר׳ שמואל בר יצחק התורה
ריבה בטהרה זרעים" [40] (מעניין ששבע עשרה פעם [כולל גם מקבילות]
נמצאת המלה סתם במובן זה אצל ר׳ יוסי ור׳ מנא, אחרוני אמוראים הקרובים
בזמן לסתמאים שבירושלמי ושלש פעמים אצל ר זירא שהזכרנו לעיל שהיה
דייקן במסירה).

במקום "גמרא" ו"סברא" שבבבלי, הלשון בירושלמי הוא "מן אולפן" ו"מן
דעה". ראה עירובין ג׳, ח׳ (כ״א, ב׳): "רבי אחא אמר לה מן אולפן, ר׳ יוסי
אמר לה מן דעה". ושם ד׳, א׳ (כ״ב, ד׳): "ר׳ אחא מן אולפן ור׳ יהודה אמר
לה מן דעה". מחלוקת כזו, שזה יאמר מגמרא וזה יאמר מסברא, לא מצינו
בבבלי. וגם בירושלמי היא נדירה. ואולי גם במקומות אחרים אמר רבי אחא
"מן אולפן", ולא מצא לנחוץ להזכיר (כי לא גרס ספקי דגברי) אלא כאן
משום שבר פלוגתיה הכחיש שיש כאן גמרא.

בעוד שבבבלי "רבנן" הם לרוב תלמידי בני ישיבה שלא זכו ששמותיהם
ייזכרו בביהמ״ד, בירושלמי רגיל אצל אמוראים "מיליהון דרבנן פליגי",
"מיליהון דרבנן מסייעין", "מיליהון דרבנן אמרין", "חמיין רבנן" ועוד.[41]
בירושלמי "רבנן" הם אמוראים ממש. ראה, למשל, ירושלמי כתובות ט׳, א׳

---

[38] אם ידוע שם אומרה אלא שאין יודעים מי הביא לביהמ״ד את המשנה (או הברייתא)
אומר "משום ר״פ אמרו" או "אמרו משום ר״פ" (יבמות ד׳, ט׳; סנהדרין א׳, ב׳; בכורות
ט׳, ח׳).

[39] שבת קי״א, ב׳; כתובות ו׳, א׳; בכורות כ״ה, א׳; ל״א, א׳.

[40] ראה גם ירושלמי, שבת ספ״י. והשווה ירושלמי מעשרות ה׳, סהל״א (נ״א, ד׳): ר׳
יוסי בשם ר׳ לא וכו׳ ו"הירושלמי כפשוטו" למהר״ש ליברמן עמ׳ 167.

[41] רשומים אצל בכר (לעיל הע׳ 16), עמ׳ 601—5.

(ל״ב, ד׳): ״ר׳ ירמיה בעא קומי ר׳ זעירא, היי לון רבנן, הא רב, הא ר׳
יוחנן, הא רשב״ל? א״ל, רבנן דר׳ יוסטינה״. וראה גם ירושלמי קידושין
א׳, א׳ (נ״ט, סע״ד): ״מאן אינון רבנן וכו׳ ״ (משמע שבשאר המקומות ידעו
מי הם הרבנן).

״חברייא״ מצוי מאד בירושלמי [42] ודומים לגמרי לאמוראים. הם אומרים
בשם אמוראים ואמוראים אומרים בשמם ואף חולקים אליבם. אנו פוגשים
אותם עם אמוראים שבכל הדורות והרושם הוא שהמתוכחים אתם ידעו בדיוק
מי הם. ואם ״חברייא״ הם אמוראים ידועים גם בירושלמי כלאים ג׳, א׳
(כ״ח, ג׳): ״וקיימנוה ולא ידעין אי חברייא קיימונה או ר׳ אימי קיימה״, אז
לפנינו שם מקרה של ספקי דגברי (ספק משמיה דרב אימי ספק משמיה
דחברייא). אבל אם חברייא שם היינו סתם (כמו״ש בקרבן העדה, והספק הוא
אם הפירוש [״וקיימנוה״] נאמר על ידי הסתמא דגמרא או על ידי רבי אימי),
אז הוא דומה למ״ש בבבלי ״אמר ר״פ ואמרי לה כדי״ (אך הדמיון אינו שלם
כי בבבלי ״אמר ר״פ ואמרי לה כדי״ נוסחאות שונות הן). [43]

בירושלמי נמצא כמה פעמים ״תלמיד ר״פ״, ״תלמידוי דר״פ״ ו״תלמידי
ר״פ״, [44] אבל בבבלי לא נמצא מלבד אולי בנדה נ״ב, א׳. בירושלמי נמצא ״חד
מרבנן״ שבע פעמים ובבבלי ליתא (ראה ירושלמי ביצה א׳, ו׳ (ס׳, ג׳): ״ר׳
יונה מפקד לחברייא וכו׳ רב מפקד לתלמידוי וכו׳ וקידושין א׳, ח׳ (ס״א, ג׳)
״רב מפקד לאילן דבי רב אחי, רב המנונא מפקד לחברייא וכו׳ ״. ״תלמידוי״
דומים לדבי ר״פ ושונים מחברייא. הם אינם אמוראים ממש). וראה ירושלמי
ר״ה ד׳, ד׳ (נ״ט, סע״ב). ר׳ שמואל בר נחמן נותן טעם למ״ש במשנה שם
״ונשתהו העדים מלבוא וכו׳ ״, ״מפני מעשה שהיה (בזמן הבית) שאירע פעם
אחת נפלה הברה בעיר וכו׳ ונתקלקלו הלוים בשיר״. והירושלמי מוסר שם:
״א״ר אחא בר נחמן בשם ר׳ זעירה חברייא בעון קומי ר׳ שמואל בר נחמן,
בשם מן, רבי אמר לה (מפני מעשה שהיה)? אמר לון דכוותכון (האם אני
כמותכם) דאית לכון רברבין סגין? בשם ר׳ יהושע בן לוי וכו׳ ״. מכיוון
שמעשה זה אירע לפני הרבה זמן ולא נזכר במשנה, רצו לדעת מאיזה רבי
שמע ר׳ שמואל בר נחמן מעשה זה.

לא ברור למה שאלו רק כאן. האם בשאר המקומות כשאמורא מוסר ״מעשה
שהיה״ הרבה זמן לפניו ידעו את כל החוליות בשלשלת הקבלה? או שמא ידעו
רק את החוליה האחרונה והסתפקו בה, משום שלא גרסו ספקי דגברי. וכאן גם

─────────────

[42] רשומים ב״חכמי התלמוד״, ירושלמי, לר׳ יוסף אומנסקי (הוצ׳ מוסד הרב קוק,
ירושלים תשי״ב) עמ׳ 1—50.
[43] ראה הע׳ 22.
[44] אומנסקי, שם עמ׳ 8—147. והשמיט פיאה ח׳, ז׳ (כ״א, א׳) ומקבילה: חד תלמיד מן
דרבי וכו׳.

את החוליה האחרונה (רבו של רב שמואל בר נחמן) לא ידעו. לכן שאלו?

בבבלי אין אנו מוצאים מחלוקת אנונימית בצורת "תרי אמוראין, חד אמר
וכו' אלא בכתובות פ', א': אמר עולא פליגי בה תרי אמוראי במערבא, חד
אמר וכו' וחד אמר וכו' ושם, כנראה (ע"פ ברכות כ"ב, א'; ל"ג, ב'; שבת
כ"א, א'; צ"ו, א'; מגילה כ"ה, א'), האמוראים הם ר' יוסי בר אבין ור' יוסי
בר זבדא (וראה גם ב"ב ע"ה, א'). אבל בירושלמי שכיח "תרי אמוראין
וכו' ". ואפילו "תלתא אמורין".[45]

בכלל שוררת פחות אנונימיות בבבלי מאשר בירושלמי. ואולי משום
שהעורכים שערכו את הבבלי עריכה יסודית וממושכת — מה שלא נעשה
לירושלמי, — זיהו אח"כ את רוב האנונימיות שבבבלי.[46]

*

ולבסוף ייאמר: דרישתם של החז"ל למסור הלכות בשם אומרן ולא להסתפק
במסירת שמות האסכולות בלבד כדרך שהקלסיקאים עושים מראה על
חשיבותו של האדם היחיד בעיניהם. ישנם מעשים שהעושה אותם נעשה שותף
להקב"ה במעשה בראשית וע"י אמירת הלכה בשמו נעשה הוא שותף להקב"ה
התורה שקדמה למעשה בראשית תקע"ד דורות. ואין לך חשיבות גדולה מזו.

[45] ראה בכר שם (לעיל הע' 16), עמ' 552.
[46] ראה סנהדרין י"ז, ב'. והשווה ירושלמי, מעשר שני ספ"ק.

דעתו של ר' יפת בן עלי הקראי על חרבן העולם באחרית הימים

מאת י' א' וידה (פאריס)

דבר ידוע הוא, שבמשך הדורות נחלקו חכמי ישראל בפתרונם של אי־אלו היגדים שבכתבי הקודש המנבאים לכאורה על חרבן השמים והארץ באחרית הימים, כששני כתובים (יש' ס״ה, י״ז וס״ו, כ״ב) מדברים אף בבריאת שמים חדשים וארץ חדשה (השווה גם כן תה' ק״ד, ל'). ישנם כמה אמרי אגדה שמביאים לכאורה את הדברים כפשוטם.[1] אולם כבר רב סעדיה גאון נוטה, כנראה, לפירוש על דרך ״העברה״ (השאלה) ומליצה,[2] שלא לדבר על דברי הביקורת החריפים של הרמב״ם במורה נבוכים, ח״ב, פ' כ״ט.

[1] עיין בר״ר מ״א (מ״ב), ג' (ת'—א', עמ' 405): כל מה שנברא ביום ראשון עתידין להבלות (במקבילה ויק״ר י״ז, ז', מהד' מ. מרגליות, עמ' רל״ה: לכלות). מקומות אלו לא הובאו אצל א. א. אורבך, חז״ל, אמונות ודעות, ירושלים, תשכ״ט. השווה ג״כ הסיפור על מותו של ר' אלעזר בן דורדיא, עבודה זרה י״ז ע״א. לפי אבות דר' נתן נוסח ב', פרק מ״ב, מהד' ש. שכטר דף נ״ט, א' (ומשם בפרק אדם הראשון, י. ד. אייזענשטיין, אוצר מדרשים עמ' י׳—י״א) הארץ עתידה שתבלה. בתנחומא, מהד' בובר, בראשית (דף ח' ע״א) מוכיח בעל האגדה מהפסוקים יש' נ״א, ו' וס״ה, כ״ב שעם ישראל עתיד להתקיים למרות כליון השמים והארץ. בבר״ר א', י״ד (עמ' 12) הובעה הדעה שהשמים החדשים כבר ברואים ועומדים משעת ימי בראשית.

[2] והנה תרגומו של רס״ג ליש' נ״א, ו' (מהדורת י. דרנבורג, פריס 1896, עמ' 78): ארפעו אלי אלסמא עיונכם ואלתפתוא אלי אלארץ' מן דונהא ואעלמו (= ודעו) אן אלסמאואת כאלדכ'אן תצ'מחל ואלארץ' כאלת'וב תבלא ואהלהא כד'אך ימותון וגות״י יכון אלי אלדהר ואהל זכותי לא יד'ערון (אין צורך בתיקון המוצע ע״י המהדיר). ברם את יש' ס״ה, י״ז הוא מתרגם (שם, עמ' 97) תוך הוספה כעין כף הדמין: פאני סאכ׳לק אלסמא כאנהא (= כאילו) ג'דידה' ואלארץ' כג'דידה' (= כחדשה). הראב״ע מצרף, כביכול, את תפיסת הגאון ופירושו של יפת (עיין להלן) בכתבו על יש' ס״ה, י״ז: יש אומרים כי טעם כאילו. ורבי יהודה המדקדק נ״ע אמר כי טעם בריאת שמים והארץ (כך) על הפרטים. והנכון כי השמים הם הרקיע, והשם יחדש אויר טוב שיהיו בני האדם בריאים בגופם ויחיו שנים רבות, וגם יוסיף בכח הארץ והנה היא חדשה. והאומר כי זה רמז לעולם הבא אינגו דבק בפרשה, כי אין לעולם הבא אכילה. וכן הורו קדמונינו ז״ל והוא אמת לבדו. השווה גם מה שפירש ביש' נ״א, ז': שאו, מזה הפסוק למדו אנשי תושיה כי נשמת האדם עומדת ודברים אמת, לכן (= ברם) אין טעם הפסוק כן. והשמים הוא הרקיע והארץ היא מיושבת וישועת השם ואמונתו וצדקתו לעולם עומדת. כנגד זה, הוא מעיר על עומדים שביש' ס״ו, כ״ב ״שלא יבלו ככקדמונים״.

כאן אנו באים לעמוד על חומר שטרם נבדק מתוך חיבורי הפרשן הקראי רב
יפת בן עלי[3].

חכם זה עורך דיון מיוחד בנושא הנ״ל בפירושו לישעיה נ״א, ו'[4].

שאו לשמים עיניכם והביטו אל הארץ מתחת כי שמים כעשן
נמלחו והארץ כבגד תבלה וישביה כמו כן ימותון וישועתי לעולם
תהיה וצדקתי לא תחת.

עלינו להזכיר את השאלות הנוגעות לפסוק זה ולהציע תשובות עליהן. אחת
מהן: מפני מה בא פסוק זה בפיסקה זו? שנית: האם יש לפרש את ההיגד כי
שמים כעשן נמלחו פשוטו כמשמעו. או אם יש לו מובן יוצא מידי הפשט?
שלישית: למי רומז ההיגד ויושביה כמו כן ימותון. ומהי הכוונה במלת
ימותון? רביעית: מה אופן החכמה בהיעשות זה (המעשה)?

התשובה על השאלה הראשונה. שני טעמים נתנו בדבר. האחד מהם: מאחר
שפעולה זו קשורה בישועה, הזכירה הכתוב תיכף ליצא ישעי (פסוק ה').
השני: שרצה (הכתוב) להראות שמי שיכול לכלות את השמים ואת הארץ,
היכולת בידו לכלות את הכופרים ואת המלכויות.

בס׳ ״האמונות והדעות״ מתבטא הגאון שלוש פעמים על הנושא הנידון כאן. במאמר ז'
(תחית המתים, מהד' לנדויר, עמ' 223, מהד' רבי יוסף קאפח, עמ' ר״ל, תרגום אנגלי
של ש. רוזנבלט עמ' 281) הוא כותב (לפי תרגומו של קאפח): ״...השמים והארץ יכלו'
והישועה תמדיד, והוא אמרו שאו... לא תחת, ואנחנו יודעים שאין הישועה עצם
שתתקיים בעצמה, אלא הכוונה בישועה אנשי הישועה״. ובאופן יותר ברור במאמר ח'
(״בישועה״ או ״בגאולה האחרונה״, ל' עמ' 246, ק' עמ' רנ״ב, ר' עמ' 311): ״...יהיה
להם עולם שכולו ששון ושמחה עד שיראו (=שיחשבו) כאלו (הפיזור שלי, במקור
כאן) שמיהם וארצם נתחדשו להם כמו כמו שפירשתי בפרשת כי הנני בורא שמים
חדשים וארץ חדשה...״ ואשר לפסוק יש' כ״ו, כ״ב, הרי הוא רומז לפי דעתו
(מאמר ט', גמול ועונש, ל' עמ' 269, ק' עמ' רע״ה, ר' עמ' 341) לעולם הבא, כשהנבואה
בס״ה, י״ז נאמרה על זמן הישועה בעולם הזה. השווה גם כן נוסח המאמר השביעי, פרק
ה', שישימש בסיס לתרגומו של ר' יהודה[ן'] תבון, המקור, מהד' ב. ז. בכר ... .Festschr
Steinschneider ליפסיא 1896, עמ' 107, אנגלית ר' עמ' 425.

כדאי להעיר שהקראי סלומון בן ירוחמ(י)ם נוטה לפרש את הפסוקים יש' נ״א, ו' ותה'
ק״ב, כ״ו–כ״ז כמורים לאפיסת העולם במועד הקבוע מראש על פי רצון האל, אולם
הייתי מהסס לחרוץ משפט בענין, כשלפנינו רק עדות יחידה (הפירוש לק' ג', י״ד,
תורגם לצרפתית ע״י כותב הטורים l'Ecclésiaste sur karaites Commentaires Deux,
לידן 1971, עמ' 95). לסוף נזכיר שהראב״ע (פירוש עה״ת, דב' ד', כ״ו) מלגלג על
הפותרים את הפסוק יש' נ״א, ו' פשוטו כמשמעו (השווה גם כן בפירוש רד״ק לפסוק).

[3] עיין עליו ... Commentaires Deux, עמ' 115.

[4] הפירוש על ס' ישעיה היה לפנינו בכ״י קובץ פירקוביץ א', כ״י 568, שנכתב בשנת
רס״ג לבריאת העולם (1503 למנינם) ע״י אלעזר בן אברהם בן אלעזר הכהן ממשפחת
בני אלכ'אזן (עיין המובא אצל Studies and Texts ,Mann Jacob, כרך ב', עמ'
270, הערה 41).

התשובה על השאלה השניה. ההיגד כי שמים כעשן נמלחו הרי פשוטו
כמשמעו. אין השכל 5 מבטלה ואין כתוב דוחה אותה. והוא, שמבחינת מה
שנוגע לבני אדם, (השאלה) היא איך ייתכן ביטול השמים והארץ כשביניהם
(נמצאות) בריות. שנית, מכיוון שה׳ ית׳ ויתע׳ ברא את השמים ואת הארץ כדי
לגלות ממשלתו, האם יש הצדקה לאבדנם מפאת חכמתו? ניפטר מהם
(בשנשיב) שהבורא ית׳ ויתע׳ יכול על ביטול הדבר כמו שהוא יכול על
המצאתו, וכמו שבריאת הבעל חי והצומח חכמה (מצידו), (כך) הוא ביטולם,
שכן החכמה נשלמה בבריאתם. (ואפשר להשיב גם כן) שכמו שהוא קבע פרקי
זמן שונים (למציאות הבעלי חיים והצמחים), כך קבע עבור השמים והארץ
פרק זמן שסופו לחלוף, אם כי היה ארוך. ובהשיבנו על השאלה האחרונה
נברר אופן החכמה בזה. ונאמר אחר כן, שה׳ ית׳ לא יחריבם בבת אחת, כדי
שלא יהיה מקום לטעון נגדנו: איפה יהיו הבריות? וזה, שהכתוב הבהיר
שחרבנם יבוצע זה אחר זה באמרו על השמים כעשן נמלחו, והעשן דרכו
להיכחד קמעא קמעא. וכן אמר בנוגע לארץ כבגד תבלה. ופירוש הדבר,
שהאל ית׳ ויתע׳ יכחיד חלק אחר חלק ויחדש במקומו ברגע קטן, ולא יהיה
חרבנם של חלקי (השמים והארץ) רצוף כי אם למקוטעין, והגלגל יהיה נע ולא
נח.6 ואם נאמר: כשחלק מסויים ייכחד, אין מקומו נע כי אם במצב אחר,7
(התשובה): אין מן הנמנע שיסוב הגלגל גם אם חלק ממנו אינו סובב כרגע. ואם
נאמר, שבאמרו כי שמים כעשן נמלחו רמז (הכתוב) לרקיע, הרי זה
פירוש מתקבל על הדעת.8 אם כן השמים העליונים יישארו כמו שהם. בעוד
שהרקיע ייחרב ותחודש תמורתו. ואשר לארץ, הרי האל ית׳ יעביר את בעלי
החיים והצמחים (שעליה) ממקום אחד למשנהו. והמקום שהחריבו׳, יעביר ממנו
את בעלי החיים עד שיחדש תמורתו (ואז) יחזירם אליה. ואם הזכיר כאן חרבן
השמים והארץ, שעה שלא הזכיר שמים חדשים וארץ חדשה, הריהו הזכיר
הללו במקום אחר כשאמר (יש׳ ס״ה, י״ז; ס״ו, כ״ב) כי הנני בורא שמים
חדשים וארץ חדשה וגו׳, כי כאשר השמים החדשים וגו׳. ועל דעת
חכמים רבים לא יחריב האל ית׳ ויתע׳ מקצת הגופים במצב אחד ומקצתם
במצב אחר אלא כשיברא את החרבן 9 יהיה זה חרבן הגופים כולם במצב אחד
ויחיד. ואם נאמר שבאמרו כי שמים כעשן נמלחו התכוון למפולת

5 ביתר דיוק: משפט שכלי.

6 ״תהיה תנועתו בלתי נפסקת״.

7 ר״ל: בכל זאת חלה איזו הפסקה בין חורבן חלק מסויים מן העולם הנידון לחורבן
לבין בריאת החלק הבא במקומו.

8 קול מסתמר (?). תירגמתי דרך השערה.

9 עיין במד׳ ט״ז, ל׳: ואם בריאה יברא ה׳ (ואולי רומז לשיטה של ה״כלאם״, לפיה כל
פעולה אלוהית – בריאה בפני עצמה).

הכוכבים, ובאמרו והארץ כבגד תבלה רומז להתפוררות ההרים ורעידות האדמה, ובאמרו השמים החדשים הכוונה לתוספת אור השמש והירח כמו ב(פסוק ישע׳ ל׳, כ״ו) והיה אור הלבנה וגו׳, ושאמרו והארץ החדשה הוא כאמרו (שם מ׳ ד׳) כל גיא ינשא, וכן (שם מ״א, י״ט) אתן במדבר ארז שטה וגו׳, (ניוכח ש)לזה ולדומה לו הוא רומז באמרו והארץ כבגד תבלה.10

התשובה על השאלה השלישית, היא (שבאמרו) ויושביה כמו כן ימותון רומז לכליון יושבי תבל, להוציא מי שנשמע לאל יתע׳, כמו שאמר (שם, מ׳, י״ח) כל הגוים כאין נגדו, זאת אומרת, שהוא ימיתם ואחרי כן יחיים ויענשם במקום העונש, כמו שאמר (שם, כ״ו, י״ט) וארץ רפאים תפיל. ואמר מפרש אחר,11 שהכוונה בכמו כן ימותון על העונש, בדומה ל(יח׳ י״ח, י״ג) החפץ אחפוץ במות הרשע. והודיע (הכתוב) שבזמן שימוגו השמים והארץ יהיה ענשם של רשעי עולם.

אשר לתשובה על השאלה הרביעית במובן השמים המדובר בם ובחידוש תמורתם, הועלו בזה אי~אלו נימוקים.12 אחד מהם (שחידוש זה יחול) מפני שחידוש העולם דבר נמנע בעיני הרבה אומות כשהן חושבות כי הוא קדמון, ויש מהן סוברות שהכוכבים שולטים בעולם. ומאחר שיש בין האומות נוהות אחרי הדעות הללו ומה שדומה להן, הרי הוא ית׳ חשב לנכון בחכמתו לכלות אותם (השמים) ולחדש תמורתם כדי להפר דעותיהן ולבטל סברותיהן ולאמת המסורת שבידינו.

ויש אומרים שהאל יתע׳ ברא את השמים ואת הארץ בששת ימי בראשית על המתכונת שידעה מראש כנחוצה לאנשי הדור שהיו עתידים למרוד בו או להישמע לו.13 אולם עבור דור ישועה, שידע (אלהים) שאנשיו לא ימרוהו, יברא שמים וארץ על מתכונת תחייבה חכמתו לפי מעשיהם. אז יהיו הטובות בשפע ולרוב ויארכו ימי חיי בני אדם בשל שיווין האויר והתמזגות הכוכבים.14

לפי סברה אחרת, מאחר ששמי בראשית וארץ בראשית נבראו בשביל העולם הזה, לא בשביל העולם הבא, והאל ית׳ ויתע׳ רצה שהגמול יתקיים בזמן הצפוי,15 הריהו ברא (כבר מראש) שמים וארץ מתאימים לגמול.

10 בנינו של משפט ארוך זה אינו מן הברורים ביותר. אולם כוונת המפרש, כנראה, לומר כי, לאמיתו של דבר, יש להבין את הנבואה על חורבן העולם כבשורה על שינוי צורה רדיקלי, לא ככליון שאין אחריו תקומה.

11 לא ידעתי מיהו.

12 מילולית: נאמרו בה כמה פנים.

13 שכן בעולם הזה הברירה ביד האדם לעבוד את בוראו או למרוד בו.

14 השווה לעיל, הערה 2, המובא מפי הראב״ע לישׁ׳ ס״ה, ה׳, ז.

15 מילולית: "לשים את הזמן הצפוי לבית הגמול", כלומר, להבדיל עקרונית בין ימות העולם הזה לבין העולם הבא, שרק בו יקבלו הבריות שכר ועונש.

מטעמים אלו ויותר מזה עתיד (ה׳) לכלות שמים וארץ ולחדש תמורתם.
ואין מ(כל) מעשי האל יתע׳ שאין הוא חכמה בעתו, כמו שאמר (קה׳ ג׳, י״א)
את הכל עשה יפה בעתו, וזה כמו החיים והמות והלילה והיום והשינויים
הדומים לאלו שכלם פעל החכמה (האלהית). ואמרו וישועתי לעולם מלמדנו
שהשמים והארץ יאבדו כשהישועה והצדקה תעמודנה. וזה (יהיה) במציאות
שמים חדשים וארץ חדשה, כמו שאמר במקום אחר (יש׳ ס״ו, כ״ב) כן
יעמד זרעכם ושמכם. הצדקה היא התורה, והודיע כי היא לא תפוג כמו
שפגה בעבר (חב׳ א׳, ד׳) על כן לא תפוג תורה.

והנה יפת חוזר אי-פעם על הרעיונות המובעים בפירוש הפסוק הנ״ל. הבה
נסדר את הטקסטים הנוגעים בעניין שידועים לנו לפי שעה.

יש׳ ס״ה, ט״ז

הפסוק הזה מודיענו שכל יושבי תבל עתידים להיכנס לדת (ישראל). ואכן
דרך כל אומה להתברך באלהיו ולהישבע בשמו. ואמר (הכתוב) יתברך
באלהי אמן משום שאלוהות הגוים פסלים ותמונות נבראים ואינם ראויים
לעבודה. ואמרו כי נשכחו הצרות, מורה בו לצרות שגרמו האומות אחת
למשניה בשל חילוקי הדעות בדת. וכאשר תהיה הדת אחת ויחידה, עתידות
הצרות לחלוף ולהתבטל מן העולם. וזה דומה ל(יש׳ ב׳, ד׳) לא ישא גוי אל
גוי חרב. ובאמרו וכי נסתרו מודיענו כי הצרות תחלופנה כליל מן העולם.
וסידר פסוק זה אחר הקודמים לו כדי להוכיח בו את הרשעים שאמר להם
(פסוק י״א) ואתם עזבי ה׳ השכחים את הר קדשי. וכשהזכיר ___ר
המתברך כלל בו את חסד (האל) והדת, שכן הם שני העיקרים הכוללי___ ___
מה שהשכל צריך לו.

יש׳ ל׳, כ״ו

הזכיר במקום זה כח הכפלת (= הגברת אורם של) שני המאורות __לו.
כשבמקום אחר הודיע שיברא שמים חדשים וארץ חדשה... [אשר ל___ר
שבעת הימים] רוצה לומר התכנסות (= התרכזות) אור של שבעה ימים __ __
שבע מנורות שאורן מתכנס (= מתרכז). וזה מורה להכפלת (= להגברת) כח
אורם לא לדבר אחר.[16]

---

[16] בפירושו לל״ד, ד׳ (דף י״ז, ב׳—י״ח, א׳) מציין יפת לפירוש לנ״א, ו׳. אחרי ש___יא
שלושה פתרונות לפסוק הנידון: א) מפולת הכוכבים; ב) ליקוי אורם של הגר___ים
השמימיים; ג) ביטולם תוך בריאת תחליפם (יג׳דד אללה תע׳ בדלהא), כשהוא מ___ר:
ובעץ׳ אלנאס יחיל אן יעדם אללה תע׳ בעץ׳ אלכ׳לק ויבקי בעצ׳הא ולנא אלי __דא
אלכלאם ר׳געﺔ פי שאו לשמים עיניכם (יש סובר שלא ייתכן שה׳ יכלה חל__ק מן
הבריאה וישאיר חלק אחר. אנו נחזור אל העניַן בפירוש שאו לשמים עיניכם).

יש׳ ס״ה, י״ז

כי הנני בורא... על לב.

אמר כי הנני, כדי לקשור הפסוק לזה שקודם. וזה, כי הודיע שביטול
הדתות יארע תוך ביטול השמים והארץ, והתגלות דת (האמת) ואחדות ה׳
תתרחש ביחד עם התגלותם של שמים חדשים וארץ חדשה. זאת אומרת,
שבשעה שיתברר אצל יושבי תבל, אחרי כליון שתי הדיוטות הללו, התחדשות
שמים חדשים וארץ חדשה, כי אז יתאשר בעיניהם חידוש העולם
וייוכחו לדעת שיש לו בורא ותוכחש דעת המחזיק(ים) בקדמות העולם
ויתר הדתות שהן נגד התורה. וכבר ביארנו (בפירוש הפסוק, יש׳ נ״א, ו׳)
שאו לשמים עיניכם איך יכלו הללו ויחודש דבר אחר במקומם כשלא יכלה
מה שבאמצע. ובאמרו לא תזכרנה הראשונות מציין למה שנברא בששת
ימי בראשית.

אמנם אין לתפוס את האמרה לא תזכרנה פשוטה כמשמעה.[17] והענין
שהתורה ״יגדיל ויאדיר״ נמצאת אצלנו ואנו קוראים אותה, אך הכתוב מכוון
לדבר מסויים. ז. א., מעשיהם של אלו כבר אזלו ומעשי ״החדשים״ הם
קיימים. ודומה לזה מה שאמר הכתוב (יר׳ ג׳, ט״ז) ולא יאמרו עוד ארון
ברית ה׳ וגו׳, שאין אנו בדעה שארון ברית ה׳ יאבד מן העולם ולא ייזכר,
רק הכתוב מכוון בזה לומר שלפנים היה מנהגם לקחת את הארון עמם בעת
מלחמה, אך לעתיד לבוא תיבטל המלחמה מן הארץ, ומשום כך אמר ולא
יאמרו עוד ארון ברית ה׳ וגו׳. וכן הזכיר בפסוק הראשון חדלון הגורמים
לחילוקי הדתות, והזכיר בפסוק זה שמים חדשים וכליון הקודמים, באופן
שתיבטל דעת אלו הדוגלים בקדמות העולם.

יש׳ ס״ו, כ״ב

כבר קדם בפירוש שאו לשמים עיניכם משמע שמים חדשים וארץ
חדשה, ואמרו עמדים לפני מורה על קיומם (= יציבותם). אחר כך צימד
קיומם של ישראל לקיום השמים והארץ כפי שנבאר ב(פירוש לירמיה
ל״א, ל״ו [ל״ה]).[18] אם ימושו החוקים, ואמר זרעכם ושמכם, והוא זרע
ישראל, כמו שאמר (ירמ׳, שם) גם זרע ישראל ישבתו. ואמר ושמכם,
רוצה לומר המלכות. צימד אפוא את קיומם זרעם ומלכותם לקיום שמים

─────────────────────────

[17] מילולית: ״מכל הבחינות״.

[18] יש להעיר שבפירושו של יפת לירמיה שפרסם Philip David Wendkos, The
Arabic Commentary of Yefet b. Ali, the Karaite on the Book of Jeremiah,
עבודת דוקטור (שרט) שהוגשה ל־Dropsie College, ב־1969, אין המפרש בפירושו על
הפסוק הנ״ל (61b) חוזר על הרעיון המובע כאן.

חדשים וארץ חדשה, שלא כזמן העבר בו נשתנו כל המצבים המעולים
להפכם.

תהלים ק״ב, כ״ז

המה יאבדו, רוצה לומר השמים והארץ הללו יתפוררו והאל יחדש שמים
אחרים וארץ אחרת, כמו שאמר (יש׳ נ״א, ו׳) כי שמים כעשן נמלחו וגו׳.
אמר יאבדו במובן השינויים (שיחולו בהם), ז. א. רעידות אדמה והתמוטטות.
כשמקומות רבים יחרבו והכוכבים יילקו (= יתקדרו), ולזה אמר כבגד יבלו.
ובאמרו כלבוש כלבוש תחליפם ויחלופו מציין לשמים חדשים וארץ חדשה
כשחַיה האל את עולמו ויביע המעינות במדברות ויטע בהם האילנות. וכן
יוסיף על אור השמש והירח, כמו שאמר (יש׳ ל׳, כ״ו) והיה אור הלבנה
כאור החמה ואור החמה יהיה שבעתים וגו׳. אשר לאמרו ואתה הוא
ושנותיך אחר אמרו המה יאבדו, הריהיו סובל אחד משני פירושים. או
רוצה לומר אתה בראתם ואתה עתיד לכלותם כשאתה תכון לעד, או יאמר: כל
מה שעובדים זולתך יחלוף עם שינוי שמים וארץ כשאתה לבדך קיים, לא
תחלוף ולא תעבור. ואמרו ושנותיך לא יתמו, מובנו, אתה הוא הקיים, אין
ראשית לראשיתך, או אפשר שר״ל אין קץ לעבודה שעובדים אותך לישועתך.
אחר כך הודיע שכמו שעבודתו קיימת לעד ולא יעבדו זולתו, כך זרע
ישראל הם שישכנו בארץ הקדושה כשאויביהם יצאו ממנה, כמו שאמר
(יש׳ מ״ט, י״ז) מהרו בניך מהרסיך ומחריביך (ממך יצאו).

פירוש ר׳ יפת בן עלי לישעיה נ״א, ו׳
קובץ פירקוויץ׳ א׳, 568 כ״י, דף 209, 212ב—212א

שאו... תחת

שילו אלי אלסמא עיניכם ואלתפתו אלי אלארץ׳ מן תחת אן אלסמא מת״ל
אלדכ׳אן תלאשת [210א] ואלארץ׳ מת״ל אלתוב תבלא וסכאנהא ענד דלך
ימותון ומגותי אלי אלאבד תכון וחג׳תי לא תנדער.

יג׳ב אן נדכר פי הדא אלפסוק מן אלמסאיל מא יתג׳ה ונג׳יב ענהא. מנהא
לאי מעני דכר הדא אלפסוק פי הדא אלפצל. ומנהא אנה הל קו׳ כי שמים
כעשן נמלחו הו עלי ט׳אהרה או לה תאויל, וכיף יתם דלך אן כאן עלי
ט׳אהרה. ומנהא אלי מַן ישיר בקו׳ ויושביה כמו כן ימותון ואיש אלגרץ׳
פי קו׳ ימותון. ומנהא מא וג׳ה אלחכמה פי פעל דלך.

אלג׳ואב ען אלמסאלה אלאולי. קיל פי דלך מעאנין: אחד [המא] הו אנה למא

---

¹⁹ מילולית: ״התמידי״.

כאן פעל דלך מקרון באלישועה ד׳כרה בעקב יצא ישעי. ואלת׳אני הו אנה
אראד אן יורי אנה אורא אן אלדי קדר עלי אפנא אלסמא ואלארץ׳ הו קאדר
עלי פַנא אלכפאר ואלדוול.

ואלג׳ואב ען אלמסאלֵה אלתאניֵה הו אן קו׳ כי שמים כעשן נמלחו הו
עלי טַהרה לא עׅקל יחﬞילה ולא נץ ידפעה. ודלך אן אלדי יתעלק באלנאס הו
אנה כיף ימכן פנא אלסמא ואלארץ׳ ובינהמא מכ׳לוקין, ואלת׳אני הו אנה
אדﬞא כאן [2210ב] אלכ׳אלק ג׳ל ועלא כ׳לק אלסמא ואלארץ׳ לאטﬞהאר חכמה
פהל לעדמהמא וג׳ה חֻכמה.

פננפצﬠל מנהם באן אלכ׳אלק ג׳ל ועלא קאדר עלי עדם אלשי כמא קדר עלי
איגﬠ׳אדה. ואנה כמא אן כ׳לק אלחיואן ואלנבﬠאת חכמה ופנﬠאהﬠם חכמה אד
אלחﬠכמה פי כ׳לקֶהﬠא קד תﬠם(!), ואן אגﬠ׳עﬠאﬠלה מקﬠאדﬠיר מﬠדﬠדﬠהﬠא מכ׳תﬠלﬠפﬠה, כדﬠאﬠן
גﬠ׳על ללﬠסﬠמﬠא ואלﬠארﬠץ׳ מﬠדﬠה תﬠתﬠקﬠצﬠ׳א ואן כﬠאﬠנﬠת טﬠוﬠיﬠלﬠה. וﬠסﬠנﬠבﬠיﬠין פﬠי גﬠ׳ואﬠב
אלﬠמﬠסﬠאﬠלﬠה אלﬠאﬠכﬠ׳יﬠרﬠה וﬠגﬠ׳ה אלﬠחﬠכﬠמﬠה פﬠי דﬠלﬠך. תﬠ׳ﬠם אﬠנﬠא נﬠקﬠוﬠל אﬠן אﬠלﬠלﬠה תﬠﬠ׳ לﬠיﬠס
יﬠעﬠדﬠמﬠﬠאﬠ פﬠי חﬠﬠאﬠלﬠה וﬠאﬠחﬠדﬠה פﬠתﬠﬠגﬠ׳ה אﬠלﬠמﬠﬠטﬠﬠאﬠﬠלﬠﬠבﬠה עﬠﬠלﬠﬠיﬠﬠנﬠﬠא אﬠﬠיﬠﬠן יﬠﬠכﬠﬠוﬠﬠנﬠﬠוﬠﬠן אﬠﬠלﬠﬠמﬠﬠכﬠ׳ﬠﬠלﬠﬠוﬠﬠקﬠﬠיﬠﬠן.
ודﬠלﬠך אﬠן אﬠלﬠﬠנﬠﬠ

ודלך אן אלנﬠע קד ביין ענד פנאהﬠא חﬠאל פﬠחﬠﬠאﬠל אﬠד קﬠﬠאﬠל פﬠﬠי אﬠﬠלﬠﬠסﬠﬠמﬠﬠא כﬠﬠעﬠﬠשﬠﬠן
נﬠﬠמﬠﬠלﬠﬠחﬠﬠוﬠ, וﬠﬠמﬠﬠן שﬠﬠﬠ שﬠﬠﬠﬠﬠﬠﬠﬠﬠﬠﬠﬠﬠﬠ שﬠﬠﬠﬠﬠﬠﬠﬠﬠﬠﬠﬠ
תﬠﬠﬠﬠﬠﬠﬠﬠﬠﬠﬠﬠ. וﬠﬠﬠﬠﬠﬠﬠﬠﬠﬠﬠﬠﬠﬠﬠﬠﬠﬠﬠﬠﬠﬠﬠﬠﬠﬠﬠﬠﬠﬠﬠﬠﬠ אﬠﬠﬠﬠﬠﬠﬠﬠﬠﬠﬠﬠﬠﬠﬠﬠﬠﬠﬠﬠﬠ גﬠ׳ﬠﬠﬠזﬠﬠﬠﬠﬠו וﬠﬠﬠﬠﬠﬠﬠﬠﬠﬠﬠﬠﬠﬠﬠﬠ
פﬠﬠﬠﬠﬠﬠﬠﬠﬠﬠﬠﬠﬠ דﬠﬠﬠﬠﬠﬠﬠﬠﬠﬠﬠﬠﬠﬠﬠﬠﬠﬠﬠﬠﬠﬠﬠﬠﬠﬠﬠﬠﬠﬠﬠﬠﬠﬠﬠﬠﬠﬠ, פﬠﬠﬠﬠﬠﬠﬠﬠﬠﬠﬠﬠﬠﬠ
אﬠﬠﬠﬠﬠﬠﬠﬠﬠﬠﬠﬠﬠﬠﬠﬠﬠﬠﬠﬠﬠﬠﬠﬠﬠﬠﬠﬠﬠﬠ. וﬠﬠﬠﬠﬠﬠﬠﬠﬠﬠﬠﬠ אﬠﬠﬠﬠﬠﬠﬠﬠﬠ קﬠﬠﬠ
מﬠﬠﬠﬠﬠﬠﬠﬠﬠﬠﬠﬠﬠﬠﬠ אﬠﬠﬠﬠﬠﬠﬠﬠﬠﬠﬠﬠﬠ פﬠﬠﬠﬠﬠﬠﬠﬠﬠﬠﬠﬠﬠﬠﬠﬠﬠﬠﬠﬠﬠ דﬠﬠﬠﬠﬠﬠﬠﬠﬠﬠﬠﬠﬠﬠ בﬠﬠﬠﬠﬠﬠﬠﬠﬠﬠﬠﬠﬠﬠﬠﬠﬠﬠﬠﬠﬠﬠﬠﬠ אﬠﬠﬠﬠﬠﬠﬠﬠﬠﬠﬠﬠﬠ אﬠﬠﬠﬠﬠﬠﬠﬠﬠﬠﬠﬠﬠﬠﬠﬠ אﬠﬠﬠﬠﬠﬠﬠﬠﬠﬠﬠﬠﬠﬠﬠﬠﬠﬠﬠﬠﬠﬠ [2211א] וﬠﬠﬠﬠﬠﬠﬠﬠﬠ כﬠﬠﬠﬠﬠﬠﬠﬠﬠﬠﬠﬠﬠﬠ
דﬠﬠﬠﬠﬠﬠﬠﬠﬠﬠﬠﬠﬠﬠﬠ אﬠﬠﬠﬠﬠﬠﬠﬠﬠﬠﬠﬠﬠﬠﬠﬠﬠﬠﬠﬠﬠﬠ. וﬠﬠﬠﬠﬠﬠﬠﬠﬠﬠ קﬠﬠﬠﬠﬠﬠﬠﬠﬠﬠﬠﬠﬠﬠ אﬠﬠﬠﬠﬠﬠﬠﬠﬠ קﬠﬠﬠﬠﬠﬠﬠﬠﬠﬠﬠ׳ כﬠﬠﬠﬠﬠﬠﬠﬠﬠﬠﬠﬠﬠ שﬠﬠﬠﬠﬠﬠﬠﬠﬠﬠ כﬠﬠﬠﬠﬠﬠﬠﬠﬠﬠﬠﬠﬠﬠﬠﬠﬠﬠ יﬠﬠﬠﬠﬠﬠﬠﬠﬠﬠﬠ בﬠﬠﬠﬠﬠﬠﬠﬠ
אﬠﬠﬠﬠﬠﬠﬠﬠﬠﬠﬠﬠﬠﬠﬠﬠﬠﬠﬠ הﬠﬠﬠ קﬠﬠﬠﬠﬠﬠﬠﬠﬠﬠﬠﬠﬠ מﬠﬠﬠﬠﬠﬠﬠﬠﬠﬠﬠﬠﬠﬠﬠﬠﬠﬠﬠ וﬠﬠﬠﬠﬠﬠﬠﬠﬠ הﬠﬠﬠﬠﬠﬠﬠﬠﬠﬠﬠﬠﬠﬠﬠﬠﬠﬠﬠ הﬠﬠﬠﬠﬠﬠﬠﬠﬠﬠﬠﬠﬠﬠﬠﬠﬠ עﬠﬠﬠﬠﬠﬠﬠﬠﬠﬠﬠﬠﬠﬠﬠﬠﬠﬠﬠﬠﬠﬠﬠﬠ בﬠﬠﬠﬠﬠﬠﬠﬠﬠﬠﬠﬠﬠﬠ פﬠﬠﬠﬠﬠﬠﬠﬠﬠﬠﬠﬠﬠﬠﬠﬠﬠﬠﬠﬠ
אﬠﬠﬠﬠﬠﬠﬠﬠﬠﬠﬠﬠﬠ וﬠﬠﬠﬠﬠﬠﬠﬠﬠﬠ. וﬠﬠﬠﬠﬠﬠﬠﬠﬠﬠﬠﬠ אﬠﬠﬠﬠﬠﬠﬠﬠﬠ אﬠﬠﬠﬠﬠﬠﬠﬠﬠﬠﬠﬠﬠﬠﬠﬠﬠ, פﬠﬠﬠﬠﬠﬠﬠﬠﬠﬠﬠﬠ אﬠﬠﬠﬠﬠﬠﬠﬠﬠﬠﬠﬠﬠﬠﬠﬠ תﬠﬠﬠﬠﬠﬠﬠﬠ יﬠﬠﬠﬠﬠﬠﬠﬠﬠﬠﬠﬠﬠ חﬠﬠﬠﬠﬠﬠﬠﬠﬠﬠﬠﬠﬠﬠﬠﬠﬠﬠﬠﬠ וﬠﬠﬠﬠﬠﬠﬠﬠﬠﬠﬠﬠﬠﬠﬠﬠﬠﬠﬠﬠ
מﬠﬠﬠﬠﬠﬠﬠﬠﬠﬠﬠﬠ אﬠﬠﬠﬠﬠﬠﬠﬠﬠﬠﬠ אﬠﬠﬠﬠﬠﬠﬠﬠﬠﬠﬠﬠﬠﬠ פﬠﬠﬠﬠﬠﬠﬠﬠﬠﬠﬠﬠﬠﬠﬠﬠﬠﬠﬠ אﬠﬠﬠﬠﬠﬠﬠﬠﬠﬠﬠﬠﬠﬠﬠﬠ עﬠﬠﬠﬠﬠﬠﬠﬠﬠﬠﬠﬠﬠﬠ יﬠﬠﬠﬠﬠﬠﬠﬠﬠﬠﬠﬠﬠﬠﬠﬠﬠﬠﬠ אﬠﬠﬠﬠﬠﬠﬠﬠﬠﬠﬠﬠﬠﬠﬠ אﬠﬠﬠﬠﬠﬠﬠﬠﬠﬠ אﬠﬠﬠﬠﬠﬠﬠﬠﬠ
יﬠﬠﬠﬠﬠﬠﬠﬠﬠﬠﬠﬠﬠﬠﬠﬠﬠﬠﬠﬠﬠﬠﬠ בﬠﬠﬠﬠﬠﬠﬠﬠﬠﬠﬠﬠﬠﬠﬠﬠﬠﬠﬠ וﬠﬠﬠﬠﬠﬠﬠﬠﬠﬠﬠﬠﬠﬠﬠﬠﬠﬠﬠﬠﬠﬠﬠﬠ אﬠﬠﬠﬠﬠﬠﬠﬠﬠﬠﬠﬠﬠﬠ. וﬠﬠﬠﬠﬠﬠﬠﬠﬠﬠ כﬠﬠﬠﬠﬠﬠﬠﬠﬠﬠﬠ דﬠﬠﬠﬠﬠﬠﬠﬠﬠ אﬠﬠﬠﬠﬠﬠﬠﬠﬠﬠﬠﬠﬠﬠﬠﬠ תﬠﬠﬠﬠﬠﬠﬠﬠﬠﬠﬠﬠﬠﬠﬠﬠ אﬠﬠﬠﬠﬠﬠﬠﬠﬠﬠﬠﬠﬠ וﬠﬠﬠﬠﬠﬠﬠﬠﬠﬠﬠﬠﬠﬠﬠﬠﬠﬠﬠﬠﬠﬠﬠﬠ וﬠﬠﬠﬠﬠﬠﬠﬠﬠﬠﬠﬠﬠ
יﬠﬠﬠﬠﬠﬠﬠﬠﬠﬠﬠ סﬠﬠﬠﬠﬠﬠﬠﬠﬠﬠﬠﬠ גﬠ׳ﬠﬠﬠﬠﬠﬠﬠﬠﬠﬠﬠ וﬠﬠﬠﬠﬠﬠﬠﬠﬠﬠﬠﬠﬠﬠﬠﬠﬠ גﬠ׳ﬠﬠﬠﬠﬠﬠﬠﬠ פﬠﬠﬠﬠﬠﬠﬠﬠ דﬠﬠﬠﬠﬠﬠ דﬠﬠﬠﬠﬠﬠﬠﬠﬠﬠ פﬠﬠﬠﬠﬠ מﬠﬠﬠﬠﬠﬠﬠﬠﬠﬠ אﬠﬠﬠﬠﬠﬠﬠﬠ כﬠﬠﬠﬠﬠ׳ﬠﬠﬠﬠﬠﬠﬠ כﬠﬠﬠﬠﬠﬠﬠﬠﬠ׳ כﬠﬠﬠﬠﬠﬠﬠﬠ הﬠﬠﬠﬠﬠﬠﬠﬠﬠﬠﬠﬠ
בﬠﬠﬠﬠﬠﬠﬠﬠﬠﬠ שﬠﬠﬠﬠﬠﬠﬠﬠﬠﬠ חﬠﬠﬠﬠﬠﬠﬠﬠﬠﬠﬠﬠﬠﬠﬠ וﬠﬠﬠﬠﬠﬠﬠﬠﬠﬠﬠﬠﬠﬠ חﬠﬠﬠﬠﬠﬠﬠﬠﬠﬠﬠﬠﬠﬠﬠﬠﬠﬠﬠ וﬠﬠﬠﬠﬠﬠﬠﬠﬠﬠﬠ׳ כﬠﬠﬠﬠﬠ כﬠﬠﬠﬠﬠﬠﬠﬠﬠﬠﬠ הﬠﬠﬠﬠﬠﬠﬠﬠﬠﬠﬠﬠﬠﬠﬠﬠﬠ הﬠﬠﬠﬠﬠﬠﬠﬠﬠﬠﬠﬠﬠﬠﬠﬠﬠﬠ וﬠﬠﬠﬠﬠﬠﬠ׳.
ועﬠﬠﬠﬠﬠﬠﬠﬠﬠﬠנﬠﬠﬠﬠﬠﬠﬠﬠד כﬠﬠﬠﬠﬠﬠﬠﬠﬠﬠﬠתﬠﬠﬠ׳ﬠﬠﬠﬠﬠﬠיﬠﬠﬠﬠﬠר מﬠﬠﬠﬠﬠﬠﬠﬠﬠן אﬠﬠﬠﬠﬠﬠﬠﬠﬠﬠﬠﬠלﬠﬠﬠﬠﬠﬠﬠעﬠﬠﬠﬠﬠﬠﬠﬠﬠﬠﬠﬠﬠﬠﬠﬠﬠﬠﬠלﬠﬠﬠ
וﬠﬠﬠﬠﬠﬠﬠﬠﬠיﬠﬠﬠ
כﬠﬠ.

ואלג׳ואב ען אלמסאלֵה אלתﬠאלﬠﬠﬠ

אלי פֵנא אהל אלעאלם אלא מן אטאע אללה תע כקו׳ כל הגוים כאין נגדו.
ודלך אנה ימיתהם ת׳ם ינשרהם ויעאקבהם פ׳ מוצ׳ע אלעקאב כקו׳ וארץ
רפאים תפיל. וקאל מפסר אכ׳ר פי כמו כן ימותון אלעקאב מתל החפץ
אחפץ מות הרשע׳ פערף אן פי וקת אצ׳מחלאל אלסמא ואלארץ׳ יכון עקאב
רשעי עולם.

ואלג׳ואב ען אלמסאלה אלראבעה פי מעני הדה אלסמא ותג׳דיד בדלהא קיל
פי דלך וג׳וה. אחד׳ הו אן אן למא כאן כת׳יר מן אלאמם יחילו חדת אלעאלם
ואנה קדים, ומנהם מן ירי אן אלכואכב מדברה. פלמא כאן פיהם מן יעתקד
הדה אלמדאהב ונט׳ראהא ראי ג׳ל ועלא בחכמתה אן יעדמהא ויג׳דד בדלהא
ליפסד מדאהבהם ויבטל אעתקאדאתהם ויצחח כ׳ברנא. ומנהא אנה כ׳לק אללה
תע אלסמא ואלארץ׳ פי ששת ימי בראשית עלי תרתיב כמא קד עלמה אנה
יג׳ב לאהל אלזמאן אלדי קד יעצונה ויטיעונה. פאמא דור ישועה אלדי עלם
אנהם לא יעצונה יכ׳לק שמים [212א] וארץ עלי תרתיב יוג׳בה חכמתה חסב
אפעאלהם, פתכון אלנעם דארה גזירה — ותטול אעמאר אלנאס לאאתדאל
אלהוא וממאזג׳ה אלכואכב. ומנהא אנה למא כאנת שמי בראשית וארץ
בראשית כ׳לקת לדאר אלעמל לא לדאר אלג׳זא ואראד אללה עז וג׳ל אן
יג׳על אלזמאן אלמנתט׳ר דאר אלמכאפאה, כ׳לק שמים וארץ אלדי יצלח
ללג׳זא. פלהדה אלוג׳וה ואכת׳ר מנהא יעדם שמים וארץ ויג׳דד בדלהא,
פליס מן פעל אללה תע שי אלא והו חכמה פי וקתה כקו׳ את הכל עשה יפה
בעתו. והדא יג׳רי מג׳רי אלחיאה ואלמות ואלליל ואלנהאר ומא שאכל דלך
מן אלתגייראת אלדי כל דלך פעל חַכִים. וקו׳ וישועתי לעולם ערף אן
אלסמא ואלארץ׳ תתלאשא ואלצדקה ואלישועה באקיתאן, ודאך בוג׳וד
שמים חדשים וארץ חדשה כקו׳ פי מוצ׳ע אכ׳ר כן יעמד זרעכם
ושמכם. פאלצדקה הי אלתורה, פערף אנהא לא תנדער כמא אנדערת פי
זמאן עָבַר כקו׳ על כן תפוג תורה.

יפת לישעיה ס״ה, ט״ז, שם, דף 340ב

הדא אלפסוק יערפנא דכ׳ול אהל אלעאלם באסרהם פי אלדין. ודלך אן מן
שאן כל אמה תתבארך במעבודהא ותחלף באסמה. פאדא קאל יתברך באלהי
אמן מן חית׳ אן מעבודאת אלגוים ה׳ תמאת׳יל וצור מכ׳לוקה פליס הי
מסתחקה ללעבאדה. וקו׳ כי נשכחו הצרות ישיר בה אלי אלצרות אלתי
כאנת תג׳רי עלי אלאמם בעצ׳ה מן בעץ׳ מן אג׳ל אכ׳תלאף אלמדאהב. פאדא
צאר אלמדהב ואחד עברת וזאלת אלצרות מן אלעאלם. והדא הו נט׳יר קו׳
לא ישא גוי אל גוי חרב. ופי קו׳ וכי נסתרו יפידנא אנעדאמהא מן
אלעאלם באסרה. ונט׳ם הדא אלפסוק אלי מא תקדם ליובך בה אלרשעים
אלדי קאל להם ואתם עזבי יוי השכחים את הר קדשי. ופי דכרה אשר

המתברך ג׳מע פיה אלנעמה̈ ואלמדהב. והמא אצלין יג׳אמען כל מא יחתאג׳
אליה אלעקל.

יפת לישעיה ל׳ כ״ו (מיספור כתב היד מבולבל)
ודכר פי הדא אלמוצ׳ע קו̈ה תצ׳אעף האדין אלמנירין ופי מוצ׳ר אכ׳ר אנה
יחדת̈ שמים חדשים וארץ חדשה [...] אלגרץ̇ פיה אג̇תמאע נור ז׳ איאם
מת̄ל סבע סרג׳ תג̇תמע אנוארהא. פהאדא ידל עלי תצ׳אעף קו̈ה נורהא לא
שי סואה.

יפת לישעיה ס״ה, י״ז, שם, דף 341א—ב
כי הנני בורא... על לב
פאן הודאני כ̇אלק סמא ג׳דיד וארץ̇ ג׳דידה̈ ולא תדכרן אלקדימה̈ ולא
תצעדן עלי אלקלב.

קאל כי הנני ליג׳עלה כלאמא מתעלקא במא קבלה. והו אנה ערּף אן זואל
אלמדאהב תכון בזואל אלסמא ואלארץ̇ וט̇הור אלדין ואלתוחיד מע ט̇הור
שמים חדשים וארץ חדשה. ודלך אן אהל אלעאלם אדא תחקקו אנעדאם
האדין אלטבקתין חדות שמים חדשים ת̇בّת ענדהם חדת אלעאלם ואן לה
כ̇אלק כ̇לקה ויפסד ענדהם מדהב מן יקול בקדם אלעאלם וסאיר אלמדאהב
אלתי הי צ̇ד אלתורה. וקד כנא שרחנא פי שאו לשמים עיניכם כיף
תנעדם הדה ותחדת גירהא ולא ינעדם מא בינהמא. וקו׳ ולא תזכרנה
הראשונות ישיר בה אלי אלמכ̇לוקה̈ פי ששת ימי בראשית. וליס קו׳
ולא תזכרנה עלי כל וג׳ה, ומעני דלך לאן אלתורה יג[דיל] ויא[דיר]
מוג׳ודה̈ פי מא ביננא ונקראהא. ואנמא יקצד בה למעני. והו אפעאל תלך קד
אנקצ̇ת ואפעאל אלחדשים הי הי מוג׳ודה̈. ולנא נט̇יר הדא, והו קו׳ ולא
יאמרו עוד ארון ברית יוי וג׳. ולים נעתקד אן ארון ברית יוי ינעדם
מן אלעאלם ולא ידכר ואנמא קצד בה מעני, והו אן כאן פי קדים אלזמאן
יוכ̇ד אלארון מעהם פי וקת אלחרב. ופי עתיד יבטל אלחרב מן אלעאלם
פלהדא קאל ולא יאמרו עוד ארון ברית יוי וג׳. וכדלך דכר פי אלפסוק
אלאול זואל אלמסבבאת לאכ̇תלאף אלמדאהב ודכר פי הדא אלפסוק שמים
חדשים וזואל אלמתקדמה̈ ליבטל מדהב מן יקול בקדם אלעאלם.

יפת לישעיה ס״ו, כ״ב, שם, דף 358ב—359א
כי כאשר... ושמכם
פאן מת̇ל אלסמאואת אלג׳דידה̈ ואלארץ̇ אלג׳דידה̈ אלתי אנא פאעל
ת̇אבתה̈ קדאמי כדאף̇ ית̇בת נסלכם ואסמכם.

קד תקדם אלקול פי שאו לשמים עיניכם מעני שמים חדשים וארץ

חדשה. וקו׳ עמדים לפני אורא ת׳באתהא, ת׳ם ג׳על ת׳באת ישראל מקרון
בת׳באת אלסמא ואלארץ׳ כמא סנשרח פי אם ימושו החקים. וקאל זרעכם
ושמכם והו זרע ישראל כמא קאל גם זרע ישראל ישבתו. וקאל
ושמכם יריד בה אלדולה. פאקרן בקא נסלהם ודולתהם בבקא שמים חדשים
וארץ חדשה לא מת׳ל זמאן עבר אלתי אנקלבת כל אלאחואל אלסנייה אלי
צ׳דהא.

יפת לתה׳ ק״ב, כ״ז (כ״י פאריס 288, דף 195א—ב)

המה יאבדו יריד בה אן הדה אלשמים ואלארץ׳ יצ׳מחלו ויג׳דד אללה סמא
אכ׳רי וארץ׳ אכ׳רי כך כי שמים כעשן נמלחו וג׳. וקאל יאבדו במעני
אלתגייר פיהא והי זלאזל ומילאן פיכ׳רב כת׳יר מן אלמואצ׳ע ותתסאקט
אלכואכב ותנכסף, ולדלך קאל כבגד יבלו. וקו׳ כלבוש תחליפם ויחלפו
ישיר בה אלי אלשמים חדשים וארץ חדשה אלדי יעמ̈ר אללה עאלמה
ויפג׳ר אלעיון פי אלבראארי וינבת פיהא אלאשג׳אר, וכדלך יזיד פי נור
אלשמס ואלקמר כך והיה אור הלבנה כאור החמה ואור החמה יהיה
שבעתים וג׳. קו׳ ואתה הוא ושנותיך בעד קולה המה יאבדו פיה אחד
קולין. אמא אן יכון יריד בה אנת אלדי כ׳לקתהם ואנת אלדי תפניהם ואנת
אלבאקי. ואמא אן יכון יריד בה אן כל מעבוד הו דונך יזול מעתגייר שמים
וארץ ואנת וחדך אלדאים לא תזול ולא תחול. וקו׳ ושנותיך לא יתמו
מענאה הו אנך אלבאקי לא אול לך. ויחתמל אנה יריד בה סנין עבאדתך
ופרג׳ך לא אנקצ׳א להא. ת׳ם ערֿף אנה כמא עבאדתה דאימא לא יעבד גירה
כדאך זרע ישראל הם אלדין יסכנון ארץ הקדושה ויכ׳רג׳ מנהא אעדאהם
כקו׳ מהרו בניך מהרסיך ומחריביך וג׳...

*

נמצאנו למדים שאחרי הבאת כל מיני טענות ופירושים שונים בא לבסוף
הפרשן הקראי לידי דעה לפיה לא תחול באחרית הימים אפיסה קוסמית
מוחלטת שאין אחריה תקומה, וכן עמדתו מתאימה עקרונית לזו המובעת
בבר״ר א׳, י״ד ובתנחומא (ב׳) בראשית, וגם אצל רס״ג.

נ. ב. עלי להעיר שהמאמר דלעיל נמסר למערכת ה-PAAJR קודם שבאה
לידי עבודת הדוקטור המצויינת והמעמיקה של חגאי בן-שמאי ״שיטות המח-
שבה הדתית של אבו יוסף יעקוב אלקרקסאני ויפת בן עלי״ (חשון תשל״ח);
עיין שם, חלק ב׳ עמ׳ ריא—ריד.

ברייתא חמורה המפיצה אור על תולדות הסנהדרין

מאת אליעזר ארי׳ הלוי פינקלשטין

א

שנינו בתוספתא סנהדרין ריש פ״ח (הוצ׳ צוקרמנדל עמ׳ 427), ״כל סנהדרין
שיש בה שנים יודעין לדבר וכולן ראויין לשמוע ראויה סנהדרי׳.
שלשה בינונית, ארבעה חכמה״.

כבר הזהיר בעל חסדי דוד שאין לדחות ברייתא זו כמשובשת שהרי היא
מובאה בירו׳ שקלים פ״ה ה״א, מ״ח ע״ד, ששם שנינו ״סנהדרין שיש בה
שנים שיודעין לדבר וכולן ראויין לשמוע הרי זו ראויה לסנהדרין. ג׳ הרי זו
בינונית, ארבעה הרי זו חכמה. וביבנה היו בה ארבעה, בן עזאי, ובן זומא, ובן
חכינאי, ור״א בן מתיה״. [במהד׳ הר״א סופר, עמ׳ 57, הגירסא ״בן עזאי ובן
זומא, ואלעזר בן מתיא, וחנניא בן חנילא״].

מן המקבילה בירושלמי ומפשוטם של הדברים משמע כי מדובר כאן
בסנהדרין הגדולה, והיא בית הדין המרכזי לישראל. הדברים מתמיהים. כיצד
ניתן לומר שהתקיימה סנהדרין בישראל שהיו בה רק שנים, שלושה, או
ארבעה שידעו לדבר? וכיצד יש לומר על סנהדרין שנמצאים בה ארבעה
היודעים לדבר שהיא חכמה? וכיצד אפשר להתאים דברים אלה עם מסורת ר׳
יוסי על תכונות חברי הסנהדרין ואופן מנוים (תוספתא חגיגה פ״ב ה״ט, מהד׳
הגר״ש ליברמן עמ׳ 384 ובמקבילות)?

נראה שרב תמה על ברייתא זו, ביארה והגיה אותה, וזהו שאמר (סנהדרין
י״ז, ב׳): ״כל עיר שאין בה שנים לדבר ואחד לשמוע אין מושיבין בה
סנהדרי. ובביתר היו שלושה. וביבנה ארבעה, ר׳ אליעזר, ור׳ יהושע, ור״ע,
ושמעון התימני דן לפניהם בקרקע״. הקשו עליו מברייתא המקבילה לתוספתא
הנ״ל, ששנו בה ״שלישית חכמה, רביעית אין למעלה הימנה״, ותירצו
מברייתא אחרת שבה נאמר ״שניה חכמה, שלישית אין למעלה הימנה״. פירש
רש״י שמדובר בסנהדרין הגדולה ו״יודעין לדבר״ (ובדברי רב ״לדבר״)
פירושו לדבר בשבעים לשון. אך מדברי הרמב״ם (ה׳ סנהדרין פ״א, ו׳) ברור
שהוא פירש את דברי רב (וכן כנראה את הברייתא בתוספתא שאף עליה סמך)
כמכוונים לבית דין מקומי, ולפיו ״יודעים לדבר״ משמעותו — ״יודעים
לשאת ולתת בכל מקצועות התורה״. לכאורה שני הפירושים דחוקים, ועי׳

המו״מ בספר מרגליות הים להרב ראובן מרגליות, סנהדרין, שם, ומה
שהביא מן הראשונים.

מן הנוסח בתוספתא מוכח לכאורה שמדובר בסנהדרין הגדולה, ופירוש
הדברים כי אין צורך שיהיו כל חברי הסנהדרין בקיאים בכל דיני התורה
ויודעים לשאת ולתת בהם, אלא די בשנים היודעים את התורה והאחרים
ראויים להבין. אם היו שלושה, נקראת סנהדרין ״בינונית״, ואם היו ארבעה
הרי היא ״חכמה״. וכך, כנראה, פירשו את הברייתא בירושלמי שקלים הנ״ל.
הזכירו בה יבנה ושם היתה סנהדרין גדולה, אלא שלפי הירושלמי היו
הארבעה בסנהדרין ביבנה כולם תלמידים שהגיעו להוראה, מן הצעירים
שבדור. ויש לתמוה שלא הזכירו את רבן גמליאל, ר׳ אליעזר, ר׳ יהושע, ר׳
יוסי הגלילי, ור׳ עקיבא שהיו גדולי הדור. ונראה שכבר רב תמה על כך ולכן
שנה ״ר׳ אליעזר, ר׳ יהושע, ור״ע, ושמעון התימני דן לפניהם בקרקע״.

כאמור, מוכח מן הברייתא המקורית בתוספתא סנהדרין — שהיא שימשה
מקור לברייתא המאוחרת המובאה בירושלמי שקלים וכן לדברי רב — כי
המדובר בסנהדרין הגדולה היושבת בלשכת הגזית.

בראשית התקופה ההליניסטית היו חכמי הסנהדרין לרוב ראשי בתי אבות
הכהנים והמשפחות המיוחסות בישראל, כפי שהוכיח כבר א. צ׳ריקובר (ספר
״ארץ ישראל״, כרך א׳, תשי״א, עמ׳ 99). הם ירשו את סמכותם של הסגנים
והחורים הנזכרים תכופות בס׳ נחמי׳. בתקופה ההליניסטית נקראה מועצתם
״גירוסיה״.

נראה שבזמנם של החשמונאים הראשונים, ואולי אף קודם לכן, בזמנו של
שמעון הצדיק, שהצטרף ל״כנסת הגדולה״ של הפרושים, הוסיפו על ראשי
בתי האבות הנ״ל חכמי פרושים אחדים, לפעמים שנים, לפעמים שלושה,
ולפעמים ארבעה.

על סנהדרין מתוקנת כזו מדובר בתוספתא סנהדרין הנ״ל. לפי דעת הפרו־
שים, כמובן, רק חכמיהם שצורפו לסנהדרין היו בבחינת ״יודעין לדבר״,
כלומר ידעו לשאת ולתת בהלכה. שאר חברי הסנהדרין היו רק ״ראויין
לשמוע״, להאזין למשא ומתן, להכריע בין הדנים בשעת הדחק, ולגזור את
הדין על פיהם.

הפרושים הסכימו אז, תמורת צירופם אחדים מהם לסנהדרין הגדולה, להכיר
בסמכותו של בית דין זה בכמה מקצועות של ההלכה שנפרטו בספרי דברים,
פי׳ קנב׳ (עמ׳ 205 ואילך, ובמקבילות), אבל לא בהלכות טומאה וטרפה (חוץ
מדיני נגעים שהיו ברשות הכהנים) ולא בעניני איסור והיתר, ולא בהלכות
אישות, שלא נזכרו שם אפילו ברמז (ועי׳ מה שכתבתי בפירוש אותה ברייתא
בס׳ השנתי ל״היברו יונין קוליג׳ ״, כרך ל״ב (1961) עמ׳ 1 ואילך).

החכם מן הפרושים שנצטרף אל הסנהדרין נקרא ״מופלא של ב״ד״. וכן

צירפו לבתי הדין הנמוכים המקומיים חכם פרושי אחד, שידע לשאת ולתת
בהלכה, וגם הוא נקרא ״מופלא של ב״ד״, ונזכר תכופות בספרות התלמודית.
בדורות מאוחרים כאשר כל חברי הסנהדרין היו חכמי ישראל, בקיאים
במסורת הפרושים, עדיין נתקיים הנוהג שאחד מהם יהיה מופלא; וזה היה
הכרח בהרבה בתי דין מקומיים, שלא היו בהם שלושה חכמים. סמכו אז על
המסורת ומינו מופלא, שהיה בקי בתורה, וצירפו לו אנשים אחרים שידעו
לשמוע, ברם לא היה בידם לשאת ולתת בתורה.[1]

בהמשך הדברים נסביר כי הפרושים לפני שהצטרפו לסנהדרי׳ הגדולה התנו
כנראה תנאים על אופן קבלת החלטות כדי למנוע מבית דין זה להכריע נגד
ההלכה המקובלת בידם.

אפשר שראשי אבות הכהנים והמשפחות המיוחסות בישראל, כאשר באו
להסכם עם חכמי הפרושים על הצטרפותם של אחדים מחכמי הפרושים
לסנהדרי׳ הגדולה מצאו סמך לדבר במסופר על יהושפט מלך יהודה שהעמיד
שופטים בארץ ״וגם בירושלים העמיד יהושפט מן הלוים והכהנים ומראשי
האבות לישראל למשפט ד׳ ולריב וישבו ירושלים״ (דה״ב י״ב, ט׳) — והם היו
בית הדין הגדול. לפי זה נתחברו חברי בית דין של המקדש, שמקודם היו רק
מראשי בתי אבות הכהנים ומראשי בתי אבות שבישראל, עם נציגי הלויים
והכהנים של השכבות הנמוכות, כלומר חכמים מן הלויים ומן הכהנים (דרך
אגב נעיר כי השבעים תרגמו כאן ״וְיֵשְׁבוּ״ כאילו היה כתוב ״וַיֵּשְׁבוּ״).

ב

על פי הסבר היסטורי זה, שבתחילה היה בית הדין הגדול מורכב מראשי אבות
הכהנים והמשפחות המיוחסות בישראל ולאחר מכן הוסכם לצרף אליהם כמה
מחכמי הפרושים, יתבארו לנו הרבה ברייתות ומשניות (ביחוד במסכת הוריות)
שלכאורה אין להן פתרון.

שנינו בירו׳ סנהדרין, פי״א, ה״ד (ל׳, ע״א) על הפסוק (דברים י״ז, ח׳) כי
יפלא ממך דבר למשפט בין דם לדם בין דין לדין בין נגע לנגע
דברי ריבות בשעריך וקמת ועלית אל המקום אשר יבחר ד׳ א׳ בו,
״ועלית זו העלייה״. פירש בפני משה ״ועלית משמעותו שיעלו״. וקשה
מאד לפירושו, מה הוסיף התנא על הנאמר בכתוב? ועוד הובא שם מיד: ״ד״א
ועלית, מיכן לבית הבחירה שלא יבנה אלא בגובהו של עולם״. הרי ברור
שנחלקו התנאים אם בנאמר ועלית הכוונה לבית הבחירה, כלומר לסנהדרין
של לשכת הגזית, או לא. על כן היה נראה לבאר ״זו העלייה״ — היא העלייה

[1] ביחס להוראת המונח ״מופלא״, ראה לאחרונה את מאמרו של צבי ארי׳ שטיינפלד,
סיני, שנה מ״ה (תשל״ח), כרך פ״ב, עמ׳ כ״ד ואילך, והספרות שציין שם; ועי׳ מה
שבארתי להלן בהמשך מאמר זה.

שבית דינם של חכמי הפרושים היה מתאסף בה בירושלים בימים קדומים,
כשם שהיה בית דין המרכזי של חכמי הפרושים מתאסף בעלייה בדורות
מאוחרים (עי׳ שבת פ״א מ״ד: "ואלו מן ההלכות שאמרו בעליית חנני׳ בן
חזקי׳ " וכו׳ ובתוספתא, שם, פ״א הט״ז, מהד׳ הגר״ש ליברמן עמ׳ 4, ובכלי
שבת י״ג ע״ב ובמקבילות; ואחרי החורבן, ירו׳ פסחים, פ״ג, ה״ז, ל׳ ע״ב:
"שכבר נמנו וגמרו בעליית בית אריס בלוד", ועי״ש חגיגה פ״א, ה״ז, פ״ו
ע״ג; בשיר השירים ר׳, פ״ב ס״י י״ד, הגי׳ "בית עליית (עריס) בלוד", ועי׳
תוספתא כפשוטה, שבת עמ׳ 30, בב׳ קידושין מ׳ ע״א: "עליית בית נתזה
בלוד"; ועי׳ סנהדרין י״א, ע״א, שנתאספו בעלייה לשם דיון בעיבור השנה;
ושם, ע״ד ע״א, כי בעליית בית נתזה בלוד נמנו וגמרו שעל כל עבירות
שבתורה יעבור ואל יהרג, חוץ מע״ז, גילוי עריות ושפיכות דמים; ובמנחות
מ״א, ע״ב: "וכבר עלו זקני ב״ש וזקני ב״ה לעליית יוחנן בן בתירא" וכו׳;
והשווה עוד מ׳ ראש השנה, פ״ב, מ״ח: "דמות צורות לבנות היו לו לרבן
גמליאל בטבלא ובכותל בעלייתו שבהן מראה את ההדיוטות ואומר כזה ראית
או כזה", משמע שקיבל עדות החודש בעלייה).

כעין שיטת הברייתא בירו׳ הנ״ל אנו מוצאים במדרש תנאים י״ז ח׳ (עמ׳
102): "וקמת ועלית, מגיד שסנהדרין בגובהה של עיר". המלה עיר כאן
משמעה ירושלים; ולכאורה בית דין של הפרושים צריך להתאסף בגובהה של
ירושלים.

הברייתות שלפיהן פונה הנבוך בעניין הלכה אל ה"עלייה", מקורן כנראה
בדורות שלפני שמעון הצדיק, שעדיין לא הכירו הפרושים כלל בסמכותה של
הגרוסיה היושבת בלשכת הגזית ושנקראה בדורות אחרונים סנהדרין של
לשכת הגזית.

ג

לפי האמור מתבארת לנו המשנה הראשונה בהוריות: "הורו בית דין לעבור על
אחת מכל מצות האמורות בתורה, והלך היחיד ועשה שוגג על פיהם, בין שעשו
ועשה עמהם, בין שעשו ועשה אחריהם; בין שלא עשו ועשה, פטור, מפני
שתלה בבית דין. הורו בית דין וידע אחד מהן שטעו או תלמיד והוא ראוי
להוראה, והלך ועשה על פיהן, בין שעשו ועשה עמהן, בין שעשו ועשה
אחריהן, בין שלא עשו ועשה, חייב מפני שלא תלה בב״ד."

הדברים תמוהים. בתו״כ חובה, ריש פרשה ד׳, מבואר שבעניייני הוריות
המדובר ב"העדה המיוחדת שבישראל, ואיזו זו? זו סנהדרי גדולה היושבת
בלשכת הגזית". וכן היא גם שיטת החכמים במשנתנו (הוריות, סוף פ״א).
וקשה, הרי לפי מסורת ר׳ יוסי בתוספתא חגיגה הנ״ל, שקיבל אותה רבי
במשנתנו (סנהדרין פי״א מ״ב), תורה יוצאה מבית דין זה לכל ישראל; ואיך

ניתן לומר עליהם שירוו לעבור על אחת מכל מצות האמורות בתורה? ואיך
אפשר לומר עליהם שהם יטעו, הלא מסקנותיהם והכרעותיהם אין לחלוק
עליהן, והן תורה. ועוד קשה סגנון המשנה ששנתה "וידע אחד מהן שטעו";
הלא במו"מ של תורה עסקינן; ואם אמנם אפשר שאחד מחברי ב"ד חשב או
החליט שחבריו טועים, איך יש לומר עליו שהוא יודע?

נראה שמשנה זו נשנתה בזמנים קדומים, כאשר חברי הסנהדרין כולם היו
ראשי בתי אבות. מלמדת אותנו המשנה שיחיד מן השוק שטעה ועשה כדברי־
הם, אף בהוראה שהיא בניגוד לקבלת הפרושים, פטור. אנוס הוא, שאין עליו
לדעת כי לבית דין זה אין שום סמכות. אבל אם אחד מחברי הבית דין עצמו
(שידועות לו הלכות הפרושים) או תלמיד שהגיע להוראה ידע שטעו, חייב,
שעליו לדעת שכאשר סנהדרין של לשכת הגזית, באותם הימים, פוסקת נגד
קבלת הפרושים, אין הוראתם הוראה כלל. ואם טעה לחשוב שאף כשהם דנים
בניגוד לדברי חכמים, יש לשמוע להם, מפני שהם יושבים בבית המקדש, חייב
חטאת.

ד

שנינו בתוספתא הוריות, פ"א, ה"ב (הוצ' צוקרמנדל עמ' 474): "הורו בית דין
ואחד מהן אין שם פטורין. רבי אומר אני עד שיהא מופלא שבהן". במשנתנו
(הוריות, פ"א, מ"ד) שנה רבי לשיטתו "או שלא היה מופלא של בית דין
שם", וכן הגירסה בתו"כ חובה, פרשה ד' ה"ד, "לא היה מופלא של ב"ד שם".
אך ברור שבתו"כ הוגהה הברייתא על פי דברי רבי, ובתו"כ המקורית גרסו
"לא היה אחד מהם שם" כמו בתוספתא, שהרי סיום אותה ברייתא בתו"כ הוא
"יכול יהו חייבין ת"ל עדת ישראל ישגו עד שיורו כולם", ממש כדברי
התוספתא.

וקשה, איך אפשר לומר שאם הורו רוב בית דין להתיר או לטהר, ומיעוטם
אסרו או טימאו, או אפילו רק אחד איסר או טימא — שהוראת הרוב אינה
הוראה?

אלא ברור שנשתמרו במסכת הוריות, וכן בתו"כ חובה פרשה ד', הלכות
שנשנו בזמנים שונים, יש מהן מדורות שלפני שמעון הצדיק, יש מהן מזמנו,
מזמנם של יאסון ומיניליאוס הכהנים הגדולים המתיוונים ומזמנם של החשמו־
נאים, ויש מהן מאוחרות יותר.

ההלכות במשנתנו (הוריות, פ"א, מ"ד) בתוספתא (שם פ"א ה"ב) ובתו"כ
הנ"ל משקפות את המצב לאחר צירופם של אחדים מחכמי הפרושים לסנהדרי
הגדולה בימי החשמונאים הראשונים או אולי קודם לכן בימי שמעון הצדיק,
כפי שאמרנו לעיל. אז, בשעה שהצטרפו חכמי הפרושים לבית הדין הגדול
שבמקדש, הסכימו שכל הוראה צריכה להיות על דעת כולם. ואם אחד מהם

נעדר, או שאמר טועים אתם, או אמר איני יודע, אין הוראתם הוראה. לאור
הסכמה זו שוב לא היה מקום לחשוש כי הסנהדרין, אם כי ברובה הגדול היתה
מורכבת מאנשים שלא היו פרושים, תפסוק בניגוד למסורת הפרושים, כי
החכם הפרושי וודאי יתנגד להוראה כזו והיא תתבטל.

ברם, כשהוצרכו הסנהדרין לדון דיני נפשות, שלא נתקיימו בהם מחלוקות
בהוראה בין הצדוקים והפרושים והיה רק צורך להחליט אם הנאשם חייב או
לא, הלכו אחרי הרוב, כמבואר בתוספתא הוריות, פ״א, ה״ג.[2]

שנינו בהוריות (פ״א מ״ג): ״הורו ב״ד לעקור את כל הגוף, אמרו אין נדה
בתורה, אין שבת בתורה, אין עבודה זרה בתורה הרי אלו פטורין [מפר העלם
דבר של ציבור, שאין הוראתם הוראה]. הורו לבטל מקצת ולקיים מקצת, הרי
אילו חייבין״.

וכעין זה בתוספתא שם (פ״א ה״ז, הוצ׳ צוקרמנדל עמ׳ 474): ״הורו ב״ד
לעקור את כל הגוף אמרו אין דם בתורה, אין חלב בתורה, אין פיגול בתורה,
הרי אילו פטורין. הורו לבטל מקצת ולקיים מקצת הרי אילו חייבין; כיצד יש
דם בתורה אבל אין חייבין אלא על הדם הקרב שלמים, [יש חלב בתורה אבל
אין חייבין אלא על חלב שלשלמים — נמצא בד״ר ובכת״י ווינא, אבל נשמט
מכת״י ארפורט ע״י הדומות] יש פיגול בתורה אבל אין חייבין אלא על פיגול
של שלמים הרי אילו חייבין״.

ויש לתמוה, וכי בתינוקות של בית רבן עסקינן שיאמרו אין נדה בתורה, אין
שבת בתורה, אין עבודה זרה בתורה, אין דם בתורה וכדומה?

אלא ברור שהמשנה והברייתא דתוספתא מדברות על סנהדרין של המתייוו־
נים, כי אז אפשר ואפשר היה שהיא תפסוק כי אין נדה בתורה, אין דם בתורה,
אין שבת בתורה, ואפילו אין עבודה זרה בתורה (ואם נניח שכבר בימי שמעון
הצדיק צירפו אחדים מחכמי הפרושים לסנהדרין, אין ספק שבימי המתייוונים
נדחו הפרושים מן הסנהדרין או פרשו ממנה מעצמם).

נראה שבאותם הדורות נשנה גם החלק השני של משנה הוריות, פ״א, מ״ד,

<hr />

[2] דעת רבי היא שהתנאי שהתנו חכמי הפרושים בדבר העדרו של אחד מן הישיבה
התיחס רק למופלא שבהם, כלומר למי שמסר את ההלכה, המפלפל בה ופוסק אותה,
כמו שביארו בבראשית רבה פ׳ ע׳, אות ח׳ (מהד׳ תיאודור־אלבק עמ׳ 807). ואם אחד
מן המופלאים, זאת אומרת, מחכמי הפרושים נעדר מן הישיבה אין הוראת הסנהדרין
של לשכת הגזית הוראה כלל.
גם לפי דעת החכמים החולקים על רבי היה תנאי חכמי הפרושים בדבר העדרו של
אחד מן הישיבה מכוון בעיקר להעדר אחד מחכמיהם הם. אך לפי דעת החכמים
הציבו חכמי הפרושים תנאי זה באופן כללי — כי ההוראה צריכה להיות על דעת כולם, כדי
שלא להבליט כי עיקר חיתוך הדין תלוי במופלא והאחרים אינם אלא שומעים.

"או שהיה אחד מהן גר או ממזר או נתין או זקן שלא ראה לו בנים הרי אילו
פטורין" שאין הורואתם הוראה (בתו״כ חובה פרשה ד׳ ה״ג נשנית הלכה זו
כבבא בפני עצמה, לפני הבבא של "אמר להן אחד טוען אתם וכו׳ ").

כבר הקשה בעזרת כהנים שם, איך אירע שמינו גר או ממזר בסנהדרין?
בירו׳ הוריות, פ״א, ה״ד, מ״ו, ע״א, אמרו: "ניחא גר. ממזר? ב״ד ממנין
ממזרין?" מבארי הירושלמי נדחקו מאד להשוותו עם הבבלי שלפיו אין
מושיבים גר בסנהדרין לדברי הכל. בעל פני משה רצה לומר כי אין
מושיבים גר בסנהדרין לדון דיני נפשות, אך ראוי לדון דיני ממונות, ועל כן
אפשר שישב לשם כך בסנהדרין הגדולה. אחרים תירצו "גר משכחת ליה שלא
ידעו, אלא ממזר לא משכחת ליה כשלא ידעו" (עי׳ גליון אפרים שם). ואין
צורך להדגיש את הדוחק שבפירושים אלה.

נראה שלפי הירושלמי היתה קיימת מסורת אחת שלפיה מותר להושיב גר
בסנהדרין,[3] והירושלמי מניח שמשמשנתנו היא לפי שי־טת האומרים שאין
מושיבים גר בסנהדרין. ולפיה סנהדרין שישב בה גר אין הורואתה הוראה;
ואילו שמינו את הגר סברו שכן מושיבים גר בסנהדרין. אך תמה הירושלמי,
היכן מצינו שמושיבים ממזר בסנהדרין? התשובה, שעברו ומינו.

ויש לתמוה על תירוץ הירושלמי, וכי בעבריינים עסקינן? אלא בווודאי לפי
הירושלמי מדובר במשנתנו בסנהדרין שקדמה לזמנו של שמעון הצדיק, או
בסנהדרין של המתיוונים, אשר בין חבריה היו כאלה שהוחזקו אצל חכמי
ישראל, והם חכמי הפרושים, כגרים וכממזרים. אצל חבריהם הוחזקו ככשרים
והם מינו אותם. לכן לפי חכמי הפרושים לא היתה הוראת הסנהדרין, אשר היו
בה חברים כאלה, הוראה.

כבר תמה רש״י, הוריות שם, על דברי המשנה "זקן שלא ראה לו בנים"
(כג׳ המשנה במשניות והמשנה בירושלמי, וכן בתו״כ כת״י רומי ב׳),
"וקשיא לי מפני מה אין ראוי להוראה?" בב׳ סנהדרין ל״ו ע״ב גרסינן "אין

[3] יש כנראה הד בדברי החכמים של הדורות המאוחרים לחילוקי הדעות אם מושיבים
גר בסנהדרין. גרסינן בספרי במדבר פי׳ ע״ח (עמ׳ 73): "ר׳ יהושע אומר וכי גרים
נכנסים להיכל והלא כל ישראל לא נכנסו להיכל? אלא שהיו יושבים בסנהדרין
ומורים בדברי תורה". ומובא ברש״י סנהדרין ק״ד ע״א, ד״ה "המה הקינים...". וכן
אמר ר׳ יוחנן בבבלי, שם, שבני בניו של יתרו זכו וישבו בלשכת הגזית. ועוד בספרי
הנ״ל: "תרעתים על שם שהיו יושבים בפתח שערי ירושלים", ששם יושב בית
הדין.
אולם במכילתא דר״י, יתרו, מסכתא דעמלק פרשה ב׳ (עמ׳ 200) מובא הסיפור על
הקינים, אך נשמט כל זכר ישיבתם בסנהדרין, וכן באדר״נ נ״א פל״ה לא הובאו דברי
ר׳ יהושע, וכן לא הובאה לא במכילתא דר״י, לא במכילתא דרשב״י ולא באדר״נ
הדרשה על תרעתים שהיו יושבים בפתח שערי ירושלים. בספרי זוטא, עמ׳ 265, נזכר
רק שישבו על שערי בית המדרש, ולא בשערי ירושלים.

מושיבין בסנהדרין זקן וסריס ומי שאין לו בנים״. פירש שם רש״י ז״ל:
״זקן, ששכח כבר צער גידול בנים ואינו רחמני, וכן סריס״ (ועי׳ במרגליות
הים להרב ראובן מרגליות, מה שהביא מן הראשונים בנידון זה). בתוספתא
סנהדרין פ״ז ה״ה (הוצ׳ צוקרמנדל עמ׳ 426) הגירסה היא: ״הסריס ומי שלא
ראה לו בנים כשר לדון דיני ממונות, ואין כשר לדון דיני נפשות״.

והנראה בזה שחשדו חכמי הפרושים בזקן שלא ראה לו בנים מעולם, שמא
הוא פצוע דכא או כרות שפכה.[4] ומכיוון שאינו ראוי לבוא בקהל הרי אינו
ראוי להצטרף לסנהדרין הגדולה. לפי זה מתבאר למה נזכר זקן שלא ראה לו
בנים יחד עם סריס: חשדו חכמי ישראל שהמתיוונים יושיבו בסנהדרין אנשים
כאלה.

לאחר שניצחו החשמונאים את היוונים בוודאי הוציאו מן הסנהדרין כל אלה
שנחשדו שהם גרים, ממזרים, נתינים, וכו׳, והחליטו כי כל הוראה שיצאה
מב״ד המתיוונים לא היתה הוראה, כי השתתפו בו פסולים; ולכן אין להביא פר
העלם דבר של ציבור על הוראותיהם, אפילו אם כל חברי הסנהדרין הסכימו
להוראותיהם, ואפילו עשו רוב הציבור כהוראותיהם. אלא כל יחיד ויחיד היה
חייב להביא כשבה או שעירה אעפ״י שעשה ע״פ הוראת ב״ד, כי שגג לחשוב
כי בית דין זה, הואיל וישב בלשכת הגזית, הוראתו הוראה; ובאמת לא היה
בית דין כלל, וחייב היחיד שעשה על פיו להביא חטאת.

בתו״כ חובה, פרשה ד׳ ה״ג וה״ד, לא נשנו, כאמור, הבבא הדנה בגר וממזר
והבבא הדנה בהעדר המופלא או שאמר אחד מהם איני יודע וכו׳, כאחת אלא

---

[4] הכלל הוא שאין מושיבים בסנהדרין אלא כהנים לויים וישראלים המשיאין לכהונה
(מ׳ סנהדרין פ״ד מ״ב), וכל שכן שאין מושיבים בסנהדרין מי שאינו ראוי לישא ישראלית
כגון פצוע דכא או כרות שפכה, וכן מבואר בירושלמי סנהדרין פ״ד ה״ה (ס״ו ע״א).
לפי האמור, תלויה המחלוקת העתיקה הנ״ל, אם מותר להושיב גר בסנהדרין, במחלו-
קת אם משפחתו ראויה להשיא בנותיו לכהונה. על כך כבר נחלקו בקידושין פ״ד מ״ו–
מ״ז. לפי ר׳ אליעזר בן יעקב, ישראל שנשא גיורת בתו כשרה לכהונה וגר שנשא בת
ישראל בתו כשרה לכהונה, אבל גר שנשא גיורת בתו פסולה לכהונה, אפילו עד עשרה
דורות. ר׳ יוסי סובר כי גם גר שנשא גיורת בתו כשרה לכהונה. אך ר׳ יהודה סובר בת
גר זכר כבת חלל זכר ואסור לכהן לשאת אותה.
לשיטת ראב״י, רק צאצאיהם של גרים שנשאו גיורות נחשבים כגרים; אולם גר שנשא
ישראלית או ישראל שנשא גיורת הרי הם ישראלים גמורים. והוא היה מסכים לדעת ר׳
יהושע כי צאצאי יונתן בן רכב, שהיה מצאצאי יתרו, היו מותרים לישב בסנהדרין, כי
הם נשאו בנות ישראל ובנותיהם נישאו לישראלים.
לפי ר׳ יוסי, המוסר כנראה את קבלתם של בית הלל, גם גר שנשא גיורת צאצאיו הם
ישראלים גמורים.
לדעת ר׳ יהודה נמנים צאצאי הגר על משפחת אבותיהם, אף אם אמותיהם הן מישראל.
הוא מוסר כנראה משנתו של רבי אליעזר, שהיא מסורת בית שמאי, שלפיה בן גר ובן בנו
של גר הם תמיד בבחינת גרים ופסולים הם לשבת בסנהדרין.

כשתים. נראה שאותה פרשה של תו״כ מקורה בימי החשמונאים. הביאו
ראשונה את ההלכה שנתחדשה בימיהם והתייחסה לב״ד של המתיוונים, ואח״כ
הוסיפו את ההלכה אשר אולי נתחדשה כבר בימי שמעון הצדיק אלא שהיתה
לה משמעות גם לגבי זמנם, כי גם הם צירפו לבית דין של לשכת הגזית אחדים
מחכמי הפרושים. ואם נעדר אחד מהם, או שאמר איני יודע, או שאמר לחבריו
טועים אתם — אין הוראתם הוראה. ומכיוון שכך, אף אם עשר רוב הקהל על
פיהם, אינם מביאים פר העלם דבר של ציבור, אלא כל אחד ואחד מן העושים
על פיהם חייב להביא כשבה או שעירה, כמבואר בתוספתא הוריות פ״א ה״א
(ע׳ 474), וכפי הגירסה הנכונה שהביאה רבינו ברוך בפירושו, המיוחס לר״ח
ונדפס בש״ס ווילנא ח׳ ע״א, וכמו שהעיר הגר״ש ליברמן בתוספת ראשונים שם.

מלבד החלוקה לבבות נפרדות יש גם הבדל עיקרי בלשון בין המשנה לתו״כ.
במשנה נאמר ״עד שיהיו כולם ראויים להוראה״, ואילו בתו״כ נאמר בבבא
דגר וכו׳ ״עד שיהיו כולם ראויים להוראה״, ובבבא דטועים אתם ״עד שיורו
כולם״.

הבבא הראשונה בתו״כ, אשר המדובר בה כנ״ל בסנהדרין של המתיוונים,
מצריכה שיהיו רק כולם ראויים להוראה. היא לא דנה כלל בתנאי שאם אחד
מהם אמר טועים אתם או אמר איני יודע, או שלא היה שם כלל. הרי בימי
המתיוונים לא מינו פרושים לבית הדין הגדול, ומה היה מועיל אז התנאי
שצריכים דעת כולם. הבבא השני׳, שהמכוון בה לבית דין שהיו בה כמה
פרושים, מדגישה את התנאי שצריכים דעת כולם.

רבינו הקדוש שגרס במשנתנו שתי הבבות יחד, שנה ״עד שיהיו כולם
ראויים להוראה״. גר, ממזר או נתין אינם ראויים להורות, וכן אם לא היה
המופלא שם, כולם אינם ראויים להוראה. רבי לא שנה ״עד שיורו כולם״, כי
לפי דעתו אם חסר אחד שאינו המופלא — הוראתם הוראה.

רבי השמיט במשנתו את המובא בתו״כ הנ״ל: ״או שאמר אחד מהם איני
יודע״, שלשיטתו אין צריכים הוראה של כל הע״א, רק שיסכימו הרוב,
והמופלא עמהם, ולא יהיה ביניהם גר, ממזר, או נתין. לא היתה קשה לו
המשנה שלפיה אם ידע אחד מחברי ב״ד שטעו חבריו ועשה כמותם חייב —
אולם אחר פטור, כי לשיטתו הוראתם הוראה, אף בהעדר אחד מהם, ובלבד
שלא התריס כנגדם, כמבואר בירו׳ ״שלא נכנס״.

בתו״כ הנ״ל גרסו ראשונה ״לא היה (מופלא) [אחד] של ב״ד שם״, ואח״כ
״אמר אחד מהם איני יודע״, ואח״כ ״אמר להם טועין אתם״. הסדר הוא זו
ואצ״ל זו. הברייתא דנה ראשונה במקרה שנעדר אחד מחברי ב״ד; אחר כך
היא מוסיפה שמכל שכן אם אמר אחד מהם איני יודע, שהרי הוא נוכח, ואינו
משתתף בהוראה; הוסיפו עוד שק״ו בן בנו של ק״ו, אם אמר להם טועים
אתם — אין הוראתם הוראה.

רבי לא ראה להפריד במשנתנו ענין גר, נתין וממזר מדין העדר המופלא.
לפי דעתו הנימוק שווה בשתי ההלכות, והוא, שנפסל בית הדין, או מפני
שאחד מחבריו היה פסול, או מפני העדר המופלא, שהוא עיקר הבי״ד. רבי
שנה משנתנו בלא זו אף זו: בראשונה שנה שאם אמר אחד מן הדיינים לחבריו
טועים אתם, אין הוראתם הוראה; אח״כ הוסיף שגם בהעדר המופלא, אף אם
לא התריס אחד נגד חבריו בכל זאת אין הוראתם הוראה; ואח״כ הוסיף, שאם
היה אחד מהם גר או נתין, אף שכולם היו נוכחים, בטלה ההוראה.

על פי דברינו מובן למה שנו בתו״כ בין במשנה גר או נתין או ממזר ולא
שנו פסול סתם. גם בזמן שלפני שמעון הצדיק וגם בימי המתיוונים לא היו
מושיבים פסול בסנהדרין. אך אפשר שהיו מושיבים מי שלפי דעת הפרושים
היה חשוד שהוא מצצצאי גר, נתין או ממזר, מפני שראשי הכהנים ובתי
האבות היו סבורים כי אדם זה אינו חשוד כלל.

ו

לפי האמור יש לבאר גם את הברייתא המובאה בירו׳ הוריות, פ״א, ה״א (מ״ה
ע״ד): ״יכול אם יאמרו לך על ימין שהוא שמאל ועל שמאל שהוא ימין תשמע
להם תלמוד לומר ללכת ימין ושמאל [הכוונה אל הכתוב לא תסור מן
הדבר אשר יגידו לך ימין ושמאל (דברים י״ז, י״א)]. הדברים תמוהים
לכאורה. כיצד אפשר לומר על בית הדין הגדול של ישראל, בין אם המדובר
כאן בבית דין של לשכת הגזית, מזמנו של שמעון הצדיק או מימי החשמונאים,
שכבר השתתפו בו חכמי הפרושים, שיאמרו על ימין שהוא שמאל ועל שמאל
שהוא ימין? הלא אם נעדר המופלא או אחד מן החברים בסנהדרין לא היתה
הוראתם הוראה כלל, וכן אם אמר טועים אתם או איני יודע. ואם היה שם
בוודאי היה מוחה על הוראה כזו.

אלא בוודאי נשנתה ברייתא זו בימי המתיוונים, וחכמי הפרושים נדחו אז
מסנהדרין זו או פרשו מעצמם כפי שאמרנו לעיל. במצב זה לא היה ראוי
לשמוע להם אף במקצועות התורה שהפרושים הסכימו להכיר שיש בסמכותם
בימי שמעון הצדיק.

ברם, בדורות מאוחרים יותר תמהו על פסיקה זו שלפיה יתכן שיאמרו על
ימין שהוא שמאל ועל שמאל שהוא ימין; וכיצד יתקיימו הכתובים שלפיהם
המסופק בדבר צריך לפנות לבית דין הגדול? ולא נראה להם לפרש שבברייתא
מדובר על בית הדין של המתיוונים, כי זה לא היה בעיניהם ב״ד כלל. לכן
הגיהו בברייתא העתיקה ושנו ״אפילו מראים בעיניך על ימין שהוא שמאל,
ועל שמאל שהוא ימין שמע להם״ (ספרי דברים פי׳ קנ״ד, עמ׳ 207).

ז

התמיהות הנזכרות על משניות מסכת הוריות ועל הברייתות המקבילות להן לא
נעלמו כמובן מתלמידי ר׳ עקיבא ור׳ ישמעאל. קשה היה להם שלפי המשניות
והברייתות הללו היה ב״ד של לשכת הגזית עלול לטעות ואפילו לעקור דבר
המפורש בתורה. ולכן פירשו ר׳ יהודה ור׳ שמעון, מתלמידיו של ר׳ עקיבא,
ור׳ יאשי׳ ור׳ יונתן, מתלמידי ר׳ ישמעאל, שמשניות אילו מדברות בבית דין
של אחד מן השבטים (עי׳ מ׳ הוריות פ״א מ״ה; וספרי במדבר פי׳ קי״א עמ׳
117). ברם לפי שיטת החכמים (עי׳ מ׳ הוריות הנ״ל) מדובר בבית דין של
לשכת הגזית, כפשוטם של דברים וכמו ששנתה בפירוש הברייתא בתו״כ,
חובה ריש פרשה ד׳.

ח

נשאר עדיין לבאר את סוף הברייתא המובאה בירו׳ שקלים הנ״ל שלפיה היו
בסנהדרין ביבנה ארבעה שידעו לדבר, והם היו בן עזאי, בן זומא, בן חכינאי,
ור׳ אלעזר בן מתיה (לפי מהד׳ הגר״א סופר, עמ׳ 57, היו הארבעה בן עזאי,
בן זומא, אלעזר בן מתיה, וחנני׳ בן חנילא, כנ״ל).

כבר הבאנו למעלה מאמרו של רב, שיסודו בברייתא זו, ולפיו היו הארבעה
ביבנה, ״ר׳ אליעזר ור׳ יהושע ור׳ עקיבא ושמעון התימני דן לפניהם
בקרקע״. ברור שרב הזכיר אחדים מגדולי יבנה כי הוקשה לו כיצד אפשר
לעבור על אלה ולמנות במקומם את התלמידים. יש גם תוספת בדברי רב,
״ובביתר היו שלושה״, שבוודאי מצאה באיזה מקור. ונראה שכוונתו היתה
לומר שבזמן מן הזמנים היתה יושבת סנהדרי גדולה בביתר.

נראה שבירושלמי ובמאמר רב נשתמרה ידיעה חשובה על התרחשויות בימי
רדיפות הדת של אדריינוס הרשע. ברור שבמקור עליו סמך רב בברייתא
בירושלמי הנ״ל תואר המצב ביבנה כאשר ר״ע היה עדיין בחיים. הרי שנינו
שמן הארבעה שנכנסו לפרדס בן עזאי הציץ ומת ור״ע נכנס בשלום ויצא
בשלום (תוספתא חגיגה פ״ב ה״ג–ה״ד, מהד׳ הגר״ש ליברמן עמ׳ 381, ובמק־
בילות). ברייתא זו בוודאי נשנתה לפני שתפסו את רבי עקיבא ונתנוהו לבית
הסוהר — כי אחרי זה בוודאי לא היו אומרים עליו שנכנס בשלום ויצא
בשלום.

מוכרחים לומר כי בן עזאי מת לפני שנעצר רבי עקיבא. וכיוון שנזכר בן
עזאי כאחד מן היודעים לדבר בסנהדרין של יבנה — מן ההכרח לומר שמדובר
במאורע שאירע בחיי רבי עקיבא וכשעדיין היה חופשי — ואם כן יש לשאול,
למה לא השתתף במושב ההוא של הסנהדרין? וכן יש לשאול על רבי יהודה בן
בבא, שאף הוא היה אז עדיין בחיים, כי הרי נהרג אחר מותו של רבי עקיבא.
בימי רדיפת הדת של אדריינוס לא גזרו את כל הגזירות בבת אחת. בראשונה

גזרו על המילה (עוד בימי רבי אליעזר, כמבואר במ׳ שבת פי״ט, מ״א); גזרו
על ק״ש ועדיין לא גזרו על תלמוד תורה, כמבואר בתוספתא ברכות פ״ב,
הי״ג (מהד׳ הגר״ש ליברמן, עמ׳ 8); גזרו על תקיעת שופר בראש השנה
ועדיין לא גזרו על התפילה (מ׳ ראש השנה פ״ד, מ״ז) ולא על אמירת הלל
(כמבואר שם, ועיין מה שהעיר על כך הגר״ש ליברמן בס׳ היובל לפרופ׳
שלום בארון, הכרך העברי, ע׳ רי״ד).

הגזירה על תלמוד תורה היתה כנראה מן האחרונות, שהרי בשעת אסיפת
החכמים בלוד דנו אם מעשה גדול או תלמוד גדול ומשמע שהיו רשאים עדיין
ללמוד תורה וללמדה, אם כי כבר נגזר שלא לקיים את המצוות.

הגזירה על הסנהדרין שלא תתאסף היתה כנראה אחת מן הראשונות, שהרי
כאשר הוצרך ר׳ עקיבא לרדת לנהרדעא לעבר השנה עדיין היה רבן גמליאל
בחיים (מ׳ יבמות פט״ז, מ״ז), ורבן גמליאל מת לפני ר׳ אליעזר (מ׳ ב״מ,
נ״ט, ע״ב). וזהו שדנו אם יש לתקוע שופר בראש השנה שחל בשבת רק בב״ד
שביבנה או בכל מקום שיש שם ב״ד, כלומר ב״ד הגדול, שגזרו עליו שלא
להתאסף; ברם היתה עדיין אפשרות להתכנס במקום אחר בארץ ישראל. לשיטת
החכמים יש לתקוע בכל מקום שיש בו בית דין, ור״א פסק שלא התקין רבן
יוחנן בן זכאי אלא ביבנה בלבד (מ׳ ראש השנה פ״ד, מ״א).

ונראה שלא רצו החכמים להעתיק את הסנהדרין מיבנה, בה נוסדה על ידי
רבן יוחנן בן זכאי אחרי חורבן הבית, אלא ניסו להסוות כינוסה על ידי
שישיתפו בה רק חכמים צעירים, תלמידים שהגיעו להוראה. נוכחותם של גדולי
הדור ביבנה היתה בוודאי מעוררת מיד את חשדם של פקידי המלכות. יסדו אז
סנהדרין חדשה שבראשה עמדו ארבעת החכמים הנזכרים, ונצטרפו להם
אנשים פשוטים שהיו יודעים לשמוע, אף שלא היו יודעים לדבר בדברי תורה.
סנהדרין זו היתה דנה בכל העניינים הרגילים. אך כשהיה צורך לדון בדבר
חשוב מאד, כמו בבעיה אם מעשה גדול או תלמוד גדול, שבה היתה תלויה
הכרעת הרבה חכמים אם לצאת את הארץ כדי שיוכלו לקיים את המצוות או
להישאר בה מפני שהיתה עדיין מרכז לתורה, או על איזה מצוות צריכים
למסור את הנפש — התאספו גדולי התורה, ברם לא ביבנה אלא בלוד, ולא
הרגישו פקידי המלכות שהיה זה מושב הסנהדרין.

החכמים מצאו סמך להחלטתם ליסד סנהדרין חדשה, בה היו רק ארבעה
שידעו לדבר, בברייתא העתיקה שמקורה בזמן החשמונאים או אפילו בזמן
יותר קדום, שלפיה סנהדרין שיש בה ארבעה היודעים לדבר נקראת חכמה,
ואף אם היו שנים ראויה להיות סנהדרין.

לפי הנמסר ע״י רב משמע שבימי מרד בר כוכבא העתיקו חכמים אלה את
מקומם לביתר מפני הסכנה, שלא ירגישו בהם פקידי המלכות. ונראה שאז כבר
יצא בן זומא מעולמו (תוספתא חגיגה פ״ב, ה״ג, מהד׳ הגר״ש ליברמן, עמ׳

371, ועי׳ בתוספתא כפשוטה, שם). כאשר אירע מקרה זה של בן זומא, היה בן
עזאי עדיין בחיים, שהרי אמר "כל שנטרפה דעתו מפני חכמתו סימן יפה לו;
נטרפה חכמתו מפני דעתו סימן רע לו" (תוספתא ברכות פ״ג, ה״ד, מהד׳
הגר״ש ליברמן, עמ׳ 12; וכבר העיר ראה״ו שכיוון בן עזאי לבן זומא
שנטרפה דעתו מפני חכמתו; ולאלישע בן אבוי׳ שנטרפה חכמתו מפני דעתו).
נשארו בביתר רק שלושה שידעו לדבר ואליהם צירפו אחרים שידעו לשמוע.

כעבור זמן רב, כראות ר׳ יהודה בן בבא שחכמי הדור או שמתו או שנהרגו,
או שיצאו לחוץ לארץ, הסתכן כדי לסמוך את ר׳ מאיר, ר׳ יהודה, ר׳ שמעון,
ר׳ יוסי, ור׳ אלעזר בן שמוע ור׳ נחמי׳ (ב׳ סנהדרין, י״ד ע״א). ר׳ יהודה בן
בבא סיכן את נפשו וגם את נפש המוסמכים, כי קיווה שתתבטל הגזרה,
ותיווסד עוד סנהדרין חדשה.

בשיר השירים ר׳ פ״ב על הפסוק סמכוני באשישות, נאמר "בשלפי
השמד נתכנסו רבותינו לאושא ואילו הן: ר׳ יהודה, ור׳ נחמי׳, ר׳ מאיר, ור׳
יוסי, ורשב״י, ור׳ אלעזר בנו של ריה״ג, ור׳ אליעזר בן יעקב. שלחו אצל
זקני הגליל ואמרו כל מי שהוא למד יבוא וילמד; וכל מי שאינו למד יבוא
וילמוד"; כלומר יסדו סנהדרין חדשה שהיו בה שבעה שיודעים לדבר וקיוו
שיצטרפו אליהם עוד זקנים שיודעים לשמוע עד שיהיו שבעים ואחד.

מובן שכל חבריה של הסנהדרין ביבנה, ביתר, ואושא, היו פרושים, אבל
הברייתא בתוספתא סנהדרין וירושלמי שקלים הנ״ל נשנתה מעיקרא על
סנהדרין של לשכת הגזית, שרוב חבריה לא היו פרושים.

פסקיו של הרמב״ם לאור גישתו לחומר הסתמי שבבבלי

מאת מאיר שמחה פלדבלום

קיימות שתי בעיות יסודיות בנוגע לסידור התלמוד הבבלי: א. איך נוצר ונערך החומר האמוראי? ב. מה טיבו וזמן יצירתו של החומר הסתמי?

הגישה הרווחת עד המאה הנוכחית היתה גישתו של רש״י כפי שנתנסחה בפירושו על המימרה בגמ׳ ב״מ פו, א: ״רב אשי ורבינא סוף הוראה.״ וכה דבריו שם: ״סוף כל האמוראין, עד ימיהם לא היתה גמרא על הסדר אלא כשהיתה שאלה נשאלת בטעם המשנה בבית המדרש או שאלה על מעשה המאורע בדין ממון או איסור והיתר כל אחד ואחד אומר טעמו, ורב אשי ורבינא סידרו שמועות אמוראין שלפניהם וקבעו על סדר המסכתות כל אחד ואחד אצל המשנה הראויה והשנויה לה והקשו קושיות שיש להשיב ופירוקים שראוים לתרץ הם והאמוראים שעמהם וקבעו הכל בגמ׳ כגון איתיביה מיתיבי ורמינהי איבעיא להו והתירוצים שעליהן...״ היוצא מפירושו הוא שעד רב אשי לא היתה יצירה ספרותית אמוראית על סדר המשניות, והרושם שמתקבל מדבריו הוא שהתלמוד שלנו כמו שהוא לפנינו הוא פרי יצירתם ועריכתם של רב אשי ורבינא. שטה זו, שרב אשי ורבינא הם מסדרי התלמוד, נמצאת ביסודה כבר אצל רב נסים גאון,[1] והד לה נשמע כבר בסדר תנאים ואמוראים.[2]

בדרך זו הולך גם הרמב״ם בהקדמתו למשנה תורה. הוא אומר: ״ורב אשי הוא שחיבר הגמרא הבבלית בארץ שנער אחר שחיבר ר׳ יוחנן הגמרא הירו־ שלמית בכמו מאה שנה.״ ובהמשך דבריו, שם: ״נמצא רבינא[3] ורב אשי וחבריהם סוף גדולי ישראל המעתיקים תורה שבעל פה... ואחר בית דין של רב אשי שחיבר הגמרא וגמרו בימי בנו נתפזרו ישראל... וכן אם למד אחד

---

[1] ר׳ הקדמתו בריש ברכות.

[2] הוצ׳ כהנא עמ׳ 31 שם: ״וכל קושיא שבכל תנויי דלא תמצא בה אביי ורבא (שמא) שמע מנה אביי ורבא תקנום וכל קושיא דתמצא אביי ורבא שמע מינה רב אשי ורבינא תקנום.

[3] רבינא זה הוא חברו הגדול של רב אשי ולא רבינא האחרון. כי לפני זה אומר הרמב״ם: ומר בר רב אשי קיבל מאביו, רב אשי, ומרבינא. ורבינא האחרון מלך אחר מר בר רב אשי. ר׳ איגרת רב שרירא, מהדורת לוין עמ׳ 95. אבל ברור שרב שרירא מזהה את רבינא של סוף הוראה עם רבינא האחרון, כי עליו הוא אומר שם דהוא סוף הוראה. וע״ע שם, עמ׳ 69.

מהגאונים שדרך המשפט כך הוא ונתבאר לבית דין שעמד אחריו שאין זה דרך
המשפט הכתוב בגמרא אין שומעין לראשון אלא לפי שהדעת נוטה לדבריו בין
ראשון בין אחרון... אבל כל הדברים שבגמרא הבבלי חייבין כל ישראל ללכת
בהם... הואיל וכל אותם הדברים שבגמרא הסכימו עליהם כל ישראל...״

הרושם שמתקבל ונתקבל הוא שרב אשי ורבינא הם האחראים לתלמוד
שלפנינו. אבל מאידך ידוע גם כן מאיגרתו של רב שרירא גאון,[4] ומעדותם של
שאר גאונים וחכמי ספרד,[5] ועל פי ניתוח ובירור של החומר התלמודי [6]
שהרבה חומר ניתוסף במשך של ארבע מאות שנה, מרב אשי עד תחילת המאה
התשיעית למנין הרגיל. בודאי שיש הבדל גדול בין סוגי החומר האחר-
תלמודי. חלק גדול ממנו, כגון זה המיוחס לסבוראים, שייך כנראה ליצירה
התלמודית. וחלק ממנו שייך לפירושי הגאונים, או כיצירה של יחידים או
כמסורת קיבוצית של הישיבות, וגם פירושים של תלמידי תרביצאי, ועוד
סוגים מסוגים שונים שנכנסו לתוך הגמרא אם במתכוון או בשגגת המעתיקים.

לאור זה ניתן לשאול שתי שאלות בנוגע להרמב״ם: עד כמה ידע או סבר
שחלק גדול מהחומר הסתמי הוא מאוחר למר בר רב אשי, ומה היתה גישתו
לחומר שכזה? האם הוא ייחס לו את סמכותה של הגמרא, או שראה בו
כפירושי הגאונים וקבלהו או הזניחהו כפי הכרעת דעתו.

אחת הדרכים לפתרון בעיה זו היא לבדוק את כל הקושיות שהקשו על
הרמב״ם בנוגע לפסקיו שאינם בהתאם לחומר התלמודי. האם פסקיו אלו
עומדים בסתירה לחומר היסודי, האמוראי, הנקוב בשם, או שהסתירה היא רק
ביחס לחומר הסתמי? ואם נסווג את סוגי הקושיות נוכל לבא לאיזו מסקנות
בנוגע לשאלות הנ״ל. ודאי שראשית כל יש לבדוק את ספרות הרמב״ם, אם
הוא דן במפורש בבעיות אלו. אבל דא עקא, שרק באי אלו מקומות, בפירושו
למשניות [7] ובהערתו של בנו ר׳ אברהם,[8] נזכרת הסתייגות מחומר תלמודי

⁴ עמ׳ 69—71.

⁵ ר׳ רבנן סבוראי ותלמודם לרב״מ לוין, והוספות מאוחרות בתלמוד
בבלי מאת יעקב שפיגל, דיסרטציה באוניברסיטת תל-אביב, תשל״ו.

⁶ מבירור וניתוח של החומר התלמודי יוצא שבכלל אין לדבר על רב אשי ורבינא
כמסדרי התלמוד. ובירור שזוהר גם שיטתו של רב שרירא גאון באיגרתו. ר׳ בירור שטתו
בהתהוות התלמוד בשלמותו לר״א וויס מעמ׳ 242, ור׳ גם ספרו של ר״י קפלן The
Redaction of the Babylonian Talmud מעמ׳ 35. אבל שטת הרמב״ם ברורה:
״...ורב אשי שחיבר הגמרא וגמרו בימי בנו...״ מה שמעניין בדבריו הוא ההיקש בין רב
אשי שחיבר הבבלי ור׳ יוחנן שחיבר הירושלמי. ובודאי ברור היה להרמב״ם שהרבה
מהחומר שבירושלמי שייך לכמה דורות שאחרי ר׳ יוחנן. וא״כ נראה שהתכוון לומר
שרק עיקר יסודו וחיבורו הוא מר׳ יוחנן ובית מדרשו. אבל בנוגע לבבלי הוא מפרש
דבריו ואומר: ״...וגמרו בימי בנו נתפזרו ישראל...״

⁷ כלאים ט:ח, בנדפס בש״ס: ״והוא שלא יהיה כלאים עד שיהיו נחברים אלו העניינים

משום שהוא רק פירוש הגאונים או סתם הוספות. ואין להוציא מהערות אלו
מסקנות כלליות על יחסו לסוגי החומר הסתמי. רק בדיקה קפדנית ומקיפה של
היד החזקה תפיץ אור על הבעיות הנ״ל.

והנה אם נגיע למסקנא שהרמב״ם לא התחשב עם אי אלה סוגים של חומר
סתמי נגיע על ידי כך לא רק לפתרון כללי של הרבה בעיות שברמב״ם אלא,
מה שעוד יותר חשוב, נוכל לנסח גישה עיקרונית איך להשתמש במקורות
התלמוד לבירור הלכות ודעות בהתאם לדרכו של הרמב״ם.

בדקתי רק חלק קטן של ההלכות שביד החזקה, ולפיכך מסקנותי הן לעת עתה
בגדר של השערות בלבד. אציג כאן רק דוגמאות מהחומר שבידי. בדוגמאות
אלו הקושיות על פסקיו של הרמב״ם יסודן בסוגים שונים של חומר סתמי. מה
שמתבלט מניתוח החומר הוא שהוא שונה בצורתו הספרותית או באיכותו
ההגיונית מהחומר האמוראי. על יסוד זה שיערתי שהרמב״ם לא התחשב עם
המסקנות היוצאות מחומר שכזה.[9]

הל׳ אישות ג, ו:

״הדברים שיאמר האיש כשיקדש צריך שיהא משמעם שהוא קונה האשה ולא
שיהא משמע שהקנה עצמו לה. כיצד... הרי את חרופתי... הרי זו מקדשת.״
והאריך הכסף משנה להקשות, שלפי סוגית הגמ׳ בקידושין, ו, א, יוצא שרק
האומר ״חרופה ביהודה מקדשת״, וז״ל הגמ׳: ״איבעיא להו: חרופתי מהו?
ת״ש דתניא האומר חרופתי מקודשת, שכן ביהודה קורין לארוסה חרופה

כולם (שוע טווי ונוז) וכל מה שאינו כך הוא כלאים מד״ס וזו הלכה פסוקה באמת ואין בו
ספק וכן אמרו בגמ׳ ואם מצאת לאחד דבר חולק על מה שאמרתי אל יכנס בלבך ספק
שהוא שכח ההלכה ההיא האמורה בגמ׳ נדה.״ אבל בתרגומו של י. קאפח כתוב אחר
המלה מד״ס: ״כן כתבו קצת מן הגאונים. וזה אצלי בלתי נכון אלא כל אחד מהם
כלאים של תורה ואותו הלשון שבגמרא נדה אינו לשון התלמוד אלא פירוש.״
ובהגהות כ״י ד׳ נאפולי: ״זהו דבר מקצת הגאונים... ומה שנזכר בנדה אינו לשון
תלמוד אלא לשון גאון.״ על המהדורות השונות, החזרות וההגהות שבפיה״מ
להרמב״ם, ר׳ את המבוא המקיף של ר״ש ליברמן להלכות הירושלמי להרמב״ם.
[8] ברכת אברהם (ירושלים תש״ך), עמ׳ 16.
[9] כי חומר סתמי, אם הוא בגדר של ״תלמוד ערוך,״ הרמב״ם יבכר אותו על משא
ומתן (אפילו אמוראי). בתשובתו לחכמי לוניל הוא כותב: ״...לא שמעתי ולא סמכתי
על קושיא זו ואמרתי לא נניח תלמוד ערוך ונפסיק הלכה ממשא ומתן של גמרא... ועל
כל פנים לא מדברי משא ומתן נפסוק הלכה...״ תשובות הרמב״ם (הוצ׳ מקיצי
נרדמים), ירושלים, תש״ך, כרך ב׳, ת׳ שמה, עמ׳ 618. ה״תלמוד ערוך״ אינו בהכרח
חומר אמוראי ומאידך המו״מ שם הוא כנראה כן אמוראי. על יחסו של הרמב״ם למו״מ
התלמוד, ר׳ גם ספרו של יעקב לוינגר, דרכי המחשבה ההלכתית של הרמב״ם,
מעמ׳ 155. אלא שהוא לא מנתח את החומר לסוגים של אמוראי וסתמא.

ויהודה הוי רובא דעלמא ה״ק האומר חרופתי... אלא ה״ק האומר חרופה
ביהודה מקודשת שכן ביהודה קורין לארוסה חרופה.״ [10]

וחשובים כאן דברי הכ״מ: ״ועי״ל שרבינו סובר דקושיית ויהודה ועוד
לקרא לאו קושיא... דלא מייתי מיהודה אלא לפרושי לישנא דקרא...,
והיותר נכון שרבינו לא היה גורס כל האי שקלא וטריא אלא גורס כגירסת
ר״ח...״ ע״ש.

בדברי הכ״מ מוצאים גישה מרחיקת לכת בשמוש במקורות התלמוד. אם
הקושיא אינה הכרחית, א״כ המסקנא שנובעת ממנה היא בבחינת לאו דוקא.

ועל זה רצוני להוסיף שתופעה זו, שהקושיא היא קלושה, נמצאת ברגיל
בחומר סתמי העומד כתוספת או כחלק בלתי אינטגרלי של החומר התלמודי.

הל׳ גירושין ב, כ:

״מי שהדין נותן שכופין אותו לגרש את אשתו ולא רצה לגרש, בית דין של
ישראל בכל מקום ובכל זמן מכין אותו עד שיאמר ״רוצה אני״ ויכתבו הגט
והוא גט כשר. וכן אם הכוהו עכו״ם ואמרו לו, עשה מה שישראל אומרין לך,
ולחצו אותו ישראל ביד העכו״ם עד שיגרש, הרי זה כשר. ואם העכו״ם
מעצמן אנסוהו עד שכתב, הואיל והדין נותן שיכתוב, הרי זה גט פסול. ולמה
לא יבטל גט זה שהרי הוא אנוס...,״ לא היה הדין נותן שכופין אותו לגרש וטעו
ב״ד של ישראל או שהיו הדיוטות ואנסוהו עד שגירש הרי זה גט פסול הואיל
וישראל אנסוהו יגמור ויגרש. ואם העכו״ם אנסוהו לגרש שלא כדין אינו גט.״

וכבר העירו מפרשי הרמב״ם [11] שפסקו אינו מתאים למסקנת הסוגיא בגיטין
פח, ב, אבל פסקו מתאים בדיוק למימרתו של רב נחמן בשם שמואל, שם: ״גט
המעושה בישראל כדין כשר, שלא כדין פסול ופוסל, ובעובדי כוכבים כדין
פסול ופוסל שלא כדין אפילו ריח הגט אין בו.״

השו״ט בסוגיא שבגמרא היא כנראה מאוחרת והרמב״ם לא התחשב בה.
ובייחוד שהרי״ף ג״כ מביא מימרתו של שמואל, וגם מהבה״ג מוכח שלא
התחשב עם הסוגיא הסתמא שלנו. [12]

---

[10] ור׳ דברי מו״ר ר״א וייס ז״ל בהערות לסוגיות הש״ס הבבלי והירושלמי
(אוסף מאמרים) (הוצ׳ אוניברסיטה בר־אילן), עמ׳ 221.

[11] ר׳ כסף משנה ולחם משנה, ור׳ גם י. לוינגר, דרכי המחשבה ההלכתית של
הרמב״ם, מעמ׳ 164.

[12] עי׳ בספרי פירושים ומחקרים בתלמוד, מעמ׳ 219. ר׳ גם דברי ר״ד הלבני,
מקורות ומסורות, נשים, מעמ׳ תר״י. ובייחוד על פסקו זה של הרמב״ם, ר׳ מאמרו
של הרב ב. ז. בנדיקט, ״הרמב״ם והפסיקה התלמודית״ בתורה שבעל פה, תש״ל,
מעמ׳ פה.

הל׳ גירושין ז, ב:

"בא הבעל וערער ואמר: לא גירשתיה מעולם וגט שהובא לה מזוייף הוא, יתקיים בחותמיו. ואם לא נתקיים ולא נודעו עדיו כלל תצא והולד ממזר שהרי אינה מגרשת."

והקשו עליו [13] שמסוגית הגמ׳ גיטין ג, א מוכח שמכיון שהעדים חותמין על השטר נעשו כמי שנחקרו עדותן בב״ד אז הפסול אפילו בערעור הבעל הוא רק מדרבנן.

אבל כבר בירתי במקום אחר [14] על התפתחותו של המושג של "נעשה כמי שנחקרה...." עיקר מימרתו של ריש לקיש הוא שהגדה בשטר היא כמו הגדה בעל פה, וכיון שהגיד שוב אינו חוזר ומגיד. אבל אם לא ידוע אם חתמו העדים על השטר, על זה לא דיבר ריש לקיש. ורק בסוגיא סתמא [15] שבגיטין הרחיבו את המושג לומר דרך כלל "כמי שנחקרה", ואפילו אם הבעל מערער ואומר שמעולם לא כתבו ולא חתמו מעיקר הדין לא מועיל הערעור.[16] מסקנא זו בנויה על קושיא שאינה הכרחית, ולפיכך נראה שהרמב״ם דחה מסקנה זו וניסח את המושג לפי מובנו הראשוני במימרתו של ריש לקיש.

הל׳ גירושין יא, כה:

"וכן גזרו חכמים שלא ישא אדם מעוברת חבירו ומינקת חבירו, ואף על פי שהזרע ידוע למי היא מעוברת. שמא יזיק הולד בשעת תשמיש שאינו מקפיד על בן חבירו."

והקשה הכסף משנה, שבגמ׳ יבמות מב, א אידחי טעם זה על פי קושית הגמ׳: "אי הכי דידיה נמי, דידיה חייס עילויה הכא נמי חייס עילוייה, אלא סתם מעוברת למניקה קיימא דלמא איעברה ומעכר חלבה." ומציע הכ״מ: "לכך נ״ל דרבינו לא גרס אלא...."

ולפי דרכנו נראה שהרמב״ם התעלם מקושיא קלושה זו שבסתמא דסוגיא. ודאי שיש הבדל בין בנו לבן חבירו, וכדברי הכ״מ, שם: "ה״מ לאהדורי ליה דלא חייס כולי האי על דחבריה כדחייס על דידיה... איכא למיחש דדחיס ליה שלא במתכוין."

---

[13] לחם משנה, שם.

[14] ר׳ ספרי פירושים ומחקרים, מעמ׳ 73.

[15] רוב הסוגיות הראשונות שבבבלי הן כנראה מתקופת הסבוראים או הגאונים. ר׳ "היצירה של הסבוראים" לר״א וויס, תדפיס מיוחד בהוצ׳ האוניברסיטה העברית, 1953 (הרצאה).

[16] אבל ר׳ מרדכי, קידושין סי׳ תקס״ט בשם ר׳ אביגדור כהן.

הל׳ איסורי מזבח ד, ח:

״אי זהו אתנן האומר לזונה הא ליך דבר זה בשכרך. אחד זונה כותית או שפחה או ישראלית שהיא ערוה עליו או מחייבי לאווין. אבל הפנויה אפילו היה כהן אתננה מותר. וכן אשתו נדה אתננה מותר אע״פ שהיא ערוה.״

ומעיר הכ״מ: ״ומ״ש וכן באשתו נדה..., שם פלוגתא דרב ולוי (תמורה כט, ב) ופסק כרב ואיני יודע למה ואדרבה משמע בגמרא דלית הלכתא כוותיה דאמרינן ורב האי תועבה מאי עביד ליה מיבעי ליה כדאביי דאמר זונה כותית אתננה אסור וכו׳ וכיון דלא קי״ל כאביי אלא כרבא וכמו שפסק רבינו לעיל בסמוך היאך פסק כרב...״

סוגיא זו בתמורה טיפוסית היא להרבה סוגיות כאלו בש״ס שבהן שו״ט איך תנא או אמורא ידרוש מדרשו של חבירו. המטבע של סוגיות אלו הוא: ופלוני? אמר לך... ופלוני? אמר לך. סוגיות כאלו הן סתמיות וטיב המדרש שבהן שונה ברגיל ממדרשי האמוראים ושונה בהרבה ממדרשי התנאים. השאלה היא אם יש הכרח לקושיות כאלו? ואם ההשלכות ההלכיות מהתירוצים מחייבות את הפוסקים להתחשב עמהן. הכ״מ מציע תירוץ אחר לקושיא: ״ורב האי תועבה מאי עביד ליה?״ כבר בגישה זו מן החידוש. אבל יותר נראה שהרמב״ם בכלל לא התחשב עם קושיות סתמיות כאלו, כי אין הכרח לומר שכל תנא או אמורא ידרוש פסוק זה לרבות שום הלכה.

הל׳ תמידין ומוספין ז, ו:

״מצותו להקצר בליל ששה עשר בין בחול בין בשבת.״

ובלחם משנה שם: ״תימא... דמאן דאית ליה דקצירת העומר דוחה שבת אית ליה דנקצר ביום פסול,... וצ״ע.״ כי הרמב״ם פסק בהלכה ז׳: ״ואם קצרוהו ביום כשר.״

והנה פסקו של הרמב״ם מפרש בכמה משניות. במשנה מנחות עא, א כתוב: ״מצותו לקצור בלילה, נקצר ביום כשר ודוחה את השבת.״ ובמשנה סג, ב: ״רבי חנינא סגן הכהנים אומר בשבת היה נקצר ביחיד ובמגל אחד,... וחכמים אומרים אחד שבת ואחד חול בשלשה,...״ ובמשנה סה, א: ״כיצד הן עושין,... בשבת אומר להן שבת זו אמר הן אקצור והם אומרים לו קצור,...״ אלא דבסוגיא עב, ב, הסיקו דנקצר ביום כשר זה לפי שטת רבי, ורבי סבר שקצירת העומר לא דחיא שבת, והמקורות שבהם קצירת העומר דוחה שבת הם דלא כרבי. אבל מסקנא סתמית זו, שרבי חולק על משניות הנ״ל, יסודה בקושיא שם, בסתמא דסוגיא. ולפיכך נראה שהרמב״ם מתעלם ממסקנות כאלו. ופלא שהסוגיא תסיק מסקנא כזו, בייחוד שבמשנה סה, א, יש כמו תיאור איך התנהגו.

הל׳ עבדים ה, ד:

"כיצד בראשי איברים... וחסרו אחד מכ״ד ראשי איברים... אבל... החותך
לשונו אינו יוצא לחירות שאינן מומין שבגלוי."

ובלחם משנה שם: "תימה דבפ״ק דקידושין השוו דין יציאת ראשי איברים
לענין מומי בכור דשם נמי בעינן מומין שבגלוי... דכל אותם המנויים
בהלכות איסורי מזבח דפוסלין את הקדשים אם נפל אחד מהם בבכור ה״ז
נשחט עליו... וכאן כתב רבינו ז״ל דלשון לא הוי מום שבגלוי לגבי ראשי
איברים וא״כ תימה דבגמרא משוה אותם וצ״ע."

אבל מכל הפרק "על אלו מומין" רואים שמומי בכור הם סוגים אחרים של
מומים ואין להשוות עם ראשי איברים שעבד יוצא בהן לחרות. וא״כ אין
להתפלא אם הרמב״ם מתעלם מהשוואה כזו שבסתמא דסוגיא דקידושין.[17]

הל׳ עבדים ו, ו:

"כל שטר שיש עליו אפילו עד אחד כותי חוץ מגיטי נשים ושחרורי
עבדים שהן כשרין בעד אחד ישראל ועד אחד כותי והוא שיהיה כותי חבר."

ובל״מ, שם: "קשה דבגמרא אמרו דחתים ישראל לבסוף... וא״כ למה רבינו
לא ביאר זה."

אוקימתא זו בגמרא, גיטין י׳, א׳, היא דחוקה ואין לה אחיזה בלשון המשנה,
והיא מסתמא דגמרא.[18] ולכאורה אוקימתא זו היתה כבר לפני רב פפא והוא
מבארה. אבל אין הכרח לזה. ובייחוד הביטוי במימרתו של רב פפא "זאת
אומרת" מכוון כנראה למשנה או למימרתו של ר׳ אלעזר שם. ולפיכך נראה
שהרמב״ם לא התחשב באוקימתא זו.[19]

כדאי להדגיש שבהרבה סוגיות הש״ס הרושם הוא שאמוראים ממשיכים
חומר סתמי, אבל אחרי העיון מתברר שהחומר האמוראי יותר מובן והגיוני אם
מקבלים את ההנחה שהוא נוצר לפני החומר הסתמי.

הל׳ מלוה ולוה יד, יד:

"שנים אוחזין בשטר המלוה אומר שלי... וישלם הלוה מחצה." ומעיר המגיד
משנה: "ואולי היתה להם גירסא אחרת בסוגית הגמ׳ שם." ובגמ׳ ב״מ ז׳ ע״ב:

---

[17] ע״ע הל׳ עבדים ד, ב... ואעפ״כ כופין את האב לפדותה אחר שמכרה משום פגם
משפחה." ומקשה שם הכ״מ שהלכה זו היא אליבא דר״ש שאינה נמכרת ונישנית, אבל
הרמב״ם פסק דמוכר ושונה. אכן מסקנא זו יסודה בקושיו של הסתמא דסוגיא שאפשר
לתרצה בקל כפי שמציע הכ״מ, שם.
[18] ר׳ ספרי פירושים ומחקרים, מעמ׳ 82.
[19] אבל יתכן גם לומר שהרמב״ם בלשונו "והוא שיהיה כותי חבר" התכוון לאוקימתא זו
אלא שניסחה בצורה כללית. "דחתים ישראל לבסוף" אומר לי שהכותי חבר.

אמר ר׳ אלעזר... ור׳ יוחנן אמר לעולם חולקין ואפילו אחד אדוק בטופס
ואחד אדוק בתורף והתניא זה נוטל עד מקום שידו מגעת לא צריכה דקאי
תורף בי מצעי.

והנה הקושי׳ אינה הכרחית כי הברייתא מכוונת לטלית, כדמוכח מדף ז, א,
וההבדל גדול בין טלית לשטר. ולפיכך נראה שהרמב״ם דחה אוקימתא זו
כהערה אחר־תלמודית.

שבסוגיא זו יש חומר אחר־אמוראי אנו למדים מעדות הראשונים: [20] ״והוי
יודע דמה שכתוב בספרים דאמר שטרא דאית ביה זמן כמה שוה אינו מעיקר
הגמ׳ אלא פירושא דמר רב יהודאי הוא ויש גמרות ישנות שאין בהן כלל...״

ובכלל יש לנו עדויות שהרבה חומר מאוחר הוכנס למס׳ ב״מ ובאופן יחסי
הרבה מחומר כזה הוכנס לפרק א׳, כפי שיוצא מהערות כנ״ל בשטה מקובצת.[21]

הל׳ סנהדרין ב, י:

״אע״פ שאין בית דין פחות משלשה, מותר לאחד לדון מן התורה, שנאמר
בצדק תשפוט עמיתך. ומדברי סופרים עד שיהיו שלשה. ושנים שדנו אין
דיניהן דין.״

והקשו עליו (כ״מ ולח״מ, שם) שלפי הגמ׳ בסנהדרין ג, א, משמע דמאן
דאית ליה דמדאורייתא בחד סגי, אית ליה שנים שדנו דיניהן דין. וראה שם
מה שתירצו.

אבל יותר נראה שסוגיא הסתמית ״מאי איכא בין רבא לרב אחא בריה דרב
איקא איכא ביניייהו דאמר שמואל שנים שדנו דיניהן דין אלא שנקראו בית דין
חצוף לרבא לית ליה דשמואל לרב אחא בריה דרב איקא אית ליה דשמואל״
היא מתקופת ראשוני הגאונים ובתקופה זו באמת פסקו כשמואל כדאיתא בה״ג
ובשאילתות.[22] אבל הרמב״ם פסק נגד שמואל, וכר׳ יוחנן וריש לקיש.[23] ובכל
זאת פסק כר׳ אחא שיחיד דן מן התורה. נראה שלא התחשב בחומר סתמי זה
שאינו לא מימרא ולא שקלא וטריא אמוראית.

ונראה שכמעט כל הסוגיות של ״מאי איכא בין...״, ״מאי ביניהו,״ ״פלוני לא
אמר כפלוני,״ הן מתקופה אחר־אמוראית.

הל׳ עדות ב, ג:

״היו העדים מרובים שנים מהם כוונו עדותן בחקירות ובדרישות והשלישי
אומר איני יודע תתקיים העדות בשנים ויהרג.״

[20] אוצה״ג לב״מ, ח׳ הפירושים. ע״ש גם הקטע בשם הרמב״ן.
[21] ור׳ ליקוט החומר ברבנן סבוראי ותלמודם לר״ב מ. לוין.
[22] ר׳ אוצה״ג לסנהדרין עמ׳ כא ובהערה 6.
[23] בירושלמי סנהדרין יח, א: ״שמואל אמר שנים שדנו דיניה׳ דין אלא שנקראו ב״ד
חצוף. ר״י וריש לקיש תריהון מרין שני׳ שדנו אין דיניהן דין.״

והקשו עליו 24 שדבריו תמוהים. בגמרא מפורש שזה ״כמאן דלא כר״ע,״
והרמב״ם פוסק כר״ע, ע״ש.

בסוגיא, סנהדרין מא, ב: ״מאי אפילו שנים אומרים... א״ר ששת אֲרֵישא
קאי, והכי קאמר בחקירות אפילו שנים אומרים ידענו ואחד אומר איני יודע
עדותן בטלה כמאן כר״ע דמקיש שלשה לשנים. אמר רבא והא עדותן קיימת
קתני. אלא אמר רבא הכי קאמר אפילו בחקירות שנים אומרים ידענו ואחד
אומר איני יודע עדותן קיימת כמאן דלא כר׳ עקיבא.״

גם פירושו של רב ששת וגם פירושו של רבא אינם מתאימים לנוסח המשנה
שלפנינו. על נוסחאות שונות במשנתנו דן רי״ן אפשטיין במבוא לנוסח
המשנה, עמ׳ 362.

והנה לפי פירושו של רב ששת, שעדותן בטלה, מובן לומר שזה בהתאם
לר״ע שמקיש שלשה לשנים.25 אבל בפירושו של רבא שעדותן קיימת אין
הכרח לומר ההפך שזה דלא כר״ע.26 דברי ר״ע הם בנמצא אחד קרוב או
פסול, אבל באיני יודע, מי אמר. וההבדל גדול בין זה לזה, ולכן נראה שזהי
הוספה משיגרא דלישנא. מכיון שכתוב בדברי רב ששת כמאן כר״ע א״כ
בדברי רבא שאומר ההפך מרב ששת הוסיפו את ההפך, דלא כר״ע. הרמב״ם,
כנראה, לא התחשב בהערה זו כחומר תלמודי.

הדוגמאות הנ״ל מעמידות אותנו על כיוון החקירה לא רק בנוגע לרמב״ם
אלא גם בנוגע לפוסקים שקדמוהו, כמו בעל הלכות גדולות והרי״ף. כדי
לעמוד על טיבו, זמנו, ובייחוד השפעתו של החומר הסתמי חשוב לא רק להבין
את התהוות התלמוד אלא גם את גדרי הפסק של גדולי הפוסקים. לפי״ז לא די
לברר את זמנו של החומר הסתמי מנקודת מבט היסטורית והשפעתו על החומר
התלמודי היסודי,27 אלא גם את גישתו של כל אחד מגדולי הפוסקים והמפר־
שים. מהם שגישתם יותר קרובה למסקנות המחקר הביקורתי ומהם שהנחתם
לגמרי אחרת.28

<hr>

24 לחם משנה, שם.   25 מכות ה, ב.
26 אבל עי׳ ברש״י ובתוס׳ ד״ה ״כמאן״ ובשאר מפרשים.
27 ר׳ מאמרי, ``The Impact of the 'Anonymous Sugyah' On Halakic Concepts'',
in *Proceedings of the American Academy for Jewish Research*, XXXVII (1969),
19–28. אבל ההפרדה בין החלק היסודי־האמוראי והחלק הפירושי היא לפעמים די
מסובכה וקשה להכריע. ר׳ ספרות שרשם שמאי יהודה פרידמן למאמרו ״הוספות
וקטעי סברא בפרק החובל״, תרביץ מ (תשל״א), עמ׳ 418, הע׳ 1, ור׳ גם מבואו
ל־״פרק האשה רבה בבבלי בצירוף מבוא כללי על דרך חקר הסוגיא״ במחקרים
ומקורות, מאסף למדעי היהדות (בית המדרש לרבנים באמריקה, תשל״ח),
מעמ׳ 283.
28 לפני עשרים שנה העירותי בספרי פירושים ומחקרים בתלמוד, מסכת גיטין,

על סמך החומר שבדקתי מסתבר שרק חלק מהחומר הסתמי שבגמרא נראה
היה בעיני הרמב״ם כחלק אינטגרלי של התלמוד, ואילו חלק ממנו היה בעיניו
לאו בר סמכא. לעת עתה אין בידי לנסח קריטריון מדויק שהרמב״ם השתמש
בו בכדי לחלק את סמכותו של החומר הסתמי, ומסופקני מאוד אם בכלל היה לו
קריטריון מדויק לחלוקה כזאת. מתקבל יותר על הדעת שהוא הכריע על
סמכותו של חומר סתמי ע״פ כו״כ סימנים, כגון: צורתו הספרותית, איכותו
ההגיונית, ובייחוד אם הוא סותר או מתאים לחומר יסודי, תנאי או אמוראי.

<hr/>

תשכ״ט, שאת הפתרון לרוב הקשיים שהעירו על הפוסקים, כמו הבה״ג הרי״ף
והרמב״ם, ״יש למצא כנראה בבירור ופירוד בין חלק ההוראה שהוא עיקר ויסוד,
לחלק הפירושי והשו״ט הסתמא שחלק גדול ממנו הוא מתקופת הסבוראים והגאונים
הראשונים, ולפעמים הוכנס משולי הגליון.״ שם עמ׳ 4. השערה זו הולכת ומתאששת על
ידי בדיקת הבעיות שבפוסקים הנ״ל לאור הגישה הנ״ל.